The Collected Works of J. Krishnamurti

Volume XV

1964–1965

The Dignity of Living

COLLECTED WORKS VOLUME 15

Photo: J. Krishnamurti, ca 1972 by Mark Edwards © Krishnamurti Foundation Trust, Ltd.

P.O Box 1560, Ojai, CA 93024

Website: www.kfa.org

Printed in the United States of America

ISBN 13: 9781934989487
ISBN: 1934989487

Contents

Preface

Jiddu Krishnamurti was born in 1895 of Brahmin parents in south India. At the age of fourteen he was proclaimed the coming World Teacher by Annie Besant, then president of the Theosophical Society, an international organization that emphasized the unity of world religions. Mrs. Besant adopted the boy and took him to England, where he was educated and prepared for his coming role. In 1911 a new worldwide organization was formed with Krishnamurti as its head, solely to prepare its members for his advent as World Teacher. In 1929, after many years of questioning himself and the destiny imposed upon him, Krishnamurti disbanded this organization, saying:

Truth is a pathless land, and you cannot approach it by any path whatsoever, by any religion, by any sect. Truth, being limitless, unconditioned, unapproachable by any path whatsoever, cannot be organized; nor should any organization be forced to lead or to coerce people along any particular path. My only concern is to set men absolutely, unconditionally free.

Until the end of his life at the age of ninety, Krishnamurti traveled the world speaking as a private person. The rejection of all spiritual and psychological authority, including his own, is a fundamental theme. A major concern is the social structure and how it conditions the individual. The emphasis in his talks and writings is on the psychological barriers that prevent clarity of perception. In the mirror of relationship, each of us can come to understand the content of his own consciousness, which is common to all humanity. We can do this, not analytically, but directly in a manner Krishnamurti describes at length. In observing this content we discover within ourselves the division of the observer and what is observed. He points out that this division, which prevents direct perception, is the root of human conflict.

His central vision did not waver after 1929, but Krishnamurti strove for the rest of his life to make his language even more simple and clear. There is a development in his exposition. From year to year he used new terms and new approaches to his subject, with different nuances.

Because his subject is all-embracing, the *Collected Works* are of compelling interest. Within his talks in any one year, Krishnamurti was not able to cover the whole range of his vision, but broad applications of particular themes are found throughout these volumes. In them he lays the foundations of many of the concepts he used in later years.

The *Collected Works* contain Krishnamurti's previously published talks, discussions, answers to specific questions, and writings for the years 1933 through 1967. They are an authentic record of his teachings, taken from transcripts of verbatim shorthand reports and tape recordings.

The Krishnamurti Foundation of America, a California charitable trust, has among its purposes the publication and distribution of Krishnamurti books, videocassettes, films and tape recordings. The production of the *Collected Works* is one of these activities.

Madras, India, 1964

First Talk in Madras

After all, in a gathering of this kind, the act of imparting, the act of listening, and the act of understanding are of great importance. Because this movement of imparting, listening, and understanding is both a part of life—everyday life—and a movement, constant, continuous, and never ending. And, especially when we are going into problems that require a great deal of understanding, not merely verbally, there has also to be that communion which comes when one goes beyond the words—not sentimentally, not emotionally—and understands the whole significance of the words, their nature, and their meaning. Then, perhaps, a gathering of this kind will have some special meaning and significance.

What we are undertaking to do together is to share, share actively; that is, there is the act on the part of the speaker, not only to impart, but also to share what is being said—not as mere information, but rather as an experimental process in which both the speaker and the listener share actively in what is being said. Most of us, unfortunately, do not share actively. We listen, agreeing or disagreeing verbally, or merely rejecting ideas; and therefore, there is hardly any sharing. Sharing comes only when both the speaker and the listener are actively participating in that which is being said. Otherwise it will be another of those innumerable talks and discourses that one, unfortunately, goes to; and it will be a waste of time on your part and on the part of the speaker if there is not an active sharing in what is being said.

Sharing implies, does it not, that you listen and do not jump to any conclusion. First, there must be the act of listening. And that act of listening depends on the listener, on the 'you' who is listening, hearing. If you accept it because it coincides with what you believe, or reject it because it does not fit in with what you believe, then sharing ceases. And what is, it seems to me, important, not only during this hour, but throughout life, is that one must have this capacity, this art of listening and therefore sharing—sharing, listening, with everything, to everything.

Life is a constant movement in relationship. And if one is at all alert, awake to all the events that are going on in the world, this movement which is life must be understood, not at any particular level—scientific, biological, or traditional, or at the level of acquiring knowledge—but at the total level. Otherwise, one cannot share.

You know that word *sharing* has an extraordinary significance. We may share money, clothes. If we have a little food, we may give it, share it with another; but beyond that we hardly share anything with another. Sharing implies not only a verbal communication—which is the understanding of the significance of words and their nature—but also communion. And to commune is one of the most difficult things in life. Perhaps we are fairly good at communicating something which we have or which we want or which we hope to have, but to commune with one another is a most difficult thing.

Because to commune implies, does it not, that both the person who is speaking and the one who is listening must have an intensity, a fury, and that there must be at the same level, at the same time, a state of mind that is neither accepting nor rejecting but actively listening. Then only is there a possibility of communion, of being in communion with something. To be in communion with nature is comparatively easy. And you can be in communion with something when there is no barrier—verbal, intellectual—between you, the observer, and the thing that is observed. But there is a state, perhaps, of affection, a state of intensity, so that both meet at the same level, at the same time, with the same intensity. Otherwise communication is not possible—especially communion which is actually the sharing. And this act of communion is really quite remarkable because it is that communion, that state of intensity, that really transforms one's whole state of mind.

After all, love—if I may use that word without giving to it any particular significance now—is only possible when there is the act of sharing. And that is only possible, again, when there is this peculiar quality of intensity, nonverbal communication, at the same level and at the same time. Otherwise it is not love. Otherwise it becomes mere emotionalism and sentimentalism, which is absolutely worthless.

Our everyday life—not the supreme moment of a second, but everyday life—is this act of imparting, listening, and understanding. And for most of us, listening is one of the most difficult things to do. It is a great art, far greater than any other art. We hardly ever listen because most of us are so occupied with our own problems, with our own ideas, opinions—the everlasting chattering of one's own inadequacies, fancies, myths, and ambitions. One hardly ever pays attention, not only to what another says, but to the birds, to the sunset, to the reflection on the water. One hardly ever sees or listens. And if one knows how to listen—which demands an astonishing energy—then in that act of listening there is complete communion; the words, the significance of words, and the construction of words have very little meaning. So, you and the speaker have completely to share in the truth or in the falseness of what is being said. For most of us, it is a very difficult act to listen; but it is only in listening that one learns.

Learning is not accumulating knowledge. The accumulation of knowledge any electronic brain can do. So knowledge is not of very great importance; it has a certain use, but not the astonishing importance that human beings give to it. But the act of learning needs a very swift mind. The act of listening demands no interpretation. You listen to that bird and you say immediately, "It is a crow," or "I wish it would be quiet, I cannot pay attention to what is being said!" So the act of listening has gone! Whereas you can listen to that bird and also listen to the speaker when there is no interpretation, when there is no translation of what is being said. Therefore, you are listening—not accepting, which is a terrible thing.

And you cannot listen if what you hear is translated in terms of your own knowledge. You know certain things by your own experience. You have gathered your own knowledge from books, from tradition, from the various impacts of life; and that remains part of your consciousness, part of your being. And when you hear something, or when you listen, then you translate what is being said through what you already know. Therefore you are not listening, and therefore there is no act of learning.

So, a mind that interprets, translates, has a tradition, or has that which it has accumulated as knowledge—such a mind is incapable of learning; it functions in a groove. A mind that functions in a groove is not a mind that is acting, that is capable of learning, that has energy, vitality. And as we are going to talk about many things during these seven talks here, what is of primary importance is this act of learning. Because, it is only the mind that is learning that is fresh, and a fresh mind can see things anew, clearly, reject that which is false, and pursue that which is true.

The truth and the false do not depend on your opinion, or on what you already know, or on your experience. Because your experience is merely the continuation of the past conditioning, modified by the present through various forms of training. Therefore, your experience is not the factor that says this is true or this is false. Nor your knowledge, because the true and the false are constantly changing, moving, active, dynamic, never static. And if you come to it with your opinions, your judgments, your experience, your tradition, then you will not be able to find out for yourself what is true, especially if you come to it with a mind that is ridden with authority, with a mind that obeys. Then such a mind is not only a juvenile mind, but it is incapable of exploring, of discovering. And truth has to be discovered every minute, and that is the beauty of it. The beauty of it is the energy of it. Therefore, one must have an extraordinarily energetic mind—not the mind that is argumentative, that believes, that has opinions, that functions in a narrow, limited groove. Such a mind has no energy. It is only the fresh mind that can inquire, that can explore, ask, demand, search out.

And we are going to search out, explore together, this question of how to bring about, in the human mind, a complete revolution. Because such a revolution is necessary for various obvious reasons. First, man has lived for two million years. He is still caught in sorrow, in fear, in despair. He is still fearful, anxious, burdened with great agony. He is still carrying on, modified, but as he was two millions years ago. The great part of the brain is still animalistic, which expresses itself in greed, ambition, envy, jealousy, violence, and all the rest of it. One has lived as a human being in this mess, in this contradiction, and the human mind has not been able to transform itself, to bring about a complete mutation within itself. And we know it can change through pressure, through circumstances, through a great many challenges, through impacts, through culture, through various tensions; it can change, modify itself—which is going on all the time, whether we like it or not. The food, the clothes, the climate, the newspapers, the magazines, the family—everything is urging, compelling, forcing us to conform to a certain pattern. And whether we like it or not, we conform, because it is much safer to conform. And in that conformity, there is a certain change. That change is merely what has been modified.

We are not talking about change. We are talking about something entirely different. We are talking about a complete mutation, a total revolution, because that is absolutely necessary if one is at all serious.

I mean by a "serious person" not one who is committed to a particular pattern of belief and functions according to that belief—he is generally thought to be marvelous and serious; I do not call him serious at all! Nor a person who is committed to a particular course of action and who does not deviate from it—one calls him a very serious person, but I do not call him serious. Nor a man who lives according to a particular principle, which is an idea, a belief, and follows it rigidly—you consider him to be a serious man, but I do not.

So, we mean something entirely different by that word *serious.* Again, unless we have the same meaning for the same word, communication becomes very difficult. I mean by "serious mind" a mind that perceives what is true—not according to any particular pattern or belief or authority—and pursues that truth endlessly. The conditions of the world—this glorification of tribalism which is called nationalism; the various forms of divisions in religion: Catholicism, Hinduism, Buddhism, and all the rest of it; the political parties: communists, socialists, capitalists, and so on; and the economic, scientific, technological divisions and the various fragmentations of life—all these demand that we approach these problems entirely differently. And to approach these problems entirely differently, one needs to have a mind that has undergone complete mutation; otherwise, we will perpetuate our problems. I think this must be seen clearly—not verbally, not theoretically, not tolerantly, but understood with fire, with enthusiasm, with vitality, with energy, with fury. Because, intellectually—that is, verbally—we can say, "We need such a change, we need such a mutation," which is fairly obvious, and remain at that level. One can intellectually accept that a mutation is necessary and let it go, and remain as static as one is. Or, one waits for circumstances, time, to bring about this mutation. And that is what most people do. By some miracle, by some chance, by some incident, accident, some kind of tremendous revolution takes place in one's being. Again, such waiting does not bring about a revolution.

The word *revolution* is used by different people in different ways. The communists use that word in one way—economic, social, dictatorial—a revolution according to an idea, according to a plan. Or, rather, one is afraid of that word revolution! If you are well-established, if you have a bank account, if you have a good job, a house, a position, you want things to go on as they are; you are afraid of that word. Or, you abhor that word because you believe in evolution, which is gradualness. But we are using that word entirely differently. We are using that word, not in the sense of revolution meaning time, according to a pattern, according to some concept, but in the sense that observing the state of the world and of oneself in the world as part of the world, and seeing totally—not at different, fragmentary levels, but totally—how imperative it is that a human mind undergo a tremendous revolution so that out of that revolution, there is clarity—not confusion, not chaos: chaos being ordered, put together, according to our conditioning.

So, we are going to ask ourselves during these seven meetings whether it is at all possible for the human mind, which is so bound, which is the result of two million years of time and space and distance, which is the result of so many pressures—whether it is possible for such a mind to bring about a mutation out of time and therefore on the instant. And to inquire into this question, one must demand freedom because you cannot inquire if you are tethered. You must have a free mind, a mind that is not afraid, a mind that has no belief, a mind that does not project its own conditioning, its own hopes, its own longings.

So, it is only through inquiry that one is going to find out, and to inquire one must have freedom. Most of us have lost—probably we never had—this energy to inquire. We would rather accept, we would rather go along the old path; but we do not know how to inquire. The scientist, in his laboratory, inquires. He is searching, looking, asking, questioning, doubting; but, outside the laboratory, he is just like anybody else—he has stopped inquiring! And to inquire into oneself requires not only freedom but an astonishing sense of perception, of seeing.

You know, it is comparatively easy to go to the moon and beyond—as they have proved. But it is astonishingly difficult to go within. And to go within endlessly, the first thing is freedom—freedom not from something, but the act of freedom which is independent of motive and revolt. When freedom becomes a revolt, it is merely a reaction to the condition it exists in; it is revolting from something and therefore it is not free. I can revolt against the present society. The present society may be stupid, corrupt, inept, ineffective. I can revolt, but that revolt is merely a reaction—as communism is a reaction against capitalism. So this revolt merely puts me in a position modified along the same pattern. So we are not talking of revolt which is a reaction, but we are talking of freedom which is not from something.

I do not know if you have ever felt this nature of freedom—not calculated, not induced—when you suddenly feel that you have no burden, no problem, and your mind is tremendously alive and your whole body—your heart and your nerves, everything—is intense, vibrating, strong. Such freedom is necessary. It is only the free mind which can really inquire, obviously, not a mind which says, "I believe and I will inquire"—it has no meaning—not a mind that is frightened of what will happen to it through inquiry, and therefore stops inquiring.

Inquiry means a mind that is sane, healthy, that is not persuaded by opinions of its own or of another, so that it is able to see very clearly every minute everything as it moves, as it flows. Life is a movement in relationship, which is action. And unless there is freedom, mere revolt has no meaning at all. A really religious man is never in revolt. He is a free man—free, not from nationalism, greed, envy, and all the rest of it; he is just free.

And to inquire, there must be the understanding of the nature and the meaning of fear, because a mind that is afraid at any level of its being cannot obviously be capable of the swift movement of inquiry. You know, because of tradition, because of the weight of authority, especially in this country, people are everlastingly boasting of seven thousand years of culture and are very proud of it! And these people who talk everlastingly about this culture probably have nothing to say, and that is why they are talking about it. Such a mind that is caught in the weight of tradition and authority is not a free mind. One must go beyond civilization and culture. And it is only such a mind that is capable of inquiry and the discovery of what is truth—and no other mind; it can talk about what is truth and have theories about it endlessly. To find out requires a mind that is free from all authority and therefore from all fear.

The understanding of fear is an enormous problem, most intricate. I do not know if you have ever given your mind to it—not only your mind, but your heart. Probably you have given your mind, but, surely, never your heart. To understand something you must give your mind and your heart. When you give your mind to something, especially to fear, you resist it, you build a wall against it, you enclose yourself and isolate yourself, or you run away from it. That is what most of us do, that is what most religions are for. But when you give your heart to understanding something, then quite a different process takes place. When you give your heart to understanding your child, when you care, then you look to every incident, to every detail; then there is nothing too small or too great; there is no boredom. But we never give our heart to anything—even to our wife or our husband or our children, and, least of all, to life. And when one does give one's heart, then there is instant communion.

When one gives one's heart, it is a total action. And when you give your mind, it is a fragmentary action. And most of us give our minds to so many things. That is why we live a fragmentary life—thinking one thing and doing another; and we are torn, contradictory. To understand something, one must give not only one's mind but one's heart to it.

And to understand this very complex problem of fear—which we shall discuss next time, I hope, that we meet here—requires not a mere intellectual effort but an approach which is total. You know, when you love something—I am using that word in its total sense, not the love of God and the love of man, or profane love and love divine; those divisions are not love at all—you give your mind and your heart to it. This is not to commit yourself to something—which is entirely different. I can give my mind and heart and commit myself to some course of action—sociological or philosophical or communist or religious. That is not giving oneself; that is only an intellectual conviction, a sense of following something which you have to do to improve yourself or the society, and all the rest of it. But we are talking of something entirely different.

When you give your heart to something, then you are aware of everything in the sphere of that understanding. Do try sometime—or I hope you are doing it now as it is being said. The man who says, "I will try"—he is lost, because there is no time; there is only the moment now. And if you are doing it now, you will see that if you give your heart, it is a total action—not a fragmentary, compulsive action, not the action according to some pattern or formula. When you give your heart, you will see that you understand that something immediately, instantly—which has nothing to do with sentiment or emotionalism or devotion; that is all too puerile. To give your heart to something you need tremendous understanding, you need great energy and clarity, so that in the light of clarity you see everything clearly. And you cannot see clearly if you are not free from your tradition, from your authority, from your culture, from your civilization, from all the patterns of society; it is not by escaping from society, going out into a mountain, or becoming a hermit that you understand life. On the contrary, to understand this extraordinary movement of life—which is relationship, which is action—and to follow it right through endlessly, you must have freedom which comes alone when you give your mind, your heart, your whole being. Therefore in that state you understand. And when there is understanding, there is no effort; it is an instant act.

And it is only such a mind which is free, clear—it is only such a mind that can see what is true and discard what is false.

December 16, 1964

Second Talk in Madras

In the modern world where there are so many problems, one is apt to lose great feeling. I mean by that word *feeling,* not sentiment, not emotionalism, not mere excitement, but that quality of perception, the quality of hearing, listening, the quality of feeling a bird singing on a tree, the movement of a leaf in the sun. To feel things greatly, deeply, penetratingly, is very difficult for most of us because we have so many problems. Whatever we seem to touch turns into a problem. And, apparently, there is no end to man's problems, and he seems utterly incapable of resolving them because the more the problems exist, the less the feelings become.

I mean by "feeling" the appreciation of the curve of a branch, the squalor, the dirt on the road, to be sensitive to the sorrow of another, to be in a state of ecstasy when we see a sunset. These are not sentiments, these are not mere emotions. Emotion and sentiment or sentimentality turn to cruelty, they can be used by society; and when there is sentiment, sensation, then one becomes a slave to society. But one must have great feelings. The feeling for beauty, the feeling for a word, the silence between two words, and the hearing of a sound clearly—all that generates feeling. And one must have strong feelings because it is only the feelings that make the mind highly sensitive.

Sensitivity in its highest form is intelligence. Without sensitivity to everything—to one's own sorrows; to the sorrow of a group of people, of a race; to the sorrow of everything that is—unless one feels and has the feeling highly sensitized, one cannot possibly solve any problem. And we have many problems, not only at the physical level, the economic level, the social level, but also at the deeper levels of one's own being—problems that apparently we are not capable of solving. I am not talking of the mathematical problems, or the problems of mechanical inventions, but of human problems: of our sorrows, of despair, of the narrow spirit of the mind, of the shallowness of one's thinking, of the constant, repetitive boredom of life, the routine of going to the office every day for forty or thirty years. And the many problems that exist, both consciously and unconsciously, make the mind dull, and therefore the mind loses this extraordinary sensitivity. And when we lose sensitivity, we lose intelligence.

As we said the last time when we met here, we are going to discuss, talk over together, the question of fear. To go into that problem really comprehensively, one must understand that all problems are related. There is no separate problem by itself; every problem is interrelated with another problem. So, a mind that seeks to solve a particular problem will never solve it because that particular problem is related to half-a-dozen other problems, conscious as well as unconscious. It is only a religious action that can solve all problems altogether.

I hope you will excuse the use of the word *religion* because for many people religion smells, and it has very little meaning in modern society! Going to the church, to the temple, hearing a psalm or a chant sung—it has very little significance; it is convenient, but no more. And we are not using the word religion in that sense at all. Organized religion, organized belief has no validity; it does not lead anywhere, it does not bring understanding or clarity, nor does it lead man to truth. Such organized beliefs and religions are really, essentially, man's incapacity to solve his daily problems, and therefore his attempt to escape from them to some form of mysticism, ritualism, and so on. We are using the word religion in a totally different sense. I mean by that word the capacity to see and understand the whole of the issue immediately, and act on that immediacy.

And I think it is rather important to understand this: to see something very clearly, intellectually or verbally, one must understand the meaning of the word and the significance of the sound of the word—the sound which evokes the symbol, the image, the significance, the remembrance, the immediate response. Unless we understand the word and see how deeply we are a slave to words, we shall not be able to penetrate into this question of what is the true significance of religion. Because the word becomes significant when the word is not a hindrance, when it opens the door—not according to one's own particular idiosyncrasy or character or inclination, or according to something that one is committed to. A word, after all, is a sound; and if that sound is merely received as an intellectual concept or as an idea or as a formula, the word loses the sensitivity of that sound. And the word becomes important when the word takes the place of, or becomes more important than, the fact.

We are sharing together this question. You are not merely listening to the speaker; you are not listening to a set of words or ideas or concepts, agreeing or disagreeing. But rather you and I are sharing together this enormous question of fear. And to share together, there must be communion—not only communication but also communion, which is much more important.

I mean by that word *communion* a state of mind that is sensitive, alert, watchful, neither accepting nor rejecting, tremendously alive and, therefore, capable of rejecting and pursuing. After all, that is what we mean by sharing. To share together a problem means, does it not, that you and I go into it together. And "together" means not that you stand aside, not that you listen to the explanation or to words that have very little meaning, but that you follow—through the words and therefore through the significance, the sound—the meaning, the sensitivity of what that word evokes. And through the communication of that word, we can establish a communion; then we can share.

And we have to share that problem together because it is a very complex problem. All problems are complex; there is no one solution to one problem. So, to share together anything, we must both meet together, we must both travel together rapidly; you not only see the significance of the word and become sensitive to the word, but also you are intellectually aware of the meaning of that word and also the feeling and the total significance that word conveys—all that is implied, is it not, when we are sharing anything together.

When you are listening to a story, you are pursuing it because it is interesting, amusing, dramatic, or tragic; you are with it, you are flowing with it. So, when we are discussing, talking about, sharing together this question of fear, we must also understand that every problem—physical pain, psychological disturbance, an economic problem, social contradiction—is interrelated with other problems, and that problems cannot be solved by themselves. A man who says, "I will solve the problems of society, or my own problems, by going within and therefore going deeper and deeper and deeper," such a man is not in relation with society, with the events that are happening. Likewise is the man who turns so, outwardly. So, to understand the problem it requires extraordinary balance, watchfulness, alertness.

And to understand this question of fear, which is not only at the conscious level but also at the deeper levels, one must understand the whole question of friction, of effort, of contradiction. Because all of our life is based on struggle, friction, effort. That is all we know: struggle, effort, friction which engender certain forms of energy, and that energy keeps us going. Ambition, greed, envy, is friction; and that keeps us on. That greed, that envy, that ambition, makes us make effort to achieve what we want; and that gives us a certain quality of energy, and that is all we know. And when that energy creates misery, confusion, sorrow, we try to escape into various forms of religious absurdities, or drink, or women, or amusement; in ten different ways we want to escape, and we do; but the problem still remains—the problem of effort, of conflict, of contradiction.

Education, society, religion, and the so-called sacred books all maintain that you must make effort, effort, effort. Man is told that he is inherently lazy, sluggish, indolent, and that unless he makes effort, he will vegetate, he will become lazy, lethargic, and incapable. That is what you are brought up on from the days of the school until you die: that you must make endless effort, not only in the family, but in the office; you must make an effort to be virtuous, to be good, and so on. We never question if there is another way of living altogether, which is without effort, without friction.

A life without friction is the religious life. And a mind without friction, without conflict, is the religious mind. When that mind acts, it has every problem dissolved; it has no problem. And we are going into that, because one must understand that first, before we go into the question of fear.

So, why do we make effort? The obvious answer is to achieve a result. And without effort, we feel we shall degenerate. But before we make an effort, we never inquire into the question: Why has the mind to make an effort at all? Is it not possible to learn without effort, to observe without effort, to listen so that that very act of listening is learning? There is effort only because we are in contradiction. If there were no contradiction at all, there would be no effort. And a man who has completely identified himself with a belief makes no effort—like those people who are unbalanced, who are psychotic; they make no effort; they are so completely identified with a certain belief, with a certain idea, with a certain concept, that there is no effort; they are that because they have no sense of contradiction. Please do follow this. We have to understand from the very beginning that a mind that makes an effort is a destructive mind and, therefore, is incapable of learning. We have gone before into the question of learning.

When do you learn? I am not asking about the accumulation of knowledge, which is quite a different thing. We are asking: When does one learn? I mean by "learning" a movement which is not accumulative, which is constantly flowing, learning, learning and never accumulating. The electronic brains accumulate knowledge; they have knowledge, but they cannot learn. And what is the state of the mind that learns? As we were saying the other day, life is a movement in relationship; and if you make that movement merely an accumulative process as knowledge, then you do not learn from that movement at all. One can learn only when there is a movement, a constant movement, either from curiosity or of exploration or of comprehension, not in terms of accumulation.

You only learn when the mind is completely quiet; then only you begin to learn. If, for example, you are listening to what is being said with ideas, with opinions, with a knowledge which you already have, or if you are comparing what is being said with what somebody else has said, then you are not learning. You can only learn if you listen. And listening is an act of silence; it is only the mind that is very quiet but tremendously active that can learn.

So, we are learning together about this question of effort. And to understand it and to learn about it—is that effort? "Life is effort. What are you talking about! We are brought up on effort, we make effort. Otherwise what you say has no meaning"—when you assert that, you have already stopped learning. To learn, which is to share, which is to communicate, you must obviously be in a state of inquiry, and, therefore, your mind must be free from the state of knowledge, of accumulation, and therefore capable of moving, living, acting. Therefore, sharing is an active process between you and the speaker. And it is only when you share that there is learning.

We make effort because we are in a state of contradiction. The contradiction is not only between the idea and the action—the idea being the belief, the concept, the formula—but also the difference between our thinking and our acting. I think one thing and do something else; I am violent and I pretend to be nonviolent—which is called the ideal. So there is always a contradiction, all our life. That contradiction is established deep down in us through society, through our own experiences, through all the innumerable accumulations of what the saints and the teachers and the books have said.

So, there is this sense of contradiction, invited or existing. We never question it. We never learn about that, so we keep on making effort. Because man does not want contradiction which brings misery, an extraordinary sense of frustration, conflict, confusion, he makes more and more effort to get out. But he never inquires or learns about this sense of contradiction.

So, is it possible to live without effort of any kind, at any level? We say it is. Do not accept it, but inquire, find out. We are going to inquire together whether it is possible.

There is the opinion and the fact, the *what is*. We have opinions, ideas, and the fact. Let us take the fact of poverty in this country. Poverty, starvation—that is a fact. But we have opinions about that; we have ideas, formulas how to resolve it—formulas as a socialist, as a communist, as a congressman, or whatever it is. Ideas, formulas, concepts, patterns are not facts but opinions, knowledge; and according to that knowledge we try to solve the problem of starvation; and so there is a contradiction. That is, if you are a socialist or a communist, whatever you are, you have a concept, you have a formula, you have a certain knowledge, you have a certain belief, and you want to fit the problem into that belief. The question of starvation, poverty, the appalling things that are going on in this country cannot be solved through nationalism nor through tribalism. No government can solve it at any level, at any time, because it is a world problem, like overpopulation and so on. It is a world issue, not the issue of a local group of people or the issue of some eccentric person wanting to do some good; and one knows that this question can only be solved as a whole, not as a part. So you have immediately a contradiction: the concept and the fact. And the same is with us, inwardly as well as outwardly. We have ideas, opinions, concepts, formulas; and there is the fact of envy, jealousy, brutality, violence. There is the idea and the fact, and immediately there is a contradiction. That is very simple.

Can one look at the fact without idea, look at something without any concept? When you approach a fact through a concept, the fact becomes unimportant and the concept becomes important; and, therefore, you increase the conflict, the contradiction. So, is it possible to look at the fact without an opinion, without an idea? Can you listen to that airplane without an idea—just listen to the sound and not let that sound interfere with the other sound of the speaker? Can you look at that tree or that sunset without a verbalization, without the memory of other sunsets? Please, we are sharing together, you are not just listening; do not go to sleep over this matter. There is that sunset; can you look at it without the word, without the remembrances of other sunsets? It is only possible to look at it, to see it completely, when there is no word, when there are no images, no symbols; then you are in direct relation, in direct contact with that sunset.

So, in the same way, can you look at a fact without bringing upon that fact all your knowledge, all your sympathy, emotions, ideas? It is these ideas, opinions, concepts, that create contradiction, not the fact; the fact never creates a contradiction. Suppose I am violent. It is the idea of nonviolence that creates a contradiction. We have been fed on ideas: that you must be gentle, that you must be good and nonviolent! And so there is a contradiction! So, can I look at my violence without the idea—which is the opposite—and merely deal with the fact that I am violent, and go into this whole question of violence, not through non-violence, but directly? What makes me violent? Either lack of calcium, or I have been frustrated in different ways, or I want something and I cannot get it. There are half-a-dozen explanations why one gets violent. You can deal with the fact and not with the idea, and you can deal with the fact immediately.

This capacity of the mind to deal with the fact instantly without bringing about a contradiction in the observing of the fact, is the real capacity of the mind that can see the whole. It is only the mind that has the capacity to see the whole thing instantly that is a religious mind. And seeing is acting; seeing is not the verbalization, not the intellectual seeing and then acting—that again creates a contradiction.

So, one has to learn that the idea, the ideal, the formula, the concept, creates contradiction—not the fact. And it is only when the mind is capable of looking at the fact that there is no contradiction, and therefore there is no effort. Please, this is very important to understand. The conflict, the friction, arises only when there is an opinion, a concept about the fact. When one says, "I want to change it, I do not like it, it must be that way, it must be this way," then contradiction arises, then one does not learn from it. And as we said, to learn is to approach any problem quietly, silently. It is only a silent mind, a quiet mind, the mind that is moving with the fact, that learns. And, therefore, in learning, there is no contradiction. It is only when one takes a position intellectually, verbally, or in experience, and from that position tries to alter the fact, that there is contradiction. I hope this is clear. If it is not, we will discuss it some other time.

So, as long as there is friction of any kind, there must be conflict, there must be contradiction. And is it possible so completely to see, to understand this whole question of contradiction, that one can live only with facts and nothing else? There is also the deeper issue involved in contradiction: there is not only the conscious and the unconscious but also the division between the thinker and the thought. Unless one understands all this, one cannot possibly go into the question of fear.

We have, as most people know, the conscious and the subconscious or the unconscious. For most of us, there is the division between the two, and therefore there is contradiction. Most of us function at the conscious level: going to an office, learning a certain technique. We spend most of our time at the level of the conscious; all our learning, all the impacts of modern civilization, and all the pressures are more or less on the surface. Then there is the unconscious which is the residue of two million years—the racial inheritance, the family, the social influence, the legends, the myths, the ideas, the formulas, the desires, the motives hidden deep down. And there is the division between that and our daily living. And occasionally that unconscious shows itself and creates havoc, creates deep disturbance, or that unconscious projects itself into dreams and so on.

We are not going into this whole question of the conscious and the unconscious, we are just pointing out the contradiction there. And one has to learn about it, not from books, not from Freud or from your recent psychoanalysts or anyone else. But one has to learn by watching every movement of one's thought. And that has much more significance than any philosophy, any teaching, any psychology, because that is firsthand—you are with it, living.

Then, there is also the contradiction between the thinker and the thought—which is between the observer and that which is observed. There, again, there is a contradiction. And one has to understand it. That is an extraordinarily complex problem. Most of us assume that there is the thinker first: the experiencer, the observer. But is that so? Not according to your Sanskrit traditions or what other people have said—Shankara, Buddha, X, Y, Z—that has no value at all because that is authority; and when you accept authority, you stop investigating, you stop sharing, learning. We are finding out together why this contradiction exists between the thinker and the thought. As long as that contradiction exists, there must be conflict, and therefore there must be the sense of infinite struggle, everlastingly.

So, one has to learn about the whole problem of thinking. Thinking is a complex problem. I am not going into that now; perhaps one day we will do it. But now we are just pointing out the contradiction which is the source of effort. And where there is effort of any kind, the mind is made dull. To learn, the mind must remain highly sensitive; and to learn implies to look at every problem not as an isolated issue but as interrelated.

Take the problem, which most people have, of sex. Why has sex become a problem? I am going to go into it. Please, this is not a matter of agreeing or disagreeing. We are going into it, exploring it. Why does anything become a problem? And what do we mean by a problem? Life is a process of challenge and response. That is, life is a constant challenge and a constant response. If the response is adequate—adequate in the sense as rich, as full, as potent, as vital as the challenge—then there is no friction. When the response is inadequate, then that inadequacy creates a problem. Right? We are not defining it. We are exploring. We mean by a problem, don't we, a human problem. Whatever the challenge may be, if the mind does not respond to the challenge adequately, completely, that challenge creates a problem in life. If I do not respond completely to the problem of death, to the problem of poverty, to the problem of my job, of my wife, of my children, of my society, the inadequacy of my response creates an issue, and that issue engenders conflict, strife, misery, confusion.

So, here is a question which most human beings have—the question of sex. Why has it become a problem? As I have said, every problem is interrelated. Sex becomes a problem when we have no other release intellectually, emotionally; or rather, when there is no sensitivity, when there is no feeling—not emotion, not sentiment, not the remembrance of a past incident, of a past sensation. That is, sex becomes a problem when your being has no release except in one direction. Intellectually you have no release because you accept, you follow; to you, the ideas are of tremendous importance, not the act, not the activity. The ideas become tremendously important intellectually, and so you have no intellectual freedom at all. Please follow all this. Intellectually you are not creative. Intellectually you are bound by authority; you are a slave to society, to respectability; you conform, and therefore there is no release through the activity of the mind. And there is no release through beauty, which is sensitivity—the beauty of a tree, of the sunset, the bird, the light, the sound. You never look at a tree, never look at the sky with stars. You may go to a concert and listen to music, but again it becomes an event; but you do not live with beauty, beauty being sensitivity—sensitivity to beauty, to squalor, to dirt, to everything. Your daily activities are a boredom. Going to the office, being insulted, the poverty of the mind and the heart, the utter insensitivity to life—through all that, you have no release at all. So, what happens? You have only one release: sex. And, because you have only one release, that becomes a problem.

So, to understand, to learn about this question, one must inquire widely into the whole problem of what it is to be creative. And you can only be creative when there is no fear.

And to inquire into the whole question of fear, one must understand the whole question of time and thought, because it is time that creates fear, and it is thought that projects fear. And a mind that is afraid is a dark mind, is a dull mind; and do what it will—it can go to all the temples and churches in the world, do all the social reforms, cultivate itself by becoming stupidly virtuous, respectable—such a mind cannot find what is truth. It is only the free mind, the mind that is highly sensitive, intelligent, clear, without any sense of conflict—it is only such a mind that can understand the ultimate.

December 20, 1964

Third Talk in Madras

We will continue with what we were talking about the other day. We were saying that learning is far more important than the acquisition of knowledge. Learning is an art. The electronic brain and the computers can acquire knowledge, can give every kind of information; and these machines, however clever, however well-informed, cannot learn. It is only the human mind that can learn. We make quite a distinction between the act of learning and the process of knowledge. The process of knowledge is gathering through experience, through various forms of impressions, through the impacts of society and of every form of influence; this gathering leaves a residue as knowledge, and with that knowledge, with that background, we function. Otherwise, without that knowledge, without all the technological knowledge that we have acquired through these many centuries, we cannot possibly function, we cannot know where we live, what to do. But the act of learning is a constant movement. The moment you have learned, it becomes knowledge, and from that knowledge you function. And, therefore, it is always functioning in the present through the past.

Whereas learning is an action or a movement always in the present, without conformity to the past. I think one should understand this rather clearly because otherwise it will lead us to all kinds of confusion when the speaker is going to go into wider things. Because learning is not listening with one's knowledge. If you listen with knowledge, with what you have learned, then actually you are not listening, you are interpreting, you are comparing, judging, evaluating, conforming to a certain pattern which has been established. Whereas the act of listening is entirely different. There you are listening with complete attention in which there is no sense of conformity to a pattern, no comparison, evaluation, or interpretation; you are listening. You are listening to those crows—they are making a lot of noise; it is their bedtime. But if you listen with irritation because you want to listen to what the speaker is saying, if you resist the noise of those crows, then you are not giving complete attention; your mind is divided. Therefore, the act of listening is the act of learning.

One has to learn so much about life, for life is a movement in relationship. And that relationship is action. We have to learn—not to accumulate knowledge from this movement which we call life, and then live according to that knowledge, which is conformity. To conform is to adjust, to fit into a mold, to adjust oneself to the various impressions, demands, pressures of a particular society. Life is meant to be lived, to be understood. One has to learn about life, and one ceases to learn the moment one argues with life, comes to life with the past, with one's conditioning as knowledge.

So, there is a difference between acquiring knowledge and the act of learning. You must have knowledge; otherwise, you will not know where you live, you will forget your name, and so on. So at one level knowledge is imperative, but when that knowledge is used to understand life—which is a movement, which is a thing that is living, moving, dynamic, every moment changing—when you cannot move with life, then you are living in the past and trying to comprehend the extraordinary thing called life. And to understand life, you have to learn every minute about it and never come to it having learned.

The life that most of us lead in society is to conform, that is, to adjust our thinking, our feeling, our ways of life to a pattern, to a particular sanction or mold of a civilized society—a society that is always moving slowly, evolving according to certain patterns. And we are trained from childhood to conform—conform to the pattern, adjust ourselves to the environment in which we live. And in this process there is never learning. We may revolt from conformity, but that revolt is never freedom. And it is only the mind that is learning, never accumulating—it is only such a mind that moves with the constant flow of life.

And society is the relationship between human beings, the interaction between human beings. It has established certain patterns to which, from childhood, we are made to conform, adjust, and in this conformity we can never be free. Society establishes a certain authority, certain patterns of behavior, of conduct, of law. It never helps man to be free; on the contrary, society makes man conform, respect, cultivate the virtues of that particular society, fit into a pattern. And society never wants him to be free; it does not educate him to be free. All religions are part of society, invented by man for his own particular security, psychologically. Religions, as they are now organized, have their dogmas, their rituals; they are ridden with authority and divisions. So religions, too, do not want man to be free—which is a fairly obvious thing.

So, the problem is, is it not, that there must be order in society. You must have order; otherwise, you cannot live—order being efficiency, order being that every citizen cooperates, does his utmost to fulfill his function without status. That is order—not what society has created, which we call order, which is status. Function gives him status; function gives him prestige, power, position. And in the battle of this competitive society, there are laws to hold the man in order.

So the problem is: There must be conformity—that is to keep to the right side of the road when you are driving—and also there must be freedom; otherwise, society has no meaning. Society does not give man freedom; it may help him to revolt—and any schoolboy can revolt! To help man to be free and understand this whole problem of conformity; to help him to conform and yet not be a slave to society; to conform to the norm, to the pattern; to adjust himself to society and yet maintain that extraordinary sense of freedom—that demands a great deal of intelligence. Man is not free, even though he has lived two million years. Unless man is free, there will be no end to sorrow, there will be no end to the anxiety, to the misery, to the appalling poverty of one's own mind and heart.

And society is not at all concerned about this freedom, through which alone man can discover for himself a new way of living—not according to a pattern, not according to a belief, not according to knowledge, but from moment to moment, flowing with life. But, if man is not free, in the deep sense of that word, not in the sense free to do what he likes—which is too simple and idiotic—but to be free from the society which has imposed on him certain conditions, which has molded his mind, then he can live for another two million years or more, and he will not be free from sorrow, from the ache of loneliness, from the bitterness of life, from all the various anxieties that he is heir to.

So, the problem is: Is it possible for man to conform and yet be free of society? Man must conform, must adjust himself: he must keep to the right side of the road for the safety of others if he is riding; he must buy a stamp to post a letter; he must pay the tax if he has money, and so on. But conformity, for most of us, is much deeper: we conform psychologically, and that is where the mischief of society begins. And as long as man is not free of society, not free of the pattern which society has established for him to follow, then he is merely moral—moral in the sense he is orderly in the social sense, but disorderly in the virtuous sense. A man who follows the morality of a particular society is immoral because that only establishes him more and more, makes him more and more a slave to the pattern; he becomes more and more respectable and, therefore, more and more mediocre.

A man who is learning is understanding, as he lives, the whole function of society, which is: to establish right relationship between man and man, to help him to cooperate, not with an idea, not with a pattern, not with authority, but to cooperate out of affection, out of love, out of intelligence. He is also understanding the heightened sensitivity of intelligence. And intelligence is only that heightened sensitivity which has nothing whatsoever to do with experience, with knowledge, because knowledge and experience dull the mind.

You know, you may pass a tree every day of your life. If you have no appreciation of the extraordinary shape of a branch, or of a leaf, or of the nakedness of the tree in the winter, or of the beauty of the sunset, or if you are not in total communion with the squalor, with the evening sunset, or with the reflection of the palm tree on the water, then, such a mind is a dull mind, however moral, however respectable, however conforming to society it may be. And such a mind can never be free. And it is only the mind that learns as it lives, every day, every minute, in the movement of life, of relationship which is action—it is only such a mind that can be free. The mind must be free—free from conflict, free from the self-contradiction that exists in man. The self-contradiction that exists in man produces everlasting conflict within himself and with his neighbor, and this conflict is called moral because this conflict helps the human being to conform to the pattern which society has established!

So conformity and desire have to be understood. Desire is unfulfilled appetite. That is what desire is—an appetite which has not been given full rein. And society says, "Hold it, suppress it, guide it, control it, sublimate it!" The religious side of society says, "Do various forms of discipline; suppress in order to find God; be a celibate; go to a monastery; do everything, but control your desires!" And, thereby one establishes within the psyche, within one's own being, this contradiction, this dual existence—desire which wants to fulfill, which is battling, boiling, longing; and on the other hand the sanction of religion, of society, which says, "You must hold, control, suppress, sublimate." So there is a contradiction, and also society says, "You must conform."

Now, what is desire? And what gives continuity to desire? Please follow this. Otherwise you will misunderstand it totally; you will say, "The speaker is encouraging appetite, asking people to indulge in their desires, in their impulses, in their longings." You will anyhow indulge, whether you listen or do not listen; you will surreptitiously, secretly, fulfill your desires in spite of your society, and therefore increase your contradiction, increase your frustration!

So we are going to learn by inquiring into this whole matter of desire. Desire means the urge to fulfill appetites of various kinds that demand action—the longing for sex, or to become a great man, the desire to possess a car, or to possess a house. We are going to go into that. What is desire? If you are asking, "What is desire?" it would be very difficult for you to answer. Desire is not desire for something. We are not talking about desire for something but about desire itself: how it arises and what gives it continuity. Do you understand? We are not talking about the fulfillment of desire in various forms, but we are talking about the nature, the meaning of desire itself, and what gives it the continuity that keeps it on endlessly. I have fulfilled there, and I have moved from one fulfillment to another fulfillment, to another demand, to another appetite, endlessly.

Sirs, may I request you not to take notes because you are not at school. You are listening, not listening to take notes. You are listening to find out for yourself as you are sitting there. To find out is to expose yourself to yourself, to find out what your desire is, how it arises, the nature of it, the meaning of it, and what gives it continuity. But if you are taking notes, you cannot listen and at the same time take notes. To listen you have to give your complete attention. If you love something, you listen—don't you? If you love your child, your wife—probably you don't love; therefore, you don't know what it is to listen—if you love somebody, if you love that tree, that bird intensely, you would listen; you would listen to the whisper, to the wind, to every movement of the leaf and the flutter of the leaf. If you love your child, you would watch all his moods, his temperament, his naughtiness, his playfulness, the joy, the curiosity, the brightness. So to learn is to love—not tomorrow; not, having taken the notes, to go back and study the notes. Love is always in the present; it is not a memory; it is not the photograph which you have in your room and which you look at occasionally—that is not love; that is the dead memory of things that have been. You can only listen endlessly. And to listen endlessly, there has to be that affection, that flame that destroys the past.

So, what is desire? You see a beautiful house or a nice car or a man in power, position; and you wish you had that house, you were that man in position, or you were riding amid applause. How does that desire arise? First, there is the visual perception—the seeing of the house. The 'you' comes much later. The seeing of the house, that is visual attraction, the attraction of a line, the beauty of a car, the color, and then that perception.

Please follow this. You are doing it, not I. I am giving words, explaining; but you are doing. We are sharing the thing together. You are not merely listening to what the speaker is saying; therefore, you are observing your own movement of thought as desire. There is no division between thought and seeing; they are one movement. Between thought and desire, there is no separate thing—which we will go into presently.

So there is the seeing, the perceiving, which creates sensation; then there is the touching; and then the desire—the desire to possess—to give to that sensation continuity. This is very simple. I see a beautiful woman or a man. Then there is the pleasure of seeing, and the pleasure demands continuity. So I think; there is thought born out of it. And the more thought thinks about that pleasure, there is continuity of that pleasure, or of that pain. Then, where there is that continuity, the 'I' comes in—I want, I don't want. This is what we all do, all day, sleeping or waking.

So, one sees how desire arises. Perception, contact, sensation; then giving to that sensation continuity, and that continuity to sensation is desire. There is nothing mysterious about desire. Now the desire becomes very complicated when there is a contradiction, not in the desire itself, but in the object through which it is going to fulfill. Right? I want to be a very rich man—that is, my desire says that I must be very rich because I see people with property, a car and all the rest of it. Desire says, "I must have, I must fulfill." And also there is a part of me which is conditioned by society and which says, "To find God, to live a noble life, to be a sannyasi, you must give that up." And so there is contradiction—which means I must conform to society through competing, through battling with my neighbor to get on the top of the heap; and also society says that to find whatever it calls "God," I must deny that. So, it tells me that, on the one hand, I must be a sannyasi—a respectable sannyasi always!—and, on the other hand, I must also be a respectable citizen, which is to compete; and competition means killing my neighbor, not physically, but by doing everything to destroy him, to get his position or go beyond it.

So, in me, there is a contradiction created by society because desire wants to fulfill itself through so many things—to be famous; to find God; to live happily; to live amidst a sense of great beauty, loveliness, and perfume, with a moment which is without the past, without regret, without anxiety; to live with a sense of great ecstasy; to live with beauty endlessly, with joy. Desire wants to fulfill itself in every direction; the objects of fulfillment are very attractive, but each object contradicts the other.

So we live, conforming, battling, fulfilling, and being frustrated. That is our life. And to find God, the so-called religious people, the saints, the popes, the monks, the nuns, the social-service people, the so-called religious people say, "You must suppress; you must sublimate; you must identify yourself with God so that desire disappears; when you see a woman, turn your back on her; don't be sensitive to anything, to life; don't hear music, don't see a tree; above all, don't see a woman!" And so that is the life of the mediocre man who is a slave to society!

Without understanding—understanding, not suppressing—desire, man will never be free of conformity or of fear. You know what happens when you suppress something? Your heart is dull! Have you seen the sannyasis, the monks, the nuns, the people who escape from life? How frigid, how hard, virtuous, saintly they are, living in tight discipline! They will talk everlastingly about love, and inwardly they are boiling; their desires never fulfilled or never understood; they are dead beings in a cloak of virtue!

What we are saying is something entirely different. Life is both challenge and response, and response means reaction. To react is to respond quickly to the beauty of a tree, to the sound of an instrument, to a lovely voice across the river; otherwise, you are dead to respond. And if that response is pleasurable, you want more; if it is painful, you want to escape. So, when you suppress, sublimate, identify the desire with something extraordinarily noble, such identification, such suppression, such control, such denial, makes the mind dull and the heart insensitive.

So, one has to find out, learn, about desire—learn, not what to do about it, not how to throttle it. And one of the most unfortunate things that has happened to this country is the innumerable saints it has had, who have said, "Suppress desire, suffocate it, destroy it." That is why you never look at a tree; that is why, to you, love is sex. You admit the squalor, the poverty, the disgrace because you are conforming to the pattern set by these saints who have never gone beyond their own conditioning.

So one must understand desire. To understand something is not an intellectual process or a verbal process. To understand something you must come to it with freshness, with an eagerness, with affection. Do you understand? If I want to understand you, I must come—not with my prejudice, not with my opinions, not with my things which I have gathered—I must come to you fresh. And to be fresh there must be a quality of deep sympathy and affection—not in some distant future, but now. Because you are burning with desire—not only to be rich, but to arrive at heaven, to come to that state of bliss. Unless one understands desire, one will always be in conflict, in frustration, in anxiety.

We see how desire arises, which is quite simple. And then we have to find out what gives continuity to desire. That is the really important question—not how desire arises. We know how desire arises. I see something beautiful, I want it. I see something ugly, painful; that reminds me of all kinds of things; I put it away. One becomes aware of the arising of desire, but one has never gone into—at least most of us have not gone into—the question of what gives it continuity and what brings, in that continuity, contradiction. If there were no contradiction—which is the battle between the good and the bad, between the pain and the pleasure, between fulfillment and frustration—if there were not this contradiction in desire and continuity in desire, if there were an understanding of that, then desire would have quite a different meaning. Then desire would become a thing of flame, would have a quality of an urgency, a beauty, a tremendous response—not a thing to be frightened of, to be destroyed, to be suffocated, to be denied.

So what gives desire continuity? You are listening to the horn of that car; it is stuck. It is making a noise, you do not like it. You wish it would stop, but your mind is there. And when that has stopped just now, you feel the relief! And what has given that irritation? What has brought about that irritation between that continuous noise and the act of listening to the speaker? What has brought about this irritation? The desire to listen quietly. You want to listen to the speaker, and that noise is irritating, interrupting. There, it is painful; you don't want it, you don't like it. But, if you see a beautiful house, a beautiful woman, or a handsome man, or a lovely tree, then the sight of that has awakened a desire, and you want that desire to continue! Please observe your own processes. You are not merely listening to the speaker. The speaker is not at all important; what is important is to understand your own desire and how it brings about conformity, contradiction, and agony—the despair of desire.

So you see desire has continuity through thought. That is, there is the perception of a house, the sensation; that sensation, thought thinks about and gives it a continuity which becomes a desire. And that desire identifies itself with the thought, which says, "It is me; that, I want." Please follow all this, step by step. It is very simple and clear. So thought gives continuity to desire. And without understanding the whole machinery of thinking, merely to suppress desire—it does not matter who tells you—is infantile, is immature.

So we have to go into that question of thought as a process of time—time as duration, time as existence, the existence of desire. Because it is desire that accumulates the pattern as memory, to which we conform. So conformity, desire, thought, and time are interrelated. Without understanding the one, you cannot possibly understand the rest. That is why we began by talking about conformity, how we conform endlessly, not only because we are so frightened to bring disorder in ourselves, but because of society which has made disorder disrespectable and so on.

So there is conformity, and there is this desire which says, "I must conform." And to that desire time gives a continuity, which is thought. So they are all extraordinarily interrelated. And if you don't understand them, you will not be able to go any further. And we have to go very much further. Because life is a movement, and to follow that movement, you must have energy—an energy which knows no conformity; an energy which has never touched conflict; an energy which is not the product of thought with all its resistances, contradictions; an energy which is not the slave of time: time, which is gradualness, " I will get it."

So unless it understands this whole movement of desire as conformity, as thought, as time, the mind cannot see itself. And it is only the free mind that is the religious mind. And it is only the religious mind that can solve all our problems—not the politicians, not the leaders, not the dictators, not any political or economical solution. It is only the religious mind that has understood this whole process, and therefore has understood conflict, that can release that energy which is spotless. And it is only that energy that can reach the highest.

December 23, 1964

Fourth Talk in Madras

If we may, we will continue with what we were talking about the other day. We were saying that unless we, as human beings, understand this whole problem of desire, there will be no order in society. We mean by "order" cooperation. And without cooperation there will be only conformity, and that conformity leads to various forms of revolt—which is not revolution. And without understanding the very complex problem of desire, there can be no freedom for man; and without freedom at every level of one's being, life becomes a series of irremediable and insoluble problems. To understand this question of desire, we ought also to understand the other complex problem of love.

For without love, as we were saying the other day, there can be no cooperation; and society that exists without cooperation must be a disintegrating society. Cooperation is one of the most difficult things—not only to understand verbally, but actually to live in a state of cooperation. We do cooperate with authority, with ideas, with a person who dominates with his ideas; therefore, cooperation is established on a basis of authority; and where there is authority, there is no freedom. To cooperate—not on the basis of a personal motive, nor out of an imperative necessity, nor for a profitable life—one must understand this question of love and desire.

We went, the other day, into the beginning of desire, how desire originates—that is, through perception, sensation, contact, and giving continuity to that sensation through constantly thinking about that particular sensation, pleasure, or pain. We went into that, and those who were here then can go into it further. We are not going to repeat it all over again because we want to go further into this matter. We see for ourselves how desire arises. Society with its saints, its religious sanctions, demands that the human being suppress these desires, control them, sublimate them, or run away from them to various forms of escapes. But when, without understanding desire, there is only mere discipline, then efficiency, order, and cooperation cease to exist.

So, we are concerned this evening with an inquiry into the ways of desire and their contradiction, and also with discipline and the question of love. We also said the other day when we met that we would go into the mechanism of thinking and of time. Because all these are related—desire, love, thought, and time. And without understanding them, one cannot follow or live in the whole field of thought, time, love, and desire.

Understanding is not mere agreeing intellectually, verbally. Understanding is the comprehension and the cognition of the words, their meaning—not only intellectually, but also with a great deal of feeling, not only mentally, but neurologically with your nerves, with your eyes, with your smell. Understanding can only take place when there is a total comprehension with all your being. Understanding is not partial, not fragmentary. "I understand what you are saying, intellectually"—such a statement has no meaning whatsoever; it means merely that I understand the words you are using; because you and I both speak English, we understand the meaning of those words. But understanding is more profound, more real, than the mere understanding of words. When we say, "we understand," it means a total comprehension and, therefore, action.

To understand is to act, not "to understand and then to act"—then understanding merely remains as an idea, which is not understanding. The idea is separate from action. And then the whole problem arises: how to bring action to conform, or bring it in approximation, to the idea. So there is always a contradiction if you do not understand this usage of words, the creation of ideas out of those words, the accepting or the rejecting of those ideas, and if you accept the ideas and try to conform, or approximate your action to those ideas—all these processes are not a state of understanding. Understanding is a state of comprehending totally, with all one's being, nervously, emotionally, intellectually, with feeling, with everything that one has. And when there is such understanding, there is action.

Life is action. These two are not separate. Life is not an idea carried out in action, just as you cannot have love as an idea. Love cannot be cultivated; it cannot be nurtured, produced; either there is love or there is not. Similarly, there is understanding, or there is no understanding. To understand something one has to listen, and listening is an art. To listen to something implies that you are giving complete attention, not only to what the speaker is saying, but also to those crows, to the sunset, to the clouds, to the breeze on the leaves, to the various colors that are here, so that your whole neurological system as well as the cells of the brain comprehend totally. Out of that total comprehension alone is there action which does not bring about contradiction and, therefore, conflict and endless pain and misery. So in that sense we are using the word *understanding.*

Now, we are trying to understand the way of desire—that is, to learn about it, not to suppress it, not to deny it, not to sublimate it. To understand something, you must give attention to it, you must learn about it, you must investigate it, you must explore it, you must go into it—which does not mean that you yield, or restrain yourself. When you understand it, you learn about it.

We said the other day that desire is the way of man. It exists in each one of us—it must exist; it is part of life. We have shown how desire arises. And people throughout the world, especially those who are concerned with religious matters, have been taught to suppress desire, to be without desire—which is absolutely impossible; one is without desire only when one is dead! But to understand desire requires a great deal of attention, a great deal of patience, inquiry.

Desire means, does it not, an unfulfilled appetite. Please, if I may point out, you are not merely hearing a talk, but you are partaking in it, sharing it. You are as active as the speaker; you are not merely hearing a few words or a few ideas, a few sentences, and then agreeing with them or disagreeing with them and then going away. We are together sharing in the investigation of the question of desire. And to investigate you must be free to find out. It does not mean that you agree or disagree. You do not say, "We have been told by the great saints—whoever those people are—that we must suppress it, we must control it, we must deny it, we must find ways of sublimating it"; that way you do not inquire, you do not learn, you do not find out. To find out, there must be freedom from traditions, from what people have said—which does not mean that you must indulge in desire.

So we are going to investigate, to find out, the ways of desire. And in the understanding of desire comes discipline—not imposed, not the way of conformity, suppression; but, in the very process of understanding desire, there comes discipline. As we said, desire is unfulfilled appetite, wish, longing. And either we yield to that longing, to that desire, or we suppress it because society says that we must suppress it, because religious organizations say that we must transmute it, and so on. And in this process there is a constant battle between the human being who is trying to understand desire or is caught in desire, and society which has established certain norms and the religious organizations with their beliefs that say that you must conform to the pattern.

Desire is not in contradiction with itself. That is the first thing we have to understand: desire is not in contradiction with itself. Desire is in contradiction with the objects of its fulfillment. You understand? I fulfill my desire in one direction; then later I want to fulfill it in another direction; the two directions, or the two states, are contrary to each other. I want to be a very rich man, and also I want to lead a saintly life—not a saintly life, but a religious life. It is one of the easiest things in the world to be a saint! All that you have to do is to conform to a pattern which is recognized by society: put on a loincloth, lead a very so-called or outwardly simple life of exhibition, showing off that you are really simple. And society says, "What a marvelous human being you are!" That is the outward show of simplicity; inwardly, you are boiling, you are tormented, you are tortured by your passions, ambitions, lust, greed, identifications with a particular society. So we are not concerned with what kind of life a saint leads inwardly; all we are concerned with is that he shall conform to the pattern of a saint, which is to be this and that. So it is comparatively easy to be a saint. But it is much more difficult, and it requires tremendous intelligence, understanding, to go into this question of desire and to be free from the conflict which the objects of desire create. To understand the whole process of desire, you need intelligence.

Intelligence is not the accumulation of experience and knowledge, but intelligence is the highest form of sensitivity. To be sensitive to everything, to the birds, to the squalor, to the poverty, to the beauty of a tree, to the beauty of a face, to the sunset, to the colors, to the reflections, to the movement of a leaf, to a bird on a wing, to the smile of a child, to tears, to laughter, to the pain, the agony, the anguish, the misery of a human being—to be totally sensitive to all that means to be intelligent. And you cannot be intelligent if you merely suppress or indulge. You can only be sensitive when there is understanding.

We have desire, which is really a response to an appetite. I want something, and I respond. This response depends upon the intensity of my feeling. If the feeling is intense, if the emotion is urgent, then there is an almost immediate fulfillment, either in thought or in action. Please, you have to follow this fairly clearly because we are going into the question of time, into the question of thought and love; and you have to follow this, step by step, not authoritatively. We are using the word *follow* in the sense of following what is being said. So far as we are concerned, there is no authority. Authority is contrary to every state of sensitivity, and a religious mind has no authority. A religious mind is a mind that is constantly in a state of learning and therefore sensitive. And learning ceases when there is authority. It does not matter who it is—the authority of a government, the authority of your priest, the authority of your guru or a Master—authority prevents your learning. Authority only makes you conform through fear. And a mind that is frightened at any level ceases to be a religious mind. As far as we are concerned, there is no authority.

Desire, which is the response of a sensation which has been given continuity by thought, seeks fulfillment; and in the various forms of fulfillment there is contradiction. And out of that contradiction there is conflict, and where there is conflict, there is effort. So desire breeds effort if we do not understand the whole process of desire.

What is desire and how does that desire continue? We see how desire arises—perception, seeing, contact, sensation. Now, what gives continuity to desire? That is the problem; that is where we left off the other day. Surely, thought gives continuity to desire. That is, I like something; it gives me great pleasure to look at the sunset, or to look at a beautiful face, or to see a man in position, status, power, money, position, and all the rest of it. It gives me pleasure to be in that man's position, and I think about that pleasure, whether that pleasure be a sensual pleasure or a subjective pleasure, or a pleasure caused by outward objects. I think about it. I like your face. You have a nice smile. And your smile, your face is attractive. I like it, I think about it. The more I think about it, the more I give strength to the desire which seeks fulfillment with that person, or through that idea, or through that object.

So thought gives continuity to desire. If there were no continuity to desire, there would be no fulfillment. It would arise and go away. It would come as a reaction—and you must have reaction; otherwise, you are a dead human being. It would come as a reaction, and there would be no continuity to that reaction if there were no continuity of thought. You observe it in your own life.

You have pleasure, sexual or ordinary pleasure; you think about it; you create, in your mind, images, symbols, words. And the more you think about it, the greater is the intensity of that pleasure. And that intensity demands fulfillment. And in that fulfillment there is a contradiction because you also want to fulfill in other directions. So, where there is fulfillment of desire, there is contradiction. Hence to escape from contradiction, from the pain of conflict, you say that you must suppress desire. But what is important is not to suppress desire, nor to shape it, nor to sublimate it, but to understand it—to understand what gives it substance, what gives it the intensity, what gives it the urgency. If that can be understood, then desire has quite a different significance.

You observe yourself: when you have a pleasure, you think about it. When you have pain, you also think about it. The thinking about it gives it vitality, gives it strength, gives it continuity. So, one has to go into the question of thinking if one would understand desire.

What is thinking? This is not an academic question. I am asking you a question: What is thinking? There is a challenge: What is thinking? And you are waiting for a response, are you not? You are waiting for a response from the speaker. You want to be told. If he does not tell it, you are trying to find out from your own knowledge, or from the knowledge of what others have given to you; or you are looking, searching in your memory, to find out what is thinking. So, when a challenge is given to you, your memory responds. Please follow this carefully, because unless you go into this very carefully, step by step, you will miss the whole sequence of what is going to be said. Life is a challenge; it is a series of continuous challenges. Life is a movement, constantly changing, constantly moving, never the same; and that is the beauty of life. It is living, not dead; and therefore it is always giving us a challenge every minute, consciously or unconsciously, whether we are aware of it or not. And when there is a challenge, we respond according to our conditioning, according to our memory, and our memory responds. In this process of challenge and response, the response is immediate, or after an interval of time; and in the interval of time there is the process of thinking.

What is thinking? Probably most of you have not thought about it at all, and you are waiting to be told! When you are told, you either agree or disagree, or your memory says, "That is not enough, that is only part of it; there must be much more to this mechanism of thought." So we are going to go into it. Where there is a challenge and a response, if the response is immediate, there is no process of thinking. If you are asked your name, you answer very quickly; because you are very familiar with your name, you reply immediately. You may have thought about it before, but the immediate response is instant. But if you are asked a much more complicated question, you take time, and there is a time interval between that challenge and response. In that time interval the mind is looking for an answer, searching, asking, waiting, questioning. That interval is what we call thinking. And that thinking depends on your race, on your family, the knowledge, the memory, the imprint of time, your experiences, the pain, the sorrow, the innumerable pressures and the agonies of life—that is the background, and from the background you respond. And so the response to the challenge is always inadequate. I hope I am making myself clear. And that inadequacy to a response creates contradiction.

So one has to understand not only the mechanism of thinking but also the storing up of knowledge as a means of response to a challenge which is always new. So you respond always to something new with the old, with your tradition if you are a Hindu; if you are a Christian, with your tradition; if you are a scientist, with your particular knowledge, and so on. Your response is never total, it is always fragmentary; and therefore there is a contradiction, a conflict, a pain, or a pleasure which you want to continue—which brings again conflict. So we live in this process: challenge, inadequate response, contradiction, conflict, pain or pleasure, and the demand for the pain to cease and the pleasure to continue. That is the cycle of our life.

If you proceed further into this question of thinking, you come to a state of mind when you actually say, "I don't know." You understand? That is the difference between the electronic computer and the human mind. The human mind can say, "I don't know," and it means "I don't know"; there is no pretense, there is no waiting for an answer. "I don't know" is a most extraordinary state of mind, if you could really understand that state. Because most of us have so much knowledge about everything! We know about God because we have been told for five thousand, seven thousand, or two million years. We are burdened with knowledge, with our experience—which is the past. We know about what we call God, love, sex, about almost everything that the human mind has invented or thought about! And we are always searching to find more; that is, adding more to our knowledge, and we never say, "I don't know." And is it not necessary always to say, "I don't know," so that the mind is always learning, is always fresh, innocent, young? It is only a young mind that says, "I don't know," and means "I don't know"—not waiting to be informed. The moment you know, it has already become the old. But a mind that is saying to itself "I don't know" all the time is not doubting. When you doubt, you are already expecting a confirmation or a denial. But when you say, "I don't know," your mind is already young, fresh, eager, ready to find out.

That is the way of thought. Thought exists only in time. We mean by time the psychological state of postponement, the psychological idea of progress, of evolution, of reaching a height, of accumulating and getting rid of a distance between *what is* and 'what should be', which is all a time interval in space. Please follow all this a little bit. A mind that has no space is a dead mind. The mind must have space, which is emptiness. And it is only in that space that a new state can come into being; it is only in that space that a mutation, a complete revolution, can take place.

We need a revolution in this world, a psychological revolution—not an economic or a social revolution, but a really deep religious revolution. Such a revolution, such a mutation, cannot take place if the mind is not totally empty, if there is no space in the mind. And the understanding of desire, the comprehension of time, brings about, without seeking, this extraordinary space. Space is not created by an object in the space. That tree, which is the object, creates space; because of that tree, there is space round it. We only know space in relation to the object and the nonobject. And a man who is caught in the space which an object creates is everlastingly a slave. It is only the mind that has space without object that is a free mind.

Now, we human beings who have lived for over two million years, according to anthropologists, have developed, progressed, evolved through time. It has taken us two million years to be what we are—two million years from the animal to the human being—and we say, "We will have more time, another two million years or more, to progress, to evolve. In those two million years we have suffered, we have lived in tremendous anxiety, with an appalling loneliness." You know what loneliness is? Most of us know what anxiety is. Most of us know what sorrow is. Most of us are familiar with pain, physical and otherwise. Most of us know the agony of uncertainty and the pain, the corruption, the disgust, the impurities of one's own thinking and life. But very few of us know that pain, the agony of complete loneliness. Man has lived with his loneliness for two million years, not knowing, escaping from it when he knows it, and inventing gods, heavens, hells, every form of fulfillment to escape from this extraordinary, intense sense of complete isolation, complete loneliness.

We have lived for two million years, and we have invented time because we are the result of time. Our brain cells, our whole structure, the organism, the brain, everything is the result of time—time being the idea: I will become; I will be; I will achieve; I will progress; I will change, from now until tomorrow, from now until the next second. That is what we mean by time. We are not talking of time as chronological time by the watch; we are talking of time as of a mind that thinks in the field of gradualness—that is an invention. Chronologically there is tomorrow by the watch; otherwise, there is no tomorrow; we have invented tomorrow. Actually when you go into it, you will see it is thought that has created tomorrow. Tomorrow is going to be uncertain, tomorrow you have to go to the office, tomorrow you have to do certain things—you are thinking about it today. Thought actually creates time as tomorrow, and so we have time. And we use time as a means of change. "I am angry, ugly, savage; but I will become something else"—that is using time as a means to become, so there is always a postponement, there is always an avoidance.

Most human beings are violent. They have never been gentle. They do not know what love is. They know what sex is, what desire is. They know the ways of agony. And being caught in agony, they say, "I must have time to get over it; I must have tomorrow, or the next life; or, I will get rid of it gradually." So thought invents time; thought is time. And a man who understands this process of desire, thought, and time is a human being who lives completely in the present. He has no time as a means of achieving.

The moment you have time, what actually takes place? You are not confronting, you are not confronted with, the actual, the factual challenge, the immediate. You act in the immediate only when you are in pain or in intense pleasure. When you are intensely sexual, or when you have intense pain, you have to act. And most of us are incapable of looking at facts as they are, seeing things as they are, the *what is*. The *what is* is the fact, and we come to that with various opinions, ideas, judgments. That is, with the past we come to the fact and therefore create contradiction or the lack of understanding of that fact.

So a mind is free only when it is capable of meeting the fact, the *what is*, meeting poverty, not some supreme challenge—there is no supreme challenge. Life is a challenge every minute—meeting poverty; meeting your boss in your office; meeting your wife, the children; meeting the bus conductor, the squalor, the beauty of a sunset; your own anger, jealousy, stupidity—which are all facts. What matters is how you meet the fact, not what you think about it, not what you should do about it. When you meet the fact, without any opinion, judgment, evaluation, then you are living completely in the present. Then for such a mind there is no time, and therefore it can act. Because the fact alone has the urgency of action—not your opinions, desires, and ideals.

Look, sirs, you have been brought up, most unfortunately, on ideals. Ideals are just words. They have no meaning whatsoever, they have no substance. They are just the barren children of a vain, thoughtless mind! You have been brought up on the ideal of nonviolence. You go round preaching nonviolence all over the world. Nonviolence is the ideal. But the fact is that you are violent in your gesture, in the way you talk to your superior or your inferior. Please listen to yourself. I am just pointing it out. You are violent—violent in your gesture, in your thought, in your feeling, in your action. Why can't you look at that violence? Why need you have an ideal of nonviolence? The fact is you are violent, and the ideal is nonfactual, so you create a contradiction in yourself and therefore prevent yourself from looking at the fact of violence. When you look at a fact, you can deal with it: you will say you are violent and accept it. You accept it and say, "I am violent and I will not be a hypocrite"; or you will say, "You are violent and enjoy it"; or you will look at it without the ideal. You can only look at an object or a fact or *what is* when there is no ideal, no opinion, no judgment—it is so. Then the fact brings about an intensity of action in the immediate. It is only when you have ideas about a fact that you postpone action. When you realize factually that you are violent, then you can look at it, you can go into it. Then you can learn all about it, the nature of violence, whether it is possible to be free or not—not as an idea, but actually.

So a religious mind has no ideals, no example, no authority, because the fact is the only thing that matters, and that fact demands urgency of action. You cannot but act immediately, without an idea, only when the mind has understood the whole question of desire, thinking, time, which prevents the mind from looking at the fact. You do it, sirs. Take your greed, take your anger, take what you like, your sexual appetite—it does not matter what it is. Look at it—not with condemnation, judgment, evaluation; not saying it is right or wrong. You know all the intellectual stuff that men invent to avoid the fact. Take the poverty in this country. That is a fact. And being caught in nationalism is going to prevent that fact from being carried out. We will discuss it some other time.

So a mind that is free from time, which is thought, which is desire, is a mind that is aware of love. For most of us love is sexual. Observe it in yourself. For most of us love is jealousy. For most of us love is a contradiction of hate and love. We really do not know what love is. We know sympathy, pity, perhaps a little generosity when it does not cost too much. Don't laugh! You are facing all this—which is yourself. You cannot laugh. If you can laugh at yourself, then it will have some meaning. But don't just laugh at facts—which means you are avoiding. We know what love is only in terms of contradiction, pain and pleasure, agony and the jealousy—the pain, the brutality of jealousy, the violence of jealousy. But you do not know what love is because you do not know what beauty is. If you do not know what beauty is, you will never know what love is—not the beauty of a woman or a man, not sex, but beauty.

You have been trained to deny beauty because beauty has always been associated with pleasure—pleasure being the man or the woman. And people have told you, especially the saints, that if you would find God, you must have no woman, no pleasure; and therefore you deny. By denying beauty you have denied also love. Beauty is not pleasure; beauty is in everything. Sirs, watch yourselves; watch the leaf there. Watch the beauty of the sunset, the beauty of the earth, the hill, the curve of a hill, the flowing water; watch the beauty of a fine, refined mind, the good mind, the beauty of a face, the beauty of a smile. You have denied all that because you have associated beauty with pleasure, and pleasure with sex and so-called love.

Beauty is not that at all. Beauty is not something merely related to pleasure. To understand beauty one must have an extraordinarily simple mind—that is, a mind unclouded by thought, that can look at things as they are, that can see the sunset with all the color, loveliness, and light, that can look at it simply, without verbalization, and be in contact, in communion with it without the word, without the gesture, without the memory, so that there is not "you" and the object which "you" are looking at.

That extraordinary communion without the object, without the thinker and the thought and the object and experience, that sense of immense space—that is beauty.

And that is also love. Without love, do what you will—you may do social work, social reforms, parliamentary government, you may marry, have children—you will find no answer to any problem in life. With love you can do what you will. With love there is virtue and there is humility.

December 27, 1964

Fifth Talk in Madras

It seems to me that one of our great difficulties is not merely that caused by words alone. Words are necessary to communicate, but communication does not merely depend on words. And however much one may be intellectual and precise in the usage of words, we cannot live by words because we have also feelings, strong emotions, violent passions, hatred, sympathy, tenderness, affection. And we seem to live at different levels of our being. If we are so-called intellectuals, we live with words, ideas, and are able to argue cleverly, eruditely. If we are emotional, we are almost on the verge of tears about everything. And the intellectual as well as the emotional are burning inside with various problems—self-created, imposed by environmental conditioning, and so on.

Our life is a torture; we try to cover it up by words, by feelings, by escapes, by every form of so-called religious as well as intellectual acts. But these do not cover our inward battle, our inward frustration, our loneliness, deep sorrows, and the sense of being completely isolated. We want to be secure, not only physically, but emotionally. We want companionship. We want somebody on whom we can rely completely, in whom we have complete trust and faith—a sense of intimate, endless contact with another human being. Not only do we seek security in another human being through relationship, but also we want security in our ideas, in our beliefs, in the way of our life. We do not want to be wrong, we want to tread the right path, whatever that may mean. We look to someone to tell us what to do. We have authority and an infinite love of tradition.

And we have to live with all this—at the intellectual level, at the emotional level, at the physical level, and at the psychological level—with loneliness, emptiness, a sense of despair. We have to live with ill-health and infinite boredom with life, with going to the office every day of our life, for the next forty or fifty years. Or one has been in the office for forty years doing the same thing over and over again, and at the end of one's life there is nothing left, one is burned out. Or one begins life with certain convictions, certain formulas, and one has great intentions; but the life about one gradually squeezes out all the energy, the vitality, the clarity, the clear perception, and one is left with oneself—empty, lonely, in despair, and in sorrow.

This is our actual everyday life. And realizing that, we try to find something transcendental, beyond, faraway, which has nothing whatever to do with our daily life. We can quote the Upanishads, the Gita, the Bible, seers, saints, and so on, away from this daily misery, horror, brutality. The wider the gap, the greater is the neurosis. And most religious people are neurotic because their life is here, and they try to have ideals, incense sticks; they go to churches, temples, rituals—anything to escape from this daily torture, daily travail of life. This is a fact. Perhaps I am not describing it too clearly, but that is our life. And we have to change here, in our daily life, in our outlook, in our activities, in our ways of thought, feeling; for this is reality, not the other. The other is merely the idea of someone who said something or other, many centuries ago; and it is no good repeating what they say, or what they said, or what the modern philosophers say, or trying to conform to modern philosophy, or to go back ten thousand years and revive the dead past which we call, unfortunately, culture.

Culture is something that grows, nourishes, moves—a thing that is nourished, functions, grows; then it becomes a dead thing. But apparently, in this country, we are very fond of this dying culture; we try to revive it through dance, through song, through music, through the temples, through various creeds; but it does not work. When it does not work, we do not abandon it, we do not come to reality and see if we cannot transform the reality that is the living, and bring about a simplicity which is the essence of harmony. We are incapable, so we look, we search, we want to find somebody to tell us what to do, and we put our faith in those people. Faith and trust have no value. You may trust a doctor because he has experience. But a theory based on another man's experience in matters of the psyche or of an inward life has no meaning at all, and apparently we cannot let that go. We have to let it go completely because we have to stand alone. And that is one of the greatest fears we have—fear being the feeling of uncertainty, the feeling of danger, the apprehension of something we do not know.

So, fear begins with the savage and with the so-called educated man, highly intellectual, verbal, capable of great efficiency and capacity. Fear is there. And apparently man who has lived for two million years cannot get rid of this fear. And I think that is one of the major problems of our existence: whether it is possible to be free of fear. Now somebody says you must be free of fear and gives you a system how to be free of fear. But one has actually to come to the realization of one's own fear, be aware of one's own fear and go into it, come into direct contact with it, be in intimate communion with it, understand it, and thereby be free of it. If the mind is afraid, it is a dead mind. You know this, you have seen this in your own life. You must have seen this: if you are afraid of something, it haunts you. You think about it, you build resistances against it; you are always watching, noticing, aggressively giving importance to the intellect or to the emotions, trying to run away with those, but never coming into contact with fear.

If you have fear of physical pain, you do something about it. Or if the pain is not too great, you put up with it. You do not make a lot of dance or song about it. You put up with it. And putting up with it is to see that it does not distort your thinking, your psyche, your affection, your forward movement—which is also very difficult because we live on our nerves, and there is the impact of pain. We want to be healthy, and perhaps we cannot be healthy. If we can, so much the better. If we cannot, there is the dread of the pain, that it might return, that it might continue. So we live in the dark corner of that fear which distorts our thinking.

There is the fear of not being secure, emotionally, psychologically, inwardly. There is the fear of not having somebody to talk to, to open your heart to, with whom to commune as though with yourself, to whom to talk whenever you want to rely on that person, to feel that he will never misunderstand anything you say, that he will know when you are angry, when you are flattering, when you do not mean what you say, so that you feel that he and you are really one with great affection, with great sensitivity. And if you find that person, you hold on to him in a deadly grip. You know very well that one day that person may turn away, may die, may lose himself in other fancies, in other people, in other illusions; so you hold when you can. And that also breeds fear because in that person you put all your faith, all your affection; and that person is like you and me, he moves away from you, he looks at somebody else, and then begins the the hate, the venom of relationship.

So we build a society in which marriage becomes most sacred. You cannot break it, you hold it tight by law, but modern pressures are breaking that law. We want permanency in that relationship, and we never realize that there is no permanency in anything. So fear darkens our days. Please I am not describing something fantastic; you do not have to conjure this up, imagining this—which is our actual daily life.

So, we seek security, physically—having a house, property, the name, the position, the status; and we push anybody that comes near it, legally, morally, religiously. And also we want security in relationship, knowing fully well, deep down, that there is no permanency in relationship. We can get used to a relationship. I can get used to my wife, to her insults, to her praise, to her nagging, to sleeping with her. I can get used to it, and that usage, that habit becomes my security, and nothing must happen to that habit. So that again breeds fear. And from fear there is sorrow. There is fear not only physically, inwardly, emotionally, but there is the fear of wanting to fulfill, wanting to do something great, to be famous, to meet a great challenge and react fully to that challenge, knowing inwardly that you are a very petty, little human being with a small mind, with an egocentric activity, and wanting to cover all that up. That also breeds fear—the desire to fulfill: sitting on a platform, talking to a big audience, getting a kick out of it; and when the audience does not come, one feels lost.

We also want to be happy. Somewhere deep down, somewhere in some heaven, we want to be happy, rested, quiet, serene, undisturbed. So we invent a heaven. Wherever we go, whatever we do, fear and sorrow pursue us, and there seems to be no end to this. We don't seem to be able to meet it with energy, capacity, efficiency, to move beyond that. And of course, there is the final fear and sorrow of death.

Death, the end of life, physical existence coming to an end—that is all we are concerned with; that is what we call death. There are so many other forms of death. A person who lives thirty or forty years, endlessly in conflict with himself and society—that is also death. To live for some years in a particular state—that is also death. There is that death of living a monotonous, stupid existence without much meaning. And that not having much meaning, we invent a purpose in life, a goal, a spiritual beauty, perception; and again there is this battle going on with sorrow, never reaching that goal because we cannot.

There are many forms of death, not merely of the physical form. A mind that lives in a narrow groove, never moving out of it, being a prisoner to ideas, to opinions, to what people will say, living according to a narrow code—which is really an unethical code of relationship with the world—that is also death. And also there is the sorrow of this extraordinary sense of loneliness. I do not know if you have ever felt this deep, apparently unending loneliness of life, of one's being.

We are going to talk, this evening, about all this and whether it is possible for you and me, for anybody, to face fear and to be rid of it. If you are not free of fear, however clever, however sympathetic you are, you are living in darkness. You watch yourself some day. When fear comes upon you unexpectedly, you are paralyzed; the greater the fear, the greater is the tension, the greater is the suffocation. And you do not know how to meet it. You never come directly in communion with it, in contact with it—as you come in contact with your food, with your sexual desires, when there is an action, an intimate activity going on. Apparently we never come into contact with this fear.

Fear does not exist by itself. It is in relation to things—to darkness; to what the neighbor says; to doing something wrong; to losing your job; the wife or the husband looking away to another; the fear of frustration; a woman who has never had a child; or a woman who has not married and does not know all that side of life; and the man, bitter, aggressive, vain, arrogant because he is very clever with his mind, with his logic.

The man who is afraid lives in darkness. It is very simple to find the cause of fear. I am afraid of my neighbor because I depend upon his good word; he might say something against me, and I might lose my job, or I cannot marry off my daughter, so I am afraid. So, I depend; I know the cause very well.

It is not so very difficult to find out the cause of fear—conscious or unconscious fear. That is very simple; if one has a fairly attentive mind, one can go into it immediately. But the discovery of the cause does not free the mind of fear; the fear is still there. Please listen to this a little bit. The mere analysis of the cause of fear does not seem to wash away fear. This is a fact; you can watch it.

One knows the cause, but one is still fearful. So the mere analysis of the cause, however deep, however intricate, however deeply analytical the discovery of that cause—the mere understanding of the cause does not free the mind, or the being, from fear. The mere uncovering of the fact does not get rid of fear. You have to come into contact with that fear. And that is the greatest difficulty—to come directly into contact with it.

And we never come into contact, directly, with almost anything, except with food and perhaps with sex. We never see the tree as tree—pure perception. We have ideas, thoughts, images—about the biological structure, the nature of that tree, and so on. And to come directly into contact is not to knock your head against the tree but to be alive to nature, to beauty, to the touch, to the smell, to the fine limb, to the leaf and the flower and the breeze among the leaves—then you are in contact. But we are never in contact with fear, and we do not know what it actually means. We have never touched it, we have never directly come into contact because we are already afraid to come into contact with fear. Please listen.

We have never come into contact with fear because there is already the fear of what it might lead to, of what might happen. If I do not really care what my neighbor says about me, I may lose my job or I may not. But my thought says, "Be careful. Don't say anything. Be dishonest, be clever, be cunning. But don't say anything against the neighbor because he is going to hurt you." So thought precedes fear, thought protects fear; and, therefore, there is never a direct contact with it. That is the first thing.

The word *fear* means apprehension, warning of danger, calamity, the loss of the good and the happening of evil. The word is not the fear itself, surely. But to us the word—the symbol, the idea—has become very important, and that word prevents us from coming into contact with the thing itself. That is fairly simple. We live by words; for us, what is important is the word, the analysis of the word, the clever usage of the word; see all the fuss we make about words. After all, what are the Upanishads, the Gita? They are just words; you don't throw them out! We use words and hope through the word to get into contact with the thing. But the word will never put us into contact with anything. We have lived not only by the word but through feeling, through temperament, through affection, through beauty, through perception: seeing the cloud, seeing the sunset. The word *sunset* is not that thing, that light, that color, that shape of the cloud, the light in the cloud. So one has to understand that the word prevents the contact. When you say, "I love somebody," you hold a hand, you kiss, you do all kinds of things. The word is not the fact.

So the word fear engenders fear. One has to find out whether the word has created fear, and whether the mind can be free of the word and come into contact with fear. I do not know if you have observed a bird, a spider, or an animal which does not think that you are watching it. Then you see every movement, you see all the design on the skin, you see every movement of the leg, you see everything. But if you have ideas about that animal or that insect, you have already lost perception, you are not seeing. So one has to come directly into contact with fear, and that is one of the most difficult things to do—that is, to look at fear nonverbally, without thought. Because thought creates fear: "My neighbor is going to make mischief,"—this thought has already bred fear in me. And thought which discovers the cause will not get rid of the fear. What brings an end to fear is coming directly into contact with it, and you cannot come into contact with it if you are running away. You must live with it. You must know all about it, you must watch it endlessly—watching, watching, watching, never running away, never putting up defenses against it, never trying to become courageous. A man who is trying to be courageous when he is frightened—he is still frightened! Fear is there! So you have to watch it as you watch a spider on the window of an evening—how it builds the web, so efficiently, so beautifully, so symmetrically. In the same way, just watch your fear: that means a mind that can look without distortion—not trying to get out of it, which is a distortion, but just to look with clarity. And there is no clarity if you are trying to run away from fear, if you are trying to use the word to cover it, if you are trying to go beyond it. You have just to watch it, to observe, to perceive every movement throughout the day, how fear expresses itself. Then the next time fear arises for various reasons, you can meet it; there is no verbal camouflage, you meet it. Therefore you are beginning to learn to meet fear. And when you have realized that thought has created fear, you put aside the thought which creates fear, and therefore you put aside also the time interval between now and tomorrow when the neighbor will say something; so you meet fear.

Fear also shows itself as the desire to be secure. One must be secure physically—must have bread, clothes, and shelter: that is obvious. Otherwise you cannot think or feel promptly. You must have physical security. The vast majority in the East have not that physical security. But it is the function of the educated, cultured man to solve this problem. Not the repetitive man who goes back ten thousand years and repeats some silly stuff, but the educated man, the man who is aware of the world situation, who is sensitive, who wants to solve it, who is eager to solve this dreadful problem of poverty—it is only that man that can solve this, it is only that man that is not afraid, and knows how to meet the situation.

There is the desire for security. And one can understand this desire to be secure when you meet a wild animal, a snake; or you watch when you cross the road. But there is no other form of security. Really, if you look at it, there is no other form. You would like to have security with your wife, children, neighbor, your relations—if you have relations—but you don't have it. You may have your mother, you may have your father, but you are not related, you are completely isolated—we will go into that. There is no security, psychological security, at any time, at any level, with anybody—this is the most difficult thing to realize. There is no psychological security with another because he is a human being, and so are you; he is free, and so are you. But we want security in our relationships, through marriage, through vows—you know the tricks we play upon ourselves and upon others. This is an obvious fact; it does not need great analysis.

We never come into contact with this insecurity. We are afraid of being completely insecure. It requires a great deal of intelligence to understand that insecurity. When one feels completely insecure, one runs away. Or not finding security in anything, one becomes unbalanced, ready to commit suicide, to go to a mental hospital, or one becomes a most devout religious person—which are all the same, forms of imbalance. To realize—not intellectually, not verbally, not as a determined, willed attitude—the fact that there is no security requires an extraordinarily simple, clear, harmonious living.

And this—not finding security—produces sorrow. You know, man has lived with sorrow for so long. You know what sorrow is—the loss of someone whom you love; the loss of prestige, position; never having a position, a status in the world, and everybody else having it; never being beautiful in face, or in gesture, or in word; never seeing the beauty of the sunset, the cloud; never feeling the wind, the night air on your face. We are not sensitive, and so we live with this, pursuing sorrow. And we never come into contact with it. We have ideas that it is past karma, that it is the result of this and the result of that. You know, a man who talks about karma is a most ignorant man. Because every cause can be changed immediately; every cause and the effect of that cause can be shattered. To keep on saying, "This is my misfortune; I did this in the past; therefore, I am this"—that is too childish! Because cause and effect are closely related together; what was the cause becomes the effect, and what was the effect becomes the cause; and that can be broken. And to break with it, you must come into contact with it, and not just live in words.

The ending of sorrow is possible. Don't say, "Have you finished with sorrow?" That is not important. It does not matter who has, or who has not. What matters is that you are in sorrow. For whatever reason, for whatever cause, the misery, misfortune, anxiety, despair you are in—you are that. To find out whether you can end it is more important than to find out whether somebody else has ended it. If I say yes, it is not important; if I say no, it has no importance. What has importance is your life, how you live. And there is also the sorrow deep down—not of the race only, of the family, but of man who has lived two million years of endless sorrow and agony and despair.

And there is the sorrow of loneliness. I do not know if you have ever been lonely: when you suddenly realize that you have no relationship with anybody—not an intellectual realization but a factual realization, a thing that is as concrete as this microphone—and you are completely isolated. Every form of thought and emotion is blocked; you cannot turn anywhere; there is nobody to turn to; the gods, the angels, have all gone beyond the clouds and, as the clouds vanish, they have also vanished; you are completely lonely—I will not use the word *alone.*

Alone has quite a different meaning; alone has beauty. To be alone means something entirely different. And you must be alone. When man frees himself from the social structure of greed, envy, ambition, arrogance, achievement, status—when he frees himself from those, then he is completely alone. That is quite a different thing. Then there is great beauty, the feeling of great energy.

But loneliness is not that. Loneliness is this complete sense of being isolated from everything. I do not know if you have felt it. The more you are aware, the more you are questioning, looking, asking, demanding, the more you are aware of it: deep down in your consciousness, at all the levels, you feel completely cut off. And that is one of the great sorrows: not being able to go beyond it, and being caught in that tremendous feeling of loneliness with its great energy. It has got vitality, a drive, an insistence, an ugliness; and we escape from it in every form. Either we are terribly clever, write books about that loneliness, and push aside that loneliness, or we run away, amuse ourselves, and never touch it. And it remains there, hidden, but like a cancerous wound; it is there, waiting. One has to come into contact with it, not verbally, but actually.

And this loneliness is a form of death. As we said, there is dying not only when life comes to an end but when there is no answer, there is no way out. That is also a form of death: being in the prison of your own self-centered activity, endlessly. When you are caught in your own thoughts, in your own agony, in your own superstitions, in your deadly, daily routine of habit and thoughtlessness, that is also death—not just the ending of the body.

And how to end it also one must find out. Not that there is reincarnation: I shall be born next life. Who cares, my friend, whether you are born next life or not? Don't you know what life is, this life? The misery, the despair, the anxiety, the little pleasures, the little affection, the sexual appetites, the confusion, the endless battle, the conflict—that is your daily life. And you say, "I will take that life and carry it over to the next life," and you are waiting to die. You believe all that, so you invent the psychological evolution of the soul: slowly, endlessly, gradually, you will get rid of sorrow, pain, travail, anxiety. You invent time to get rid of sorrow, or you worship sorrow in a church! And one realizes you have to meet death, you have to come into contact with it, as you come into contact with that tree, the sunset, the beauty of a face, with squalor and the tawdriness and the shoddiness of the human mind. You have to come into contact with death—not the ending of the body only, the mechanism wearing itself out; that can be understood. The organism can be prolonged; the scientists are investigating into whether it cannot be prolonged for another fifty years. We will prolong it for another fifty years or more—the same self-centered and brutal activities: ambition, competition; seeking status, position, power, greed, envy. But we never come into contact with death.

Do you know what it means to come into contact with death, to die without argument? Because death, when it comes, does not argue with you. To meet it, you have to die every day to everything: to your agony, to your loneliness, to the relationship you cling to; you have to die to your thought, to die to your habit, to die to your wife so that you can look at your wife anew; you have to die to your society so that you, as a human being, are new, fresh, young, and you can look at it. But you cannot meet death if you don't die everyday. It is only when you die that there is love. A mind that is frightened has no love—it has habits, it has sympathy, it can force itself to be kind and superficially considerate. But fear breeds sorrow, and sorrow is time as thought.

So to end sorrow is to come into contact with death while living, by dying to your name, to your house, to your property, to your cause, so that you are fresh, young, clear, and you can see things as they are without any distortion. That is what is going to take place when you die. But we have limited death to the physical. We know very well logically, sanely, that the organism is going to come to an end. So we invent a life which we have lived of daily agony, daily insensitivity, the increase of problems, and its stupidity; that life we want to carry over, which we call the "soul"—which we say is the most sacred thing, a part of the divine; but it is still part of your thought, and therefore it has nothing to do with divinity. It is your life!

So one has to live every day dying—dying because you are then in contact with life. You have to come into contact with your everyday life—not some sublime life, which is all nonsense—with every movement of thought, with every word, every feeling, the agony, the despair, the loneliness, the fears, the sorrows, so that your mind is highly sensitive. But the mind cannot be sensitive when it is burdened with the past.

Only when the mind knows how to die to itself is there love. And love is very simple. That is the only thing that brings harmony in life—not all your intellectual arguments, not all the philosophies, not the sacred books or the unholy books. A mind that has understood all this, that has gone through it and meets it every minute of the day—it is only such a mind that can know what love is. And when there is love, do what you will, there is virtue, goodness, beauty.

December 30, 1964

Sixth Talk in Madras

I would like this evening, if I may, to talk about something about which you may have heard, or which you may have practiced or gone into deeply—the question of meditation. I would like, if I may, to cover a great deal, a great territory, the full significance of that extraordinary word. But before we go into it or rather into the nature and the significance of it, we have to understand not only beauty but also that generic word called *love.* In most of our lives, there is so little beauty and so little love. We see things like the trees, the squalor, the poverty, the hunger. We see our own sordid, narrow, petty life, and battle within a small area of our mind. And we do not know actually the depth and width of love. We know sympathy; we are aware occasionally of great affection, without any motive, for another; we also know generosity, kindliness, gentleness, but these words do not really cover the full meaning of that word love. All the practices which we shall go into, all the virtues that we try to cultivate and practice endlessly, and the social reforms and the opinions and characteristics of those people who are supposed to be saints—all these, it seems to me, lack this essential thing, love. And without it life has no meaning at all, has hardly any significance.

So, we shall this evening, go into "love" and "meditation." We are not indulging in words. Words are only useful to communicate. Words have a certain definite meaning when we use words which both you and I understand—not the whole argumentative and dialectical and logical meaning of each particular word, but we more or less grasp the meaning of each word. And if I may suggest, while we are talking this thing over—which is actually sharing together—this whole extraordinary problem of love and meditation, we should also learn the art of listening. We hear a great many things, like that crow; we hear what the speaker says, the words he uses. But hearing is not listening. To listen, there must be not only the verbal communication but also neither agreement nor disagreement; there must be just the act of listening—not translating what you hear into your own peculiar vocabulary, or translating what you hear according to some tradition or what someone has said; those prevent the act of listening.

The act of listening is always in the present. It is a movement always in the present. And the moment you translate what you hear in terms of your own understanding, of your own tradition, of your own culture—if you have a culture—you merely prevent listening. If one is listening, then one can go on in an extraordinary movement endlessly, not only listening to the speaker, but listening to everything: to those crows, to that bus, listening to the movement of the breeze among the leaves, seeing the sunset. It is a total act, it is not a partial act. And if we could listen that way all our life, not just for a few minutes, but right through our life, listening to every sound, not only to the sound of a voice with which one is familiar, but also to every movement of thought and word, then life would become an endless action of learning and listening.

And as we are going to talk over together, share together, this love and meditation, one has to listen not only to the words but to much more than the words; not only on the surface, but beyond the surface. The quality of love is cooperation. We only know one kind of cooperation—cooperation through reward or punishment, or through necessity. That is the only cooperation we know. Cooperation, that is, working together to produce a thing, is either through gain or through loss or through conformity to authority—authority being an ideal, or tyranny of a person, an example, and so on. That is the only cooperation which we know. If you observe yourself, you will see, when you go to the office, in everything, when you have to do things together, there is this cooperation through reward or punishment, or with necessity. Such cooperation is really primitive; it is not cooperation at all.

We must cooperate; otherwise, we cannot exist. There is no society, no relationship, when there is no cooperation. And that is what is happening in this country: there is no cooperation; each group, each part of the country, is thinking of itself. And this way of fragmentation—with which one is so familiar, which is so tribal, which is so nationalistic—is obviously a state of noncooperation, and therefore disintegration, a destruction, a deterioration. And we can only live when there is cooperation, working together.

Is it possible to work together without punishment, without reward, without compulsion? It seems to me, by the very nature of that word and the meaning of that word, cooperation can only exist when there is affection, when there is love. And that ceases the moment there is a vested interest, there is a tribal activity of a petty little mind, conditioned by a particular language, by a particular country, by a particular section. And so, most of us who talk of cooperation are very primitive people because our cooperation is based on fear, necessity, gain, and pain. And, it seems to me, really to cooperate, to work together, demands a great deal of affection, a great deal of this generic word which we are shy in using: *love.*

So, we are going, this evening, to find out, to discover, for ourselves, the state of mind that knows the meaning and the nature of that word. For it is this one act that will liberate man, that will completely bring about a mutation. This sense of affection, this love, this quality, cannot be cultivated, cannot be practiced, cannot be brought about; but it must happen as naturally as breathing, as fully, with great joy and delight, as the sunset.

And to explore that, one must inquire into this question of space and the object within the space. When we are using the word *space,* we mean, don't we, a continuous state, looked at with or without object, in reference to that thing round the object, or without the object. I will go into it a little bit. What we are going into is real meditation, and we have to understand this thing. We know space only because of the object that lives within the space. I know space only because of the four walls of the room. There is space because of the object which you call the tree; the tree creates the space round it. There is space, an interval, distance, between you and the speaker. There is space as a time interval; there is space between two points—the point as the observer and the thing observed which creates space. That most of us know.

This is a serious thing—what we are talking about. This is not for children, and if you have children, please take them away; let them enjoy themselves playing in the garden. You have to give your total attention; otherwise, you will not be able to understand what we are going into.

Space is also that interval between two thoughts. Space is also that state of mind when there is the thinker and the thought. So we only know space because of the object within that. There is space because of the speaker as an object—the space round him. And that is all we know. Always the object, the observer; and because of the object and the observer, there is space. And within that space is all communication and desiring. And as long as space is brought about by the object, the human mind will always be a slave; it will never be free because it is only the object that creates the space, and to live within that space created by the object or by the thinker will never bring about freedom.

It is only when there is space without the object, without the thinker, that there is freedom. This requires a great deal of inquiry, and this is important to understand. You must have space—space in the mind, space in the heart. Otherwise you are closed; otherwise there is no freedom. And if the space in the heart and the mind is only created by the thinker or by the object which creates space, then the mind remains petty, narrow—however erudite, however clever, however logical.

I do not know if you have noticed, observed, a chair in a room. It is the chair in the room that creates the space, and it is the four walls of the room that create the space. And within that we live. And living there in the space created by thought or by the object, we struggle endlessly; we move the furniture from place to place; we expand the room; we extend, through various forms of drugs and so on, our sensitivity; we heighten our sensitivity. But it is still living within the space created by thought. And living in that way, as most of us do, the movement is always from the object towards another object, within the space which those objects make. And, therefore, we have never that sense of freedom, and without freedom there is no love.

So the whole inquiry, which is meditation, is to find out, is to come upon that space, which the thought or the thinker or the object does not create. I hope I am making this somewhat clear. For this, there has to be love. When we use that word, we wonder if it awakens in you a sense of vast expanse, without the entity who looks at that space. We are going to go into it. That is, space can only exist when there is silence. And there is silence only when there is love.

So what we are going to inquire into is this whole process of silence. First of all, a man who sits deliberately to meditate, who takes a posture deliberately and sets about to meditate, will never be free to come upon this strange thing of silence. We will explain why. You only know that you are breathing when your lungs are clogged and are heavy, when you have a heavy cold; otherwise, you are totally unaware that you are breathing. Deliberately to sit down to meditate is to force the mind to function along a pattern, established either by yourself or by another, in order to achieve a silence, to have some peace in the mind which is called the "peace of mind"—as most of you call it—which is just a "piece of mind," nothing else; just a sound, a word. A deliberate act of meditation is an act of noise, the noise being controlled according to the characteristic or idiosyncrasy or tendency of the hypnotic process of that noise.

So the following of any particular method of meditation is deadly, destroying, whether you invent it for yourself, or whether the ancients have invented it or thought it out for you to meditate so as to arrive at that particular state called "silence"—which is non-silence, which is the result of a deliberate act to silence your mind in order to arrive at a particular space called silence. Because that only makes the mind more and more narrow.

And if you watch, this process of so-called meditation is a form of escape from reality—the reality being the everyday living, not the escape into some form of mysticism which you think you will get or find by forcing, by control, by the repetition of words, by concentration on a picture or an image or a symbol. After all, a method only trains the mind to function along a certain line. And that practice brings about self-hypnosis: you have visions, you have all kinds of things in that state, and therefore it gradually helps you to run away from life. So there is a distance between living and the pursuit of meditation. Living is real—the battle, the jealousies, the anxieties, the hopeless despairs, the monstrous competition, the brutality, everything; these are real. The other is a fanciful escape through hypnosis, through verbalization, through some state which has no reality whatever. And the more you conform to the pattern, the more you think you are achieving. Obviously you are achieving—which is to bring about an imbalance, a contradiction between living, the reality, and fiction.

So one has to understand this process and put away completely this whole idea of practicing meditation. I know it goes against your grain completely because that is what you have learned. Look at what is implied in that. When you practice meditation, you are trying to concentrate on an object, on an idea, on some vision, on some image; and therefore you push away every other intrusion. So your concentration is a form of resistance, and you spend your energy—which is required to find out this extraordinary thing called "silence"—you waste it in trying to concentrate; your mind wanders off, and you spend endless years trying to bring your mind to concentrate on something in which it is not interested. You observe it yourselves, sirs.

So concentration, which is brought about through practice, makes the mind more and more dull, more and more insensitive. Because it creates endless conflict, and a mind in conflict is obviously insensitive. And you need the highest form of sensitivity, which is intelligence, to discover, to come upon, this thing called silence.

And for most people meditation is self-absorption. I do not know if you have watched a child or a boy playing with a toy. The child is completely absorbed in that toy, he is completely concentrated, he is altogether with it. There is no mischief. He does not do anything mischievous; he is not naughty; he sits quietly; he sits endlessly playing with that toy, until he breaks it—then he wants a new toy. And most of us are like that, we want to be absorbed by something, absorbed by the image which we have created—the image of our tradition, of our eccentricity, of our tendency, our devotion; and we are absorbed by that, and we call that meditation! Surely, it is not meditation; it is the projection of your mind which absorbs your thinking. You are not interested whether that image, that symbol, that vision, is projected by you; you think that is real.

So meditation is neither concentration nor absorption by the image or the symbol, nor prayer. You know what prayer is: the endless repetition of words; the quicker the word, the better it is! You hear that, or, sitting in front of a picture or an image—an image graven by the mind or by the hand—you endlessly repeat words, words, words; naturally that repetition quietens the mind. This quietening of the mind is to make the mind dull, to hypnotize it by words, whether those words have any meaning or not; it has no reality; you just repeat "Coca-Cola" endlessly—that has as much significance as your mantra, as your Latin repetition. And this goes on—this prayer, being absorbed by an image which you have created, the vision, or concentration. This is generally called meditation! There are various schools which say, "Be aware of the movement of your toe, watch it and follow the distractions, and go back to the toe." There are various forms of methods, systems, ideas—how to meditate!

And as we said, a man who deliberately sits down or practices meditation is as far away from reality as a man who has no idea of living. We are concerned with living—that is, our everyday activity, our everyday life, our sorrows, our despairs, our agonies, the brutality of life, the ruthlessness of it all. Unless that is changed, do what you will, you can never find out what is the real. So it must begin there; there one must find the beauty of existence, the extraordinary delicacy of existence. And the so-called meditation is a way of distraction, is a way of escape from reality.

And to bring about a total mutation, a total revolution in daily life, is the way of meditation. Not to sit down and meditate and then act, but living, understanding, being aware of everything that you do—your words, your gesture, the way you talk, the whole existence of every day—that is meditation. That is to be aware of the spider, the web it creates, the efficiency of it, the color of it, the beauty of it, the delicacy of it; to be just watching. And as you are watching, your mind wanders off. Pursue that wandering, do not deny, do not call it distraction and force yourself to look at the spider. Go after that distraction. Then you will find there is no distraction at all; there is only a state of continuous awareness about everything.

Then you will find, in that awareness, there is always the observer, the entity who is aware; the entity that says, "I must practice awareness; I must look; I am learning; I am feeling more; I am becoming more sensitive." That is, in that awareness there is choice. That is, "I" choose to look at that spider, "I" choose to say, "This is good and this is bad; this is right and this is wrong."

So with most of us awareness is of choice. And if you penetrate still further, you will find you can look, you can observe, you can be aware, without any choice. You can look at that tree, at that sunset, completely, without word, without thought—it does not mean that you are asleep. You are completely watching—not "you" are watching, but there is complete watchfulness of that sunset. As we said, you are only aware that you are breathing when there is some impediment; you are only aware that you are breathing heavily when you have got a cold; otherwise, you are not aware of it. As you are sitting there, you are not aware that you, as an entity, are breathing. It is a natural process. So is meditation a natural process—not a deliberate act. When it becomes a deliberate act, there is the chooser, the censor; and then that entity remains. But in watching that censor, watching that tree, that face, watching your thought it is only when you choose or deny or suppress or alter that thought that the entity comes into being as the watcher. But if you merely watch, without any interference, there is no watcher at all. So, immediately you have space.

You are following all this, I hope! Not verbally, but actually doing it, because we are sharing together, at this moment, meditation—understanding it, moving with it. As long as there is a censor, an entity that translates what he sees in terms of his own conditioning, which is the past, as long as there is interpretation of what you observe, of what you see, of what you listen to, there must be the center, the object, which creates space round it, and therefore a duality. And once you have established duality, then there is conflict. But if you merely observe, then you will find that there is space without the object. It is as simple as that. But we do not like simplicity, we want to complicate all this. It is extraordinarily simple. And it is only a very simple mind that can see clearly, that can listen completely, that is aware without choice.

And simplicity is not mere outward show. The conformity of simplicity is exhibitionism; it becomes respectable by putting on a loincloth. Becoming a sannyasi is a form of bourgeois respectability! But the saint will never know simplicity because he is not simple; he is in perpetual battle within himself. And to find what is truth, to discover it, to come upon it, is to understand the nature of observation, to observe without thought, without the interference of thought, without time.

And one has to understand this space of silence. One has to understand also the whole question of experience. We all want experience—the more, the better. Because we are fed up with the daily experience of life. We do not see in it any beauty, any loveliness; we see only the routine habit, dreariness, the boredom of life. We are used to that, so we say, "We must have more experience: going to the moon, living under the sea—more and more experience." And the mind that seeks experience or is saturated with experience has no space, and therefore no silence.

We mean by experience, don't we, a response to a challenge. I see the sunset as an experience. I walk along the road and I tread on some filth—that is an experience. I get into the bus, and the bus conductor is rude—that is an experience. I talk to my wife—that is an experience. Life is a process of challenge and response, endlessly. And you get used to that challenge and response—as most of us do. Going to an office for forty years—just think of it! Every day of your life being bored, or being excited because you are doing a little better than somebody else, getting a little more pay, having a little more drink or a better car, a better house! That is all part of experience. And when at the end of it all, when you—your brains and your heart and your mind—are burned out by routine, then you want a little more; then you seek God, whatever that thing is you call "God."

So you want more and more and more! You get that "more" through drugs, which give you an astonishing sensitivity. And in that heightened sensitivity you have an experience which you have never had before, according to your temperament, according to your idiosyncrasics, according to your conditioning. If you are a priest, you get an extraordinary experience, and that little experience alters your whole life. But it is still living in the search for experience, and that is what most of us do. When you deliberately sit down to meditate, that is what you want. And a mind that is groping after more experience, more excitement, more sensation—such a mind is not silent; and, therefore, it experiences only within the borders of its own conditioning and within its own knowledge.

So one has to understand this whole process of experience, and only then is the mind no longer seeking experience—not because it has become stupid, not because there are no more experiences, not because it is satisfied with the one experience which is so supreme that it says, "No more." The search for experience is another form of greed. And wisdom is not come by through experience. There is wisdom only when there is response out of silence.

So it is none of these things. Yet, for most of us, space exists only because of the object—the 'me', the 'I', the 'watcher', the 'experiencer'. And naturally, according to his little mind, according to his pettiness—whether it is poetic pettiness, or artistic pettiness, or the pettiness of a housewife everlastingly occupied with cooking, breeding children, and so on—such a petty mind has experience. However much it may experience, however much it may control, however much it may practice endlessly, such a mind is still petty.

The mind—we mean by mind, not only the brain, but the whole organism, the totality of one's being—has space only when this thing called the "object" ceases. And you cannot make it come to an end by any form of trickery. It comes to an end only when you watch endlessly every movement of its activity, every thought, every feeling—just watch it; do not interpret it, do not say, "It is right, it is wrong; this must be, this must not be." Out of that watchfulness comes choiceless awareness—not as step by step; it happens naturally. When the water of a river goes by the bridge, through a dirty town, cleansing itself, it moves, moves, moves endlessly; it does not go step by step; it is a movement. From that choiceless awareness comes attention—not about anything, but just to be attentive, to be in a state of attention; there is no desire for experience, you are completely attentive. There is no desire to change, to become something noble or ignoble. You are completely attentive. And you will see, when there is such complete attention, there is no object; therefore, there is space. And because of that space, there is complete silence.

Silence is not only of thought but also of the brain. I will not go into all that; there is no time to go into all that. The brain, which is the nerves, the cells, everything, is quiet, but terribly awake, attentive—it must be. Then because of this silence, there is space; and because there is space, there is love. You cannot come to it by practice, by saying, "I will first attempt to be aware, then choicelessly aware, then attentive, then silence." Minds are so petty! You want it all on a blueprint, and all that you have to do is just to follow. It does not work like that. Either you see the whole thing, the whole beauty of the sunset, of the tree, and the whole beauty of this meditation, completely and at once, and therefore flow with it, or you do not see at all.

Then you will see that love does alter immediately every action of life. That is the only catalyst, the only thing—nothing else—that will bring about a total mutation of the mind. And we need such a mutation. Because man has lived so long in his misery, with the everyday torture of existence, the uncertainty, the confusion, the conflict, and the supposed meaninglessness of life. But there is an extraordinary meaning to living. Living—going to an office, talking to your wife, doing everything that you do—has tremendous meaning, if you know how to look at it, how to come upon it. And to come upon it, to know it, to see the beauty of it—that can only take place when there is silence, when there is space and love. And that is truth, and that is the only thing that matters in life. Then all the heavens and all the hells are open. Then you do not have to seek God. Then you do not have to go to any temple or any church; you do not have to be a slave of any priest or of any book or of any authority. Then there is only light, and that light is love and silence.

January 3, 1965

Seventh Talk in Madras

As this is the last talk, at least for this year, I would like, if I may, to talk about what is a religious mind. I would like to go into it rather deeply and investigate together into this whole question of man's search for something beyond his own petty limitations, trying to find something beyond his own measure. And to share, to go into it together, the word *religion* must be clearly understood both by the speaker as well as by you who are listening.

From what anthropologists have discovered, man has always sought, through two million years and more perhaps, some deity, some divinity, something other than this transient world, and always he has created, out of his imagination, out of his search for something permanent, something which is not easily destructible. He has created images or symbols, which he has carved according to his own image, according to his own imagination, according to his poetry of life, according to his limitations, fears, hopes, and all the travail of life. And having established an image carved by the hand or by the mind, he began to worship it, to give it, day after day, flowers; to go to it regularly; to look to it as protection against the weather, against death, against disease, against various calamities that man is heir to.

And out of this constant search for a savior, for a God that is not bred by the imagination, by thought, he has always sought—through rituals, through going to the temple, day after day, following certain modes, certain patterns, certain formulas—and has got himself lost, if necessary, in some form of mysticism, some vision, some heightened sense of intelligence.

And one has really to find out, and not merely revive the dead past of a culture. Because what is revived is something that is already gone, dead, buried, withered; and to worship that and try to revive it in the modern world has very little meaning, or hardly any meaning. And yet that is what we do. When we cannot find an answer to the agony of our life, we try to go back to something far away, and try to revive, to catch hold of it through memory, through deep remembrances, through every form of deceit and habit.

But it seems to me this revival of the past, this adherence to something that has been well established for centuries, this resorting to the temples—their rituals, their organized beliefs, their dogmas, with their property, with their enormous wealth—is utterly fantastic; it has really no meaning at all. If you go into it deeply and observe it for yourself, there is no meaning in our life, our daily, active life of misery, despair, insufficiency, and fear.

Therefore, one has to find out for oneself if there is such a thing as a religious mind—not a religion. To find that out one must put aside all the nonsense which the priests have invented, along with their saviors, with their rituals, with their everlasting repetition of words; we must put all those aside completely and start as though anew. And that is the only way to find out: as though organized belief, rituals, the so-called sacred books never existed, and as though you have never read them. Actually, they have no meaning in daily life. What has meaning is our daily life of struggle, of misery, of pain, of not being able to go beyond our own limited activities of the body, of the heart, or of the mind.

Our life is very limited, very petty, circumscribed by so many things, by circumstances, by fears. Is it possible for man to go beyond that? That is really the fundamental issue—not whether there is God or no God, whether you believe or don't believe. It does not make any difference whether you believe or do not believe. Your belief is the result of your conditioning. If you are born a Muslim, a Christian, a Hindu, your society shapes your thinking, your belief, your thoughts, your feelings. And in the communist world, they do not believe in it at all; they think you are talking sheer nonsense.

So really to find out, one must put away from oneself, operate surgically on, all this nonsense. One must put away the absurdities of so-called religion with its rituals, with its mutterings, whether in Latin or in Sanskrit, so that one can face the reality of *what is*.

So, we have to take this journey together—not abstractly, not in theory, not listen to a talk and follow the words and think perchance you have got something out of it; all that has no meaning at all. What has meaning is to explore and, in the very act of exploration, to bring about a radical change in daily living. For that is the basis, that is the foundation, on which one can build—the daily living with its agony, with its boredom, with its loneliness, with its fear, with its unseeable future. It is the daily living that we have to investigate, to explore.

And to explore, you need passion; you need tremendous vitality, energy. And very few have the energy, or rather the passion, to inquire because we are so easily satisfied! We are, most of us in the modern world, discontented with almost everything—with the family, with the job, with the routine of life, with loneliness. If we are completely discontented, we try to find an action through an organization, through social reform, through political reform, or through religious reform—always reforming. Or, not entering that kind of activity, one goes within oneself, as the monks are supposed to do. But the monks do not go within themselves at all; they have all the outward appearance of a simple life! But a simple life begins only when you have put away dogma, belief, and authority; then you can go within. But the going within is very difficult; it requires energy. And, as we were saying, very few people have the energy of this kind.

There is energy created through friction, through resistance, through battle with oneself, through conflict—that engenders a certain form of energy, as one can see. You want something, you go after it. You are miserable; you are unhappy; you cannot get on with your wife, your husband; you battle; and from that resistance, battle, comes a form of energy which is really hate, envy, greed. And discontent is so easily satisfied. You find some channel through which you can fulfill yourself, or your hopes, or your fears; and you are satisfied immediately. But to keep this discontent at its height, to keep it hot, burning, without finding any channel, to keep it terribly alive, one must inquire into oneself and discover that energy which has no motive.

And that is what we are going to do, if we may, this evening. We are going to discover for ourselves if there is a passion, an energy, a very simple way of looking at life, without battle, without conflict, without seeking an end. To do that one must go within oneself. And one cannot go within oneself, except by going through outward activity and then moving from there inwardly. Without understanding the world, society; without understanding your relationship as a human being to that world, to that society; without understanding your job, your wife, your family, your word, your gesture, outwardly, you cannot begin to go inwardly. And that is very difficult to do. Nothing is easy in life—nothing. But most of us want a quick answer, a quick way of getting all this over and coming to some extraordinary mystical stage, which is all illusory.

So one must begin to find out the meaning and the significance of our outward activities because that is the only test one has. You cannot deceive yourself there. Whether you hate, whether you are bored, whether you are deceiving others or deceiving yourself, whether you are frightened, whether you are happy, whether you are creating, in this world, something out of your own self-centered activity, if you have no criterion as a test from the outside, how can you go within yourself and discover the most extraordinary complex entity with all the deceptions, motives, anxieties?

So to go within and to go very far within, you must look to the outside and find it. That is, as the tide goes out and the same waters come in, so must we: we must rise on the tide which goes out, which is our relationship to the world and, having understood that, ride on that water and move within.

So, you have to look to your relationship to the world. Your relationship begins with the family, the wife, the husband, the children: that is the world you live in. You have to find your relationship, you have to find out what it is based on—not deceive yourself. What is it actually based on? Habit, a certain tradition, a narrow little circle—and we live in that. The family is composed of the husband, wife, and children; and there we dominate or are dominated, sexually, emotionally; there we are dependent.

Please, observe yourself. You are not merely listening to a lot of words. One can build on a lot of words, but that does not get you very far. But the words reveal the state of your own relationship, the actual relationship—not what you would like your relationship to be, with your wife, with your children, but the actual fact. Then, from there, one can move.

The family is against society; the family is against human relationship as a whole. You know, it is like living in one part of a big house, in one little room, and making an extraordinary thing of that one little room, which is the family. The family has only importance in relation to the whole of the house. As that one room is in relation to the whole of the house, so is the family in relation to the whole of human existence. But we separate it, we cling to it. We make much about the family—my relations and your relations—and we battle with each other everlastingly. And the family is like the little room in relation to the whole house. When we forget the whole house, then the little room becomes terribly important; so also the family becomes very important when you forget the whole of human existence. The family has only importance in relation to the whole of human existence; otherwise, it becomes a dreadful thing, a monstrous thing.

So, one has to find out for oneself the fact of the actual relationship, and discover through that relationship the relationship with your neighbor, with the world, with the extraordinary human beings who are cantankerous, who are mischievous, who are ugly, brutal, tyrannical. And to find that out, you must start very near.

And there is this problem also of sex, which has become so astonishingly important for most people—such a complex thing. As we were saying the other day, we cannot find other ways of releasing ourselves, and so we turn to the one thing, sex, and make a monstrous issue of it. And when we say, "We love the family," we do not really love that family; we do not love our children—actually we do not. When you say that you love your children, you really mean that they have become a habit, toys—things of amusement for a while. But, if you love something, your children, then you would care.

You know what caring is? If you care, when you plant a tree, you care for it; you cherish it; you nourish it; you find out the right soil, the right fertilizer; you care, you watch it infinitely. I do not know if you have ever planted a tree, a seedling, and watched it every day. You have to dig deep before you plant, then see the soil is right, then plant, then protect it, then watch it every day, look after it as though it were a part of your whole being. But you do not love the children that way. If you did, then you would have a different kind of education altogether. There would be no wars, there would be no poverty. The mind then would not be trained to be merely technical. There would be no competition, there would be no nationality. And because we do not love, all this has been allowed to grow.

Therefore, one has to begin with the very near thing, and discover from there the actual state of one's mind and one's being. And that is very difficult to do because we find in ourselves so many ugly things, conscious as well as unconscious. And we cannot face them; we rather run away to a temple, or to a church, or to a cinema, or to some other organized amusement—and the temple or the church is also an organized amusement. And to face something actually demands energy. You have no energy if you are battling uselessly about nothing—and that is what most of us are doing!

So to bring about this passion, this energy, which one needs to go into something very deeply, endlessly, every day and every minute, there are certain things one has to do, obviously. One has to eat the right food, not what one's tongue dictates. You can study and find out what is the right food; we do not have to go into it. Then, one has to understand the urge to obey. Most of us so easily obey. A man who obeys easily or with great difficulty is seeking power. Please follow this. Why should you obey anybody? You obey your boss in the factory, in your office, because you may lose your job. If you show yourself a little more intelligent than the boss, you might lose your job—and there are so many people waiting to get that job. So there is this fear built up, and therefore you obey. Your intelligence is downgraded because every one of us is seeking power, position, prestige, status. Watch it, you are doing that in your life, every day.

You are not concerned with function alone, but you use the function to arrive at a status. And, therefore, the status becomes far more important than the function. And hence there is the battle for status—not for the efficiency of function, but for what you get out of that function, what position, what power, what prestige, what status. And hence there is competition for status, not for functioning efficiently. So, most of us obey because we want power, position, status; and we will gradually climb to that status through obedience and therefore cultivate inefficiency, cultivate this obedience and the fear that goes with it.

To find out what is the religious mind, you must understand not only the relationship of yourself with the family, with society and beyond, but also this whole process of the search for power—which is to dominate, either in the family or in society, or to be the dominating authority in an organization, religious or otherwise.

So the mind must investigate this whole process of authority in which is included law. You must obey law: you must keep to the left side of the road, here; you must buy a stamp. But every other form of authority, psychological authority, must be understood completely so that the mind never seeks authority of any kind.

So one begins to discover for oneself the nature of the religious mind. One may have a family, but that family is in relation to the whole and not separate. And because it is not separate, it has to be looked after, cared for. And therefore a totally different kind of education is called for. And the inquiry which begins very near shows this desire for power, for dominance, and this urge to obey, which manifests itself in so many ways—which is disrespect for many people and respect for a few. If you have no disrespect for anybody, you need not have respect for anybody.

So, then one can begin to go within oneself, beginning outwardly, being aware of the outward things—of the trees, of the poverty, the reason for the poverty, the whole social and economic structure as it is—and understanding those outward things.

When we use that word *understand*, we mean not merely analytically, intellectually, verbally, but understanding it with your blood, with your heart, with your mind, with everything. And you have to understand your relationship with your family; you have to understand your relationship to power, position, authority, status.

Then you can go within. And to go within one must first understand the principal thing, which is to be terribly honest to oneself so that there is no deception whatsoever. We deceive ourselves so easily! We would not look. We would rather talk about something transcendental: God, theories, atma, anything.

You know, when you enter a room, you are so concerned about discussing reality—if there is this, if there is that—and you never watch the furniture, the color of the carpet, the flowers, the shape of the window; you watch nothing, you are so consumed by the other. One has to watch, one has to observe everything: watch the sunset, watch the tree against that sunset, the darkness, the casuarina with its delicate foliage, the light through it, the leaves, the trunk. And if you do not watch that, you cannot watch this. If you do not know how to look without, you cannot look within. And we have tried to look in by denying the outer, by denying the outward beauty of life. All the saints, all your literature, never talk about the beauty of life; they tell you how to escape from this misery.

And there is tremendous beauty in living. And that beauty is shown in nature—in watching a tree, in being in communion with a tree. And if you do not know how to look there, to look where you are walking, to observe what you are saying, outwardly, the gestures you make, the way you show respect and disrespect—if you do not watch that, how can you watch within? So you must begin again outwardly; then you can go within.

And to observe there must be no deception. What is the power that creates, breeds deception? You understand? Why do we deceive ourselves? Why do we put on masks? You know what a mask is? When a human being is capable and efficient in technology, that is a particular mask; he lives in that; he does not want to know what is behind that mask. He may be a first-class engineer, a first-class bureaucrat: and that is a mask. That mask becomes respectability which the world accepts as a marvelous human being. But remove the mask; then, whether he is a scientist or an astronomer, he is just like everybody else.

So one has to find out for oneself what is the power, what is the energy, that creates deception. You know what I mean by "deception"? Never to see actually what we are—actually, not theoretically. Not to be able to see clearly, definitely, what we are. Because we are frightened, because we want to change what we are into something noble, or whatever it is, we want to make it supreme; we want to be everything.

So the motive of deception begins when you want to change *what is*, when you are discontented with *what is*. We are going to go into that. But, first, we are showing how necessary it is to remove every deception and the means that create deception, so that your mind can look clearly.

Most of us live in deception, which is, living on the surface. Just amusing ourselves if we have money, or going to an office, day after day, just living on the superficial things and never inquiring—that also is a form of deception. Because we do not live by bread alone, we live at other levels, a deeper existence. But if we deny all that, we are also deceiving ourselves. So one must become aware of this power to deceive oneself. And that power to deceive oneself comes to an end, deception comes to an end, when there is no end, when there is no desire to reach any end, and when one moves from fact to fact.

And to look at oneself is possible only when there is no interference by deception. You have to look without the word, without the desire to translate it according to your own past memory. And that is one of the most difficult and arduous things to do—to look: to look at a tree, at a woman, at a man, to look at the squalor, merely to observe.

If you can observe without any interpretation, without any translation, then from that observation you will find you have tremendous energy. Because, now, that energy is being wasted through interpretation, through translating what you see into like or dislike, or trying to alter it according to your social, economic, religious, or moral pattern.

So this desire to change *what is* is dissipation of energy. Whereas if you look at *what is* actually—at your anger, at your jealousy, at your lust, at your violence—without any interpretation, then you have energy.

So the religious mind is a mind that has no deception whatsoever, that does not seek any status, that has no desire or urge for power of any kind. And the religious mind understands its relationship with the family and with the whole of man. Then it can go deeply. We have only the intellectual instrument—at least, that is what is said. But there is the instrument of observation, which is to observe every movement of thought, to observe every movement of feeling, and so uncover the fears that are hidden, the secret desires that are never looked at, that are never explored. And to explore, as we said, needs tremendous energy. And this energy is released when you are moving with what you are discovering, when you are not translating or interpreting what you are seeing in terms of the past.

Have you ever wondered how the scientists have extraordinary energy? When you go into a laboratory, if you have ever gone into a first-class research laboratory, there you will see the scientist completely full of energy, active. Because he is dealing with outward things, there is no resistance; he is moving from fact to fact; he does not indulge in theories, hypotheses, speculations; he is not a theoretician. He is a pure, clearsighted technician, watching everything under the microscope. Therefore he has tremendous energy there, in the laboratory. But let him go outside, he is just like everybody else—anxious, fighting for position, competing, nationalistic, caught in religious beliefs, or inventing his own particular belief, and so on. There is a waste of energy.

And to look, the mind must be completely silent. After all, if the scientist is looking through the microscope, or whatever he is doing, he is observing from silence, not from knowledge. What he sees, he then translates in terms of knowledge, and therefore there is action. But he sees from silence—it may be that silence may last a split second or an hour. And that is the only way to observe.

So the cultivation of a silent mind becomes stupid. You cannot practice and arrive at a silent mind. But, to look, to observe, you must have silence. Do look at that sunset. You cannot look at that sunset, you cannot see it, if your mind is chattering. You can see it completely only when the mind is extraordinarily quiet and intense. After all, that is beauty. That is, the perception of beauty or nonbeauty is only possible when there is passion, when you look at that sunset with complete intensity. And you cannot be intense if you are not silent. So you begin to see how extraordinarily silent the mind becomes when you observe. When you are observing, you do not have to discipline the mind to be silent—then it is a dead mind. But the mind that is observing out of a silence creates its own discipline; it does not need discipline because it is observing.

So this observation out of silence is passion, is energy. Then you can observe your fears. Most people are frightened—frightened of death, frightened of this empty, useless life. And one has to meet that fear, and to observe it without any movement, without trying to go beyond it or to resist it, without trying to get rid of it. To go beyond it, to overcome it, to suppress it—these are a waste of energy. Whereas if you observe the whole movement of fear, then that observation out of silence gives energy; then that problem of fear ceases.

Then the question of time enters into it, and the whole implication of time that we have already talked about.

So there has to be this observation of daily events. When we are using the word *observation*, we mean the observation which is not critical, which is not the outcome of discontent or conformity or suppression, but which is the observation out of silence, the observation of fact only, not the translation of that fact or the opinion about the fact. Then you will see, out of this observation, there is no effort necessary to do, to resist, to overcome or to deny; effort altogether goes away. And one can live one's daily life—going to an office, cooking, doing everything—without effort.

The religious mind is the mind that understands the family and its position relative to the whole; the mind that does not seek power, position; the mind that is not caught in any ritual, any dogma, any belief, any organized church or temple; the mind that has no power whatsoever to create illusion. And the religious mind is the mind that looks at facts and, therefore, does not make any effort at all, whatever it does.

Then one goes still further. That is, by observing the outward things, one has come to the inner. And the outer and the inner are not two different states; they are the same state of observation out of silence.

This silence is space. We live in a very small space, in the space created by the mind with its own ideas. And the mind is the result of its own conditioning in a particular society and culture; it lives in a very small space; and all the battles, all the relationships, all the anxieties are within that little space. But the moment the mind, through observation, becomes naturally, easily, without effort, silent, that little space is broken. The moment the mind is completely quiet, you will see that there is no limitation to space. You will then see that the object does not create the space; there is space—endless space.

And when that takes place, the mind is the truly religious mind; and from that mind there is activity. You can be a super-citizen—not running away to a monastery, not becoming a sannyasi, or a complete technician, or a mechanized human being. But from that effortless, silent observation, there is action; and that is the only action that does not breed hatred, enmity, competition. Then through observation and silence you will see that because there is space, there is love.

Love is dying every day. Love is not memory, love is not thought. Love is not a thing that continues as duration in time. And, through observation, one must die to the continuity of everything. Then there is love, and with love, there comes creation.

Creation is one of the most difficult things to understand. The man who writes a poem, however beautiful, thinks he is a creative being. The man and the woman who breed children think that they are creative. The man or the cook who makes bread thinks, perhaps, he is also creative. But creation is something far more. That man is not creative who merely writes a book or fulfills himself in some petty, little ambition. Creation is not a man-made structure, or man-made technological knowledge and the result of technological knowledge, which is merely invention. Creation is something that is timeless, that has no tomorrow and yesterday; it is living timelessly. And you come to it very naturally if you understand this whole problem of existence.

So a religious mind is all these things, and then it knows, or rather it is in, a state which is creative from moment to moment. It is always acting from that extraordinary sense of emptiness.

I do not know if you have ever noticed how a drum is always empty. When you strike on it, it gives the right tone; but it is empty. Our minds are never empty; they are always full. Therefore, our action is always from this dreadful noise of thought, of memory, of despair; and, therefore, action is always contradictory, leading to great misery.

But a mind that is completely empty, empty in the sense of observation, silence, and, therefore, love and the whole understanding of death—such a mind is creative. And a creative mind is empty all the time; it acts from that emptiness, it speaks from that emptiness. And, therefore, it will always be true, it will never bring about a deception within itself. And it is only such a religious mind that can solve the problems of misery in this world.

January 6, 1965

Bombay, India, 1965

First Talk in Bombay

I think most of us seek some kind of mystery beyond life; we want something mysterious, occult, hidden, beyond existence; and it seems to me that there is a great mystery and an extraordinary beauty in the way of life, in the way that we live that life. For most of us, living—that is, everyday living: going to the office, the dreary house, the petty quarrels, and the innumerable ambitions and trials of life—is a degradation; it is boring and tiresome. And so we try, I think, rather vainly to go beyond the very nature of existence, and to find something that will give us complete satisfaction, gratification. And so we never know how to live, we never seem to understand the whole depth, the beauty, and the dignity of living.

And during these talks it is the intention of the speaker not only to explore, if we can, verbally, rationally, and sanely, but also to penetrate, through the word, something that lies beyond the word.

To find the full significance of living, we must understand the daily tortures of our complex life; we cannot escape from them. The society in which we live has to be understood by each one of us—not by some philosopher, not by some teacher, not by a guru—and our way of living has to be transformed, completely changed. I think that is the most important thing we have to do, and nothing else. In the process of transformation, in the process of bringing about, without bargaining, a change in our life, there is beauty; and in that change we shall find for ourselves the great mystery that each mind is seeking. Therefore, we must concern ourselves not with what is beyond life, or what is life, or what is the purpose of life, but rather with the understanding of this complex existence of everyday life, because that is the foundation upon which we must build. And without understanding that, without bringing about a radical change in that, our society will always be in a state of corruption, and, therefore, we shall always be in a state of deterioration.

We are society; we are not independent of society. We are the result of the environment—of our religion, of our education, of the climate, of the food we eat, the reactions, the innumerable repetitive activities that we indulge in every day. That is our life. And the society in which we live is part of that life. Society is relationship between man and man. Society is cooperation. Society, as it is, is the result of man's greed, hatred, ambition, competition, brutality, cruelty, ruthlessness—and we live in that pattern. And to understand it—not intellectually, not merely theoretically, but actually—we have to come into contact directly with that fact, which is, a human being—that is you—is the result of this social environment, its economic pressure, religious upbringing, and so on. To come into contact with anything directly is not to verbalize it but to look at it.

And, apparently, it is one of the most difficult things to do, to come directly into contact with the fact. There is the fact of that tree—the fact, but not what you think about the tree. What you think about the tree is not the fact, which is the tree. Please follow this. For most of us, fact is nonexistent. We live with ideas; we live with our memories, with our experiences; and in the shadow of those experiences and memories we approach the fact, and thereby transform the fact, or rather hope to transform, hope to change the fact. Whereas to look at the fact, in itself, brings about the energy that is necessary to transform that fact. We are going into this a little bit.

You know, we never look at things. We never look at the sky. We never look at the shape of a building or at our neighbor—what he looks like, what he thinks, what he feels—we never observe. We are too occupied with our own miseries, with our own worries; and we are so self-centered, so enclosed in our own problems that we never see anything. But to observe means to learn. It is only through learning that you can bring about a radical change. The very act of learning is the act of change. So to look, to observe, is the primary necessity of a religious man, not what he thinks, not what he feels, not what his reactions are. We will come later to those reactions, to those beliefs, to those environmental influences which condition the mind and distort what he observes.

I do not know whether you have looked at a sunset, or the quiet dignity of a tree, or the line of a bird on the wing. To look demands quiet; it demands a quality of the mind that is quiet, that is not incessantly chattering with itself. There must be a certain silence to observe. And you cannot have silence if your mind, when it is observing, is projecting its own ideas, its own demands, its hopes, its fears. So, to observe the social structure in which we live, and to bring about a radical change in that society, we must first observe *what is,* not what we want that society to be.

Because this society in which we live, we have created, we are responsible for it—each one of us. It has not come into being because of some fictitious, spiritual forces. It has come about through our greed, through our ambition, through our personal likes and dislikes and enmities, through our frustrations, through our search for pleasure and satisfaction. We have created the religions, the beliefs, the dogmas, out of fear. It is in that society that you live. Either you run away from that society because you cannot understand it, or cannot bring about a change in that society of which you are a part; or you become so completely engrossed in your own particular travail that you lose complete interest in the radical demand of a human mind that says that it must change.

So, existence is relationship, existence is a movement in relationship, and that existence is society. And we cannot possibly go beyond the limits of our mind, of our heart, unless we understand the structure of our own being, which is society. The society is not different from you—you are society. The very structure of society is the structure of yourself. So when you begin to understand yourself, you are then beginning to understand the society in which you live. It is not opposed to society. So a religious man is concerned with the discovery of a new way of life, of living in this world, and bringing about a transformation in the society in which he lives, because by transforming himself, he transforms society. I think this is very important to understand.

Most of us are concerned with finding a way of living harmoniously, without too many conflicts, without the barrenness of modern existence. But without understanding existence, our life, there is no way out of our confusion, out of our misery, out of all the travail of man. I think that is the first thing to face. That is the fact. You have to face that fact objectively as you would face the fact of that palm tree; you have to look at it. Now, to look at a tree—you can easily do it because the tree does not interfere with your life. You can look at the lovely clouds full of life and gaiety and extraordinary vitality because it has no significance in your daily life. You can see the light on the water and enjoy the beauty, the quickness, the dance; and again that has no significance in your daily life. You can read all the sacred books in your country, quote them everlastingly; and again, that has no significance in your life.

And to understand the tree, the cloud, the light on the water, you must look. And when you do look, your mind must be empty to look. I do not know if you have ever looked at a flower—not casually, not in passing by—ever observed it. To observe a flower is as important as to observe yourself. Because in observing a flower, you begin to learn how to observe. While observing a flower, most people bring forth into that observation the naming. They say it is a rose, a violet, or a primrose; and thereby they have stopped looking. The verbalization of the fact is a distraction away from that fact.

But to observe demands a quiet, nonverbalizing mind, a mind that looks without opinion, without judgment. And that is one of the most difficult things to do—to look at an objective thing, nonverbally. You try, as you are sitting there, to look at that palm tree or to listen to the speaker objectively, putting aside your opinions, your ideas, the reputation of the speaker, and so on—to nonverbalize. Then you will find, if you do look, that your mind must be somewhat quiet; otherwise, you cannot see. If I look at that palm tree thinking of other things, I cannot possibly see the beauty, the stillness, the depth, the quality, the nature, the totality of the tree.

And to observe something totally, your mind must be completely empty to observe. And it is very difficult to observe things outwardly, if one has ever tried it. It is much more difficult to observe the social structure, the environmental influences, the state of your mind as part of your society. To observe—that requires enormous attention; and that is what we are going to learn during these talks—to learn, not to acquire knowledge.

There is a vast difference between learning and acquiring knowledge. Acquiring knowledge is mechanical. The computers, the electronic brains, are full of knowledge. Knowledge has been fed into these machines, as you have been fed from childhood to acquire knowledge. Knowledge is not merely book learning, but knowledge is experience, knowledge is memory. That is one thing—acquiring knowledge. Such knowledge in certain circumstances is necessary. But learning is something entirely different because the moment you have learned, it has become knowledge. But a mind that is learning endlessly—such a mind alone can bring about the necessary transformation within itself.

So both of us, the speaker and you, are going to learn—learn about ourselves. Not coming with knowledge and thereby acquiring more knowledge about ourselves—that is fairly easy. But to learn about yourself is entirely a different thing. Because knowledge is acquired, added, through experience, through reaction, through every form of influence, pain, suffering. And when you look at yourself or at society with that knowledge, then there is distortion; then there is no freedom to observe and therefore to learn.

I feel that the most important thing to understand in the first talk is to look and thereby to learn. To look is not merely with your eyes but also with your ears—to listen with your ears. Probably most of us never listen. Again, to listen demands attention, not concentration—just attention to listen to the crows, to listen to the breeze, to listen to the murmur of a big town, to listen to the distant sea, and to listen to the speaker; just to listen without interpreting, without translating, without saying, "I have already heard that before, last year, when he came." Because when there is learning about listening, then you will see that you can listen to all the intimations of your mind and also listen to all the hints of your own existence; and without listening you cannot learn. Because we have to learn about ourselves, we have to learn anew about society.

As an individual, it is your responsibility to bring about a tremendous change in the world. It is your responsibility because you are part of this society, because you are part of this tremendous sorrow of man, this constant effort, struggle, pain, and anxiety. You are responsible. Unless you realize that immense responsibility and come directly in contact with that responsibility and listen to the whole structure, the machinery of that responsibility, do what you will—go to every temple, to every guru, to every Master, to every religious book in the world—your action has no meaning whatsoever because those are mere escapes from actuality.

So we have to understand this existence, this life, our relationship to society. We have not only to understand our relationship with each other, with society, but to bring about a radical change in that relationship. And that is our responsibility. I do not think we feel this urgency. We look to the politicians, we look to some philosophy, we look to something mysterious that will bring about an alteration within ourselves. There is no way out except that you become aware of this immense responsibility as a human being, and becoming aware of that responsibility, you learn all about it and do not bring all your previous knowledge to learn. And to learn there must be freedom; otherwise, you will repeat the same thing over and over again. You cannot learn ahimsa.

I do not know if you have noticed that there is so much confusion, misery, and sorrow in the world, and that man—the modern-day man—has not been able to find a way out of it. So he resorts to the past. He thinks he must go back five thousand or seven thousand years and resuscitate that past to bring about a revival. And again, there is no answer that way. There is no answer through time. Time can make life more happy, more comfortable; but comfort and pleasure are not the absolute answers to life. Nor does the answer lie through some reform. Nor is there a way out through any temple, through any sacred books. I think one has to realize the seriousness of all this, and put away all that nonsense, and come face to face with facts—which is our life, our everyday, brutal, anxious, insecure, cruel life, with its pleasures, with its amusements—and to see if one can bring about, as a human being who has lived for two million years, a radical transformation within oneself, and therefore within the structure of society.

To be aware of this responsibility means great, arduous work. We have to work not only within ourselves but also in our relationship with others. I mean by "work" not the practice of some silly formula, some absurd theory, some fantastic assertions of some philosopher or of some guru or teacher. Those are all too infantile, immature. When we talk about work, we mean by that becoming aware of the responsibility, as a human being living in this world, that he has to work to bring about a change within himself. And if he really changes, if he brings about a mutation within himself, then he will transform society. Society is not transformed through any revolution, economic or social. We have seen this through the French

Revolution, the Russian Revolution. The everlasting hope of man—that by altering the outward things, the inward nature of man can be transformed—has never been fulfilled, and it will never be. The outward change, the economic change, which is bound to come to this country which is so poor—that is not going to change man's attitude, the ways of life, his misery, his confusion.

So to bring about a total change of man, man has to become aware of himself—that is, he has to learn about himself anew. Man, according to the recent discoveries of anthropology, has lived for two million years; and man has not found a way out of his misery. He has escaped from it, he has run away through some fanciful illusion. But he has not found it, has not built a society that is totally free; he has not built a society which is not a society of conformity.

You know, if you observe, there are those societies which through necessity cooperate. Through necessity, through compulsion, through an industrial revolution, people must live together; they must cooperate, they must conform, they must follow a pattern. And in that society, as one can observe, there are still conflicts; each man is still against the other because he is ambitious, he is competitive, though he may talk about the love of the neighbor. By force he must cooperate, but through that cooperation, through that assertion of loving the neighbor, he is competitive, ruthless, ambitious. Therefore such a pattern of society brings about its own destruction.

Then there is a form of society where there is no civic consciousness at all; each man is out for himself. As you observe in this country, each man is concerned with his family, with his group, with his class, with his particular part of the country, with his linguistic divisions; and he has no civic consciousness. He is not at all conscious of what is happening to his neighbor; he does not care; he is totally indifferent to what happens. But yet, if you observe, his religious books have told him that perhaps he will live the next life, therefore, he must behave; that there is karma: what he does now will matter, how he talks, how he tells things, it does not matter to whom; that behavior is righteousness, and if he does not behave now, he pays for it next life—this is the crude form. On that you have been brought up for centuries, and yet, such beliefs, such ideas have no importance through your life because you do not believe. You still carry on as though this is the only life that matters. Because you are competitive, you are ambitious, you destroy your neighbor; you are not at all civic minded socially.

So there are these two forms of society. One form of society is such that the human being that lives in it is made to conform, made to cooperate out of necessity. Thus the human being becomes civic minded: he does not throw things out on the road because he would be punished; there is order. But within that order, within that framework, each man is against the other. In the other form of society, as in this country, there is no framework. Here you have no civic consciousness at all because you do not believe one bit in what you think you are being told.

You have these two forms of society, and each of these societies, inherently within itself, has the seed of its own destruction. So, a religious man is concerned with creating a new society which is neither this nor that, but something entirely different—which is, each human being behaves righteously every minute because he understands his responsibility as a human being. He alone is responsible and no other—how he behaves; what his activities are; whether he is ambitious, cruel, destructive, hating, jealous, competitive; what his fears are. It is only such a mind that can bring about a new society.

And we do need a new society, and that society is not going to be created by anybody except by you. I do not think we feel the immense responsibility of this. That is the first thing that matters. Because that is the foundation, which is righteous behavior, right conduct—not the conduct of a pattern, but the conduct which comes about through learning. If you are all the time learning, that very learning brings about its own righteous action. Therefore it is only the religious mind that can create this new society.

And, as we said, you must learn about yourself—not what you have been told about yourself, not what your sacred books have told you about yourself, because they are irrelevant, they have no meaning. You have to learn anew about yourself. Therefore, you have to learn how to observe yourself. As you observe that tree, so you have to observe yourself. As you observe that tree without distortion, so you have to observe yourself without distortion—and that is the greatest difficulty. Because we do not observe the fact, but we rather know what gives us pleasure or pain and therefore avoid the fact.

You know, if I want to know about myself, to learn about myself, I have to watch every movement of my mind, every feeling I have—not say that it should not exist or must exist, not deny it or try to modify it, but just to observe what I am. And that demands a certain discipline. Because to observe the fact is in itself a discipline. Please do look at it. Look at a flower and see how difficult it is to look at it without naming it, without bringing all your reactions upon it, without saying you like or dislike—just to observe. Then you will see how extraordinarily difficult it is to look at something which is totally outside objectively. And then, when you turn inward, it is much more difficult because you have opinions about yourself: what you should be or what you should not be; what you are; that you are the highest self, the atma, the God, or what you think you are—all the fantastic ideas and memories about yourself. It is these memories, these fancies, these illusions, these experiences—this acquired knowledge—that prevent you from looking at yourself. And to be aware of these—knowledge and the various forms of knowledge—and not allow them to interfere with your observation of yourself brings about a discipline in itself.

You know, to go very far, you have to begin very near. You must begin here, not beyond existence. You must begin with the earth, with us, with human beings, with ourselves, and not try to find what is the transcendental beauty of life. To find the transcendental beauty of life, we must begin with life itself. It is only through the daily existence and the understanding of the beauty of that life in our daily ways—it is only through that door that we can find that which is not measurable.

Our minds seek always something not transient, something called God, something called truth. And we are so desperate, we are so anxious, we are so surrounded by fear that we make every effort to find something which we call truth, which we call God. But to find that, we must lay the right foundation; and the right foundation is right action in our behavior. So we must lay the foundation, not on sand, but on the responsibility of our daily life, and try to bring about a tremendous revolution in that life.

You know, for most of us, change implies a bargaining process. I would like to change, and so I begin to bargain with myself whether it is profitable or not, whether it is worthwhile or not, so change implies a bargaining. Please think about it and feel how extraordinarily our mind works with regard to change. We change if it is profitable, if it is pleasurable, or we change when it is painful. But any change with bargaining is no change at all. So our mind that wishes to find the reality must begin with itself.

And there is something that is not measurable by the mind or by the instruments invented by man. There is truth, there is benediction. But we must come upon it not through prayers, not through hope, but by becoming totally responsible for every action, every day and every minute of the day. Then out of that responsibility comes the flower of understanding, and that understanding is the way of life. And there has to be that discovery, for each one, of the way of living; and it is only that way that can bring about reality, clarity, and the great depth of the mind.

February 10, 1965

Second Talk in Bombay

It is always rather difficult to communicate, through words, what one wants to convey. And it is especially difficult, not when we use technological words, or words that have special forms or meanings according to a certain formula, but when we are using everyday words, as we are going to do—then it becomes much more difficult to convey the meaning and the significance of what one wants to say. Most of us, unfortunately, think in formulas. We have certain concepts of freedom, of society, of what is goodness, of what is virtue, and so on. On these patterns we think. And if one uses words that have ordinary meaning, not belonging to any particular formula, then communication becomes much more difficult because you have certain concepts, ideas, and the speaker has to battle through your concepts and formulas to convey what he wants to convey.

This is an inevitable process of communication: you have certain ideas, and the speaker has to force his way, as it were, through what you have already come to, through what your conclusions are already. So, knowing that you have your special formulas—and I am going to use ordinary words with ordinary dictionary meanings which both of us know—we can proceed and find out how far we can communicate with each other.

We are going to deal with very complex problems during these talks, issues that need a great deal of investigation, insight, that need a mind that is willing to put aside its own particular opinions, conclusions, and experiences, and is willing to explore. And to explore we must have, obviously, not only the freedom from the verbal conclusions that one has, but also the freedom to inquire, the freedom and the urgency to find out. Because it is only in freedom that one can find out about anything, about scientific matters, or about psychological matters. And as we are dealing with psychological matters, we need much greater insight, freedom, and the urgency to discover.

So, words have certain definite meanings. And we must always bear in mind that the word is not the thing. The word *sea* is not the sea, the ocean, the vast water, any more than the word *tree* is the tree. That must always be borne in mind if we are going to investigate into something extraordinarily complex, that demands all your attention. By attending one or two talks you are not going to find out the whole structure of your thinking, feeling; you have to take the whole series and go into it critically, sanely, with balance.

As we were saying the other day, we have to find order in society and in freedom. Society is the organized relationship of man with man. In that organization we must find freedom, and that freedom must be in society, and it must be orderly. Otherwise it is not freedom; then it is merely a reaction against society. That is, most of us are caught in the environment, and we react, we revolt; and that revolt, we take it, is freedom. But that revolt which is born of reaction does not bring freedom; it brings disorder. So freedom is a state of mind, which is not the result of a reaction, just as communism is a reaction to capitalism; and such a reaction in daily life or in organized society only leads to further disorder.

There is technological order in society, and that is what is taking place throughout the world. Order is necessary to work together, to live together, to function together; to cooperate together, order is necessary. But that order is the outcome of technological necessity and of the necessity born of convenience, of fear, and so on. In that technological order there is disorder because man is not free. And it is only when we understand the psychological relationship of man with man, and bring order in that psychological relationship, that there is freedom. This must be clearly understood between the speaker and yourself.

When we talk of freedom, we are not talking of reaction; we are talking of order born out of understanding the whole psyche of man, the whole total essence of man, the whole sociological, psychological structure of man. And in the understanding of that structure, there is freedom which brings order, and only within that order can men live together peacefully. So, our concern throughout these talks is to bring about order in freedom, or rather to bring about a transformation of the human mind which can come through the understanding of its social relationship with man and the psychological relationship of man, which will bring about freedom—out of which freedom there is order. So our concern is how not to be slaves to society, and yet establish a relationship in a new world which will be orderly and not produce disorder in relationship with man.

As society exists now, man's relationship to man is organized; in that there is disorder because we are in conflict, not only within ourselves, but with each other: as communities dividing themselves linguistically, nationally, religiously; dividing itself as family opposed to a community, the community opposed to a nation, and so on—outwardly. Inwardly, there is a tremendous urge to succeed, to compete, to conform; there is the drive of ambition, the despair, the boredom of everyday existence, and the despair of every human being when he discovers himself to be utterly, irredeemably lonely. All this, consciously or unconsciously, is the battleground of relationship. Unless we bring order in that relationship, whatever the economic, the social, or the scientific revolution may produce, it will inevitably disintegrate because the whole structure of the human mind has not been understood and resolved and made free.

So our problem is that we are responsible to bring about a complete psychological revolution because each one, each human being, is part of society, is not separate from society. There is no such thing as an individual. He may have a name, a separate family, and all the rest of it, but, psychologically, he is not an individual because he is conditioned by his society, by his beliefs, his fears, his dogmas, all those influences which are exercised by society, by the circumstances in which he lives. That is fairly obvious. He is conditioned by the society in which he lives, and the society in which he lives is created by him. He is responsible for that society, and he alone, as a human being, must bring about a transformation in that society.

And that is the greatest responsibility of every human being—not to join certain social reforms; that is totally inadequate, totally absurd; that is a fancy of some people according to their eccentric ideas. What we, as human beings, have to do—and to do this is our responsibility—is to bring about a psychological revolution so that the relationship between man and man is based on order. That order can only come about through a psychological revolution, and this revolution can only come about when each one of us becomes gravely and tremendously responsible.

Most of us feel that someone else will bring about this revolution; that circumstances, God, beliefs, politicians, prayers, reading some books called the "sacred books," and so on will somehow transform our minds—that is, we shift our responsibility to someone else, to some leader, to some social pattern, to some influence. Such ways of thinking show an utter irresponsibility and also a great sense of indolence.

So this is your problem. I am not imposing this problem on you. You may not be aware of it, and the speaker is merely trying to point it out to you; he is not imposing the problem on you. If you are not hungry, no amount of anybody else's saying that you are hungry will make you hungry; but to be healthily hungry, your body must have a great deal of exercise. You have to be aware of this problem: that economic, political, scientific revolution is not the answer; that no leader, however tyrannical or beneficial, no authority, can bring about psychological order except you yourself, as a human being—not in the world of heaven, even if there is such a world, but in this world, and now.

So it is your problem. You may not want it. You may say, "I wish somebody else would show me the way; I will easily follow." Because we are used to following people—in the past, religious teachers; now it is Marx, or your particular guru, or some saint with his peculiar idiosyncrasies—we are always bound to authority. A mind enslaved by authority for centuries, through tradition, through custom, through habit—such a mind is willing to follow and therefore shifts the responsibility on to somebody else; such a mind cannot, under any circumstances, bring about psychological order. And that psychological order is imperative because we must lay the foundation in our daily life—that is the only thing that matters. From there, from the solid foundation, you can go very far. But if you have no foundation, or if you have laid your foundation on belief, on dogma, on authority, in the trust of someone else, then you are completely lost.

So we have to bring about a psychological transformation in our relationship with the society in which we live. Therefore, there is no escape from it into the Himalayas, into becoming a monk or a nun, and taking up social service and all the rest of such juvenile business. We have to live in this world; we have to bring about a radical transformation in our relationship with each other, not in some distant future, but now; and that is our greatest responsibility. Because if you cannot alter the psyche, the inward structure of your mind and heart, then you will be everlastingly in confusion, misery, and despair.

So, if it is a problem to you, not imposed by me, and if you are at all alert, if you are at all taking note of everything that is happening in the world, inevitably you will have this problem facing you. You may run away from it and, therefore, become irresponsible. But if it is a problem to you—as it must be to every thoughtful, intelligent, sensitive human being—then the problem is: How is one to bring about this radical transformation in the psyche, in the psychological structure of the human mind?

I, as a human being, am living in a particular society, and that society is not different from me. I am part of that society, I am conditioned by that society. That society has encouraged my greed, envy, jealousy, ambition, brutality; and I have contributed to that society my brutality, my ambition. We are both in it. I am part of it, I am part of the psychological structure of that society, which is me. Now, how am I to bring about a tremendous revolution within myself?

I see that any revolution—economic, social, scientific—only affects the periphery, the outward boundaries of my mind, but inwardly I am still the same. I may put on different clothes, acquire different forms of technological knowledge, work only a few hours in a week, and so on. But inwardly, I am still in conflict; I am still ambitious, frustrated, under a terrific strain. Unless there is a tremendous transformation there, I cannot be orderly in living; there can be no freedom, no happiness, no escape from sorrow.

So how is a human being to bring about this transformation? The way for most of us is through the will. That is, we exercise our will as a means of achieving a result—the will expressing itself in different ways: through resistance, through control, through conformity, through suppression, through sublimation, through denial. Exercising the will, we have considered, is the way to bring about a psychological change. To discipline oneself endlessly, or to deny oneself endlessly—that is to exercise the will in order to bring about a desired result. Now, to the speaker, the way of the will is the way of destruction. But please do not go to the other conclusion that somebody else is going to do all the work, and that all you have to do is not to exercise your will but to accept, be so devoted or be so sentimental that you will follow the way of the Lord, and all the rest of it.

So most of us are used to the way of the will. Now what is will? Please follow this because we are going to show to you that the way of the will is the way of the most destructive process of a mind. We are going into it logically, not irrationally; we are going into it sanely, and you also must follow it. That is, we are both going to investigate into this question of will. You are not going to accept what I am saying, but we are both going into it, to find out the whole structure of this extraordinary thing called "will" which we exercise in so many ways.

Will is effort. To me, effort under any circumstances perverts the mind. We are going to go into that, and I hope we will be able to communicate with each other. You are used to the action of the will. So when I talk about it, do not translate what you hear in terms of what you have already learned or read, do not resist it. We are, both of us, going to investigate the nature and the significance of the will because we think that by exercising will, we will bring about a psychological change or transformation within ourselves. We are going to show that is not the way.

So, what is will? Whether you exercise it weakly or very strongly, it is still the same process; whether you exercise it negatively or positively, it is still will. When you say, "I must not," and begin to discipline on the most absurd things—such as, "I will not smoke"—there you are exercising the will; there you are making effort. Because there is a contradiction in desire—to smoke and not to smoke—and that contradiction implies effort; and effort means the will to achieve that or this, negatively or positively.

So we are going to find out what we mean by the will. After all, will is the extension of desire—that is clear. I desire something, and I go after it. If it is pleasurable, I go after it much more strongly and push aside anything that stands in the way in order to achieve it. Or, if it is painful, I resist it. The resistance and the pursuit, pleasure and pain, the pursuit of the one and the denial of the other—both involve the action of the will.

So, what is will? Now, probably you have opinions or ideas about the will—your books have told you. Or you have no idea about what will is. For the moment set it aside because I want to convey something to you. You have taken the trouble to come and sit here, so, please listen.

You know, it is one of the most difficult things to listen. We never listen. Now, to listen without resistance is one of the most difficult things to do—to listen to those crows and at the same time to listen to the speaker. Please follow this: to listen to the crows and at the same time to listen to the speaker demands attention. You want to listen to the speaker, but the crows are interfering. So, you resist the noise of the crows, and you say, "I must not listen to the crows, I must pay attention to what the speaker says." What have you done in that process? You have exercised the will to resist the noise of the crows and tried to concentrate on listening to the speaker, so you are not listening. You are making an effort to listen, and all your effort has gone into resistance and concentration; and, therefore, you are not listening at all. Please observe this process in yourself. Whereas if you listen without resistance to the crows and without intense concentration to the speaker, then your attention is not divided; then you listen both to the crows and to the speaker. In that there is no concentration because you are sensitive to both.

You know, it is very difficult to talk about these matters when there is what is generally called distraction. That lady is getting up and wanting to find her way out; and the crows are cawing and saying good night to each other before they go to sleep; and you have to listen to the speaker. To listen to all these at the same time, without any distraction, is a most excellent way to listen—it is the most supreme way to listen with the highest sensitivity.

We are going to listen to the whole structure of the will. As we say, the will is the extension and the strengthening of desire—which is fairly obvious. I want something and I go after it. Now, what is desire? Please listen. We are not saying that you must be without desire, or that you must suppress desire, as all your religious books say, or as all your gurus say. On the contrary, we are going to explore together into this question of desire. If you suppress desire, then you are destroying yourself, you are paralyzing yourself, you are becoming insensitive, dull, stupid—as all religious people have done; to them beauty, sensitivity, is denied because they have suppressed. Whereas if you begin to understand the whole subtlety of desire, the nature of desire, then you will never suppress desire, you will never suppress anything—I will come to it later.

What is desire? Desire arises when you see a beautiful woman, a beautiful car, a well-dressed man, or a nice house. There is perception, sensation through contact, and then desire. I see you wearing a nice coat. There is perception, seeing; the attraction—the cut of that coat—and the sensation; and the desire to have that coat. This is very simple.

Now, what gives continuity to desire? You understand? I know how desire arises—that is fairly simple. What gives continuity to desire? It is this continuity of desire that strengthens, that becomes the will, obviously. Right? So I must find out what gives continuity to desire. If I can find out that, then I know how to deal with desire; I will never suppress it.

Now what gives continuity to desire? I see something beautiful, attractive; a desire has been aroused. And I must find out now what gives it vitality, what gives it the continuity of its strength. There is something pleasurable which I feel desirable, and I give it continuity by thinking about it. One thinks about sex. You think about it and you give it a continuity. Or you think about the pain you had yesterday, the misery; and so you give that also continuity. So the arising of desire is natural, inevitable; you must have desire, you must react; otherwise, you are a dead entity. But what is important is to see, to find out for yourself, when to give continuity to it and when not to.

So you have to understand then the structure of thought, which influences and controls and shapes and gives continuity to desire. Right? That is clear. Thought functions according to memory and so on—into which we are not going now. We are just indicating how desire is strengthened by thinking about it constantly and giving it a continuity—which becomes a will. And with that we will operate. And that will is based on pleasure and on pain. If it is pleasurable, I want more of it; if it is painful, I resist it.

So the resistance to pain or the pursuit of pleasure—both give continuity to desire. And when I understand this, there is never a question of suppression of desire, because when you suppress desire, it will inevitably bring about other conflicts—as in the case of suppressing a disease. You cannot suppress a disease; you have to bring it out; you have to go into it and do all kinds of things. But if you suppress it, it will gain in potency and become stronger and later will attack you. Similarly, when you understand the whole nature of desire and what gives continuity to desire, you will never, under any circumstances, suppress desire. But that does not mean that you indulge in desire. Because the moment you indulge in desire, it brings its own pain, its own pleasure, and you are back again in the vicious circle.

So most human beings are used to this: if they want to change, if they want to drop a habit, they exercise their will. And that will is engendered through contradiction, and therefore, there is a battle going on all the time within one. Is there another way of bringing about a radical transformation within oneself, to find oneself in a totally different dimension, not in the old dimension?

And to explode into the new dimension, one must understand the nature of the old dimension—what is involved in it, what are all the structures, the pains, the nuances, the subtleties of the old dimension. One of the things of the old dimension is the will. So one must understand it, and one must be free of it. That is, one must be free of this idea of effort. And that is one of the most difficult things to do because all our life, from childhood until we die, we are making efforts to be good, to achieve, to become a great man or a little man, to go to heaven or to find God; we say we must do this and we must not do that—we are continuously making effort. You know, goodness flowers naturally. If you make an effort to be good, you are no longer good. But to flower in goodness is the very nature of a mind that is religious. Therefore, a mind that is called religious, that makes an effort to be good, is irreligious.

To find out for oneself and not to accept or deny a way of life in which there is no effort at all, whatever you do in the office, in your home, while walking, while thinking—that demands great investigation, great understanding, immense insight within oneself. When you make effort, what is involved in that effort? First of all, there is strain, physical strain—more and more strain, not because of work or food. But this constant strain—the strain brought about by our ambition, by our disorderliness, our greed, our competition, our brutality, our insensitivity—affects the heart.

Why is it that we have been brought up to make effort? I do not know if you have ever asked yourself this: Why do you make effort? To better yourself? To be better in your office? To control yourself? To change the psyche, the psychological thoughts and feelings, and all the rest of it? Have you succeeded in changing yourself through effort, radically, not superficially? Or is there a different approach to this thing altogether? Because all effort destroys spontaneity. If you are not spontaneous, then you are mechanical, you become dull, you become insensitive. You become insensitive to that moon, and when you cannot see the beauty of that moon spontaneously, naturally, with vitality, with vigor, then such a mind is a dead mind, is an inefficient mind, is a disorderly mind, is an irreligious mind.

But we never look at the moon, we never see the beauty of it. Passing by occasionally, if somebody points it out and asks you to look at it, you turn your head up and look at it; but your thoughts, your worries, occupy greater space, and so you never look. You never look at the beauty of the sea or the river, of a tree in another's garden. You never look at the beauty of the face of a child, of a women, of a man. Because, to you, beauty is always associated with sex; and all your religious books have said, "Have nothing whatever to do with woman if you want to find God." So in denying beauty you have denied life, and when you have denied life, you cannot find life everlasting. Life is here, not in the hereafter.

So it is imperative that you find out for yourself why you make effort. I can explain, but explanations, words, are not the facts—just as the word *tree* is not the tree. The explanation is not the fact of your own discovery. When you discover it for yourself, then it becomes tremendously vital; then it has significance; then it gives you vitality to meet that fact. Look! If I tell you to look at that moon, you will look; but you have not looked at all because you have been told to look. But if you are listening to the speaker as well as looking at that moon, then you will see how extraordinarily united the attention is which looks at the moon and listens to the words of the speaker—they are not two different things, two different activities. It is the same energy that looks, and it is the same energy that listens. But when you divide it as an act of listening and as an act of looking, then you have created a contradiction. Then, in that contradiction, there is effort. Then, you exclude the moon and listen to the speaker. When you exclude the moon and listen to the speaker, you are not listening to the speaker.

And the beauty of listening lies in being highly sensitive to everything about you—to the ugliness, to the dirt, to the squalor, to the poverty about you, and also to the dirt, to the disorder, to the poverty of one's own being. When you are aware of both, then there is no effort. That is, when there is an awareness which is without choice, then there is no effort. If you say, "I will be aware of the moon," you choose to be aware of that; then, you will also choose not to be aware of the speaker and what he says; so there is a division—the one you exclude, and the other you are aware of. In that exclusion and in that division there is a contradiction. It is this contradiction that breeds conflict and therefore effort. Whereas if you listen and if you observe without any choice, without any exclusion, without any contradiction, then there is no effort at all.

We will go into this question of effort perhaps at the next meeting. But what is important is to understand this: Will inevitably creates contradiction, whether it is a positive will or negative will, and when the mind is in contradiction, outwardly or inwardly, there must be effort; and where there is effort, there is no attention, there is no awareness, and hence all the problems arise.

So a mind that listens and at the same time looks at the moon without a contradiction—such a mind is sensitive to everything; and such a mind learns, learns indefinitely, never accumulating what it has learned as knowledge. Because a mind that is merely accumulating knowledge and storing it up is a dull mind, an insensitive mind. But a mind that is learning is highly sensitive.

And you can only learn when you observe, when you see, when you hear, when you feel, when you have this extraordinarily complete feeling and, therefore, high sensitivity. It is only such a mind that has no conflict; and therefore such a mind, when it goes very far and very deeply, is an untortured mind; it is not marked, it is not distorted. And it is only such a mind that can see what is truth; and it is only such a mind that can live beyond time.

February 14, 1965

Third Talk in Bombay

I do not think you have tried to understand the meaning of the word *share.* Sharing does not imply any credit, nor is there, in the act of sharing, you or I. There is no consciousness of giving or taking; there is only the act of sharing in which there is no credit for the giver or the taker. And to share—that is, to partake—implies a great deal: that both of us, the speaker as well as you, the listener, are in a state of mind where there is only the sense, or the feeling, or the affection, or that love that, unknowingly or without any identification with any personality, shares. It is not that, in that sharing, there is no instruction. There is neither the teacher nor the pupil, neither the giver nor the taker, but only an act of complete communion in that sharing. I do not know if you ever have had that feeling of complete union, complete communion in the act of sharing, which is really an act of great affection, compassion.

And we are going to go into something that demands not a merely verbal, dialectical explanation, or the exchange of opinions, or one idea opposed to another idea—when these are there, this act of sharing becomes very poor. We are talking this evening about the question of action. But to understand it, not merely verbally, not merely intellectually, but with a totality of one's whole being, one has to go beyond words. It is only then there is communion, there is sharing, there is partaking together of something vital. And this question of action needs not only a verbal explanation but, rather and much more, a moving together, feeling our way hesitantly together into this question of what is action.

So to commune with one another there must be, surely, not only a verbal comprehension but also an intensity, an intensity at the same time and at the same level; otherwise, no communion, no sharing is possible. There must be an intensity, at the same time, at the same depth, at the same level—which is, after all, love; which is compassion. And to understand this problem of action, one needs not only an objective mind, an objective examination, but also a great deal of subtlety, a sensitivity—not the mere acceptance or denial of a certain definition of what it is to act, but rather the discovery for oneself of this extraordinary thing called "life," which is action. Existence is action. There are two states—at least it seems to me—in existence. There is that state which is static—which is to exist. There is that movement which is dynamic, which is existence.

Life is existence, is a movement, and this movement is action. Life—the totality of life, not parts of it, the whole state of existence—is action. But when we merely exist, as most of us do, then the problem of action becomes complex. Existence has no division; it is not a fragmentary state of mind or being; in that a totality of action is possible. But when we divide existence into different segments, fragments, then action becomes contradictory.

We have divided life as business, religious, worldly, psychological, artistic, literary, and so on. It is broken up into various fragments: the tribal division, which is glorified into nationalism; the tribal leaders; the tribal religions; the various fragments of our life, such as going to an office, and there acting, thinking, and feeling differently from the acts when you come home; the act when you get into a bus; the act when you are walking; the act when you try to do some social work; and the worship—religious pursuit. The various fragments of our life, because they are fragmentary, are, and must inevitably be, in conflict with each other; therefore, our actions inevitably contradict each other. This is our life. This is your everyday life. Your behavior at home is different from the behavior in the office or at your club or when you are meeting some friends; or the behavior, the idea of action—which is behavior—is different when you are by yourself, alone in your room.

So our life, as one observes, is fragmentary, broken up. And we try to integrate all these different parts together. But one can never integrate. To integrate is to bring together. When you do integrate the different parts, it breaks apart again. So, what we are going to discover is not how to integrate the parts but rather what is total action—whether in the office, or when you go to the church or temple, or when you are at home, or when you are by yourself, or when you are looking at the sea or when you are communing with nature; the totality of it. We are going to find out if there is such an action, and therefore, if we can live in a state of constant action which is existence, which is a movement, which is life, and which is not fragmentary. That is our issue for this evening.

Most of us want to live, if we can, a fairly peaceful, intelligent, harmonious life, with a certain integrity, not being controlled by environment, not everlastingly being in battle with another or with oneself. One wants to live a fairly intelligent, integrated life. And that is not possible because all our activities are in a state of contradiction, not only consciously, but also unconsciously. If one observes oneself—which is, after all, what we are doing at these meetings—one will find that one is not merely listening to the speaker but rather using the words of the speaker as a mirror to examine the ways of one's own mind, and then to discover for oneself what is true and what is false—not because somebody else points it out—and, in that state, to see for oneself the contradictory nature of one's activities.

Now why is life so contradictory? Why is there such contradiction in ourselves, in our outlook, in our feeling, in our behavior, in our ideas? And why is there this fragmenting of life—in the office, at the home, the religious and the nonreligious, the mundane, and so on—each activity contradicting the other.

We were discussing the other day "desire." Desire is there when there is a feeling of missing something, wanting something. That is, when you desire something, it is an indication, is it not, that you are missing something. But desire, in itself, is not contradictory. But there is contradiction when the objects of desire are contradictory or different or opposed. Desire is constant, but the objects of desire change, vary, or are opposed; and hence every activity of desire breeds contradiction. That is, every act of desire is a state of wanting, missing, in relation to the object; then one feels desire is contradictory. I want peace, and also at the same time I am full of competition. I want to be good, and at the same time I have a great feeling of antagonism. The ideas, the objects of desire, are contradictory, not desire itself. I think this is important to understand. Most people believe that desire, in itself, is contradictory; hence they try to suppress, sublimate, or control, or do all kinds of things with desire.

So the sense of missing, the sense of insufficiency, makes us compare; and out of this comparison arises the urge, the desire, the longing for that which will fill that emptiness, that sense of missing. It is very simple. I am not trying to complicate it. Because the whole thing is very complicated, one has to look at it very simply.

We said, the other night, that desire is the outcome of perception—seeing, sensation, contact, and then desire. This is what happens: there is a beautiful car—seeing it, touching it, the sensation, the desire. And that desire is strengthened and perpetuated by thought, and hence the conflict to achieve or to have that car. That car gives fulfillment, filling that emptiness, that sense of missing—if I had that car, I would do this and that; I would have more power, more money. The sense of missing is the state of desire. So, then, there is the conflict. That is, most of us are insufficient in ourselves—at least, we think we are—and we try to fill that insufficiency, which is a form of desire; and that insufficiency breeds this contradiction, and hence contradictory activities arise.

Please, as I said, you are not listening merely to the words of the speaker. You are listening to your own mind, observing your own state of being. Then you will see, for yourself, how contradiction arises. I think the car will give me happiness, power, position, status. And also, deep down within me, there is the feeling of affection, sympathy, kindliness; and also there is the feeling that I must achieve, I must be somebody—which is contradictory. And this contradiction arises out of the enormous sense of insufficiency, the sense of emptiness, the sense of loneliness. So we make constant effort—effort being struggling, striving. That is our life: constantly striving to become, to achieve, to be good, to fulfill, to have status, position, power, to dominate, to become clever. This is our life: a constant struggle, an endless struggle until we die; and to escape from this struggle we invent gods, temples, a way of life away from this. Until you understand the struggle, do what you will, you will have no peace. You may have superficial peace—superficially, taking a pill tranquilizes—but that will not solve your problem. The problem is much deeper.

So, to understand what is action—not right action or wrong action—one has to understand this vast process of desire; and also one has to understand this division between idea and action. And also one has to understand the contradictory nature of the thinker and the thought, or the observer and the thing observed.

So, first we are going to examine this contradictory nature of idea and action. That is, we have a formula of what is right action—the ideal, the pattern, the image, the symbol, the 'what should be', the 'what must be'; and there is the fact, *what is*. That is clear, isn't it? There is the ideal, the hero, the example, the 'what should be', and there is the *what is*. *What is* is entirely different from 'what should be'. And we are always approximating *what is* with 'what should be'. We are violent; that is a fact. That is, we are actually violent; the ideal is nonviolence, and so we are always trying to approximate *what is* with 'what should be', and hence there arises a contradiction.

And so, the idealist is always in conflict, is always battling with "I must not" and "I must"—suppressing, driving, struggling to transform *what is* into 'what should be'. The whole of our life is this battle, as the life of most of us is. I have been, I am, and what I should be—the "what I should be" is the ideal, the pattern, the formula; the "I am" is the result of "what I have been"; and so, there is this constant battle maintained. Please observe yourself. We use the ideal as a means of changing *what is,* as an incentive. Please do follow this because we are going to go into something that demands your attention. We use the ideal as an incentive to transform or change or modify *what is,* hence the conflict, and hence the struggle.

So, we never know *what is,* but only in relation to or with 'what should be'. So we never observe *what is.* We never come into direct contact with *what is,* but we come into contact with *what is* through 'what should be' or 'what should not be'. Therefore, there is no complete communion with *what is,* and hence the conflict. Because we are trying to change *what is* into something which we imagine will give us greater pleasure or avoidance of pain, there arises the battle, the conflict, the struggle, the everlasting brutality of trying to do something with an ideal.

So there is this division: the fact, the *what is,* and the pattern or the formula or the ideal, the 'what should be'. But yet, the *what is* must change. We have used the ideal, the example, as the means or as an incentive to alter the facts, the *what is,* and hence we live in conflict. And a mind that lives in conflict is a dead mind, is an insensitive mind, is a brutalized mind. A mind that has suppressed suffers infinitely. And a mind that is a tortured mind cannot possibly see what is true, cannot possibly discover something beyond time—if there is such a thing. So it is only a mind that is fresh, innocent, young, vital, that can face the fact, that can see what is true—not a tortured mind. All the saints, all these mahatmas, gurus, have tortured minds; and, therefore, they never see what is true.

A mind is meant to be fresh, young, innocent—not to be tortured, bullied, twisted. And yet the *what is* must be changed; that is important, obviously. Suppose one is greedy; the ideal is to be nongreedy. Or, take a much more religious problem with which we are acquainted—to find God you must be a saint. So there is the ideal and there is the fact, and then there is the battle—which is to suppress, control, everlastingly be in battle with what is called "sex," and therefore the escape from that fact. One does all kinds of absurd social reforms, runs away to the Himalayas, shuts oneself up, brutalizes everything, to escape from the fact. And yet, the fact must be understood and transformed without conflict. Am I making myself clear? The fact—which is the *what is* as violence, as lust, as greed, and so on—must be changed without effort; the moment you make effort, the moment you strive or struggle, you have twisted the mind; you have made the mind dull, insensitive.

To live, you must be extraordinarily sensitive—sensitive to beauty, sensitive to ugliness, to the squalor, to the brutalities, to the dirt, to the filth of the street in this town, to the clouds full of an evening with the light of the sun, to the reflection on the water, to a lovely face, to a beautiful smile. To be sensitive to everything is the very nature, the very existence of life. But when a mind is brutalized by effort, by constant battle, through suppression or sublimation or an escape, such a mind becomes a dull, dreary, stupid mind, without any sensitivity. So, to bring about a mutation in the fact, in the *what is* without effort—that is the issue. Is it possible to look at that fact, the *what is,* without the desire to transform it, without the desire to change it, without identifying yourself with it?

You know, I was told that an electron, measured by an instrument, behaves in one way—which can be measured on the graph. But when that same electron is observed by the human eye through a microscope, that very observation by the human mind, through the microscope, alters the behavior of that electron. That is, the human watching the electron brings about in the electron itself a different behavior, and that behavior is different from the behavior when the human mind is not observing it.

We have been talking for many years about seeing, observing, looking. Is it possible to look at a flower, a tree, or a face without naming it, without identifying yourself with it through condemnation, or justification, or explaining? That is, is it possible to look at it without thought? This does not mean that you go blank, but you look at it. And it is only possible to look when there is no sense of the 'me' interfering with the look. You understand? That is, there is the fact that I am violent. And I have pushed away from me the silly idea of not being violent, as that is too juvenile, too absurd, and has no meaning. *What is* is the fact—that I am violent. And also I see that to struggle to get rid of it, to bring about a change in it, needs effort, and that the very effort which is exercised is a part of violence. And yet, I realize that violence must be completely changed, transformed; there must be a mutation in that.

Now, how is it to be done? If you just push it aside because this subject is very difficult, you will miss an extraordinary state of life: existence without effort, and therefore, a life of the highest sensitivity, which is the highest intelligence. And it is only this extraordinarily heightened intelligence that can discover the limits and the measure of time, and can go beyond that. Do you understand the question, the problem? So far, we have used the ideal as a means or as an incentive to get rid of *what is,* and that breeds contradiction, hypocrisy, hardness, brutality. And if we push that ideal aside, then we are left with the fact. Then we see that the fact must be altered, and that it must be altered without the least friction. Any friction, any struggle, any effort, destroys the sensitivity of the mind and the heart.

So what is one to do? What one comes to do is to observe the fact—to observe the fact without any translation, interpretation, identification, condemnation, evaluation—just to observe. It is fairly easy to observe a flower without naming it, without saying, "I like" or "I don't like." Just to observe—one can do that with outward things which do not interfere psychologically, emotionally. But it is different to observe violence in that manner—which is, not to name that feeling of violence, not to condemn it, not to judge it, not to evaluate it, not to identify it, but just to observe it. When you just observe the fact, then you will see that there is a different behavior, as there is when the electron is observed. When you look at the fact without any pressure, then that fact undergoes a complete mutation, a complete change, without effort.

We dissipate energy by denying the fact, by suppressing it, by wishing to escape from it or dominate it or control it or suppress it. We are exercising energy in doing this. And when we stop doing that, naturally, without effort, then we have all that energy to observe; and that very energy of observation, with the fact—which is also energy—becomes a total energy, and therefore, there is no contradiction.

Then there is the fact: the thinker and the thought. You observe this in yourself as the experiencer and the experienced. Again, there is the division, a contradiction, a duality and, therefore, a conflict. What we are trying to do is rather to share together, which is really a sense of real affection, a great sense of love in which there is no sense of conflict at any time—when you are in an office, when you are at home, with your family, with your wife, with your husband, doing anything, any action, without effort. And it is possible only when every contradiction is understood, is observed.

And one of the major contradictions in our life is this: the division between the thinker and the thought. The thinker for most so-called religious people is the atma and all that stuff; something that is first, and thought afterwards. But if you observe, there is no first, there is only thinking; thinking invents the thinker, and the thinker assumes a permanency in time, as the supreme, the higher self, the atma; but it is invented by thought. Without thought, there is no thinker, so we have this contradiction not only at the conscious level but at the unconscious level. There is this division—mine and not mine; having experience and to experience more; to change the thought by the thinker. So there is this duality, a battle that is going on consciously or unconsciously, all the time. And as long as we maintain the thinker as the center, as the observer, there must be conflict, and hence action breeding further conflict. So one has to observe thought without the thinker—that is, not to condemn thought, not to change it, not to suppress it, not to say this thought is good, that thought is right, this thought is noble, that thought is ignoble; but just to observe thought.

Then, you will say, "Who is the observer who observes thought?" The observer, the thinker, exists only when there is the idea to transform the thought, to suppress the thought, to change the thought, to dominate the thought, to control the thought. Only when there is the activity of doing something about the thought, is there the thinker. But when that whole activity stops, there is thinking, and not the observer thinking. And when you so observe, you will see that, in the observation, the thought undergoes a fundamental revolution; and, therefore, life, existence, is such that there is no contradiction in action. This is not an ideal; this is not something for you to achieve. Do not think in that way anymore. This is a natural process, if you understand this extraordinary phenomenon of observation: to observe oneself without any desire, without any sense of wanting to change, to mutate, to suppress—just to observe.

You know, we observe or we have the habit of observing, looking, seeing, and hearing at the level of dimension which is time. We look at everything through time—not only chronological time, but the time which the mind has invented as tomorrow. Actually, there is no tomorrow. We have invented it psychologically. There is only tomorrow in the sense of chronological time. We look at thought, at greed, at envy, at ambition, at our stupidity, at our brutality, at violence, at pleasure and love through this dimension of time, and we use time as a means to transform the thing that we observe. Hence the contradiction between the fact which is living, and time which is fixed.

So one has really to look at life, this vast field—not the tribal life of an Indian, or a Christian, or a Buddhist, or a German, or a Russian, or a communist, which are all tribal with their witch doctors; but the life which is enormous, palpitating, vital, immense—with eyes that are merely observing, and therefore act totally, act with all one's being, at every minute. Then there is no contradiction because one has understood the whole nature of duality or contradiction.

We explained the feeling of insufficiency, emptiness, missing, as desire—desire to which thought gives continuity—and escaping from it as a form of action, or filling that emptiness as another form of action. We also explained the contradiction between the thinker and the thought, and the contradiction between the fact, the *what is,* and the ideal. When you have understood this whole process by observing—not intellectualizing, not getting emotionalized, but just by observing—then you will see that life is action, not different actions at different levels contradicting each other, but a total activity as existence, as a movement; then you can go to the office, you can do everything totally, not contradictorily.

Only a mind that has observed all its activities, all its behavior—it is only such a mind that can live without effort; and therefore its action is not contradictory; and therefore it is not in bondage to time.

February 17, 1965

Fourth Talk in Bombay

If I may, I would like to talk about something that may be considered rather complex. But it is really quite simple. We like to make things complex, we like to complicate things. We think it is rather intellectual to be complicated, to treat everything in an intellectual or in a traditional way, and thereby give the problem or the issue a complex turn. But to understand anything rather deeply, one must approach the issue simply—that is, not verbally or emotionally merely, but rather with a mind that is very young. Most of us have old minds because we have had so many experiences, we are bruised, we have had so many shocks, so many problems; and we lose the elasticity, the quickness of action. A young mind, surely, is a mind that acts on the seeing and the observing. That is, a young mind is a mind to which seeing is acting.

I wonder how you listen to a sound. Sound plays an important part in our life. The sound of a bird, the thunder, the incessant restless waves of the sea, the hum of a great town, the whisper among the leaves, the laughter, the cry, a word—these are all forms of sound, and they play an extraordinary part in our life, not only as music, but also as everyday sound. How is one to listen to the sound around one—to the sound of the crows, to that distant music? Does one listen to it with one's own noise, or does one listen to it without noise?

Most of us listen with our own peculiar noises of chatter, of opinion, of judgment, of evaluation, the naming, and we never listen to the fact. We listen to our own chattering and are not actually listening. So, to listen, actually to listen, the mind must be extraordinarily quiet and silent. When you are listening to the speaker, if you are carrying on your own conversation with yourself, turning out your opinions or ideas or conclusions or evaluations, you are actually not listening to the speaker at all. But to listen not only to the speaker but also to the birds, to the noise of everyday life, there must be a certain quietness, a certain silence.

Most of us are not silent. We are not only carrying on a conversation with ourselves, but we are always talking, talking endlessly. Now to listen, we must have a certain sense of space, and there is no space if we are chattering to ourselves. And to listen demands a certain quietness, and to listen with quietness demands a certain discipline. Discipline, for most of us, is the suppression of our own particular noise, our own judgment, our own evaluation. To stop chattering, at least for the moment, we try to suppress it, and thereby make an effort to listen to the speaker or to the bird. Discipline, for most of us, is a form of suppression; it is a form of conformity to a pattern. To listen to the sound, every form of control, suppression, must naturally disappear. If you listened, you would find it extraordinarily difficult to stop your own noise, your own chattering, and to listen quietly.

I am using the word *discipline* in its right sense, its right meaning—which is, to learn. Discipline does not imply, in the original sense of that word, conformity, suppression, imitation, but rather a process of learning. And learning demands not mere accumulation of knowledge—which any machine can do. No machine can learn; even an electronic computer or electronic brain cannot learn. The computers and the electronic brains can only accumulate knowledge, information, and give it back to you. So the act of learning is the act of discipline, and this is very important to understand.

We are going to go into something this evening that demands the act of learning each minute—not a conformity, not a suppression, but rather a learning. And there can be no learning if you are merely comparing what you hear with what you already know or have read—however widely, however intelligently. If you are comparing, you cease to learn. Learning can only take place when the mind is fairly silent and out of that silence listens; otherwise, there is no learning. When you want to learn a new language, a new technique, a new something which you do not know, your mind has to be comparatively quiet; if it is not quiet, it is not learning. When you already know the language or the technique, you merely add further information; the adding of further information is merely acquiring more knowledge, but not learning.

And to learn is to discipline. All relationship is a form of discipline, and all relationship is a movement. No relationship is static, and every relationship demands a new learning. Even though you have been married for forty years and have established a comfortable, steady, respectable relationship with your wife or husband, the moment you have already established it as a pattern, you have ceased to learn. Relationship is a movement, it is not static. And each relationship demands that you learn about it constantly because relationship is constantly changing, moving, vital; otherwise, you are not related at all. You may think that you are related, but actually you are related to your own image of the other person, or to the experience which you both had, or to the pain or the hurt or the pleasure. The image, the symbol, the idea—with that you approach a person, and therefore you make relationship a dead thing, a static thing, without any life, without any vitality, without passion. It is only a mind that is learning that is very passionate.

We are using the word *passion* not in a sense of heightened pleasure but rather that state of mind that is always learning and, therefore, always eager, alive, moving, vital, vigorous, young, and therefore passionate. Very few of us are passionate. We have sensual pleasures, lust, enjoyment; but the sense of passion most of us have not. Without passion, in the large sense or meaning of that word, how can you learn, how can you discover new things, how can you inquire, how can you run with the movement of inquiry?

And a mind that is very passionate is always in danger. Perhaps most of us, unconsciously, are aware of this passionate mind which is learning and therefore acting, and have failed unconsciously; and probably that is one of the reasons why we are never passionate. We are respectable, we conform. We accept, we obey. There is respectability, duty, and all the rest of those words which we use to smother the act of learning.

This act of learning, we said, is discipline. This discipline has no conformity of any kind and therefore no suppression because when you are learning about your feelings, about your anger, about your sexual appetites, and other things, there is no occasion to suppress, there is no occasion to indulge. And this is one of the most difficult things to do because all our tradition, all the past, all the memory, the habits, have set the mind in a particular groove, and we follow easily in the groove, and we do not want to be disturbed in any way from that groove. Therefore, for most of us, discipline is merely conformity, suppression, imitation, ultimately leading to a very respectable life—if it is at all life. A man caught within the framework of respectability, of suppression, of imitation, conformity—he does not live at all; all he has learned, all he has acquired is an adjustment to a pattern; and the discipline which he has followed has destroyed him.

But we are talking of the act of learning which can only come about when there is an intense aliveness, passion; we are talking of discipline which is an act of learning. The act of learning is every minute, not that you have learned and you apply what you have learned to the next incident—then you cease to learn. And this kind of discipline, which we are talking about, is necessary because, as we said, all relationship is a movement in discipline—which is in learning. And this discipline, which is the act of learning every minute, is essential to inquire into something which demands a great deal of insight, understanding.

For most of us pleasure is of the greatest importance, and all our values, our longings, our search is for more pleasure. And pleasure is not love. To understand pleasure—not to deny it but to learn about it—demands that you come upon pleasure with a fresh mind. Pleasure is enjoyment, a delight; and it is sensual enjoyment also. When you see a cloud full of light of an evening, it is a great delight. If at all you look up at the sky, if you are not caught up in your daily worries and amusements and aches, there is a delight in looking at that cloud, at the sky, at the light on the water; there is the enjoyment of seeing a fine face full of smiles and innocency; and there is also the sensual pleasure, the sensual enjoyment, having a good meal, hearing good music—both intellectual as well as physical, the sensation of taste, of sex, of ideas, and so on. There is intellectual pleasure, emotional pleasure, and physical enjoyment in all that; and that is pleasure. But love is something entirely different. Probably we are going to discuss that this evening.

First of all, to understand pleasure we must come to it to learn, not to suppress it, not to indulge in it. To learn about it is a discipline, which demands that you neither indulge nor deny. The learning comes when you understand that if there is any form of suppression, denial, control, you cease to learn, there is no learning. Therefore, to understand the whole problem of pleasure, you must come to it with a fresh mind. Because, for us, pleasure is extraordinarily important. We do things out of pleasure. We run away from anything that is painful, and we reduce things to the values, to the criteria of pleasure. So pleasure plays an extraordinarily important part in our life, as an ideal, as a man who gives up this so-called worldly life to find another kind of life—it is still the basis of pleasure. Or when a man says, "I must help the poor," and indulges in social reform, it is still an act of pleasure; he may cover it up by saying "service," "goodness," and all the rest of it; but it is still a movement of the mind that is seeking pleasure or escaping from anything that causes a disturbance which it calls pain. If you observe yourself, this is what we are doing in daily life, every moment. You like somebody because he flatters you, and you do not like another because he says something which is true and which you do not like, and you create an antagonism; and therefore you live with a constant battle.

So it is very important to understand this thing called pleasure. I mean by "understand" to learn about it. There is a great deal to learn because all our sensory reactions, all the values that we have created, all the demands—the so-called self-sacrifice, the denial, the acceptance—are based on this extraordinary thing: a refined or a crude form of pleasure. We commit ourselves to various activities—as communists, as socialists, or what you will—on this basis. Because we think that by identifying ourselves with a particular activity, with a particular idea, with a particular pattern of life, we shall have greater pleasure, we shall derive a greater benefit; and that value, that benefit is based on the identification of ourselves with a particular form of activity as pleasure. Please observe all this.

You are not listening to the words merely, but actually listening to find out the truth or the falseness of what is being said. It is your life; it is your everyday life. Most of us waste this extraordinary thing called life. We have lived forty or sixty years, have gone to the office, have engaged ourselves in social activity, escaping in various forms; and at the end of it, we have nothing but an empty, dull, stupid life, a wasted life. And that is why it is very important, if you would begin anew, to understand this issue of pleasure. Because the suppressing or the denying of pleasure does not solve the problem of pleasure. The so-called religious people suppress every form of pleasure, at least they attempt it, and therefore they become dull, starved human beings. And such a mind is arid, dull, insensitive, and cannot possibly find out what is the real.

So it is very important to understand the activities of pleasure. To look at a beautiful tree is a lovely thing; it is a great delight—what is wrong with that? But to look at a woman or a man with pleasure—you call that immoral because to you pleasure is always involved in, or related to, that one thing, the woman or the man; or it is the escape from the pains of relationship, and therefore you seek elsewhere a pleasure—in an idea, in an escape, in a certain activity.

Now, pleasure has created this pattern of social life. We take pleasure in ambition, in competition, in comparing, in acquiring knowledge, or power, or position, prestige, status. And that pursuit of pleasure as ambition, competition, greed, envy, status, domination, power, is respectable. It is made respectable by a society which has only one concept: that you shall lead a moral life, which is a respectable life. You can be ambitious, you can be greedy, you can be violent, you can be competitive, you can be a ruthless human being; but society accepts it because at the end of your ambition, you are either a so-called successful man with plenty of money, or a failure and therefore a frustrated human being. So social morality is immorality.

Please listen to all this, neither agreeing nor disagreeing; see the fact. And to see the fact—that is, to understand the fact—don't evolve ideas about it, don't have opinions about it. You are learning about it. And to learn you must come with a mind that is inquiring, therefore passionate, eager, and therefore young. Morality, which is custom, which is habit, is considered respectable within the pattern as long as you are conforming to the pattern. There are people who revolt against that pattern—this is happening all the time. Revolt is a reaction to the pattern. This reaction takes many forms—the beatniks, the Beatles, the Teddy boys, and so on; but they are still within the pattern. To be really moral is quite a different thing. And that is why one has to understand the nature of virtue and the nature of pleasure. Our social custom, habit, tradition, relationship—all this is based on pleasure. I am not using that word *pleasure* in a small sense, in a limited sense; I am using it in its widest sense. Our society is based on pleasure, and all our relationship is based on that: you are my friend as long as I comply with what you like, as long as I help you to get better business; but the moment I criticize you, I am not your friend—it is so obvious and silly.

Without the understanding of pleasure you will never be able to understand love. Love is not pleasure. Love is something entirely different. And to understand pleasure, as I said, you have to learn about it. Now for most of us, for every human being, sex is a problem. Why? Listen to this very carefully. Because you are not able to solve it, you run away from it. The sannyasi runs away from it by taking a vow of celibacy, by denying.

Please see what happens to such a mind. By denying something which is a part of your whole structure—the glands and so on—by suppressing it, you have made yourself arid, and there is a constant battle going on within yourself.

As we were saying, we have only two ways of meeting any problem, apparently: either suppressing it or running away from it. Suppressing it is really the same thing as running away from it. And we have a whole network of escapes—very intricate, intellectual, emotional—and ordinary everyday activity. There are various forms of escapes into which we will not go for the moment. But we have this problem. The sannyasi escapes from it in one way, but he has not resolved it; he has suppressed it by taking a vow, and the whole problem is boiling in him. He may put on the outward robe of simplicity, but this becomes an extraordinary issue for him too, as it is for the man who lives an ordinary life.

How do you solve that problem? You must solve it. It is an act of pleasure. You must understand it. How do you solve it? If you don't solve it, then you merely become caught in a habit. It means a routine; your mind becomes dull, stupid, heavy; and that is the only thing you have. And you have to solve the problem. First of all, do not condemn it, as you are going to learn about it. Please learn about it. That is why we talk about learning. When intellectually, emotionally, you are throttled, you have merely a repetitive mind, intellectually; what other people have said or done, you copy, you imitate; you quote endlessly the Gita, or the Upanishads, or some sacred book; intellectually, you are starved, empty, dull. In your office, you are intellectually imitating, copying day after day, doing the same thing whether in your office, or in your factory, or whatever you do in your home—the constant repetition. So, the intellect, which must be vital, clear, reasonable, healthy, free, has been smothered; otherwise, there is no outlet there, there is no creative action there. And emotionally, aesthetically, you are starved because you deny emotion with sensitivity—sensitivity to see beauty, to enjoy the loveliness of an evening, to look at a tree and be intimately in communion with nature. So what have you left? You have only one thing in life which is your own, and it becomes an immense problem.

So a mind that would understand that problem must deal with it immediately because any problem that goes on day after day dulls the spirit, dulls the mind. Haven't you noticed a mind that has a problem which it is not capable of resolving? What happens to such a mind? Either it is going to escape into some other problem, or it suppresses it, and therefore it becomes neurotic—so-called sanely neurotic, but it is neurotic. So each problem, whatever it is—emotional, intellectual, physical—must be resolved immediately and not carried over for the next day because the next day you have other problems to meet.

And therefore you have to learn. But you cannot learn if you have not resolved the problems of today, and you merely carry them over to tomorrow. So each problem, however intricate, however difficult, however demanding, must be resolved on the day, on the instant. Please see the importance of this. A mind that gives root to a problem because it has not been able to tackle it, because it has not the capacity, it has not the intensity, it has not the drive to learn—such a mind, as you see in this world, becomes insensitive, fearful, ugly, concerned with itself, self-centered, brutal.

So this problem of so-called sex must be solved. And to solve it intelligently—not run away from it, or suppress it, or take a vow of some idiocy, or indulge in it—one has to understand this problem of pleasure. And also one has to understand the other issue—which is, most human beings are secondhand people. You can quote the Gita upside down, but you are a secondhand human being. You have nothing original. There is nothing in you which is spontaneous, real, either intellectually or aesthetically or morally. And there is only one thing left: hunger, appetite as food, and sex. There is compulsive eating and compulsive sex. You have observed people eating, gorging themselves—and the same thing, sexually.

So, to understand this very complex problem—because in that is involved beauty, affection, love—you have to understand pleasure, and to break through this conditioning of a mind that is repetitive, of a mind that merely repeats what others have said for centuries or ten years ago. It is a marvelous escape to quote Marx or Stalin or Lenin, and it is a marvelous escape to quote the Gita, as though you have understood any of it at all. You have to live, and to live you cannot have problems.

So, to understand this problem of sex, you must free the mind, the intellect, so that it can look, understand, and move; and also emotionally, aesthetically, you have to look at the trees, the mountains, and the rivers, the squalor of a filthy street, to be aware of your children, how they are brought up, how they are dressed, how you treat them, how you talk to them. You have to see the beauty of a line, of a building, of a mountain, of the curve of a river; to see the beauty of a face—all that is the releasing of that energy, not through suppression, not through identification with some idea, but it is the releasing of energy in all directions so that your mind is active, aesthetically, intellectually, with reason, with clarity, seeing things as they are. The beauty of a tree, of a bird on the wing, the light on the water, and the many other things in life—when you are not aware of all that, naturally, you have only this problem.

Society says that you must be moral, and that morality is the family. The family becomes deadly when it is confined to the family; that is, the family is the individual, and the individual which is the family is opposed to the many, to the collective, to society; then there begins the whole destructive process. So virtue has nothing whatsoever to do with respectability. Virtue is something like a flower that is flowering; that is not a state that you have achieved. You know goodness; you cannot achieve goodness, you cannot achieve humility. It is only the vain man that struggles to become humble. Either you are or you are not good. The 'being' is not the 'becoming'. You cannot become good, you cannot become humble. And so is virtue. The moral structure of a society which is based on imitation, fear, ugly, personal demands and ambitions, greed, envy—that is not virtue, nor is it moral. Virtue is the spontaneous action of love—spontaneous, not a calculated, cultivated thing called virtue. It must be spontaneous; otherwise, it is not virtue. How can it be virtue if it is a calculated thing, if it is practiced, if it is a mechanical thing?

So you have to understand pleasure, and you have also to understand the nature and significance of pleasure and sorrow—perhaps we shall discuss this some other day. And also you have to understand virtue and love.

Now, love is something that cannot be cultivated. You cannot say, "I will learn, I will practice love." Most idealists, most people who are escaping from themselves through various forms of intellectual, emotional activities, have no love. They may be marvelous social reformers, excellent politicians—if there is such an excellent thing called politician—but they have no love at all. Love is something entirely different from pleasure. But you cannot come upon love without understanding it with the depth of passion—not denying it, not running away from it, but understanding it. There is a great delight in the beauty of pleasure.

So love is not to be cultivated. Love cannot be divided into divine and physical; it is only love—not that you love many or the one. That again is an absurd question to ask: Do you love all? You know, a flower that has perfume is not concerned with who comes to smell it, or who turns its back upon it. So is love. Love is not a memory. Love is not a thing of the mind or the intellect. But it comes into being naturally as compassion when this whole problem of existence—as fear, greed, envy, despair, hope—has been understood and resolved. An ambitious man cannot love. A man who is attached to his family has no love. Nor has jealousy anything to do with love. When you say, "I love my wife," you really do not mean it because the next moment you are jealous of her.

Love implies great freedom—not to do what you like. But love comes only when the mind is very quiet, disinterested, not self-centered. These are not ideals. If you have no love, do what you will—go after all the gods on earth, do all the social activities, try to reform the poor, the politics, write books, write poems—you are a dead human being. And without love your problems will increase, multiply endlessly. And with love, do what you will, there is no risk; there is no conflict. Then love is the essence of virtue. And a mind that is not in a state of love is not a religious mind at all. And it is only the religious mind that is freed from problems, and that knows the beauty of love and truth.

February 21, 1965

Fifth Talk in Bombay

There is a creeper—I think, it is called the morning glory—which has that extraordinary pale blue color that only flowers have, or a deep purple with a touch of mauve, or a peculiar white. Only living flowers have those colors. They come, they bloom in the morning—the trumpet-shaped flowers—and then within a few hours they die. You must have seen those flowers. In their death they are almost as beautiful as when they are alive. They bloom for a few hours and cease to be, and in their death they do not lose the quality of a flower. And we live for thirty, forty, sixty, eighty years in great conflict, in misery, in passing pleasures, and we die rather miserably without delight in our heart, and in death we are as ugly as in life.

I am going to talk this evening about time, sorrow, and death. We must, I think, be very clear that we are not talking about ideas, but only about facts. That flower, blooming, full of beauty, delicate, with delicate fragrance—that is a fact. And the dying of it after a few hours when the wind comes and the sun rises, and the beauty of it even in death—that is also a fact. So we are going to deal with facts and not with ideas.

You can imagine, if you have got imagination, the color of those flowers. Have a picture, mentally conjure up an image of that creeper with its delicate colors, the flowers of delicate colors, the extraordinary beauty of the flowers. But your image, your idea about the creeper, your feeling about the creeper, is not the creeper. The creeper with its flowers is a fact. And your idea about the flowers, though it is a fact, is not actual. You are not actually in contact with the flower through an idea. I think this must be borne in mind throughout this talk: that we are dealing with facts and not with ideas, and that you cannot touch intimately, directly, concretely, come into contact with a fact through an idea. Death cannot be experienced. One cannot come directly into contact with it through an idea. Most of us live with ideas, with formulas, with concepts, with memory; and so we never come into contact with anything.

We are mostly in contact with our ideas, but not with the fact.

And I am going to discuss, rather I am going to talk about, time, sorrow, and that strange phenomenon called death. One can either interpret them as ideas, as conclusions, or come directly into contact with the whole problem of time and the dimension of time. One can come directly into contact with sorrow—that is, that sense of extraordinary grief. And also one can come directly into contact with that thing called death. Either we come directly into contact with time, sorrow, love, and death, or we treat them as a series of conclusions—the inevitableness of death or the explanations. The explanations, the conclusions, the opinions, the beliefs, the concepts, the symbols have nothing whatsoever to do with the reality—with the reality of time, with the reality of sorrow, with the reality of death and love. And if you are going merely to live or look or come, or hope to come into contact with the dimension of time, sorrow, or death through your idea, through your opinion, then what we are going to say will have very little meaning altogether. In fact, you would not be listening at all, you would be merely hearing words; and being in contact with your own ideas, with your own conclusions, opinions, you would not be in direct contact.

I mean by contact: I can touch this table, I am directly in contact with the table. But I am not in contact with the table if I have ideas of how I should touch the table. So the idea prevents me from coming directly, intimately, forcefully in contact. And during this hour, if you are not directly in contact with what is being said, then you will continue living a wasteful life. We have this life to live. We are not discussing the future life—we will come to that presently. We have this life to live. We have lived wastefully, without life itself having any significance. We live in travail, in misery, in conflict, and so on, and we have never been in contact with life itself. And it would be a thousand pities—at least I think so—if you are merely in contact with ideas and not with facts.

We are going to talk about time, first. I do not know if you have thought at all about this thing called time—not abstractly, not as an idea, not as a definition—if you have actually come into contact with time. When you are hungry, you are in contact directly with hunger. But what you should eat, how much you should eat, the pleasure you want to derive from eating, and so on—those are ideas. The fact is one thing and the idea is another. So to understand this extraordinary question of time, you must be intimately in contact with it—not through ideas, not through conclusions, but intimately, directly, with tremendous intimacy with time. Then you will be able to go into the question of time, and see whether the mind can be free from time.

There is obviously the question of time by the watch, chronological time. That, obviously, is necessary. In that is involved the question of memory, planning, design, and so on. We are not discussing that time, the chronological time of every day. But we are going to talk about time which is not by the watch. We do not live only by chronological time; we live much more by a time which is not by the watch. For us, time which is not chronological is much more important, has much more significance, than time by the watch. That is, though chronological time has importance, what has much more importance, greater significance, greater validity for most people is psychological time—time as continuity; time as yesterday, a thousand yesterdays and traditions; and time not only as the present but as the future.

So we have time as the past—the past being the memory, the knowledge, the tradition, the experiences, the things remembered—and the present, which is the passage of yesterday to the time of tomorrow, which is shaped, controlled by the past through the present. For us that has tremendous significance, not the time by the watch; and in that dimension of time we live. We live with the past, in conflict with the present, which creates the tomorrow. This is an obvious fact. There is nothing complex about it. So there is time as continuity and there is time as the future and the past; and the past shapes our thinking, our activity, our outlook, and so conditions the future.

We use time as a means of evolving, as a means of achieving, as a means of gradual changing. We use time because we are indolent, lazy. Because we have not found the way of transforming ourselves immediately, or because we are frightened of immediate change and the consequences of the change, we say, "I will gradually change." Therefore we use time as a means of postponement, time as a means of gradually achieving, and time as a means of change. We need time by the watch to learn a technique; to learn a language we need time, a few months. But we use time—psychological time, not time by the watch—as a means of changing, and so we introduce the gradual process: "I will gradually achieve; I will become; I am this and I will become that, through time."

And time is the product of thought. If you did not think about tomorrow or look back in thought to the past, you would be living in the now; there would be neither the future nor the past; you would be completely living for the day, giving to the day your fullest, richest, complete attention. As we do not know how to live so completely, totally, fully, with such urgency, in today, bringing about a complete transformation in today, we have invented the idea of tomorrow: "I will change tomorrow; I will; I must conform tomorrow, and so on." So, thought creates psychological time, and thought also brings fear.

Please follow all this. If you do not understand these things of which I am talking now, you won't understand them at the end. They will be just words, and you will be left with ashes.

Most of us have fears: fear of the doctor, fear of disease, fear of not achieving, fear of being left alone, fear of old age, fear of poverty; these are outward fears. Then there are a thousand and one inward fears: the fear of public opinion, of death, of being left completely alone so that you have to face life without a companion, the fear of loneliness, the fear of not reaching what you call God. So, man has a thousand and one fears. And being frightened, he either escapes in a vast network, subtle or crude; or he rationalizes these fears; or he becomes neurotic because he cannot understand it, he cannot resolve it; or he completely runs away from fear, from various fears, through identification or social activities, reformation, joining a political party, and so on.

Please, I am talking not of ideas but of what actually is taking place in each one of you. So you are not merely listening to my words, but through the words that are being used, you are looking at yourself. You are looking at yourself, not through ideas, but by coming directly into contact with the fact that you are frightened—which is entirely different from the idea that you are frightened.

So unless you understand the nature of fear and are completely free of it totally, your gods, your escapes, your doing of all kinds of social work, and so on, have no meaning because you are then a destructive human being, exploiting, and you cannot resolve this fear. A neurotic human being with his innumerable fears, in whatever he does—however good it may be—is always bringing to his action the seed of destruction, the seed of deterioration, because his action is an escape from the fact.

Most of us are frightened, have secret fears; and being afraid, we run away from them. The running away from the fact implies that the objects to which you run away become much more important than the fact. You understand? I am frightened; I have escaped from it through drink, through going to the temple, God, and all the rest of it; so the god, the temple, the pub become far more important than the fear. I protect the god, the temple, the pub much more vigorously because to me, they have become extraordinarily important, they are the symbols which give me the assurance that I can escape from fear. The temple, the god, nationalism, the political commitment, the formulas that one has become far more important than the resolution of the fear. So unless you totally resolve fear, you cannot possibly understand what fear is, what love is, or what sorrow is.

A mind that is really religious, a mind that is really socially minded, a mind that is creative, has completely, totally, to put away, or understand, or resolve this problem of fear. If you live with fear of any kind, you are wasting your life because fear brings darkness. I do not know if you have noticed what happens to you when you are frightened of something. All your nerves, your heart, everything becomes tight, hard, frightened. Haven't you noticed it? There is not only physical fear but also psychological fear, which is much more. Physical fear, which is a self-protective physical response, is natural. When you see a snake, you run away from it, you jump—that is a natural, self-protective fear. It is not really fear; it is merely a reaction to live, which is not fear because you recognize the poison, and you move away. We are talking not only of physical fear but much more of the fear that thought has created.

We are going into this question of fear. Unless you follow it step by step, you won't be able to resolve it. We are going to come into contact directly with fear—not what you are frightened about. What you are frightened about is an idea, but fear itself is not an idea. Suppose one is frightened—as most people, the young and the old, are—of public opinion, of death. It does not matter what they are frightened of; take your own example. I will take death. I am frightened of death. Fear exists only in relationship with something. Fear does not exist by itself but only in relation to something. I am frightened of public opinion. I am frightened of death, I am frightened of darkness, I am frightened of losing a job. So fear arises in connection with something.

Let us say I am frightened of death. I have seen death. I have seen bodies being burned. I have seen a dead leaf falling to the ground. I have seen so many dead things. And I am frightened of dying, coming to an end. Now there is this fear in relation to death, loneliness, a dozen things. How do I look at, or come into contact with, fear as I come into contact with this table? Am I making myself clear? To come directly into contact with fear—I hope you are doing it, not merely listening—to come directly into contact with that emotion, with that feeling called fear, the word, the thought, the idea must not come in at all. Right? That is, to come into contact with a person, I must touch his hand, I must hold his hand. But I do not come into contact with that person, though I may hold his hand, if I have ideas about him, if I have prejudices, if I like or dislike. So, in spite of my holding his hand, the image, the idea, the thought, prevents me from coming into contact directly with that man. So, in the same way, to come directly into contact with your fear—with your particular fear, conscious or unconscious fear—you must come into contact with it, not through your idea.

So one must first see how the idea interferes with coming into contact. When you understand that the idea interferes with coming into contact, you no longer fight the idea. When you understand the idea—the idea being the opinion, the formula, and so on—you are then directly in contact with your fear, and there is no escape, either verbal or through a conclusion, or through an opinion, or through any form of escape. When you are in contact with fear, in that sense, then you will find—as you are finding when we are discussing what we are talking about—that fear altogether disappears. And the mind must be free of all fears, not only the secret fears, but the open fears, the fears of which you are conscious. Then only can you look at the thing called sorrow.

You know, man has lived with sorrow for millennia, many thousands, millions of years. You have lived with sorrow, you have not resolved it. Either you worship sorrow as a means to enlightenment or you escape from sorrow. You put sorrow on a pedestal, symbolically identified with a person, or you rationalize it, or you escape from it. But sorrow is there.

I mean by sorrow the loss of someone, the sorrow of failure, the sorrow that comes upon you when you see that you are inefficient, incapable, the sorrow that you find when you have no love in your heart, that you live entirely by your ugly little mind; there is the sorrow of losing someone whom you think you love. We live with this sorrow night and day, never going beyond it, never ending it. Again, a mind burdened with sorrow becomes insensitive, becomes enclosed; it has no affection, it has no sympathy; it may show words of sympathy, but in itself, in its heart, it has no sympathy, no affection, no love. And sorrow breeds self-pity. Most of us carry this burden all through life, and we do not seem to be able to end it. And there is the sorrow of time. You understand? We carry this sorrow to the end of our life, not being able to resolve it. There is a much greater sorrow: to live with something which you cannot understand, which is eating your heart and mind, darkening your life. There is also the sorrow of loneliness, being completely alone, lonely, companionless, cut off from all contacts, ultimately leading to a neurotic state and mental illness and psychosomatic diseases.

So, there is vast sorrow, not only of a human being, but also the sorrow of the race. How do you resolve sorrow? You have to resolve it, just as you resolve fear. There is no future—you can invent a future. There is no future for a man who is living with intelligence, who is sensitive, alive, young, fresh, innocent. Therefore you must resolve fear, you must end sorrow.

Again, to end sorrow is to come into contact with that extraordinary feeling, without self-pity, without opinion, without formulas, without explanation—just to come directly into contact with it, as one would come into contact with a table. And that is one of the most difficult things for people to do: to put away ideas and to come into direct contact.

Then, there is the problem of death—and with the problem of death, the problem of old age. You all know that death is inevitable—inevitable through senility, through old age, through disease, through accident. Though scientists are trying to prolong life by another fifty years or more, death is inevitable. Why they want to prolong this agonizing existence, God only knows! But that is what we want. And to understand death, we must come into contact with death; it demands a mind that is not afraid, that is not thinking in terms of time, that is not living in the dimension of time—which I have explained. To live with death—I am going to go into it.

You know, we have put death at the end of life—it is somewhere there, in the distance. And we are trying to put it as far away as possible, as long away as possible. We know there is death. And so we invent the hereafter. We say, "I have lived, I have built a character, I have done things. Will all things end in death? There must be a future." The future, the afterlife, reincarnation—all that is an escape from the fact of today, from the fact of coming into contact with death.

Think of your life, what is it? Actually look at your life which you want to prolong! What is your life? A constant battle, a constant confusion, an occasional flash of pleasure, boredom, sorrow, fear, agony, despair, jealousy, envy, ambition—that is your life actually, with diseases, with pettiness. And you want to prolong that life after death!

And if you believe in reincarnation—as you are supposed to believe, as your scriptures talk about it—then what matters is what you are now. Because what you are now is going to condition your future. So what you are, what you do, what you think, what you feel, how you live—all this matters infinitely. If you do not even believe in reincarnation, then there is only this life; then it matters tremendously what you do, what you think, what you feel, whether you exploit or whether you do not exploit, whether you love, whether you have feeling, whether you are sensitive, whether there is beauty. But to live like that, you have to understand death and not put it far away at the end of your life—which is a life of sorrow, a life of fear, a life of despair, a life of uncertainty. So you have to bring death close; that is, you have to die.

Do you know what it is to die? You have seen death enough. You have seen a man being carried to the burning place where he will be destroyed. You have seen death. Most people are frightened of that. Death is as that flower dies, as that creeper dies with all the morning glories. With that beauty, with that delicacy, it dies without regret, without argument; it comes to an end. But we escape from death through time—which is, it is over there. We say, "I have a few more years to live, and I shall be born next life"; or, "This is the only life, and therefore let me make the best of it; let me have all the greatest fun, let me make it the greatest show." And so, we never come into contact with that extraordinary thing called death. Death is to die to everything of the past, to die to your pleasure.

Have you ever tried without argument, without persuasion, without compulsion, without necessity, to die to a pleasure? You are going to die inevitably. But have you tried to die today, easily, happily, to your pleasure, to your remembrances, to your hates, to your ambitions, to your urgency to gather money? All that you want of life is money, position, power, and the envy of another. Can you die to them, can you die to the things that you know, easily, without any argument, without any explanation? Please bear in mind that you are not hearing a few words and ideas, but you are actually coming into contact with a pleasure—your sexual pleasure, for example—and dying to it. That is what you are going to do anyhow. You are going to die—that is, die to everything you know, your body, your mind, the things that you have built up. So, you say, "Is that all? Is all my life to end in death?" All the things you have done—the service, the books, the knowledge, the experiences, the pleasures, the affection, the family—all end in death; that is facing you. Either you die to them now or you die inevitably when the time comes. Only an intelligent man who understands the whole process is a religious man.

The man who takes the sannyasi's robes, grows a beard, goes to the temple and runs away from life—he is not a religious man. The religious man is one who dies every day and is reborn every day. That is, his mind is young, innocent, fresh. To die to your sorrow, die to your pleasure, die to the things that you hold secretly in your heart—do it; thus you will see you will not waste your life; then you will find something that is incredible, that no man has ever perceived. This is not a reward. There is no reward either. You die willingly, or you die inevitably. You have to die naturally, every day, as the flower dies, blooming, rich, full, and then to die to that beauty, to that richness, to that love, experience, and knowledge—to die so that, every day, you are reborn, so that you have a fresh mind.

You need a fresh mind; otherwise, you do not know what love is. If you do not die, your love is merely memory; your love is then caught in envy, jealousy. You have to die, every day, to everything you know—to your hatred, to your insults, to flatteries. Die to them; then you will see that time has no meaning; there is no tomorrow then, there is only the now that is beyond the yesterday and the today and the tomorrow. And it is only in the now that there is love.

A human being that has no love cannot approach truth. Without love, do what you will—do all your sacrifices, your vows of celibacy, your social work, your exploitations—nothing has any value. And you cannot love without dying every day to your memory. For love is not of memory; it is a living thing. A living thing is a movement, and that movement cannot be caged in words, or in thought, or in a mind that is merely self-seeking. Only the mind that has understood time, that has ended sorrow, that has no fear—only such a mind knows what death is, and therefore for such a mind there is life.

February 24, 1965

Sixth Talk in Bombay

I would like this evening to talk over with you, or rather communicate to you, a rather complex problem. To communicate, one has not only to listen with one's ears but also to see with one's eyes; and really to communicate, one has not only to see with one's eyes, to hear with one's ears, but also to see and feel with one's mind and heart. Because one sees much more with one's mind—much more rapidly, much more quickly—than the eyes see; and the mind hears much more quickly, with greater precision, than the ear. And to feel, one must see and hear, not only with one's mind, but also with one's heart—that is, be very sensitive. Most of us, unfortunately, have become insensitive through our education, through modern life, through everyday turmoil, the ugliness and the despair of life, the routine, the boredom, and senseless existence.

And to listen, to see, demands that the mind be astonishingly precise and sharp; that there must be a great sensitivity, not only to the word, but to the feeling, to the beauty of something that you hear to be true; and that the mind be equally sensitive when you hear something false, something not right. As most of us are so indifferent, have no time or patience to consider deeply, to investigate profoundly, we resort to the quickest way of communication—that is, just hear a few words, and oppose them or agree with those words, opinions, or terms; we deny or accept. This is what we generally do. But when we are discussing something that demands not only that the ear pay attention but also that the mind and the heart be at attention, sensitivity is necessary if we would communicate together something that demands careful attention.

We are not going to talk about something. "About something" is always an idea. I talk about politics, about religion, about a particular problem. But the "about" is the idea—about politics, about a particular problem, about a particular issue. But when we are communicating together, when we are in communion together, there is no such thing as the "about"; there is no idea. You and I are in communion directly, here—in the world, seeing, feeling; and the mind listening much more, nonargumentatively, neither accepting nor denying. If you accept or deny, you are not in communion. We must establish communion. And to establish communion, we must not talk about something because always the "about" is the unessential: the word, the opinion, the belief, the dogma. But if there is communion between the speaker and the listener, then both will go through the words, the terminology, the opinions, the ideas, and come to something which will have tremendous significance to both. What I wanted to talk about—again "about"—what I wanted to commune with you—which is the better word—is the nature and significance of meditation.

First of all, the word *meditation* naturally evokes certain images, certain reactions, pleasant or unpleasant. And as we are going to commune together, as we are trying it, as you are feeling your way with me into this extraordinary thing called meditation, you must naturally, easily, willingly, put aside your opinions, your practices, your disciplines, to find out what the other man is trying to convey. It is one of the most difficult things to find out for oneself what is meditation.

Now, first of all, to enter into an immense problem like that, you need to be very sensitive. You cannot come to it with clear-cut ideas, opinions, and judgment; but you must be sensitive. We are rarely sensitive to beauty. Beauty means nothing for most of us. Personal adornment is not beauty. Beauty is not a reaction to some kind of stimulation. You listen to good music, and tears come to your eyes; and such a feeling you call a beautiful feeling. You call that an experience. That is, you are stimulated by an outward incident, by an outward occurrence, such as seeing a statue, seeing a sunset, seeing a beautiful woman or the clean, healthy smile of a child. You feel that is beautiful; that is, you are stimulated. The reaction of that stimulation is either pleasurable or not pleasurable. If it is pleasurable, you call that beauty.

But there is a beauty that is not the outcome of a reaction or a stimulation. Now that sense of beauty is not merely color, proportion, texture, quality, but it is something far greater, much deeper; and it has nothing whatsoever to do with a passing stimulation. It is difficult to convey that feeling, the feeling of that sense of beauty where the mind, the heart, the nerves, the whole sensory organism is in complete coordination. That feeling is not induced or brought about by any stimulation but actually is there because you are throughout the day sensitive to everything—to your word, to your gesture, to your walk, to the dirt on the road, to the squalor of a house, to its disorderliness, the ugliness of the office, the brutal travail of man. You are aware, sensitive; and because you are so sensitive, you have activated every field of your being, activated every corner of your consciousness, of your state. It is only then that there is a sense of beauty, not stimulated by the lake, or by the mountain, or by a poem, or by the movement of a bird on the wing.

Now to communicate that feeling, if really you and I both feel that beauty which is not adorned, which is not a stimulation, which is not an intellectual concept, but an actual state—to communicate that, you and I must both not only be intense but meet at the same level, with the same intensity, at the same moment. Otherwise communication ceases. And such communication is necessary to understand what we are going to go into.

You know, we rarely are in a state of communion. You may hold the hand of your wife or your friend or your child, but you are not in communion; you are only physically in contact. Communion implies that there is no division—not a physical division but, much more, a mental or an emotional division which each one of us has. Because each one of us is struggling to assert himself, to fulfill himself, to be something, to strive, to try to become famous, ambitious, competitive; and in that state there is no communion. There may be a physical communication. But communion is something far more deep, much more intense, where you and the speaker are both in contact with something that is real—not imagined, not dialectical, not with mere reason—where both of us see the same thing, at the same moment, with the same intensity. Then there is an extraordinary relationship established between you and the speaker. This happens very rarely for most of us. To communicate with another is part of the thing about which we are going to talk.

Most of us are burdened with tradition—not good tradition or bad tradition, but tradition. The word *tradition* means to carry over from the past generation to this generation; from time immemorial, to carry over from father to son and on and on, a certain custom, a certain idea, a certain concept. And that tradition conditions the mind.

Just listen, this evening. Don't argue with me, don't discuss with me; just listen. I feel that you must listen just, actually, with your ear—not listen to your opinion, to your experiences, to your ideas. You must actually listen to the speaker because that is what you are here for, obviously. And what we are saying is not irrational or insane or nonsense; we are just stating facts. If you listen to a fact, if you listen actually with your ear, then you will see that that fact has an impact on a mind that is conditioned. It is necessary to have that impact. That impact does everything, if you let it. But if you begin to argue—"Should we keep certain traditions? Are not certain traditions necessary? Otherwise we would be this and that"—the argument with yourself and with the speaker prevents you from listening and, therefore, you are not meeting the fact. Your meeting the fact will have tremendous effect if you will actually listen.

We know what we mean by tradition; custom, habit, has shaped the mind—that is a fact. And that tradition has established certain methods, certain specialized processes; it says you must meditate in this way. And organized thought, a method, has been established or is being established by people who think they know how to meditate and want to teach others. It is based on a tradition, or on their own experience; or they have borrowed it from others and put it together; and they want you to practice it in order to arrive at something which they call peace, God, truth, bliss, and all the rest of it.

So the religious people throughout the world have, through tradition, established a method or methods in order to arrive at that state which they call peace, or God, or some extraordinary experience. That is a fact: a method, a system, a practice. Please listen. What is implied in the practice and in the method? There is the method, and then there is the carrying out of that method, which is called the practice. We are examining these two: the method and the practice. What is implied in the method? An organized system of ideas: If you do this, this, and this, you will arrive there. It is an organized, specialized procedure in order to help you to arrive; and the procedure you begin to practice, day after day, slowly, purposefully—in which is involved great effort. So there is the method and there is the practice. Through a method or methods you will arrive only at a state which must be static. If you have a method, that will lead you somewhere; that somewhere must be static; it cannot be moving, dynamic; it cannot be living; it is not a movement; it is static.

Some people say that if you do certain specialized, organized things, you will have peace. That peace is an idea which becomes static. But peace is never static; it is a living thing; it comes only when you understand the whole of man's struggle—not just one particular struggle, but the whole of existence—which is, his daily bread, his feelings, his ambitions, his sexual appetites, his competitiveness, his despairs, and his fulfillments; the vast complex network of escapes. In understanding all that, out of that understanding you may have peace. But if you follow a method in a particular direction, through a particular system, which will promise you or guarantee that you will have peace, then such peace is merely an idea, a static concept, which is not real at all. That is what you are doing. You want peace of mind—whatever that may mean—and you practice it day after day. But you will get angry, you will be ambitious, you will be greedy, you will talk roughly with your servant—if you have a servant—you will be competitive. So you divide life; you practice a particular method, which you call meditation, in order to have peace; and all your life destroys what you are seeking. So that is what is involved in practice and in method.

And also, in a method, in a system, there is implied authority—"You know, I don't know. You have realized the self, whatever that may mean, and you are going to tell me what to do. I will get it." So there is established this thing called the guru—the authority, the enlightened, the self-realized, the man who knows—and you who do not know; and you want *that*, whatever *that* may mean. The guru looks fairly happy, fairly quiet, secluded; and he talks a great deal about self-realization and all that stuff. And you say, "How good it will be to have it!" You want it; you begin to practice, and he becomes your authority. So the method, the practice, implies authority.

We are again dealing with facts. I am not trying to tell you something which is not. Therefore, listen to it so that it has an impact, not of agreement or disagreement. Now, what happens in an authority? You have not understood yourself, your life, your behavior; whether you have affection, love, sympathy, does not matter; you have not explored your extraordinary being, yourself; you deny all that, and you follow somebody else. And by following somebody else, you have added an extraordinary layer of fear because you might not follow according to the sanction of those people, and so on.

So practicing a method implies authority. Practicing a method implies mechanical procedure, it becomes mechanical. It is not a living thing which you are examining, watching, exploring. You are merely practicing like a machine—you go to the office, there you do something; you get into a habit, and that habit carries on. In the same way, you practice a system which you hope will lead to peace; you merely practice and establish a habit; thereby your mind becomes dull and insensitive, mechanical. All these are implied when you are practicing a method; there is authority; there is a mechanical cultivation of habit which suppresses, which helps you to escape from yourself. See the fact of it. When you see the fact of it, the impact of it, then your mind is no longer concerned with practice, no longer concerned with habit, no longer concerned with authority—spiritual authority—at all. Then you are concerned with exploration, investigation, understanding. Then you are concerned not with a result but with the whole of existence—not one part of existence.

For most of us, meditation means prayer; it means repeating certain words endlessly, or taking a certain posture, breathing in a certain way. Do you follow what you are doing? You are giving importance to outward activity, sitting very straight—which is fairly simple. Why should you sit straight? Because blood flows more easily to the head; that is all. And when you breathe deeply, the blood gets more oxygen. There is nothing mysterious about it. But we begin with the outward signs of meditation: sitting quietly in a room, and you know every outward gesture. But there is no inward comprehension at all. Everything is from the outside.

So meditation is not practice, is not following a system. System implies authority. Therefore, meditation is not the result of authority. Nor is it a collective prayer or an individual prayer, prayer being a supplication, an asking. Because you are miserable, you pray for some entity or some being to give you help. You have reduced your life to a terrible chaos, misery. You have built this social structure, this environment that is destroying human beings. You are responsible for your greed, for your activities, for your ambition—which have created the society in which the human being is caught. So you are responsible, and therefore it is no good asking somebody to help you. When you do ask, it is an escape.

There are prayers for peace in Europe, in America, and in this country—not in the communist world where there are no prayers for peace. To have peace, you must live peacefully; that is, no ambition, no competition, no nationality, no class division, no petty, little division of race, of country—linguistic or nonlinguistic. To live peacefully you must be at peace with yourself. And if you cannot be at peace with yourself, it is no good praying for peace, because everything that you are doing is bringing about disorder, bringing about conflict.

So meditation is not prayer, nor is it repetition of words. You know that one of the most astonishing things is how this word *mantra* gives people such fantastic ideas. You use any word—it does not matter what word—or use a series of words, give it a special meaning, and repeat it. What happens when you repeat over and over again a series of words in English, or in Sanskrit, or in Latin, or in any other language? Repeat, repeat, and your mind becomes gradually quiet, gradually dull; and you think at last you have quietened your mind.

So meditation is not prayer, not a repetition of words, not practice, not pursuing a particular method or a system in which is implied authority. If you listen to this fact, then you will never go back to that. Then you become completely responsible for yourself. Therefore, you have no guru; you do not rely on anybody, including the speaker. You are then responsible for everything that you do. Therefore, what is necessary is that you have an abundance of self-knowledge, that you must be completely rich in knowing yourself; that is the only basis from which you can proceed. And for most of us, this knowing oneself is so arduous, so difficult, that we would rather take a pill, hoping that everything will be all right, that we shall get something for nothing. That is how you practice and do all the innumerable things which have no meaning, because you do not know how to look into yourself.

So, one has to know oneself, not the higher self, not the atma, not God; all that is theory, absurdity, invented by some people; it is not a fact; you just repeat what is merely a tradition; therefore, you must be free from the authority of tradition to find God. To know yourself is to be aware. Do not give a mystical meaning or some complicated meaning to that very simple phrase "to be aware"—to be aware of those crows, to the noise of those crows. Just listen; please listen; be aware of the light that is in the sky; be aware of the dark trunk of the mango tree; be aware of that palm; be aware of your neighbor, his color, his dress; just be aware—not condemning it; not comparing;

not saying, "This is good, that is bad"; not explaining; not justifying—just be aware.

Most people are not aware at all even of outward things. I am sure you pass every day, in the bus or in the car, various houses, the road, the trees. But you have never watched those trees, you are never aware of those trees, the outline of those houses, how many floors there are in that apartment house; you are never aware of the tree, of the flower, or the child that goes by. Please be aware outwardly, without comparing, without judging, without evaluating; then move with that awareness inwards.

Please listen to this. Do it, as I am talking. Do not think about doing it, but actually do it now. That is, be aware of the trees, the palm tree, the sky; hear the crows cawing; see the light on the leaf, the color of the sari, the face; then move inwardly. You can observe, you can be aware choicelessly of outward things. It is very easy. But to move inwardly and to be aware without condemnation, without justification, without comparison is more difficult. Just be aware of what is taking place inside you—your beliefs, your fears, your dogmas, your hopes, your frustrations, your ambitions, your fears, and all the rest of the things. Then the unfolding of the conscious and the unconscious begins. You have not to do a thing.

Just be aware; that is all that you have to do, without condemning, without forcing, without trying to change what you are aware of. Then you will see that it is like a tide that is coming in. You cannot prevent the tide from coming in; build a wall, or do what you will, it will come with tremendous energy. In the same way, if you are aware choicelessly, the whole field of consciousness begins to unfold. And as it unfolds, you have to follow, and the following becomes extraordinarily difficult—following in the sense to follow the movement of every thought, of every feeling, of every secret desire. It becomes difficult the moment you resist, the moment you say, "That is ugly; this is good, that is bad; this I will keep, that I will not keep."

So you begin with the outer and move inwardly. Then you will find, when you move inwardly, that the inward and the outward are not two different things, that the outward awareness is not different from the inward awareness, and that they are both the same. Then you will see that you are living in the past: there is never a moment of actual living, when neither the past nor the future exists—which is the actual moment. You will find that you are always living in the past: what you felt; what you were; how clever, how good, how bad; the memories. That is memory. You have to understand memory, not deny it, not suppress it, not escape. If a man has taken a vow of celibacy and is holding on to that memory, when he moves out of that memory, he feels guilty, and that smothers his life.

So you begin to watch everything and, therefore, you become very sensitive. Therefore by listening, by seeing not only the outward world, the outward gesture, but also the inward mind that looks and therefore feels, when you are so aware choicelessly, then there is no effort. It is very important to understand this.

Most of us make effort in meditation because we want experience. It is a simple fact. Please listen to the fact—not my judgment of the fact, not your opinion with regard to the fact. The fact is that most of us want some kind of spiritual experience and the continuity of that experience. So you have to examine the whole content of experience, and the mind that desires experience.

What is experience? The word *experience* means to go through. We want experience, the so-called spiritual experience—which is, a vision, a heightened perception, a heightened understanding. We want a deep, wide, profound experience that will shatter our way of living. And by experience we mean, don't we, a challenge and a response. I ask and you answer, or you see and there is a response. Life is a constant series of experiences, conscious as well as unconscious, pleasant or unpleasant. This is a fact. Whether you recognize those experiences or not, they are going on all the time. When you are riding on the bus, when you are sitting quietly at home, when you are working in the office, when you are talking to your wife or your husband, when you are walking by yourself, this experiencing is going on all the time.

Most of us, not being aware of this extraordinary interaction of life, get bored with the few experiences that we have—sexual experiences, the experiences of going to the temple, and the ordinary experiences—and so we want something more, much more. So we turn to meditation. And because we want greater, heightened emotion and experience, we resort to drugs. There are various new drugs in America and Europe, which, when you take them, momentarily give you a heightened perception. If you are an artist, if you take that drug called LSD, that gives you an astonishing feeling of color; you have never seen color before as when you take this drug; color then becomes alive, vibrant, infinite; and you can see the tree as you have never seen before; there is no division between you and the tree. If you are a priest, and if you take that drug, then you have priestly experiences, and that gives you greater conviction that what you are doing is perfectly right. Or it alters your life in the field of your conditioning. So, man, being bored with his own life, with his daily experiences, wants a greater experience. So he tries to meditate, or to take drugs, or to do innumerable things to get more.

So when the mind is seeking more, it indicates that it has not understood the whole structure of its own being. Without understanding yourself or laying the right foundation—which is the only foundation, which is to understand yourself, do what you will, sit in any posture, stand on your head, repeat, follow, or do anything—you will never find peace, you will never come by that which is true.

So without understanding yourself, there is no righteous behavior. Without understanding yourself, there is no action which does not breed more conflict, more misery, more confusion. Without understanding yourself, do what you will, there is no wisdom. And only when you understand yourself, is there the intimation of life.

Now what we have done so far, in this talk, is to put away all the things which are not true; negatively, we have denied. The denial is factual. It is not my denial; it is the denial of something which is not true—it does not matter who says it: Shankara, the Buddha, your guru, or anybody else. So we have pushed negatively aside everything that is not true. Then, let us find out what it means to meditate.

We are starting with having laid the foundation of self-knowing. If you have not done it, you cannot proceed; and it becomes a theory only. If you live by a theory, then you are a dead human being; you are living with ideas and not with facts. It is only a mind that is very sharp, very clear, a heart that is alive, that can deal with facts and nothing else. A mind that sets about to meditate ceases to meditate because it is a deliberate action. A deliberate action in order to achieve a result, in order to gain something, is a desire, an urge, to escape from the fact of your daily life.

Therefore, a mind that deliberately practices meditation is not in a state of meditation, do what it will. Therefore, there must be no deliberate act of meditation. If there is a deliberate act of meditation, then it becomes an effort, and therefore a pressure on the mind. So, meditation is not a deliberate act, it is not continuity. Because the moment it has continuity, it has time value; and therefore, it has been created by the mind as a means to achieve something, or as a means to retain something.

So meditation is an act which ends each minute and has no continuity. One can see that a healthy mind is not under any pressure—the pressure of any desire or of any compulsive urge. Nor is it influenced by any outward movement: political, revolutionary, economic. It is a healthy mind that is not influenced, that is not under the compulsion of any desire. And it can only be healthy when there is self-knowledge, when it has understood the whole business. Then the mind, being under no pressure, under no compulsion—the brain must also be very quiet, not induced to be quiet.

Listen to those birds. You are listening. If you are listening, then there is no reaction. You are listening obviously through the brain, which reacts. The function of the brain is to react. But now you are listening without any reaction, but yet you are listening because your mind, your brain, is quiet, receptive, sensitive, alive. But if it reacts, it follows a certain pattern.

So the brain must be sensitive, quiet, alert and without any pressure of like or dislike; this again depends on the depth and the abundance and the richness and the fullness of self-knowing. Then also, naturally, your body must be very quiet. But do not begin with the body, making it quiet at first—that means nothing. All this comes naturally. You do not have to induce, you do not have to say, "I will sit quietly; I will try to train my brain to be alert, without reaction; or I will watch so that no influence enters." Then you are lost completely. But if you begin with self-knowing, then these things will follow naturally, like the sun rising after it has set; it will follow as sweetly and as naturally.

Then you come, naturally again, to the sense of being silent. You cannot be silent if you have no space. Most of our minds have no space at all. Our minds, our brains—everything is so full, overcrowded. In a town like this, you live in a flat, in one room; and you have no room outwardly; everything is round you. Inwardly, too, you have no space because your mind is cluttered with your ideas, your beliefs, concepts, formulas, "must not" and "must"; there is never a space where you can completely be free, where the mind can be open, quiet. So silence goes with space, and silence is not an end, the result of a particular practice, or a wish or the demand of a particular desire. It comes about naturally, and therefore effortlessly. Don't practice silence, because in that silence, there is nothing to practice.

I am not giving you a method, I am not telling you what to do. You are doing it. We are communicating together. Therefore, you can go to it naturally. Then you will be a light to yourself, a free human being; then you will have no fear; there is no guru, there is no tradition—you are a human being alive. These things follow as naturally as the day follows the night.

In that silence there is a movement which is not made of the energy of conflict. All our life is conflict, and through that conflict we derive energy. But when the mind has understood the whole nature of conflict in the world and within oneself, then out of that understanding comes silence. And therefore in that silence there is tremendous energy. It is not the silence of sleep, stagnation, but it is a silence of tremendous energy.

I do not know if you have seen a machine or a dynamo, something that is moving with terrific speed, full of energy. In the same way the mind that is completely silent is completely full of energy. And that energy, because it is not named, has no nationality, no conflict. That energy is anonymous; it is not yours or mine. And therefore that energy, when allowed to move freely, goes very far; it can go beyond the measure of time.

And this whole process which we have communicated to you is the act of meditation. When there is such an act, there is benediction. Such an act is love. And it is only such a mind that can bring order to the world. It is only such a mind that can live peacefully. It is only such a mind that does not bring confusion in its activity. And it is only such a mind that can find what is true.

February 28, 1965

Seventh Talk in Bombay

This is the last talk this year, at least in Bombay. It seems to me that man for so many centuries has always sought peace, freedom, and a state of bliss which he calls God. One has sought it under different names and at different periods in history, and apparently, only a very few have found that inward sense of great peace, freedom, and that state which man has called God. And in modern times it has become of such little importance; we use the word *God* with very little meaning. We are always seeking a state of bliss, peace, and freedom away from this world, and we take flight in various forms from this world, to find something which will be enduring, which will give us sanctuary and sanctity, which will give us a certain sense of deep, inward quietness. Whether one believes in God or not depends on mental influence, tradition, climate. To find that state of bliss, that freedom, that extraordinary peace—that must be a living thing—one must understand, I think, why one is not capable of facing the fact and transforming the fact and thereby going beyond it.

I would like this evening, if I may, to talk about, or rather communicate together, this feeling of why we always give such great importance to idea and not to action. Though we have talked about it in different ways and at different times and also here in Bombay, during these talks, I would like to go into it in a different way. Because it seems to me that we are responsible totally, completely, for the society in which we live. For the misery, for the confusion, for the utter brutality of modern existence, each one of us is totally and completely responsible. We cannot possibly escape from it; we have to transform it. And the transformation of the human being who is part of society and has created this society—for this he is totally and completely responsible. And to bring about a mutation, a transformation within himself and thereby within the pattern of society, is only possible when he ceases completely to escape into ideas.

God is an idea depending on the climate, the environment, and the tradition in which you have been brought up. In the communist world, they do not believe in God—again dependent on circumstances. Here you are dependent on your circumstances, on your life, and on your tradition, and you have built up this idea. One must liberate oneself from these circumstances, from society; and only then is it possible for a human being, in his freedom, to find that which is true. But merely to escape into an idea called God does not solve the problem at all.

God—or any other name you would like to use—is the cunning invention of man; and we cover that invention, that cunningness, by incense, by ritual, by various forms of belief, dogmas, separating man as Catholics, Hindus, Muslims, Parsis, Buddhists—all the clever, cunning structure invented by man. And man, having invented it, is caught in it. Without understanding the present world, the world he lives in, the world of his misery, the world of his confusion, sorrow, anxiety, despair, and the agony of existence, the complete loneliness, the sense of utter futility of life—without understanding all that, the mere multiplication of ideas, however satisfactory, has no value at all.

It is very important to understand why we create or formulate an idea. Why does the mind formulate an idea at all? I mean by "formulating," a structure of philosophical or rational or humanistic or materialistic ideas. Idea is organized thought, and in that organized thought, belief, idea, man lives. That is what we all do, whether we are religious or nonreligious. I think it is important to find out why human beings throughout the ages have given such an extraordinary importance to ideas. Why do we formulate ideas at all? Why is it not possible to meet or rather act—always acting? We form ideas, if one observes oneself, when there is inattention. When you are completely active, which demands total attention—which is action—in that there is no idea; you are acting.

Please, for this evening, if I may suggest, just listen. Don't accept or deny; don't build defenses so as to prevent listening by having your own thoughts, beliefs, contradictions, and all that. But just listen. We are not trying to convince you of anything; we are not forcing you through any means to conform to a particular idea, or pattern, or action. We are merely stating facts whether you like them or not, and what is important is to learn about the fact. "Learning" implies total listening, a complete observation. When you listen to the sound of the crow, do not listen with your own noises, with your own fears, thoughts, with your own ideas, with your own opinions. Then you will see that there is no idea at all, but you are actually listening.

So in the same way, this evening, if I may suggest, just listen. Just listen, not only consciously, but also unconsciously—which is perhaps much more important. Most of us are influenced. We can reject conscious influences, but it is much more difficult to put aside the unconscious influences. When you are listening in the manner of which we have talked, then it is neither conscious nor unconscious listening. Then you are completely attentive. And attention is not yours or mine—it is not nationalistic; it is not religious; it is not divisible. Hence when you are so completely listening, there is no idea; there is only a state of listening. Most of us do this when we are listening to something rather beautiful; when there is lovely music; or when you are seeing a mountain, the light of the evening, or the light on the water, or a cloud; then in that state of attention, in that state of listening, seeing, there is no idea.

In the same way if you could listen with that ease, with that effortless attention, then perhaps you would see the great significance of idea and action. As I was saying, most of us formulate ideas when there is inattention. We create or conceive ideas when those ideas give us security, a sense of certainty. And that sense of certainty, that sense of being safe, brings about ideas; and into those ideas we escape, and therefore there is no action. And we create or formulate ideas when we do not completely comprehend that *which is.* So ideas become much more important than the fact.

To find out, actually, to find out the fact—if there is God or if there is no God—ideas have no meaning whatsoever. Whether you believe or don't believe, whether you are a theist or an atheist, it has no meaning. To find out you need all your energy—your complete, total energy; energy that is not spotted, that is not scratched; energy that has no twist, that has not been made corrupt. So to understand, to find out if there is such a thing as that reality which man has sought for so many millions of years, one must have energy—energy that is completely whole, uncontaminated. And to bring about that energy, we must understand effort.

Most of us spend our life in effort, in struggle; and the effort, the struggle, the striving, is a dissipation of that energy. Man, throughout the historical period of man, has said that to find that reality or God—whatever name he may give to it—you must be a celibate; that is, you take a vow of chastity and suppress, control, battle with yourself endlessly all your life, to keep your vow. Look at the waste of energy! It is also a waste of energy to indulge. And it has far more significance when you suppress. The effort that has gone into suppression, into control, into this denial of your desire distorts your mind, and through that distortion you have a certain sense of austerity which becomes harsh. Please listen. Observe it in yourself, and observe the people around you. And observe this waste of energy, the battle. Not the implications of sex, not the actual act, but the ideals, the images, the pleasure—the constant thought about them is a waste of energy. And most people waste their energy either through denial or through a vow of chastity, or in thinking about it endlessly.

And as we were saying, man is responsible—you are responsible, and I—for the condition of the society in which we live. You are responsible, not your politicians, because you have made the politicians what they are—crooked, glorifying themselves, seeking position and prestige—which is what we are doing in daily life. We are responsible for society. The psychological structure of society is far more important than the organizational side of society. The psychological structure of society is based on greed, envy, acquisitiveness, competition, ambition, fear, this incessant demand of a human being wanting to be secure in all his relationships, secure in property, secure in his relationship to people, secure in his relationship to ideas. That is the structure of society which one has created. And society then imposes the structure psychologically on each one of us. Now greed, envy, ambition, competition—all that is a waste of energy because in it there is always a conflict, conflict which is endless as in a person who is jealous.

Jealousy is an idea. The idea and the fact are two different things. Please listen. You approach the feeling called jealousy through the idea. You do not come directly into contact with the feeling called jealousy. But you approach jealousy through the memory of a certain word which you have established in your mind as jealousy. It becomes an idea, and that idea prevents you from coming directly into contact with that feeling which you call jealousy. Again, this is a fact. So the formula, the idea, prevents you from coming directly into contact with that feeling, and therefore the idea dissipates this energy.

As we are responsible for the misery, for the poverty, for wars, for the utter lack of peace, a religious man does not seek God. The religious man is concerned with the transformation of society which is himself. The religious man is not the man that does innumerable rituals, follows traditions, lives in a dead, past culture, explaining endlessly the Gita or the Bible, endlessly chanting, or taking *sannyasa*—that is not a religious man; such a man is escaping from facts. The religious man is concerned totally and completely with the understanding of society which is himself. He is not separate from society. Bringing about in himself a complete, total mutation means complete cessation of greed, envy, ambition; and therefore he is not dependent on circumstances, though he is the result of circumstances—the food he eats, the books he reads, the cinemas he goes to, the religious dogmas, beliefs, rituals, and all that business. He is responsible, and therefore the religious man must understand himself, who is the product of society which he himself has created. Therefore to find reality he must begin here, not in a temple, not in an image—whether the image is graven by the hand or by the mind. Otherwise how can he find something totally new, a new state?

Peace is not merely the expansion of law or sovereignty. Peace is something entirely different; it is an inward state which cannot possibly come by the alteration of outer circumstances, though the change of outer circumstances is necessary. But it must begin within to bring about a different world. And to bring about a different world, you need tremendous energy; and that energy is now being dissipated in constant conflict. Therefore, one must understand this conflict.

The primary cause of conflict is escape—escape through idea. Please observe yourself: how, instead of facing—let us say—jealousy, envy, instead of coming directly into contact with it, you say, "How shall I get over it? What shall I do? What are the methods by which I cannot be jealous?"—which are all ideas and therefore an escape from the fact that you are jealous, the going away from the fact that you are jealous. The going away from the fact through ideas not only wastes your energy but prevents you from coming into contact directly with that fact. Now, you have to give your complete attention, not through an idea. Idea, as we pointed out, prevents attention. So when you observe, or become aware of, this feeling of jealousy, and give complete attention to it without ideas, then you will see that not only are you directly in contact with the feeling, but because you have given your complete attention, not through ideas, it ceases to be; and you have then greater energy to meet the next incident or the next emotion, the next feeling.

To discover, to bring about a complete mutation, you must have energy—not the energy which is brought about through suppression, but that energy that comes to you when you are not escaping through ideas or through suppression. Really, if you think of it, we know only two ways to meet life—either we escape from it altogether, which is a form of insanity leading to neurosis, or we suppress everything because we do not understand. That is all we know.

Suppression is not only putting the lid on any feeling or any sensation but it is also a form of intellectual explanation, rationalization. Please observe yourself, and you will see how factual it is—what is being said. So it is necessary that you do not escape. And it is one of the most important things to find out, never to escape. It is one of the most difficult things to find out because we escape through words. We escape from the fact not only by running to the temple and all the rest of that business but through words, through intellectual arguments, opinions, judgments, evaluations—we have so many ways of escaping from the fact. For example, take the fact that one is dull. If one is dull, that is a fact. And when you become conscious that you are dull, the escape is to try to become clever. But to become sensitive demands that all your attention be directed to that state of mind which is dull.

So we need energy—which is not the result of any contradiction, any tension, but which comes about when there is no effort at all. Please do understand this one very simple, actual fact—that we waste our energy through effort, and that waste of energy through effort prevents us from coming directly into contact with the fact. When I am making a tremendous effort to listen to you, all my energy is gone in making the effort, and I am not actually listening. When I am angry or impatient, all my energy is gone in trying to say, "I must not be angry." But when I pay attention completely to anger, or to that state of mind, by not escaping through words, through condemnation, through judgment, then in that state of attention there is a freedom from that thing called anger. Therefore that attention which is the summation of energy is not effort. It is only the mind that is without effort that is the religious mind. And, therefore, such a mind alone can find out if there is, or if there is not, God.

Then there is another factor: We are imitative human beings. There is nothing original. We are the result of time, of many, many thousands of yesterdays. From our childhood we have been brought up to imitate, to copy, to obey, to copy tradition, to follow the scriptures, to follow authority. We are not talking of the authority of law which must be obeyed, but we are talking of the authority of the scriptures, the spiritual authority, the pattern, the formula. We obey and imitate.

When you imitate—which is to conform inwardly to a pattern, whether imposed by society, or by yourself through your own experience—such conformity, such imitation, such obedience, destroys the clarity of energy. You imitate, you conform, you obey authority, because you are frightened. A man who understands, who sees clearly, who is very attentive—he has no fear; therefore, he has no reason to imitate. He is himself—whatever that "himself" may be—at every moment.

So imitation—conformity to a religious pattern, or nonconformity to a religious pattern, but conformity to one's own experience—is still the outcome of fear. And a man that is afraid—whether of God, whether of society, whether of himself—such a man is not a religious man. And a man is only free when there is no fear. Therefore, he must come into contact with fear directly, not through the idea of fear.

Again, the coming together of that unspotted, uncorrupted, vital energy can only happen when you reject. I do not know if you have noticed that when you reject something, not as a reaction, that very rejection creates energy. When you reject, let us say, ambition—not because you want to be spiritual, not because you want to live a peaceful life, not because you want God or anything else, but for itself—when you see the utter destructive nature of conflict involved in ambition and when you reject it, that very act of rejection is energy. I do not know if you have rejected anything. When you reject a particular pleasure—for instance, when you reject the pleasure of smoking, not because your doctor has told you that it is bad for your lungs, not because you have no money to smoke umpteen cigarettes a day, not because you are caught in a slavish habit, but because you see it has no meaning—when you reject it without a reaction, that very rejection brings an energy. Similarly, when you reject society, not run away from it as the sannyasi, the monk, and the so-called religious people do, when you reject the psychological structure of society totally, out of that rejection you have tremendous energy. The very act of rejection is energy.

Now you have seen for yourself or understood or have listened this evening to the nature of conflict, effort, which dissipates energy; and you have understood or realized, not verbally, but actually, this sense of energy which is not the outcome of conflict but which comes when the mind has understood the whole network of escapes, suppression, conflict, imitation, fear. Then you can proceed, then you can begin to find out for yourself what is real, not as an escape, not as a means of avoiding your responsibility in this world. You can only find out what is real, what is good—if there is good—not through belief, but through transforming yourself in your relationship with your property, with people and with ideas, and therefore being free from society. Only then have you that energy to find out, not by escaping or suppressing.

If you have gone that far, then you must begin to find out the nature of the discipline, the austerity which one has, either traditionally or because you have understood. There is a natural process of austerity, a natural process of discipline, which is not harsh, which does not conform, which is not merely imitating a particular pleasurable habit. And when you have done this, you will find there is an intelligence of the highest form of sensitivity. Without this sensitivity, you have no beauty.

A religious mind must be aware of this extraordinary sense of sensitivity and beauty. The religious mind of which we are talking is entirely different from the religious mind of the orthodox. Because to the religious mind of the orthodox, there is no beauty; he is totally unaware of the world in which we live—the beauty of the world, the beauty of the earth, the beauty of the hill, the beauty of a tree, the beauty of a nice face with a smile on it. To him beauty is temptation; to him beauty is the woman, whom he must avoid at all costs to find God. Such a mind is not a religious mind because it is not sensitive to the world—to the world of beauty, to the world of squalor. You cannot be sensitive only to beauty; you must also be sensitive to squalor, to dirt, to the disorganized human mind. Sensitivity means sensitivity all round, not just in one particular direction. So a mind that is not in itself aware of its beauty cannot proceed further. There must be this quality of sensitivity.

Then such a mind, which is the religious mind, understands the nature of death. Because if it does not understand death, it does not understand love. Death is not the end of life. Death is not an event brought about by disease, by senility, by old age, or by accident. Death is something that you live with every day because you are dying every day to everything you know. If you do not know death, you will never know what love is.

Love is not memory; love is not a symbol, a picture, an idea; love is not a social act; love is not a virtue. If there is love, you are virtuous; you do not have to struggle to be virtuous. But there is no love because you have never understood what it is to die—to die to your experience, to die to your pleasures, to die to your particular form of secret memory of which you are not aware. And when you bring out all that and die every minute—die to your house, to your memories, to your pleasures, voluntarily and easily and without effort, then you will know what love is.

And without beauty, without the sense of death, without love, you will never find reality; do what you will—go to all the temples, follow every guru invented by every unintelligent man—you will never find reality that way. That reality is creation.

Creation does not mean producing babies or painting a picture or writing a poem or producing a good dish of food—that is not creation; that is merely the result of a particular talent, a gift, or learning a particular technique. An invention is not creation. Creation can only come about when you are dead to time—that is, when there is no tomorrow. Creation can only take place when there is complete concentration of energy, which has no movement at all within or without.

Please follow this. Whether you understand it or not—it does not matter. Our life is so shoddy, so miserable; there is so much despair and so much misery. We have lived for two million years, and there is nothing new. We only know repetition, boredom, and the utter futility of every act that we do. To bring about a new mind, a sense of innocence, a sense of freshness, there must be this sensitivity, this death and love and that creation. That creation can come about when there is this complete energy which has no movement in any direction.

Look! When the mind faces a problem, it is always seeking a way out by trying to solve it, to overcome it, to go round it or beyond it or above it—by always doing something with the problem, moving out or within. If it did not move in any direction—

when there is no movement at all, within or without, but there is only the problem—then there would be an explosion in that problem. You do it sometime and you will see the actuality of what is being said—about which you need not have to believe, to argue, or not to argue. There is no authority here.

So when there is this concentration of energy, which is the outcome of no-effort, and when that energy has no movement in any direction, at that moment there is creation. And that creation is truth, God, or what you will—it has no meaning then. Then that explosion, that creation, is peace; you do not have to seek peace. That creation is beauty. That creation is love.

And it is only such a religious mind that can bring about order in this confused, sorrowing world. And it is your responsibility—yours and nobody else's—while living in this world to bring about such a creative life. And it is only such a mind which is the religious mind and the blessed mind.

March 3, 1965

London, England, 1965

First Dialogue in London

How shall we proceed with a gathering like this? Shall we discuss? Or would you like to ask questions? Or would you like me to talk a little while, and then discuss?

I really feel, after having been practically all over the world, that a tremendous inward revolution in every human being must take place, and not just an ideological revolution, or a mere intellectual change of concepts and formulas. I feel we are coming to an impasse, intellectually, emotionally, sentimentally. There is no future in that direction at all. Intellectually one sees the utter hopelessness of the useless life that one leads, a life that has no meaning whatsoever; and sentimentally, emotionally, it is very shallow, empty. There is no significance at all in becoming sentimental, devotional, or in accepting religious concepts, gods and images, worship and ritual—all this has utterly no meaning.

So what is one to do? Most thoughtful people have put aside religious beliefs, dogmas, gods, rituals—all the circus that goes on in the name of religion. And when one does put aside those things, one feels tremendously empty, lonely, and in despair. One is ready to commit suicide, or join some mystical association, or create something within oneself. If one does deny literally everything, as one must—one's own concepts, formulas, projections, ideas, fears, hopes, and all the rest of those things which we hang onto in our daily life—and if it is possible to reject all that intelligently, not as a reaction, and not commit oneself to any particular political or religious party, or idea, or action, then where is one? I don't know if you feel that way at all. And if you do, if one does, without throwing oneself into the lake, is there anything more? After all, that is what we are trying to find out, isn't it? Not accepting any authority, any personal salvation, and all that—that is too immature.

When one does arrive at that position, is there anything more which is not self-projected, which is not an imagination, a vision, a heightened sensitivity? All of these are fairly simple to explain, to understand, and to bring about. If one is at all serious, how does one proceed further? That I would like to discuss. I don't know if you want to discuss that.

The fairly obvious things, I think, one can grapple with—like wars, the terrible starvation in the East, poverty, the enormous technological revolution that's going on, the electronic brain and automation giving enormous leisure to man. Not immediately, but perhaps in fifty years, or twenty years, man is going to have a great deal of leisure. He is going to be freed from labor, from incessant toil. And what is going to happen then?

If one is at all serious, what does one do? I mean by that word not a determined seriousness, which is brought about by will, but a seriousness that comes naturally. When one observes all the superficial tendencies of man, what's going on in the world and in ourselves, one inevitably comes, I think, to a certain quality of seriousness. And if one is serious in that sense—and one must be after all these years of discussion, talking, listening, struggling with life—one must naturally, I think, have come to certain rejections, certain denials of the things which have been imposed on man by his own ambition, greed, and so on, and by the society which he has created. When one rejects all that, one does become rather serious. By seriousness I do not mean going to various groups of meditation and schools of yoga, all that stuff.

If one is at all serious, what actually takes place? I think it would perhaps be worthwhile to discuss, to go into that in these six meetings. Because we can go on plowing everlastingly, and never sowing; and most of us, I'm afraid, do that: keep on plowing, not knowing how to sow, not having the capacity to proceed intelligently after plowing.

Comment: Krishnamurti, you talk about preparing and sowing. The point is, we don't know what to sow. We get to the point where we don't know what to do.

KRISHNAMURTI: The lady says we don't know what to do. We think we have plowed, but after that, we don't know how to sow, or what to do.

Comment: It is very easy to do things, but it is not so easy just to be able to be.

KRISHNAMURTI: The lady says it is a matter of being, not plowing or sowing, but we don't know how to be.

Question: What do you mean by "sowing," Krishnaji?

KRISHNAMURTI: That's only a simile, sir. Don't run the simile to death. To me, sowing, plowing is really like going within oneself. And the very plowing, if one goes within oneself very deeply, is the sowing. It is not that they are two different things. So we can't carry on with that simile.

After all these years of struggle, sorrow, searching, joining this group and that group, seeking the Masters, seeking something mysterious, trying to find something permanent, some hope, something called the eternal, the out of time, and so on and so on, we must find out whether we can throw them aside. We have played with all these things, searched for them, struggled for them, gone after them, joined the communist party, the socialist party, or led a very, very simple life, as they do in India with a loincloth and one meal a day, thinking that is the religious life, and sitting on a riverbank, meditating endlessly. We have played with all this. You may not have directly done these things, but you have observed them; and if one has observed them intelligently, without reaction, one rejects them. There are the various schools where they teach you how to be aware, to practice; and you see through that too. You see where communism has led. And if one is at all aware of all this, one wants peace, one wants a certain quality of mind, without deceiving oneself endlessly. I am sure you have done all this. If not, one has to start all over again from the beginning about unconditioning the mind, how to uncondition the mind, whether it is possible to uncondition the mind, whether it is at all possible to be free from fear, despair, anxiety, greed, envy, the seeking of power, position, prestige—all those things.

Question: There are many young people today who have traveled throughout the world and who feel they have reached something. They have not settled in any society. What about them?

KRISHNAMURTI: Leave the others alone. If one has done all this oneself: joined the communist party, gone out of it; become a religious person, gone out of it; gone to a monastery for a month or two and seen the whole business of it, left it; read all the clever books, and so on and so on and so on; if one has done some of that, or at least felt one's way through all that, not necessarily joined them, then what? Do we look to another to tell us what to do? Obviously not. Obviously, if you have gone through all this, you throw all authority aside, authority in the sense of law. Then what do you have to do? You can't look to another; you can't put your faith in another; you have no trust in another. You have yourself—yourself in relation to society. Or rather, you are society because you are a human being—a human being who has lived for two million years, creating this appalling world. You are that, you are society, which you have created. Realizing that, what is one to do? There is no authority outside oneself to tell one what to do. Any hope, any despair is part of oneself. Either one creates, in hope, great things, great images and utopias and gods, and all the rest of it; or, being in despair, joins some footling, little society or jumps in the lake. If one does not do any of those things, which is very difficult, perhaps one has not reached a point where one has completely rejected everything, without cynicism, without bitterness, without despair. That may be the real crux with all of us, the real issue. It may not be possible to reach such a point without any distortion, without any reaction. That demands tremendous discipline in oneself, tremendous attention, alertness, and one may not want all that.

So, if one has come to that point where there is no distortion, if it is at all possible, where the mind can function very clearly, not in departments, but as a whole—if one can come to that with energy, with vitality, with freedom, is there anything more? And is it possible to come to that point? Knowing what society is, the influence of society, one's own background, tradition, influences, and conditioning, and how cunning and subtle the mind is to slip through, is it humanly possible?

Comment: Most of us have to function within society simply to earn our daily bread.

KRISHNAMURTI: That's what I mean. Living in society, and being out of it in another sense, can one come to that point? Because living is action. Living is relationship. Living is a movement—not business and living. Taking the thing as a whole, is it possible to live in this world and come to that point—not escaping into monasteries and all that stuff, which has no meaning, or identifying oneself with a particular nation or group, working for communism or some other cause? Can one, living in this world, come to that point? If one can't, then one must make the best of this world, and therefore there is no significance in this appalling boredom and monotony of life. Going to an office for forty years to earn a livelihood, and that's the end of it. Seeing that, one revolts; one becomes a beatnik and all the rest of it, or one becomes extraordinarily superficial, wanting to be entertained endlessly.

You must also have seen and read and heard or been told, as I have, that automation and the computer are going to give man tremendous leisure. What is he going to do with that leisure? They are already talking about a twenty-hour week.

Comment: You just have to reach that point, and then remain there.

KRISHNAMURTI: That's what I mean.

Comment: And find out what it is for yourself.

KRISHNAMURTI: Yes. How do we come to that point? You follow, sir? Most of us are groping in the dark. We read so much. So many religious people, all the clever writers, the existentialists, and all the others have said so many things.

Comment: From what you're saying, then, there is no answer in words.

KRISHNAMURTI: Let's think about it; don't let us come to any finality, any decision yet. I feel it is very important how we come to that point.

Question: Do we come to it, or is it that we are never really out of it?

KRISHNAMURTI: We are always in it.

Comment: We are not aware of it.

KRISHNAMURTI: Ah, that's right, sir. We are always in it, but we are not aware of it. But we are aware of our misery, of our despair, of our endless conflict with ourselves, and when we are free of these, perhaps we are *that,* whatever that may be.

Comment: I think we are trying to come to this position, but we always see that it is a reaction; we are not coming to it spontaneously or freely. It is always an attempt through reacting to something else.

KRISHNAMURTI: Yes, sir. Here is one: thirty years, or forty years, or eighty years, one has lived. Where is one? Still in the same cage? Or, as a reaction, gone out of it, created another cage; or, not finding an answer to life, just drifting? So would it be right to ask oneself where one is, not as a reaction, just as a challenge? It would be very interesting to find out one's response to that challenge.

Comment: You don't mean the place where one is, you mean the state of mind.

KRISHNAMURTI: Yes, sir. Not at Wimbledon! (Laughter)

Comment: Sir, the whole problem is: One arrives at a point where one suddenly feels, "I am here, out of everything," and suddenly one is afraid of this void. This void naturally remains a concept; one doesn't get a chance to analyze it. Before it actually comes upon you, you think it is going to swallow you up, and then you set off another reaction all over again, which creates fear, and off you go all over again.

KRISHNAMURTI: So, if you asked yourself, that would be your response.

Comment: One probably can't remain continuously in that state.

KRISHNAMURTI: No, sir, no. It is not continuously remaining in a certain state.

Comment: You see, one comes to it; one doesn't give it a chance. One comes to something unknown, and just as one is going to approach it, one thinks, "Let me look back."

KRISHNAMURTI: I understand. Quite.

Comment: The thing that one thinks one wants with one hand, the other hand is fighting against.

KRISHNAMURTI: All that implies conflict, doesn't it?

Comment: Exactly.

KRISHNAMURTI: And conflict is contradiction—contradiction, conflict, and effort. That's our circle.

Comment: It's important to have this concept about an ideal.

KRISHNAMURTI: No, no, no concept at all. Sir, look; we live with love and hate, with anger and pleasure, don't we? The conflict goes on in us, always, endlessly. And that is contradiction, which breeds effort; and effort is a reaction. You know all this.

Comment: You asked the question whether it is possible.

KRISHNAMURTI: Let's leave that question aside. Let's put the question differently. I've lived for forty years, let's say. Where am I? I'm married, with a child, sex, anger, jealousy, ambition, a house, a family, the quarrels, the mistakes, the failures. I'm all that, wanting more, fighting for more. And I say, "Now where am I at the end of forty years, or eighty years, where am I? In the same old grind?"

Comment: Not quite the same, but almost.

KRISHNAMURTI: Modified.

Question: Sir, isn't the problem that one's mind is like a tape recorder? One records everything for so many years, the same thing.

KRISHNAMURTI: Yes, sir, yes!

Comment: One comes to oneself, and one says, "It is all rubbish." The answer is to rip it out. So what is one to do? At the moment of ripping it out, it records a bit more on it, with a little bit more variety, perhaps, so you go shooting off on the thing, undecided whether to rip it up, or not rip it up.

KRISHNAMURTI: So one says to oneself, "I am a machine that's endlessly repeating"—repeating modified, not always the same gramophone, the same sound. It's modified, changed, but it's in the same pattern. Then what is one to do? If one realizes that, what is one to do? Break it? And how to break it without creating another pattern?

Comment: One doesn't have to break it if one realizes and says to oneself, "I am a machine repeating this, that, or the other." The minute one has that realization, because one is looking at it, one simply stops going on being it.

KRISHNAMURTI: So, how do you look at it? How do you become aware that you are a machine, and not let the recorder create another pattern of machine, another recorder, and so on and so on, the endless repetition modified? How is one to be so aware of one's own mechanical ways of thinking that one will be completely free and not set another mechanism going? I don't know if I'm making myself clear.

Comment: What one has to do, it seems to me, is to become more aware of any environment in which one is living at any given time, because by doing that, one is more in the present.

KRISHNAMURTI: All right. Then what do you mean by "aware," being aware? I am aware of the environment I live in—the society, the family, the friends, the business.

Comment: No, I didn't mean just the immediate environment, but the whole.

KRISHNAMURTI: Let's just begin slowly, shall we? When we talk about being aware, what do we mean by that word?

Comment: Looking.

KRISHNAMURTI: Looking. How do you look?

Comment: In order to look, there must be no looker.

KRISHNAMURTI: That's right, sir. Are we exchanging words, or facts? You follow, sir, what I mean?

Comment: I think that to be aware implies the establishment of a relationship.

KRISHNAMURTI: No, sir, just a minute, sir. I'm first of all asking the meaning of those words, *to be aware.* I am aware that I am sitting in front of this microphone. And I say, what do I mean by being aware of that? I see it, and I know it's a microphone; and that's very simple. There is nothing to it. But I am aware of you sitting there and of me sitting here. Is there any relationship between you and me? That's part of awareness, isn't it? Do I look at you with my peculiarities, idiosyncrasies, tendencies, prejudices? Or do I look at you without all that? If I look at you with all the content of my mind, then I'm not looking at you; I'm not aware of you. I see; is it verbal or factual? I have an intellectual concept that I'm not aware of you when my mind is crowded. Is that just a concept? Or is it a fact, a realization that I'm not aware of you when I am full of my own fears, hopes, problems, and all the rest of it? There can only be a contact, an awareness, a communion between you and me when you and I both, at the same time, at the same level, with the same intensity, are free of your background and of my background. Then we can communicate. And after all, that is love. All that is awareness, surely. Not only am I aware of the colors of the walls, and the people, the color of dresses, and so on and so on, but also of my inward reaction to all that, my reaction based on my conditioning, and whether it is possible to be free of that conditioning. Verbally you can go on endlessly talking about this; but to actually be aware of my conditioning, stepping out of it, as it were, if it is possible, and seeing what the relationship is then, that is the movement of life—not my prejudices meeting your prejudices, which stops everything.

So, can I take stock of myself without any "kick," without pleasure or pain? Just to take stock of myself as I am, first superficially, that is, consciously, at the conscious level, and then at the deeper level. And, in taking stock of myself, am I the observer taking stock? As long as there is an observer taking stock, he becomes the censor. And is it possible to take stock without the censor? I don't know if you are following. All this demands tremendous vitality, energy, and attention. And if one can't do it, one is not serious. Then one can go on playing around. That is why I suggested finding out where we are. Am I still caught in my own problems: sex, financial, oh, a dozen problems, conscious or unconscious? If I have conscious problems, perhaps I have not the capacity to deal with them. And if I have the capacity and haven't dealt with them, and pushed them aside, then there are also the unconscious problems—problems which are deeply seated, problems which are so in the recesses of one's mind, so secret, that one has never looked at or exposed them, or one is frightened to look at them. Can one bring all these out, recognize them as they are, not as one wishes them to be? And can one deal with them not bit by bit but totally?

It seems to me that is the major issue with most of us—that we don't seem to be able to meet life as a whole, or ourselves as a whole. We are life, we are society, we are the human being who has lived for a million years and more, perhaps two million years. We must take this whole entity, not the intellectual entity, the emotional entity, the physical entity, but the total thing. Each reacts on the other, each is related to the other in a most intricate manner. We must take the whole thing, and be with it as a whole.

Question: Am I right in saying that fundamentally there is only one thing? It may be in a thousand forms, but the only thing in the world is primeval fear. Everything else, even love, is just some aspect of it.

KRISHNAMURTI: Yes, partly, yes. That's right, fear.

Comment: Negative fears.

KRISHNAMURTI: The animal is afraid, and we are part of that animal because we are born with all these fears and anxieties. Take fear as a whole—not just I'm afraid of my wife or husband, or my boss—deal with it as a whole, and be rid of it so completely inwardly that it never touches one. Is it possible?

Comment: There is fear of making mistakes.

KRISHNAMURTI: I don't mind making mistakes; that's a very small affair. That's part of our fear—making mistakes, not always being right.

Comment: Then we must be rid of fear inwardly and outwardly.

KRISHNAMURTI: Yes, that's what we said; we must look out, and then from that outward place, approach within. It is not just to keep looking out, it is a movement, surely. It is a tide that goes out and comes in, not two different things. It is an endless process, to begin with the outer, come in, and from the inner, go out.

Comment: You mean, sir, there is no distinction really between the inside, which is the mind, and the outside?

KRISHNAMURTI: Yes, sir, yes, sir. Inside the skin, and outside the skin.

Comment: There is very little distinction.

KRISHNAMURTI: Sir, I'm coming to that. Look, can we deal with life as a whole, which is the inner as well as the outer?—not the intellectual concept, and another concept, not dividing consciousness into the intellect, the emotions, and so on, but the whole thing, the conscious as well as the unconscious. Because if we don't take it as a whole, but break it up, and then try to solve the problems which each broken part or fragment creates, there is no end to it. We live in fragments. I am one thing at the office, I am another thing in the family, and I am totally another thing when I am by myself, or in the bus, or walking in the woods.

Question: Is not the whole problem in that?

KRISHNAMURTI: That's what I'm saying. That's the whole problem. Consciously I am one thing, unconsciously I am another. Now, is it possible to look at this whole as a whole, not as fragments, dealing with each other separately?

Question: Is it not very difficult, sir, to look at it as a whole?

KRISHNAMURTI: I would not call it difficult. We are so conditioned, we are so used to dealing with life in fragments. What I want to get at is whether it is possible for a human being to take life as a whole and look at it as a whole.

Comment: We mustn't have the idea that it is difficult. That is what prevents us from doing it.

KRISHNAMURTI: I don't know yet. I don't know whether it is difficult or easy. All that I know is that we have dealt with life in fragments. We don't know what it means to look at life as a whole. We can't call it difficult or easy. All we know is that our life is fragmentary.

Comment: If we were to remove the idea of difficulty, perhaps we could see it.

KRISHNAMURTI: Yes, sir. But you see, we are not concerned that our life is fragmentary. During working hours I am a scientist, a professor, a biologist, a businessman, a technician, and I am something else the rest of the time. We live that way, in compartments. First I have to realize that. First I have to realize the way I live, not whether or not it is difficult to look at life as a whole. Now, how do I realize it? Do I realize it because you tell me that I live fragmentarily? And because you have told me, do I then realize it? Or do I realize it without your telling me? You don't have to tell me that I'm hungry. I know it when I'm hungry. So, how does one realize it? Does someone tell you, or is it through your own direct experience, your own, not someone else's?

Comment: No, it is a fact, isn't it, for yourself.

KRISHNAMURTI: Ah, wait, sir. It's terribly difficult. Don't be too quick at this. It's terribly difficult for me to realize that I'm a liar. I can find out that I'm a liar because of circumstances, pressures, fears, and all the rest of it. That's still a reaction, not a realization. I must first find out or learn as a thing for myself, an original thing, and realize my fragmentary way of life.

Question: Why do you say it's the central problem? The most important, the core?

KRISHNAMURTI: Because I am trying to solve problems fragmentarily, and hence increasing my problems. When I look at life as a whole and deal with it as a whole, then my whole way of living, thinking, feeling, is totally different. Then I'm terribly honest. Do you follow?

Comment: It's a principal barrier that keeps us from realizing.

KRISHNAMURTI: And all the rest of it. That's one of the major issues. So, how does one realize anything? How do I realize that I am living a fragmentary life, which brings about innumerable problems, and hence contradictions, and hence conflict and effort? The cycle goes on and on and on.

Comment: As ordinary thought is limited, it must necessarily bring a fragmentary life. We can only think in small parts.

KRISHNAMURTI: At present, yes; but perhaps there is a different way of thinking, or not thinking, which will solve this fragmentary problem.

Comment: You said that to look at life totally, one has to be aware of oneself totally, and that, for me, is the question.

KRISHNAMURTI: No, no, sir. I am aware that I live a fragmentary life. Now, how am I aware of it? That's very important for me to find out.

Comment: If I watch myself, I see that I am awake, and then I sleep, and then I go deeper and I don't sleep, I don't dream, and then I find myself.

KRISHNAMURTI: No, madame, let us stick to this one thing for a minute, if you don't mind. I realize, I see my way of life. The way of my life is fragmentary: office, house, family. Now, how do I realize it? How do I know it? Is it an intellectual concept, or a reality?

Comment: It creates conflict, the fragments get in conflict with one another. That creates a disturbance, and I recognize that there are these fragments.

Comment: The fragments are a chronic situation of which we are always aware.

KRISHNAMURTI: Sir, we are trying to establish, if it is possible, what we mean by realizing.

Comment: One looks to see them as one wishes to see them, instead of seeing them as they are. And it is that wishing to see that is really the conditioning factor. One must get rid of that conditioning.

KRISHNAMURTI: Not "get rid."

Comment: I think one must realize the conditioning.

KRISHNAMURTI: You know, there is a difference between when somebody tells me that I am in conflict because of a fragmentary way of living, and when I, without being told, realize it. Then it is not an intellectual thing; I know my life is fragmentary.

Question: How do I know if I am realizing this directly?

KRISHNAMURTI: Please, let's keep it simple at first; it becomes complicated a little later. Let's begin slowly. You see, we are secondhand human beings. Our experience, except perhaps for hunger and sex, is secondhand. And is the realization that I am fragmentary secondhand or original? If it is original, then it has quite a different vitality. It brings a tremendous energy.

Comment: It is just that point, that to realize, more must take part in it; and my thought, it isn't a thought.

KRISHNAMURTI: So, what is it? No, sir, just a minute. What is the "more" that takes part?

Comment: My feeling.

KRISHNAMURTI: Your feeling, your nerves?

Comment: My whole body.

KRISHNAMURTI: Your whole body. That means what?

Comment: The totality of it.

KRISHNAMURTI: Go on, sir, go on a little more. Proceed. Do we look at anything with all our being—with our mind, with our heart, with our body, with our nerves, with our eyes, with our smell—with everything? Does it ever happen?

Comment: It is a paradox because we actually are content with what is. *We realize that we are fragmentary because while we are doing one thing, a part of thought is doing something else, like you are looking, but you may be thinking in another direction. Your hands are doing a job, and you are thinking of something else. You realize this because of the intrusion of something which is not a part of the problem. When you are whole, there is not a realization of the part. You are the whole; there is no part to realize.*

KRISHNAMURTI: Yes, sir. But how do I come to that? How does the mind come to that state where there is no intrusion? Everything is part of the whole. I don't know if I am conveying anything.

Comment: When you are doing something, if you are totally interested in doing it . . .

KRISHNAMURTI: No, you're not. That, the total interest, is merely a concentration. Look, I am afraid we must go very, very slowly, step by step; otherwise, we can't understand, we are jumping.

Comment: In a moment of crisis.

KRISHNAMURTI: But life is a crisis. Not a moment of crisis. Everything in life is terrible.

Comment: All the time there is an evaluation going on, and that has to stop.

KRISHNAMURTI: Sir, will you give me two minutes, let me talk a bit, a little bit? One knows that one lives a fragmentary life, and one also knows in a sense, intellectually, verbally, that these fragments create the opposites and hence contradiction, conflict, and effort. One knows that verbally, intellectually. To know it completely, not through intellect, not through mere words, demands quite a different approach, surely. What does it mean to know somebody? I know you because we are friends, we have met sometimes before. I have certain memories, certain reactions; and according to those memories, reactions, prejudices, and experiences, I say I know you. I really don't know you. I only know the past of which I am aware. I only know you when the past doesn't interfere. So, in the same way, I lead a fragmentary life; and any effort on my part to integrate the fragments creates another fragment. There is no integration of fragments. So I must look at it in a totally different way; I must approach this problem entirely differently. Now, how am I to do it? No action of will at any level is going to bring the fragments to an end, but all my life I have exercised will. Now to suddenly deny that will is almost impossible. It is this will that has created the fragments: I will, and I will not. I have to look at it quite differently. I have to understand the nature of will so that will doesn't interfere.

What is will? Don't define it to find out what will is because we are coming to something, which is to live a life without will.

When do you say, "I will" or "I must," with determination, a drive, a resistance? When does this will come into operation—when you desire something very strongly or when you don't desire? Surely it is when you desire strongly, which is based on pleasure or displeasure; when you want something, that will comes into operation. When there is the urgency of desire, when that desire meets resistance and there is no easy way out, then there is that will. This is fairly simple and clear.

Now, what is desire? Without understanding desire, which breeds will, which separates life into fragments, I shall not be able to solve this whole fragmentary issue. So I must learn about desire and become completely familiar with it, not destroy it, not resist it, not say to myself, "I must be without desire," which is too silly. I must be completely *au fait* with it, I must know all the movements of it: the physical desires, the emotional reactions which we call desires, and the intellectual concepts, the goals, the objectives, that create desire. I must know the whole of it, not just one fragment of desire.

Comment: It is only when there is opposition that we are conscious of desire.

KRISHNAMURTI: Ah, no, sir; not only when there is opposition. I see a beautiful car, I want it. There is no opposition. I see a beautiful person, and I rejoice in it. If you are very sensual, you say, "I want that person."

Comment: If fear is fundamental to all life, then living is only a procession of more or less futile efforts to escape from fear. Each effort to escape brings a sort of reaction, so life is a series of conflicts.

KRISHNAMURTI: We will come to the understanding of fear through the understanding of desire. You will see the connection. I must find out what desire is, how it comes into being, and what gives continuity to desire. Please, I am not against desire. I am not saying one must live a life without desire. All that has no meaning. I must know for myself the origin, the beginning of desire, how it comes into being, how it takes hold, and what gives it a process which as it moves gathers strength. I must then understand the battle to resist it. I must learn about the whole phenomenon.

So, what is desire? I think it is fairly simple, isn't it? Seeing, contact, sensation, and the feeling from that sensation either, "I like to have," or "I don't like to have."

Comment: There is no problem if you've got the money. (Laughter)

KRISHNAMURTI: No, I want to know how desire arises. Of course, if I have the money, or if I have no money, I live with it. But I want to know how it comes into my being, how desire exists, how it flowers, what gives it nourishment. This is fairly simple. I see a beautiful thing, a beautiful house, a beautiful woman, a beautiful car—it doesn't matter what it is, a flower, a lovely garden. Obviously there is sensation—seeing, sensation, contact, and desire. This is a fact which you know for yourself. This is so obvious. What is not obvious is, what makes it flower? What gives it strength, endurance, nourishment, and vitality, with a tremendous drive behind it? What brings about the flowering of desire?

Comment: Thinking about it.

KRISHNAMURTI: Right—thinking, thought. I can look at a car, see the desire arise, and if I don't "think," then there is no nourishment, there is no vitality behind it. But wait a minute. A car is something quite objective, but subjectively, inwardly, it is much more. I see, I observe, I perceive, I understand the fact that desire is sustained and nourished by thought.

Comment: It's not just thought. It's thought in combination with the feeling of myself.

KRISHNAMURTI: Just begin little, sir. Begin with little things and then go into bigger things. I know thought is the giver of nourishment to desire. I know desire can be pleasurable or painful. I know also that I would like to keep the pleasurable desires and throw away the desires that cause pain. If I say, "I'll keep these and throw away those," I'm dealing with fragments. So I have now to find out why thought interferes.

Comment: Because it isn't necessarily true; it doesn't necessarily relate to the object.

Question: Isn't it because we feel insecure?

KRISHNAMURTI: Sir, look. I am asking you a question.

Question: And I am trying to answer it. Why shouldn't it interfere?

KRISHNAMURTI: Now, sir, look. I am asking you a question. Or rather you are asking me a question. I know I can answer. Ten different words will come out, but can I listen to you without answering, and try to find out what is the fact? If I answer immediately, I'll answer in the good old way. I'll bring it out from my habit, from my repertoire of words. But if you have asked me and I don't know the answer, I listen and I am silent. I really don't know why thought interferes, or why it should not interfere. I know it interferes, and I say to myself, "why?" Don't I wait to find out? Don't I feel around, make my mind be quiet, not always throwing up words? Don't I just find out myself why thought interferes? Actually, I've never thought about it. This is the first time I have asked myself why thought interferes. I am waiting.

Question: Is it a matter of time?

KRISHNAMURTI: No. I am not waiting to find the answer. I really don't know.

Question: Does thought interfere?

KRISHNAMURTI: Yes, sir, it does interfere. So how do I find out what is the truth of the matter—infallible truth, not opinion; not according to Jung, Freud, the mahatmas, the gurus? I just want to know why it does interfere. And not knowing, I become silent. My body, my nerves, my mind, my heart—everything is quiet because I really don't know the answer.

April 22, 1965

Second Dialogue in London

The other day we were saying how important it is to be serious, to be earnest in everything that we do, especially in matters that concern much deeper understandings and perceptions. I think one has not only to understand words and their significance, but also to go beyond mere words, explanations, and intellectual concepts. We live by formulas, and it is very difficult to free oneself from an ideation, a concept. If one would understand the whole of existence, one must not only understand the meaning of words but also one must realize that the word is not the thing. The word is never the thing, but for most of us the word is the thing, so communication becomes rather difficult.

We were also saying that to live means to treat life as a whole and not fragmentarily. We do treat life in fragments: intellectually, emotionally, sensually, or merely sensorially. There isn't a total approach to life. We mean by life not only earning money, satisfying some sexual appetites and some superficial sensory desires, but something much deeper, much more vital, much more significant. To live that way, one must approach life as a total thing. That is not possible when we live in departments, trying to solve problems fragmentarily, or as long as we approach life through the action of will.

Will is the result of intense desire. Desire arises naturally and inevitably when there is contact, sensation, and perception. We asked what gives desire continuity and intensity. Someone suggested thought. Desire has a continuity when thought interferes or identifies itself with it. Why does it identify, why does it interfere, and why shouldn't it interfere? That is what we are going to discuss today.

Living in this world, not in a monastery, not in an ivory tower, not in some region of isolation, but living in this world, carrying on with our daily activities, is it possible to live without effort? Effort implies will. Will is the outcome of contradiction. Unless we understand this whole question of desire, not suppress it, not deny it or transcend it, or try to control it and drive it in a certain direction, it will not be possible to solve our problems totally.

Comment: When you use the word desire, *I take it that you mean the feeling of "to want." You say we see something; there is contact, and then sensation.*

KRISHNAMURTI: It is not a question of what I say, sir. This is what takes place, isn't it?

Comment: Well, no, I don't think so.

KRISHNAMURTI: How does desire arise? How does it come into being?

Comment: It is from the memory of sensation.

KRISHNAMURTI: Go on, sir. Proceed; dig deeper.

Comment: I don't really know the source of the original desire. All my desires apparently are; they have occurred previously.

KRISHNAMURTI: Almost everything we do is the result of effort. We try, we struggle, we adjust, we compromise; and in that, there is always effort. Is it possible to live without effort, spontaneously, and yet be intensely active—have all one's faculties heightened and live completely, but not vegetate? Effort involves dissipation of energy. When all energy is concentrated, without effort, and there is no movement in any direction, then that energy explodes, and that explosion is creation.

Comment: When one is interested in something, there is no effort involved.

KRISHNAMURTI: Then how is one to be totally interested? I have no interest. How am I to arouse interest? That poses a problem, doesn't it? Life is routine, a bore, filled with constant strife and struggle. All our relationships create tensions. We fall into mechanical and superficial habits and simply carry on, consciously as well as unconsciously. How is a human being to break away from this mechanical existence and make life a creative thing? To find that out, one surely must inquire into how one dissipates energy. Because one needs tremendous energy, energy without movement, for something new, for an explosion to take place. So I must find out how the mind dissipates energy.

The ancients have said that one dissipates energy by being worldly, by being sensual. Therefore, one leaves the world, treats it as illusory, and goes into a monastery where one is trained, controlled, subjugated, and suppressed. Or one accepts the world as it is and lives a very superficial life, with no interest in any of the wider and deeper things. The escape from life into a monastery, or into a religious concept, a religious dedication to an ideal, is still a waste of energy because it breeds conflict. Conflict at any level, whether physical, emotional, or intellectual, is the essence of wasted energy.

Is it possible to end all effort? Will cannot do it. If I exercise will to stop it, again there is a battle. That very exercise breeds conflict. An effortless life is the only creative life. To live that kind of a life, one has to understand the structure of desire because desire breeds conflict of the opposites, duality, the want and the not-want, the pleasure and the non-pleasure. One has to find out how desire arises, from the very beginning. One must understand the foundation and the whole structure of desire, neither suppressing it, transmuting it, trying to control it, nor attempting to shape it.

We see that thought gives desire shape, continuity, and vitality. Why does thought interfere with desire in this way? I see something beautiful: a woman, a car, a house. Desire begins and thought gives it duration. If thought did not interfere with it, there would be an end to desire. If you have experimented with it, you know. What we are afraid of is the ending of something, isn't it? If desire ended, and there were no continuity to it, what would happen? Time is involved. Because we are afraid to come to an end of everything, we use time, not chronological time, but psychological time, which is not a fact but is invented by the mind. For us time has become extraordinarily important. If one were really confronted with the fact that psychologically there is no tomorrow, one would be horrified.

Question: Isn't it also that we use our thought to locate ourselves? We are so uncertain as to where we are that by having our thought in past time, we can locate ourselves there and feel more secure.

KRISHNAMURTI: This is the same, surely. We cling to time. Thought, giving duration to desire, is the prolongation of oneself, of one's desire, one's future.

Comment: The feeling that you are the same person you were a moment ago is so ingrained, and so automatic, that I don't see how it can be broken through.

KRISHNAMURTI: Let's put the question differently. One sees that one's daily life is mechanical, repetitive, with false desires, activities, and habits. Is it possible for a human being to break away from that and be fresh each moment, each minute of the day? That is the real issue, isn't it? How is that to come about?

Comment: We have to see that we really do live mechanically.

KRISHNAMURTI: If we see that our life is mechanical, that our pleasures, our sorrows, and our anxieties are a repetition, how can it all be ended?

Comment: It ends sometimes, but starts again.

KRISHNAMURTI: I don't think it ends sometimes, and starts again.

Question: If we continue to see every day, don't you think we begin to distance ourselves from the conditioned mind?

KRISHNAMURTI: That means you are looking to time as a means of destroying the mechanical process.

Comment: Yes.

KRISHNAMURTI: If one eventually comes to it by slow degrees, by being aware, by freeing oneself from conditioning, that implies time. One looks to time as a means of ending this mechanical way of living.

Comment: Except that I feel it puts one into another dimension of time. It isn't the dimension of time of the conditioned mind. But I agree it is still time.

KRISHNAMURTI: I don't know what this other dimension of time is. I may invent it, I may speculate about it, I may hope for it; but the actual fact is that I don't know it. I am not with it; it's not part of me. I have to find it, I have to come into it. I must not use time because time implies effort and continuity. The mechanical process goes on and on. Is it possible to live in such a way that there is no tomorrow? Inwardly, psychologically, the thing we really want is the continuity of pleasure, pleasure that has a tomorrow.

Comment: The subconscious conviction that it is you who will suffer or have pleasure the next moment is so strong, I don't know if it is possible to do as you say.

KRISHNAMURTI: It is not "Do what I say," but "See what happens," sir.

Question: Sir, is the psychological freedom from tomorrow possible when one lives under natural law? That is, it is day and then it is night; there is light and then there is darkness. That goes very deep into one, surely, even deeper than the conditioned mind.

KRISHNAMURTI: I don't quite follow, sir.

Question: How is it possible to be free of wanting, to be free of the waiting for tomorrow and the continuity of time, since one lives under the natural laws of day and night, darkness and light? All that makes one aware of time.

KRISHNAMURTI: Does the succession of night and day make one aware of time?

Comment: That only makes one aware of change, not time.

Comment: I see that it need not make one aware of time.

KRISHNAMURTI: I look to tomorrow because I am going to enjoy tomorrow. Thinking about tomorrow gives me pleasure. I am going to meet someone—the whole round of pleasure.

Comment: But I might not be enjoying tomorrow. I might think of something which I would be afraid of.

KRISHNAMURTI: If I am afraid of tomorrow, it is the same thing.

Question: How is it possible to fear tomorrow if I do not know what tomorrow is?

KRISHNAMURTI: Surely you have some fear of tomorrow, fear of death, of not being, of losing a job, or of your wife running away. Also, we all know very well the pleasure created by thoughts of tomorrow.

Comment: Following what that gentleman said about this natural law, we are like a goldfish in a bowl. We are so surrounded by things which continually remind us of time that we have to consider it constantly. Even our posture is a habit, and the way we balance. It seems to be rather difficult to separate psychological time from actual time, clock time, and the natural living process of our own body.

KRISHNAMURTI: All right, sir, let's look at it again differently. What is the act, the moment of learning? What is the act of seeing and of listening? When you are listening, are you listening in time? Are you listening with concepts, with formulas, with ideas, or are you merely listening? There is that noise of traffic going on outside the room. How do you listen to it? Do you listen with irritation, with memories, with distaste, or do you merely listen? When you see, do you see with time, or out of time? Do you see only with your eyes when you see your wife or your husband, or when you see yourself in the mirror? Or do you also see in time, with distaste, despair, depression, or some other reaction based on memory?

Comment: You asked about the act of learning, but I don't think we do learn. We try to bring time into it. We look into the mirror and we see more gray hairs. We compare them with how many were there yesterday, and find we're getting older. That is the way we learn, but I don't think it is real learning.

KRISHNAMURTI: Then what is learning?

Comment: I think it is seeing without time.

KRISHNAMURTI: Don't speculate about it! What is learning? When do you learn?

Comment: When you become aware of your conditioning.

KRISHNAMURTI: When do you learn? Don't answer immediately, please. Just look at it. What is the act of learning? What is the state of the mind when it is learning?

Question: Do you mean learning apart from seeing?

KRISHNAMURTI: For me, seeing and learning are the same.

Comment: It is experiencing.

Comment: To be open.

Comment: By concentrating. To be eager to find out.

KRISHNAMURTI: When do you learn? Learning is different from knowing, isn't it? Accumulating knowledge is different from learning. The moment I have learned, it becomes knowledge. After I have learned, I add more to it. This process of adding we call learning, but that's merely the accumulation of knowledge. I am not against the accumulation of knowledge, but we are trying to find out what the act of learning is. The mind is really learning only when it is in a state of not knowing. When I do not know, I am learning. The moment I have learned, what I have learned takes its place in time; it becomes knowledge, and with that knowledge I function. Can I function also in the act of learning?

Comment: I think that sometimes one just says in words that one doesn't know, but it is not the real thing. I may say that I don't know, but it is something else to perceive that it is actually a fact.

KRISHNAMURTI: There can be learning only when there is an actual ending.

Question: Why shouldn't it be the real thing?

KRISHNAMURTI: Sir, what are we trying to find out? Aren't we trying to find out, not verbally or theoretically, but actually and factually, whether it is possible to live in this world at a different dimension in which there is no effort at all involved? This means living at a level where there is no problem; or, if a problem arises, it is met so completely that it is over the next minute. We can go on spinning a lot of theories, but that is too stupid and infantile. To find out anything, there must be an end to the things I have known, or the things I have known must not be allowed to interfere. I must learn what it is to end, and to end, the ending must be in complete energy.

Question: Are you meaning something more than to forget?

KRISHNAMURTI: Of course. To forget is very simple.

Question: Could you make it a little clearer what you mean by ending?

KRISHNAMURTI: Look, sir, it is very simple. Have you ever experimented with ending a pleasure?

Comment: Yes.

KRISHNAMURTI: Without effort?

Comment: Yes.

KRISHNAMURTI: Without any form of restriction, not knowing what will happen afterwards?

Comment: Yes. I have become bored.

KRISHNAMURTI: Oh, no, not bored! Take your own particular pleasurable habit, whether it is sex, smoking, drinking, ambition, or something else. End it without a struggle, without knowing what is going to happen next. Take the habit of smoking as an example. End it immediately without rationalizing, without fear of the harm of smoking, without fear of the kind of cancer you are going to get if you continue smoking. End the habit.

Question: While you still enjoy it?

KRISHNAMURTI: While you still enjoy it, of course. (Laughter) How does one come to the point where, in the full enjoyment of something, one ends it?

Comment: If one remains inactive when one would normally take some action to satisfy desire, and instead of taking that action, just watches the desire . . .

KRISHNAMURTI: How do you watch? Please, don't theorize. The moment you theorize, you won't be able to proceed. Take a particular pleasure which you are enjoying. You are having a good time with it. Why should you stop it?

Eventually this repetitive pleasure becomes mechanical. You get disgusted with it, and get hold of another pleasure which you enjoy until that, too, becomes distasteful.

Comment: You wouldn't give it up unless you saw that it binds you.

KRISHNAMURTI: I don't want to give up anything. I see life is so terribly mechanical: pleasure and pain, and boredom with pain and with pleasure. Being bored, I attempt to use as an escape the temple, the church, meditation, the Masters, or the pursuit of knowledge. It is all an attempt to escape from this mechanical process of living.

I do not want to theorize. I want to find out if one can really live in a different way which will not be mechanical. How is one to do it? The only way, as far as I see it now—I may change as I go further into it—is that there must be a cessation of every waste of energy; because to end anything, one needs tremendous energy. To listen one needs energy. To see without the interference of thought, without the interference of my conditioning, without prejudice, the very seeing is total energy. To listen to that car going by, one needs attention in which there is no interference; and to attend completely demands great energy. Total attention demands energy, not only neurologically, but also mentally.

I am dissipating energy now. How am I to stop this dissipation without effort? The moment I make an effort to stop it, that breeds other forms of contradiction, other waste. The mind realizes that it has to stop the waste of energy. How can it be done?

Comment: I see that the mind by itself cannot. Unless I as a whole am convinced, know, see, and understand that it has to be, I will not stop it.

KRISHNAMURTI: The mind itself, which is the result of time, cannot stop it because the mind is made up of prejudices, idiosyncrasies, temperaments, and experience. The mind itself, using time, is wasting itself; so it cannot operate, it cannot end the waste of energy. When you are listening, or seeing, or learning, are you using just the mind, or are you using your whole being—the mind, the intellect, and the emotions?

Comment: Total awareness.

KRISHNAMURTI: Is a total awareness, a total attention, a total intensity in operation when one is listening? One never listens that way all the time, obviously. There are moments when one is completely attentive, completely aware, and there are gaps, long periods of time, in which one is not attentive, in which one is not so completely aware. What is one to do? One generally says, "How is one to be continuously aware?" I think that is a wrong question, a wrong demand. What one has to do is to be attentive to inattention. Because it is the inattention that is breeding problems and conflict, not attention.

Question: When there is no attention, who is there to be attentive?

KRISHNAMURTI: When there is no attention, who is there to be attentive to that inattention? That's the question. When you are attentive, when you are listening, when you are learning, when you are seeing, is there an entity which is observing? As you listen to the speaker, find out. When you give your complete attention, with your body, with your mind, with your nerves, with your eyes, is there an observer, a censor?

Comment: No.

KRISHNAMURTI: It is only when you are inattentive that the thing comes in. This inattention breeds problems, and the solutions of the problems are still sought in inattention. If one has a problem, and one listens to the problem completely, totally, without trying to find an answer, without rationalizing, without trying to find an escape from it, but lives totally with it, then one will see that there is no problem at all. The problem arises only when there is no attention.

Comment: It is quite likely, I feel, that this form of attention needs tremendous energy.

KRISHNAMURTI: Yes.

Comment: That is true. I cannot be in this form of attention except for a moment. I lose it. I cannot renew this attention.

KRISHNAMURTI: Attention cannot be renewed.

Comment: During those moments of attention, one sees there is something there all the time.

Comment: The problem, as you say, is that we must have close attention in order to conserve our forces, yet there seems to be something which is about my mind continuously. The reason I don't have total attention is not that I can't, but I don't want to. That is my problem.

KRISHNAMURTI: Then keep it your problem. (Laughter) The way we live, life is full of problems, isn't it? And if you like it, live with it. Go on with it. Suffer pain and despair, the whole fear that is our life.

Comment: No, it is not exactly that. What I meant was, I have a fear of what that total attention would do. There is this burst of energy.

KRISHNAMURTI: But sir, you can't have a fear of something which you don't know.

Comment: All right, it is a fact that you can't, but it is possible to choose.

KRISHNAMURTI: So you say, "I cannot be totally attentive because I am afraid."

Comment: Exactly.

KRISHNAMURTI: So we have to examine fear, not how to get rid of fear, not all the intellectual concepts and escapes. What is fear? Try this with me: listen to it completely, giving your full attention to it. You can't give full attention if your body is not completely relaxed, if your mind is not completely quiet. Physically, emotionally, and mentally it must be completely rested. Psychologically there must also be a quietness in order to listen. Listen in that state. What are you listening to, an explanation, a series of words, or the thing of which you are afraid? If you are listening in that way, is there fear? You can listen to the unconscious promptings of fear, can't you? And then, is there fear?

Let us take the fear of loneliness, this sense of isolation. Though one may be related to many people and have a great many friends, there is a sense of complete loneliness. One knows it, and that is probably the major cause of fear. To listen to that feeling of loneliness, to see it, feel it, and learn about it, one must have tremendous energy, energy which is not disciplined. There is no rationalization, no explanation. In that state of listening the mind is completely quiet with regard to that loneliness. If one is so attentive and learning about it, there is no entity who is accumulating knowledge about it. There is not the observer and the thing observed. This is the most difficult thing. This contradiction, this division as the observer and the thing observed, creates the problem of conflict. Is it possible to look at something so completely that the observer is not?

What is communication? How do you communicate? Words or gestures are necessary in order to be understood. If there is to be communication, both the speaker and the person communicated with must be at a certain intensity. In that state of intensity there is not someone listening, and the speaker. There is only the act of listening. In that state the mind is in communion. Communion implies space.

A mind that has problems becomes a dull mind, and a dull mind cannot possibly be attentive. When any problem arises, only a mind that is attentive, intense, learning, listening, can meet it, dissolve it, and move on. How is a mind, which has so many problems, to meet new problems? There is the problem of death, there is the problem of time, the problem of space, the problem of relationship, the problem of living, of earning a livelihood, the problems of disease, health, and old age. How is the mind to meet all these problems at once, not one by one, but the whole of them at once, without effort?

The way we meet them now, our problems are all fragmentary. There is the problem of fear, the problem of boredom, the problem of enjoyment—a multitude of problems, one after the other. Is there a way of meeting all these problems, not separately, but totally? If I deal with each problem separately, each is going to take time; so I have to understand time.

Comment: If you can deal with all problems at once, then that implies that they have a common root.

KRISHNAMURTI: That is partially right.

Comment: If you are living in the present, you only have one problem at a time. In fact, all the problems coalesce into one problem.

KRISHNAMURTI: The existentialists say, "Live in the present." What does it mean to live in the present, the active present?

Comment: It means the past doesn't take you away from it.

KRISHNAMURTI: Do go into it a little more, sir. How can I live in the present when I am the result of the past, and am using the present as a means of getting to the future? It means that I have to bring all of time, the past, the present, and the future, into the immediate present. To live in the present, time must collapse.

Comment: I should say, sir, that it is direct perception, without endeavoring to do anything about it.

KRISHNAMURTI: Yes, madame, but do look at the immense difficulty. How is time to collapse? How is space to collapse? How is the distance between here and the moon to collapse? Don't say, "Well, if I am attentive, it will"; that's not the answer. When we say, "Live in the present," it must be something extraordinary. Because I am the result of two million years, my mind, my brain, and my habits all are of time. You tell me to live in the present. I ask what you mean by it. How can I live in the present when I have an immense history behind me which is pushing me through the present into the future? How am I to live in the present with the past? I can't. Therefore there must be a collapse of time. Time must come to an end; time must stop.

Comment: I feel that I live in the present when I have no memories, when I'm just there—at those moments when I have experience.

KRISHNAMURTI: Yes, but those moments come and go. It's not good enough. We have all had those moments when time has no meaning at all.

Comment: One sees the interrelatedness of all the problems, and then there is an action which arises from that.

KRISHNAMURTI: What do you mean by action? Is it to do, to be, to function, to think, to act? Does action mean getting up, going to work, and all the rest of it? That action is based on the past, on idea, on memory. For us, action is related to time. We are now trying to make everything fit into time. To find out, to live and act in the present—all of these demand the understanding and the ending of time.

Comment: For time to collapse, it must mean the collapse of the entity.

KRISHNAMURTI: Yes, sir, collapse of the entity.

Question: Would you explain why it is that the past and the future always seem to be so much more interesting than the present?

KRISHNAMURTI: The lady wants to know why the past and the future are much more interesting than the present. That's fairly obvious. (Laughter)

Question: Well, may I ask this question: Why is the present so difficult to confront?

KRISHNAMURTI: That's what we're trying to find out.

Comment: I mean, one may be in a safe environment, but it is still difficult to confront the present.

KRISHNAMURTI: If we really understand something, if we see some fact truly, then that very fact, that very observation brings its own action. I don't have to find out how to act. What we are trying to find out, what we are trying to discover for ourselves is whether it is possible to live in the present at all.

Question: Isn't it impossible not to? That is the only place we can live.

KRISHNAMURTI: That's an idea, sir. All my acts are based on ideas, on a formula, on an experience, on knowledge, all of which are of the past. I know no action which is not related to time. Then someone comes along and tells me to live in the present. I say, "What do you mean by it? How can I live in the present?" If it is a theory, it is valueless; it has no meaning at all. To find out what it means, I have to discover, understand, and be totally aware of time—time as space, time as distance, time as a gradual achievement; using time as a means of getting rid of something or of gaining something. In order to live in the present, that way of thinking, that way of looking, that way of living, must collapse. But my whole being, conscious as well as unconscious, is of time. How is the mind to step out of it?

Comment: All images of oneself must collapse.

KRISHNAMURTI: That is an idea, sir. It is not a fact.

Comment: The fact is that I don't know enough.

KRISHNAMURTI: You have no time to know enough.

Comment: But I see myself creating time whenever I think. Every moment that I am not at full attention, which is practically all the time, the clock goes on.

KRISHNAMURTI: Yes, sir.

Comment: So all through my life I create time.

KRISHNAMURTI: How are you going to end it?

Comment: I could just arbitrarily stop thinking.

KRISHNAMURTI: Of course not. The question is: Can time collapse? To live in the present means there is no tomorrow. That means there is an ending of pleasure, there is an ending of pain, an ending of sorrow—not tomorrow, but now. One cannot live in the present with sorrow, with despair, with hope, with ambition. One has to come to this ending of time, this stopping or collapse of time, not directly but in a different way. One has to come to it negatively. One does not know what the ending of time means; so one has to come to it by being aware of how the mind thinks, and how the mind uses time, negatively or positively, as a means of achievement.

There is the question of peace. How is one to be peaceful, not theoretically, not as some ideal to be achieved, but actually? How is one to be peaceful when there are wars, contentions, quarrels? Everything in this world is based on violence. For peace to be, there cannot be a tomorrow.

Scientists are inquiring into this question of the collapse of space, which is the collapse of time, because rockets will take so many months, or years, to go to Mars. There may be a way of getting to Mars much quicker. There are tremendous things involved in this. Can a mind like ours, which has been used to time, having lived that way for two million years, suddenly collapse? Can we eliminate endless arguments, realizations, fears, and hopes?

Next time I would like to discuss whether it is possible to stop time. Perhaps that is creation.

April 26, 1965

Third Dialogue in London

We were talking, the last time we met here, about time; but before we go into that, I would first like to talk about freedom and order. We seem to think that freedom is a matter of time, growth, and evolution, that freedom is a reaction. As we have to live in a society, the problem then is: Can there be freedom and yet order? When we look to time to bring order, we find that time invariably breeds disorder. Our society is not orderly; within it there are all the elements of destruction and violence. The social structure is based on acquisitiveness, competition, and ambition, with all the signs of disorder. I think one more or less accepts that as inevitable, and lives in that pattern. Freedom within such a society cannot be, nor is freedom possible outside that society. If freedom is merely a reaction, then it breeds disorder, as time does. But if we understand freedom not as something that you cultivate, not as a process, nor a thing to be achieved, then freedom has a quite different meaning. To understand this thing called freedom, one must also understand the nature of time, both physical and psychological time.

One has to accept physical time. One can't do otherwise. But when one looks to psychological time as a means of achieving freedom, or peace, one finds that such time only breeds disorder because it is not based on a structure of reality.

What we are discussing is not a theory, a concept, something with which one can play intellectually. We are dealing with facts. In a society such as ours, freedom means disorder because it is conceived of as a reaction. But if one understands the nature and the structure of time, perhaps one can see that there is a kind of freedom which is not a reaction. It is not freedom from something.

There are two obvious times: physical or chronological time, and the time which is constructed by thought, by the psyche, which is psychological time. We are not dealing with physical time, but we are trying to determine whether through psychological time one can have freedom and therefore order. It is very important to have freedom from fear. One must understand fear and be totally free of it; otherwise, there can be no order structurally, either outwardly or inwardly. One must understand not only the nature of fear but also whether it is possible to be free of it immediately and not through the process of time. If we can free the mind, it will free itself of fear. We have used time as a means by which the mind can free itself. We hope to be free from fear through a process, whether it be analysis, discipline, or understanding. We use time as a means of trying to rid ourselves of fear, of a habit, or of the poison of nationalism. Is it possible? Can one be free of fear through time, by saying to oneself, "I will be free tomorrow"? Is it possible to be free of fear tomorrow, whether you restrict that tomorrow to a day, to a second, or to many years?

Is there a different approach to the problem altogether? Fear in any form distorts, breeds illusion, brings about confusion. It is very destructive for a mind to be afraid and live in a state of fear. It breeds every form of illusion and conflict. Is it possible to be free of fear totally, completely—not tomorrow, but in the now, which is not of time? Can one understand the whole structure, the nature, and the significance of fear immediately, and be free of it instantly? If not, then one must depend on time to free the mind from fear. This dependence on time, this usage of time, only breeds disorder. Whether one is afraid of one's neighbor, or of ideas, or of any form of social or psychological disturbance, it does breed fear, and that does bring about disorder.

Is it possible to be free of fear, not only consciously, but also at the deeper levels of consciousness? Without freedom from fear, there is no peace, either among nations, races, or continents. Peace is not possible when the world is divided, not only politically and economically, but also religiously. If one would understand what peace is, actually, not theoretically—not as an idea, as something to be pursued, lived up to as an objective or a directive—one must be within oneself totally at peace psychologically, not having any form of conflict.

All religions have maintained that time is necessary, the psychological time we are talking about. Heaven is very far away, and one can only come to it through the gradual process of evolution, through suppression, through growth, or through identification with an object, with something superior. Our question is whether it is possible to be free of fear immediately. Otherwise fear breeds disorder; psychological time invariably does breed extraordinary disorder within one.

I am questioning the whole idea of evolution, not of the physical being, but of thought which has identified itself with a particular form of existence in time. The brain has obviously evolved to come to this present stage, and it may evolve still further, expand still more. But as a human being, I have lived for forty or fifty years in a world made up of all kinds of theories, conflicts, and concepts; in a society in which greed, envy, and competition have bred wars. I am a part of all that. To a man who is in sorrow, there is no significance in looking to time for a solution, in evolving slowly for the next two million years as a human being. Constituted as we are, is it possible to be free from fear and from psychological time? Physical time must exist; you can't get away from that. The question is whether psychological time can bring not only order within the individual but also social order. We are part of society; we are not separate. Where there is order in a human being, there will inevitably be social order outwardly.

Question: Isn't the basis of fear the unconscious demand to be free from conflict?

KRISHNAMURTI: Sir, one can find out fairly easily the cause of conscious or hidden fears through analysis, through observation, through introspection, through examination, or by going into oneself very deeply. Will that help to be free of fear? Will discovering the cause, either by being told or by discovering it oneself, free the mind from fear? If one discovers it for oneself, it is much better than being told. To find out the cause through analysis implies time, doesn't it? And if one uses time as a means of discovering the cause of fear, what has one actually done? When one finds the cause, what has happened?

Comment: Nothing.

KRISHNAMURTI: Just nothing?

Comment: Certain kinds of discovery about oneself can come as a revelation. It can be very dramatic, not something one learns.

KRISHNAMURTI: Yes, it can be very dramatic and all the rest of it, but the fear still remains. Look, sir, someone I like dies. I feel terribly upset about it, and I call that sorrow. I know why I am in sorrow; it is because I have lost a friend. I have lost someone whom I liked very much, and I'm lonely. I'm suddenly bereft of a companion with whom I used to discuss things. Knowing all that, does it free me, free my mind from sorrow? Do please observe a little more closely.

Comment: Surely what makes one feel sorrow is a feeling of guilt because one has been so inadequate in one's relationship.

KRISHNAMURTI: Yes, inadequate, repentant, and all the rest of it.

Comment: I keep thinking about it.

KRISHNAMURTI: That's analysis, thinking about it, investigating it with regret and repentance, with a feeling of "I wish it hadn't been that way." But at the end of this long journey of discovery, is one free of fear or of sorrow? We have explanations: religious, psychological, and factual. Will they bring about freedom from fear?

Comment: One can look at the fact and be aware of it.

KRISHNAMURTI: I feel that there is a different way of tackling this problem altogether. There must be. The way we have lived, we have not solved any problem. We still have the problem of fear, the problem of sorrow, and the problem of anxiety. We still go on living in that mess. I feel there is a real way out, if we can approach this whole issue differently.

I see for myself that mere discovery of the cause of sorrow doesn't end sorrow. The explanations, the regrets, the thought of "I wish I had treated that friend better"—none of these resolve and finish my sorrow. Now, what have I done? In examining, in searching for the cause, I have wasted time, and energy. I need energy to meet something which I don't understand. I see that time as a process of analysis and investigation of the cause only breeds disorder and wastes energy. So I will not dissipate my energy looking for the cause. I know very well that the cause is self-pity. I push all of that completely aside—the explanation, the cause, the regret, the self-pity—I deny it and reject it totally because I see the stupidity of it. It has no meaning.

Comment: By trying to understand any problem, or feeling, or sorrow, I see that state of mind.

KRISHNAMURTI: Look, sirs, I would like to convey something; I would like to tell you something. In order to understand what the speaker is saying, you must listen. You must not only listen to the words, but you must also get the feeling, the structure, the nature, and the significance of what lies behind the words. To listen, you have to be tremendously attentive. Of course you have your own ideas, your own opinions, your own experience; put those aside for the time being; don't let them intervene and prevent listening. This does not mean that you must accept what is being said, but quite the contrary. You are not being mesmerized, or being made to accept something which is totally different from your own ideas. You are just listening to find out. We are saying that perhaps there is a totally different approach to the problem of sorrow, or of fear. To understand and to find out for yourself, you are not only listening to the speaker, but you are using the speaker, if I may employ the word *use,* to see either the truth or the falseness of what he is saying. He is saying something very simple: that one has used time while searching for an explanation, in order to discover the cause of sorrow, thereby hoping to be free from it. That is what one has done. I say that is not the way to be free from sorrow.

You have to find out what the speaker means, what he wants to say. Therefore you have to listen. He says that when you are analyzing, being introspective, and examining into causes, it is a waste of time and a waste of energy. To meet the challenge of fear or of sorrow, you have to have all your energy, and therefore you cannot afford to waste it in trying to find out what the cause is.

I will not waste one second of time or one iota of energy on analysis or on self-pity. I want to be free from fear. I see what happens if one is afraid. I see how fear distorts, how it prevents, how it corrupts, and how it creates illusions. We have a network of escapes, and all that is a waste of energy because it involves time, and time is disorder.

I have said that. Is it a fact to you, or do you have merely a verbal understanding? Is it a fact in the sense that the microphone in front of me is a fact? If I do not see the microphone and someone describes to me what it is, what its function is, and its structure, with me it is merely a verbal statement; but when I see it directly, it is factual. When you are hungry, that is a fact. No one has to tell you that you're hungry, or describe what hunger is. The fact reveals the structure of disorder, of time. Unless one comes to the point where this becomes a fact to oneself, one can't proceed further. When the mind realizes that time breeds disorder, and that this is a fact, not a theory, a verbal statement, or an intellectual concept, the very realization brings about a tremendous revolution because one has denied psychological time.

Question: How can you hold this realization?

KRISHNAMURTI: It is not a question of holding it. If you realize it, it is so.

Question: Does the environment help you to realize?

KRISHNAMURTI: No, it has nothing to do with environment. It has nothing to do with what one is or what one is not. Simply, does one see the fact? Sir, in your bathroom you have a bottle marked "poison," and you know it is poison; you are very careful of that bottle, even in the dark. You are always watching out for it. You don't say, "How am I to keep away, how am I to be watchful of that bottle?" You know it is poison, so you are tremendously attentive to it. Time is a poison; it creates disorder. If this is a fact to you, then you can proceed into the understanding of how to be free of fear immediately. But if you are still holding time as a means of freeing yourself, there is no communication between you and me.

You see, there is something much more; there may be a totally different kind of time altogether. We only know two times, physical and psychological, and we are caught in time. Physical time plays an important part in the psyche, and the psyche has an important influence on the physical. We are caught in this battle, in this influence. One must accept physical time in order to catch the bus or the train, but if one rejects psychological time completely, then one may come to a time that is something quite different, a time which is not related to either. I wish you would come on with me into that time! Then time is not disorder; it is tremendous order.

Comment: Sir, in psychological time I see that my mind has projected forward a future that doesn't exist. That creates disorder because I respond to something that does not exist.

KRISHNAMURTI: Quite.

Comment: However, this occurs on two levels, the conscious and the unconscious, and it is very hard to penetrate into the unconscious.

KRISHNAMURTI: Sir, we give tremendous importance, it seems to me, to the unconscious. Freud and company have given us an extraordinary thing, and weighted us down with this terrible thing; but I don't think it's important at all. It is such a trivial affair, and the conscious mind is also a very trivial affair. Why do we give such significance to the unconscious, and why don't we give significance to the conscious mind? Is it because we don't see that thought itself is insignificant?

Question: Is there not a better use of time, which will dissolve fear?

KRISHNAMURTI: Look, sir. You are in sorrow. I am not wishing you to be in sorrow. Will tomorrow help you to get rid of it?

Comment: Tomorrow it may be gone, and often it is.

KRISHNAMURTI: It may or it may not be gone. Generally it is not. The idea that it may be gone is just an idea. It is not a fact. Man has lived with sorrow, or deified sorrow. The Christians have worshiped sorrow. In India and in the East they explain it away, for they have the doctrine of karma. Explaining sorrow away or deifying it is a form of escape. One can also escape through drink or through drugs. You are asking if there is a right usage of time. Obviously there is.

Comment: I think that my use of time in the past has been faulty because I have used time stupidly.

KRISHNAMURTI: What is right usage of time? Apart from physical time, time by the watch, what does time mean?

Comment: Time means a change.

KRISHNAMURTI: Time does mean a change. I am in sorrow. I need time, either tomorrow or the next moment, to change that whole. Does that take place? When one is hungry, when there is a real demand, does one say, "Well, I'll wait until tomorrow"?

Comment: Yes, but there are many other illustrations that show it would work. For example, I feel a desire. If I don't do anything about it, it passes away, and I am not bothered by having to fight the thing.

KRISHNAMURTI: Quite. Discuss it, sir; go on.

Comment: As an illustration, the passage of time results in desires being eliminated because they become painful.

KRISHNAMURTI: Look at what you are saying. You are saying that time, which is part of pleasure, can be used to get rid of nonpleasure. So time gives you pleasure. That's all we want.

Question: Is not the dream state a state of the mind in which there is no psychological or physical time?

KRISHNAMURTI: Dreams are something entirely different. I think dreams are a waste of time, a waste of energy. Why does one dream? It is fairly obvious, isn't it? One is so terribly occupied all day long, the conscious mind caught up in its quarrels and in all the other activities of one's waking hours. When one goes to sleep, the conscious mind is somewhat less active, and the so-called unconscious projects all its intimations as dreams. We don't have to glorify dreams, for then we get the interpreters of dreams and all the rest of it. (Laughter)

If one is awake all day, watching everything, watching the way one walks, talks, dresses, and thinks, watching one's relationship to people and to nature, giving attention to all that is hidden below, then the so-called unconscious comes up, and one does not have to dream at all.

Question: Can you point out why time, per se, can never solve sorrow?

KRISHNAMURTI: I've been showing this. Look, sir. I lose my son. I investigate what is happening in my mind. I see that I am bereft of something upon which I relied. I have lost a companion, I have lost a son in whom I have invested not only money but also hopes, fears, and longings. I cannot immortalize myself in him. I wallow in self-pity and regrets. Now, that has taken time. It has taken a day or a year; whatever it is, it has taken time. While I have been taking time, other influences, other strains have come into being. It is not just one continual discovery. There are other things interfering. But the cause never brings about the right effect. When there is a cause and an effect, there is a time interval. In that time interval there are all kinds of strains; therefore, the effect is changed, and what was effect becomes the cause of a new series of changes. There is never a precise cause and a precise effect. So mere investigation of the cause which has produced my sorrow is a waste of time. If that is clear, is it a verbal clarity or a factual clarity?

Comment: In the particular illustrations which you give, it is obviously a factual clarity.

KRISHNAMURTI: So you are no longer depending on time.

Comment: I say to myself that if I were aware over a period of time, then . . .

KRISHNAMURTI: You cannot be aware through a period of time. Then it becomes mechanical. Sir, look. I come into the room, and I see the colors of the various dresses, the door, the windows, the disproportionate shape of the room, the light, and all that. I see it immediately, and I am aware of my reactions to all of it. I am aware of how those reactions arise, and I am aware of my conditioning, whether it be classical, Victorian, or something else.

Comment: Yes, you are aware, but I am not.

KRISHNAMURTI: If you proceed that way, you will discover, won't you? But if you come into the room, look around and try to discover your reactions, your conditioning, it takes time. And when you have taken time, there are other factors involved in it, not just one thing, and that is a waste of time. Now is it a fact that you are no longer using time as a means of being aware, of being rid of fear, or of sorrow?

Question: Doesn't time only come in when one starts thinking of oneself?

KRISHNAMURTI: No, please, that is not the question. You are introducing something else. All right, I'll say yes, of course. Then what are you going to do about it? Again investigate how to get rid of that thought which thinks about itself?

If it is a fact, not an idea, not a word, not an intellectual concept or a theory, but something that is real, as it must be to some who are here, then we can proceed. There is no time at all through which I am going to be rid of something, and I know there is fear. I am afraid of public opinion, death, darkness, or my grandmother. I am also aware that I am in sorrow. I have to meet it without time. That means I have to meet it with all the energy I have. I have the energy now, you understand. I did not have it before because I used time as a means of escape. It brought disorder because the fact is sorrow, and I introduced other factors which had no value at all. The other factors were mere escapes from the one fact. When I really reject time as an idea, a concept, or as something which I use in order to get rid of fear, then I have the energy to meet this thing, and all this requires enormous energy.

I am afraid, but I am not looking any more to time as a means of dissolving that fear. I have to meet it. Now, how do I meet it? All escapes, explanations, causes, all the ways to get over it: restraint, suppression, control—all those have gone. They all imply time and a waste of energy. Then how do I meet it?

Comment: If all escape is gone, surely the fear itself is gone.

KRISHNAMURTI: Don't come to that. Because if you go into it, you will see something else taking place.

Comment: But if I don't know how to do that, then . . .

KRISHNAMURTI: Then it means you have not rid yourself of the concept of time at all. The concept of time as thought is pleasure; you want pleasure, and you continue that pleasure in different forms, and therefore you are not rid of time.

Comment: You have to meet it directly.

KRISHNAMURTI: To meet it directly, you have to know, you have to understand the structure and the nature of pleasure. Because pleasure is what we want.

Comment: The emphasis is on pleasure.

KRISHNAMURTI: That's what we are looking for; that's what we want. We want pleasure; we want the continuation of pleasure, not the understanding of sorrow, not the understanding of fear or time. We use time as a means of continuing pleasure and avoiding sorrow; that's all we are concerned with.

One has an experience of pleasure: a lovely sunset, a beautiful tree, a scene, a beautiful face; one gets a tremendous pleasure, and one wants that to be repeated. The repetition is time, not the instant of pleasure.

Comment: It is a very difficult point because if one feels fear or sorrow, then the mind is pulled away from it by all these influences; and if you reject them, then . . .

KRISHNAMURTI: No, no! When you reject time, you reject it because it is a fact. You are never pulled towards its effect because you know its effect. It is only when your pleasure comes in looking at that precipice that you are pulled towards it.

Question: Is rejecting this concept of time a return to pleasure?

KRISHNAMURTI: No, quite the contrary; time is the invention of thought as pleasure.

Comment: No, I don't mean thought; I mean as an experience.

KRISHNAMURTI: You have to understand pleasure. Let's go into it. What do we want? Really, what do all of us want?

Comment: We want to be happy.

KRISHNAMURTI: Happiness is pleasure, a continuation of pleasure, a repetition of something which is pleasurable: sex, an image, an experience, an idea, anything that gives pleasure.

Comment: You want freedom.

KRISHNAMURTI: No, sir! (Laughter)

Comment: I mean freedom from unhappiness. If one thinks of happiness, one automatically thinks of unhappiness.

KRISHNAMURTI: Freedom, not freedom from—just freedom.

Comment: Just freedom.

KRISHNAMURTI: If you are free from something, are you free?

Comment: No.

KRISHNAMURTI: Please. We have so little time left. I am not impatient, or anything of that kind, but you are missing so much by just going back and back.

Comment: Carry on without the interruptions, sir.

KRISHNAMURTI: Sir, it's no good my carrying on because, after all, we want to communicate with each other. Verbal communication is no communication at all. There is communication when we are dealing with facts, which is real communication. When you hate me, you are in communion; when I love you, we are in communion; but if you are indifferent, and I am something else, we have no communion. So, look at it, sirs. As we said in the beginning, time breeds disorder. You can see what is happening in the world. There is starvation in India and other parts of Asia, unemployment in many places, and other terrible things, including war, going on in Asia. Science could feed man, clothe and shelter him, but cannot because of the poison of nationalism, because of politicians and their ideas, their concepts. They say, "Belong to this party, that party," and the whole of the East starves. They say, "Well, we must go through nationalism, through our particular party," and in the meantime people starve. So we can see that time does breed disorder, not only politically, but inwardly. I see that. I see for myself as a fact that time breeds disorder, and that man must live in order. Otherwise we create illusions, we live in despair. I see that as a fact, and time no longer exists for a man who sees it. I am not a nationalist and belong to no party. I am not a Catholic, a Protestant, or a Hindu. I have the energy to meet the fact, which is fear, because I have understood pleasure. But most of us want just one thing: pleasure. If it is not sexual pleasure, it is some other form of pleasure. One gets fed up with different kinds of pleasure as one grows older, and then eventually seeks God (Laughter) or something else.

One has to understand this extraordinary drive of pleasure, and when one understands it, one also understands the nature of time which gives it duration as thought. It is all so simple, sirs—simple if you really see the truth of the nature of time. If you do, then what takes place? You are no longer shaped by time or pleasure as a principle. You can look at the fact, not in terms of pleasure and pain and therefore of time. Then what happens? When you meet a fact completely, as a whole, you meet the fact with peace, which is not pleasure. Peace is affection, isn't it? Don't agree, please; just examine the statement. Peace never has pleasure in it. That's the most beautiful thing about peace. And when time has been rejected, then you have energy to meet the fact. This means that the mind has undergone a revolution and therefore is meeting something in a totally different dimension. If one has only known pleasure, and the continuation of pleasure as time, as thought, one has only known the conflict which is disorder. One tries to escape from it, to mesmerize oneself with all kinds of activities, but that's the only thing one knows. One sees that and rejects it completely. Then the mind is not swayed by pleasure. It has a tremendous energy which is peaceful; it has no conflict, and it can meet fear.

How do we meet fear? That's what I want to know. We generally meet fear by trying to escape from it; therefore, we never do actually meet it. We escape it through verbalization, through innumerable networks which man has made. We know all this: God, drink, sex, amusement, literature, painting, art—anything but the fact. When we stop all that, the mind becomes extraordinarily alert and very quiet. It cannot be quiet when it is always, everlastingly, seeking different ways of pleasure. Please don't misunderstand. There is nothing wrong with pleasure. To look at something beautiful is a lovely thing. But to get the right pleasure from it, one must not insist that it continue—that is where disorder comes in.

When you have rejected time, not as a reaction, but because you realize that it creates disorder based on the principle of pleasure, then you have the energy to meet the fact. Then there is no distortion. The pleasure which creates illusion and distortion has come to an end; therefore, the fact can be met.

One of the most difficult things to understand is the whole principle or structure of pleasure. When you are highly sensitive, your whole being is sensitive, your body, your nerves, your eyes, your ears—everything about you is sensitive. The mere seeing of something very beautiful, or very ugly, is a moment of pleasure, but it should have no continuity. The moment it has continuity, one becomes insensitive; and being insensitive, there is disorder.

What takes place when one rejects time, when one rejects pleasure and its continuity, is that the mind is completely still, the brain is completely still; and this stillness, this quietness, this intensity, is the outcome of the fact which one has seen; and therefore there is no effort involved in it at all. There is effort when there is pleasure. If one has really grasped this, the mind has stepped out of the rut of the time-pleasure principle and therefore is no longer looking to time as a means of evolution, of getting rid of something, or of achieving. When there is the death of someone, the mind meets that challenge, that incident, without any movement. This does not mean a lack of sympathy; it does not mean cruelty. Death is an immense thing, too vast to be understood by a puny, little mind. You can only meet something immense when the mind is quiet.

April 29, 1965

Fourth Dialogue in London

Shall we continue with what we were talking about the other day—time? We were saying that time, apart from physical time by the watch, creates disorder; and to be sane, factual, unemotional, and unsentimental, one has to understand the whole structure of time. We went into that somewhat, and I think perhaps this evening we can approach it from a different angle.

Conflict in any form is the illusion of time, and we are all in conflict, different kinds of conflict at different levels of our being. We accept the conflict of life as inevitable, and we adjust ourselves to that conflict. One can see that conflict in any form distorts and perverts thought, and therefore thought becomes the breeder of illusion, which is time.

We are not talking about something. We are not talking about an idea. It is not like looking at a picture someone else has painted and saying, "I like it," or "I don't like it," wondering who has painted it, if it has any monetary value, and so on and on and on. We are not doing that. We are not looking at a verbal picture. We are actually living the thing that is being said, and the thing that is being said is not foreign, it is not something strange. That's why it is very important, I think, to listen attentively, not only to the speaker, but to everything in life, listen without any distortion, listen without time.

Then perhaps we will find out for ourselves whether it is at all possible to live in this world—earning a livelihood, having a family, living a life of continuous movement in relationship—without effort, and therefore without time.

Time also implies space. We only know space from a center which is the observer, and therefore our space always has a limit, a boundary, a frontier. Actually, not as a theory, we only know the space within a house because of the four walls of the house. Within ourselves, when we look at ourselves and consider what space is, there is always a center from which we are looking; and therefore space is limited, and its limitation is bred by the observer. In the modern world, where the amount of physical space available is becoming less and less, if one has to have space, one must go to the moon or to the other planets. Space without the center, space without the boundary, is freedom; and that freedom is not possible when there is time which creates the illusion of the observer, who limits space by his thought. The observer divides himself from the thing which he has observed, and therefore there is a space between the thing observed and the observer, which is still of time.

It is very interesting, if you go into it for yourself, to find out what space is, whether you can have space, not only outwardly, but inwardly, without going crazy. It is only in space that there is no influence, no pressure, no civilized entity as the observer, the center, who discriminates, who exercises will to achieve or not to achieve. So in understanding time, not physical time, we have also to understand this question of space—whether there is space without the observer and the thing observed. Since the observer and the thing observed are separate, there is conflict; and to understand conflict and so to be free of conflict, neither the observer nor the observed must exist.

We know space because of the four walls of the house which enclose the space, and because of the chair which creates space around itself. We also know space as distance in time. We know space because we exist as human beings, with all our turmoil, conflicts, miseries, and sorrow; and we also know space from the struggle, the conflict, the drive to achieve, from the center to that which is projected by thought as the end. That center becomes the experiencer, the observer, and from that center one knows space, but one doesn't know space without that center. Therefore, without discovering that space without the center, one is always a slave to time, and hence the constant strain, the conflict of the duality of the observer and the observed.

The observer, which is the 'me', the thought, the center, creates a space around himself either to ward off, to push away, to resist, or through identification, to establish another center. The experiencer and the observer cannot exist without creating another center. He may reject his center because his center is the result of time and experience and knowledge. Unless he completely understands and rejects it, he is not free of that center and invariably creates another outside of himself as an ideal, as a utopia, as a symbol, as God, as what you will, and proceeds to identify himself with that. He still creates space as time, and time to achieve.

One has to understand the question of time and space if one would understand this matter of a life without effort, which is really quite extraordinary, demanding great sensitivity and great attention. It is not just saying, "How can I live without effort in the modern world?"—just brushing it off, or trying to make living without effort into an ideal and living according to that, because it then becomes an effort. And action which is really spontaneous, and not instinctive, not impetuous, is not limited by time.

If the mind is crowded and has no space, one cannot look, one cannot really observe. To observe totally demands a looking, a seeing, a hearing in which distance is not, and therefore space is not—space created by the center. If I would see you and you would see me, your mind cannot be crowded with problems, with every kind of question and doubt and misery, for then there is no space in which to look. Most of us don't want space because space means fear.

Is it possible to live in this world, not escaping from it, but without experiencing? Because the moment there is experiencing, there is the experiencer, who prevents space from being.

This is not as crazy as it sounds. It is only in space that anything new can take place. As long as one is experiencing everything, and therefore translating the new in terms of the old, which is experience, the space created by the experiencer is always limited because it is in the field of time. I have accumulated a great deal of information, knowledge, and experience. That experience has created a space around itself, and therefore has limited space. In that limited space I live with my identification with all the things which I have experienced, with all my memories, with the past. How can I be free of it? How can I so completely reject it that the very rejection is an explosion? When we ask how, the "how" is disorder because it is of time.

The fact is that each human being, who is really not an individual at all, is held in time, as the experiencer projecting his own space around himself. That center is the observer, and whatever he looks at is still the observed, and therefore there is no relationship between the observer and the observed, that is, no real communion. Communion exists only when the center is not, and that takes place when, if I may use the word without distorting it, there is love. And love is not of time, it is not a remembrance, it is not of the past. As a human being who has lived a life of experience, accumulating knowledge, whose center creates the space of time and its bondage, how is it possible for me to cease and therefore for space to exist?

You see, death must be something extraordinary, yet nobody wants to know what it is. Nobody wants to find out the enormous significance of something one doesn't know. I know there is death, and I see others going by, going to their graves; I see myself becoming old, losing my capacity, not only physical capacity, but emotional and mental capacity as well, with a lessening of sensitivity, and a quickening of deterioration. Anything I experience as the unknown, which is death, is still in the field of time if I experience it. But to find out what death is, not only must there be the end of fear, which is fairly obvious, but also one has to really understand this complex thing called time and the space which one cannot experience as an observer, an experiencer.

After all, we know nothing about peace; we don't know what peace is. We talk about it, and the politicians everlastingly play with the word. Actually we don't know what it means. I am not referring to the verbal meaning of the word *peace* but to that state of peace where there is tremendous activity without conflict, without time. To find out how to achieve it, what does one do? Please don't put to yourselves the question, "How am I to do it?" or "How am I to achieve it?" The moment you ask the question, "How?" you are already bringing in disorder because you are introducing time as a means of achieving peace, and that which is achieved through time is no longer peace; it is only disorder, confusion. We don't know what it means to be really peaceful, which means no violence at all. Violence not only includes killing animals for food, killing each other, wars, and the conflict of nationalities, but also ambition, greed, envy, the discipline of society which becomes immoral, and the disciplining of oneself, as one tries to conform to an idea, to imitate a pattern, or to pursue a symbol, which are all in the structure of violence. So we don't know what this extraordinary thing called peace is. We think that if we can ban the bomb we'll have peace. Certainly not! Or we try to control anger, or to get rid of this or that. That doesn't bring about peace. We don't know what it is, as we don't know what love is, or death. We know love as jealousy and as pleasure, the conflict of jealousy, and the sexual relationships of pleasure, which are all of time. But we don't actually know—not as an experiencer, because that's too immature, if I may use that word, and too limited—what it is to be aware of this extraordinary thing called love, or to be aware of peace or of death.

There is this thing called death. I'm not talking about it because I'm getting old! One avoids it because one can't understand it, or one has theories about reincarnation or resurrection. One tries to brush it away and lock it up. It is something unknown, like love and peace, and life without effort. One doesn't know it. One cannot approach it through time as experience, and one cannot approach it through disorder. We must have order to be free from experience. It is only the disordered mind that seeks experience, or wants more experience. I don't know if you have gone into this matter of experience at all. Would you like to ask questions? There is a danger of your merely listening and my going along alone.

Question: When you say "experience," do you mean "conditioning"?

KRISHNAMURTI: No, please don't. We are asking if one has gone into and explored this question of experience. Experience is a reaction to a challenge, adequate or inadequate. Experience is to go through something—anger, jealousy, sex, what you will—and to go through it as an experiencer. We say, "I had a marvelous experience yesterday when I was out walking; the beauty of the clouds, the light in them, was something extraordinary." I've experienced; it has become a memory. There was that beautiful sunset; I have responded. One has to respond; otherwise, one is dead. If a needle is put into me, I must react, unless I am paralyzed. But when the experiencer draws from that pinprick, or from that sunset, a memory of pleasure or pain, then one has set the pattern of experience going. And it is this pleasure and pain that translate every reaction as experience. If one is surfeited with experience one wants a greater experience, a wider, a more significant, a more meaningful experience because this life is terribly boring, seeing the same wife or husband, working in the same office year after year, living in a crowded little, tight little island, very bourgeois. One gets very tired of all that. One either becomes a beatnik, a Beatle, or one takes to drugs because what one wants is more experience. And the "more experience" is always the demand for the same in terms of the new. If we had no experience at all, most of us would go to sleep. If there were no challenging on the part of the state, of our neighbor, of the computer, of automation, we would all go to sleep. We depend on experience to keep us awake in that sense.

If you have gone beyond that a little bit, not in time, but if you understand it, then you create your own challenge; the challenge is much more acute, much more vital, than the challenge which is given to you from outside. However, that challenge which you yourself have posed is still within the field of time because you as the experiencer responded to it.

There is an outward challenge or an inward challenge to that outward response. One can put aside the outward challenge because that has very little meaning for the really serious man. One has one's own challenge, which becomes much more acute, much more vital; and when one understands that too, then is there any challenge at all? Because every experience is still the experiencer and the thing experienced in time; therefore, it creates illusion and creates a space which is time-bound. To see, to observe without the experiencer, is to create order—which is really virtue.

The mind, which is the result of time, the brain, the nerves, everything that I know, experience, think, feel, and strive after—all are from a center of experience. With that I try to discover the unknown as death, as love, as peace; the very attempt to find out is disorder. This is terribly important to understand. Order is peace, but not the social order. That of course you must have. It is not the order of relationship between husband and wife. That also is necessary. But the order which we want to establish in the world is based on time, and therefore it is everlastingly producing disorder.

Look at all the politicians, the lawyers, the businessmen, look at them! They want order on their terms; what they want is disorder. To have order, which is really an extraordinary structure of understanding, there must be an understanding not of time, and you cannot grasp this understanding as an experience.

So there is, like death, something new: the unknown. I cannot possibly approach that thing with the known, as the known. So you see the problem: How am I, who am a bundle of the known, to end it, without introducing time, without experiencing the dying of the known? I cannot possibly conceive of or formulate the unknown. No symbol, no word can be that. The word is not that.

So, is it possible to die to the known—the known as the memory of my wife and my children, the pleasures which we have had together, the problems? Is it possible to die without experiencing death, without effort, and therefore without time?

Let's look at it differently. Life is a movement—action in relationship. It is a movement without a beginning and without an end. But all our actions spring from the known as an idea, and from carrying out that idea in action. Is this getting too complicated? When one says to oneself, "I will do this tomorrow," one has already projected the tomorrow and the idea, as well as the action which is going to follow from that idea, not only physical action—that of course must be, so we won't bring it in, because that would make things more confusing—but the psychological action, which involves time. That's what we do.

I have an idea about myself; I think I am that. Or I have symbolized my concept of myself in words or in an image; and that idea I want to alter, I want to change; and the change of that idea is still another idea—idea being organized thought. And thought is of time. So time, thought in time, as time, creates disorder. I see all my activities—trying to be great, trying to become a saint, trying to be successful, trying to be famous, trying to be, trying to change, trying to do this and do that. There is a division between the concept and the act; there is a division between the concept and the experiencer who is acting. My whole life is: "I am going to be; I will give up," and "I must be." This same thing is carried out politically, as they do in the communist world, with their utopia. Our action is always divided, an image conforming to the pattern of an idea. Therefore there is conflict, and total disorder. There is disorder the moment will operates as pleasure in time.

I see all this. It is not that someone has told me, or that I have read a book about it. I see all this, I observe it all around me, in myself; wherever I go, this is the nature of conflict. The very essence of it is this observer and the thing observed; and hence the disorder of time, and the bondage of space to time. The problem then arises: How does one see? I see this, I say I understand it; at least intellectually and verbally I do understand it. Then the question arises: How am I to put it into action? I see it. It seems so terribly sane, rational, and logical, structurally as well as verbally. How am I to give it action which is not of me? I have to find out what it means to see, what it means to listen, and what it means to listen and learn, because learning, listening, and seeing are the same. They are not three separate things. When I listen, I'm learning, and therefore I'm seeing. Seeing is acting—not I see first, and then act later. If there is an interval of time between seeing and acting, the seeing and acting result in disorder.

There is no "how"; there is no machinery, no formula explaining how I am going to do it. That must be completely wiped out. One can see why. The moment one says, "How am I to do it?" one has already created a division between the experiencer and the thing experienced, and therefore one is already caught in time as practice. I am trying to do that—there is this habit, and I am going to break it, which is a division. But seeing a habit, whatever it may be, is the ending of that habit. So, it is very important to find out for oneself what it is to see. Seeing is not only visual; seeing is also much more of the mind.

When you are driving a car, your mind sees much more than your eyes. It is already aware of the car coming around the corner before the eye sees it; and if the mind is not really sensitive, and the brain also is not very sensitive, there is no seeing. They cannot be sensitive if the body and the nerves are not sensitive. So, one has to have the body and the nerves highly sensitive, not sodden with drink, food, and all the rest of it; therefore, right food—I'm not advising, please! (Laughter)

So, the body, the nerves, the brain, the mind, the total entity, which includes the unconscious as well as the conscious, must have great sensitivity. You must be aware of your likes and dislikes, of how you walk, how you talk, how you listen, so that the unconscious is activated.

Seeing, listening, learning is total attention, in which there is no experiencer; therefore, there is no question of, "How am I to be aware?" or "How am I to be attentive?" The "how" is the most disorderly demand. Either you see or you don't see. If you don't see, leave it alone; don't beat yourself in order to see.

The structure of our being is based on the known, and that known cannot know the unknowable, the unknown. Yet that is what we are trying to do all the time.

Question: What is silence?

KRISHNAMURTI: The gentleman asks what silence is. Silence is that which has been going on while there was talking. (Laughter) I am not saying something absurd. Don't you know what silence is? Not a silence created by the mind, by the brain; not put together by discipline or by the absurd artificial practice of meditation, which we will go into another time. Is there silence apart from the entity who experiences silence? I don't see how you can separate silence from peace, from death, from beauty, from love. If you have touched one of them, the others are. Some astronauts say there is extraordinary silence in outer space.

Question: Could we describe silence as equilibrium?

KRISHNAMURTI: I'm afraid you can't describe it. How can you describe something which you don't know?—and if you know it, you'll not describe it. To most of us, expression becomes extraordinarily important. The painter insists on expression; otherwise, he says, "What's the good of living?" But to express, there must be creation; and creation is something which may not demand expression at all.

Question: Krishnaji, to come back to time: Is it not possible that it is physical time that pulls us into this whole mess?

KRISHNAMURTI: We have gone into that, sir. We said physical time is necessary.

Comment: But it pulls us into it.

KRISHNAMURTI: Wait. Physical time is necessary. Does it pull us back? No. Physical time is necessary. Then what's the problem?

Comment: Physical time demands that we think.

KRISHNAMURTI: All right. Physical time demands, the gentleman says, that you think.

Comment: And when we think, we create psychological time.

KRISHNAMURTI: We do at present. It is not necessary, is it? Somebody puts a pin into me. I react, which is normal, healthy, and sane. But why do I build psychologically the whole process of time? I dislike you because you have hurt me, verbally or in other ways. So physical time is a pain, and I must react to it. The reaction is all over; when you hit me, I withdraw. That's normal. But the disorder comes in when the mind begins to create the experiencer. This is very simple, isn't it? Must I explain it?

All right, all right. Let's go into it. You hit me, you flatter me; physically you harm me, put a pin into me. I react. That's physical time, that's physical response. That's normal, right? Why don't I stop there? I'll be very careful next time that I don't come too close to you (Laughter) because you may put a pin in me. Wait. But I have nothing against you. I don't say, "Well, last time he hit me, and this time I'm jolly well going to take care I'm going to hit him." I stop with the pain, full stop. I don't build. The building up is the coming into time.

I want to say something; I say it. But I say it because I'm vain; I want you to flatter me. The demand for the continuance of pleasure, or the avoidance of pain, is time, and time is disorder. I can live in this world without creating disorder, which is pleasure and time.

Comment: It's simple to see.

KRISHNAMURTI: Ah, no. If it is simple to see, it is simple to act.

Comment: It's so simple and natural that the pull of physical time, as it goes on, pulls your mind into planning and avoiding.

KRISHNAMURTI: No. I said, "If you see that, you are not attracted to it." You are not attracted to an abyss unless you are somehow mentally unbalanced. You are not attracted to some poison because you understand it. However, it is not a question of being attracted or not being attracted but of seeing the fact of pleasure and pain, that's all; seeing the fact that pleasure gives continuance to time and illusion. If I see that, I can look at a beautiful tree, or a woman, or a man, or a child, and say, "How beautiful," and there it is. But if I can't leave it there, and say, "Well, I wish I had that tree in my garden," I have begun the whole business. Therefore, this demands extraordinary attention to facts only, not to your emotions and your pleasures and all the rest of it. But there is a time in which there is a different kind of joy, which is not pleasure. I can't go into it now; it's not the occasion.

Comment: It seems to me that physical time is the villain in the piece.

KRISHNAMURTI: The gentleman says that physical time is the villain in the piece, in the play. Is it, sir? Look. I fall ill; I may die. That's a physical fact. But I don't stop there. I say, "I'm afraid"; I wonder if I will live. I wonder what's going to happen to my family, to my husband, to my wife, to my children, to my property, to my estate. I wonder if there is a life hereafter, if there is a God who is going to be kind. I am lonely.

You see, the fact is that we are afraid of facts—the fact that I'm old, the fact that I'm stupid. We are afraid to face facts because we cannot look at anything except in terms of pleasure and pain. This is so obvious. You're not asking the right question; that's why you keep on going round in a circle, if I may kindly point it out.

What is the question? Not that physical time draws you in, puts you in a net; physical time doesn't. It is psychological time that creates the net. I have to go to Paris next week. I'll go. But I don't like to go to Paris because of this, that, and the other.

Question: Is that the way to stop making karma all the time?

KRISHNAMURTI: Ah, karma! (Laughter) You know the word? I've been told by Sanskrit scholars that the word *karma* means cause-effect, which is action. Can you stop action? Obviously one can't stop action. But action as an idea, or imitating an idea, a formula, is of time, and creates disorder all our life. Oh, this is all so clear!

I don't know if you have observed something. The acorn will always produce an oak tree. It can't produce a pear tree. There is a definite cause, and there is a definite, fixed result. But we aren't like that. I did something yesterday. That is the cause, but today there is a time interval during which other factors enter in; and therefore the effect is entirely different; and that effect becomes the cause of the next action. So there is never a definite cause-effect, except in nature. What becomes very important is not the avoidance of cause and effect, or the cessation of an act which has done harm to myself or to someone else, but an understanding of the whole structure of action in relation to time as an idea. If one sees that very clearly, then one acts without all this inward structure of the past which otherwise shapes action.

May 3, 1965

Fifth Dialogue in London

I would like this evening, if I may, to talk about change and about meditation. One must have asked oneself, I'm quite sure, whether one changes at all. I know that outward circumstances change; we marry, divorce, have children; there is death, a better job, the pressure of new inventions, and so on. Outwardly there is a tremendous revolution going on in cybernetics and automation. One must have asked oneself whether it is at all possible for one to change at all, not in relation to outward events, not a change that is a mere repetition or a modified continuity, but a radical revolution, a total mutation of the mind. When one realizes, as one must have noticed within oneself, that actually one doesn't change, one gets terribly depressed, or one escapes from oneself. So the inevitable question arises: Can there be change at all? We go back to a period when we were young, and that comes back to us again. Is there change at all in human beings? Have you changed at all? Perhaps there has been a modification on the periphery, but deeply, radically, have you changed? Perhaps we do not want to change because we are fairly comfortable. We have a government that looks after one, a welfare state, an assured job, old age pensions, and all the rest of it; so perhaps there is no motive to change. And when there is a motive to change, it is change within the field of the known.

I would like to have you find out for yourselves this evening whether it is at all possible for you to bring about a real revolution. I am not talking about a change from house to house, from country to country, or going from one type of religious bigotry to another; that's no change at all. I am talking about a deep, psychological mutation, a transformation, a new mind, a totally different existence, which is not in the field of time. One must listen, not sentimentally, not aggressively, not doubting or questioning, but simply listen, in order to discover for oneself the art of learning about oneself. This act of listening will perhaps reveal that there is no change at all in our life. We go on as we are, a little bit discontented, depressed, lonely, miserable; going on to old age, full of sorrow, with unresolved problems; and that's our life. Most of us get used to all that; our minds get dull, heavy, stupid; we accept the inevitable and thereby get terribly bored with life, its routine, and its apparent utter lack of significance. Or we invent a purpose, a significance, and according to that significance and that purpose, we try to bring about a pattern of existence; but it is still, as one observes, no change at all.

So, do we change? Is there a change at all? And if we do change, is it a movement which is not in time? A change in space, in time, created by thought, or put together by thought, is no change at all. Because change brought about through an act of will, which is the space between what I am and what I should be, is still within the field of time.

I want to change. I see that I am terribly unhappy, depressed, ugly, violent, with an occasional flash of something other than the mere result of a motive; and I exercise my will to do something about it. I say I must be different, I must drop this habit, that habit; I must think differently; I must act in a different way; I must be more this and less that. One makes a tremendous effort, and at the end of it one is still shoddy, depressed, ugly, brutal, without any sense of quality. So one then asks oneself if there is change at all. Can a human being change? A change within the field of time, one observes, is no change.

I want to be peaceful; I want to be quiet, inwardly silent, aware, intelligent, vital; I want to have a sense of beauty, and I strive after it all. This striving becomes an effort, and I am never actually what I want to be. I am always just groping after it. So, at the end of a few years or a few months or a few days, one gives it up and goes back to the old pattern. One is depressed, becomes cynical, gets irritable, takes to drink or to church, or whatever it is that one does. Or one goes to an analyst and explores the unconscious, taking months, or years, if one has the money. We carry on that way, endlessly, with a terrible sense of fear, anxiety, and dread, until we die in despair. We are fairly familiar with all that. So one asks oneself, "How is it possible to change, without all this process, and suddenly find oneself in a new dimension?"

As we said the other day, the "how" is disorder; disorder arises from asking the question, "How am I to jump from this to that; how am I to bring about a change within myself so fundamental, so radical, that I have a new mind, that I am a new human being?" Scientists are talking about the coming of the new man, with a new mind. I don't know what they mean, and I am not concerned. I am concerned, if I am at all interested, not about the coming generation, not with what is going to happen in a hundred years, or twenty years, or tomorrow, but with what I am actually, and whether it is possible to change and dissolve this helpless, hopeless endeavor that has no meaning. So I ask myself, "How am I to do it?"

Now, the "how" is very important to understand. When we put to ourselves the "how," it implies time, practice, method, system, a pattern to be followed and struggled after; therefore, it involves time, time being the space between me as I am and what I should be, or something which I cannot imagine myself to be. That implies space; therefore, to cover that distance, time is necessary: a second, a day, or even a year. When we ask how, and seek a method, we think that by pursuing a system, a method, a pattern of discipline, of order, we can forget all the other pressures that exist around us, which are always influencing and modifying. There is always a contention, a battle, a conflict, a question; and therefore the "how" essentially brings about disorder. One must be completely free and understand all this. The "how" implies either going back to an old pattern or creating a new pattern and following it; hence the battle between what I am and what I should be.

So, it is a stupid question on my part to ask, "How am I to do it; how am I to change?" Of course, if one is a little bit neurotic, a little unbalanced, one goes to various analysts. Perhaps one gets a little change, and adjusts oneself to a society that is always in decay. We are not concerned for the moment with the people who are unbalanced.

So, how is—I am using the "how" merely as a question—how is one to find oneself in that? I think that here the question of meditation comes in. I am not talking of meditation as a method. It has nothing whatever to do with method because method is the "how," and we have pushed that aside as being inadequate, immature, juvenile. To put the same question differently, any change in time is no change. We are talking of fundamental change: fundamental, radical mutation; so the mind must discover a new movement, which is out of time. All movement of the mind is in time, as thought, as pleasure and the duration of pleasure. I know this time, and I see that in it no change is possible. There must be a movement which doesn't belong to this time.

I see that the time which mind and thought have built, put together, is a movement which breeds sorrow, pleasure, agony; it has its own movement, its own evolution; it grows and decays. I know that very well. The mind cannot ride on that movement. There must be a movement which is not of this nature; and the mind must discover it, a movement which is not of this time, but of a different time altogether—if I can use the word *time* to indicate a movement which is not sullied by the psychological time which I know. There must be a time which has no beginning and no end. It is a movement which does not belong to this dimension at all. That's speculation. When I say, "There must be," that is a speculation. So I go off on that. I want to discover that time; I pursue it. That demands a heightened sensitivity, so I play with drugs, with every form of stimulation, hoping to capture it; and having captured it, to repeat the pattern.

So I see that any movement of the mind must always be in time. Yet my mind wanders, tremendously active, projecting ideas and visions, struggling, trying to concentrate, trying to restrain; it is endlessly in movement. It sees itself in movement, and therefore it makes a tremendous effort to be quiet. This enforcement, this discipline, this conformity to a pattern in order to arrive at quietness is generally called meditation—which of course is too childish, too absurd.

Yet I see that the mind must be extraordinarily quiet because I know that movement in any direction, at any level—movement towards God, towards peace—any movement is always within time. You see the problem? Here I am, having a mind which is fairly sane, fairly rational, healthy, and it wants to change. It must change. The way I live is too stupid, too unintelligent; it has no meaning. So the mind says, "I must change," and it tries to change gradually. It rejects that way, if it is intelligent; it says, "That's too absurd. I only repeat the pattern over and over again, modified." It sees that there is a possibility of a change that is completely quiet; so it struggles to be quiet, which again is within the borders of time. It must change immediately, or not at all.

I can't look to tomorrow, I can't practice, I have no time for discipline or to conform to a pattern which is supposed to give me that peace, or that sense of silence. So I reject all that, not only verbally, but actually. By understanding all this, my mind has become astonishingly sensitive and alert, tremendously aware of itself. The difficulty is that very few come to this with terrific energy; because when you reject time in the sense in which we are using the word, all movement—conscious or unconscious movement in any direction—has come to an end.

May I go on with this?

Comment: Yes, yes.

KRISHNAMURTI: No, no! Are you doing it, actually following it inwardly, or are you merely following the words? Because this implies a tremendous, nonexperiencing mind which is completely alone because it has understood loneliness, its own loneliness and isolation, its self-centered activities which create walls around itself, its moralities which are immoral, its virtues which are not virtues at all but mere adjustments to a pattern. It has finished with ambition, greed, envy, and all the things that we go after: pleasure, the sense of power, domination; otherwise, it can't proceed. How one finishes with these things is very important. If one says, "I will do it gradually," that of course has no value. They must drop away immediately, without any effort.

Let's examine the habit of smoking and the habit of envy. Smoking gives you certain sensations of pleasure, something to do with your hands; everyone does it, it is socially accepted. Can you—if you are a smoker or a drinker or whatever your particular habit is—can you drop it completely, immediately, without the exercise of will, without motive? If there is a motive, then it is pleasure or pain, and therefore one is back again. So can you drop that habit completely, immediately? If you cannot, you are caught in time, and therefore there is no release from the habit.

Envy is deeply ingrained in most people. It takes so many forms, not only envy of a man who is more intelligent, who is famous, but also the envy which is always comparing. For it, the 'more' is important: more learning, more information, competition, trying to struggle, trying to understand, trying to become intelligent, trying to find God, doing this and doing that—eternally more, more—not only more and better bathrooms and refrigerators, but psychologically more. Can one see the implications of it instantly and drop it, without analysis, without seeking the cause of envy, which we've gone into, not allowing time to interfere with it at all, and therefore ending it immediately?

To end this thing, this habit immediately, there must obviously be a sense of awareness.

You must know what you are doing with your hands. You must be aware of how deeply ingrained this envy is—aware without judgment, without choice; with an awareness which merely sees and acts. It can only see and act instantly when it is aware of the whole implication of envy, and the understanding of that envy. The structure, the implication, is not of time. You can see instantly.

I do not know if you have gone into this matter of being aware and what it means. There is nothing mysterious about it; you don't have to practice it. It begins with outward things: being aware of trees, people, colors, noise, endless chatter, outward escapes, the shape of a room and its color—begin there and ride on that tide; come in, go inward. You can only ride on that tide which is coming in when there is no choice, no comparison, no condemnation. Just ride it. Out of this there is physical order, which is obviously necessary. Physical order which is austere. For most of us austerity is harsh, a disciplined result, a denial, a sacrifice, a conformity; and therefore, when there is discipline, a conformity, a forcing, it becomes violent; and generally all austerity is the denial of affection. But when one is very much aware of the words, thoughts, the whole structure of the mind, then there is order. One must have order because that is the essence of virtue. It does not matter how many clothes one has, or how many houses, or if one has no houses and just a loincloth. Out of this austerity there is simplicity—not in things, not in clothes, but inwardly. So the mind, having brought order, is very sane and therefore has no illusions—it is only time that creates illusion, as thought. Then there is a movement which is silence.

Now, all this is meditation. It doesn't matter where you are. You can do this when you are riding in a bus. You don't have to take a special posture, take deep breaths; all that has very little meaning because a stupid mind can sit very erect and practice breathing indefinitely; it will still remain a stupid mind, and its gods will still be stupid.

We are talking about a meditation which is a natural thing. If one has gone that far, one will know for oneself—no, one won't know for oneself! A mind that is aware of itself as silent is not a silent mind. It is a mind which is experiencing, and therefore there is the observer, the experiencer—and the thing experienced. When the experiencer experiences silence, it is not silence; therefore, the question becomes: Can the experiencer cease to be, immediately? To understand that, one has to understand pleasure, which we tried to go into the other day. You can see what gives continuity to pleasure; it is thought, thinking about it. I take pleasure in something or other, and I think about it; by so doing, I give strength, vitality, and nourishment to that which has been pleasurable. If thought does not give continuity to pleasure, there is an immediate end to it. You cannot deny a reaction, but to give continuity to reaction in the form of pleasure or pain brings about the duration of time.

Conceit and vanity have gone. The mind becomes extraordinarily quiet, and so do the body, the nerves, and the brain cells themselves. With most of us the brain functions only along certain lines, in certain grooves, which we are constantly using as memories, as routines, as habits, as reactions—the familiar grooves. So the brain becomes more and more insignificant, dull, weary—the brain itself, and the individual cells. I don't know if you have observed it. I may not be talking in scientific language, but you know what I'm talking about. That brain has to be activated, that brain has to become tremendously active; and to bring about this intense activity, one has to be aware of everything one does.

So the mind, the brain, the nerves, the body, everything is full of energy because the mind has brought about order; and because it has order, it is virtuous—not the foolish thing called virtue. One has order, an order which has come about through awareness without any sense of conflict.

Up to now we have used time, and that's all we know: time as pleasure, as pain, as a movement to bring about a change, and so on. Psychologically I have used time in order to become something, in order to change, in order to establish a better relationship with my wife, with my neighbor, with my husband. If there is an understanding of all this, there is a total rejection, not a partial rejection; a total rejection of it all, of time. Not of physical time, because you will miss your train or your bus if you reject physical time.

Because the mind has rejected psychological time, there is tremendous order, and the mind naturally comes to a point where it has no movement of any kind because it is no longer experiencing itself as a movement or not as a movement. It is silent because it has tremendous energy, because it is tremendously active—not in doing something, not in pursuing something, not in trying to transform. It has no movement, it is completely still; and therefore, being active, it is full of energy without motion, without movement. Then what takes place? In this stillness, which is full of energy, in a mind which is completely still, there is an explosion; and this explosion is movement in a different dimension of time.

After all, what is creation? I am not talking about the ability to paint, a talent to write, or the capacity to do great research and to invent. I don't mean that kind of creation at all.

Question: Do you mean existence, or living?

KRISHNAMURTI: I asked, "What is creation?" Because most of us are secondhand people. What we create, what we bring out, what we express is still secondhand. You may be a marvelous painter, well known, selling your pictures for an enormous price, but is that creation? Is that the expression of a creative mind? Yet everyone wants to express. If you have talent, you burst to express it. If you are a secondhand writer, you will push it out. We think we are very creative people, but all that is not creation. We don't know what creation is. Creation is something that must be explosive each time. My mind is not only secondhand, a thing that has lived for two million years, but it has nothing new in it. If I have talent as an artist, I try to find a new expression—without arms, with one eye, or whatever it is—nonobjective painting, and so on and on and on, but there is nothing new inwardly. As long as the mind does not discover that, it must live in routine, in boredom, and in repetition.

Creation is very important, and to explode in this creation, the mind must be completely quiet, all energy without any action. It is like a kettle in which water is boiling; if there is no escape for the steam, the kettle bursts. And it is only then that there is something totally new.

Comment: If I may make a suggestion, Krishnaji, I think we all are potential gods.

KRISHNAMURTI: There is nothing to be said to that. You see, madame, we may be gods, we may be eternal, we may be this, and we may be that. The Indians, the Hindus, have a marvelous system for all that, but that isn't good enough. It is what I actually am now that matters—my state as a bourgeois, with a secondhand mind; with my miseries, anxieties, quarrels, prejudices, and battles; my agony, despair, hopes. I am all that. I can imagine what I am supposed to be, but the "supposed to be " is not a fact. Every day I am torn to pieces by my own thoughts. I am depressed and I am concerned about changing that completely, that's all. What happens after that, when there is such a tremendous, radical change, you will find out.

Comment: If once there has been an explosion, you want it again.

KRISHNAMURTI: There is no explosion if there is an experiencer. Full stop. That is why I explained all that very carefully.

Comment: Sir, if there is no effort, if there is no method, then any transition into the state of awareness, any shift into a new dimension, must be a completely random accident, and therefore unaffected by anything you might say on the subject.

KRISHNAMURTI: Ah, no, sir. I didn't say that. (Laughter) I said one has to be aware. By being aware, one discovers how one is conditioned. By being aware, I know I am conditioned: as a Hindu, as a Buddhist, as a Christian; I am conditioned as a nationalist: British, German, Russian, Indian, American, Chinese. I am conditioned. We never tackle that. That's the garbage we are, and we hope something marvelous will grow out of it, but I am afraid it is not possible. Being aware doesn't mean a chance happening, something irresponsible and vague. If one understands the implications of awareness, one's body not only becomes highly sensitive, but the whole entity is activated; there is a new energy given to it. Do it, and you will see. Don't sit on the bank and speculate about the river; jump in and follow the current of this awareness, and you will find out for yourself how extraordinarily limited our thoughts, our feelings, and our ideas are. Our projections of gods, saviors, and Masters—all that becomes so obvious, so infantile.

Comment: This brings a most unfamiliar state of mind.

KRISHNAMURTI: That's just it, sir. This brings about a very unfamiliar state of mind.

Comment: One is not at all certain whether there is an inside or an outside.

KRISHNAMURTI: There is definitely an outside. There is no uncertainty about the outside.

Comment: One is not certain whether the consciousness is outside or inside.

KRISHNAMURTI: There is outside: the land, the trees, the houses; I see these things. There is a body; I see the outside. But we don't know what is the inside, what is inside the house. Since what we want is only to breed more security, we are afraid to be uncertain. We only want security; that is why we become very familiar with the things we know, and why we hold on. For any creation to take place, mustn't there be emptiness, which is space? You can't be sure and certain of space. You can't be sure and certain that in this space something will happen. That's just it; we are so frightened to be alone. One can understand that one can't live in complete insecurity, physically. One must have food, clothing, and shelter. That is accepted; we won't even discuss it. But to assure food, clothing, and shelter for everybody, the inward mess must come to an end. We can't be divided into nationalities—all that stupid stuff. We want outward security without doing anything inwardly; and when there is outward security, as there is in this and other countries, the mind soon begins to decay. People commit suicide; there is violence and delinquency, adult delinquency as well as juvenile delinquency; every form of amusement and entertainment—you know what is going on. So, one must have this extraordinary sense of alertness and awareness, not something vague and irrational, but very factual.

Comment: Sir, what you say can only be a hypothesis for someone who hasn't explored where you have explored.

KRISHNAMURTI: Obviously, sir, obviously.

Question: And to someone who does know that state of awareness, it adds nothing. So, why do you go on talking, sir? (Laughter)

KRISHNAMURTI: Why do I go on talking? First of all, it is not because I get a kick out of talking. When one addresses an audience, a small one like this or a larger one, as is generally the case in India, it is difficult not to get a kick out of it, not to feel tremendously important. I don't. You will say, "How do you know that you don't?" (Laughter) Because I've gone into it. I have stopped talking, watched myself, and I've never got a kick out of this talking to people. Never. So it is not of great importance. Then, is it to help people? Please listen carefully. Is it to help people? No. That would imply a form of conceit: "I know, and you don't; therefore, let me teach you." Then there is the relationship of teacher and disciple, leader and follower, which is abhorrent, which is Hitler and all that business, religious or political. It is not that either. So it is not as an amusement, an entertainment, for satisfaction or fulfillment, nor to help people that one talks. If you do not help yourself, no one is going to help you. Then is it to express oneself, like a poet or an artist? No. When one denies all that, what is left?

Comment: Nothing! (Laughter)

KRISHNAMURTI: Please, this is very serious; it is not amusement.

Comment: Communication.

KRISHNAMURTI: No, I'm not concerned with that. That gentleman asked, "Why do you speak?"

Comment: Sir, you speak because a friend asks you to.

KRISHNAMURTI: No, I don't.

Comment: Because people want to listen to you.

KRISHNAMURTI: That is, if they want to. No, sir. When you are not using the audience for your satisfaction, when you are not talking in order to help another, in order to feel yourself a helper, doing good—move away all those, what have you left?

Comment: Love.

KRISHNAMURTI: Ah, wait a bit, wait a bit! Love. Are you doing it out of love? Is that it?

Comment: Yes.

KRISHNAMURTI: Oh, Lord! (Laughter) No, sir. You are asking questions that have no meaning.

Question: Is it that you want to share it?

KRISHNAMURTI: What does that mean? Are you suggesting that one should exploit people, using the audience, appearing to help them and thereby becoming important?

That's all one knows: help, service, doing good. When you see the absurdity of all that, what is there left? When you have done that, ask the question. Ask it then. But if you have done all that, you won't ask the question. Then our relationship is entirely different.

May 6, 1965

Sixth Dialogue in London

Our lives are so superficial; we have most of the things we want physically, and most of us are easily satisfied with little pleasures or with intellectual concepts, theories, and arguments. If we have read a great deal, it gives us a certain sharpness of mind, a disputatious mind, and we are able to quote and give an impression that we are very deep and very vital. Is it possible for a very clever mind, or a mind that has a great deal of knowledge and information, to go very deep? Most of us live for intellectual or sensual pleasure, and we seek its prolongation. When it wanes, we seek other forms of pleasure, but there is very little joy in our lives, in our relationships, in our activities. I don't think we will be able to find joy through pleasure; the two things are entirely different. The difference is not in words, in actions, or in having a great deal of knowledge. It is a matter of understanding pleasure and going beyond it. Then only is it possible to have joy, or bliss, or whatever word you like to use.

The world being what it is, most of us seem to find it very difficult to go very deep within ourselves; and I don't see how one can find this joy, or be in that state of mind, unless one goes profoundly within oneself. As we were saying the other day, the understanding of pleasure ends all illusion. Because if one has illusions of any kind about oneself, and identifies oneself with a joy, an image, a pleasure, a vision, an idea, a theory, it gives a certain satisfaction, a certain quality of pleasure. But this self-identification with something is still the pursuit of pleasure. How is one to go within oneself so profoundly, so deeply, without effort, without the time-binding nature of time? Is it a matter of time, of constant awareness, constant examination, constant watchfulness, of making a continuous effort to put away the things that one knows are rather stupid, to go into oneself and so perhaps discover? Do time and pleasure make the mind non-religious? Religion, for most of us, is authority, ritual, repetition, and acceptance. When one has brushed all that aside, as most so-called intellectual, modern people have done, does one find something much more significant? To me the religious quality of the mind is very important. I mean by the term *religious mind* a mind that has understood the nature of pleasure, that has freed itself from fear, and therefore has no illusions, does not create illusions for itself, and so is capable of living with facts, with *what is,* and of going beyond. Such a mind, it seems to me, is a religious mind—a mind that fundamentally has understood the nature of pleasure, of time, and of fear.

As we were saying the other day, fear in any form, conscious or unconscious, breeds darkness, breeds illusion. One seeks an escape from the network that man has developed in his effort to be free of fear. To be aware of the network, and so to be free, demands an awareness in which there is no effort, but merely observation. Most of us, I'm afraid, are not serious enough to pursue to the very end. We are so easily put off, we are so easily satisfied with a little experience, with a little knowledge, with a little understanding.

What is a human being to do who is in agony, who is in sorrow, fearful, striving after position and prestige, in order to cut through all this so that fear doesn't ever arise again? How is one to be instantly free of fear—not merely physical fear, which does affect psychological fear, but the psychological fear, which breeds physical fears? We are using the word *how* not as a question, not as a means or as a system through which to be rid of fear, because, as we said the other day, the "how" is disorder; for the "how" implies time, and time does breed disorder.

Being aware, one knows that one is afraid of so many things inwardly; how can one step out of it? It seems to me that this is one of the major problems of our life. Time will never resolve fear. Time is used by the mind to create tomorrow as a means of getting rid of something through a gradual process of examination and analysis. This utilization of time does not free the mind from fear. So what is one to do? One must understand the whole problem of pleasure—not fear—because pleasure is the central factor, the guiding principle of our life.

Please do not merely listen to words but be aware of the nature of pleasure, actually, factually; and be aware of how all our thoughts and all our activities are based on this extraordinary, intricate desire for pleasure. When there is an understanding of this, fear comes to an end. Because it is pleasure that breeds illusion—not the ultimate, deep psychological pleasure, but the everyday pleasure to which thought gives continuity.

In order to understand pleasure, one has to examine and be aware of the whole process of thinking. We give such extraordinary significance to thought, to ideas, to concepts, to formulas. There are physical formulas which are necessary, but are psychological formulas at all necessary?

I am not saying that we should be stupid, uninformed, dull; but why do we give such extraordinary importance to the mind, to thinking, to the intellect? If one doesn't give importance to the intellect, one gives importance either to sensate values or to the emotions. But as most people are ashamed of emotions and sensate values, they worship the intellect. Why? Please, when I ask a question, let's all of us find the answer together. Books, theories, and the whole intellectual field are considered so important in our life. Why? If you are clever, you may get a better job. If you are highly trained technologically, that may have certain advantages, but why do we give importance to ideas? Isn't it because we cannot live without action? All relationship is a movement, and that movement is action. Ideas become important when separated from action. To most of us action is not important, relationship is not important; ideas are much more important than all these other factors.

Our relationships, which comprise our life, are based on organized memory as idea. Idea dominates action, and hence relationship is a concept, not actual action. We think relationship should be this or that, but we don't actually know what relationship is. Not knowing what relationship is, actually, factually, ideas become all-important to us. The intellect becomes all-important, with its beliefs, ideas, and theories as to what should be and what should not be. Action is of a time-binding nature; that is, action involves time because idea is of time. Action is never immediate, never spontaneous; it is never related to *what is,* but to 'what should be', to an idea, and hence there is a conflict between idea and action. We make life such an extraordinarily complicated thing. There is idea, followed by action based on pleasure, duty, or responsibility. The pleasure breeds illusion, which is incapable of meeting the fact, *what is;* and hence we have fear.

It is not a matter of your agreeing or disagreeing with what is being said. If one observes, one sees that it is so. The intellect is not a total thing; it is a fragment of our life. Yet that fragment takes on tremendous importance. Since a fragment has such tremendous importance, our life, our living is fragmentary; it is never a complete thing, a whole.

Probably most of us are aware of all this, and know or feel that there is constant conflict going on between idea and action. We are conscious of the fact that the separation between idea and action involves time, and that when there is the question of time, there is disorder. We know all this. Perhaps some of us know this directly, watch and see it as a fact. But apparently we don't seem to be able to go beyond this. We know very well that it's no good being too clever, being able to quote, with all the cerebration that goes on. We know very well that it does not have tremendous importance, yet we play with it. We also are aware of the nature of pleasure as habits, sexual and otherwise. Also, we are inwardly, deeply anxious. There is a deep sense of guilt, and a desperate loneliness. We know there is fear, and yet we don't seem to be able to go beyond all this.

How is it possible for a human being to step out of this circle, this everlasting, vicious circle? That's the major question, not investigating and analyzing needless words and definitions of words. Is there a different approach to this problem? It seems to me that we are always approaching life from the periphery, from the outside to the inner, making things complex, hard, intricate. Let's approach it differently.

Pleasure is not love; it is the continuation of memory, which feeds and sustains it. Pleasure is not love. If there is what we call love, it is surrounded by jealousy, anxiety, loneliness, and the fear of losing, which is what we call love. Beauty, for us, is again pleasure. Beauty is the result, for most of us, of stimulation: a beautiful baby, a beautiful sunset, a cloud in the sky. We call them beautiful because they act as stimulants. Is there beauty which is unrelated to pleasure, which is not the result of a stimulant? Our life is without love, and most of the time we are secondhand human beings. There is nothing original, nothing actual, and therefore we never know what it is to be creative. We all want to express ourselves in different ways, as artists, as technicians, and this expression is what we generally call creativeness. How can there be creation when there is fear, pleasure, and the involvement of time? Surely creation means ending, not the continuation of something I have known, however pleasurable, however significant it may have been. It is only when there is a complete ending that there is something new. We are afraid to end; we are afraid to die—die to all pleasures, memories, experiences. So we continue, never ending; therefore, we are never creative.

It seems to me that beauty, love, death, and creation all go together. But they obviously cannot exist when there is fear in any form. Having heard this statement, you may approve, agree, or disagree; it doesn't matter which. These facts are obvious; one can observe them.

Is it possible for you and me to step completely out of this system of time and pleasure? Is it possible to look out of silence at fear, without thought and without feeling, and not look upon it as something that one must find the cause of, analyze, and eliminate? It is fairly simple to look at a flower nonbotanically, without thought and feeling, because the flower is not of great importance in one's life; it doesn't interfere, it doesn't mess up our life. But to look at our activities, at our problems as they arise, without thought or feeling, and therefore to observe without time, is not so easy.

We look at things from a center which creates space around itself. I look at you from my center of memory; that center creates a space around itself, and through that space I look. I never look at you directly; I only observe you through my space, which has been created by my center, which is experience, knowledge, memory. I can really look at you, as I can look at the flower, only when there is no center, but I never observe without that center, which is time-binding in nature, which is the result of pleasure. That center is always creating illusion, and therefore I never come face to face with fact.

I can look at a flower, a cloud, or a bird on the wing without a center, without a word, the word which creates thought. Can I look without the word at every problem—the problem of fear, the problem of pleasure? Because the word creates, breeds thought; and thought is memory, experience, pleasure, and therefore a distorting factor.

This is really quite astonishingly simple. Because it is simple, we mistrust it. We want everything to be very complicated, very cunning; and all cunning is covered with a perfume of words. If I can look at a flower nonverbally—and I can; anyone can do it, if one gives sufficient attention—can't I look with that same objective, nonverbal attention at the problems which I have? Can't I look out of silence, which is nonverbal, without the thinking machinery of pleasure and time being in operation? Can't I just look? I think that's the crux of the whole matter, not to approach from the periphery, which only complicates life tremendously, but to look at life, with all its complex problems of livelihood, sex, death, misery, sorrow, the agony of being tremendously alone—to look at all that without association, out of silence, which means without a center, without the word, which creates the reaction of thought, which is memory and hence time. I think that is the real problem, the real issue: whether the mind can look at life where there is immediate action, not an idea and then action, and eliminate conflict altogether.

Question: Do you mean that you can look at something the same way you look at a flower, without using it, without making use of it? Is that what you had in mind?

KRISHNAMURTI: Sir, you look at a flower, actually look at it. There is no thought behind it. You are looking at it nonbotanically, nonspeculatively; you don't classify it, you just look. Have you never done this?

Question: Doesn't the mind enter in?

KRISHNAMURTI: Wait, wait, no, don't talk about the mind. That's a little more complicated. Begin with the flower. When you look at a flower, do not let thought interfere; then see if you can look at your wife or husband or neighbor or country in the same way. If one cannot, one says, "Is there a method, a system by which I can train my mind to look without the interference of thought?" It becomes too absurd. The fact is that we do look at a flower without the interference of thought as memory or as pleasure. Can there be observation in the same way of everything that arises in us and outside us—the words we use, the gestures, the ideas, the concepts, the self-identifying memories, the images that we have of ourselves and of others? To be so widely aware is only possible when there is an observation of things external, when one can look at a cloud, a tree, without the interference of words.

Comment: It is not just the interference of words or associations; it is the swiftness of associations.

KRISHNAMURTI: Yes, sir, the swiftness of association; therefore, you are not looking. If I want to see you, or see the cloud, see my wife or husband, I must look and not let the association interfere; but the word, the association interferes instantly because behind it there is pleasure. Do see this, sirs; its's so simple. Once we understand this thing clearly, then we will be able to look.

Comment: You said that we should look at the flower without thought and without feeling, and if one is able to do that, one gets tremendous energy. This energy, as we use the word, is thinking and feeling. I wonder if you would clarify this.

KRISHNAMURTI: Ah, you see, sir, I purposely said thought is feeling. There is no feeling without thought, and behind thought is pleasure; so those things go together: pleasure, the word, the thought, the feeling; they are not separated. Observation without thought, without feeling, without word is energy. Energy is dissipated by word, association, thought, pleasure, and time; therefore, there is no energy to look.

Comment: If you see that, then thought is not a distraction.

KRISHNAMURTI: Then thought doesn't enter into it, sir. It is not a question of distraction. I want to understand it. Why should thought interfere? Why should all my prejudices interfere with my looking, my understanding? It interferes because I am afraid of you, you might get my job—ten different things. That's why one must first look at a flower, a cloud. If I can look at a cloud without a word, without any of the associations which come in so swiftly, then I can look at myself, at the whole of my life, with all its problems. You may say, "Is that all? Haven't you oversimplified it?" I don't think so, because facts never create problems. The fact that I am afraid doesn't create a problem, but the thought that says, "I must not be afraid," brings in time and creates illusion—that creates a problem, not the fact.

Look, sir. There is a problem, the question of death. We all know it. We may prolong life for another 150 years, but still at the end of it there is that thing, waiting. Now, look at it as a fact; do not rationalize it, nor escape from it through belief or through the various other escapes that one has, but just be in contact with the fact. You cannot, if you don't know what ending is—ending to all pleasures, not certain pleasures. Then the mind can look at the issue in a totally different way.

Take the question of affection, love. How can there be love when there is competition, ambition, fear, jealousy? Obviously there cannot be. Yet without it our life is extraordinarily shallow and empty. Can I look at my jealousy without the word, without thought, without association; can I live with it and just look at it as a fact? This demands energy, so dissipation of energy as thought, as an avoidance, association, or word must not come in. I see that to observe a fact demands tremendous energy. Because I understand it, all dissipation of energy ceases; I don't have to struggle against it.

Comment: When a real, genuine quality in relationship arises, I notice in myself that there is immediately a strong rush of emotions, which involves thought and brings me right into the whole thing. What you are saying is that this process arises because I don't bring enough energy to the observation.

KRISHNAMURTI: You cannot bring enough energy to the observation because you are dissipating it through thought, through words, through emotions, through feeling. Sir, just look at a flower. Apparently it seems to be a most difficult thing to just observe it. We never look from silence; we look out through a lot of noise and disturbance. If one can look at a flower out of silence, therefore without thought and all the rest of it, one can look at oneself and at all the problems which exist within.

Question: Does that dissipate the problems, sir?

KRISHNAMURTI: How you look at it is of the highest importance. Do you look at it as an experiencer observing that thing? Is the observer different from the thing observed? I am jealous, I am envious, I hate somebody. Now, in that there is the hater and the hated, the experiencer and the thing experienced. Are the two separate? Is the observer separate from the thing observed? I observe the microphone; it is separate because I know the nature of the microphone, what it is; it is something different from me. I am jealous; the feeling of jealousy is different from me. That is true for most of us. I am jealous. That is, the observer is separate from the thing observed, which is jealousy. But is it separate? Is not the observer himself jealousy? Is he really separate from jealousy?

Comment: Then you are not looking at the thing you hate; you are looking at your hate.

KRISHNAMURTI: No, no. Look at it a little more, please. Consider it a bit more. Let's go back. Look at a tree. You observe the tree with your experience, and there is the tree. The tree is different from you. Now, can you look at that tree not as an observer? You don't know what that means?

Comment: No.

Comment: Yes, you can. Yes.

KRISHNAMURTI: Wait, wait. Do go slowly; don't be so quick. What does it mean to look at a tree without you as the observer? Have you ever done it?

Comment: Sometimes.

KRISHNAMURTI: Sometimes?

Comment: I did with a flower this morning. I was rather taken by surprise, but I couldn't describe any reaction at all.

KRISHNAMURTI: Sir, we are not talking about reaction. Please, just keep to one thing. Look at a tree, not from a center, not as an observer. Look at your wife, your friend, your husband, not as an observer, not as the husband, or the friend, or the wife, with all your memories; just observe. This is one of the most difficult things to do; you can't just use words, you have to look.

Comment: Well, when I look at a tree, it gives me a feeling of pleasure, so that shows that I am looking as an observer.

KRISHNAMURTI: Therefore, to look at a tree, or at a person, without being the observer, is to commune with that person, or with that tree—commune. I generally look at my wife, husband, at a person, with all my prejudices and memories. Through those memories I look; that is the center from which I look. Therefore the observer is different from the thing observed. In that process thought is constantly interfering, through association, and with the rapidity of the association. Now, when I realize the whole implication of that instantly, there is an observation without the observer. It is very simple to do this with trees, with nature; but with human beings, what takes place? If I can look at my wife or my husband nonverbally, not as an observer, it is rather frightening, isn't it? Because my relationship with her or with him is quite different. It is not in any sense personal; it is not a matter of pleasure, and I am afraid of it. I can look at a tree without fear because it is fairly easy to commune with nature, but to commune with human beings is much more dangerous and frightening; my relationship undergoes a tremendous revolution. Before, I possessed my wife, and she possessed me; we like being possessed. We were living in our own isolated, self-identifying space. In observing, I removed that space; I am now directly in contact. I look without the observer, and therefore without a center. Unless one understands this whole problem, merely to develop a technique of looking becomes frightful. Then one becomes cynical, and all the rest of it.

Comment: It is more difficult to look at one's boss in that way.

KRISHNAMURTI: Do it.

Question: Sir, if I look at anything, look at a tree, and know that I am looking, am I not the observer?

KRISHNAMURTI: You can't help that, can you, sir? Visual looking you can't help, unless you are blind. You see that tree. But why must all the past come into your looking? If I listen, why should all my past come when I am listening? When I am listening, I am learning. Learning is entirely different from accumulating knowledge. In accumulating knowledge, the center is established; but if I am learning, which is listening, there is not the listener. Try; do it; be completely attentive. Be attentive to the speaker, to what he is saying; be attentive to the way you are listening; be attentive to that noise outside, the bus or the cars going by; be attentive to someone coughing—totally attentive. Then is there a center? Is there an observer who is attentive? There is only a state of attention.

Comment: There is the observer if one thinks one might miss something.

KRISHNAMURTI: No, you're not doing it! Sir, for two seconds do this: be attentive to the colors, to the walls, to the noise; attentive to your thoughts, to your feelings, the way you're sitting, standing, listening. Be totally attentive, not fragmentarily attentive—completely, with all your being: your nerves, your body, your eyes, everything attentive. Then is there a center from which you are being attentive? But if you say, "I must be attentive," and then, "How am I to be attentive?" you begin the whole circle.

Comment: Within that awareness, complete awareness, is communion, as far as I understand.

KRISHNAMURTI: Yes, sir.

Comment: But this complete awareness also includes the complete awareness of everything, not only outside, but inside as well.

KRISHNAMURTI: Ah, no, sir. When you are attentive, there is neither outside nor inside. You listen to that car going by, to that cough; you are attentive to the color, to what you're thinking, feeling—just be attentive, not saying that you like or dislike, just be attentive.

Question: That is always so, isn't it, sir?

KRISHNAMURTI: It is not always, sir. Sir, do it!

Question: And you will also be attentive to the apparent impossibility of being totally attentive. Is that right?

KRISHNAMURTI: Yes, sir. Be attentive to inattention; do not try to become attentive.

May 9, 1965

Paris, France, 1965

First Talk in Paris

Perhaps after I have talked a little, you will be good enough to ask questions and to discuss what we have already talked about. I understand French quite well, so you can ask in French; but unfortunately my French isn't good enough to reply in French, so I will answer in English—and perhaps you might like to ask questions after I have talked.

It seems to me that we go through life having made problems and never resolving them; and, finding these problems so extraordinarily difficult, intricate, and sometimes very subtle, we avoid them and seek escape in all forms, through religion, through drink, through sex, and in innumerable other ways which man has invented—a network of escapes. And, it seems to me, unless we solve all our problems psychologically, our minds will always be confused, always be in a state of misery, constantly eaten up with uncertainty and a demand for certainty, stability, security. So it is necessary that we do solve our human problems.

We have problems: economic, social, emotional, intellectual, and religious. We live in different departments, divided, and each division, each segment, each fragment has its own problem or problems; and these problems, born of different fragmentations of the mind, naturally are in contradiction with each other. One wants to fulfill intellectually, become famous as a good writer, as an artist—to fulfill in one way or another in life. And this urge to fulfill contradicts other forms of existence. We are uncertain and we seek certainty, we seek a permanency; we want to understand immortality, and old age creeps up, and we wither away emotionally and psychologically, as well as physically.

So, all our life—however well off we are financially, and even though we may be in somewhat good relationships with one another—we have problems. And unless we resolve them totally—and it is possible to resolve them totally—however clever we are, however intellectually, argumentatively brilliant, however capable we are, these problems eat our minds and hearts away. And how is it possible for a human being living in this world and not escaping from it—not escaping to some monastery, into some fanciful, mythological seclusion, not escaping into some belief, dogma, ritual, into some fanciful, nonsensical visions—how is it possible for such a human being to clear the mind of all problems so that it is fresh, young, and innocent?

Now, to understand what we are talking about, one has to listen, and that is one of the most difficult things to do: to listen. It is an art. Because we don't ever listen. You are not actually listening to what is being said. Actually, you have your opinions, judgments, evaluations, conclusions; you have certain ideas about the reputation of the speaker. You wait, you are expecting something to happen, and that prevents you from actually listening, obviously. Of course that acts as a screen, and so that prevents you from actually listening with all your intensity. And it is only when you listen in the sense of listening without any strain or effort, neither agreeing nor disagreeing, but just observing and seeing the fact, and not bringing in your opinion about the fact, your conclusions, your intellectual concepts, formulas about the fact—it is only then, it seems to me, that you can really listen quietly, easily, and penetrate what is being said, find out for yourself whether it is true or false. And it seems to me that is one of the most important things to do if we are to communicate with each other. Because, after all, we are here, you and I, to communicate, to commune with each other. You have not come here to listen to my talk, and go away either agreeing or disagreeing, offering your opinions, contradicting, and so on and so on. You and I are here to commune with each other about the extraordinary problem of life; and to communicate with each other, we will not only have to use words but also understand the meaning of words, knowing that the word is not the thing, and the word is never the thing; and also, as you listen, knowing or being aware of your own prejudices, your questionings, your bargainings, your deceits, your whole psychological structure through which you listen.

So it is quite an art, and probably one of the most difficult arts, not only to observe, to listen, but also to learn. Learning is something entirely different from knowledge. It is very easy to accumulate knowledge, to gather information, store it up through experience, through reading, through reactions, and so on—store it up and from that knowledge act, which is what most of us do. But to learn is something entirely different because the moment you have learned, which is the past, it has already become knowledge. Learning is a constant process, a movement in which there is no accumulation at all. Most of us look at any problem through what we already know—through our accumulations, through our knowledge, through our remembrances, through our experience, through our conditionings—and so we prevent ourselves from learning about the problem.

Learning is an act—an act of the active present. It is the verb *to learn;* it is a movement. But that which has been learned has already become a static thing. So in the same way, if we could listen, not only to what the speaker is saying, but also to everything in life—to all the intimations of one's own demands, urges, the hints of one's own desires, secret longings, to listen to another, whether it is your husband, or a child, or a wife, or a neighbor, so that the mind becomes sharp, clear, dealing only with facts and not with emotional opinions and prejudices—then perhaps we can come to understand the very complex problems that life hides.

We live in fragments. There is the fragment of the so-called spiritual life, the fragment of the intellect, the fragment of the emotions, the fragment of the physical senses. So the mind is broken up into various fragments, each in a watertight compartment having very little relationship with the others, and so there is a constant conflict between them; and we are always avoiding that conflict by escaping. But to understand anything, one must look at the fact, one must come immediately and directly into contact with the fact. But we do not come into contact with the fact because we either try to analyze it or to avoid it, or to find the cause of it; or, if we do none of these things, we escape from it completely and live a very, very, superficial life, being satisfied with the little things, with the bourgeois life that most of us do lead.

So the question is: Is it possible to come into contact directly with a problem? You know, when you come into direct contact with something—direct contact—then perhaps you will see the full significance of that fact. And we never do come into direct contact with anything, except perhaps physically, sensuously. I have touched that microphone, and that is a direct contact. There is nothing, no verbal conclusion which prevents me from coming directly into contact with it. But to come into contact or to commune with myself so directly, with all the problems that a human being has, is probably very difficult—and so the problems not only multiply and increase but they take root in the mind; and the mind acts as a soil in which all the problems, from childhood until now, exist.

Please, you are not listening merely to a lot of words, for that would be absolutely useless. You are surely listening to words which have significance as a direct contact with your own problems; that is, you are using the words as a mirror in which you are aware of yourself, of your problems. If there is such awareness, a direct contact with your own problem or problems, then this talk will have some meaning. Otherwise, if you treat it merely intellectually or verbally, then one goes away with an empty hand and a lot of ashes which have no meaning at all. So I hope that you are listening, not merely to gather some information, but actually to come directly into contact with your own problems as a human being.

To come into contact with a problem, as you come into contact when you touch a physical thing—whether that problem be intellectual, emotional, psychological, physical, or so-called spiritual—one must first understand, surely, the meaning and the significance of words, because words prevent us from coming into contact with the problem. If one is anxious—full of that sense of guilt, fear, despair, which is anxiety—to come into contact with anxiety, one must see the significance of the word *anxiety* because the word creates the feeling. I don't know if you have ever noticed how words in themselves instigate a particular feeling. So one has to be quite cognizant of the word itself. When you are so aware of the word and see that the word is not the thing, that the word anxiety is not the fact at all, then you are more or less in contact with that feeling. I hope I am making myself clear. It doesn't matter; we will talk about it.

So, one has not only to understand the word, and how the word creates, or dominates, or gives color to the feeling, but one also must be aware that the word is not the thing, the word is not the feeling. For most of us, the word is the feeling; there is an instantaneous response between the feeling and the word. So, if one wishes to come into contact with the fact, one has to see the significance, the importance, the nature, and the meaning of the word.

Then one has to be aware of the various escapes because a problem becomes intensified, acute, only when it is something immediate that demands all our attention. And most of us do not want to live with such intensity—so problems increase, multiply, and take root. So one must not only be aware of the word but also of how the mind escapes, because we are very good at escaping from life. We have the churches, literature, our own experiences, our knowledge, our particular ways of looking at life, our various forms of psychological escape, and so we never come into contact with the fact.

You know, we think that if we can understand the cause of a problem, we have solved the problem; or if we analyze the problem, we think we have understood it. But is that so? I know the cause of fear or anxiety; and knowing the cause does not prevent fear—

my being anxious, fearful. I can also analyze the nature of fear, of anxiety, of guilt, and so on; and yet my mind is not free of it. So mere examination, analysis, seeing the cause of a thing, does not free the mind from the fact; and the search for the cause, the analysis, becomes an escape from the fact. So, if one would really resolve all the problems of life, then one must come directly into contact with the problem; and to be directly in contact with it is to understand the word, and also to understand the nature of escapes. Then one comes into contact with the problem directly.

We are talking about problems because it seems to me that a mind that has a problem, of whatever nature it be, becomes a dull mind, a mind that is afraid of death, of old age, of—oh, so many things! A mind that is afraid, or acquiesces to the various forms of life without any struggle, soon becomes very confused, dull, insensitive. Have you not noticed how extraordinarily inefficient, unclear, dull the mind is when it is afraid? And most of us are afraid of so many things: of living, of death, of the neighbor, of losing a job, of never having a full moment in life. The innumerable frustrations all bring fear, and fear then becomes an intense problem, of which you may be conscious or unconscious. Consciously you may be able to resolve fear, escape from it, smother it, put it away; but it is still there, and to come into contact with that fear so that you can put your teeth into it, requires, as we pointed out, the understanding of the word and the nature of the escape.

Our problems are increasing. Though we may have security—physical security, social welfare, and so on—psychologically a great part of us is still the animal; and unless we understand this whole psychological structure of society—as well as of ourselves, which is part of society—the mind can never be free; it will always be tortured by fear. That is why, it seems to me, a mature human being who would go very far—not to the moon, but very far into himself to discover what is true—must have a very clear, uncontaminated, unspotted mind. And a mind is unspotted and clear only when it is free—free from fear, for example. It is only then that one can find out—without any dogma, without any belief, without any effort—what is true.

So, if we are at all serious, our first concern, it seems to me, is to persevere with this question: the question of whether the mind can ever be free from problems. Living in this world, going to the office every day, being married and having children, or not being married—you know, the whole business of life, without my going into too many details—can one be in this world, in the twentieth century with all its fantastic technological developments, and live a life in which there is no problem at all? That, it seems to me, is the most essential thing because a mind that has a problem is in conflict. All problems mean conflict. And can the mind be active, energetic, efficient, clear, vital, without effort—which means being without a problem? Because, if you are making constant effort in any direction, at any level, such effort, obviously, makes the mind dull, incapable of dealing with life; and life is always throwing up problems. I mean by a problem something that we don't understand, a challenge to which we respond inadequately, insufficiently, without complete attention, and so there is a contradiction between the challenge and the response; and it is only when the response is adequate that there is no problem. But to live adequately so that one meets every form of challenge requires a mind that is not constantly in battle.

We must be aware that we have not only conscious challenges, demands, questions, but there are also challenges, experiences, to which we respond unconsciously. I really don't like the word *unconscious* because that is one of the most empty words one can use. It seems to me that the unconscious is such a trivial affair, and one has given such significance to it. But the unconscious is what we are. The unconscious is the past, the traditions, the various accumulations of knowledge, of experience, the racial inheritance, what we have been told—the whole of consciousness is that, but we are aware of only certain parts of it, while of other parts we are not aware. We are aware of the conscious because that is the only part we use in our daily activities, in our life at the office, and so on and so on. The other part is dormant, and we have carefully put it aside. But to be aware of the total thing is not to give continuity to the past, to the unconscious. Most of us live in a state of dreaming. We are not aware of the total content of our dreams; we live at a certain level, in a certain part; and that part, that fragment, reacting to a particular challenge, can only create contradiction. It is only when there is a total response to a challenge that there is no contradiction and hence no problem.

So our question is this: Is it possible for each one of us as a human being who has lived two million years and perhaps more, who has an extraordinary past, a great history of the past, whether as a Frenchman, an Englishman, an Indian, or whatever one is, with all its accumulated knowledge and experience—can one be free of all that, which is the past, and meet the challenge which is always in the present? Otherwise life becomes a frightful conflict, a misery, a confusion. You can pray to all the gods that have been invented by man, run to all the organized religions, beliefs, rituals, but the problem will never be solved that way. That is an escape, and a futile escape. You might just as well take a drink. What matters is to understand this whole structure, not as an intellectual process, but to be totally aware of all this—the past, the present—and not escape from it, but come actually into contact with it. Then perhaps we shall know what it is to live. We shall find out for ourselves as a human being—not as an individual, but as a human being—because the human being is far more important than the individual; the human being is the total entity of two million years, with all that he has gathered; he is not an isolated individual in a little corner. Then perhaps we shall know for ourselves how to live a life without conflict—and in that there is great beauty. It is only a mind that has freed itself from every kind of problem, and therefore from every kind of effort—only such a mind can discover something that is not projected by itself, something which is not mere word, mere sentiment, emotion.

Perhaps now you would like to ask questions.

Questioner: What can we do to be aware, to be attentive?

KRISHNAMURTI: I don't think you can do anything. All that you can do is to be attentive to inattention. Do you understand? If you are trying to be attentive, trying to be aware, then it becomes a conflict, a battle, a process which involves time. I won't go into the question of time now—I will do that another day. What most of us want is a continuity; we think, "If I could only be attentive all the time, then I could solve my problems." But we are not attentive all the time, it is impossible; our nerves won't stand it—our physical brain itself is incapable of maintaining a continuous alertness. But if one were attentive to inattention—you know what I mean, if one were totally attentive to inattention—then one would find out for oneself, naturally, how attention comes about without trying. Please listen; don't say, "I will try," but do it. That is, pay attention to your own inattention, which breeds conflict. It is only inattention that creates problems, isn't it? If I am attentive even if only for a minute, in that minute of attention there is no problem—the problem simply doesn't exist. I mean by attention not only being attentive with the nerves, with the body, with the eyes, with the ears, but attentive also with your mind, with your feeling; and in that moment of complete attention, there is nothing that has been experienced, and therefore no experiencer. But most of us are not attentive to inattention, which breeds conflicts. When we are inattentive, we say things we don't mean, we do things halfheartedly, we react according to our conditioning; so it is this inattention that creates problems. But when one is attentive to inattention, then inattention will not breed any problems.

I do not know if you follow this.

Question: Even though the mind is broken up into fragments, isn't there a relationship, a great deal of interplay, a great deal of influence between the different fragments?

KRISHNAMURTI: Surely. There is a great deal of influence, a great deal of relationship between the fragments. That is an obvious fact, isn't it?

Comment: Yes. But when you spoke about the difficulties which arise, whether they are material, emotional, social, and so on, you spoke as if the solution were a compartmental thing.

KRISHNAMURTI: No, sorry. If I said that, I didn't mean it. I mean something entirely different.

Question: Then what do you mean?

KRISHNAMURTI: I am going to explain it. First of all, I am no authority. If you take me as an authority, then we will not understand each other. But if you and I are trying to understand each other, then our relationship is entirely different. Don't take just one part of a statement and throw it at me.

We are human beings, all broken into interrelated fragments, each fragment influencing the others. If we are very intellectual, we translate the whole of life in terms of the intellect, and that intellect is related to other factors. If we are very emotional, again we go through that fragmentary process, knowing that the fragments are all interrelated. We give predominance to one fragment, which then dominates our life; and all that I am saying is that as long as we live in these departments, compartments, or broken fragments, even though they are subtly interrelated, intercommunicating with each other, our life becomes a contradiction, a hypocritical life, and hence a battle, a conflict. I am pointing out that when there is no conflict of any kind, it is only then that we are total human beings; and then we shall have a mind that is capable of going very far, without projecting illusions.

May I ask a question? You have been listening to me for forty-five minutes. Perhaps most of you, or some of you, understand English; and in those forty-five minutes you have been listening, what has happened to you? It seems to me much more important to inquire into that than for you to ask me questions. Actually—not theoretically, not problematically, not hypothetically—what has taken place? That is the only significant thing, nothing else. I ask this question, and I hope you will not think it to be impudent. That is not at all my intention. I ask this question because I think it is important for each one of us to find out for ourselves whether a talk of this kind—call it a conversational talk, or a lecture, it doesn't matter; it is really an informal affair—whether such a talk has any significance, any vitality, so that one's mind is shaken up and sees something new. Otherwise these talks become so utterly futile, because one can pile up words—write, read, listen—indefinitely. If one listens in the sense we have been talking about, listens without effort, with clarity, then I think that very listening is the vehicle of action. You do not have to do anything about it—the very act of listening is action.

It is like seeing something, it is like looking at a flower. We never actually look at a flower because we look with our minds, with our thoughts, with our ideas, opinions, with our botanical knowledge of that flower. So it is thought that looks—not so much the eye, as thought. Our thoughts, ideas, opinions, judgments, botanical knowledge—these interfere with our looking. It is only when you can look at something completely that you are in direct contact with that thing; and to look completely demands a great deal of energy—not words, words, words; they don't create energy. What brings energy is this observing, listening, learning, in which there is not the observer; there is only the fact, and not the experiencer looking at the fact.

Question: Does that mean that when you are in contact with things, facts, problems, there is nothing to do but just accept them as they are?

KRISHNAMURTI: Sir, if you look at something out of silence—I don't know if you have ever done it—if you look at your wife, at your husband, at a flower, or whatever it is, without the interference of the past as knowledge, as ideas, as a conclusion, as an experience, then surely you are directly in contact with the fact; you are not concerned with whether it's pleasant or unpleasant. If you look so attentively, you will find that there is no experiencer and the thing experienced; there is no center from which you are looking. You must have felt this very simple phenomenon. When you see something very beautiful, that very thing which you call beautiful has pushed away all your thoughts for a second, and you are just absorbed by that beauty, by that sense of immensity; the mountain, the lake, or whatever it is, absorbs you. For a second or two you are not there—only that thing is there. But then what happens? The thing has absorbed you, has pushed you aside, has knocked you out, if I can use that word. But to observe without being absorbed by that which is observed is quite a different matter. If you can look at and be completely attentive to every problem that arises, you will find that there is no observer and the thing observed; there is only attention without a center.

Question: It seems that then there is no effort.

KRISHNAMURTI: There is no effort—but that requires a great deal of going into. Perhaps we will be going into it the next time we meet here—into the whole question of effort.

Question: How do you define the word fact?

KRISHNAMURTI: How do I define the word *fact?* I will put it into words, but we are not seeking definitions. The dictionary meaning of a fact is that which is observable, knowable, capable of being experienced by all. It is a fact that that microphone is there. Then what is the fact when I am angry? It is not a matter of who has made me angry, or of my response to that anger as a conditioned human being. The fact is *what is,* which is anger, and the word *anger* is used to recognize that fact. I use the word to define, to classify a certain feeling which I call anger. So there are physical facts, there are psychological facts, and perhaps there are intellectual ideas which we call facts.

Comment: When one observes one of those facts, there is a response to it; one doesn't just sit still and look.

KRISHNAMURTI: That's right, that's right. When one observes a fact, there are reactions to that fact. You say something to me which hurts me, or gives me pleasure. If I don't react, I am a dead human being, I am paralyzed, obviously. If you call me an idiot, I must react—that is, I must find out, I must observe the actual fact, and not just call back to you, "You also are one." Through my reaction I observe what actually is the fact. I may be an idiot, and probably I am, so I look to discover the fact, and not to give sustenance to my reaction.

May 16, 1965

Second Talk in Paris

Unless one is completely satisfied with things as they are—with oneself, with world conditions, and with the general misery and confusion of man—unless one is satisfied with it, one must have asked oneself whether it is possible for a human being to change totally, to bring about a transformation within himself so that his mind and his whole being are totally new, fresh, young, and innocent, vital. One has to ask oneself that question without quarreling with the world and therefore with oneself—because quarrels with oneself don't produce much. What gives understanding, depth, is to put to oneself the right question; and to question is rather difficult because when we do question, most of us want an answer, a satisfying, pleasurable, agreeable answer, so our questions invariably produce a static state where the mind no longer functions freely.

So, one has to ask oneself whether it is possible for a human being to change, not merely superficially, but deeply, because superficially we are always changing. Outwardly we are being influenced by new inventions, by the computer, by automation, by the explosion of population, and by the demand for economic welfare and a good outward life. Those influences do bring about a certain superficial change. But what happens if one has gone beyond all that and is aware that one is so easily influenced? Because we are influenced by climate, by food, by clothes, by the society, the culture in which we live; these things do influence superficially our character, our outlook, our various thoughts. But if we have gone a little bit further than all that and—without escaping into monasteries, into isolation, into the dogmas, beliefs, and rituals which the churches and the various religions offer—have asked ourselves whether it is possible to bring about within oneself a radical change, then perhaps we can go into it together and discover for ourselves the whole significance of what is implied in that word *change,* and whether a radical change is at all possible.

Mere discontent brings about a revolt against society. A revolt is a reaction, and any action, any deep, fundamental questioning born of reaction, can only produce a further series of reactions, and therefore cannot bring about total understanding. So one has to be rather aware of one's own discontent. Because most of us are discontented, and being merely discontented we are easily satisfied; and that satisfaction is again a reaction. So we spin along from satisfaction to satisfaction, thinking that is a change.

Now, may I here point out that we are not discussing or talking things over together merely intellectually, that is, verbally, argumentatively. Rather one is trying to find out for oneself the truth of the matter, and therefore one has to listen without necessarily accepting what is being said, or rejecting it. You know, when one does listen intimately, as it were, one gets much more out of it. Because we are going to talk about something rather difficult, perhaps, and it would be rather futile if we treated what is being said as a mere intellectual entertainment, a thing to be argued over. But I think it would be significant if we could listen with a certain sense of ease, with a quality of attention in which there is neither effort nor resistance because, for most of us, resistance is a defense mechanism which comes into operation so instinctively, so naturally. We instinctively withdraw when anything doesn't please us; we become defensive verbally, argumentatively, intellectually, in different ways, and such defensiveness prevents us from listening, investigating.

To investigate there must be a certain sense of freedom—freedom to inquire—and that is what we are going to do. We are going to inquire. But to inquire, the mind must have the inclination to be free; otherwise, one can't discover. There must be a certain intensity to search out what is true. But that inquiry ceases when we want a particular answer—an answer which will be satisfactory, or which will satisfy a projected desire. So one has to be rather aware of all this if one would really inquire into the question of whether there can be a fundamental change in human beings such as we ourselves are—with our traditions, our enormous past history—whether it is at all possible to bring about a radical revolution within oneself.

But perhaps most of us are not so keen to have such a revolution because we are satisfied with things as they are; we prefer to patch up our relationships, to cover things over so that we shan't have more trouble, more anxiety, more quarrels and escape into our beliefs. So most of us don't want a fundamental revolution within ourselves. But I am afraid one has to have such a revolution—a revolution which is not a reaction, a transformation which is not a calculated risk.

The world, technologically, is progressing enormously; there are vast changes going on, incalculable changes. A new society may come out of it, while we as human beings continue to be more or less the same, though a little more polished, a little more clever, a little more adjusted; but we shall not have resolved our sorrows, and there will be no ending to loneliness, to fear, to the understanding of mortality. Most of us are inclined to be easygoing, to be very easily satisfied, and so this question of whether it is possible to change fundamentally never arises.

Now, when the speaker puts this question to you, either it becomes your own question and is therefore intimate, vital, or when it is put to you, you merely accept it and look at it as something outside of you. When you are hungry, no one need tell you. You know it for yourself. Similarly, when you ask yourself whether it is at all possible to bring about this radical change, it is your question, not my question. It then becomes your problem, not imposed by another. So if it is your own human problem, then you can look at it quite differently, not as an issue put before you by somebody else.

Change, surely, implies order. We are now in a state of disorder, and to change from disorder implies order—order in society, order within ourselves, and order in our values, our outlook. So to change, in the sense in which we are using that word, is to be free to bring about order. But society does not want freedom because it is afraid that freedom implies disorder. That is why there is always imposed on the individual human being by society the restriction that he must not escape from the psychological structure of society. Society is afraid that freedom will bring about disorder because society is satisfied to live in the disorder which it calls order; therefore, it cannot experiment totally. It is only the individual human being who can experiment and discover for himself the total revolution which is order.

So when I use the word *change,* I am using it to imply a change from disorder to order because as individual human beings, we are not in order. We are in conflict, we are miserable, we are confused, we are ambitious, greedy, envious—you know, the whole human structure. We are afraid, terrified of so many things; and to change this whole structure of fear is to bring about order. So order is not the product of revolt because revolt against society is a reaction, which will only produce a series of actions within the frontiers of society; and, like communism, or any other reaction, it will eventually come back to what has been.

I am talking about the change which is not a reaction—which is not a reaction against society, against this so-called order, but is rather a process of understanding the whole structure of disorder; and the understanding of the structure of disorder brings about order, which is radical revolution.

I hope I am making myself clear, but if not, we will discuss it after I have finished talking.

Change, we say, implies time. I am *this,* and to bring about a change within myself, which is to become *that* in the future, involves time, doesn't it? That is very simple. I am what I am, with all my anxieties, fears, despairs, hopes, miseries; and I want to change, to bring about order in all that; and to bring about order demands time. There is fear, and to be free of fear, we consider, will take time. I am afraid, and to overcome, or to understand, or to be rid of fear, involves time. That is fairly obvious—at least, that is what we think.

Now, what is time? Please, we are not discussing this philosophically, as an idea, as something which you have to learn; but one can understand, observe this thing for oneself.

Take fear. One is afraid of so many things, the ultimate fear naturally being death. But there is also fear of public opinion, fear of losing a job, fear of being dominated—the whole network of fear that one has. One sees, one is aware that fear does breed every form of escape, and that fear does breed darkness, uncertainty, anxiety. So the mind gets confused, uncertain, and therefore escapes because it has not been able to resolve this question of fear. It escapes in dogmas, in drink, in sex, in a dozen different forms of escape.

Now, to be totally free of fear at every level of one's consciousness, not just superficially, but right through, one has to understand the nature, the structure, and the meaning of fear; and this process of understanding, we consider, takes time. Please do listen to this. We say, "I am afraid, and I will find out the cause of fear." So we investigate into the cause of fear, or we analyze fear, or we ask an analyst, or otherwise escape from fear. All this implies time, doesn't it? We say, "I am not free, but one day I will be free from fear."

So time means moving from *what is* to 'what should be'. I am afraid, but one day I shall be free of fear; therefore, time is necessary to be free of fear—at least, that is what we think. To change from *what is* to 'what should be' involves time. Now, time implies effort in that interval between *what is* and 'what should be'. I don't like fear, and I am going to make an effort to understand, to analyze, to dissect it, or I am going to discover the cause of it, or I am going to escape totally from it. All this implies effort—and effort is what we are used to. We are always in conflict between *what is* and 'what should be'. The 'what I should be' is an idea, and the idea is fictitious, it is not 'what I am', which is the fact; and the 'what I am' can be changed only when I understand the disorder that time creates. Do you follow? When I am afraid, that is a fact: I am afraid. If I introduce the element of time, I give a continuity to *what is,* and therefore that creates disorder. Am I making myself clear?

You see, we are conditioned to think that time is necessary, that the gradual process is necessary to bring about any kind of change within oneself. For example, we all want to fulfill ourselves in different ways—as an artist, or in any one of ten different ways; we all want to fulfill, and in that fulfillment, which involves time, there is pain, there is anxiety, there is fear. I want to be that, but I am not that.

Our question then is: Is it possible for a human being to change without introducing time at all? Can one be rid of fear totally, completely, immediately? Because if I am not free of fear immediately, I introduce the element of duration, which means that fear will continue; and where there is a continuity of fear, there is disorder.

So, is it possible for me to be rid of fear totally, completely, on the instant? If I allow fear to continue, I will create disorder all the time; therefore, one sees that time is an element of disorder, not a means to be ultimately free of fear. So there is no gradual process of getting rid of fear, just as there is no gradual process of getting rid of the poison of nationalism. If you have nationalism and you say that eventually there will be the brotherhood of man, in the interval there are wars, there are hatreds, there is misery, there is all this appalling division between man and man; therefore, time is creating disorder. So when you introduce time as a means to bring about a radical change, you are furthering disorder, and not order. And if one understands that, not just verbally, but if one sees the truth of it, the fact of it, then that very discovery is a revolution in itself—because we are used to time.

Look: we know what jealousy is. Most people are jealous about something or other, and by allowing it to continue, there is pain, there is anxiety, there are quarrels, hatred, and so on. The continuity of jealousy produces more confusion. So, is it possible for a human being to be free of fear, or jealousy, completely and immediately? If you say, "No, it is not possible," then you have already made up your mind. The moment you say it is not possible, you have stopped experimenting, discovering; and most of us are apt to say it is not possible because we are so lazy, so indifferent, that we would rather go on with our pain and pleasure, our jealousy and fear. We are so used to jealousy, to fear, that we would rather put up with the thing than find out whether it is at all possible to be totally rid of this extraordinary burden of fear.

Why do we introduce time at all, in the sense we are talking about? Why do we accept the continuity of fear? Why? Please don't answer me—nor is this a rhetorical question. We have probably never asked ourselves why we allow fear to continue even for a day, even for a minute, knowing what damage, what hatred, what lies, what hypocrisy, what confusion and conflict it creates. We accept it, probably, because we are used to it, and because we don't know any other way except the gradual process of getting rid of it—at least, we think the gradual process is a way of getting rid of fear. But now one sees that when there is a duration of fear, during that period there is hatred, there is confusion, there is effort, there is misery. We accept it only because we are so conditioned to it. So one asks oneself: Is it at all possible, without allowing time to interfere, to look at thought, to look at fear, and to understand the nature of fear—not the symptoms of fear, not the various forms of expression or the causations of fear, but fear itself?

Now, what is fear? It is very important to understand this because most of us are afraid; not only at a superficial level of one's consciousness, but deep down, one is afraid. There are many forms of fear, and we needn't go into all of the forms; but every fear is the outcome of relationship. Fear has a cause, it doesn't exist by itself, and we think that by understanding the cause, we will be rid of fear; but that is never possible. You know why you are afraid. You have probably thought about fear, looked at it, and you know the cause that gives rise to your fear; but though you know the cause, you are not free of the symptom. So one discovers that the mere finding of the cause does not necessarily free one of fear, nor does analysis free one of fear. Again, analysis implies time.

So, how is one to be free of fear immediately? That is really the tremendous question that one puts to oneself. And you can put that question to yourself only when you have understood the implications of the gradual process of time.

How is one to be free of fear immediately? When I use the word *how,* it is not to suggest an inquiry to find a process because a process, a method, a system implies time, and therefore disorder. So, is it possible to be free of fear immediately?

Now, does thought deal with fear, or does thought create fear? Thought itself is the ground upon which fear grows. Please listen carefully, and don't say at the end of it that I am advocating thoughtlessness, or asserting that we mustn't think.

Let us suppose I am afraid of death—that is, of tomorrow, of old age, pain, suffering, and the inevitable end. Because it has had experience of pain, disease, and the pleasures of youth, thought looks to the future; it projects or puts death at a distance, and whenever it thinks about death, it breeds fear. Or, because it has not understood this whole question of fear, it seeks beliefs, hopes, and all the rest of it. So, can I look at fear without the mediation, without the interference of thought?

Am I making this clear enough? Verbal clarification is one thing, and actual clarification is another. You may tell me something verbally, and I may say, "Yes, I agree with you, verbally I see what you mean." But seeing verbally is not seeing. I can look at a flower, and though I see it with my eyes—the light, the color, and all the rest of it—I see it only verbally. Seeing the flower with the eye is one thing, and seeing it with the word is another. Most of us see the flower with the word, and we don't see the flower actually. We have all kinds of ideas, knowledge, information, botanical concern, and so on and so on, when we look at a flower. Similarly, you may understand the verbal explanation up to now, and you may agree or disagree with that explanation; or you may not understand the words which have been used, or substitute your own words and translate what is being said into your own particular language. And therefore what happens? You are not actually looking at the nature of your own fear. So when you say, "I understand what you are talking about," is it that you are actually in contact with fear—with your own particular form of fear—or are you merely in contact with the word which gives you the indication that you are afraid?

You know, to be physically in contact with something is very easy. I can touch that microphone, and I know I am in contact with it. There is no time interval; there is a definite action taking place. But we are never totally in contact with another human being, or with anything at all. If you will observe, this is not just a generalization but an actual fact. I can come physically into contact with something, but to be in contact with fear is one of the most difficult things to do because it requires tremendous attention—attention in which there is no waste of energy through words, through explanations, through escape. Only then are you directly in contact with fear—and that is what it means when we ask ourselves whether it is possible to be free immediately of fear. It means that all escape from fear has come to an end—all verbal escape. Because the word not only gives strength to the thing which we call fear by identifying itself with that thing, but also the word itself may be the cause of fear. We can see how the word *death,* for example, awakens images, causes fear. So the word itself creates fear; and when we want to come into contact with fear, the word then becomes an escape. In touching that microphone, there is no escape, there is no word, there is no thought attached. But to come into contact totally with fear, one has to understand the structure, the meaning, the significance of the word. One has to be aware that thought is brought about by the word. Thought is a reaction to the word, and one has to be aware of that fact. I hope you are doing all this with me.

When I say that one can be completely free of fear, I do not mean freedom from the desire to avoid being knocked down by a bus or a lorry—that is the natural instinct to protect the physical organism. But when thought builds up a picture of it, then that picture creates fear. So, can the mind look at fear without the word—without allowing itself to escape by saying, "I will get rid of fear eventually"—and thereby come totally into contact with the thing which is called fear?

You know, we are never really in contact with anybody, are we? I may be in contact physically with my wife or husband, or with my children, but there is no other contact, is there? I have memories of my wife, of my husband, of my children, of my neighbor, and it is with these memories that I have contact. I have pictures, images, remembrances, both pleasant and unpleasant, and these interfere and prevent my being in contact directly with another. To be in contact with another is to have no intervening screen of remembrance.

So, is one directly in contact with fear? I wonder if you understand the question, and all that is involved in it. Are you looking at fear as an observer, fear being the observed? Are you the thinker, observing the thing which is called fear? Or are you looking at fear, but not as an observer, and therefore there is no censor, no center from which you are looking, so that fear is the only fact?

Let me put the thing differently. Most of our life is a conflict, a struggle between *what is* and 'what should be'. And we are used to effort, to this constant battle which is going on within the skin, within ourselves, this adjustment, this quarrel between the *what is* and the hoped-for 'what should be'. We are used to this constant battle, and that is all we know; we are conditioned to it from childhood. Our whole social structure—our religious concepts, our morals, everything—is based on this constant effort to become.

Now, don't say, "If there were no effort, if there were no striving, what would we be? We would be monkeys as before, we would stagnate." That is the usual response. But in our very striving there is a great part of us which is the animal, the monkey, and it is this constant greed, envy, fear, anxiety, this tremendous demand to be satisfied with pleasure and the continuation of pleasure. The demand for the continuation of pleasure brings effort, and our social, moral, religious, ethical values are based on pleasure. We know what love is only because of pleasure. Perhaps, when we understand the significance and the structure of pleasure, then love will have quite a different meaning in which there is no jealousy, no possessiveness, no domination. But to come to that, one has to see the nature of this effort which is transforming *what is* into 'what should be'. The 'what should be' is the continuation of pleasure. We call it the noble, the good, the virtuous, but behind the façade of words there is this pursuit of pleasure.

So, is it possible to change, to bring about a radical revolution within ourselves? And there must be such a revolution; otherwise, our life remains so shallow, empty, dull, stupid, mediocre; there is nothing new. Is it possible, without effort, to end fear? You can end fear only when there is direct contact with that feeling which is called fear, without the intervention of thought as the word; and this happens immediately if one has understood the whole nature of time, pleasure, confusion, and disorder.

All this requires great energy. After all, to attend to anything, to attend to what is being said, requires energy. But if you are not interested in what is being said, if you are looking at somebody else, if you are thinking—goodness knows what—or clinging to some complicated way of approaching life, then all this is a bore, and you are dissipating energy; therefore, you are not giving complete attention. Complete attention demands energy, both physical and neurological—energy in which there is no dissipation through words, through escape, through trying to get beyond *what is*. It is only when there is this total energy that the mind can look at *what is;* and by the very fact of that attention—which is total energy applied to this thing called fear—you will find out for yourself that one can be completely free of fear.

Perhaps you will ask questions, or we can discuss this matter.

Question: What about fear related to daily happenings, to the events of daily life?

KRISHNAMURTI: Surely, one meets the daily happenings, but we generally meet them with fear and apprehension because we already know the pain or the pleasure that a particular event has previously brought about. So we meet the daily events already conditioned by fear. You see, I am afraid we are not quite understanding this issue—probably I have not made it clear.

You know, we approach every event of life, every happening, with the past, with a memory, with the knowledge of yesterday, with all its pleasures, pains, fears, hopes. We meet every happening through the past, and so we are never directly in contact with anything. We are always in contact with the past, and that past is what meets the present, which creates contradiction and therefore effort, fear, and so on and so on.

What is it that we are trying to do in this talk? Are you trying to find out from me how to meet life? Are you looking for a method, a system, a standard of conduct, of behavior? Or are you and I together investigating the problem, going into this whole question of fear? If you are merely listening to discover a method which will end your fears so that you can live differently, and so on, then I am afraid you and I will have no relationship at all; there can be no communion or communication between us because you want one thing, and I am talking about a different thing. But if what we are doing is taking a journey together, then it is your discovery, not mine.

Throughout the world there is domination and tyranny—the tyranny of governments, the tyranny of churches in the name of God, in the name of love and peace. We have every form of authority thrust upon us, and most of us accept it because it is satisfying. But the man who would discover what is true, what is real, must put aside all authority—obviously including the authority of the speaker—so that his own mind begins to unfold itself, and see all the dark recesses of itself; and that, surely, is the only intelligent and creative thing to do.

May 20, 1965

Third Talk in Paris

Perhaps at the end of the talk we can really talk things over, not argumentatively, but as two friends discussing to find out for themselves how to live in a monstrous world that is so brutal, a world which we have created ourselves, a world in which we are caught socially, economically, and in every form of relationship. We are caught in this society, which we have put together through centuries; and to talk it over together in a friendly manner requires clarity, not only on the part of the questioner, but also on the part of the speaker. We must both be very simple, and that is one of our great difficulties. We are intellectual, clever, cunning, verbally secretive; we don't mean what we say, we take poses. But if we can put all that aside and talk things over, then perhaps we shall be able to find a way—not as an escape—out of this dreadful confusion and misery that exist within and without.

What I would like to talk about this morning is quite simple, though the very simplicity is made complicated when we use words; and unfortunately one has to use words because that is the only means of communication you and I have. And communication through words is not necessarily communion. There is a difference between communication and communion. One can communicate through a telephone, through books, through words, through a gesture. But communion is something entirely different. Communion can take place only when you and I are at the same intensity, at the same level, at the same time, when we both feel these things strongly, vitally, at the same depth and at the same moment. Then there is communion, and then words become so utterly useless, empty. But that communion cannot take place if we do not verbally understand each other.

So, words being necessary, and knowing the difficulty in the usage of words, which are quite complex things, one has to be aware of words; one mustn't be caught in words, or intellectually spin a lot of theories. Because we are not talking out of cleverness about something that can be theoretically approached. You can't approach life theoretically, intellectually, emotionally. You can only approach it totally, that is, with all your being—intellectually, emotionally, physically. You can't just take one fragment of it and then try to solve the problem through that one segment. Life is much too vast, too immense to be approached through a theory, through a hypothesis, through a pattern. One must come to it like a flood that comes down the mountains. Then one understands the extraordinary quality of living.

This quality of living is obviously action. You can't live without action. All our relationship is action; it is a movement. But out of our sorrow, our personal pleasures, our likes and hatreds, and all the petty incidents of our life, we want to make in this vast stream a particular little groove, a static little shelter, and live there, and then try to understand the whole process of living.

So one has to understand relationship because that is life. We can't exist without relationship of some kind. You can't withdraw into isolation, build a wall around yourself, as most people do, because that act of living in a sheltered, secure, isolated state of resistance only breeds more confusion, more problems, more misery. Life is, if one observes, a movement in action, a movement in relationship, and that is our whole problem: How to live in this world, where relationship is the very basis of all existence;

how to live in this world so that relationship doesn't become monotonous, dull, something that is ugly, repetitive.

Our minds do conform to the pattern of pleasure—and life is not mere pleasure, obviously. But we want pleasure. That is the only thing we are really seeking deeply, inwardly, secretly. We try to get pleasure out of almost anything, and pleasure, if one observes, not only isolates and confuses the mind, but it also creates values which are not true, not actual. So pleasure brings illusion. A mind that is seeking pleasure, as most of us are, not only isolates itself, but must invariably be in a state of contradiction in all its relationships, whether it is the relationship with ideas, with people, or with property; it must always be in conflict. So that is one of the things one has to understand: that our search in life is fundamentally the demand, the urge, the seeking of pleasure.

Now, this is very difficult to understand, because why shouldn't one have pleasure? You see a beautiful sunset, a lovely tree, a river that has a wide, curving movement, or a beautiful face, and to look at it gives great pleasure, delight. What is wrong with that? It seems to me the confusion and the misery begin when that face, that river, that cloud, that mountain, becomes a memory, and this memory then demands a greater continuity of pleasure; we want such things repeated. We all know this. I have had a certain pleasure, or you have had a certain delight in something, and we want it repeated. Whether it be sexual, artistic, intellectual, or something not quite of this character, we want it repeated—and I think that is where pleasure begins to darken the mind and create values which are false, not actual.

What matters is to understand pleasure, not try to get rid of it—that is too stupid. Nobody can get rid of pleasure. But to understand the nature and the structure of pleasure, is essential; because if life is only pleasure, and if that is what one wants, then with pleasure go the misery, the confusion, the illusions, the false values which we create, and therefore there is no clarity. It is a simple fact, psychologically as well as biologically, that we are seeking pleasure, and we want all relationship to be based on it; and hence, when relationship is not pleasurable, there is a contradiction, and then the conflict, the misery, the confusion, and the agony begin.

I am not saying anything extraordinary, I am just pointing out a fact. And having been trained, having been so heavily conditioned in this pursuit of pleasure, can the mind see the limitation of pleasure, understand it, not just verbally or intellectually, but see the nature of it, the inward significance of pleasure—and in that very act of seeing, put itself in a different dimension altogether?

That is, we are communicating with each other now; and not only are we communicating, but we are also trying to find out for ourselves, as we go along, whether this is what is actually taking place in our lives. Does one understand the pleasure of self-fulfillment, the pleasure of being somebody, of being recognized in the world as an author, as a painter, as a great man? Does one understand the pleasure of domination, the pleasure of money, the pleasure of taking the vow of poverty, the pleasure that one experiences in so many things? And does one see that when pleasure is not fulfilled, then begins the frustration, the bitterness, the cynicism? So one has to be aware of all this, not only physically, but psychologically; and then one begins to ask: What place has desire with regard to pleasure?

You know, there has to be freedom from illusion, that is, freedom from the power of the mind to create values which are not actual, values which have no reality with regard to life, to actual living. The mind has an extraordinary power to create illusion through beliefs, through escapes, through dogmas. It projects every kind of pattern, goal, ideal, through which it hopes to fulfill, and this identification with something it has projected, it calls becoming the 'greater'. Now, unless we are totally free from this power of illusion, and the breeding of illusion, we can never find out what is real, what is true, or whether there is God, something much more than this dreadful, superficial existence.

After all, most intellectual and fairly intelligent people want to discover something beyond the monotonous, exhausting routine of their own daily life. Because there is this tremendous longing, one goes to churches, where one is given false coin; one reads, one escapes through literature, through ideas, through various forms of Eastern and Western theology. But to find out for oneself what is true—not as an illusion, not as an escape, but actually to know it as one knows what it feels like to be hungry—one must have immense freedom. This freedom is not some extraordinary state, but it is freedom from creating any form of illusion through the movement of pleasure. If there is a movement of pleasure—whether it be the pleasure of having sexual relationship, or the pleasure of seeing a sunset, or the pleasure derived from going to Mass, or the pleasure that one experiences in the search for something beyond the mind—it does inevitably breed an illusion which gives you satisfaction, and which you want to hold on to; and then the whole trouble begins.

So it seems to me extraordinarily important to understand the nature and the significance of pleasure. The world outwardly is becoming more and more prosperous, more and more efficiently organized; the computer and automation are going to take over and give man almost complete leisure from work. It is not going to happen tomorrow, it may not happen for twenty years, but that is what is coming. Man is going to have a great deal of leisure—and leisure means pleasure for most people. Hence, though outwardly we may have everything we want, inwardly we shall be in turmoil, and to escape from it we shall have still other forms of pleasure. So it is very important, if one would understand this whole process of living and not escape from it into some fantasy, myth, or some absurd dream, that one be brutally—brutally in the sense of vitally—aware of this structure of pleasure.

Pleasure also means desire. You know, throughout Asia and Europe those who seek what they call God—the monks, the so-called religious people—have been advised by their traditions to put away desire, and they say that one must be without desire. You have probably read all about it—and I think it is totally wrong because it means to cut, to suppress, to operate on desire. You can't put away desire that way. You can never put away desire—but one can understand the inwardness of it, its limitations. I do not mean by the word *understand* mere intellectual understanding. One can never understand anything intellectually; do what it will, the cunning intellect can never grasp the quality of love, for example. The intellect can talk about it, write volumes about it, but the intellect cannot possibly feel it, or sense the quality, the perfume, the nature of love. And the intellect is all we have. We have so cunningly, so cleverly developed the intellect, that when we use the words, *I understand*, we mean that we understand intellectually—which is sheer nonsense. Nobody can understand anything merely intellectually. Either one understands or one doesn't understand. You can understand only when you give your whole being—body, mind, heart, everything that you have—to understand, including the intellect. But when the intellect is separate and says, "I understand," it doesn't. That is sheer nonsense.

So, to understand desire, which is pleasure, one has to go into it, feel it out, learn all that one can about it, and not say, "This is right desire, that is wrong desire; this is good desire and that is bad desire." There is neither good nor bad, neither noble nor ignoble desire. There is only desire, and to understand it is to feel your way into it in a nonverbal sense, without cunningly trying to avoid it, or not to have it, or to go beyond it—because you can't. One has to understand desire—and I have explained what I mean by "understand." One has to go into the structure of desire, not according to your fancy or my fancy, but actually understand what it irrefutably and irremediably is. And when that is very clear, then one will know the limitations of desire, and therefore understanding its whole structure, one is out of it—the mind is no longer caught in desire, or in the process of pleasure.

So we are going to examine together the very structure of desire, and not think in terms of your opinion or my opinion, or quote what some biologist, or some psychologist, or some religious quack has said about desire. We are going to find out what desire actually is—and it seems to me to be so extraordinarily simple. I see something, and I want it. I see a beautiful tree in your garden, lovely, full, rich, and I would like to have that tree in my garden—that's all. In seeing something, there is the reaction, the sensation of pleasure, and out of that sensation there is desire. It is as simple as that, if you watch it in yourself. You don't have to read any book to find out this very simple fact. There is the perception of a beautiful house, or a nice flat, clean and empty, with but few things; you enter it and say, "I wish I could live here." First there is visual perception, or seeing, then the reaction, the sensation of pleasure, and out of that, desire. This is the whole process of desire. It becomes more complicated, naturally; it becomes much more subtle. But if you understand the beginnings of it, the roots of it, then you don't have to climb every branch, examine every blossom, tear every leaf from that tree. You know the quality of desire, how it happens, and when you know that, then you need never suppress desire because you understand all its implications.

But for most of us desire means self-indulgence, self-expression: I desire that, and I must have it. Whether it is a beautiful person, or a house, or an idea, I must have it. Why? Why does the "must" come into being? Why does desire say, "I must have that"—which brings about the agony, the drive, the urge, the demands of a compulsive existence? It is fairly simple, fairly clear, why there is this insistence on self-expression, which is a form of desire. In self-expression, in being somebody, there is great delight because you are recognized. People say, "By Jove, do you know who he is?"—and all the rest of that nonsense. You may say that it isn't just desire, it isn't just pleasure, because there is something behind desire which is much stronger still. But you cannot come to that without understanding pleasure and desire. The active process of desire and pleasure is what we call action. I want something, and I work, work, work to get it. I want to be famous as a writer, as a painter, and I do everything I can think of to become famous. Generally I fall by the wayside and never get recognized by the world, so I am frustrated, I go through agony; and then I become cynical, or I take on the pretense of humility, and all the rest of that nonsense begins.

Now, why is there this tremendous demand for fulfillment? I hope you are going along with me, and not merely listening verbally; because if you are merely listening verbally, then our communication, or our relationship of communion, has come to an end. As I said at the beginning, we are taking a journey together into your life, not mine.

So we are asking ourselves: Why is there this insistence on desire being fulfilled? If you want a coat, a suit, a shirt, a tie, a pair of shoes, you get it—that is one thing. But behind this persistent drive to fulfill oneself, surely, there is the sense of complete inadequacy, loneliness. I can't live by myself, I can't be alone, because in myself I am insufficient. You know more than I do, you are more beautiful, more intellectual, more clever, you are more this and more that, and I want to be all those things and more. Why? I do not know whether you have ever asked yourself this question. If you have, and if for you it is not just a clever theoretical question, then you will find the answer. But you can find the answer only when your mind is not projecting an answer.

Are you following me? Am I making myself clear?

I want to know why one craves many things, or one thing. One wants to be happy, to find God, to be rich, to be famous, to be complete, or to be liberated, whatever that may mean—you know all the things, a craving for which one builds up. One wants to have a perfect marriage, a perfect relationship with God, and so on. Why? First of all, it indicates how shallow the mind is, doesn't it? And doesn't it also indicate our own sense of loneliness, emptiness?

You know, there are two kinds of emptiness. There is the emptiness in which the mind looks at itself and says, "I am empty"; and there is the real emptiness. There is the emptiness I want to fill because I don't like that emptiness, that loneliness, that isolation, that sense of being completely cut off from everything. Each one of us must have had that feeling, either superficially, casually, or very intensely; and becoming aware of that feeling, one obviously escapes from it, one tries to cover it up with knowledge, or by means of relationship, the demand for a perfect union between man and woman, and all the rest of it. This is actually what takes place, isn't it? I am not inventing anything. If one has observed oneself, gone into oneself a little bit—not tremendously, that comes much later—one knows this to be a fact. So one begins to find out that where there is this sense of inexhaustible loneliness, this emptiness created by the mind's looking upon itself as being empty, there is also an urge, a tremendous drive to fulfill, to get something with which to cover it up.

So, consciously or unconsciously, one is aware of this state of—I don't like to use the word *emptiness* because emptiness is a beautiful word. A thing like a cup, or a room, is useful when it is empty; but if the cup is full, or the room is crowded with furniture, then it is useless. Most of us, being empty, fill ourselves with all kinds of noise, with pleasure and every form of escape. There is a sense of emptiness, and we have the urge to fill that emptiness with the objects of desire, with pleasure and the continuity of pleasure, which in turn create false values and hence conflict in all our relationships. I want pleasure in my relationship with my wife and husband, and when that wife or husband turns to another, I am jealous, I hate. I take pleasure in my nationality, in the position I have attained in the country with which I have identified myself; and when that country "defends" itself, as it is called—which is to attack another; there is no defense apart from attack, it is all the same—and the butchery begins, I am inevitably caught in it.

So we all know this emptiness, and the escape from it through pleasure, the fulfillment of desire, and so on.

Now, why is there this emptiness? I hope you are nonverbally pursuing it with me. Why is there this emptiness? Is it inevitable, or is the mind creating it? When we use the word emptiness, it is comparative, is it not? I see that you are rich—not just physically, that is nothing at all; any man who works a little bit hard, and who is clever and cunning, can be fairly well off. But you are rich in other ways: you have knowledge, you know what it means to feel, to live richly inwardly, and I am nothing, I am stupid, ugly. So comparison is the beginning of this emptiness. I know we say that if there is no comparison, there is no progress. Progress in what? Not all technological progress is due to one man; it's the result of effort by a whole group. The splitting of the atom, the perfection of the car—such things are not brought about by one person but by a whole group of people. But we as individuals compare and say, "You are somebody; I am not, and I want to be." So one begins to see that comparison invariably breeds the feeling of emptiness and this is one of the most intricate and subtle things to understand because we are brought up from childhood and taught in our schools to compare, compare, compare. You are beautiful, I am not. You get higher marks and I get lower marks. So we are conditioned that way from childhood.

So the mind's comparing itself with some other mind is the beginning of this sense of emptiness. Please look at it, don't push it aside. It is so simple.

And must we compare? Must I compare myself with you, who are so this or so that? And is there progress, evolution through comparison? Inwardly, obviously there is not. If I compare my painting with your painting, I have ceased to be a painter. If I love, and compare my love with your love, it is not love. This is what is happening all the time. But if you can live without comparison—which is one of the most subtle things to understand, and the most marvelous—then you will find that the mind is no longer creating this emptiness; it is then not comparing itself with another and thereby making itself either small or great. And one can live that way, without any sense of comparison with anybody. Then one begins to understand this whole process of the mind's looking at itself through comparison and thereby reducing itself to something small; and being small, it wants to become great; and being great, it wants to be greater. Hence it breeds within itself this feeling of insufficiency, this sense of emptiness, loneliness, and so all the misery and the travail begin.

Then you will see, not tomorrow, but now—if we are still in communion with each other—the significance of action. Our life is action: going to the market, cooking, breeding children, thinking, going for a drive, looking at a tree, going to the office. All life is tremendous action. If you sit quietly in a forest in springtime, you see that everything is burstingly alive. You know, most of us never die, and therefore we never produce. The trees bring forth new leaves, and when the leaves die, they are marvelous to look at. But we live on in the past; we never die, and therefore we never renew; our action is always imitative, conforming, following the pattern of pleasure, and hence there is agony. That is the only action we know, and from that we try to escape—the action born of idea. What we call pleasure is an idea. There is pleasure, actual pleasure, and that is one thing. But to breed out of pleasure an idea of pleasure, and then act from that idea—that is quite a different thing. Action is entirely different from idea, and so there is a contradiction between idea and action.

This is very simple, if we are still in communion with each other.

If you are no longer comparing, if you are no longer driven by the desire for pleasure—which is very subtle, it is not so easy to understand; you have to apply your whole being to understand it—then you will find that action is never conforming to a pattern; it is new all the time, it is not born of an idea. Thus you will discover a way of living in this world and being free from the psychological structure of society—and one must have this freedom from the psychological structure of society, with its greed, ambition, ruthlessness, brutality, and all the rest of it. Then one can go far, for then begins real meditation. What has been called meditation up to now is all too childish.

When the mind is no longer seeking pleasure, and no longer caught in the contradiction between idea and action, then it is active—not "I was active," or "I shall be active," but active. There is only the verb "to act," not in the past tense or the future tense, but in the active present. But that is possible only when one has understood the nature of greed, envy, ambition, competition, jealousy. And to understand all that is not a matter of time, because if you use time to understand it, you only create further disorder.

So one must lay the foundation—and this is the foundation—of real meditation by finding out how to live in this world without escaping from it. This means having your relationships, your sex, your work, your miseries, your conflicts, and living with them, understanding them. Without understanding the nature of pleasure, of loneliness, of emptiness, without understanding the insistence of desire on various forms of fulfillment, of becoming, and all the rest of it, one can never go beyond the limitations which the mind makes for itself. That is why the search for God by a man who is greedy, violent, is nonsense. His God will be of his own making: a petty little god, a petty little savior.

When one begins to understand all this, not as a theory, but in actual life, in living, then one can go into the nature of meditation. But I am afraid we shall have to leave that until the next time we meet because it is nearly twelve, and there will be no time for discussion. So we will stop here, if you don't mind.

Comment: One comes to understanding slowly, little by little.

KRISHNAMURTI: Do you? I know that is the obvious statement everybody makes: that we come to understanding by slow degrees. We say and we live by that, but is that a fact? Though you may say it, and a hundred million people may say it, that doesn't mean it is true. One must find out. Does time bring understanding? You see, if I may respectfully point it out, you are not inquiring, you are just agreeing or disagreeing. Does time bring understanding—a duration, a period, a length of time? I may learn a language in four months. Learning a new technique, a new craft, a new way of doing things, takes time. But is understanding a matter of time?

Do we come to understanding through experience? What is experience? And do we learn anything through experience? We have had two bloody, dreadful wars. Have we learned anything—except perhaps new techniques, like how to build better airplanes? Have we learned not to kill each other, physically, mentally, verbally, nationally, comparatively? Obviously not.

Now, take a simple thing like nationalism. Why are we nationalists? We are discussing this in relation to understanding. I identify myself with my country, which is greater than myself, because from that identification I derive a certain satisfaction. You do the same as a Frenchman; somebody else does it as a German or an American, with all the rest of that silly nonsense, and we are ready to go to battle—over what? Over our identification with an idea. We say that because you and I are human beings, with our passions, with our hatreds, with our agonies, with our nationalism, really to become a united Europe, a united world—to become united human beings—will take time. What does that mean? It means that we don't want to give up our particular little idiosyncrasies, our identifications—which we could give up tomorrow, immediately. When you see something to be a poison, you give it up instantly.

But we like to be called a Frenchman, or an Englishman, and all the rest of it, and therefore we cling to our nationalism until circumstances gradually force us to become united. So we say, "By Jove, it will take time to get united."

In the same way, we say that time is necessary to come to understanding. Is it? We say it is because we never give attention to anything. We give attention to something only when there is a tremendous crisis. And the world is in a state of crisis all the time, not just when you want it to be. As you sit in this hall there is a crisis, there is misery, there is starvation in the world—not in Paris, perhaps, not in France, but go in an airplane eight hours away and you will know all about starvation, misery, disease, ugliness. Yet you sit quietly back in your comfortable chair and say it will take time to understand! The crisis is there, but we don't want to face it. For God's sake, do see that understanding doesn't take time! Time, as we saw the other day when we talked about it, only creates more disorder. It is very simple, and I don't want to go into it again.

Understanding comes when you give your mind and your heart and your body to something; and when you don't, you won't have understanding. Either you do it voluntarily, easily, happily, or you are compelled; and when you are compelled, you resist, and therefore you say, "Well, it will take time."

You know, most of us are jealous, envious, and we like it. We like it because it involves possession, domination, comparison, the feeling that we own, that we are somebody, and all the rest of it. When you see what is actually involved in the whole comparative structure, either you like it and go on with it or you don't. And if you don't, you understand it immediately. Because you understand it, you don't go that way.

Question: Who is it that understands?

KRISHNAMURTI: Who is the entity that understands? Is there an entity when there is understanding? We say, "I understand," but that is only a form of communication. I say to you, "I understand what you are talking about"; but at the actual moment of understanding, is there an entity who says, "I understand"? At the moment when there is joy which has no cause, and which is completely different from pleasure—at that moment, is there an entity who says, "I am joyous"? And when you do say, "I am joyous," then joy ceases. I do not know if you have noticed this. The moment you say, "I am happy," are you happy then?

It is the same when you are completely attentive. Do try it for yourself, and you will see. Look at a flower, or a tree, or a cloud, or what you will. Look at it nonverbally, that is, without naming it, without saying it is good, bad, beautiful, this or that. Look at it nonverbally and therefore attentively—attentively in the sense of completely, with your whole mind, with everything. There is then a state of attention in which there is no effort, and in that state of attention, is there an entity who is attentive? The entity who is attentive, and who is aware that he is attentive, is born of memory, which is inattention; and it is only in that state of inattention that there is an entity who observes.

If you ever go into a wood, and I hope you do, look at a tree quietly. Just look at it. By looking I do not mean looking with your mind only—the mind thinks much more than the eye—but look at the whole tree with your whole being so that you are in communion with the tree. This is not some mysterious or mystical phenomenon. You know, there is something tremendously mysterious in life which is not created by the ugly, stupid little mind. Sit down and look at that tree, or at that flower; look at it attentively, without concentration. Concentration limits, concentration is exclusive. A businessman or a merchant concentrates when he is bargaining to get something. When you want this or that, you concentrate, and thereby limit the mind; the mind fixes itself on a certain point—but that is not what I mean by attention. When you look at a flower or a tree, look at it attentively, easily, and you will find that there is no entity as the observer, as the experiencer, as the thinker, because then the observer is the observed.

May 23, 1965

Fourth Talk in Paris

It seems to me that one of the most difficult things in life is to communicate sanely with each other because we have to use words, and we interpret those words according to our pleasure, our pain, our dislike; we translate them always in terms of our particular knowledge and information. And so communication becomes rather difficult, especially when we are going into matters not actually physical, for then one needs a greater sharpness and clarity, not only in listening, but also in expressing.

I would like, if I may this evening, to talk about something which may be a little foreign to you—not that I represent the country I come from; but I would like to go into the question of what is that state which is called sanity.

To be completely sane is extremely difficult, and very few of us are really balanced, sane, rational, clearsighted. To be sane is to be without self-contradiction; it is to be inwardly and outwardly extraordinarily balanced, which means that psychologically everything is in order; and this state of sanity, it seems to me, is very difficult. One of the indications of sanity is that there is no contradiction within oneself, there is no imbalance. It is a state in which thought and action correspond to each other, actually, not theoretically. What you think is what you do; there is no contradiction between them, and belief is nonexistent because you are dealing with facts, with *what is*, and not with 'what should be'. 'What should be' is not real; *what is* is real. A mind that would understand the nature of sanity and order must surely be free from every kind of belief, dogma, superstition, and ideal because they obviously contradict what one actually is; and when there is such a contradiction, as there is in the life of most of us, then out of that contradiction arise various forms of disharmony and imbalance.

So it seems to me that to find out for oneself if there is such a thing as that which may be called truth, something far beyond the mere projections of a clever, cunning, philosophical mind, or of a mind that escapes from the daily routine of physical existence, with its boredom and conformity—to find that out for oneself, surely one must have extraordinary order in one's life, order in the sense that there is no contradiction of any kind. Because contradiction does breed imbalance—like the man who wants peace, but does everything in actual life not to have peace. The two cannot possibly go together, and the disturbance, the strain of this contradiction does breed enmity within oneself and brings about a lack of balance, a lack of sanity.

Now, I would like to talk about something which is neither Eastern nor Western, and the word generally applied to it is *meditation*. Because it seems to me that if one does not know how to meditate, or if the mind is not in a meditative state, one misses a great deal in life. Our life at present is pretty shallow, rather empty, dull; and when the petty little mind tries to divine the mysterious, the unknowable, obviously it merely creates an image of its own pettiness. So the question is whether a little mind, a mind that is full of worry, despair, anxiously striving to change itself, to become something—whether that petty little mind can transform itself, break through its own limitations and be open to wide horizons; because unless it does, sanity is almost impossible. Sanity is order, not only outward, but inward—inside the skin, as it were; and it matters a great deal how this order is brought about.

Inwardly most of us are very disorderly. We may have a great deal of knowledge, well-ordered information, outward clarity; we may have outward purpose and be capable of argument, but inwardly most of us are confused, in conflict. This may be seen in the case of many clever writers. Because they have a gift and are in contradiction with themselves, under great strain and tension, they produce all kinds of literature, but it is basically the work of a sick mind. And most of us, I am afraid, are confused; there is in us no clarity. This clarity cannot be discovered through another, nor by following some authority or system of thought, ancient or modern. This clarity is order, and order in its ultimate, subtle sense, is virtue. The morality which society imposes is not morality at all. Social morality is immorality because it breeds every form of contradiction, every form of ambition, competition. Society by its very nature, whether in the communist world or in the Western world, does breed an outward, social conformity which is called morality; but if one goes into it very deeply, one sees that such morality is immoral.

I am talking of virtue, which has nothing whatsoever to do with society and its so-called morality. Virtue can come about only when there is psychological order within oneself. When we understand the whole social structure—the psychological structure of society, of which we are a part—in that understanding there is order, which brings about virtue. Without virtue, the mind cannot possibly have clarity, sanity, and therefore sanity and virtue go together. I think it is very important to understand this because for most of us, virtue has become very tiresome, a rather silly, old-fashioned thing without much significance, especially in the modern world. Not that I am advocating the superficial morality of society, but we are inquiring together, I hope, into this whole question of what is true virtue.

As one keeps a room orderly, tidy, neat, clean, and one does this every day, so there must be inward order; but inward order demands much more attention; it demands awareness of what is taking place inwardly. The mind has to be aware of all its own thoughts and feelings, of the open as well as the secret desires and pursuits; and out of this awareness comes order, which is virtue.

If one inquires into virtue still more deeply, one sees that it is not a thing that you can have permanently—and that is the beauty of virtue. You cannot say, "I have learned what it is to be virtuous, and it's all over." Virtue is not a continuous, fixed phenomenon. Virtue is order reborn from moment to moment, and therefore there is freedom in virtue, and not a revolt. As I pointed out the other day, revolt is not freedom; revolt is still within the pattern of society, and freedom is outside the pattern of society. The pattern or mold of society is psychological; it is the envy, greed, ambition, the various conflicts of which we are a part. We are the society which we have made, and if one is not free from it, there cannot possibly be order. So virtue is of the highest importance because it brings freedom. And one must be free—but that is what most people don't want. They may want political freedom—freedom to vote for some politician, or nationalistic freedom; but that is not freedom at all.

Freedom is something entirely different, and most of us do not want freedom inwardly, in the deep sense of that word, because it implies that we must stand completely alone, without a guide, without a system, without following any authority; and that requires enormous order within oneself. Most of us want to lean on somebody, and if it's not a person, then it's an idea, a belief, a way of conduct, a pattern established by society, by some leader or so-called spiritual person, or by oneself.

So most of us accept authority. And here one must be clear that the authority we are talking about is not the law of the land. What we are talking about is the authority we follow through fear of being alone, through fear of standing on our own feet and not looking to anyone for the way of our life, of our conduct, or for inward clarity. Because such authority breeds contempt, it breeds enmity and division between man and man. A man who seeks truth has no authority of any kind, at any time, and this freedom from authority is one of the most difficult things for most of us to grasp, not only in the Western world, but also in the East, because we think that somebody else will bring about order in our life—a savior, a Master, a spiritual teacher, and all that business—which is absolutely absurd. It is only through our own clarity, through our own investigation, awareness, attention, that we begin to learn all about ourselves; and out of that learning, out of that understanding of ourselves come freedom and order, and therefore virtue.

So, the realization that one must be completely alone comes when you begin to understand yourself. Self-knowing is the beginning of wisdom, and wisdom is always alone because it cannot be bought through books, through the quotations of another. Wisdom is something that has to be discovered by each one, and it is not the result of knowledge. Knowledge and wisdom do not go together. Wisdom comes when there is the maturity of self-knowing. Without knowing oneself, order is not possible, and therefore there is no virtue.

Now, learning about oneself, and accumulating knowledge about oneself, are two different things. Please listen to this a little bit. Not that you are following me, or merely accepting what I am saying, which I hope you are not, but we are investigating, discovering together. We are taking a journey together, and therefore you are as much aware as the speaker, you are working as hard as the speaker, which means that we are both together inquiring.

Learning and accumulating knowledge are two different things. A mind that is acquiring knowledge is never learning. What it is doing is this: It is gathering to itself information, experience as knowledge, and from the background of what it has gathered, it experiences, it learns; and therefore it is never really learning, but always knowing, acquiring.

When I have talked a bit, I hope you will ask questions about this. But I must proceed.

Learning is always in the active present; it has no past. The moment you say to yourself, "I have learned," it has already become knowledge, and from the background of that knowledge you can accumulate, translate, but you cannot further learn. It is only a mind that is not acquiring, but always learning—it is only such a mind that can understand this whole entity that we call the 'me', the self. I have to know myself, the structure, the nature, the significance of the total entity; but I can't do that burdened with my previous knowledge, with my previous experience, or with a mind that is conditioned, for then I am not learning, I am merely interpreting, translating, looking with an eye that is already clouded by the past.

So there is a vast difference between knowing and learning. Knowledge binds, whereas the movement of learning frees the mind. I have to be learning about myself all the time because the 'myself' is an extraordinary, living thing. Every moment there is a change, there is a mutation, there is a variety of intimations, a variety of reactions, and I have to observe all this, learn about it. But if I come to it with previous experience as knowledge, I am not learning. I hope this is somewhat clear.

Learning about oneself—not only about one's physiological reactions, one's biological compulsions, demands, but also about the whole inward movement of one's thought—is necessary to bring order; and only then can you proceed with meditation. You know, there are so many books on meditation, so many teachers and clever people who have written about how to meditate, what to do. I don't know if you are interested in this. If you are not, you must be, because not to know the meaning of meditation is like having only one arm, or no arms at all.

Most of us are seeking the mysterious because we see that our life has very little meaning, very little significance. The routine of going to the office, of doing something over and over and over again, whether it's pleasurable or not pleasurable, the incessant conformity to a pattern—we get rather tired of all that, and therefore we seek something mysterious, something not of this world, an otherworldliness. So we think that through what we call meditation—which is one of the inventions of Asia—we shall come upon this extraordinary thing, a reality which is not put together by the mind.

Now, it is very important to understand what meditation is because in real meditation there is great beauty, there is a sense of great intensity, and it is only the meditative mind that knows what love is. Most of us do not know what love is. We know love in relation to pleasure, but we don't know the nature of that love which is not born of pleasure. That is, if one has observed, one sees that love as we know it is always related to pleasure: physical pleasure, the pleasure of companionship, the pleasure of association, the pleasure derived from so-called loving another, loving a country, and so on and on.

Now, pleasure, as I pointed out the other day, is the outcome of desire; but there is a slight, subtle difference between desire and pleasure. I do not know if you have noticed for yourself that when desire arises, thought gives it continuity. I see something beautiful—a house, a car, or whatever it is—and there is the reaction of desire; and then thought gives continuity to desire, which is pleasure. I can look at a beautiful tree, or person, and there is a reaction which is normal, healthy, sane. But what gives continuity, duration, to that reaction is thinking about it; and therefore thinking about desire is pleasure. And the continuity of desire as pleasure obviously denies love.

So, again, to bring order within oneself requires attention, an awareness of what is taking place from moment to moment within oneself, and never denying it, never escaping from it, but merely being aware of it choicelessly.

You know, there is a great deal of difference between attention and concentration. When you concentrate, your whole mind is focused on one particular thing, and if you are very good at it, you can build a wall so that nothing else comes in. Concentration is an exclusion, a resistance, and therefore a contradiction, whereas attention is a state of awareness, which is something entirely different. Do you know what it is to be aware? One is aware of the size of this hall, aware of its ugliness or disproportion; one is aware of the people, of the colors they are wearing; one is aware of what is taking place outwardly. But one is not aware if one says, "I don't like that color, that person," for then one has stopped the movement of awareness. One has to be aware of this place, the colors, and so on, without any choice. Then you are learning much more; your mind is much more active.

From outward awareness, riding as it were on that wave, the mind begins to be aware inwardly. Observe yourself, observe the movement of your own thought; see how it is conditioned, see its nature, its subtlety, its background. If you concentrate on it, you can't observe. If you take one segment of the total and try to learn about that one particular segment, you are in a state of contradiction. But if, being choicelessly aware outwardly, the mind begins to move inward, then out of that choiceless awareness comes, naturally, attention.

You know, when you are attentive to something, as perhaps you are now to what is being said, you are attending with your whole being, aren't you? You are completely aware, totally attentive with your body, with your nerves, with your eyes, with your ears, with your emotions, with your intellect. In that state of attention there is no entity who is attentive; there is only attention. I am not talking Greek, or some fantastic stuff. It is very simple if you actually do it. When there is concentration, which is a process of exclusion, there is a resistance and therefore a contradiction. But when there is attention, there is no contradiction because an attentive mind can concentrate without exclusion. This attention is not a state to be developed through time because, as I was pointing out the other day, time breeds disorder.

I don't know if you want me to go further into it. We have done it sufficiently, haven't we?

If I postpone action, if I say I will change tomorrow, between now and tomorrow every kind of pressure, influence, every kind of movement is taking place. Therefore time does not produce order. It is only in the immediate that there can be order, not through time. There can be order only when onc understands the whole structure and nature of time.

So you have to understand the outward nature of life, be in communion with it, and then move from the outer to the inner, to the psyche, to that bundle of memories which is yourself, with all your conditionings, your traditions, your hopes, your fears, your despairs, your longings; and to be aware of all that, to be attentive to and therefore to dissolve and be free of all that, is not a matter of time. When one does this, the mind itself becomes very sharp, clear, subtle, because there is no contradiction, no effort to be or to become. Contradiction means effort. A mind that is making an effort to be this or that is in a state of confusion, and whatever effort it may make in order to clarify and bring depth to itself will only produce greater dullness, greater confusion.

This total process is meditation.

For most of us, beauty is a stimulation, a reaction. We depend on a stimulus to make us feel beauty, or to see beauty. We say, "What a lovely sunset," or, "What a beautiful building." But there is a beauty which is not a stimulus at all, which is not the result of a stimulant, and that beauty cannot exist without great simplicity. Simplicity is not a matter of how much or how little one has, but it comes about when there is the clarity of self-knowing, self-learning; and this simplicity is the nature of humility, which is austerity.

All this is necessary to go beyond the limitations of the mind. Now, who is the entity that goes beyond? As I said, when one is intensely aware, attentive, there is no entity at all. Do it sometime—I hope you are doing it now—and you will see. If you are completely attentive to what is being said, there is only the hearing of the word, not a 'you' who is listening to the word. When the mind is inwardly attentive, and has come to that state of complete attention through outward understanding of the nature of the word, there is then no entity who says, "I will go further." You know, when you are very attentive, there is a great deal of silence inside you, isn't there? When you are actually listening to what is being said with all your being—not accepting, translating, denying, or trying to understand, but merely attentive—then your mind is extraordinarily quiet, isn't it? There is a silence which is not artificial, which hasn't been put together by will, by force. That silence comes when the whole structure of the self is understood, and where there is silence, there is space. The mind that is silent, that has space—it is only such a mind that knows the beauty which is not a stimulus.

This whole process is meditation.

Perhaps you will ask questions, and we can talk together about what has been said if you are interested.

Question: Is it possible to go beyond oneself without suffering?

KRISHNAMURTI: Now, let's find out what suffering is. What is suffering? What is sorrow? There are certain things which produce sorrow: the death of someone you like, not being able to fulfill, not having a good, strong, healthy mind, not being loved. There are so many ways, so many symptoms of suffering; but when you look at all the symptoms, what do you find out about suffering? Actually, what is suffering? I lose somebody I like—my son, my wife, my father—and I am in sorrow. What does that imply? First of all, in that sorrow there is a great deal of self-pity because I have lost somebody on whom I depended, somebody I loved, and I now find myself without a companion. I am left alone. So one of the factors of sorrow is self-pity. Please don't deny it.

Comment: I don't mean the suffering that is caused by the self; I mean the suffering that comes when the self ceases.

KRISHNAMURTI: Oh, I beg your pardon. I will come back a little later to what we were talking about. When I see myself as I am, the gentleman says, it breeds sorrow. Is that the question you are asking, sir?

Comment: No, sir.

KRISHNAMURTI: I am sorry, sir, I don't understand. The difficulty here is a matter of communication. I really don't understand what you are trying to tell me. You are saying, sir, aren't you?—I am putting it very briefly—that when I actually see what I am, it brings suffering. Now, why should it bring suffering? Suppose I am a liar, and I see myself as I am; why should it bring suffering? It is a fact. But I have an image of myself; I think I am a very honest man, and therefore the image is in contradiction with the fact. This contradiction brings conflict, which I call sorrow. But seeing the fact, the *what is,* can never bring suffering. When the image which I have of myself is in contradiction with *what is*—it is only then that conflict, which I call suffering, begins.

Comment: I only wanted to ask you whether it is possible to have self-knowledge without this kind of suffering.

KRISHNAMURTI: Absolutely. If there is any kind of suffering, there is no self-knowledge. If there is any kind of suffering when self-inquiry begins—that is, if self-inquiry brings about suffering—it is no longer self-inquiry.

Question: When a spectator who is watching a play is completely absorbed in the play, is that the state of total attention?

KRISHNAMURTI: You are watching a play, and the play is so interesting that you are completely absorbed. There is no 'you' for the moment because the play has absorbed you, with all your worries, anxieties, fears. Now, what is the difference between your absorption, and that of a child who is absorbed by an amusing toy? The child may have been naughty, mischievous, doing all kinds of restless things, but give that child a toy which is very interesting, and he is completely absorbed in it. The toy is so interesting that he forgets all about his restlessness. What is the difference between the two? A play, a book, a church service, an idea, a belief, a piece of music, a picture, or what you will absorbs you, and you forget yourself. So what has become important is the picture, the toy, and not the understanding of yourself. You may be absorbed for an hour by the play, but when you go back to your home, you have your old self again. So if one is absorbed by anything, by propaganda, by nationalistic demands, or if one identifies oneself with something, which is another form of absorption, in that state there is no learning; therefore, there is no freedom, and hence no virtue. A mind that is absorbed by a toy, however gracious, however beautiful, however supposedly important, is obviously escaping from itself. Such a mind is always in disorder, and its actions produce further disorder, further confusion in the world.

Question: Doesn't the knowledge that life is impermanent bring suffering?

KRISHNAMURTI: Right, sir. But it is a fact that life is impermanent, isn't it? Your relations are impermanent, your thoughts are impermanent, your self-fulfillments, your ambitious drive and achievements are impermanent, because there is death. And why should one suffer because of impermanency? The fact is that there is impermanency. It is so. But you don't want to accept that fact; you say, "There must be something permanent." You have a picture of what permanency is, and therefore, when you are faced with impermanency, there is a feeling of despair. You put death, which is the essence of impermanency, in the distance, so there is an interval, a gap, between you and that which you call death. Here you are, living every day, carrying on with your routine, your worries, your frustrations, your ambitions, and there is death in the distance; and you think about that. You have seen death, and you know that you also will die one day, and you think about it. It is the thought of the future as impermanent that breeds fear. Please listen to this. But if you bring death—which you have put in the future—into the present while you are active, vital, strong, not diseased, then you are living with death; you are dying every minute to everything you know. After all, only that which ends can have a new beginning. Look at the spring. When the spring comes after the long winter, there are new leaves, there is something fresh, tender, young, innocent. But we are afraid to end; and ending, after all, is death. Take just one thing, something that gives you great pleasure, or great pain; take a memory that you have of somebody, a memory which causes you pain or pleasure, and end it, die to it, not tomorrow, but instantly. When you do that, you will find a new thing is happening, a new state of mind is coming into being. So there is creation only when the old has ceased.

May 27, 1965

Fifth Talk in Paris

The word is never the thing it represents; the word is not action. But most of us live in words, in images, in symbols, and therefore action doesn't bring about energy; and we dissipate whatever energy we have through contradiction within ourselves. We seldom realize that energy, or the passion of energy, comes through action; that action is energy. It is not that one must have energy first in order to act, but when one realizes that the word is not the thing, is not the act, and therefore begins to understand the structure, the meaning, the significance of the word, then there is action—and it is this action that brings about the passionate, sustained energy which has nothing whatsoever to do with enthusiasm. We cannot have the action which brings about energy as long as there is contradiction within ourselves; and most of us, consciously or unconsciously, do have many forms of self-contradiction, some of which we are aware of, and others of which we are unaware. Our whole life is caught up in this state of contradiction, and therefore there is no clear, direct action, which alone can bring about energy. And energy is necessary, not only physical energy, but also a sustained, passionate energy which enables the mind to go right through any one action completely. So it seems to me very important to understand the nature of this contradiction: the contradiction between the word and the act, the contradiction between the conscious intentions and pursuits on the one hand, and the unconscious urges, the hidden demands, the secret desires and pursuits, on the other. This contradiction, in various forms, exists in all our activities, in all the desires and pursuits of human existence.

I think most of us are aware of this contradiction within ourselves, if we are at all conscious of our own activities, of our own thoughts and state of being. Therefore one tries to bring about an integration within oneself, and I think such an act of attempted integration is sheer folly. You cannot integrate the opposites; you cannot possibly integrate love and hate. Either you hate or you love—there can be no combination of both, no integration of the opposites. So I think we should be very clear, at least for this morning, that the attempt to bring about integration within oneself has no meaning at all. What has meaning is the understanding of contradiction, and therefore being free of it.

To be free of contradiction, one has first to be aware of it; and perhaps some of us are not aware of it. We just carry on. And when we are aware of this extraordinary contradiction, which exists not only in our outward life but also very deeply within us, what happens? We find no solution for it, no freedom from it, so either we turn to what we call God, to the whole structure of belief, dogma, ritual, and authority which generally goes by the name of religion, or we take life as it comes and give it no significance at all—which is what many modern writers are trying to do. They have denied the whole structure of the church, of organized religion—which any intelligent man must do, for it has no meaning whatsoever—but then they are forced to face their own contradictions, their own hates, hopes, frustrations, their utter helplessness, and so they say, "This life has no meaning; let's make the best of it," and they invent a philosophy of despair. So there are these two extremes, which are in contradiction with each other.

Now, I feel it is possible to totally eradicate all contradiction—but not by an act of will because will again breeds contradiction in itself. Will is in essence contradiction. I think one has to understand this fact very deeply because we are brought up to exercise every form of will; we are taught to overcome, to deny, to assert, to determine. And if one observes the nature of will, one sees that will is in itself a form of resistance, and therefore it is inherently a state of contradiction.

So, living in this world, carrying on with one's job, one's family, going through the whole business of modern life, is it at all possible to live without any contradiction whatsoever, at any level of one's being, either outwardly or within the skin? Is it possible to have no contradiction at all, and therefore to act in such a way that action itself is energy? If one observes oneself, one sees that the more physically active one is, the more energy one has. It is not the other way around; it is not that you must have energy to act. On the contrary: the more you act, the more energy there is, biologically as well as psychologically. Action itself is energy—it's not a matter of action and then energy, or energy and then action. It's not idea first, and then action. Idea never gives this sustained energy, though it may give a stimulation, a momentary enthusiasm. It is action which brings about the energy from which further action derives.

To understand the contradiction in our life, one has to go into it very deeply—and that is our difficulty. We want to be told what to do; we want to conform to a pattern, or follow somebody, hoping thereby to sublimate, deny or suppress every form of contradiction—all of which is very superficial. So, to go into this question of contradiction, one must penetrate much deeper. You know, the depth is not comparable to the surface. The surface is one thing, but the depth is another. Most of us live on the surface, and therefore, when we try to move inward, we merely go through the motions; there is an activity which we call going inward, and that in itself breeds a contradiction. I hope I am making myself clear.

When I use the words *to go deeply,* I do not mean going from the outside to the inside. If you do that, then there is immediately a contradiction between the outer and the inner. To go deeply is to understand contradiction—and it is necessary to understand contradiction if we are to bring about peace, not only within ourselves, but in the society of which we are a part. We must have peace, not war and peace. Peace now is only an interval between two wars. To understand this extraordinary state of contradiction, which is very complex and very subtle, we cannot just deal with it outwardly, or try to patch up the symptoms, but one has to go to the very root of it.

The root of contradiction is the division between the thinker and the thought. For most of us there is a wide gap between the observer and the observed, between the thinker and the thought, between the center which experiences and the thing which is experienced; and it is this interval, gap, or time lag which is the real source of contradiction.

I hope that you are not merely listening to the words—which is not an act of listening—but are using the words of the speaker to discover for yourself this wide gap between idea and action, this actual state of division between the thinker and the thought, with the thinker trying to control, dominate, change, or suppress thought, trying to be peaceful. As long as there is a thinker, a censor of the good and the bad, there must be this constant division which the thinker creates and which obviously gives nourishment to contradiction. This is a fact which you must discover for yourself, and not merely accept because someone else tells you it is so; and the very act of discovery is the beginning of that energy with which you can approach the root problem of contradiction. There is a vast difference between being told what it is like to be hungry, and the actual hunger which you know for yourself. Similarly, if you merely accept this division between the thinker and the thought because you are told it exists, then it will have no revealing vitality. But if you discover the division for yourself, if you see it as an actual fact, then that very perception of the fact brings the energy that is necessary to deal with this contradiction.

I hope it is fairly clear so far.

You see, when there is a great contradiction in the mind, it brings about a certain tension. The greater the tension, and the greater your capacity to express yourself—as a writer, as an artist, as a politician—the more misery you create, not only for yourself, but for the public also. I do not know if you have observed this fact. Being in a state of contradiction, if one has the capacity to write, or to paint, or if one is unfortunately a politician, then one creates greater misery for man and also for oneself.

So one has to understand the enormous depth and the significance of contradiction, and thereby be completely free of it, because otherwise there is no love. All that we know of love is a state of contradiction, with its jealousy, hate, antagonism. Love is not the sensual pleasure which we call love, nor is it the so-called love that goes with hate, envy, ambition. An ambitious man can never know what love is, obviously. When an ambitious man, a man who is competitive, talks about peace, it has no meaning. There is peace only when your mind is noncompetitive, noncomparing, and therefore there is no contradiction within yourself. So, to bring about a different structure of society, a different social existence, one must inevitably understand the nature and the significance of this contradiction within oneself.

Most of us are trying to fulfill ourselves, whether through painting, through writing, through doing this or that, or through the family—which is again an indication of contradiction. Then you will say, "Mustn't man express himself? Isn't it his nature to do so?" But surely we are putting the cart before the horse, aren't we? Why this extraordinary insistence on expression? You may or may not express yourself, but if you insist on expressing yourself objectively—in painting, in writing a poem or a book, in a gesture, or what you will—then that very insistence is an indication of contradiction.

So, as I was pointing out, the root of contradiction is this division between the thinker and the thought; and the two cannot be integrated. But if you observe the structure of the thinker, you will see that the thinker is not, when thought is not. It is thought that breeds the thinker, the experiencer, the entity who creates time and is the source of fear.

Most of us have many forms of fear. Please watch your own fears as we are talking about it; deeply inside, see your own secret fears. Obviously, there is the ultimate fear of death. Being afraid of death, we try to escape from it through belief, through such ideas as resurrection, reincarnation, and so on and on. Either you rationalize death or you have a belief; and both rationalization and belief are an avoidance of death, an escape from it, and that creates a contradiction.

We regard death as something opposite to living. But to understand death, we must understand life, which means that we must examine our life and find out what it is. What is our life—not theoretically or hypothetically, not as it should be, but what is it actually? It is a series of memories, a bundle of accumulated experiences, of misery and pain, of joy and despair; it is the agony and longing of loneliness, the turmoil of the good and the bad, of health and disease. That is what we call our life, and that is all we know. Our life is endless conflict, endless misery and confusion. I am not exaggerating. This is the actual fact, and we do not know how to solve it, how to understand it. We do not know how to go beyond this misery, how to end sorrow; so we escape either through religion, or through the assertion that life has no meaning at all, no significance whatsoever, therefore let us live for today.

So one has to understand life totally to free oneself from all this misery—and it is possible to do that. Then living is not different from dying. Then there is not this gap, this wide interval of time created by the thinker, in which the thinker is always breeding fear. To understand what living is, is to die every day, without argument, to all your misery, to all your problems, to all your pleasures. That is what is going to happen when you die physically. You die without argument; you can't discuss with death. Similarly, one must die to sorrow. But we never die to sorrow because we do not know what real joy is, nor have we the capacity or the understanding to end suffering; and we prefer to be in sorrow, with all its self-pity, commiseration, and so on and so on, rather than to enter into something we do not know.

Please observe these facts for yourself. I am not trying to impose anything on you, the listener. We are neither agreeing nor disagreeing. We are just observing the facts, the actual *what is;* and that very observation of *what is* brings the energy which is action.

So one has to understand the nature of self-contradiction, and one can understand it only when one observes the whole structure of the thinker with his thoughts, with his hopes, with his despairs—the thinker who is creating a constant contradiction between himself, as the censor, and the thing in himself which he observes. Therefore to observe *what is* requires great seriousness, not a flippancy of observation. It is only the serious person who is living; the superficial person is not really living at all. He may have wealth, property, position, but he knows nothing of life. He knows only the surface of life. To understand this whole structure of oneself, one must come to it, not with a determination to change, not with an effort to be different, but merely with a willingness to observe *what is.* Then there is no contradiction because the observer is no longer acting as a censor, as one who condemns, who denies, who says what is right and what is wrong, what is good and what is bad. This doesn't mean that you live a most superficial life. On the contrary, to come to that point when there is no censor, you have to understand your whole conditioning. It is not just a matter of assertion. To understand it, you have to work at it; and then you will see that the mind becomes merely an observer. Such a mind is no longer in a state of contradiction, and therefore it has tremendous energy. That energy is love, passion—not physical passion, that is fairly easy, fairly common, that is the lust everybody knows. What I am talking about is the passion which has no cause and therefore no contradiction, no motive and therefore no end. Where there is love, there is also death; the two cannot be separated because love has no ambition.

Please, I am stating these things, but they will have value for you, actual meaning, only if this contradiction totally comes to an end.

Love and death must be, for creation to be. Do you know what creation is? Not the expression of capacity—that is very simple to understand. You may express yourself as a writer, as a poet, as an artist, but that is not creation. Creation is something entirely different. You know, creation can come about only when there is energy which has never been contaminated by will, which is not the result of effort—that energy which action itself brings. At present all our activity is more or less self-centered—it is centered upon ourselves in relation to various things; and this self-centered activity, which is the activity of the thinker, invariably breeds contradictions. Being in a state of contradiction, the mind demands some form of expression: I must escape, I must write, I must do this or that. The man who is in a state of self-contradiction, which is a state of self-centered activity, and who happens to be a painter, an artist, a musician, may call what he does creation, but it is not. Creation must be, and is, something totally different.

Now, as I have said, the mind which is untouched by contradiction, having understood the whole structure of it, conscious as well as unconscious, is completely still because any movement is a dissipation of energy. It is only when the mind is completely still with tremendous energy that there is an explosion; and that explosion is creation, which may or may not express itself. A mind that is afraid, ambitious, greedy, envious, jealous, competitive—such a mind can never have this energy which is brought about by action without a motive; nor can it ever know what love is, obviously. Where there is love, there is a constant dying to all the memories of every day's experience, and therefore love and death always go together. Love is always fresh, new, young, innocent, uncontaminated by the past, because it dies to every day's past. Love and death exist in this tremendous energy when this energy is completely quiet. Then there is creation—or call it by whatever name you will. The name has very little importance. Unless this transformation comes about in each human being—who is part of society, who is society itself—there cannot be a new society.

Question: Will it not take time for the individual human being to come to this transformation?

KRISHNAMURTI: No, it is not a question of time. Through time you will never come to anything. Time will only breed disorder.

Question: What do you mean by self-knowledge?

KRISHNAMURTI: I think I have made it sufficiently clear, sir, but let me explain it once more.

We have always used time as a means of achievement: I am this, and I will become that. There is an interval between *what is* and 'what should be'. We say that to achieve 'what should be' takes time; one needs many days, many years, or many incarnations, as they believe in the East. So we use time as a means of achieving the 'what I will be'. The 'what I will be' is a projection of what I am; or it is the opposite of what I am, a contradiction of *what is.* So between *what is* and 'what should be' there is a time interval, and during that interval many other factors come into play. The 'what should be' isn't a static thing because there are other factors all the time operating. All kinds of influences, pressures, changes are happening in the interval, and therefore the 'what should be' is always altering; and the *what is* is also undergoing a tremendous change. So the 'what should be' is not important at all; the ideal, the end, the purpose, the hoped-for achievement, has no meaning because it is fictitious. It has no reality, it is nothing but an idea. What has reality is *what is.* I am miserable, I am suffering, I am confused—that is the only significant factor, and to understand *what is,* time will not help. Time is merely an avoidance, a postponement, an escape into unreality. To understand *what is,* there must be no hypothesis, no looking to the future. But you see, that means we have to apply ourselves to the problem, to the *what is,* immediately, with our whole being—and that is something we don't want to do. We say, "I will do it tomorrow." We are frightened, miserable, unhappy, jealous, but we don't say, "I want to end jealousy immediately." We want to find out how to end it eventually, and therefore time becomes a means of escape from *what is.* But time will never change *what is,* and therefore time brings disorder, not order. This is so simple.

To understand all this is self-knowing. Self-knowing is not something extraordinary;

it is the perception of what is actually going on. I am in misery, I am anxious, frustrated, in despair—don't you know all these things? So what happens? I use tomorrow, the 'what should be', as a means of escaping from *what is,* or I look to the past. I am not healthy today, I am ill, but I have been healthy in the past, so my mind goes back in memory to the state which I called health and says, "I wish I could be healthy again." Therefore there is a strain, there is an effort, there is the pressure of past remembrances. Whereas, if I do not bring in past remembrances at all but see the actual fact that I am ill, and not let thought—with its memories of how good it was when I was healthy—interfere with the organism, then the organism brings into play its own curative powers.

Again, to understand all this is part of self-knowing—it is self-knowing. It is not an imposed self-knowledge, but you understand for yourself this process of thought, of thinking, the whole structure of your own being. And self-knowing is not a matter of time. I don't say, "I will understand myself little by little, day after day; self-knowledge will come gradually." It never comes gradually. You have to see the self, the 'me', with all its struggles, completely; and it can only be seen completely now, not tomorrow. To see it completely, you must give your whole energy to it.

Question: What is the relationship between action and meditation?

KRISHNAMURTI: What is action for most of us? Action is based on an idea, on comparative values. We say, "I should do this," so the only action we know is a contradiction between the idea and the act. That much is clear, isn't it? I won't go into detail; we have not the time, but that is what is actually taking place. I have an idea brought about through experience, through thought, through knowledge or information, through fear and escapes, and I approximate my action to that idea. That is the only action we know. Now, action without idea, action which does not create contradiction and is not the result of contradiction—to understand the nature of such action is part of meditation.

I do not know to what extent you are familiar with that word *meditation.* In the East it is a very familiar word, and being very familiar, it is also very traditional. Meditation, there, is a thing that you can practice. You discipline, control, you shape your thought according to a pattern. There is a set of rules for it: the way you sit, the way you breathe, the way you move. There are various systems of meditation, and if you follow this or that system, they say you will get results. Of course you will get results. That is fairly obvious, isn't it? If I do something over and over and over again, day after day, month in and month out, I am bound to get a result; but the result is a projection of a mind which is petty, small, stupid. The mind is conforming to a pattern; therefore, there is no freedom, and such meditation is no meditation at all. It is merely conformity to a pattern through which you hope to achieve peace, God, or whatever else it is you are after. A petty, bourgeois, frustrated little mind may sit down to "meditate"; it may practice discipline, control, and shape its activity according to a pattern; but it will always remain petty, and its "God" will be equally petty. When once you see the truth of that for yourself, you reject that whole approach to meditation, and in the very rejecting of it, you are free from this old idea that you must conform to what has been established. Being free, enormously free, for you there is no longer any contradiction in action; there is no conformity to an idea, or to the pattern which has been established by tradition, by the sayings and the habits of innumerable people. When you are free of all that because you understand it, then you begin to meditate; and meditation is one of the most marvelous things if you know how to do it—not "how," but if you do it.

Meditation requires the total understanding of the self, and therefore freedom from the psychological structure of society. This means that you are no longer ambitious, greedy, envious, trying to achieve, trying to become, and hence there is no effort; therefore, the mind is completely still, not made still by discipline, control, breathing, and all the rest of those stupid, little tricks, nor by drugs. Then the mind becomes extraordinarily active and quiet. To be active and quiet, the mind must be silent; it must be full of energy and yet empty.

But you see, most of us want experience. Of course, and that is why people try to meditate. They have had all the usual physical, intellectual, and emotional experiences, and they want more, so they take drugs. There are several drugs on the market to give you a stimulus and enable you to have certain unusual experiences. Now, one has to understand the nature of experience. If you had no experiences at all, you would go to sleep. If there were no pressures on you, if you were not being pushed around by society, by books, by every form of influence, you would go to sleep immediately because what you want is safety, comfort, security. Having had all the ordinary kinds of experience, you are fed up, bored with it, and being fairly sensitive and subtle, you now want wider, deeper experience; but it is still the same movement.

Now, when you understand the whole nature of experience, you no longer pursue the outward stimuli which give you experiences. Having rejected all that, you then have an inward stimulus, which creates its own experience. That is why in what they call meditation many people see visions—and they love to see visions, and experience all the other childish things which are the result of their own conditioning. When you have understood all this, it is only then that the mind is still, quiet. In that silence there is no experiencing at all because such a mind is alive, clear, it is a light unto itself; being totally awake, it is beyond all experience—and all of this is meditation.

May 30, 1965

Saanen, Switzerland, 1965

First Talk in Saanen

As there are going to be several talks here, I think it would be good to begin with the understanding of what is communication. I feel it is very important to see the nature and the structure of verbal communication. We have to use words, but unfortunately each word is interpreted by you as well as by the speaker according to a certain reference, or a memory, or an incident, or an experience; we are always using words and translating them according to our pleasures, our likes and dislikes, and so communication becomes extremely difficult. If we don't commune or communicate with each other, then there is no point in meeting at all, or getting together for a talk like this. So it seems to me that it is vitally important to understand each other.

Communication is not one-sided. It is not that you are merely listening to the speaker and trying to understand what he is talking about, but rather communication is a two-way process: you have to communicate with the speaker, and the speaker has to communicate with you. Communication can exist only when both of us intend to communicate and are so much with our intention that we are capable of real intensity at the same time and at the same level. Otherwise communication is not possible. Unless we are both looking in the same direction, you and I cannot see the same thing. So we must be quite sure that we are looking together in the same direction, and then what we talk about is communicable. Otherwise it becomes extremely difficult to communicate what one wants to convey. So, from the very beginning, we must be very clear in what direction we are looking, and whether both of us are looking in the same direction. You may be looking south, and I may be looking north, and then communication is not possible.

To communicate with each other, we must find out what it is that we are seeking, what it is that we are both looking for—if we are looking, if we are seeking. Life has so many problems, both individual and collective, conscious and unconscious, so many tortures, such despair, anxiety—the conflict in the family, the uncertainty of a job, the ceaseless effort to adjust oneself to a particular relationship—and you may be seeking a way out of it. Or, being tortured, being in despair, uncertain, one seeks a certainty, a hope, a something that will give comfort. Perhaps that is what most of us are doing—perhaps that is what you are doing—and the speaker may not be doing anything of that kind at all. You may be seeking something, and the speaker may be saying, "Don't seek at all." If you are seeking, and the speaker is saying, "Don't seek," obviously there is no communication. So you have to understand what the speaker is saying, and the speaker has to understand what you are trying to do—and that is what we are both going to do this morning.

How are you going to find out what the speaker wants to convey when he says, "Don't seek at all"? The speaker is saying, "Don't inquire, don't look around, don't look to any teacher, to any group, to any organization, to any particular system of thought; don't go to any analyst, don't seek any help from outside"—and you will have to understand what he means by that, why he says it. Is it irrational, unreasonable, stupid? Has it no meaning? You will find out when you and the speaker have established a relationship, that is, when both of us are looking in the same direction, for then communication becomes extraordinarily simple, easy, and vital.

Another difficulty in communication is that we don't listen. It is possible to listen to that airplane that is coming back, without any resistance, without any annoyance or irritation; you can just listen to it. But it is very difficult to listen in that way, and particularly to somebody who is saying something entirely the opposite of what you think, or what you want to hear. To listen without judging, without evaluating, without accepting or denying, but just to listen—that is one of the most difficult things to do because how can one listen when one is tortured, when one is caught in the net of uncertainties, when one is angry, furious with oneself, with society, with the environment in which one lives? So it is extremely difficult to listen quietly, and it seems to me that one can learn really deeply and profoundly only when one does listen quietly, without any demand, without asking a question and waiting for an answer; just to listen.

So we have several things to do together. Although it's hot in the tent, we have to work hard together this morning, not casually, but seriously and with full intent. But very few people are serious. One is serious about one's own personal, limited problems, but that seriousness is a very trivial affair. There is a deep seriousness which is not personal, particular, but which arises when you have a certain anxious problem. It is this quality of deep seriousness that is required to find out, to communicate—not the superficial seriousness of a mind that says, "I must tackle my problem and resolve it," or, "I must find the truth, I must do this and that," which seems to me such a trivial affair when there is a tremendous issue involved.

So this morning, and every morning that we meet here, we are going to work together. It is not only the speaker who is going to work but you also because, as I said, communication is a two-way process. The speaker is not conveying something to you, nor are you trying to understand the speaker, but we are trying to understand together the extraordinary problem of living as a total human being, caught as we are in a particular society, in a particular environment, entrapped in religious organizations, caught up in family life with all its problems, its jealousies, its fears, its acceptances, its dominations—a life which seems to indicate that there is no meaning at all to existence, a life which has become a routine, a habit. Caught in all that, we try to solve our problems within the limitations of our own thoughts, our own conditioning. But this whole problem must be approached as a movement of life, and in understanding the total problem, perhaps we shall then be able to resolve our own particular little problems. That is, one has to understand the total rather than the particular. The understanding of the particular will not lead to the understanding of the total. After all, our life is broken up into various fragments. There is the fragment of the nationalists, the fragment of a mind that is seeking peace outside of society, outside of the family, the fragment that goes to church, that follows a particular doctrine or philosophy, the fragment that believes, that has tremendous hope in some fantastic mystical affair, and so on; and we approach the total through the fragment. We look at the whole from the periphery, and the speaker is saying that it is not possible ever to understand this totality of living, which includes all the fragments, from a fragmentary or peripheral outlook.

So, caught in the fragment of a particular problem, of a particular issue, of a particular torture, despair, as most of us are, how is one to look at the total, at the whole of life? It is only by looking at the whole that you can really understand and be free of the particular. But merely to understand the particular, and then try to grasp the whole through the particular, has no meaning at all, and it can never be done. When you look with clarity at those marvelous mountains, at the trees, at the river, at the extraordinary light of an evening, at the moon over the snow, as one could do last night, you see it all as a whole; and if you don't see it as a whole, you don't really see it at all. If you are merely concentrating on a particular pine tree, then you miss the beauty of the whole scene—the extraordinary vitality of the mountains, of the light of the moon, of the forest, of the river.

So, for a mind which is caught in the network of a particular problem, of a particular individual, it becomes extremely difficult to see the whole. And how is it possible—I am using the word *how,* not to offer a method, but merely as a question—how is it possible for a fragment, for a mind that is caught in a particular issue, to see the whole and therefore to act, not from the particular, but as a whole?

I hope I am making the issue clear. My point is this: You have to see the whole map of life—the whole of it. The absurdities, the chicanery, the brutality, the appalling wars, the so-called peace, the uncertainty, the fear of death, the beliefs, the gods, the saviors—you have to see all that, not from the particular point of view of a Christian, of a Hindu, of a Zen Buddhist, or God knows what else, but you have to see the whole of it; and if you see the whole, then I think you will be able to answer the particular. You have to see the whole picture, but not just intellectually, verbally, not as an idea, not as a concept. You can't have a concept of those mountains: you either look and see or you don't see. You can't have a concept of the beauty of the moonlight on the snow. If you have a concept of it, you don't see it, you are not directly in communion with that light, with that beauty. Similarly, you must see the whole picture of life, and in seeing the whole picture, you will then be able to answer the particular, the personal issues, problems, tortures, miseries, and all the rest of it.

That is what I am going to talk about this morning.

A mind that is very personal, that is concerned about itself, caught up in its problems, its tortures, its beliefs, its vanities, its despairs, its experiences, its pettiness—such a mind cannot possibly see the whole. And unless you see the whole, you cannot answer your particular problems. You may think you can, but you will only create more misery, more confusion, more torture. I think this is fairly obvious—that unless you see the totality of existence, do what you will, there is no way out of your confusion.

Take a nationalist, for example. He is a stupid entity because he is trying to solve his problems in a narrow little field called nationalism. He is like the man who is caught in a particular system of philosophy or religion, and who is trying to find truth through that system—which is impossible. He may become very clever, cunning, or philosophical within the limited space of his own intellect; but to be free of confusion and misery, he must understand the whole of life, nonverbally, nonconceptually, nonideationally.

So, is it possible to see the whole of life, not through analysis, not through intellectual concepts, not through intellectually breaking up the whole into various parts and then joining them together, but can one see the whole of life at once? Is such a thing possible? Now, to understand the possibility of it, one has to go beyond the various states in which the mind says, "I understand, I see." That is, you can only see the totality of something nonintellectually, nonconsciously. When you make an effort to listen, for example, you miss half of what is being said; but if you listen unconsciously, as it were, then you are taking in much more than you do through conscious or calculated listening. Am I conveying anything at all?

If I consciously make an effort to listen to what you are saying, most of my energy has gone into that conscious, concentrated effort; but if I am listening to you very casually, that is, attentively but easily, then what you are saying goes much more into the unconscious, and it takes root. I don't know if you have experimented with this—you must have.

We are trying to find out whether it is possible to see the totality of life, and not be caught in the particular, because it is only when we understand the totality, the whole picture of life, that the particular issues and problems can be resolved. If that is true, factual, as I think it is, then the question is: How is the mind to see the totality of existence?

The conscious mind can never see the totality. The conscious mind is the individual mind, whereas the unconscious mind is never individual. The unconscious mind is the race; it is the collective experience of man. Outwardly the various races may have different colors, and you may live in America, in Russia, or in India, but in essence the unconscious is everywhere the same; therefore, in the unconscious there is no individuality. It is shaped and limited by the racial or collective tendency, the vast, hidden inheritance of man, and therefore it is not an individual, a separate entity.

Please, this requires a great deal of thinking, of going into, so don't accept or deny it, but rather inquire into it.

If we look at the whole of life through the conscious mind, what happens? Listen, for example, to that airplane—do listen to it. If you listen to it consciously, then you are limited, and you are irritated by it. But if you listen to it with all your being, then you will find that something quite different takes place.

Now, the conscious mind is the educated, the modern, the technically-trained mind.

Please do listen to this; don't agree or disagree, but just listen. For goodness' sake, somebody is already shaking his head! If you immediately say that it cannot be, or that it is or is not so, then you are obviously not listening. What is being said may be totally wrong, but to find out you have to listen without saying, "Sorry, I don't agree"—which is so stupid. To find out the truth of the matter, you have to listen, and to listen, you can't have an opinion, you can't have a concept—and that is where our trouble is going to be from now on. If you have a concept of the conscious mind as being this or that, and of the unconscious as being something else, then that concept is guiding you, shaping your thought, and therefore you are not listening. Hence you say, "Well, I agree with what you are talking about," or, "I disagree"; but it is not a matter of agreement or disagreement. We are trying to find out what is the fact, and when something is found to be a fact, there is no question of agreement. What is being said is so, or it is not so; but to start right off by saying, "I disagree"—well, that is too juvenile.

You see, we are trying to look at the totality of life; and life is immense, it is not just the superficial layers of our daily existence. Life is something immense, extraordinarily subtle, fluid, moving, it has no static position; and it is not possible to understand the totality of this extraordinary movement of life through the conscious mind, with all its beliefs, concepts, idiosyncrasies, with its fragmentary outlook, because such an outlook does not give you a total perception. That is all I am saying.

Now, if you understand that when the conscious mind makes an effort to look at the whole picture of life, it has no value at all, then you stop looking in that way. This means that you no longer have concepts, beliefs; you are just looking. You do not look through a concept, through a philosophy, through a system of thought, through a particular hope; but that, of course, is up to you. And if one doesn't look through the conscious mind, then how is one looking? Then one has the unconscious, but the unconscious is still the reservoir of the past, isn't it? It may no longer be "my" reservoir, "my" storehouse, but it is still the storehouse of man. That collective experience of man through millions of years I may now interpret differently, and that interpretation may give me pleasure or pain; but as long as I am burdened with this collective content of the unconscious, obviously I cannot see the whole.

Am I making something clear—that you cannot see the totality of life, the whole picture of life, either consciously or unconsciously? Do you understand what I am saying? That is, to look at the totality of life, at the whole immense, marvelous picture of life, there must be no platform from which you look—no background of belief, experience, or knowledge, either conscious or unconscious.

You know, most of us are not aware of how we look at somebody. How do you generally look at a person sitting next to you? Either you don't like him—he is hot, bothersome, fat, ugly, smelly—or you like him or her. You look with dislike or with pleasure—and your dislike or your pleasure prevents you from looking. Or you are totally unaware that you are sitting next to a person because you are so consumed with your ideas. Surely, you can look at a person sitting next to you, or opposite you, only when there is no pleasure or dislike. The pleasure or dislike may be conscious or unconscious; it may be positive, or it may be negative, a feeling of which you are not aware; but really to look at somebody, there must obviously be freedom from all this. Only then are you capable of looking.

So looking is neither conscious nor unconscious. If you make an effort to look at a person, it becomes conscious, and then you say, "I don't like him, but I must treat him as my brother." What nonsense that is! You are making a positive effort based on a conclusion, a concept, and therefore you have no relationship with that person except as an idea. And if you unconsciously draw away from him because you are intellectually superior, emotionally more refined, and God knows what else, then again you have no relationship with that person. So to look, to listen, is an act which is beyond the conscious as well as the unconscious; and when the mind is capable of looking in that way, then the barrier to total perception ceases; and from there you can act about your particular problem.

I hope we are both communicating with each other—which means that you are actually doing this and are not just listening, hearing, understanding verbally, and then trying to put it into action. There is only action, which is the act of listening.

So one's personal problems as a human being cannot be resolved totally unless one understands the immensity, the complete picture of life; and one can see the totality, the immensity of life only when one perceives the futility of every belief, every dogma, every experience, every philosophy.

Comment: In completely listening to the speaker, one becomes the speaker.

KRISHNAMURTI: The speaker is not important. What is important is that one understands this immensity of life. If you have listened rightly to all that the speaker has said this morning, really listened to it, you have seen the totality, and from there you will act. That is why I have pointed out how important it is to communicate. I believe they are making a great study of communication, because to communicate needs sanity. If we don't know how to communicate with each other—if I don't know how to communicate with you, and you don't know how to communicate with me, or with your husband, your wife, or your child—then we live in a world of mounting confusion, which leads to more misery. So communication becomes extraordinarily important, even about the tiniest little thing, like where the salt is. If you don't give me exact directions where the salt is, I shall wander around looking for it, whereas if you tell me exactly and clearly where it is, the matter is finished.

So it is very important to be able to communicate with each other clearly because that is the basis of sanity. It may take time. We may have to use different words; we may have to deny one thing and assert another, and then deny what is asserted. We have to keep moving together because communication is not a static thing, it is a movement, and both of us must be capable of moving with it. Therefore there is not at any time either agreement or disagreement—and that is the beauty of listening.

Question: To see the totality of life, must there not be attention?

KRISHNAMURTI: When you see something, what actually takes place? There is the observer and the thing observed, isn't there? You see the speaker sitting here, which means there is a 'you' who is looking, seeing; so you are the observer, and the speaker is the thing observed. In what we call seeing, there is this division between the seer and the thing seen. Now, is that seeing? When I look at a tree, there is the tree and the 'me' who is looking at it—we are two separate facts. In looking at that tree, I am the observer—with all my memories, my misfortunes, the whole human business—and that tree is the thing observed. Surely, that is not really seeing the tree, though it is a visual fact. To actually see the tree in the sense I am talking about, the observer must come to an end.

What is communion? When you and your husband, or your wife, or a friend are communing together, are there two separate entities? When you love somebody, if you do, is there you and that person? If there is, it ceases to be love. As long as I am conscious that I am looking at that tree, I am not looking at it, though I may identify myself with it and think I am that tree—which is too silly.

So it requires tremendous attention, a tremendous understanding of oneself, of the totality of life, to look at something—at a tree, or a mountain, or a person. Then communication is possible.

If I may suggest something—and please don't do it just because I am suggesting it—look at a tree this afternoon, be quiet with a tree. Don't take a novel, or a radio, and then sit under a tree, but go to it alone; be quiet with it, just sit and watch without thought, without anxiety, without fear, without loneliness. And if you watch, you will see how disturbed you are, how restless, how "city-sophisticated" your mind is. But if you can put all that aside and sit quietly—not dreamily, not in a state of ecstasy about some nonsense, but just look—then you will see for yourself that there is neither the observer nor the thing observed; and it is only then that there is beauty. Beauty is neither subjective nor objective, it is not a thing that is made by man or by nature. Beauty exists only when the mind is completely quiet, neither personal nor impersonal; and out of that silence an immensity comes.

July 11, 1965

Second Talk in Saanen

Shall we continue with what we were talking about the other day? I was saying that individual problems have no meaning in themselves except in relationship to the total process of life; and it is only when we understand the whole structure and meaning, the whole picture of life, that individual problems have significance and can be resolved. That is what I was saying the other day when we met here.

It is one of the most arduous and difficult things to perceive the total picture of life. Life is a continuous movement in relationship, and it is only when we understand that relationship as a whole—not in fragments, but as a whole—that we shall perhaps be able to resolve our individual problems. By problems I mean the difficulties that arise in one's life—the lack of understanding, the innumerable doubts and questions, the imbalance, the constant struggle to adjust oneself to a pattern of belief, or to an experience, or to a particular social norm. All these struggles create problems, difficulties, do they not? We know life only as a series of emotional, psychological, factual difficulties, and we are never able totally to resolve them. If we are at all aware of ourselves, we know that, on the contrary, we would rather run away from them. We are never capable of looking at our difficulties with cleareyed insight; we are never able to examine the pattern of our existence totally. When our innumerable hidden problems become acute and there is a crisis, we do become aware of them; but even then we do not know how to resolve these problems; we do not seem to have the intensity, or the clarity, or the knowledge to resolve them.

So what I am going to talk about this morning, if I may, is whether it is at all possible to be free of these problems in our daily life. When the mind is caught in any problem, whether one is conscious of it or not, it does affect the clarity of thought, it does affect one's daily activity. So it seems to me very important to understand these problems and be free of them, rather than to escape from them, or try to find a definite answer. One has to be aware of them first, one has to know what one's problems are—and even that requires a certain attention, an awareness. To resolve one's own problems, one must know what they are. It is no good going to an analyst, to a confessor, to this person or to that, all of which indicates an escape from the fact, from one's own actual problems.

So, as we are going into it, I hope you are listening to what is being said, not just as an objective, verbal statement, but in order to become aware of your own problems.

Do you know what I mean by a problem? It is something you have not understood, something that gnaws at the heart and mind, some torture that goes on repeating, repeating, repeating, and of which you are afraid. You have a dream that is repeating night after night, a dream which influences your activities during the day and from which you are trying to escape, or for which you are seeking an answer, an interpretation. Or you are afraid of death, of poverty, afraid of not being loved, of relationship. Or, driven by ambition, by vanity, there is the feeling that you are never fulfilled. One has so many problems, some of which one is not conscious or aware of, and one does not even know the limits of those problems. And one has to understand, surely, that a mind that is ridden by problems—however small, however petty, or however intense, vital, significant—cannot go far. Whatever the problems, they inevitably influence our thought, our activity; they shape our life, and unless one is extraordinarily free from problems, one cannot go very far.

Our problems are concerned with daily living: everyday activity, sex, love, the job, the fear of not being loved, loneliness, the sense of utter despair, the boredom of a life which has no meaning at all. Surely one has to be aware of all this because these things do influence the course of our action. We cannot possibly escape from them, and we cannot have worldly problems, daily problems, and yet try to find a deep inner life, a spiritual life, or whatever you wish to call it. The worldly life and the so-called inner life are not two separate strata, they are intimately related to each other. Without understanding and being free from the daily problems of life, however petty, however small, tyrannical, ugly—without this freedom, your search for a spiritual, inner life has no meaning whatsoever.

You can see the rationality of this. It is logical. It is not just my statement, which you can accept or deny, but it is so. Unless one's mind is free from worrying about money, about whether one is loved or not loved, about whether one will make a name in the world or not, with all the accompanying temptations, ugliness, and brutality; and unless one understands all the superficial problems of daily living, one's mind is utterly incapable of penetrating deeply into something that demands complete energy, something that is not to be sought after, that has no cause, no motive.

So one has to be aware of one's daily problems, of one's daily activities. And I hope you are becoming aware of them with me, because unless you are, we can't go very far this morning, or even during these talks. I would like to go very deeply, but you cannot go very deeply when your problems are choking you, blinding you. If you do, it is a mere escape, a verbal pursuit of some myth which has no reality whatsoever.

So, if one is aware of these problems, what is one to do? First of all, what do we mean by awareness—being aware of our problems? Please take your own particular problem, by which you are tortured. When you say, "I know I have a problem," what do you mean by that? You mean that you have a difficulty, a pain, or a pleasure you are afraid won't continue, don't you? In avoiding that pain, or in seeking the continuity of that pleasure, you say, "I am aware of my problem." Well, what do we mean by being aware of it? Are you aware of it as you are aware of that microphone? Is it something outside of you which you are looking at, or are you aware of it without any space between you and the thing which you are observing, without the division as the observer and the observed? If you are the observer, then you are trying to do something about the thing which you observe; you want to alter it, you want to bring about a situation in which that thing will not give you any more pain, or will give you a continuity of pleasure.

So a great deal depends on how you look at your problem, how you are aware of it, how you know it. Usually you know it as an outsider looking in, which means that what you look at is different from the image which you have of yourself. Each one of us has an image of himself, generally a rather pleasurable image, and from that image we look at the thing which gives us pain or pleasure.

Please do this as I am talking, because it will then become very interesting if we go further into it afterwards, as I hope we shall do this morning.

So you have an image of yourself as you are, or as you should be, or must be, and from that image you look at the thing which you call a problem. So there is the image, and the problem; and then you try to approximate the problem to that image, or you interpret the problem according to the pattern which the image has established. Is that not so? You, who have a particular image of yourself, look at the problem, which is not you; so there is a division, a contradiction between the problem and what you think you are, or what you think you should be; there is a constant conflict between what your image represents and the problem which contradicts that image.

May I proceed? Is it clear so far?

Now, the problem can never be resolved as long as the image exists—the image of what you should be, or the image which the mind has created of itself through knowledge, through history, through family tradition, through every form of experience. You are aware, not of the image, but of the problem. Whereas, what we are trying to do here is not to resolve the problem but to understand the structure of the image; because if you have no image of yourself, then you can deal with the problem.

One generally has an image of oneself as an extraordinary human being, or as a man who has failed, a man who is miserable, who must fulfill, who is vain, ambitious—you know the image which most people have of themselves. They think that they are God, or not God, that they are merely environment, that they are this or they are that. They have a dozen images of themselves, or one predominant image. Now, if I have an image of myself, then that image will contradict the facts of daily existence, and I am incapable of looking at the daily facts except through the eyes of that image. Therefore the problem is created by the image, and not by the fact itself.

Listen to what I am saying; don't deny it, don't accept it, take it in, but just look at it.

So then, why do I build an image of myself? I see that as long as I have a concept, an image, a conclusion about myself, problems will exist. So I am no longer concerned with the problem, with the difficulty; I am concerned now with understanding why I have these images, these concepts, these conclusions about myself. In the East people have the idea that they are God, they have innumerable concepts; and here in the West you also have your concepts, your images. Go to the communist world, and they have their images, too. Now, why do we build these images, these concepts?

Please, I am putting the question, and do try to find out. We are asking a fundamental, not a superficial, question. Most of us never ask ourselves a fundamental question, but this is a fundamental question we are asking ourselves now.

Why have I, who have lived forty, fifty, sixty, or whatever number of years it is that I have lived—why have I gathered this storehouseful of what I think, what I feel, what I am, what I should be, this accumulation of experience, knowledge? And if I had not done that, what would happen? Do you understand? If I had no concept about myself, what would happen to me? I would be lost, wouldn't I? I would be uncertain, terribly frightened of life. So I build an image, a myth, a concept, a conclusion about myself, because without this framework life would become for me utterly meaningless, uncertain, fearful. There would be no security. I may be secure outwardly; I may have a job, a house, and all the rest of it, but inwardly also I want to be completely secure; and it is the desire to be secure that compels me to build this image of myself—which is verbal. Do you understand? It has no reality at all; it is merely a concept, a memory, an idea, a conclusion.

Now, I see that to be a fact. That is, I am aware of it. Please proceed with me, let us do this together. I know why I have built up an image of myself, whether through conscious effort, or unconsciously, through the innumerable influences of society, of organized religion, of books. I know all that. I have built it up, and I see why I have built it up. Society demands it; and also, apart from society, I want to be completely sure of myself. Society helps me, and I help myself, to be that image, that idea, that conclusion, and I am aware of this whole process.

Now, I want to know what we mean by being aware of something. You are aware that you are hungry, nobody need tell you; it is not a secondhand experience. It is not something you have learned from a book. No teacher has taught you that you are hungry; no philosophy, no method, nothing has intervened. There is a reaction inside you which you call hunger—it is a firsthand experience. And are you aware of the structure, the meaning, and the nature of this image, as you are aware of your hunger? Do you understand what I mean? Is it something which you have realized, discovered for yourself, and nobody need tell you because it is your own perception, and not my description of it, which you have accepted? You know, when you have a toothache, or any other kind of pain, it is yours. Similarly, if you are aware of that image as something you have discovered for yourself, then nobody can take it away, dissipate or add to it. It is so. They may describe it, they may add more detail, but for you the fact is there. So, can we proceed?

Now, what happens when I am aware of the fact that I have built an image of myself—as aware of it as I am aware of hunger? You know, we are so used to making effort. From childhood we are encouraged to make effort, struggle, because we must be better than somebody else, do better than our uncle—you know, all the rest of that stupid stuff. We worship success, so we make effort. But here there is no effort needed at all because there is nothing to make effort about. Are you following? So I am just observing the fact that I have an image of myself. Any effort to change, to encourage, or to dissipate that image is to conform to another image which I have of myself. Is that clear? If I make an effort to dissipate or destroy the present image, that effort springs from still another image which I have made of myself, and which says that this present image must not be.

Am I mesmerizing you all, or are we actually doing this?

As I said at the beginning, there must be freedom—not just freedom from some stupid, little anxieties and all the rest of it, but complete freedom. And freedom is not a reaction. A reaction is merely a revolt within the prison, it is not freedom. A mind that is crippled with problems can never be free. Whether it is the problem of death, the problem of your dreams—whatever the problem may be, as long as it exists there is no freedom. The problem is not important at all, but what is important is the image which you have of yourself. If you have no image at all, if the mind is completely free of all images, then you can deal with any issue that arises, and it is no problem at all. Are you following?

So the mind is aware that it has created an image of itself, and that to try to dissipate, or to resolve, or to do anything about that image, springs from still another image which is much deeper and which says, "I must not create an image." Any effort to alter the present image is the outcome of a deeper image, a deeper conclusion. I see that to be a fact; therefore, the mind is not making any effort to dispel the image. Are you following? So the mind is completely aware of the image without any desire, without any effort, without any alteration; it is just aware of it, just looking at it. I look at that microphone, and I can't do anything about it. It is there, it has been put together. Similarly, the mind looks at the image, at the conclusion it has about itself, without any form of effort; and that is real attention. In that observation you will discover there is tremendous discipline—not the silly discipline of conformity. Because there is no effort to alter it, the mind itself is that image. It is not the mind and the image, but the mind is the image. Any movement on the part of the mind to identify itself with that image or to destroy it is the creation or the urge of another image. Therefore the mind is completely aware that it is itself the creator of the image.

If you really see this fact, then the image loses its significance altogether. Then the mind is capable of dealing with any issue, any crisis that arises, without a previous conclusion of the image from which it tries to answer. The mind is now clear of all images, and therefore it has no static position, no platform from which it observes, no belief, no dogma, no experience as knowledge from which it is approaching the issue. So the mind can now be completely with any issue that arises, and doesn't treat it as a problem. Problems exist only when there is a contradiction. But here there is no contradiction. I have no image, no center, no conclusions from which I look; hence there is no contradiction, and therefore no problem.

As I said at the beginning, life is a movement in relationship, not only with people, but relationship with everything—with nature, with money, with ideas. Life is a movement, and when you are moving with life, it has no problem. It is only when there is a static state from which you are trying to understand that life becomes a problem. The worldly life is the only life which you have to understand, not the spiritual life. When you are no longer driven by ambition, greed, envy, no longer seeking fame, and when all the things that go to make up what we call the worldly life are completely in order—and they must be in order—then there is a totally different movement which the mind cannot previously imagine, believe in, or come to a conclusion about. There is only the movement of life, but we have divided it as the worldly movement and the spiritual movement, the outer life and the inner life. We have made the inner life something apart. Because we are tired of this worldly life, with its ugliness, its brutality—you know what is going on—we try to escape from it, try to establish within ourselves a spiritual life, which is so silly. You can't establish a spiritual life for yourself without first having complete order, and order means freedom. Then you will find that there is a totally different kind of life, not created by the mind—a life that has no cause, no end, no beginning; it is a movement. But do what you will—sit in any posture, do all the tricks that you like—you cannot possibly come to or understand that movement unless there is complete order, which means freedom from the outward, everyday struggle, pain, sorrow, greed, ambition.

Comment: There are many problems—social, economic, national—which I am not responsible for.

KRISHNAMURTI: There is starvation in Asia; there is misery, poverty, disease, terrible things of which you know nothing here. But who is responsible for it? You know, through automation, through the perfection of the computer, through cybernetics, and so on, science is now able to free man from the drudgery of certain kinds of work. Science can give food, clothing, and shelter to the whole world; but why isn't it being done? Don't agree with me, for God's sake. Just look. It is because we are nationalistic. The glory of France, the way of life of the Americans, the Indian nationalism, the African nationalism, the imperialism of the communists as well as of the capitalists—all these things are separating man economically. And religiously man is separated by his beliefs. Here in the West you believe in Catholicism, or in a particular savior, and in the whole of Asia they don't believe in any of that. They have their own beliefs. So man is divided by nationalism, by racialism, by economic pressures, by so-called religion. And we are all responsible for it, aren't we? You are a nationalist, you are very proud of being English, proud of your tradition as a Frenchman, or God knows what else. It is this that is separating people, isn't it? So you and I will cease to be responsible for the misery in the world only when we are free from nationalism, from racialism, only when there is order in ourselves.

To put it differently, we are human beings, not individuals. Individuality is an old-fashioned idea, a stupid idea. We are human beings, burdened with all the problems of every other human being, whether he is in Asia, in Europe, or America. But if as a human being I understand the whole structure of my society, of my way of life, with its problems and everything else, then there is freedom from that image. Therefore order is brought about, and then I am no longer responsible for the world's misery. I am outside society, and therefore I can help society. I don't want to reform society. Do you understand? I am not a social reformer. One must extricate oneself, be free from society, so that a new group of human beings will arise, and therefore a new structure of society can be formed. You can't reform the old society; that is merely retrogression.

Comment: You have built up an image of yourself, and you are jolly well satisfied with it.

KRISHNAMURTI: Then there is nothing more to be said. That is what most of us have done, sir. Most of us are happy with the images that we have, and therefore we are happy with the problems that we have. Therefore our minds are dull, heavy, stupid, and when we revolt we become beatniks, or the other kind. That's all.

Question: Is the gentleman speaking for himself?

KRISHNAMURTI: I don't know. He may be speaking for himself, or for others. It is all part of our daily life; we are all satisfied with our own images.

Comment: If I have no image of myself, then I am nothing.

KRISHNAMURTI: But are you anything anyhow? (Laughter) Please don't laugh; this is much too serious. Are you anything in yourself? Strip yourself of your name, title, money, position, your little capacity to write a book and be flattered—and what are you? So why not realize and be that? You see, we have an image of what it is to be nothing, and we don't like that image; but the actual fact of being nothing, when you have no image, may be entirely different—and it is entirely different. It is not a state that can be realized in terms of being nothing or of being something. It is entirely different when there is no image of yourself. And to have no image of yourself demands tremendous attention, tremendous seriousness. It is only the attentive, the serious, that live, not the people who have images of themselves.

July 13, 1965

Third Talk in Saanen

We were talking the day before yesterday about the approach to a problem. The problem ceases to exist, as I said, when the image, the formula, the concept, is no longer the center from which we look at a crisis. The image which each one creates for himself depends on his own temperament, circumstances, and the various pressures and experiences that shape his thought. That is what we were discussing the day before yesterday.

I would like this morning, if I may, to talk about something which is more or less the same issue, but perhaps we can approach it differently.

When there is greater outward security for the individual as a social entity—as in the Western world, where there is security for practically everyone—there is a correspondingly greater demand for inner security, isn't there? And inner security is sought through organized religions, through various forms of escape, through entertainment, through political dogmatism either of the extreme left or of the extreme right, and so on. Whatever it is, in that we take shelter, and thereby create a certain sense of inner security. Having created that sense of security in ourselves, we resist every form of change; and I would like this morning to talk about the implications of that word *change*.

Most of us resist change, outwardly as well as inwardly. Outwardly there are extraordinary changes going on, changes of which you are probably not fully aware, particularly in the scientific and technological fields, and in the field of cybernetics; but inwardly there is hardly any change at all. We are what we have been, and we strengthen what we have been.

Please, again let me repeat that you and I are in communication with each other. Communication is not one-sided; it is a movement in which both of us are taking part. You are not merely listening to a series of words with which you agree or disagree, a series of ideas which you can refute or accept. If you listen thus, then there is no possibility of our communicating with each other.

We are going to consider something which demands a great deal of intelligence, insight, and inquiry. Therefore, it seems to me, one has to be conscious of one's own desire to be secure; one has to be aware that one is seeking something permanent, which is the image that most of us create. And when you become aware that you are seeking a sense of being secure in that image, there is a revolt; but that revolt has very little meaning because it is only the response of another form of image. So we go from one conclusion to another, from one belief or dogma to another, from one system of philosophy to another—or we cling to our own experience, and there we settle down, crystallize. Most of us become neurotic, quite unbalanced, when we have these mythical, unreal images; we do not want to examine these images, we do not want to be aware of what is actually going on. When we do become aware of it, there is a great conflict, from which we try to escape, and we resist every form of change.

Now, I think it is very important that we should change, but not just outwardly. Outwardly there are a great many pressures and influences—political, scientific, economic—going on all the time, to which we are consciously or unconsciously responding; we are resisting, or flowing with them. To me, that is no change at all. Mere outward adjustment to a social pattern, however revolutionary it may be, is not change because one has to adjust oneself; otherwise, one will be destroyed. One is compelled to accept the situation, to conform or adjust oneself to certain outward changes, and live with them. All forms of pressure to make one change outwardly have no significance inwardly. They may influence one superficially, but fundamentally they do not bring about a change in oneself. That is obvious; we don't have to labor the point.

So we have to consider what it is that changes, and what that word *change* fundamentally implies. As I said, each one of us has an image of himself, pleasurable or painful, flattering or condemnatory. Please follow this with me, become conscious of your own image and observe it. Don't say, "It is my nature to have an image of myself. I was born with it, it is part of me, and I cannot change"—which is sheer nonsense. Human nature can be changed radically, fundamentally, deeply. There is no such thing as an image which is "natural." So please be aware of the image you have of yourself.

Then the next step is choice. You choose what you will be, or what you will not be, according to the image you have of yourself. That image dictates your activities. Outwardly you may conform, you may go to the office, be with the family, and all the rest of it, but inwardly that image dictates your activities, your way of thinking and feeling, your motives, your energy, your drive. Where there is the exercise of choice, there is will in action, isn't there? You have an image of yourself, and that image helps to bring about your various forms of choice; and the carrying out of choice in action is will. Are you following this?

For most of us, will in action is necessary. We do not know any other action. We only know action as will—"I will" and "I will not." We say, "This is pleasurable and I will pursue it; that is not pleasurable and I will avoid it." Please observe yourself, don't merely listen to me, because I want to go into this very deeply if I can.

We know action only as will, and from will there is so-called virtue. We say, "I will be this, and I will not be that." Our virtue, our morality, our ethics are based on choice, which is will in action.

Is it all right so far? Please don't agree with me, don't accept or deny what I am saying, but see what is actually taking place in yourself.

So our morality is based on choice, on the action of will, behind which there is the image. Now, any change which we consciously bring about is within that pattern, so our action is always contradictory, isn't it? When action is based on choice and will, it can only be in a state of contradiction; for behind it there is the image of ourselves, the image of what we would like to be, whether neurotic or merely fanciful, pleasurable or painful. According to that image we act, and as action must constantly vary, it contradicts itself. You cannot follow one uniform action because life won't permit it, so your action is always in a state of contradiction. If this is not clear, we will discuss it a little later on.

Now, we can see that order is necessary, not only outwardly, but inwardly. There must be order, not only outwardly in the room you live in, but also inwardly. Order is virtue, obviously, but order cannot be brought about by will. Will in action is immoral because it brings contradiction, which is disorder.

Let me put it around the other way. I see some of you are not clear about this.

In the room in which I live, I must have some degree of cleanliness, order, tidiness, so that it doesn't disturb me. But I have not only to be sensitive to outward things, I must also be sensitive inwardly. If there is outward disorder, confusion, then sensitivity is not possible. In the same way, inwardly I must have great order if I am to be greatly sensitive. When there is disorder inwardly, it creates confusion, contradiction; it keeps the mind constantly agonized, in travail, in misery. So I must have inward order. But I see that inward order cannot be brought about by will because will is resistance. If I say, "I shall create order within myself," the "order" I create is according to the pattern, the image which thought has established; therefore, there is contradiction, which is disorder.

But I must have order, and order is virtue. Not the virtue of society, not social morality, the behavior of respectability, and all the rest of it—I am not talking about that. That is not virtue, it is immorality. Social morality is no morality at all. I am talking about order inwardly, and how I am to bring it about.

Please see the problem. I have an image of the kind of order I want, and according to that image, I choose, I exercise will to bring about order. But now I see that to do this is not to bring about order at all. It is merely creating in myself a fortress of resistance—and therefore there is disorder. So I must find a way to bring about order in which there is no choice. Choice in any form is the action of will, or choice brings about the action of will, according to the image, the background, the conclusion, the experience, the ideas that I happen to have.

So I see that there must be order which is not resistance, which is not isolation, which is not an escape, and that such order must come about through a choiceless state in which no will as resistance operates. I see that the order I have created before, inwardly and outwardly, is really disorder. Outwardly I conform to the accepted pattern, the social norm; that is, I am ambitious, envious, greedy, competitive, and this creates terrible disorder in the world. Inwardly I want peace and quiet. I want serenity, security; and there too—because my desire is to find pleasure—I create disorder. So I see that all my action, inwardly as well as outwardly, is productive of disorder. Though what I do outwardly may be called moral, ethical, and all the rest of that nonsense, it actually brings about disorder. I see this very clearly. Any form of choice and the exercise of will based on pleasure do breed resistance, and therefore disorder.

Now, is there another kind of action which is not derived from choice or will? Don't say, "How am I to act without will? How am I to live in this world without choice? Everything I do is based on choice, whether it is choosing the color for my trousers, or something else. If there is to be no choice, and therefore no exercise of will, then I shall just float; there will be no stability, no anchor." That is your natural reaction, isn't it? You say, "If I don't exercise will, what shall I do?" You put that question only when you don't see the implications of the whole activity of will. Will is essentially based on pleasure and resistance, and whatever order it may bring about is actually disorder; and when once you understand this whole process of will, then you won't touch it, you won't go near it, because fundamentally you want order.

So, do we understand the nature of will? Will is based on pleasure and resistance to pain; it is based not on fact but on pleasure. I wonder if you understand! Are you following me? Please, you are not my disciples—don't follow me in that way! But we are moving together in the discovery of something; we are trying to find out if there is a new way of living. That is a natural, essential demand on the part of every intelligent human being—to find a new way of life so that one will not be tortured, will not be in agony, will not have these terrible fears, anxieties, this endless confusion. There must be a new way of living, and to find the new way, you must discard, reject the old completely. But you cannot reject the old without understanding it. You can't just say, "Well, I won't live in that way"—it has no meaning. Whereas, if you understand what is implied in the whole pattern of the old, which is thought and action derived from will and choice, then it naturally drops away.

But, you see, most of us are very lazy, physically as well as inwardly. All this demands a great deal of going into, searching out, breaking down, not accepting; it means living with tremendous energy to find out, and because most of us are lazy inwardly, we don't want to do that. We would rather live happily in the neurotic state of our image—or live unhappily, hoping that circumstances will somehow change the image and bring about a happy, new image.

This whole structure of image, choice, and will is based on holding on to pleasure and discarding pain. Please understand what we are talking about in referring to pleasure and pain. One must resist physical pain, but we are speaking of the fear of psychological pain. Do you understand? Being afraid of inward or psychological pain, we are not facing facts but are looking at everything with an eye to avoiding that pain, or maintaining pleasure.

So, if one understands this whole process, then what is action without will? And what then is change? When you change consciously by saying, "I will not smoke, I will not drink; I will not do this, I will not do that," when you deliberately set out to bring about a change in yourself, don't you find that in this deliberate change there is a great deal of resistance and waste of energy? You are resisting, battling with the old habits, the old patterns of thought, hoping thereby to find a new way of life. This is quite a familiar pattern, isn't it? Where there is a deliberate choice, a deliberate intention to bring about a change, there is not only resistance but a waste of energy, and therefore there is no change at all.

I wonder if you are getting all this? Is it somewhat clear so far?

So I see that where there is deliberate action to bring about a change in myself, there is no real change at all, but only a waste of energy. Therefore change can take place only when there is no conscious effort to change. Change must happen without your deliberately wanting to change. Change comes when you understand the whole pattern of the image, and how it has been created—the image based on the pursuit of pleasure and the avoidance of psychological pain, from which there is choosing, exercising the will in action. This pattern repeats over and over again, and within the field of this pattern we want change; but any such change is still a resistance, a waste of energy, and therefore it is no change at all. Change in the real sense of the word means an explosion, and to explode you need energy, and to have energy there must be no resistance. It is a change into which thought as will has not entered at all. Change is like virtue. Virtue that is cultivated ceases to be virtue. Being full of vanity, when I deliberately set about being humble and practice the virtue of humility every day, it has no meaning. But to explode vanity without the exercise of will, unconsciously, is to have complete energy with which to look at the quality called vanity; and in that there is humility.

So virtue is order brought about without a deliberate thought or intention—and in that there is great beauty. Order is not of time. Time breeds disorder. So I have to be aware of this whole cycle, without pushing it aside, or running away from it, or otherwise doing something about it; I have to be aware of it as a fact, without choice, as I am aware of that microphone. That microphone is a fact, isn't it? It is so, and I can't alter it. It is there in front of me. Similarly, I have to be choicelessly aware of this whole process of thinking in terms of the image, which so far has brought such immense disorder and misery to man, to each one of us. And when one is choicelessly aware of it, one will find that there is an action into which time and will do not enter.

I have said that time breeds disorder, but I do not want to go into the question of time this morning. We will go into it another day because one has to spend a great deal of time on that—time by the watch—and perhaps this is not the occasion for it. But when you really understand that immense order is necessary inwardly, then outwardly, in all your relationships, there will be order—order in your relationship with your family and friends, with your property, and with ideas.

Order—which is essentially the beginning and the end of virtue—does not come about through a deliberate act in any form. Any deliberate act to bring about order is immoral—and that is what we see in the world. The social order which we have established in various parts of the world is based, as you well know, on competition, greed, envy, brutality; and on Sunday, or whatever day it may be, we talk about brotherly love. But the two cannot go together. Our social order is disorder, and therefore immoral. I am not condemning society. I just see the facts.

So, to bring about order in myself as a human being—not as an individual in isolation, but as a human being who is part of the rest of humanity—I must understand this extraordinarily complex and subtle process of will, choice, and the image.

Comment: The moment one becomes conscious of the image that one has built up, it causes pain, a disturbance, and the thought that looks at it stops.

KRISHNAMURTI: First of all, are we conscious of the image for ourselves, or have we become conscious of it because somebody has told us about that image? Do you see the difference? Am I conscious of the image that I have in me, without anybody telling me? Or am I conscious of that image only because you have told me about it? Surely there is a difference. I know when I am hungry, nobody need tell me. But if you say to me, "You are hungry," and I react and say, "By Jove, I am hungry," then that is something entirely different.

So, are you aware of the image that you have built up through the years, the image that society has given you, and so on? Are you aware of it without being told? Or are you aware of it only because somebody has told you? Please find out. If it is your own discovery, it has vitality; but if you are merely told about it, and you say, "Yes, I have an image," then that has not the same vitality, the same energy.

Question: What happens when it is neither?

KRISHNAMURTI: When you have neither discovered it for yourself nor found it because somebody has told you about it, then what happens? Well, then I am afraid that either one is asleep or one doesn't want to discover it, or one says, "It is part of my sublime self, the supreme"—whatever that may be. Please, this is fairly simple; why do we complicate it?

If I don't want to discover that I have an image, any amount of your telling me that I have an image will not make me see it; and most of us don't want to discover it because it is such a safe, satisfying, gratifying image. We don't want to be questioned about it, so we turn a deaf ear. But if you discover it for yourself, that has much more vitality than being told what is wrong.

Now, let's proceed. I have discovered that I have an image. I have suddenly become conscious of the fact that I have an image of myself—an image which has been built up through my vanity, through my pleasure, pain, conclusions. It is an image put together by thought, by experience, by life, by my relationships, by my activities, sorrow, disgrace—everything has put together in me this image, and I have become aware of it. Then what happens? Am I choicelessly aware of it as a fact—as a fact which I can't alter? Do you understand what I mean? It is a fact that the sun rises and sets, and I can't do a thing about it. Similarly, this image is a fact, and I see it as a fact without saying, "I want to get rid of it," or "I want to change it," or "I must do something about it."

Are you following this? Do you see the image of yourself which you have built up through centuries—see it as a fact? Do you understand? Are you looking at it choicelessly, and not according to your pleasure and pain? If you look at it without choice, then it is a fact, isn't it? The image is a fact, it is so. Now, are you looking at it as an outsider who is observing it—or are you the image? Do you understand what I mean? I hope I am making myself clear.

I have discovered this image unconsciously. Am I looking at it as an observer apart from the observed? Am I separate from that which I am observing? Is there a space between the observer and the thing observed? Actually, the observer is the image, the two are not separate—and that is where our difficulty is going to come in, because I have treated the image as a thing outside of myself, a thing to be observed, to be altered, to be added to, to take something away from. I have never seen it as 'me' as the observer itself, but always as the thing observed. To see the image as the observer itself demands complete attention. When you are merely the observer apart from the thing observed, it is a form of escape from the fact, and one has to become aware of this. That is to say, there is only the image, and not the observer.

Now, take a flower, a tree, a face—it doesn't matter what it is—and look at it. When you look at the flower, you are looking at it biologically, botanically; that is, you are looking at that flower with all the knowledge that you have about it. Is that not so? And do you ever look at a flower nonbotanically, or does all the information you have about that flower always interfere? When your knowledge interferes with looking, then you are merely the observer looking at that flower. That is fairly simple.

You have probably never looked at the image without the interference of choice, so you don't know that there is then only the image and not the observer. When that happens, there is no question of getting rid of the image, or adding to it, or denying it. It is a fact. But as long as you are the observer looking at the fact, you are dissipating the very energy which is necessary to understand completely, or be, or see that fact without the observer.

Now, what happens when there is only the image, and not the censor who says, "I like," or "I do not like" that image? What happens when there is only the fact, and there is no escape from the fact; when the fact is neither pleasurable nor painful, but is simply so, and you are therefore able to look at it completely, with all your energy? Do you understand? Energy is dissipated when there is an observer, a censor. But when there is only the fact, which demands all your energy and attention, then you will find that the image explodes; it has no validity at all, no substance. It has gone completely. Then you start a new life, for there is no longer a censor dictating what you should or should not do. There is a complete revolution, a total change, and therefore great order.

July 15, 1965

Fourth Talk in Saanen

We have been talking, the last three times we have met here, about the necessity for a fundamental and radical revolution within oneself. It is not a revolution within oneself as an individual that we are talking about—a matter of saving your own particular little soul—but a revolution within oneself as a human being totally related to all other human beings. We may consciously separate ourselves into petty, little individualities, but deep down, unconsciously, we are the inherited human experience of all time; and mere superficial changes on the economic or social level, though they may provide a little more comfort and convenience, are not productive of a new society. We are concerned, not only with the human being's transformation of his total nature, but also with bringing about a different society, a good society; and a good society is not possible if there are no good human beings. Good human beings do not flower in prison. Goodness flowers in freedom, not in tyranny, not in one-party systems, either political or religious.

Freedom is considered by society to be dangerous to society because in freedom the individual pursues his own particular enterprise. Through his own cleverness, cunning, the individual dominates others who are less enterprising, and so there is generally a feeling, an idea, a judgment that freedom is contrary to a good society. Therefore political tyrannies try to control, religiously as well as economically and socially, the human mind; they penalize the mind, trying to prevent man from thinking freely. In the so-called democratic societies there is greater freedom, obviously; otherwise, we would not be sitting here discussing this matter. It would not be allowed in some countries. But freedom is also denied in the democracies when it takes the form of a revolt. Now, we are not talking about revolt in the political sense but rather of a complete flowering of human goodness, which can alone produce a creative society.

This goodness of the human being can flower only in freedom, in total freedom; and to understand the question of freedom, one has to go into it, not only in terms of the social order, but also in terms of the individual's relationship to society. Society survives through maintaining some semblance of order. If one observes the society in which one lives, whether it be of the left, of the right, or of the center, one sees that society demands order, a social relationship in which the individual does not rampantly exploit others. But order is denied because of the very structure, the basic psychological structure of society. Though it may proclaim otherwise, society as we know it is based on competition, greed, envy, on an aggressive pursuit of one's own fulfillment, achievement; and in such a society there can be no real freedom at all, and therefore no order. Society as it is, whether of the left or of the right, is disorder because it is not concerned with a fundamental transformation of the human mind. This inner transformation or revolution can take place only in freedom—and by freedom I do not mean a reaction, a freedom from something. Freedom from something is a reaction, and that is not freedom at all.

If the mind merely frees itself from a certain attitude, from certain ideas, or from certain forms of its own self-expression, in that freedom from something, which is a reaction, it is driven into still another form of assertion, and hence there is no freedom at all. So one has to be very clear what one means by the word *freedom*. I know this problem of freedom has been discussed in a great many books; it has given rise to philosophies, to religious ideas and concepts, and to innumerable political expressions. But living as we do in a world which is so destructive, so full of sorrow, misery, and confusion, and being so ridden by our own problems, by our own frustrations, despairs, unless you and I—as human beings in total relationship with other human beings—find out for ourselves what freedom is, there can be no flowering of goodness. Goodness is not a mere sentimental word; it has an extraordinary significance, and without it I do not see how one can act without reaction, in which there is misery, fear, and despair.

So I think it is necessary for the human mind to understand totally this question of what goodness is. The word *goodness* is not the fact; the word is not the thing, and we should be extremely watchful not to be caught in that word and its definition. Rather we must be, or understand, the state which is goodness. Goodness cannot flower and flourish except in freedom. Freedom is not a reaction, it is not freedom from something, nor is it a resistance or a revolt against something. It is a state of mind, and that state of mind which is freedom cannot be understood if there is no space. Freedom demands space.

There is in the world less and less space; towns are getting more and more crowded. The explosion of population is denying space to each one of us. Most of us live in a little room surrounded by innumerable other rooms, and there is no space except perhaps when we wander into the country, far away from towns, smoke, dirt, and noise. In that there is a certain freedom, but there cannot be inward freedom if there is no inward space. Again, the word *space* is different from the fact, so may I suggest that you don't seize upon that word and get caught in trying to analyze or define it. You can easily look up the word in a dictionary and find out what it says about space.

Now, can we put to ourselves the question "What is space?" and remain there, not trying to define the word, not trying to feel our way into it or to inquire into it, but rather to see what it means nonverbally? Freedom and space go together. To most of us, space is the emptiness around an object—around a chair, around a building, around a person, or around the contours of the mind.

Please just listen to what is being said; don't agree or disagree because we are about to go into something rather subtle and difficult to express in words; but we must go into it if we are to understand what freedom is.

Most of us know space only because of the object. There is an object, and around it there is what we call space. There is this tent, and within and around it there is space. There is space around that tree, around that mountain. We know space only within the four walls of a building, or outside the building, or around some object. Similarly, we know space inwardly only from the center which looks out at it. There is a center, the image, if I may go back to that word—and again, the word *image* is not the fact—and around this center there is space; so we know space only because of the object within that space.

Now, is there space without the object, without the center from which you as a human being are looking? Space, as we know it, has to do with design, structure; it exists in the relationship of one structure to another structure, one center to another center. Now, if space exists only because of the object, or because the mind has a center from which it is looking out, then that space is limited, and therefore in that space there is no freedom. To be free in a prison is not freedom. To be free of a certain problem within the four walls of one's relationships—that is, within the limited space of one's own image, one's own thoughts, activities, ideas, conclusions—is not freedom.

Please, may I once again suggest that through the words of the speaker you observe the limited space which you have created around yourself as a human being in relationship with another, as a human being living in a world of destruction and brutality, as a human being in relationship to a particular society. Observe your own space, see how limited it is. I do not mean the size of the room in which you live, whether it is small or big—that is not what I am talking about. I mean the inner space which each one of us has created around his own image, around a center, around a conclusion. So the only space we know is the space which has an object as its center.

I don't know if I am making myself clear. I am trying to say that as long as there is a center around which there is space, or a center which creates space, there is no freedom at all; and when there is no freedom, there is no goodness, nor the flowering of goodness. Goodness can flower only when there is space—space in which the image, as the center, is not.

Let me put it another way—you look a little bit puzzled. You know, it is the very nature of a good, healthy, strong mind to demand freedom, not only for itself, but for others. But that word *freedom* has been translated in various ways—religious, economic, and social. In India it has been translated in one way, and here in another. So let us go into the question of what is freedom for a human being. Isolating oneself in a monastery, or becoming a wandering monk, or living in some fanciful ivory tower—surely, that is not freedom at all. Nor is it freedom to identify oneself with a particular religious or ideological group. So let us inquire into what is freedom, and how there can be freedom in every relationship.

Now, to understand freedom in relationship, one must go into this question of what is space, because the minds of most of us are small, petty, limited. We are heavily conditioned—conditioned by religion, by the society in which we live, by our education, by technology; we are limited, forced to conform to a certain pattern, and one sees that there is no freedom within that circumscribed area. But one demands freedom—complete freedom, not just partial freedom. Living in a prison cell for twenty-four hours a day and going occasionally into the prison yard to walk around there—that is not freedom. As a human being living in the present society, with all its confusion, misery, conflict, torture, one demands freedom; and this demand for freedom is a healthy, normal thing. So, living in society—living in relationship with your family, with your property, with your ideas—what does it mean to be free? Can the mind ever be free if it doesn't have limitless space within itself—space not created by an idea of space, not created by an image which has a certain limited space around itself as the center? Surely, as a human being one has to find out the relationship that exists between freedom and space. What is space? And is there space without the center, without the object which creates space?

Are you following all this? It is very important to find out for ourselves what space is; otherwise, there can be no freedom and we shall always be tortured, we shall always be in conflict with each other, and we shall only revolt against society, which has no meaning at all. Merely to give up smoking, or to become a beatnik or a Beatle, or God knows what else, has no meaning because those are all just forms of revolt within the prison.

Now, we are trying to find out if there is such a thing as freedom which is not a revolt—freedom which is not an ideational creation of the mind, but a fact. And to find that out, one must inquire profoundly into the question of space. A petty, little, bourgeois, middle-class mind—or an aristocratic mind, which is also petty—may think it is free; but it is not free because it is living within the limits of its own space, the confining space created by the image in which it functions. Is that clear?

So you cannot have order without freedom, and you cannot have freedom without space. Space, freedom, and order—the three go together, they are not separate. A society of the extreme left hopes to create order through dictatorship, through the tyranny of a political party; but it cannot create order, economically, socially, or in any other way, because order requires the freedom of man within himself—not as an individual saving his petty, dirty, little soul, but as a human being who has lived for two million years or more, with all the vast experience of mankind.

Order is virtue, and virtue as goodness cannot flower in any society which is always in contradiction with itself. Outside influences—economic adjustment, social reform, technological progress, going to Mars, and all the rest of it—cannot possibly produce order. What produces order is inquiry into freedom—not intellectual inquiry, but doing the actual work of breaking down our conditioning, our limiting prejudices, our narrow ideas; breaking down the whole psychological structure of society, of which we are a part. Unless you break through all that, there is no freedom, and therefore there is no order. It is like a small mind trying to understand the immensity of the world, of life, of beauty. It cannot. It can imagine, it can write poems about it, paint pictures, but the reality is different from the word, different from the image, the symbol, the picture.

Order can come about only through the awareness of disorder. You cannot create order—please do see this fact. You can only be aware of disorder, outwardly as well as inwardly. A disordered mind cannot create order because it doesn't know what it means. It can only react to what it thinks is disorder by creating a pattern which it calls "order" and then conforming to that pattern. But if the mind is conscious of the disorder in which it lives—which is being aware of the negative, not projecting the so-called positive—then order becomes something extraordinarily creative, moving, living. Order is not a pattern which you follow day after day. To follow a pattern which you have established, to practice it day after day, is disorder—the disorder of effort, of conflict, of greed, of envy, of ambition, the disorder of all the petty, little human beings who have created and been conditioned by the present society.

Now, can one become aware of disorder—aware of it without choosing, without saying, "This is disorder, and that is order"? Can one be choicelessly aware of disorder? This demands extraordinary intelligence, sensitivity; and in that choiceless awareness there is also a discipline which is not mere conformity.

Am I driving too hard? Am I putting too many ideas into one basket, as it were, presenting them all at the same moment?

You see, for most of us, discipline—whether we like it or not, whether we practice it or not, whether we are conscious or unconscious of it—is a form of conformity. All the soldiers in the world—those poor, miserable human beings, whether of the left or of the right—are made to conform to a pattern because there are certain things which they are supposed to do. And although the rest of us are not soldiers trained to destroy others and protect ourselves, discipline is nevertheless imposed on us by environment, by society, by the family, by the office, by the routine of our everyday existence; or we discipline ourselves.

When one examines the whole structure and meaning of discipline, whether it is imposed discipline or self-discipline, one sees that it is a form of outward or inward conformity or adjustment to a pattern, to a memory, to an experience. And we revolt against that discipline. Every human mind revolts against the stupid kind of conformity, whether established by dictators, priests, saints, gods, or whatever they are. And yet one sees that there must be some kind of discipline in life—a discipline which is not mere conformity, which is not adjustment to a pattern, which is not based on fear, and all the rest of it; because if there is no discipline at all, one can't live. So one has to find out if there is a discipline which is not conformity because conformity destroys freedom; it never brings freedom into being. Look at the organized religions throughout the world, the political parties. It is obvious that conformity destroys freedom, and we don't have to labor the point. Either you see it or you don't see it; it is up to you.

The discipline of conformity, which is created by the fear of society and is part of the psychological structure of society, is immoral and disorderly, and we are caught in it. Now, can the mind find out if there is a certain movement of discipline which is not a process of controlling, shaping, conforming? To find that out, one has to be aware of this extraordinary disorder, confusion, and misery in which one lives; and to be aware of it, not fragmentarily, but totally and therefore choicelessly—that in itself is discipline.

I don't know if you are following all this.

If I am fully aware of what I am doing, if I am choicelessly aware of the movement of my hand, for example, that very awareness is a form of discipline in which there is no conformity. Is this clear? You cannot understand this just verbally; you actually have to do it within yourself. Order can come about only through this sense of awareness in which there is no choice, and which is therefore a total awareness, a complete sensitivity to every movement of thought. This total awareness itself is discipline without conformity; therefore, out of this total awareness of disorder, there is order. The mind hasn't produced order.

To have order, which is the flowering of goodness and of beauty, there must be freedom; and there is no freedom if you have no space.

Look, I will put a question to you—but don't answer me, please. What is space? Put that question to yourself, not just flippantly, but seriously, as I am putting it to you. What is space? Your mind now knows only the space within the limitations of a room, or the space which an object creates around itself. That is the only space you know. And is there space without the object? If there is no space without the object, then there is no freedom, and therefore there is no order, no beauty, no flowering of goodness. There is only everlasting struggle. So the mind has to discover by hard work, and not just by listening to some words, that there is in fact space without a center. When once that has been found, there is freedom, there is order, and then goodness and beauty flower in the human mind.

Discipline, order, freedom, and space cannot exist without the understanding of time. It is very interesting to inquire into the nature of time—time by the watch, time as yesterday, today, and tomorrow, the time in which you work, and the time in which you sleep. But there is also time which is not by the watch, and that is much more difficult to understand. We look to time as a means of bringing about order. We say, "Give us a few more years and we will be good, we will create a new generation, a marvelous world." Or we talk about creating a different type of human being, one who will be totally communist, totally this, or totally that. So we look to time as a means of bringing about order; but if one observes, one sees that time only breeds disorder.

That is perhaps enough for this morning, so let us discuss what I have talked about. I hope you are not too hot.

Question: Can one share the misery, the tortures, the despairs of another?

KRISHNAMURTI: What do you mean by the word *share?* I can share a few francs with you; I can share with you the few things that I possess—shirts, trousers, the extra room that I have. I can share an experience verbally; I can tell you about my misery, the things I have lived through, the beauty I have seen. So where does sharing end? Where does it begin? I love my wife or my husband, my children, my family, my neighbor—no, sorry, I don't love my neighbor. Even though I talk about loving my neighbor, and the priests shout about it every day, it is all nonsense because I compete with him, I destroy him through business, through war. I say that I love my family. And do I share anything with them, apart from things, possessions? Do you understand? Can I share my sorrow, my misery, with another? I can tell him about it, and he may say, "I am so sorry, old chap, you are having such a bad time"; he may pat me on the shoulder, hold my hand, but can I actually share with him the agony, the anxiety I am going through?

Have you ever shared anything with anybody? Do you understand? When does one actually share with another—not financially, not in words, not through ideas or the exchange of ideas, not through arguments, and all the rest of it, but when is one really open to another nonverbally, not through the mere sharing of things, but actually? Surely, we share with another, commune with another, only when there is love. But wait a minute. That word has so many meanings for so many different people. I don't want to go into all this now because it is too complex. You know, we share something together—something which is nonverbal, and which is not a matter of giving or receiving things—only when both of us are intense about it at the same level and at the same time. Otherwise there is no communion—which means there is nothing to share but things, words, explanations, knowledge, or stupid experiences. That is not sharing.

Can two people have this communion? Can you and I have it? You don't know me, I don't know you. You may know your wife or your husband, but I doubt it. To know another implies a great deal. Can you and I live for a few hours, or even for a minute, with an intensity, an urgency which is at the same depth and at the same time? Only then is there communion, only then is there sharing. Otherwise there is merely an exchange, a thing of the marketplace, or a sentimental, emotional thing which has no meaning at all. To share, there must be no emotionalism, no sentimentality, but only a state of mind in which both of us are serious, intense, alive. Then there is no question of sharing anything with anybody. A flower doesn't "share" with you or with me its beauty, its perfume. It is there for all to see, for all to smell.

July 18, 1965

Fifth Talk in Saanen

I would like, if I may this morning, to talk about time. It is rather a complex problem needing careful inquiry, and a subtle insight is required to find the truth, or to put a stop to time. Most of us, I think, are tortured by the conflict and confusion that arise in the everyday living of our lives. We haven't been able to find a way out of our misery in all the two million years of man's existence. In spite of the many technological advances, in spite of the innumerable drugs and opiates, in spite of the analysts, priests, saviors, Masters, and gurus, and in spite of these talks also, we don't seem able to throw off our accumulations easily, without the least effort, as a leaf drops from a tree in the autumn and is blown away. We apparently have not the capacity, the know-how to free the mind—or for the mind to free itself—from its various entanglements, from its conscious or unconscious problems, travails, from its undiscovered despairs and secret miseries; and we think that time—tomorrow multiplied by a thousand—will somehow bring about a miraculous change.

Now, I feel that there is a totally different way of living—a way of living which has nothing to do with escaping, with running away into monasteries, or taking vows, or joining some particular social, political, or economic activity. I feel that there is a different approach, a different way of resolving the mountainous difficulties of our daily life; and I would like to talk about it, if I may, and request you to listen—not in order to agree or disagree, but just to listen quietly, as you listen to that airplane passing overhead. Listen intently, but effortlessly, if that is possible. Because it is fairly obvious that by mere intellectual probing, examination, and analysis, we are not going to be able to solve this problem of human misery. For so many years, for so many lives, for so many centuries we have been trying to find a way out of our misery through discipline, through sacrifice, through control, through forgetting oneself and being identified with something that we have called the greater. We have tried innumerable systems, followed innumerable paths, and yet at the end of it all we are still as we were—fearful, anxious, tortured, full of sorrow. So there must be a totally different approach to this problem.

I am going, if I can this morning, to wander into this different approach—not just verbally or intellectually, because verbally or intellectually one can't enter into this realm of clarity, nor can one do so with any sort of sentiment or emotionalism. One must come into it unknowingly, without effort, without any deliberate intention; and if you will quietly listen, then perhaps we shall move together. But if your inquiry is merely intellectual, analytical, then I am afraid you and I will lose our communication, our communion with each other.

So there must be a different approach altogether to this monstrous way of living, with its wars, its competition, its dreadful ambition to be somebody, its constant battle with one's neighbor, with society; and to understand it, one has to go into the question of what is freedom. We talked about this a little the other day, but it is an inexhaustible subject, and being inexhaustible, we must come to it without any effort—and that is going to be the most difficult task for each one of us. You see, most of us do not want freedom because we do not know what it is, and we would rather put up with the painful, sorrowful things that we have than to abandon them, because the things of the future we don't know.

We don't know what freedom is. We have an idea, but the idea is not the fact, and no amount of experience or knowledge will lead to freedom. As I was saying the other day, freedom demands order; and order brought about deliberately, purposefully, is disorder. Order established by the will is merely a form of resistance, and with this so-called order we are very familiar because man has indulged in it for centuries.

Where there is freedom, there must be space. Space implies a sense of solitude, a sense of aloneness. This is not something mystical, a mere abstraction, but a very definite reality—as definite as your sitting in this tent in Switzerland.

There cannot be immense space in which the mind can function if the mind is not completely alone. Aloneness and loneliness, surely, are two different states. We all know very well what loneliness is: the sense of being isolated, cut off from everything, without a companion, without any relationship, even though one may be surrounded by one's family and be living an active and prosperous life. In spite of all that, there comes an extraordinary sense of loneliness which most of us—or at least those of us who have inquired into the ways of life—have discovered.

Now, loneliness and aloneness are two different states. Loneliness is the result of everyday activity in which action springs from the center or the image. The image is in essence a center put together through discarding pain and not discarding pleasure. Our values are based on what will give us pleasure, and not on fact, not on *what is.*

Please listen to what is being said, not as you would listen to an outsider, but as you would listen to one with whom you are talking about yourself. After all, that is what we are doing here in all these talks. Each one of us is observing himself, exposing himself, not neurotically, emotionally, sentimentally, but factually. Each one of us is discovering himself, and therefore understanding himself.

So, as long as there is this image whose values are based on pleasure, there must be the loneliness of the center, which creates its own space. The center creates space around itself in its relationship with people, with things, with ideas; and this center, which creates space around itself, is loneliness—a state of which we are either conscious or unconscious. Loneliness is entirely different from being alone. Aloneness is not the result of any activity of the mind.

The mind, after all, has evolved through time. It has grown into its present state, like the animals have, through the cultivation of values based on pleasure. If you have watched an animal, you will know how it takes delight in pleasure and avoids every form of pain. Similarly, the human mind, which has developed through many centuries, is still based, not on fact, not on *what is,* but on the evaluation of *what is* according to pleasure. Such a mind wants to live continually in a state of pleasure, and therefore the very space it creates around itself is its own limitation. Aloneness, on the other hand, is not the product of pleasure at all. Therefore we must understand very deeply this whole question of pleasure. I am not saying that pleasure is right or wrong. I am only pointing out that if the mind is evaluating everything in terms of pleasure, which means there is a center whose values, judgments, concepts, activities are all based on pleasure, then that very center is productive of conflict and contradiction; and as long as there is contradiction within itself, all action on the part of the mind, and all its relationships, are bound to create more conflict, more confusion.

Now, if we are at all aware, we may know how to deal with a problem as it arises. By watching a problem and not running away from it, by being totally attentive to that particular problem, it is possible to end it. If you smoke, for example, it is possible to be so aware of the habit that a crisis is reached. When the craving is at its highest point, if you are totally aware of that craving without running away, it soon dissolves, withers, disappears. If you have tried it, you will know this is so. Which means what? That we have learned a certain trick, if I may use that word—how to dissolve a particular problem. But we have many, many problems, both conscious and unconscious.

(An interruption is caused by latecomers.)

Sirs, this is a very difficult subject, and what we are now going to go into together demands your full attention, which means there can be no disturbance. Or, if there are disturbances, like the noise of the passing airplane, and you are distracted by them, be aware of your inattention; and if you are aware of your inattention, you will be attentive. Do you follow? Don't try to force yourself to pay attention because then you won't be attentive. But if you are aware of a particular noise—of the river, of the wind, of the people who come in and go out—and if it is interfering with your attention, then be fully aware of that noise, of that movement, and of your inattention. In this way you will naturally come to be attentive.

I don't know quite where I was, so I will start over again.

You see, we have many problems, both hidden and open—problems with which we can communicate, and problems with which we cannot. And should we go through, open up, investigate, root out every problem? That involves time, doesn't it? We have innumerable problems—economic problems, social problems, problems of relationship, problems of sorrow, doubt, uncertainty, the demand to be completely secure, and so on. Now, should we take these problems one at a time and understand them, resolve them? Have we the time to deal with each problem separately? What is implied in that process? If we try to deal with each problem separately, we need time, we need energy, and there is a constant battle to be aware of and not to miss one single problem. So what happens? We say to ourselves, "Problems will never end. I shall not be able to resolve all my problems before I die, there are too many of them," and so we try to escape into some mystical, fanciful, idiotic nonsense. Whether we smoke marijuana, or go to church, it is all about the same.

Now, there may be a totally different way of looking at our problems, and that is what I want to go into. I have, say, ten problems or more, and if I take each problem separately, I must understand each one so completely that it doesn't interfere with my understanding of the next problem. Do you follow? And I know very well that all problems—economic, social, personal—are interrelated. There is no separate problem, independent of the others. I see that. And I also see that I must have freedom immediately—not tomorrow, or when I am about to die, but immediately. With an intensity, with a drive, with complete energy there must be a sense of freedom—freedom from all problems, for that is the only freedom.

Freedom implies action—freedom is action; it is not that I derive action from freedom. But most of us say, "I must be free to act." We say, "I must be free to think what I like, politically, economically, socially"—but very few of us say, "Religiously I must be free," because there we are caught. We demand what we call freedom, from which we hope to act; or having so-called freedom, we choose how to act. If we are caught in the tyranny of a party system—of a dictatorship in the name of the people, and all that silly nonsense—then we want freedom to act. So for most of us freedom is something different from action. Whereas, I am saying that freedom is action, and action then is not based on an idea. When action is based on an idea, it is the organized pursuit of pleasure, is it not? It is the outcome of the desire for satisfaction. Therefore action based on an idea is really inaction leading to bondage, not to freedom. There is the action which is freedom only when there is a release from, or a complete understanding of, the action which is based on idea.

So, I see that freedom is action, and that action is not of time. And is it possible not only to dissolve immediately the many problems which I have but also to prevent further problems from arising? There are two things involved: to deal immediately with the problems I already have, and to prevent further problems from arising, so that my mind is at no time entangled in a net of problems. It is only then that there is freedom, and freedom then is action.

To understand all this, one must understand time. Time is duration, a continuous existence. Time as we know it is a movement from here to there. Time is the interval between a thought and its achievement through action. Time is the postponement of a problem, the gap between the arising and the ending of a problem. Time implies a gradual process of action which is supposed ultimately to resolve the problem. So we use time as a means of achievement, like an ambitious author who wants to fulfill himself through his sordid, little book, or big book, and who therefore says, "I must have time to complete it." We all use time in this way—as a means of achievement, of changing, of cultivating a certain capacity. We use time to bring about happiness, or a better relationship, and all the rest of it.

Now, what is involved in this gradual process? You see, every problem is related to another problem, and if you try to resolve a particular problem gradually, during that period the tensions, the influences, the pressures of other problems come into play and further complicate the original problem; therefore, you can never solve any one problem by means of a gradual process. Am I making myself clear?

Look, if thought attempts to move from here to there over a period of time, other influences, other drives, other causes arise which divert thought; therefore, thought never comes to that particular point. And yet that is what most of us are doing continually. We are using time as a means to achieve a result, to bring about a fundamental change psychologically, and therefore we never complete anything, we are always modifying and being modified. So to me time breeds disorder, it can never bring about order. If I understand this, not just verbally, not as a mere picture or image, but if for me it is so, I act immediately. If I am hungry and I have food, I eat. There is no postponement of action.

Now, if I understand very clearly that time breeds disorder, then how am I to deal with all the problems that are totally related to each other? Do you understand the question? I see very clearly that time has no meaning, except chronologically. Time is necessary for the acquiring of knowledge, and so on, but time has no meaning in any other direction. And yet I have problems that must be dealt with, problems of which I may be conscious or unconscious. I know that my problems cannot be resolved separately, that they must all be resolved at once. I cannot resolve my economic problems apart from my psychological problems without creating still more problems. So problems must be resolved totally, not fragmentarily. I cannot resolve them in one particular area, and then move on to another area of problems. They must be resolved completely. How is this to be done? Do you understand?

There is the problem of old age, disease, and death, the problem of suffering, of loneliness; there are the travails, the tortures, the sense of despair. How will you deal with it all? If you don't know how to deal with it immediately, you depend on time to bring about a change—and then you are tortured until you die. So you are now faced with a question to which no one can give you the answer; no book, no philosopher, no teacher, no church can tell you what to do. If another tells you and you follow him, then you are lost, you are back again in the turmoil and the conflict. Since there is nobody to tell you, what will you do?

In a situation of this kind, don't you stop all activity of the mind? You have looked in every direction, tried to solve this one fundamental problem in ten different ways, and you are still faced with it. What will you do? Surely, there is only one state of mind. As you don't know the answer, as you don't know what to do, the mind completely stops all its activities. You don't know what to do, yet you must find a way out. Books and all that rubbish have been thrown away. You are faced with this problem; what are you to do with it? You know you can't go back the old way. You are confronted with a positive question, and any positive approach to it is a matter of time; therefore, your mind must become completely negative. Do you know what I mean by the negative and the positive approach? The positive approach is the process of analysis, examination, asking, tearing to pieces, following, destroying—and you have done all that. You have gone to this or that church, followed this or that guru, priest, or philosopher, read certain books, practiced a particular system; and you have now discarded that whole positive activity. Therefore your mind, when confronted with this fundamental issue, is in a state of negation, is it not? Negation in the sense that it is not expecting an answer, not looking for a way out.

Do follow this. If you can understand it, you will be able to resolve all your problems with one breath.

Having inquired, analyzed, having wandered around, tried all the positive ways, followed the various paths, and not having found any answer, your mind is now completely in a state of negation. It is not waiting for an answer, not hoping, not expecting that someone will tell you. Isn't that right? Please don't agree—for God's sake, don't agree! Now, when your mind is in that state of complete negation, you can approach anew all your problems, and then you will find that they can be resolved totally and completely because it is the mind itself that has been creating the problem. The mind has been treating each problem as a separate, fragmentary issue, hoping thereby to resolve it. But when the mind is completely quiet, negatively aware, it has no problems at all. Don't think problems won't arise—it is inevitable; but as problems arise, the mind can deal with them immediately. Do you understand?

After all, what is a problem? When there is a crisis, a challenge which the mind is incapable of meeting totally—it is then that a problem arises, is it not? There is an inadequate response to a challenge, and that brings about a problem.

Please follow this, it is quite interesting. Most of us need challenges; otherwise, we would fall asleep. There is the Common Market, which de Gaulle is trying to break up—that is a challenge. The events that are taking place in Algiers, in Vietnam, and so on are all challenges, and we must find an adequate response. If there is not an adequate response, then the inadequate response creates a problem because it is inadequate. Challenges are being thrown at us all the time, consciously or unconsciously, and without them most of us would go to sleep. Or we are so tired, so worn out, that we don't want challenges, so we escape from them by living in some mythical world of our own devising.

Now, if you see this process of challenge and response, and are aware of the necessity of keeping the mind awake, then you will also see that the mind can keep awake without any outward challenges at all. This requires a great intensity; and if you once awaken that intensity, then you don't depend on the challenge of de Gaulle, of Algiers, of Vietnam, of the communist tyranny, or whatever it is; you don't depend on any outward challenge to keep the mind awake because you are aware of the whole issue of challenge and response, and you see it is the inadequacy of response that creates the problem. Then, having rejected the outward challenge, and because your mind is immensely more awake then ever before, it creates its own challenge. Do you follow? That inward challenge is much greater than any outward challenge because your mind is now being questioned by its own doubts, its own inquiry; its own energy is driving it to ask, to look. And if the mind has been through both of these types of challenge and has responded adequately, then it can be awake without any challenge at all. That which is clear, that which is light, has no challenge—it is what it is. But if you merely say, "Well, I have reached that state, it has become part of my nature," then I am afraid we shall have to begin all over again at the beginning.

The mind that is in a state of complete negation because it has understood the whole process of following, denial, acceptance, the process of positive inquiry, positive assertions—it is only such a mind whose action is freedom, and therefore it has no problem.

I am surprised that you seem to accept all that has been said. Perhaps you don't accept or deny it, but you just haven't thought about it. You must be asking yourself, "What the dickens is he talking about? How can I live, do, be, without a formula, without a concept, without a future? How can I act without idea?" Don't you ask yourself that? Because your action is at present based on a formula of what you should do. Your action is based on a technique, or on the various experiences you have accumulated as memory, which then becomes action. Now, the speaker is saying that as long as your action is the result of an idea, you will have a contradiction, and therefore pain, misery. But you just listen and accept it! You don't say to me, "Look here, what am I to do?"

I know the way I act, the way I live. I am aware that I want to be famous. If I write a book, I am frustrated if that book is not recognized. If you have insulted me, I am stuck with all the memories of that experience; and how am I to put them aside? Similarly, if you have given me delight by flattering me, I have as a result certain ideas about you, and according to those ideas, I act.

Now, is it ever possible for the mind to be free from idea, and therefore always to be in a state of action? Are you following? Instead of there being idea and then action, can the mind be always in a state of complete action? Surely, it cannot be in a state of complete action unless it is in a state of negation.

After all, one wants to live with great sensitivity and intelligence; and they are both the same: to be completely sensitive is to be completely intelligent. And can one be so intelligent in life that one lives without conflicts, without miseries, without effort? Surely, to be so tremendously intelligent and sensitive as that, there must be no interval between idea and action. If there is an interval between idea and action, then in that interval, which is time, there is conflict, and therefore the deterioration of energy. If you understand this really, deeply, then you will see that your mind is in a state of complete action all the time. The inaction of such a mind is complete action. The mind can be active, and also be aware of its inaction; but its inaction is not inattention. The mind is capable of living, working, acting, without an interval between idea and action, only when it has understood this whole process of breeding problems through experience, through the inadequate response to challenge, and all the rest of it. Such a mind is completely alone—which has nothing whatsoever to do with loneliness or isolation. And only the mind that is completely alone is free.

July 20, 1965

Sixth Talk in Saanen

It seems to me that we very rarely ask ourselves a fundamental question; and when we do, we generally answer it according to our particular pleasure, fancy, or belief, and therefore the original question—the essential, fundamental question—never gets answered.

We answer it in terms of a particular religion, or a particular branch of knowledge, or according to some mythical, theological conception of life. And I think that we must not only ask fundamental questions but also try to discover the true, original answers.

This morning I would like to talk about conformity; that is, I would like to find out if there is anything original, anything which is free of conformity, and which is not a mere abstraction, not just an idea, but as actual as any fact in daily life. So the fundamental question we are asking ourselves is this: To what extent can conformity be ended? Is it possible to end conformity altogether, and thereby allow the original to be? I think this is a fundamental question because most of us do conform endlessly. We shape ourselves according to a particular pattern, according to an established ideological mold, whether imposed by society, by economic, social, and environmental pressures, or by our own experience. We are always shaping ourselves in one way or another—I think this is an obvious fact. And can this process of conformity—which is so deep-rooted, and which is conscious as well as unconscious—come to an end?

Surely, it is only when we are free of conformity that we can find out for ourselves what is the original, the essential, the true; and unless we find that out for ourselves, we shall always live a counterfeit, secondhand life, a life of imitation. Therefore it seems to me a valid, fundamental question to ask ourselves whether conformity can ever end. By conformity I mean the process in which thought and the thinker are always shaping themselves to a pattern, always imitating, repeating, always complying with an idea, a concept, a belief, a dogma, always adjusting to a particular standard or ideal in relationship. Such conformity is the norm of our life; it is the everyday pattern of our existence, and we are now asking ourselves whether that conformity can come to an end. And we should ask ourselves also whether the ending of conformity breeds disorder, so that we must conform; or whether, with the ending of conformity, there is the discovery of something totally original, not counterfeit, not secondhand.

Most of our lives are secondhand. We do not know for ourselves what the original is, or even if there is that which may be called the original. To me, the word *original* is ordinarily rather misused. We talk about original writing, an original painting, an original way of thinking or expressing oneself; we say that an author has written an original book. I do not think the word original is aptly used in such matters. There is an original something which religion throughout the world—however organized, repetitive, however stupidly ritualistic it may have become—has always sought. But apart altogether from organized religion, with its dogmatism and complex theology, with its absurd ceremonials, and all the rest of that nonsense—apart from all that, can you and I as human beings living in this world, surrounded by all the complexities of modern existence, discover for ourselves something which is really original? Otherwise life becomes terribly monotonous, a boring routine that has very little significance.

So this morning I would like, if I may, to go into this question of conformity, in which is implied imitation, molding thought according to a certain pattern, whether imposed by society or put together by our own experience, and thereby never coming near the original. When I use the word *conformity,* all this is implied—the counterfeiting process, the desire to conform to a particular pattern, to imitate, to accept, to obey.

Now, first of all, are we totally aware of this conforming process that is going on within each one of us, whether we are conforming to the past, to a present concept, or to some future ideal or utopia? And if we are aware of it, then should we not ask ourselves whether it is possible to end this conformity? Surely, to be free of the whole process of conflict, effort, we must first understand and be free of conformity; and because effort implies conformity, we must find out whether it is possible to live in this world without conformity, and therefore without effort. One can see that the more effort one makes, the more conflict and confusion there is, and hence the greater the sorrow, the greater the pain. So we must find out whether it is possible to live without effort, that is, to live originally and therefore to be free of all conformity.

Now, to come to that point, I think one must first be aware—which seems so obvious—of the nature of a mind that conforms. Why do we conform at all? Please bear in mind that when I use the words *to conform,* I mean to counterfeit, to imitate, to obey authority, to adjust oneself to a pattern—all this is implied. So, why do we conform? Conformity implies effort, does it not? And when there is effort in any relationship, there is no relationship. If I make an effort to be kind, to be affectionate, or to be polite to you, it has no meaning. Kindliness, gentleness, and affection spring from a state of mind in which there is no effort; and to understand that state of mind, one must understand fundamentally this question of conformity.

One naturally conforms in certain outward, superficial things, but that is not what we are discussing. I conform here when I put on this kind of clothing, whereas in India I conform in another way, I put on something else. When I drive a car, I conform by keeping to the right side of the road here, and to the left side in England. I conform in a certain way when I have to post a letter, and so on.

But have I to conform to the poison of nationalism? Must I conform to a particular pattern of existence, to a particular way of thinking which society seeks to impose on me and through which my mind is shaped by organized religion, by economic and social influences? So, if I would live a life in which there is the establishment of right relationship, right conduct, right behavior, I have to find out whether it is possible to live without effort; because where there is effort, all that is denied.

Where there is effort, there must be conscious or unconscious conformity. I see that. I may see it verbally, intellectually, but that is too easy, it has very little meaning. I have to be aware of it in myself. Am I aware, in my daily activities, in my daily relationship with my family, with my friends, to what extent I conform? Being aware of it means knowing that I do conform, not merely superficially, but very deeply, because it is the very nature of the unconscious to conform, and one has to be aware of all that. In talking together this morning, the speaker may be aware of conformity, but that awareness becomes useless unless you also are aware of your own unconscious conformity. You have to be aware, not merely of your adjustments to superficial things but also of your deep-rooted conformity.

As we have seen, conformity implies effort, and where there is effort, there is no real relationship of any kind, but only imitation and a secondhand kind of life. One is aware of this—it is all so obvious. Then one asks oneself whether it is possible to be totally free from the deep cause of conformity. Do you understand? Superficially we have to conform in certain things. You have to sit there, and I have to sit here, unfortunately. We have to put on this or that article of clothing, and so on. Very superficially it is necessary to conform. But to search out this question of conformity in the deep psychological sense, and to find the right answer—not an answer according to one's pleasure, or according to a particular concept, formula, or religious dogma, which is no answer at all, and which becomes so utterly meaningless and stupid—one has to inquire into the question of fear. We are afraid, and that is why we conform. If one had no fear of any kind, would one conform?

So, one sees why one conforms, imitates, adjusts. Superficially a certain conformity may be necessary, and perhaps it is necessary. But deep down, inside the skin, as it were, we conform because there is fear of not doing the right thing, fear of going wrong, fear of not living a complete life, fear of not finding reality, God, and all the rest of it. So in all of us there is the root of fear, and I think it is very important to understand that fact before we try to answer the question as to whether it is possible to end all conformity.

I do not know whether you have ever actually experienced fear. Apart from the instinctive fear which arises upon meeting a physical danger of some kind, have you ever realized what it is to be afraid? It is generally an idea which makes you afraid, is it not? Or rather, the idea creates the fear. Do you understand? I am afraid, let us say, of what you might think of me. That is an example of an idea creating fear; and when an idea creates fear, I am not in relationship with the fact of fear itself. Are you following me? Am I making myself clear?

You know, an idea can cause fear, and with most of us, it is the idea which causes fear. The concept of what tomorrow might bring causes fear, with the result that the concept becomes much more important than the actual fact of fear. So we try to change the concept, the idea, the cause, and we are never directly in relationship with fear itself. Either one is made fearful by an idea, a concept, or one is in immediate contact with fear, and not through an idea. But is there fear without idea?

Please don't just listen to me; don't accept or reject what is being said, but actually go through this with me. Most of us have our own peculiar fears, and it is an idea that is creating them. Perhaps you are afraid that you might lose your husband, your wife, your job; you may be afraid of what will happen tomorrow, afraid that you will fall ill again, and so on. These are all ideas. So we must find out whether it is always an idea that creates fear, or whether there is fear independent of idea. Is there fear independent of idea? Until I find that out, I cannot possibly understand this question of conformity.

Are you following this? It is not really very intricate, but it demands attention and penetration.

I see that there is no fear without idea. I see that thought creates fear, and that fear in itself is nonexistent; so I have to find out why thought, idea, creates fear. Am I making myself clear?

Does thought create fear? Or is it that thought, having created the thinker, then creates fear? Surely, thought in itself does not create fear. Fear arises when there is a thinker separate from the thought, a thinker who is conforming, and who therefore creates fear.

Let us look at it differently. There is the censor, the observer, apart from the thing censored, the thing observed; there is the experiencer apart from the experience, the thinker apart from the thought. And it is thinking that has created the thinker because without thinking, there would be no thinker.

Please, this is not some fanciful theory or mystical philosophy—it is nothing of that kind at all. We are just observing our own daily life. The thinker is the idea, the memory of pains and pleasures, the bundle of recollections, which responds, when there is a challenge, in terms of thought and action.

So I see, as you also must see, that the thinker is the center of ideas based on the pursuit of pleasure and the avoidance of pain. He is the originator of all effort to conform, and that effort is based on fear. As long as there is fear, there is the urge to conform, and so there must be effort. Effort then is always the struggle to imitate, to become, to shape, to adjust oneself to a pattern, and all such effort is obviously based on fear. So merely to cultivate courage, which is part of the effort to become something, has very little meaning. But when one understands this whole structure of fear, then one is confronted with quite a different problem.

As long as there is a thinker separate from thought, there must be not only fear but also effort based on the urge to conform; and when one is aware of that, is it possible to think without creating the thinker? Are you following me? Does this mean anything, or is it just a lot of words being put together? I see you are all puzzled about this, sirs, so let us begin again.

One sees that one's whole life is a routine, a conformity, a repetition, and therefore it is boring. One is aware of that fact. Then one asks oneself: Can there be an ending to all this conformity, not ultimately, at the time of death, but while one is living? To inquire into this, one has to find out what is the nature of conformity, and why the mind always conforms, whether it be to a past experience or to a present pattern of action, or to some future ideal. Conformity, as we have seen, implies imitation, repetition, adjustment, and all the rest of it. I see that where there is conformity, there must be effort; and when there is the effort to conform in relationship, all relationship ceases. My life is a constant repetition, a ceaseless effort to conform, and therefore there is no relationship at all. So I must find out whether it is possible to end the effort of conformity, and therefore to have relationship. But to find out what is implied in the cessation of this effort, I must first find out whether fear, of which one may be conscious or unconscious, can come to an end—totally, and not just partially. This means that my mind must inquire into the depths of the unconscious.

Now, is the conscious mind capable of inquiring into something it has never touched? You know, there are experts—Freud, Jung, and many others—who have described the unconscious, attributing to it various characteristics; but if one is at all aware of one's own inward activities, one need not go to the experts at all. It is fairly obvious that the unconscious is the residue of the past, and the past includes the inherited as well as the acquired memories. There are the family memories, the racial memories, the communal memories. Man's total existence of two million or more years—it is all there in the unconscious. And that unconscious is part of one's fear. I may not be consciously afraid of anything, but deeply I am afraid of so many things. I may have rationalized death most beautifully, but deep down there is still this extraordinary fear of coming to an end. So in the unconscious there is fear; and to understand it, you must come to it, not consciously, not deliberately, but with sensitivity, with freshness, with eagerness, with intensity. In other words, you must come to it with affection, with love, for that is the only way you can understand anything.

So, is it possible to end all fear? One may be afraid of the dark, or of coming suddenly upon a snake, or of meeting some wild animal, or of falling over a precipice. It is natural and healthy to want to stay out of the way of an oncoming bus, for example, but there are many other forms of fear. That is why one has to go into this question of whether the idea is more important than the fact, the *what is*. If one looks at *what is*, at the fact, and not at the idea, then one will see that it is only the idea, the concept of the future, of tomorrow, that is creating fear. It is not the fact which creates fear.

Conformity, adjustment, and adaptability are superficially necessary; but inwardly, deeply, conformity brings about effort, and therefore imitation. As long as the mind is imitating, making effort to conform, it is isolating itself; therefore, it has no relationship, and only breeds greater fear.

Now, I have somewhat analyzed this thing. One could go into it much more deeply, in more detail, and at a greater length, but we have more or less touched upon the important facts. However, the description is not the fact. The word is not the thing. When you are hungry, I can describe food to you, but the words are obviously not the food. Similarly, one has to be directly in contact with this whole question, not just verbally, but actually, and then one begins to find out what freedom is, which is not conformity. One begins to discover for oneself that as long as there is the thinker apart from thought, there must be fear, there must be effort, there must be conformity. Then effort is conformity. And is it possible—please listen to this—is it possible only to think, and not create the thinker? Is it possible to think intensely, reasonably, sanely, logically, without the thinker, whose values, ideas, concepts are all based on pleasure, and therefore the whole process of effort and imitation begins? Is it possible to think only when necessary, not otherwise? That is, can one think only when a question is asked, and the rest of the time be in a complete state of negation—which is a most positive state?

Am I making myself clear? Please don't agree. This is a most difficult thing to inquire into, or to feel one's way into. You can't just say, "I agree"—that has no meaning.

It is the center as the thinker, the censor, that breeds time, and therefore the center is the origin of disorder. It is not thought that creates disorder, but the center, the censor, the thinker who has been put together through time. And as long as there is this censor, this center, this maker of effort, do what you will, there can be no end to fear.

So, for a mind burdened with fear, with conformity, with the thinker, there can be no understanding of that which may be called the original. And the mind demands to know what the original is. We have said it is God—but that again is a word invented by human beings in their fear, in their misery, in their desire to escape from life. When the human mind is free of all fear, then, in demanding to know what the original is, it is not seeking its own pleasure, or a means of escape, and therefore in that inquiry all authority ceases. Do you understand? The authority of the speaker, the authority of the church, the authority of opinion, of knowledge, of experience, of what people say—all that completely comes to an end, and there is no obedience. It is only such a mind that can find out for itself what the original is—find out, not as an individual mind, but as a total human being. There is no "individual" mind at all—we are all totally related. Please understand this. The mind is not something separate; it is a total mind. We are all conforming, we are all afraid, we are all escaping. And to understand—not as an individual, but as a total human being—what the original is, one must understand the totality of man's misery, all the concepts, the formulas which he has invented through the centuries. It is only when there is freedom from all this that you can find out whether there is an original something. Otherwise we are secondhand human beings; and because we are secondhand, counterfeit human beings, there is no ending to sorrow. So the ending of sorrow is in essence the beginning of the original. But the understanding that brings about the ending of sorrow is not just an understanding of your particular sorrow, or my particular sorrow, because your sorrow and my sorrow are related to the whole sorrow of mankind. Do you understand? This is not mere sentiment or emotionalism; it is an actual, brutal fact. When we understand the whole structure of sorrow and thereby bring about the ending of sorrow, there is then a possibility of coming upon that strange something which is the origin of all life—not in a test tube, as the scientist discovers it, but there is the coming into being of that strange energy which is always exploding. That energy has no movement in any direction, and therefore it explodes.

(Pause)

Sirs, as you seem disinclined to ask questions, may I ask you a question? Have you ever experimented with gathering all your energy—physical, emotional, mental, visual, every form of energy—and being with it completely, quietly? Do you understand? You know, when energy has movement in any direction, that energy is being dissipated. But when all one's energy is completely still, there is a movement which is original and therefore explosive. Are you getting this? Try it sometime and see if you can do it. But it requires a great deal of intelligence, a tremendous awareness—it is not just a matter of pleasure and pain. If you can gather all your energy without effort, the mind is then completely full of energy without friction of any kind. Then there is an explosion, and in that explosion there is the original.

July 22, 1965

Seventh Talk in Saanen

In an extraordinarily changing world, in a world of scientific revolutions, economic pressures, and impending wars, it seems to me that our own lives must undergo a tremendous change. The change that is needed is not merely outward, it is not just a matter of acquiring more and better food, clothing, and shelter, but it is necessary to find out what one actually needs apart from food, clothing, and shelter. Life in the modern world is becoming very, very complicated, and one must therefore make one's own human life extraordinarily simple; and that simplicity demands a great deal of intelligence. As a human being living in this changing world, where there is every kind of pressure, anxiety, trouble, sorrow, it seems to me that one has to find out for oneself what one actually needs.

Now, confronted with this question, each person will say what his needs are according to his particular temperament, economic position, social prestige, and so on. But I think that to find out what one needs, one must have peace. It is not that one first finds out what one needs, but rather one must first have peace. Most of us want peace outwardly, in all our relationships; but I think peace begins somewhere else, not outwardly; and without peace, nothing can flourish, nothing can blossom.

Peace is not an escape from the world, from our everyday activities, but rather one has to find out, while actually living in this world, what peace is. As a human being living in a confusing, contradictory, suffering world, how deeply does one demand peace? Surely, the manner of our life, the way of our conduct, the nature of our daily activities, will spontaneously bring about peace, if we want peace. But I am afraid very few of us want peace; and when we do want peace, what we really want is security, comfort, a state of not being disturbed at all. Obviously we cannot go on as we are, with the way we think, the way we act; we cannot possibly go on in the way we are going now. Either there is going to be a terrific crash or human beings will awaken to a different way of thinking, a different way of living.

And that is what I would like to talk about this morning. As human beings totally related to all other human beings, and living in the actual world of everyday events, can we discover for ourselves a different way of living, a different way of thinking, acting? To find that out, one must inquire into the actual state in which we as human beings are now living; one must be conscious of the everyday movement of one's own life—not as a theory, not as a concept, but as an actual fact. And one not only has to be conscious of that but also has to end sorrow, because a mind in sorrow cannot think clearly, cannot see clearly. The ending of sorrow is the beginning of wisdom, and it is only in wisdom that a new thing is born.

So one must inquire very deeply into the ending of sorrow, because if we can end sorrow, we have solved all our problems. For most of us, if we are at all awake to anything in life, that is the one central demand—how to end sorrow so that a new beginning can be made. I think that is a fundamental question which one has to ask oneself. Is it at all possible for a human being to end sorrow altogether, and not escape from the world of actuality, from the world of daily activities? Can one be totally free of sorrow, and not just escape from sorrow through drugs, through religious beliefs, through philosophical concepts, or through some kind of mystical bent of one's own mind that gives one complete satisfaction?—for that too is an escape from actuality.

So, living in this world, living our daily life of relationship, we must find out whether it is possible completely to end sorrow. Consciously we can rationalize sorrow, we can see the causes of it; but mere rationalization does not bring sorrow to an end. Sorrow is grief, uncertainty, the feeling of complete loneliness. There is the sorrow of death, the sorrow of not being able to fulfill oneself, the sorrow of not being recognized, the sorrow of loving and not being loved in return. There are innumerable forms of sorrow, and it seems to me that without understanding sorrow, there is no end to conflict, to misery, to the everyday travail of corruption and deterioration.

This is one of the fundamental questions, it seems to me, that one has to ask oneself and find an answer to. There is conscious sorrow, and there is also unconscious sorrow, the sorrow that seems to have no basis, no immediate cause. Most of us know conscious sorrow, and we also know how to deal with it. Either we run away from it through religious belief or we rationalize it, or we take some kind of drug, whether intellectual or physical; or we bemuse ourselves with words, with amusements, with superficial entertainment. We do all this, and yet we cannot get away from conscious sorrow.

Then there is the unconscious sorrow which we have inherited through the centuries. Man has always sought to overcome this extraordinary thing called sorrow, grief, misery; but even when we are superficially happy and have everything we want, deep down in the unconscious there are still the roots of sorrow. So when we talk about the ending of sorrow, we mean the ending of all sorrow, both conscious and unconscious.

To end sorrow, one must have a very clear, very simple mind. Simplicity is not a mere idea. To be simple demands a great deal of intelligence and sensitivity. We think that to be simple is to return to nature, or to have only one or two articles of clothing, or to eat very few meals and have only just enough shelter. We are familiar with all the outward show of simplicity, but I do not know if we have ever really thought about this matter at all. What does it mean to be very clear, very simple?

Now, let us differentiate here between what we mean by simplicity, and what is generally regarded as being simple. Nowadays more and more facts are being accumulated. There is a computer-like acquiring of information, knowledge, and with this knowledge we hope to arrive at a better understanding of life, a greater expansion of wisdom. But the more knowledge one has, the less simple life becomes.

Please, you and I are both learning; and to learn, one must listen. Listening is learning. There is not first listening and then learning, or first listening and then acting. Listening is action. If you and I know how to listen to human events, to all that is taking place in the world, to the philosophies, the dogmatisms, the rituals, the religions, the television—if we know how to listen to all that, then the very act of listening is doing; and that, I think, is the art of listening. If you can listen to the train that goes by, to that rushing water, to your neighbor, to the radio, to yourself; if you can listen to what is going on in the world: the misery, the confusion, the extraordinary conflict between man and man—listen to it totally, completely, and not translate it in terms of your own knowledge, in terms of the information gathered by your own petty, little mind—then perhaps that very listening is acting. And that is what we need: action. But to act you must have simplicity, and simplicity is not derived from the complexity of knowledge. Simplicity comes with great sensitivity, and with the understanding of sorrow.

What is sorrow? Why do we suffer, not only physically, organically, but inwardly, psychologically? Why do we suffer, and what does this suffering mean? Apparently very few human beings have escaped from this suffering—escaped in the sense that they have brought suffering to an end. Throughout the history of the world, probably only one or two have gone beyond this ache. And unless we human beings find out for ourselves how to end sorrow, all our lives will be dull, empty, confused, conflicting, and we shall everlastingly be making effort to do or not to do something. So we must find out, learn what sorrow actually is, and not interpret it in any way, not search for the cause of it. We know the cause of sorrow. Someone dies, and you feel terribly lonely, miserable, full of self-pity; so death brings sorrow. Or there is sorrow because you have not been able to fulfill yourself in life, you have not become known, important, famous. You want to do certain things, but you are not able to do them because you are physically incapacitated in some way, so again there is sorrow. Or you use time as a means of endgaining, and in that process of time there is sorrow. So we all know that the mere search for the cause of sorrow does not end sorrow. I know why I suffer, and you know why you suffer, but that knowledge does not bring sorrow to an end. So either one becomes cynical, bitter, hard, or one escapes from sorrow, or one just lives with it, and therefore the mind becomes more and more dull, insensitive.

Knowing all this, what is one to do? You understand my question? It is very important to answer this question because a mind that is worn out by sorrow, conscious or unconscious, is a dull mind, an insensitive mind; it is a mind that is incapable of learning. And life itself is a movement of learning. It is not a process of acquiring knowledge from which you subsequently act—learning is action, and in acting you are learning. But if you acquire knowledge or information with which to shape action, or have a formula from which you act, then there is bound to be conflict, and that conflict also is sorrow.

This is one of the major problems of life, and how is one to resolve it intelligently, sanely, completely? To answer this question, not just verbally, but actually, and therefore to end sorrow, one must have great inward peace.

Now, what do we mean by the word *peace?* Most of us want peace in terms of our own pleasure. Please listen to what is being said—listen to it neither agreeing nor disagreeing, but as you would listen to that water rushing by. It rained a great deal last night, and that river is swift, rich, full of silt. You can't alter it. It is there, running, and you can only listen to it; and the more you listen, the more sensitive you become to all the noises, to the murmurings, to the quietness, to the solitude, to the immensity of life. In the same way, listen now to what is being said, and discover as we go along.

You know, we all want peace: peace in our relationships, in our work, in our surroundings; peace inwardly and outwardly. But for most of us peace means being completely satisfied, accepting things as they are and remaining with them. We don't want to be disturbed. But life is always disturbing us. There is the war going on in Vietnam, there is the war in our hearts. The armies and the generals are preparing for war in every part of the world, though they talk of peace. The politicians talk of peace, and yet they are seeking power, position, national prestige. We want peace in terms of our own pleasure, but pleasure and peace cannot go together because pleasure prevents the mind from seeing the actual, the factual, the *what is*. So to understand peace, one first has to understand pleasure.

We translate what we call peace in terms of our own pleasure, and therefore, without understanding the whole structure of pleasure, we cannot possibly have peace. And one must have peace. That is, one must have peace in the sense of having immense space inwardly, space without limitation. Peace means space in which there is no center to create a boundary. This is very difficult to go into and to understand. Peace is a state of mind which gives no boundary to space. And to understand peace, we must understand what pleasure is, because it is pleasure that creates the image, that center which projects a limited space around itself. It is pleasure that dictates the terms and translates the values of every act. Please observe yourselves, see your own conscious and unconscious ways of thinking and feeling, your self-created values.

So what is pleasure, and why does the mind cling to pleasure? The animal avoids pain and wants only pleasure—and there is a great deal of the animal in each one of us. If we observe ourselves, we will see that we don't want anything but continuous pleasure in different forms. We want excitement, amusement, knowledge, information, prestige, fulfillment; we want to be known, to carry out what we think is right, trying in the process to control others. The cycle or the wheel of pleasure—that is what dictates our values, our standards, our activities, our relationships. What is pleasure? It is sensation—the sensation which is pleasurable, and from which there is desire. And what gives continuity to desire? There is perception or seeing, sensation, contact, and desire.

Are you following me? Please watch this. It is nothing mysterious that we are talking about; it is a very simple fact. You see a fine car, or a beautiful woman, or a splendid house, or a precious jewel, or a man who has great power in the world—whatever it is—and you want that too. You see something so-called beautiful, attractive, and from the perceiving, the seeing of it, there is sensation, followed by contact and desire. That is the cycle, is it not? And then the question is: What gives a continuity to that moment of desire? Because if I understand what gives continuity to desire, then perhaps I shall know how to deal with desire, how to come to grips with it and not merely suppress, control, or try to destroy it.

So the mind knows how desire arises. That much is clear. But what gives desire a continuity? Surely it is thought. When there is perception of a car, followed by sensation, contact, and desire, if thought does not give continuity to that desire, the desire ends, does it not? We see, then, that desire is given continuity by thought. The more I think about that car, the more the desire to possess it is strengthened—which is the desire for pleasure. So without understanding the machinery of thinking, I cannot possibly understand the nature of pleasure, or of peace. Therefore I must understand the machinery of thinking.

Please, we are trying to find out what peace is, because without peace our life is dreadfully confused, miserable, anxious, as we know all too well. And to find out what peace is, we must not only understand sorrow, but we must also understand what is pleasure, what is desire, and what is thinking. We cannot skip any phase of it; we have to understand the process as a whole, and not in fragments.

So we are now inquiring into what thinking is. Putting it very simply, thinking is obviously the response of knowledge and experience as memory. The computer stores up a great deal of information on its electronic tape, and when you ask it an appropriate question, it will give you the right answer. Similarly, a great deal of inherited and acquired knowledge has been stored up in the human brain as memory, and when it is challenged, it responds according to its stored-up knowledge, according to the memory of its various activities and experiences. Whether memory is conscious or unconscious, it is always conditioned. Like the computer, it cannot go beyond itself, beyond the information that has been given to it. We as human beings cannot go beyond ourselves because we are conditioned; we are tethered to our knowledge, to our information, to our experience, to our past. It is the past that responds to any question, and that response is what we call thought. The response may take a long or a very short time, and this process is fairly simple and clear. A familiar question may be answered immediately, whereas a question which is not at all familiar will take a greater length of time—the interval between the question and the answer will be greater.

So what we call thought is always conditioned. The more one thinks about pleasure, and avoids pain, the more the values and images of desire take root in the mind. Surely that is very simple. Yet it is right and natural to respond to what one sees. When you see a beautiful car, for example, you respond, and that response must exist; otherwise, you are blind, or paralyzed, or insensitive. But why should one think about it? If you want the car and have the means, you get it. If you don't have the means, why should you keep on creating in your mind the image of pleasure? So one begins to see that desire is not a thing to be abhorred, controlled, or suppressed, but rather one must understand how it comes into being, and what gives it continuity. When we understand this whole picture, then desire has quite a different meaning. Then desire no longer tortures the mind.

Now, if that much is clear, then one sees that what we call thought is the origin of conflict. Our thought being the response of the past, it meets the challenge of the present inadequately, and therefore there is conflict. Then we say that thought must be controlled; but that very control of thought only increases our conflict with life, which, like that stream, is constantly moving. So thought does not bring about the understanding of life; thought does not free the mind from sorrow; thought will never bring about peace. Thought is the response of the past, and therefore thought must always be limited, conditioned. As long as the mind is translating all the activities of life in terms of thought, and as long as thought is creating action, it will only breed more conflict, more misery.

Then what is peace? Is peace to be sought through thought, through the pleasure of organized idea? Obviously not. Peace is a state of mind in which the image, or the idea, or the pleasure of organized idea, does not arise.

Please, we are asking the mind to do a most extraordinary thing, a thing which it has never done before. We are used to having a series of thoughts, conclusions, formulas, from which we act. But I say such a process will not bring about peace at all. What brings about peace is to understand the total machinery of thought, pleasure, and idea. When that machinery is completely understood, then there is a quietness with which thought does not interfere. Then there is no thought except when thought has to act.

I wonder if I am making myself clear? No, please don't nod your heads in agreement, because this is one of the most difficult things to understand. We are trying to find out how to end sorrow. You are not agreeing or disagreeing with my words or ideas. We are trying to find out how a human being, who has lived in sorrow for two million years or more, can end sorrow; because without the ending of sorrow, there is no light, no clarity, no intelligence. Man may be very clever; he may go to the moon, photograph Mars, invent new machinery, new techniques to kill and to preserve; but as long as there is sorrow, there is no ending to conflict, to misery, to confusion. That is why we are inquiring into sorrow and trying to find out whether one can actually be free of sorrow.

As I said, without understanding the nature of thought, the nature of pleasure as organized idea, there is no peace. We have to live in this world, which is becoming more and more complex, more and more tyrannical. The radio, the television, the newspapers, the politicians, the priests, the organized religions with their beliefs, dogmas, rituals, are all conditioning us, and their propaganda is becoming more and more cunning. Psychologically they know all the tricks, how to control the mind of man. So one has to be aware of all these processes, aware of these innumerable influences that are always impinging upon us, and be free of them. And that is where simplicity begins. It is not a cunning mind, not an informed mind, but only a very simple mind that sees directly, without distortion; and there will be distortion as long as there is in the mind the image of pleasure.

The simple mind is an austere mind. Do you know what it means to be austere? An austere mind is generally understood to be one that is harshly self-disciplined, controlled, suppressed, a mind that ruthlessly conforms to a pattern. But such a mind is neither simple nor austere; it is really a frightened mind, and because it is frightened, it conforms. Its conformity is called austerity, but we are talking of an austerity in which there is no conformity of any kind at all. We are using the word *austere*, not in the sense of being disciplined according to a pattern, but in the sense of being aware of all the implications of pleasure, and of the image or the center. That very awareness brings about a spontaneous discipline—which is the austerity I am talking about.

You cannot be austere if you are not passionate. You know, for most of us passion is translated as lust, or we talk about having a passion for work, a passion to express oneself, or a passion to become something. But I am using the word in the sense of intensity. There is a gathering-in of energy, which becomes tremendously intense—and that is passion. Without this passion, there is no austerity, and therefore no simplicity. You must have tremendous passion to be simple; and with that passion, with that intensity, you can approach sorrow. You cannot resolve or end sorrow without passion, without great energy; and energy is dissipated when there is conflict, that is, when you say, "I must not suffer," or try to find the cause of sorrow, or try to escape from sorrow. You need all your energy, all your attention to face sorrow. There is a state of intense, passionate attention which, while not conforming, is highly disciplined, and is therefore extraordinarily austere. In that state your mind is very simple, and therefore you can meet this thing which is called sorrow. Then the mind will discover for itself that sorrow has an end, and therefore despair, frustration, loneliness—all these things also come to an end. It is only when there is the ending of sorrow that there is freedom, and it is only when the mind is free that it is both wise and active.

Question: Is there any difference between individual suffering and the suffering of mankind?

KRISHNAMURTI: Is your suffering as an individual different from my suffering, or from the suffering of a man in Asia, in America, or in Russia? The circumstances, the incidents may vary, but in essence another man's suffering is the same as mine and yours, isn't it? Suffering is suffering, surely, not yours or mine. Pleasure is not your pleasure, or my pleasure—it is pleasure. When you are hungry, it is not your hunger only, it is the hunger of the whole of Asia too. When you are driven by ambition, when you are ruthless, it is the same ruthlessness that drives the politician, the man in power, whether he is in Asia, in America, or in Russia.

You see, that is what we object to. We don't see that we are all one humanity, caught in different spheres of life, in different areas. When you love somebody, it is not your love. If it is, it becomes tyrannical, possessive, jealous, anxious, brutal. Similarly, suffering is suffering; it is not yours or mine. I am not just making it impersonal, I am not making it something abstract. When one suffers, one suffers. When a man has no food, no clothing, no shelter, he is suffering, whether he lives in Asia, or in the West. The people who are now being killed or wounded—the Vietnamese and the Americans—are suffering. To understand this suffering—which is neither yours nor mine, which is not impersonal or abstract, but actual, and which we all have—requires a great deal of penetration, insight. And the ending of this suffering will naturally bring about peace, not only within, but outside.

I think we should stop now because I have talked for over an hour. But if you have really listened, then that very act of listening is the act of doing. To listen is to act. If you have listened this morning really deeply, listened with full attention, with clarity, then you will see that sorrow will never touch you again—which doesn't mean that you don't love. When we have ended sorrow, then perhaps we shall know what love is. But without ending sorrow, love becomes tyranny, love becomes pain, love becomes a thing that has no meaning at all, except as memory, as pleasure.

July 25, 1965

Eighth Talk in Saanen

I would like this morning to go into a question which I think is most important in the lives of all of us: the question of love and death. But before I go into that, I would like to make certain things clear.

Communication is comparatively easy when we both know the same language and give the same meaning to the same word. If both of us have the same reference, and it is constant, then communication becomes possible, as was demonstrated by the Mariner II, which passed fairly close to Mars and sent photographs and messages back to earth. As long as verbal communication is necessary, we must both be very clear in the understanding and use of words.

But communion, I think, is much more difficult because in communion we are not sharing—even though that word, according to the dictionary, implies sharing, partaking. I think sharing is possible only with regard to things, experiences, ideas; but if you go beyond all that, sharing becomes really impossible. You and I can't share the beauty of those mountains. One may talk about them, one may write a book about them, or put words together to make a poem; but you and I can't share their extraordinary beauty. That beauty is there for each one of us to look at, to delight in, but we are not sharing that beauty. Beauty cannot be shared because beauty is not a stimulus. If we understand the meaning of that word *sharing,* we can see very clearly that sharing implies that one who has experience, or knowledge, is willing to allow another to partake of it with him. That is generally what is called sharing—and with that goes the whole hierarchical system of division. Sharing implies that you know and I don't know, does it not? You share with me what I do not know, what I have not experienced, what I have never felt. You are good or generous enough to be willing to share something with me.

But pure beauty cannot be shared because you can't own it, and I can't own it. It isn't an item of personal property; it isn't a thing which you or I can possess, and then share with another. Beauty is simply there, like the sunset, like the mountain, like the flowing of a river, like the quietude of an evening. Because beauty is there, you can look at it and delight in it; but you cannot share that beauty with another. The other also must be deeply aware; he must be equally sensitive, intelligent. Then beauty is not to be shared but rather to be looked at, to be enjoyed. It is there for each one to revel in, to take delight in.

So when we use the word share, it generally implies that one possesses and another does not, that one has something and another has not. That attitude, that feeling of sharing, reflects the hierarchical approach of life: the top brass and the common soldier; the Pope and the ordinary priest; the cardinal in his magnificent robes and the lowly monk in his black cloth; the one who knows and the one who does not know. Such an attitude breeds authority, ambition, struggle, great pain, and infinite sorrow.

Please listen to all this very carefully because we are going into something which cannot be shared, and therefore there is no partaking. You must really understand this dreadful evil—if I may use the word—of the hierarchical division of life as the one who knows and the one who does not know. Truth cannot possibly be divided as the high and the low; therefore, there is no authority, no hierarchical approach. The hierarchical division of life is a poisonous, dreadful thing.

So what we are going to do this morning is not a matter of sharing, but both of us are going to inquire; we are going to move together into something which we don't know. Please do not wait for me to tell you, or to share something with you which you have not; do not wait for me to give you enlightenment, or freedom. No one can give you freedom, nor can anyone share it with you. But most of us are used to this attitude of someone giving and another receiving, and it creates a division in life which brings about authority with all its evils. In truth there is not the follower and the one who leads, there is neither the teacher nor the taught; and that is a marvelous thing, if you realize it for yourself. In that there is great beauty, in that there is freedom, in that there is the ending of sorrow because one has to work, to inquire, to break through, to destroy all that is false, and thereby find out for oneself.

Now, this morning we are going to inquire into two things which for most of us are of the utmost importance in life: love, and the thing called death. To inquire, to find out, to discover, there must obviously be freedom—not freedom at the end, but freedom right from the beginning. Without freedom you can't look, you can't inquire, you can't move into the unknown. For a mind that would inquire, whether in the complicated field of science or in the complex and subtle field of human consciousness, there must be freedom. You can't come to it with your knowledge, with your prejudices, with your anxieties and fears, for these factors will shape your perception; they will push you in different directions, and therefore all real inquiry ceases. Similarly, when we are trying to see what this extraordinary thing means—this thing that we call love—we cannot come to it with our personal prejudices, with our conclusions, with our preconceived notions that it must be this way or it must be that way; we cannot say that love must be expressed in the family, between husband and wife, or that there is profane love and spiritual love, because all this prevents us from going into the question profoundly, freely, and with a certain breathless pursuit.

So, to inquire we need freedom, and therefore we must be aware from the very beginning of how conditioned we are, how prejudiced we are; we must be aware of the fact that we look at life through the desire for pleasure, and thereby prevent ourselves from seeing what actually is. And when we are free of these things, then perhaps we can inquire into this extraordinary thing called love.

We live in this world in a state of relationship—relationship between man and woman, between friends, between ourselves and our ideas, our property, and so on. Life demands relationship, and relationship cannot exist when the mind is isolating itself in all its activities. Please watch this process in yourselves. When there is self-centered activity, there is no relationship. Whether you are sleeping in the same bed with another, or going in a crowded bus, or looking at a mountain, as long as your mind is caught up in self-centered activity, obviously it can only lead to isolation, and therefore there is no relationship.

Now, it is from this turmoil of self-centered activity that most of us begin to inquire into what love is, and this again prevents real inquiry because all self-centered activity is based on the pursuit of pleasure and the avoidance of pain. As long as we are inquiring from a center which exists for its own pleasure, our inquiry will be useless and vain. To really inquire, there must be freedom from this self-centered activity—and that is extremely difficult. It requires great intelligence, great understanding, great insight, and therefore one has to have a very good mind: a mind that is not sentimental, not emotional, not carried away by enthusiasm, but a mind that is very clear, aware, sensitive all around. It is only such a mind that can begin to inquire into what we call love.

Now, what is love for most of us, actually?—not what we would like it to be. What we would like love to be is merely an idea, a concept, a formula, and therefore it has no validity at all. We must start with *what is*, and not with 'what should be'. We must start with the fact, and not with opinions, conclusions. Conclusions, opinions, formulas, are utterly misleading and destructive. A marvelous utopia, conceived or formulated by a few clever, cunning minds, can twist and destroy the lives of thousands and millions of people because they are willing to kill or be killed for that one idea. And we do the same, inwardly, with ourselves. We have a formula, a feeling, a belief that to love we should be this or that, and we torture our lives, live in agony, because we are trying to approximate the fact of what we are to the ideal of what we should be, which is an illusion, a mere invention of the mind, which has no reality.

So we are now going to inquire, not from 'what should be', but from *what is*. What actually is our love? There is in it pleasure, pain, anxiety, jealousy, attachment, possessiveness, domination, and the fear of losing that which we possess. There is the love which exists in the relationship between two people, and there is the love of an idea, of a formula, whether it be the nation, a utopia, or God. Now, when we talk about love, we are only talking about the love that actually exists in relationship, and not about the poisonous thing called love for one's country, that nationalistic patriotism which is exploited by the politician and the priest. We are talking about the fact of love as it actually exists between human beings. In that love there is pain, there is the torture of uncertainty, jealousy, the fear of loneliness, and therefore the urge to possess, to dominate, to hold. These are facts, are they not? And therefore we have the legal marriage, which society has established for the protection of the children. But the family as a unit is opposed to every other family unit. "My family" is competing with all the other families of the world. And in the family itself there is a battle going on incessantly: the desire to possess, to dominate, and hence fear, jealousy, anxiety over whether you are loved or not loved, and so on and so on. That is what we call love. And though one must have a family, we try in various ways to escape from this torture: through social activity, or by becoming terribly religious, which means that we join some ugly, little organization and believe in a particular formula about God, or Jesus, or Buddha, or what you will. Or else we treat the whole of family relationship as something very superficial, just a passing burden which we have to put up with, so we grit our teeth and carry on.

All this is what we call love. Becoming dissatisfied with so-called family love, we turn to the love of God, or the love of humanity, or the love of one's neighbor. We don't really know what love is, but we love God, we love our neighbor—at least we say we do. And all the while we are destroying our neighbor through ruthless ambition, through cunning business practices, through all the competitiveness of modern society. Then there is the so-called love of parents for their children—and you know the real structure, the torture of that possessive game.

Now, if one is at all sensitive, watching, feeling, looking, one knows all this. One is intimately and painfully aware of it all; and then one asks: Is it possible to live in a family, to live with one's wife or husband, with one's children, without this torture? If one can do that, then perhaps one begins to find out what love is. Love demands, really, that we see the actuality of our daily life, doesn't it? The petty, everyday incidents that take place in the family, in the office, on the bus, in the car, on the road; the disrespect we feel for people—knowing the torture of all this, is it possible to let it all go, actually and not just theoretically? Is it possible actually not to be attached, not to be possessive, not to dominate or be dominated? And if your wife or your husband wants to go away with someone else, is it possible not to be jealous, not to feel hate, antagonism? Surely it is only then that there is a possibility of something unknown coming into being.

The love that we have is the known, with all its misery, its confusion; there is in it the torture of jealousy, the ugliness and pain of violence, the pleasure of sex. That is all we know, and we are unwilling to face that fact—the fact of what we know.

You know, you can live with the beauty of those mountains, and get very used to it.

After a week or ten days, you will no longer even notice that beauty. You will be like the villagers, who don't look at the mountains for a second, they are so used to them. We get used to beauty, as well as to ugliness. What is important is not the beauty or the ugliness but the fact of getting used to anything. We get used to our own lives, to our tortures, to our miseries, to our petty, little houses, to all the ugliness of our narrow, little minds. We don't want to look beyond, we don't want to tear through all this confusion and find out, so we just get used to it. And when one gets used to anything, it doesn't matter what it is—whether it is beauty or torture or anxiety or ugliness—the mind becomes dull, insensitive, unaware, and in that state it occupies itself with all kinds of things: with God, with religion, with entertainment, with social work, with gossip, with accumulating knowledge, or looking at television.

So what is important is to be aware of the facts of our life, of the tortures, the possessiveness, the domination, the interference, the constant corrections, the criticisms, the demands—to live with all that and not get used to it, to be aware of it and not just accept it. I do not mean that we should put up with it, embrace it, but that we should look at it and not avoid or escape from it. We should look at the facts of our daily relationships without giving reasons why this should be and that should not be. To look at the facts of your own life in this manner demands great energy, and you have that energy only when you are not escaping from those facts, either through belief, through explanations, through trying to find the cause, or in any other way. If you are completely aware of *what is,* which is to know all the intricacies, all the subtleties of it, if you are totally familiar with the known, then perhaps there is a possibility of being free of the known.

If we do not know what love is, then we shall never know what death is. We have got used to death. Hundreds are now being killed in Vietnam. We have had two terrible world wars, and untold thousands of people have been killed in Russia for the sake of ideas. We have got used to all this killing, and to the starvation, the poverty, and the degradation in Asia, which exist side by side with the prosperity in Europe and America. We have got used to this thing called death, and we accept it. We say that death is man's inevitable end—old age, disease, and finally the grave or the crematorium, whichever you prefer. We don't revolt against death because we can't; it is coming nearer every day, as we grow older. We have misused the physical organism, so there is disease. One may die young, or die old, but either way there is disease, pain, torture. Through the demand for good health people may eventually live for 150 or even 200 years, but there is always death at the end of it.

Knowing that death is inevitable, most of us have faith in reincarnation, in resurrection, or in some other form of continuity after death because continuity is all we want; so belief, formula, hope, dogma again play an extraordinarily important part in our life. We are not concerned with the fact of death but with whether there is a life hereafter. We say, "What is the point of struggling, cultivating virtue, trying to become godlike"—you know all that silly stuff that one does—"only to end in death?" Therefore we say that there must be something hereafter.

Now, what is the "something" that we want to continue? Do you understand? In different words, in different spheres, in different types of hope, and so on, all the religions throughout the world promise some kind of continuity after death. But when we put all that away, what is it that we want to continue? It is our daily life, isn't it? The life that we know. And what is the life that we know? It is the life of companionship, the life of daily torture, uncertainty, hope; the agony of loneliness, the quarrels, the going to the office day after day for thirty or forty years; the petty, little mind that we have, the conditioned life, the pleasures of traveling and seeing something new; the disease, the pain, the empty boredom of our existence—that is all we know. And now we also know how to go to Mars and take photographs. We know more and more of external things.

So, what is it that we so desperately cling to? Obviously, it is the memory of things that have been; and is it not a terrible thing to realize that we cling to something that is past, gone, finished, dead? That is all we know, and to that we cling. We cling to the known. One's character, one's books, the paintings one has done, the experiences, the pleasures, the anxieties one has had, the guilt one has felt—all that is the past, and that is what we are clinging to. That is all we know, and so we want that to continue after death. If I have lost my wife, I want to meet her on the other side, and so on. So what we are afraid of is losing the known, which is the past—the past which, moving through the present, creates the future; and that is what we are clinging to.

Please do listen to this. I am not doing propaganda for something, I am just pointing out the facts.

Now, when you cling to something that is past, then your mind, your heart, your whole being is already dead. It may have been a deep delight, a thrilling pleasure, but the moment you cling to it, your mind becomes an ugly, little thing that cannot really live. And that is our life. Being afraid that our so-called life is going to end, we invent or we hope for a continuity after death. But when you are aware of all that and are no longer escaping, when you are looking, observing, listening, being choicelessly aware of everything that is going on inside you, then you are faced with the question of death, which is actually the unknown. You don't know death; you merely have ideas about it. You have ideas, fears, anxieties, and there is this tremendous sense of loneliness, of being alone, in solitude. And when one is aware of all that, then one asks oneself, "Can I die to everything known? Can I die to the past, not bit by bit, not keeping the pleasurable and rejecting the unpleasant, but dying to pleasure as well as to pain, which is to end the past without argument?"

You know, when death comes you don't argue, you don't say, "Give me a few more days." When death is there, you have gone. In the same way we must empty the mind of all the past. In emptying the mind willingly, naturally, effortlessly, then perhaps there is freedom from the known, and therefore there is an understanding of the unknown.

Most of us don't know what love is. We know the pain and the pleasure of love, but we don't see the fact of love as we see the fact of a mountain; so for us love is something unknown, as death is. But when the mind is free of the known, then there is the coming into being of that which is not knowable through words, through experience, through visions, through any form of expression. Without knowing love, without knowing the extraordinary fullness, the richness of death, we shall never know what it is to live without torture, without anxiety, without the pain of everyday travail.

Shall we discuss, or will you ask questions on what I have talked about this morning?

Question: What is the origin of continuity?

KRISHNAMURTI: It is fairly simple, isn't it? You have had a pleasure you want it to continue, and thought gives it the nourishment to continue. If thought did not interfere with that pleasure, it would have no continuity, no endurance. Do see this, it is so simple. Let us say you have written a book and put your name to it. That gives you pleasure because you have become known; you are praised, criticized, publicized, and all the rest of that nonsense, which you like, and so you think about it. You meet your friends, who say, "What a marvelous book you have written"; you delight in it, you think about it, and all this gives continuity to your pleasure. It is really very simple. What matters is to be aware of this total process, and then you can put your name to the book, or not put your name to it, and it has no meaning. Then you function as a human being, anonymously; and anything that is great must be anonymous.

(Pause)

Since you are not asking any more questions, I would like to ask you a question. By now you must be asking yourself, "How is one to die to anything?" Do you understand? How is one to die to a pleasure that one has had, or to the insults that one has received? How does one put away, easily, happily, without the least effort, the remembrance of an experience that has given one tremendous pleasure? It is easy to put away something that has given pain—one forgets it very quickly. The pain you had a week ago when your tooth was bothering you, you have already forgotten. You have forgotten the intense pain you had when your baby was born; but the pleasure of that baby, the delight in seeing it grow and all that business, you cling to. Now, how is one to die to all of the known, the pleasurable as well as the painful, and yet live and function in this world reasonably, efficiently, going to the office, and all the rest of it? Don't you want to know? Why don't you ask? Is it that you have merely accepted all this? You see, there is great sorrow in not asking, in not finding out. It is not a matter of finding out from me but of finding out for yourselves by asking fundamental questions and going through to the very end of the problem, whatever it is, irrespective of your family, and of all the paraphernalia of society that surrounds you.

How does one totally reject the past—which, after all, is dying?

You know, forgiveness is a dreadful thing. Do you understand? No? All right, I will explain. First you accumulate the insults, the angers, and after accumulating all that, you forgive. But if you never accumulate, there is nothing to forgive, is there? So the first thing to find out is whether it is at all possible never to accumulate the past. If you don't accumulate the past, there is no need to die to the past. In the same way, if you don't accumulate the pain, the insults, the angers, then there is nothing to forgive. A mind that is forgiving is a cruel mind. So that is one problem: How not to accumulate the past, as most of us do, but to reject it instantly and totally? To use time as a means of dying to the past, or of rejecting it bit by bit—that is the greatest sorrow of man. One can do it in a completely different way. We will go into that presently.

Please, I am not giving you a method or a formula. Don't say, "I have learned something, and I am going to apply it." If you have learned some formula from what I have been saying, and you are going to apply it, then you are like the man who accumulates and forgives, and therefore you are back again in the same old torture of conflict and effort.

Now, I have accumulated pleasure in different forms; I have remembrances of pleasure in its different aspects, its different nuances, subtleties; and how am I to end all that? We know how to get rid of pain; the mind somehow always gets rid of pain quickly because it is pursuing pleasure. Its main concern is pleasure; all its evaluations are based on pleasure, and therefore it can very quickly reject anything that is not pleasurable; it happens almost unconsciously. But how am I, who have accumulated pleasure, with all its subtleties and values, to die to that pleasure, to reject it, not piecemeal, but totally? Do you understand my question?

Comment: By letting go.

KRISHNAMURTI: Who am I to let go? Who is it that is letting go?

Comment: The maker of that habit.

KRISHNAMURTI: Who is the maker of that habit? It is still the essence of pleasure. You don't listen to yourself as you are saying things, you don't learn from what you are saying. You say, "Let go." Who is it that is letting go? The image that is the essence of pleasure says, "I will let that go because I want a greater pleasure, which is the understanding of the unknown." Previously it was the toy, the house, the wife, sex, the family, the nation; and now, because you are a little older, a little bit senile and fed up with the whole thing, you say, "Well, I'll let go to get the unknown."

No, sir, you are not learning. You are not learning from your own observation. Please just listen to me. I know all the questions you would like to ask. I have talked for an hour, I am sorry, and I don't want to be the only person who talks; but please just listen quietly to what is being said.

How am I, who have gathered so much pleasure, and have thereby invited so much pain—how am I to die to all that, let it drop away? First of all, why should I let it drop away? Why should I drop my pleasure? Is it because someone has told me that pleasure breeds pain? Or do I see for myself the significance, the nature, the structure of pleasure? Seeing the nature of pleasure is like seeing the nature of a tree, and how it grows. One does not see it verbally, as an idea, but one is actually living with it. One is not accepting or denying pleasure, one is not thinking about it, or pushing it away. No positive action is taking place: One is merely looking at it. One is looking at the memory of pleasure, completely, quietly, without any movement of the mind. Do you understand?

Sir, when you look at that mountain, if you look at it very quietly, it will tell you a lot of things. You then look more deeply, you feel the nature of it, you see the beauty of its soaring peak and curving lines. But if your mind is chattering, asking, demanding, pushing—you know all that it does—then you are not looking.

So, to understand and therefore to be free of the past, you must know the nature, the structure, the whole meaning of pleasure. To watch, to be aware of pleasure, is not to say, "I will keep this pleasure and throw away that pleasure." Just watch the whole structure of it. Then you will see that pleasure no longer has any significance. You have to remember certain things, but pleasure has nothing to do with it, and therefore you die to the things that have given pleasure. You must have a certain amount of technical knowledge, and you may have to add more to it, but that accumulation of knowledge does not give you pleasure, even though technical knowledge can be used to derive pleasure. For the mind that is alertly aware of itself, that is fully conscious of its own activities, there is self-knowing; and self-knowing is the beginning of wisdom. Self-knowing brings freedom; and when there is freedom from the known, which is the very image of pleasure, then the mind enters into quite a different state, into quite a different dimension.

July 27, 1965

Ninth Talk in Saanen

We have had eight talks here in the tent this year, and we have touched upon many points concerning human thought, feeling, and action; and we have seen the necessity for a total mutation of the human mind. Most of us, I think, do not realize how extraordinarily important it is to feel our way hesitantly, persistently, and seriously into this question of a total mutation, rather than to make a determined effort to pursue a certain type of activity. The mind has been heavily conditioned for millennia, and is it at all possible to break through this conditioning and come upon a way of living which is totally different, a way of living in which there is no sorrow, no conflict, and in which all the travail that human beings are heir to has completely ceased? Surely, one must find out whether it is possible to have a fresh mind, a new mind, a mind that is good, strong, healthy, reasonable, a mind that can function in the various aspects of our daily living—having a family, holding a job, going to the office—as an integrated whole, and not as a series of fragmentary problems.

We have gone into all this, more or less, taking each time different points; and this morning I would like to consider with you, if I may, the question of deterioration. We can see that everything in the world—artistically, politically, morally—is going downhill. I know that as we get older we tend to compare the present conditions with those we knew when we were younger, and we deplore the present because of something that we enjoyed in the past; but that is not what I mean. If one observes, one sees that throughout the world there is a great deal of deterioration, not in any particular sphere, but in all the areas of human activity, both individual and collective. After all, each human being is totally related to all other human beings. The individual may consciously separate himself from others, but unconsciously, deeply, he is totally related. Your sorrow, your misery, your anxiety are essentially the same as those of a man living far away. And being, as we are, so totally related, being so subject to influence through propaganda, through suggestion, through literature, through every form of persuasion and dissuasion, is it at all possible for us as human beings to see in ourselves the fact of deterioration and put an end to it?

There is inevitably physical deterioration, the natural process of getting old; the organism, even when it is rightly used, gradually wears itself out; but need the mind and the heart of man deteriorate? And since with most of us they obviously do deteriorate, is it possible to understand and put an end to that deterioration? Merely to revolt against society is a form of deterioration; and to accept the norm of society, conforming, adjusting to the pattern of the left, of the right, or of the center, is also a form of deterioration. If one is at all aware of human events, of what is happening in literature, in aesthetics, in morality, one knows that in all the various expressions of man, except perhaps scientifically, there is a great deterioration taking place. And as each one of us is a part of the whole structure, we must find out for ourselves whether it is possible to end this deterioration, and thereby be free of sorrow. That is what I would like to talk about this morning.

Now, there are two ways of listening to what is being said. Either you hear only words and, translating what you hear according to your particular conditioning, you act if it happens to please you or you listen totally, neither accepting nor rejecting what you hear. When you listen to something totally, you listen to it as you would listen to that river flowing by. The murmuring of the river is a fact, and in listening to it there is neither acceptance nor denial. To listen in that way to what is being said, you must close your eyes, figuratively speaking, and listen only through your ears. When you listen with your eyes closed—please don't actually do it, but just listen quietly to what I am saying—then you listen much more intently. In listening to that river flowing by, or to the voices of the boys behind the tent, if you listen with your ears and do not turn to look with your eyes, then you listen much more intently because your whole nervous organism is relaxed, not under a strain. You just listen.

So I would suggest this morning, as I have suggested almost every morning, that the act of listening in itself should be a total action. What is required is not fragmentary action, not action shaped to a formula and carried out by will, but action which is total, because it is total action that puts an end to all deterioration.

Now, why do we deteriorate? Why do we decline, grow dull, insensitive, unaware, unperceptive? Why do we become ridden by formulas, ideas, creeds, dogmas, by patterns of long-established thought? When we are very young, the mind has a certain brightness, a clarity, a frankness; we see things differently. There is a sense of revolt, a sense of not accepting things as they are. But as we grow older, the mind becomes dull, the heart becomes weary. Not only physically, but emotionally and mentally we lose that quality of innocence, clarity, freshness, vitality. Why? I do not know if we have asked ourselves this question. If we have asked it, probably we have done so only superficially, and we have not the time, or the inclination, or the energy, to tackle the problem and go into it fully. But this morning we are going to go into it honestly and rather deeply; and to go deeply into anything one needs energy, a passionate intensity. We can't sit down and merely accept or argue about something—which is blatantly obvious. We have to grapple with the thing, not just verbally or intellectually, but actually, as a vital problem which each one of us has to solve.

When you are hungry and without a job, or when there is any other immediate, intense crisis, you can't escape from it, you have to grapple with it. To grapple with any vital problem, you need energy, you need passion; and for most of us, it seems to be one of the most difficult things to awaken passion or energy. You don't get passion, energy, by merely analyzing the issue. You get energy be acting, by doing. It is not that you have energy first, and then act. But you do have passion, you do have the clarity of energy when you are acting—not when you are merely speculating about the cause of deterioration. When the mind is out to discover for itself the cause of deterioration, then you have energy.

Now, what is the cause of deterioration, not only in every human being, but also in the group, in the family, in society? How does one discover the cause of something without too much investigation and analysis—which again is a waste of time and energy?

I hope I am making myself clear. I want to find out why there is deterioration in oneself. Is it possible to see the whole structure of deterioration at one glance, or must I go through a long series of analyses and examinations, asking, probing, studying, investigating? Surely, merely to investigate, to probe, to study, to analyze, is a waste of energy. I think it is possible to see for oneself the nature of deterioration—to see it totally, not just partially or intellectually; but if you proceed to create an idea as to why you decline, then the idea becomes dominant, and trying to battle with that idea in action again destroys energy. I do not know if you are following all this.

What I am asking is this: Is it possible to see the total cause of human deterioration, not just physically or fragmentarily, but completely—see it without analysis, without taking time over it? Because, as I have said on other occasions, time breeds disorder. I think that is clear, and I won't go into it now. If you are here for the first time, I am sorry, but I can't help that. Anything that involves psychological time breeds disorder, whether it is moral disorder, physical disorder, or conceptual disorder; and disorder is one of the factors of deterioration. All concepts are disorderly, so I must not cling to any concept but see the total structure of deterioration. And I must see it immediately; otherwise, if I take time to perceive, then time depletes energy.

Now, what is it that brings about in us deterioration, which is also disorder? What is it that breeds in you and me disorder and therefore deterioration? Having put that question, I must see the total answer immediately. I have no tomorrow because to see the answer tomorrow, or an hour later, breeds still further disorder and other forms of wasting energy. So I must discover the answer as instantly as I put the question. Do you follow? The moment I have put that question to myself, I must see the total answer immediately. The immediacy, the urgency of the answer is passion and therefore energy.

So, I am putting that question to you, and it is a fundamental issue. It is not something that you can escape from; you have got to answer it for yourself. The total structure of deterioration is the self-centered activity of the human being. He may expand his activity through knowledge, through social service, through trying to create a good society; but if consciously or unconsciously he is seeking fame, prestige, status, or if his activity is in any other way self-centered, then that activity breeds disorder and therefore deterioration.

Please, as I explained, you are listening with your ears, not with your eyes. You are listening, not to agree or disagree, but to find out if what the speaker is saying is true or false in itself. In listening to the murmur of that river flowing by, you are not listening with your eyes, you are not listening partially or indifferently. You are listening totally with your ears, with your whole being; and you should be listening in the same way to what is being said. The speaker is saying that deterioration takes place, disorder comes into being, when there is either self-improvement or self-expansion, which is a self-centered activity that may be carried on through good works, through the acquisition of knowledge, through identification with something greater than oneself—whether it be a nation, a community, a family, or an organized belief which is called religion.

Every form of identification with something which one considers greater than oneself is still the pursuit of pleasure, and therefore it breeds disorder, deterioration. I see that to be a fact. Then I ask myself, "How is this disorder to come to an end?" Do you understand? My demand is that the mind shall be young, fresh, alive, innocent, active, without creating disorder. And how is disorder to come to an end? It cannot come to an end if this self-centered activity, which is based on pleasure, says, "I must end disorder because in that way I shall have greater pleasure." Do you see what I mean? I identify myself with order, which is greater pleasure, and therefore I want to put an end to disorder; but in that pursuit of order there is effort, struggle, pain, determination, and all the rest of it, which only creates greater disorder.

So I must find a way—a "way" does not mean a method because a method implies continuity, and therefore disorder. But there must be, not a "way," but a catalyst that will put an end instantly to this self-centered activity which breeds disorder and deterioration. All self-centered activity is based on pleasure, and pleasure, as I said the other day, does breed sorrow, pain. Enjoyment is one thing, and pleasure is another. Yesterday was a lovely day. There were clear, intensely blue skies, and every tree, every blade of grass, every buttercup in the field was full of light and delight. One sees all that with a pulsating feeling of enjoyment. But when that enjoyment is translated as pleasure and I say, "I wish today were another day like yesterday so that I could have more enjoyment, greater pleasure," then the pain begins.

So there is an enjoyment which is natural, spontaneous, healthy, immediate; but when that enjoyment is translated by memory into pleasure and there is the demand for its continuity, which breeds the avoidance of pain, then there is sorrow. Now, I see this whole process, and I also see that it must end—but not because I want something more, not because I want greater pleasure. It must end because it is natural to have a very good mind, a mind that is young, healthy, reasonable, sane, strong. When I see the truth of this, then what takes place?

Thought is of time. Thought, as we use it to get rid of something we don't like, is based on an idea—the idea being the continuity of pleasure; and so thought says, "I must end deterioration." But when thought intervenes to bring about the ending of deterioration, it only adds more confusion.

This requires a great deal of clarity, and I do not know if I am making it really clear.

You see, we have thought as the only means of giving a continuity to, or ending, something. And thought is the response of the past, of experience as memory. So when thought intervenes in the ending of deterioration, it only intensifies deterioration.

Please do listen very carefully to this. It is not a question of your agreeing with the speaker.

We are used to thought because thought is the only instrument we have. And I see that when I use thought—with its cunning, its ideas, its pursuits, its determination, avoidance, resistance, escapes—as a means of ending deterioration, it only creates more disorder, more deterioration. Therefore there must be a way of stopping thought.

Are you following all this? Please, I am talking very objectively. This is not some oriental or mystical nonsense. It is not a fancy of the speaker which he wants to impose on you. He is talking about two facts: the fact of deterioration, and the fact that it is necessary to put an end to deterioration. And he is also pointing out that we use thought as a means to put an end to deterioration because thought is all we have. We exercise thought in so many cunning ways, hoping to put an end to it by escaping, by saying, "I am the soul, I am the atma, the higher self," and all that stuff. Or we escape through using thought to identify ourselves with a belief, an idea which we call God, or with a country, a party ideology, and so on. In these and other ways we have used thought to put an end to deterioration. And now I see clearly, not argumentatively, but as a fact, that when thought interferes in any way, it only adds to the deterioration. To me this is as factual as that river running by, murmuring with delight. When thought is challenged, it must obviously function clearly, reasonably, logically, sanely, nonneurotically. But there is the essential fact of human deterioration, with which thought cannot interfere; and when it does, it increases the deterioration. So the mind must discover how to end thought—which does not mean becoming vague, blank, or plunging into some mystical, nonsensical fancy. Thought is the response of the past; it is based on an image which is essentially pleasure and the avoidance of pain; and if that pleasure principle tries to put an end to deterioration, it only adds more deterioration. So the mind must discover for itself the total ending of thought with regard to deterioration. But the mind must nevertheless be full of energy as thought functions when you go to the office, and all the rest of it. So I am not saying that you must end thought in everyday living. I am saying that thought must end totally when you are faced with a fundamental problem.

So the mind must find out what it is to be silent. It is only when thought comes to an end that there is silence. You know, when you are listening without resistance to the flowing of that stream, or to those boys playing football, and there is not the principle of pleasure as thought, you are then listening out of silence, aren't you? Please do it as I am talking. Listen to that river completely. Do not resist it in order to hear what the speaker is saying—that is irrelevant for the moment. You are listening completely to that river; therefore, you are attentive with your whole being; there is no forcing of the mind to concentrate. And if you are totally attentive, not resisting, not forcing, are you not listening out of total silence? To be silent, there must be freedom; and to have freedom, you must have inward space.

So there is this fact of deterioration, and there is also the fact that for untold centuries man has been using thought as a means to put an end to deterioration—thought being will, resistance, avoidance, escape. But now one has discovered that thought does not put an end to deterioration, and so one is asking oneself: Is it possible for the mind to be completely quiet, totally silent? Because total silence means a total renewal. The mind is completely quiet, totally still, but not through determination, not through wish, not through the desire for pleasure, not through the avoidance of pain. It is a total stillness in which thought is absent. Thought is of time, and therefore this stillness is not of time. And when the mind is totally still, completely free of thought, it has within itself immense space, without a center that is making space.

Now, all this demands a clarity of perception, of hearing, a spontaneous discipline. When you are listening to that stream attentively, completely, without resistance; when you are not resisting the shouting of those boys playing football; when you are listening completely to every noise and are not resisting anything at all, then that listening in itself is a discipline in which there is no conformity, no adjustment to a pattern, because your mind is then completely alert, your whole being is intensely alive and therefore silent. But the discipline that we generally have is based on conformity, and hence it is total disorder. To come upon this silence, the mind must be extraordinarily sensitive, alive, active; and when there is this silence, there is no deterioration at all.

But one has to understand that when once there has been this silence, the mind craves for more of it. You know, the mind is used to pleasure, and it always wants more pleasure, and therefore it subjugates itself, controls itself, hoping thereby to have the continuity of pleasure. To me, subjugation of the mind, controlled concentration, is another factor of deterioration—which doesn't mean you can do whatever you like, lie down on the floor smoking, or kick off your shoes in a drawing room. One has to understand the whole nature of control, and why the mind constantly demands to control itself, or to be controlled; why it wants to be engaged in an activity which will absorb it, or be occupied with something so completely that it can forget itself. One has to understand all that if one is to understand the nature of control and concentration. When once you have felt a moment of this silence, you want it to continue, and you will discipline yourself to death to get it back. We want every experience of pleasure to continue and be intensified, and in the hope of getting it back we will do almost anything, from taking a drug to imposing on ourselves some austere discipline of harshness. But this silence has no continuity, and that which has continuity is the self-centered activity of pleasure dictated by thought.

So this silence is not to be cultivated; it cannot be come by through any system of meditation, through any method or formula. You may sit cross-legged, breathe in different ways, stand on your big toe, or do anything you like, but you will never have it, because this silence demands a great understanding of life, not your escaping from life. It demands a tremendous sensitivity of your whole being, of your heart, your mind, your body. Therefore the way you live matters immensely—what you eat, everything becomes intensely important. As long as one is a slave to society, as long as one is greedy, envious, ambitious, pursuing pleasure, prestige, seeking status through function—as long as one is not free of all that, there can be no renewal, no freshness, no rejuvenation, no silence, no freedom, and therefore no space in which creation can take place.

Comment: While I am here listening to you, I seem to understand; but when I am away from here, I don't understand, even though I try to apply what you have been saying.

KRISHNAMURTI: I hope you will not think I am rude, but you are not listening to me. That is where the mistake is. What is the speaker saying? He is just pointing out certain things. The speaker is yourself speaking aloud. For God's sake, do please understand that simple fact! You are listening to yourself, and not to the speaker. If you are listening to the speaker, he becomes your leader, your way to understanding—which is a horror, an abomination, because you have then established the hierarchy of authority. So what you are doing here is listening to yourself. You are looking at the picture the speaker is painting, which is your own picture, not the speaker's. If that much is clear, that you are looking at yourself, then you can say, "Well, I see myself as I am, and I don't want to do anything about it"—and that is the end of it. But if you say, "I see myself as I am, and there must be a change," then you begin to work out of your own understanding—which is entirely different from applying what the speaker is saying. If you want to work hard, you go at it; if you don't, that is your affair. But you have to create a new world, a new society, a new group of people, and you cannot do that by saying, "I have listened to the speaker, and I want to know how to apply what he is talking about." You are listening, not to the speaker, but to yourself; and you can listen to yourself either casually, indifferently, curiously—or attentively. If you are really attentive, then you have the energy, the passion to go on listening to yourself; and that is all you have to do. To listen to yourself means having no resistance to what you are listening to. There is no comparison, no saying, "This is good and that is bad," or "I must be this and not that"—all such stupid, petty nonsense is gone. Out of that passion and energy there is action—the total thing is action. You don't say, "Having listened to the speaker, I want to apply it." You cannot apply what you are listening to—if you do, it becomes tawdry, juvenile. But if, as the speaker is speaking, you are listening to yourself, then out of that listening there is clarity, there is sensitivity; out of that listening the mind becomes healthy, strong. Neither obeying nor resisting, it becomes alive, intense—and it is only such a human being who can create a new generation, a new world.

Question: If we can understand what you are saying, will there not be freedom?

KRISHNAMURTI: Madame, it is not a matter of understanding anything I say but of understanding yourself. You know, your "self" is a living, moving thing. It is never the same; it is active, pushing, driving, changing, never constant. To look at that self, to go into it, to understand it, your mind also must be fluid; and it cannot be fluid if there is a pattern according to which it is functioning. You see, jealousy, envy, greed, ambition, the desire to become great, to fulfill, to avoid despair—these things are all interrelated, and this interrelation is brought about by the center, the self. The center is memory, with its conformities, its images; and that center, consciously or unconsciously, is always seeking pleasure and therefore breeding pain. This is what you are actually doing; it is what is taking place in each one of us, so you are not understanding me. The speaker is only a sounding board; he is not important at all. He is pointing out how to listen to yourself; and if you know how to listen to yourself, you can go on a journey that has no end, a journey that penetrates further and deeper than Mars. Out of the understanding of yourself there comes order, virtue, the cessation of conflict, and in that state there is great beauty.

July 29, 1965

Tenth Talk in Saanen

I would like this morning, if I may, to go into something which I consider very important. We have so far dealt with many sides, aspects, or fragments of a total life. But it is very important—at least I think so—to come to the essence of that totality rather than to deal with peripheral activities. We have been considering up to now the activities that lie on the boundaries of our thinking, of our feeling, and the various activities that go on in our daily life. But it seems to me essential to find out the essence of life, and to function from there. However, to go into that, one must first clear away a great deal of verbal confusion. Many words and symbols are heavy with superstition, with tradition, and one has to use certain words that are loaded, unfortunately, with Christian or Hindu symbolism, and so on. The word is never the thing; the symbol is never the essence, the truth. It would be very unfortunate if we were to be caught in symbolism, in words, because the symbol or the word is never the real. When the word or the symbol becomes important, the real thing has disappeared; it has ceased to have any substance, any validity.

This morning we are going to discover for ourselves the essence, the truth, and not be caught in the symbol or the word. To come to that reality, which cannot be grasped through words or through symbols, we must obviously put away from our minds the traditional meaning, the religious implications of certain words. Man throughout the centuries has sought something beyond himself, something that he could use as a means of escape from his ugly, tyrannical, sorrowful world, or something to compensate for his aching, miserable, confused existence. In order to live in this world somewhat sanely, if we can, you and I have created—out of our vanity, out of our fear, out of our anguish—an image, a personal God, a superhuman power which is supposed to act as a guiding principle and make us behave. That image is somewhat different in the Orient from what it is in the Occident, but it is everywhere a creation of the human mind. There is nothing sacred about it. There is nothing sacred in the rituals of the West or of the East, for they have all been put together by man in his despair, in his torture, in his fear, in his anxiety; and what is born of fear, of anxiety, can never lead man to truth. His rituals, his symbols, his prayers may be amusing, they may be exciting, they may give him a certain inspiration, a certain sense of well-being; but they have no truth behind them at all because they are put together by human beings in utter agony.

Man has always sought, and apparently found; so we are now going to examine those two words, *seeking* and *finding*. We seek because of our own confusion. We seek something permanent because we see that everything about us is impermanent. We seek a spiritual love, a heavenly comfort, a divine providence, because in ourselves there is so much confusion, so much sorrow, so much agony. In other words, we seek out of chaos, and what we find is born of this chaos. So one must understand this fact—that to seek and to find is not only a waste of energy, but it is an actual hindrance, an actual detriment.

Please, you may not agree with what is being said, but this is not something with which you can agree or disagree. We are inquiring into something that demands a great deal of energy, a great sensitivity, an intense awareness and attention. This means that we have to put aside everything to find out—every assertion, every dogma, every sanction. All the religions throughout the world have established certain formulas, certain methods and traditions which they insist must be practiced in order to find out. Man has always sought, hoping to find something original, something beyond his own imagination, beyond his own vanity: God, a Supreme Being, a divine essence that will guide, help, comfort him. But behind his urge to find some comfort, there is this vast reservoir of man's ignorance of himself, of the cause of his despairs, and of his everlasting demand to find something permanent.

If one is somewhat intelligent or aware, and if one is dissatisfied with this transient world, one wants something permanent, and therefore one is constantly seeking—joining this movement, committing oneself to that party or activity, and so on. One is always active in this search. But this search invariably leads to a predestined end. What one wants is comfort, permanency, a state of mind that will never be disturbed, which one calls peace; and one will find what one is seeking, but it will not be the real, it will not be truth.

So a mind that would discover what is the real, what is truth, must totally end this seeking, this demand to find. Being confused, anxious, miserable, laden with sorrow, we seek reassurance outside of ourselves in books, in teachers, in gurus, in saviors, in organized religions; and once having found some comfort, some reassurance, we cling to it desperately. But this seeking and this finding invariably bring about the deterioration of the mind because the mind needs to be intensely active, supremely sensitive, aware, vitally energetic. So to put an end to seeking and finding is to put an end to sorrow because then the mind is unfolding and understanding itself, which is the very essence of religious activity.

Without knowing oneself, mere search only breeds illusion. Human beings want more and more experience. We all want more experience—not only the experience which is to be derived from going to Mars, or discovering new galaxies, but we also want more experience inwardly because the experience of everyday living has no meaning any more. We have had sex, and that pleasure, repeated day after day, has become slightly monotonous, boring, so we want some other form of experience, some new social activity. We want the praise of the community, we want to become world famous, we want to have prestige by deriving status from function. And it is because we want more experience that we take drugs like LSD, which make the mind much more sensitive, much more active, and thereby give us wider, deeper, more intense experience.

Please, as I said the other day, the speaker is not important, but what he says is important because what he says is the voice of your own self talking aloud. Through the words which the speaker is using, you are listening to yourself, not to the speaker, and therefore listening becomes extraordinarily important. To listen is to learn, and not to accumulate. If you accumulate knowledge and listen from that accumulation, from your background of knowledge, then you are not listening. It is only when you listen that you learn. You are learning about yourself, and therefore you have to listen with care, with extraordinary attention; and attention is denied when you justify, condemn, or otherwise evaluate what you hear. Then you are not listening, you are not perceiving, seeing.

If you sit on the bank of a river after a storm, you see the stream going by carrying a great deal of debris. Similarly, you have to watch the movement of yourself, following every thought, every feeling, every intention, every motive—just watch it. That watching is also listening. It is being aware with your eyes, with your ears, with your insight, of all the values that human beings have created, and by which you are conditioned; and it is only this state of total awareness that will end all seeking.

As I said, seeking and finding is a waste of energy. When the mind itself is unclear, confused, frightened, miserable, anxious, what is the good of its seeking? Out of this chaos, what can you find except more chaos? But when there is inward clarity, when the mind is not frightened, not demanding reassurance, then there is no seeking and therefore no finding. To seek God, truth, is not a religious act. The only religious act is to come upon this inward clarity through self-knowing, that is, through being aware of all one's intimate, secret desires and allowing them to unfold, never correcting, controlling, or indulging, but always watching them. Out of that constant watching there comes extraordinary clarity, sensitivity, and a tremendous conservation of energy; and one must have immense energy because all action is energy, life itself is energy. When we are miserable, anxious, quarreling, jealous, when we are frightened, when we feel insulted or flattered—all that is a dissipation of energy. It is also a dissipation of energy to be ill, physically or inwardly. Everything that we do, think, and feel is an outpouring of energy. Now, either we understand the dissipation of energy and therefore, out of that understanding, there is a natural coming together of all energy, or we spend our lives struggling to bring together various contradictory expressions of energy, hoping from the peripheral to come to the essence.

The essence of religion is sacredness—which has nothing to do with religious organizations, nor with the mind that is caught and conditioned by a belief, a dogma. To such a mind nothing is sacred except the God it has created, or the ritual it has put together, or the various sensations it derives from prayer, from worship, from devotion. But these things are not sacred at all. There is nothing sacred about dogmatism, about ritualism, about sentimentality or emotionalism. Sacredness is the very essence of a mind that is religious—and that is what we are going to discover this morning. We are not concerned with what is supposed to be sacred—the symbol, the word, the person, the picture, a particular experience, which are all juvenile—but with the essence; and that demands on the part of each one of us an understanding that comes through watching or being aware, first, of outward things. The mind cannot ride the tide of inward awareness without first being aware of outward behavior, outward gestures, costumes, shapes, the size and color of a tree, the appearance of a person, of a house. It is the same tide that goes out and comes in, and unless you know the outward tide, you will never know what the inward tide is.

Please do listen to this. Most of us think that awareness is a mysterious something to be practiced, and that we should get together day after day to talk about awareness. Now, you don't come to awareness that way at all. But if you are aware of outward things—the curve of a road, the shape of a tree, the color of another's dress, the outline of the mountains against a blue sky, the delicacy of a flower, the pain on the face of a passerby, the ignorance, the envy, the jealousy of others, the beauty of the earth—then, seeing all these outward things without condemnation, without choice, you can ride on the tide of inner awareness. Then you will become aware of your own reactions, of your own pettiness, of your own jealousies. From the outward awareness, you come to the inward; but if you are not aware of the outer, you cannot possibly come to the inner.

When there is inward awareness of every activity of your mind and your body; when you are aware of your thoughts, of your feelings, both secret and open, conscious and unconscious, then out of this awareness there comes a clarity that is not induced, not put together by the mind. And without that clarity, you may do what you will, you may search the heavens and the earth and the deeps, but you will never find out what is true.

So a man who would discover what is true must have the sensitivity of awareness—which is not to practice awareness. The practice of awareness only leads to habit, and habit is destructive of all sensitivity. And habit—whether it is the habit of sex, the habit of drink, the habit of smoking, or what you will—makes the mind insensitive; and a mind that is insensitive, besides dissipating energy, becomes dull. A dull, shallow, conditioned, petty mind may take a drug, and for a second it may have an astonishing experience; but it is still a petty mind. And what we are doing is finding out how to put an end to the pettiness of the mind.

Pettiness is not ended by gathering more information, more knowledge, by listening to great music, by seeing the beauty spots of the world, and so on—it has nothing to do with that at all. What brings about the ending of pettiness is the clarity of self-knowing, the movement of a mind that has no restrictions; and it is only such a mind that is religious.

The essence of religion is sacredness. But sacredness is not in any church, in any temple, in any mosque, in any image. I am talking about the essence, and not about the things which we call sacred. And when one understands this essence of religion, which is sacredness, then life has a different meaning altogether; then everything has beauty, and beauty is sacredness. Beauty is not that which stimulates. When you see a mountain, a building, a river, a valley, a flower, or a face, you may say it is beautiful because you are stimulated by it. But the beauty about which I am talking offers no stimulation whatsoever. It is a beauty not to be found in any picture, in any symbol, in any word, in any music. That beauty is sacredness; it is the essence of a religious mind, of a mind that is clear in its self-knowing. One comes upon that beauty not by desiring, wanting, longing for the experience, but only when all desire for experience has come to an end—and that is one of the most difficult things to understand.

As I pointed out earlier, a mind that is seeking experience is still moving on the periphery, and the translation of each experience will depend on your particular conditioning. Whether you are a Christian, a Buddhist, a Muslim, a Hindu, or a communist—whatever it is you are—your experiences will obviously be translated and conditioned according to your background; and the more you demand experience, the more you are strengthening that background. This process is not an undoing of, nor a putting an end to, sorrow; it is only an escape from sorrow. A mind that is clear in its self-knowing, a mind that is the very essence of clarity and light, has no need of experience. It is what it is.

So clarity comes through self-knowing, and not through the instruction of another, whether he be a clever writer, a psychologist, a philosopher, or a so-called religious teacher.

As I said the other day, there is no sacredness without love and the understanding of death. You know, it is one of the most marvelous things in life to discover something unexpectedly, spontaneously—to come upon something without premeditation, and instantly to see the beauty, the sacredness, the reality of it. But a mind that is seeking and wanting to find is never in that position at all. Love is not a thing to be cultivated. Love, like humility, cannot be put together by the mind. It is only the vain man who attempts to be humble; it is only the proud man who seeks to put away his pride through practicing humility. The practice of humility is still an act of vanity. To listen and therefore to learn, there must be a spontaneous quality of humility; and a mind that has understood the nature of humility never follows, never obeys. For how can that which is completely negative, empty, obey or follow anyone?

A mind that out of its own clarity of self-knowing has discovered what love is will also be aware of the nature and the structure of death. If we don't die to the past, to everything of yesterday, then the mind is still caught in its longings, in the shadows of memory, in its conditioning, and so there is no clarity. To die to yesterday easily, voluntarily, without argument or justification, demands energy. Argument, justification, and choice are a waste of energy, and therefore one never dies to the many yesterdays so that the mind can be made fresh and new. When once there is the clarity of self-knowing, then love with its gentleness follows; there comes a spontaneous quality of humility, and also this freedom from the past through death. And out of all this comes creation. Creation is not self-expression; it is not a matter of putting paint on a piece of canvas, or writing a few or many words in the form of a book, or making bread in the kitchen, or conceiving a child. None of that is creation. There is creation only when there is love and death. Creation can come only when there is a dying every day to everything, so that there is no accumulation as memory. Obviously you must have a little accumulation in the way of your clothing, a house, and personal property—I am not talking about that. It is the mind's inward sense of accumulation and possession—from which arise domination, authority, conformity, obedience—that prevents creation because such a mind is never free. Only a free mind knows what death is and what love is, and for that mind alone there is creation. In this state, the mind is religious; in this state there is sacredness.

To me, the word *sacredness* has an extraordinary meaning. Please, I am not doing propaganda for that word, I am not seeking to convince you of anything, and I am not trying to make you feel or experience reality through that word. You can't. You have to go through all this for yourself, not verbally, but actually. You actually have to die to everything you know—to your memories, to your miseries, to your pleasures. And when there is no jealousy, no envy, no greed, no torture of despair, then you will know what love is, and you will come upon that which may be called sacred. Therefore sacredness is the essence of religion. You know, a great river may become polluted as it flows past a town, but if the pollution isn't too great, the river cleanses itself as it goes along, and within a few miles it is again clean, fresh, pure. Similarly, when once the mind comes upon this sacredness, then every act is a cleansing act. Through its very movement the mind is making itself innocent, and therefore it is not accumulating. A mind that has discovered this sacredness is in constant revolution—not economic or social revolution, but an inner revolution through which it is endlessly purifying itself. Its action is not based on some idea or formula. As the river, with a tremendous volume of water behind it, cleanses itself as it flows, so does the mind cleanse itself when once it has come upon this religious sacredness.

In a few days we are going to have discussions, and we can start those discussions this morning. But if you assert and I assert, if you stick to your opinion, to your dogma, to your experience, to your knowledge, and I stick to mine, then there can be no real discussion because neither of us is free to inquire. To discuss is not to share our experiences with each other. There is no sharing at all; there is only the beauty of truth, which neither you nor I can possess. It is simply there.

To discuss intelligently, there must also be a quality not only of affection but of hesitation. You know, unless you hesitate, you can't inquire. Inquiry means hesitating, finding out for yourself, discovering step by step; and when you do that, then you need not follow anybody, you need not ask for correction or for confirmation of your discovery. But all this demands a great deal of intelligence and sensitivity.

By saying that, I hope I have not stopped you from asking questions! You know, this is like talking things over together as two friends. We are neither asserting nor seeking to dominate each other, but each is talking easily, affably, in an atmosphere of friendly companionship, trying to discover. And in that state of mind we do discover, but I assure you, what we discover has very little importance. The important thing is to discover, and after discovering, to keep going. It is detrimental to stay with what you have discovered, for then your mind is closed, finished. But if you die to what you have discovered the moment you have discovered it, then you can flow like the stream, like a river that has an abundance of water.

Question: You are advocating that we liquidate the environment within us. Why do you advocate that? What is the use of it?

KRISHNAMURTI: I am not advocating anything. But you know, the cup is useful only when it is empty. With most of us, the mind is clouded, cluttered up with so many things—pleasant and unpleasant experiences, knowledge, patterns or formulas of behavior, and so on. It is never empty. And creation can take place only in the mind that is totally empty. Creation is always new, and therefore the mind is made constantly fresh, young, innocent; it doesn't repeat, and therefore doesn't create habits.

I don't know if you have ever noticed what sometimes happens when you have a problem, either mathematical or psychological. You think about it a great deal, you worry over it like a dog chewing on a bone, but you can't find an answer. Then you let it alone, you go away from it, you take a walk; and suddenly, out of that emptiness, comes the answer. This must have happened to many of us. Now, how does this take place? Your mind has been very active within its own limitations about that problem, but you have not found the answer, so you have put the problem aside. Then your mind becomes somewhat quiet, somewhat still, empty; and in that stillness, that emptiness, the problem is resolved. Similarly, when one dies each minute to the inward environment, to the inward commitments, to the inward memories, to the inward secrecies and agonies, there is then an emptiness in which alone a new thing can take place. I am not advocating it; I am not doing propaganda for that emptiness—good God! I am only saying that unless that emptiness comes into being, we shall continue with our sorrow, with our anxiety, with our despair, and our activities will bring more and more confusion.

To bring about a different human being, and therefore a different society, a different world, there must be the ending of sorrow; for it is only with the ending of sorrow that there is a new life.

August 1, 1965

Saanen, Switzerland, 1965

First Dialogue in Saanen

Before we begin to ask questions, I think we should find out what these meetings are for. One can examine argumentatively or dialectically, that is, discover the truth of opinion; or we can talk things over, not to be instructed, not to be taught, but to learn. I wonder what is the state of the mind that learns? If we could go into that a little, and then talk things over, then perhaps we shall be able to find out for ourselves about the act of learning. During these seven morning discussions we are going to investigate—not theoretically, not in any abstract sense, but actually—the mind that is in a state of constant learning. The active present of the verb "to learn" is "learning"; "learned" is the past, and "I will learn" is the future. We are trying to find out what is the actual state of the mind that is learning. What I have learned from the experiences of yesterday, from the opinions I have gathered, selected—all that becomes the past, the storehouse of knowledge. Will that help me to bring about a mind that is actually learning? I think we should be rather advisedly watchful about this thing because most of us function or think or act from a mind which has learned, which has accumulated; and that may be a hindrance to the active present of learning.

When one is learning a technique or a language, one must accumulate as one is learning. If I don't know a certain job and start, in doing it I begin to learn. I have to be very much alive to do a job I don't know, and in the doing I'm learning. So the doing is the learning. That's what we are going to do. We are going to be doing, and in the doing, learning. That becomes extraordinarily interesting and vitalizing. But before we do that, the doing and the learning, shouldn't we find out what is the state of the mind that is doing, and in the doing, learning?

Please don't wait for me to tell you. We are going to discover it together.

You have come this morning in haste, and have met in the tent, talking and saying good morning to each other. You may sit quietly and listen quietly, but your minds are still agitated. When the mind is agitated, when the brain is reacting very quickly and very sharply, critically, is the mind in a state of doing and learning? Or is a totally different state necessary to do and to learn?

Question: Sir, I have gathered from your talks that you advocate becoming aware of all conditions, all things, all actions and feelings. Can you say something on the apparent fact that once we have heard what you say, and have become aware of it, it all passes into the realm of knowledge? From there we act and try to become aware of all that is going on. Is there any conflict between what

I have learned, which has become knowledge, and my acting in the present?

KRISHNAMURTI: That's right, sir, we are going to find that out. We have been talking about awareness; the accumulation of what I have learned, which becomes knowledge, and is stored up; and the fact that from that knowledge, or with that knowledge, I act. Between the acting, which is the present, and the accumulated awareness, accumulated knowledge, is there a conflict? Before we enter into that, we must find out what learning is.

To me this act of learning is one of the most important things in life. One wakes up on a morning like this and sees the sky, the beauty of the hills and the trees, the river and the flowers. One looks at it all, not with a freshness, not with élan, not with a fury, or with passion, but one compares it with something that happened yesterday, judging, evaluating. When one does that, all learning has stopped. So, one asks oneself, "What is the actual fact of learning, and what is the actual state of the mind that learns, not accumulates?"

As I said, you come here rather agitated, sit and try to listen to the speaker. Before you listen, mustn't you find out for yourself what is actually taking place in the mind which is listening, or which is going to listen? If you are going to listen with an agitated mind, full of chatter, then you have no space in which to learn. Say all your good mornings outside the tent. Leave the "How are you? You look very nice this morning; that's a nice dress; that's a nice hat; oh, I love that dress," and all that stuff outside. Come in and sit very quietly, not with a forced quietness, not saying, "I must." If you do it naturally, your mind becomes extraordinarily silent and quiet.

You discover the state of the mind that learns; you find that there must be a great silence, a great quietness which is not forced, not premeditated, but really quiet. Then when you listen, that very listening is learning and doing. If we can, every morning, come and sit with that alert silence, not a blank silence, then perhaps our talking things over will be an extraordinary event. I won't talk very long; we'll ask questions and talk things over. If one listens with this complete quietness and stillness, then one begins to find out the nature and the quality of silence. That silence, that quality of a still mind, is a positive activity, in a negative sense of not letting anything pour into it.

Sir, I know you have a question to ask me, but the moment you get up and ask, your mind is not quiet; you are not doing what we are talking about.

Coming here this morning you must have seen those trees, very still, with a light on them, against the blue sky, against the river. Did you look at all, and if you did look, how did you look at them? Our minds are so heavy, so dull, so petty, so narrow and limited that how the mind looks is far more important than what it looks at. During this hour, we are going to learn how the mind works rather than what the question is, or what the answer to that question is.

Have you ever experimented with having a few seconds of silence, a few minutes of inward quiet, before doing anything, no matter what—cooking, washing dishes, making the beds, or talking to someone? When there is that natural, spontaneous, energetic silence, efficiency has a totally different meaning; it is not mechanical, it is a movement.

Now, sir, what were you going to ask?

Question: Is it possible for me to live every moment in this other dimension, with this openness, this newness?

KRISHNAMURTI: I'm sure many are going to ask questions. How shall we approach this problem? Shall we answer each question separately, or shall we take one subject, one question, and go through with it to the very end? We have seven mornings, and if we could put several questions together, make one question out of them all, and go right to the end of it, it might be more worthwhile than asking, answering, and asking and answering, or talking things over one question after another.

If you all agree, then what question shall we take up and go right through with to the end? One question is, as that gentleman asked: "How can I, having experienced, having known, having tasted, having smelled that dimension, how can I live in it all the time in spite of my daily difficulties?" Let many ask questions; we'll put them all together into one question, and then go into it.

Question: Is there a difference between being aware of the object of thought, and being aware of thinking?

Comment: All day long we are busy knowing our environment, and we know it in ways that involve the thinker. So perhaps it would help if we could find out how we can know our environment in ways that do not involve the thinker.

Comment: When I have no purpose, I feel a certain silence; but the moment I start to act, to have a purpose, there comes a tenseness in the middle of my brain, and I cannot relax that, and the silence is gone.

Question: Is searching only an accumulative process, or is it life itself?

KRISHNAMURTI: Now, that's enough. (Laughter) After hearing these questions, what would be the central question which would contain them all? Please, we are working together; you are not just listening. I am not the only speaker. What question would elicit an answer to all of them together? We want to find a central issue that will include all those questions. I may be mistaken, but I think the central issue in all that is the division between the thinker and the thought—the thinker, who is trying to be aware, and the thought, which wanders off, or is shaped by circumstances, by influence, by environment. I am just inquiring; I am not stating yet. If we could discuss the question of why this division exists between the thinker and the thought, then perhaps awareness, the effort to be aware, and trying to maintain that awareness will have a different meaning.

Comment: Yes.

KRISHNAMURTI: Several issues have been raised, apart from the neurotic. One wants to live, as that gentleman pointed out, in a different dimension. One has perhaps felt a certain quality during these talks, or when walking by oneself in the woods, or when in relationship with some person, and one says, "If I could only maintain that, and not slip back." There is a contradiction between the experience, that feeling of a different dimension, and the actuality. If we can wipe away the contradiction, then we shall not have a moment during which there is a feeling of a different dimension, and an attempt to reach it all the time. If we approach these questions and try to find out whether it is possible to eliminate this contradiction altogether, both at the conscious and at the unconscious level, then perhaps we shall be living, and not comparing. Shall we go into that one question this morning?

How is one conscious of this contradiction, if one is at all aware and sensitive? What tells you that you are in a state of contradiction? Do you become aware because someone tells you, or because it brings pain?

Do you want to pursue a pleasure, and in the very pursuit of that pleasure you become aware that there is a contradiction? Do you want to pursue one thing, yet your activity, your daily life pulls you away from it? One must find out how one becomes aware.

We are going into this step by step. We are not going to come to any conclusion. We are going to learn as we are watching, as we are examining, and therefore there is no conclusion at the end. Because if someone tells me that I'm in a state of contradiction, that has a totally different effect.

I have an idea of peace, an image of peace, and I am violent; I get angry, irritable, furious. I am in a state of contradiction. There is the established ideal, and I do something which contradicts that ideal. How do I become aware of a state of contradiction? Do I see that I am in a state of contradiction, or does someone point it out to me? This is of very little importance, but it too has significance.

I have an ideal of nonviolence, of peace, and I am violent, so there is a contradiction; or two desires pull in opposite directions, and there is a conflict. Life points out to me, or someone tells me, that I'm in a state of contradiction. I may become aware of this contradiction through an effort, through a pain, through making an adjustment between the fact and the ideal, through something. An incident or an experience tells me that I am in a state of contradiction. That's one state. Or there may be an awareness of this contradiction without any stimulus. Now which is it for most of us? Does an incident awaken the mind to its contradictoriness, or is the mind, without incident, aware of its own contradictions? Let's deal with the first now, and come to the second afterwards.

We know contradiction through an incident, either pleasant or painful. I have an image, an ideal, a settled pattern of conduct; and some incident takes place which contradicts all that. Then I'm in pain. I say, "I am in a state of contradiction," and nervously try to get over that contradiction, either by making the fact, which is my violence, adjust itself to the ideal or by wiping away the ideal, leaving only the fact.

Through the established formula of conduct, or my own habits, there is an image of what I should do, what I must be; and then an incident outside that image takes place which contradicts the image. Because the contradictoriness creates pain, I want to get rid of it. I either adjust the fact, the incident, to the image or I remove the image altogether and leave no center at all.

Who is the entity that says, "I must adjust the fact to the ideal," or says, "I must wipe away the ideal"? I have three things involved: the fact, the ideal, and the entity who says, "I must get rid of the contradiction, either by wiping away the ideal or by merely accepting the fact." Now I must find out who that entity is. As long as the entity exists, there will be contradiction.

Comment: Contradiction is not connected with anything. Contradiction exists in itself.

KRISHNAMURTI: We are coming to that presently. First, let's be clear, sir, on this point. There is the image, the 'what I should be', the ideal, and there is the fact that I am violent. I will wipe away that ideal which I have created, and therefore deal only with the fact. Who is the entity that says, "I must wipe away, and deal only with the fact"? If I don't understand the entity, the center which dictates, that center will always be in a state of contradiction, or create contradiction. Now, who is that center? What is that center?

Question: Isn't that part of yourself?

KRISHNAMURTI: Yes, madame, but what is yourself, what is that?

Comment: Something which stands in the way, which must be overcome.

KRISHNAMURTI: Look, madame, we are asking ourselves what that center is which says, "I must not be in a state of contradiction. I will wipe away the ideal, in order not to be. I will accept the fact." Yet the center is still there, and we are asking what is its structure, its nature.

We are going to find out, learn about it afresh. That's the only way to learn. You may have thought about it, you may have come to conclusions about it; but if you have, you have stopped learning. We are now going to learn about the center which creates contradiction, whether you wipe away the ideal or neglect the fact. The state of the mind that is going to learn about it must be that it really does not know what that center is. We may have known it yesterday, but if we come with that knowledge of yesterday, we shan't be able to discover what it actually is today. It might have moved, it might have changed, it might have transformed itself, it might not exist at all. So, to find out, to learn about that center today, we must be free of yesterday, free of the conclusions of yesterday. Therefore our minds must be silent, completely silent, still, with that question. Then we shall be able to learn about it; then we're learning about it.

What is that center which is always creating contradiction—the censor who says, "This is right, this is wrong; this I must do; this should be; I am not loved; I must love; I am unhappy; I must live in a different dimension; I have listened, but I have not got"? What is that movement?

Comment: It is the movement of knowing.

KRISHNAMURTI: It is a very difficult question we are asking. The ancients have said it is the soul, it is the atma, it is God, it is goodness, it is the original sin. And do you mean to say that you are going to quickly brush all that aside, and say it is this? First you must know what others have said about it, and discover whether there is any truth in that. If you merely repeat what the theologians say, the people who believe in God, in truth, in the soul, in the atma, in the permanent, then you'll get nowhere. You are not interested in the repetition of some authority. If it is merely tradition, you throw it out. You investigate and come to a certain point; you come to it completely not knowing, silent. You want to learn about it, and to learn, you see that a complete quietness is necessary before you can look. Can you be silent, without being forced and driven to be silent, but spontaneously silent, to find out what that movement is?

Comment: I think that knowledge becomes the center.

Question: Why have discussions at all? It becomes useless.

Comment: It is in accordance with the principle of harmony.

KRISHNAMURTI: I am afraid, sirs, you're not going into this question. You are merely stating what you feel, what you think.

Comment: The mind is the center of contradiction—the mind which has accumulated knowledge, the mind which has created images, the mind which has established a savior and the world, the mind which thinks that there is the permanent and the impermanent—the mind itself is in a state of contradiction.

KRISHNAMURTI: Now, wait a minute. You have stated that. What have you learned about it? You have analyzed it, felt your way to it, and said it is the mind. You have verbalized and made a statement. What have you learned? Have you learned anything? You say that it is the mind that is in a state of contradiction—the mind which has acquired knowledge, the mind which believes, the mind which is the Catholic, which is the Protestant, which is the communist, which is the nonbeliever, the believer, which creates the image—the mind, the mind. Is that an actual fact, or an idea?

Question: Is it the unconscious desire for freedom?

KRISHNAMURTI: No, madame. There is a statement made that it is the mind, mind including knowledge. What makes you say it is the mind?

Comment: I have investigated.

KRISHNAMURTI: I am asking you. One mind is asking another mind. How do you know that it is the mind? What makes you say it is the mind?

Comment: We have been told.

KRISHNAMURTI: You have been told? I have also been told that there is a marvelous world when I die, but I have to live in this world. When you say "the mind," either you have realized the fact—realized it, as you realize hunger, and therefore the realization has validity—or you are merely speculating and saying that it is the mind. In that case you're not learning. So, before any of us answer that it is the mind, the image, the conditioning, the pattern which has been established as a Catholic, as a Protestant, as a communist, we must learn about it—learn, not merely make a statement. Before we understand this particular issue, we must first find out what the mind is that is going to learn about it.

Look, sir: my son, my sister, my mother, my grandmother, whoever it is, is not well, is unhappy, is not acting properly, and I am disturbed; from that disturbance, I want to do something—help her, hold her hand. But if I am disturbed, I cannot deal with the fact as a fact, unemotionally, unsentimentally, unstupidly. So it matters very much, when this question is put to you, how you are listening. Either you listen with a conclusion, with an idea which you already have about what that center is, or you say, "I really don't know; let's go into it." If you really don't know, you come to the question with a fresh mind, not with a jaded mind which has already speculated, which is already conditioned.

So, what is much more interesting than the issue, which in this case is contradiction, is that state of the mind that looks at it. If I look at a tree, what is much more important than the tree itself is how I look at it. What is the state of the mind when confronted with this question of contradiction?

Comment: That is where the difficulty is, because it seems very plain that the mind has to be silent.

KRISHNAMURTI: Be silent! Be silent! Be, be, don't talk! You see, you all talk, you don't do. Be silent!

Comment: It's ignorance.

Comment: When you say "Be silent," you are trying to impress upon us the importance of being silent.

KRISHNAMURTI: I am not impressing it on you. Look, I don't know Chinese. What do I do? My mind is empty; I don't know. I begin to learn as I go along. But you are not doing that.

Comment: I think that if you watch your mind, in that same moment you get silent.

KRISHNAMURTI: Madame, *be* silent, not you get silent. Look, the issue is contradiction, why human beings live in contradiction. We said there is a permanent image established, a formula, and the daily fact contradicts that formula. If the mind wants to learn how to live without contradiction—learn, and actually live without contradiction—then it must approach with hesitancy, with silence, with quietness. And when it does, as I am doing now, there is the problem and there is the mind that's completely quiet, not knowing about the problem. I ask what this strange quietness is, this strange stillness which is looking at the problem. Is it induced? Has the mind induced that silence in order to get rid of the problem and live in a state of harmony without contradiction, or is that silence natural? If it is natural, not induced, not made to be natural, then is there a center? Is there a center which is in a state of contradiction? The center inherently is contradiction. And if there is only silence which looks at that contradiction, at that problem, is that silence a natural state, or is it induced because the mind wants to live in a state of harmony? If it is not natural, the contradiction begins again.

So, can the mind approach any problem—life, the tree, the wife, the husband—completely with silence? This is one of the most difficult things to do, yet one sees that any other approach must breed contradiction. We have always approached the issue through positiveness: it is knowledge, it is the image, it is the mind, it is this, it is that, and so on and so on. But this time we have gone a little further. We have said silence. Is silence the negation of noise, the negation of rumor, the rejection of this and that, in order to be silent? I must find out what this sense of negation is which is not positive, directive, but which must exist in life.

A really good mind is both positive and negative; it is both the woman and the man—not just the man, or just the woman. The Greeks had a word, and so had the Hindus. They symbolized it in their images, and therefore have lost it. The moment you put it into words, into an image, it's gone. But if you begin to learn—and keep on learning, learning, learning, you may then put it into words, but it will never die.

So, we are going to understand a silence which is not the opposite of noise, not the opposite of this perpetual battle; and to understand that, one must understand the whole structure of negation.

August 4, 1965

Second Dialogue in Saanen

I think we shall continue, if we may, where we left off yesterday. We were saying yesterday that doing is learning; not that you learn first, and then do afterwards. If there is the idea first, and then action, in that there is contradiction and therefore conflict. But if acting is learning, then there is a constant process of understanding in which there is no conflict and no contradiction whatsoever. We also said that to learn is to have a silent mind; there must be a silence, a stillness which is not induced, which is not put together by thought in order to acquire silence. But invariably, if there is intensity and attention in everything we do, there comes that quality of silence from which learning and acting take place.

We said also that it is very essential to understand contradiction; and contradiction within ourselves will always exist as long as there is a center, the censor, the observer who is judging, evaluating, creating images, and so on. We were inquiring into what that center is; we were examining the whole structure of the positive, directive activity of a center that is always guiding, shaping, controlling, changing.

Question: Since this state of silence seems to be a precondition to everything, would you please describe it in terms of what you do not mean by the word? What kind of activity do you not mean by silence? Approach it that way.

KRISHNAMURTI: I wonder if we can't approach the whole issue differently. I think most of us are aware that we are in a state of contradiction. One doesn't have to go into the details of that contradiction. Because that contradiction causes pain, various forms of destructive activity, one says to oneself, "Is it possible to be free of all contradiction, not only conscious, but also unconscious contradiction?" That is the principal question. I want to learn about it. I do not want you to tell me what silence is, or what it is not, but I want to understand, I want to learn in the very process of observation. I observe that I am in a state of contradiction; and also I know very well that as long as there is a center, a form, an image, whatever it may be, it will always breed contradiction. Then what is the mind to do? How is it to learn about contradiction without creating another center which would in turn become a further source of contradiction? I see that I must have a certain passive, quiet, still awareness in order to learn, in order to understand anything. That passive awareness is not a thing which I can cultivate. To understand this vast stream of life which is myself, with my various centers—business, spiritual, family—is the act of silence itself.

What is this silence? You are not going to cultivate it by listening to me, getting a pattern of silence, or of what silence is not, and then working up in it and capturing the silence—you never can do that, obviously. What is this silence? Can it be described? If it is described, either positively or negatively, there is still an observer, there is still a center which looks at it as silence; that center creates contradiction by saying, "How am I to cultivate that silence?"

First of all, are we clear that the mind must be somewhat quiet if it would listen to that stream, if it would look at a tree, if it would look at another's face? To look, to listen, to learn, there must be a certain quiet, there must be a certain passive attention—not a blankness, not a determined quietness, nor a cultivated quietness. If we inquire what that silence is, what that quietness is, we'll invent images, symbols, words, which become the center.

What is this quietness? What is the nature and the structure of the silence itself, not the structure of the words which describe the silence? Please, again let's be very clear. You are not listening to me, trying to understand me, the speaker. The speaker is not at all important. What is important is to understand the nature and the structure of the mind which is quiet, and out of that quietness to learn and act. The learning is the acting.

We have used three expressions: silence or stillness, passive attention, and negation. What do we mean by a passive mind? To understand the nature of the passive mind, we must understand what we consider to be positive. The positive is not in contrast to the passive. If the negative, passive state is the opposite of the positive, there is a contradiction, and therefore it is not passive or negative. What constitutes, or what is the structure of, or what is the nature of a mind that is always functioning in the positive?

Shall we describe the things that constitute the positive, or shall we come to the essence of it? Shall we describe in detail the positive mind that follows, that accepts, that obeys, that creates authority and therefore fear, that is always looking for someone to tell what it should do, that lives and has its being in experience as knowledge?

Comment: No.

KRISHNAMURTI: Wait, please. You are so impatient. Shall we go through all the detailed description—and it may be necessary because we haven't really understood—or shall we come to the essence of what a positive mind is? If you say, "Yes, get to the essence as quickly as possible," you will not have understood the nature and the structure of a positive mind. But if you have understood, examined, approached, learned about the positive mind, then you would put to yourselves the question of what the essence of it is.

Our minds, our brains, our whole organisms are the result of time. During the course of time the mind has established certain patterns of behavior, conduct, thought, activity; and the pattern, the formula, is the positive. Am I working and finding it out, and you are listening and accepting, or are we working together, with you finding it out also? If we are working together, there is a learning together about what we call a positive mind, a mind which is aggressive, which is assertive, which is dominating, and which, because it dominates, accepts being dominated. It functions within the pattern of knowledge because it wants to be sure.

So the essence of a positive mind is a demand for security at any price, for complete security, not only outwardly, but also very deeply inwardly; for something which will give it permanency. I've just learned, the mind has just learned that as long as it is seeking and therefore finding permanency, security, certainty in relationship, in activity, in anything, the seeking and the finding make up the essence of a positive mind.

Question: Is there a way to suppress contradiction in the positive mind?

KRISHNAMURTI: Sir, you're not even listening! Look, please, I understand what you are saying. I am not trying to deviate from it. We are trying to find out, and learn; in the very finding is the learning, not that I find, and then act. We are trying to learn about the nature and the structure of the positive mind, and after examining the details, I see. I may be wrong. Don't accept what we are talking about as the final word of the oracle that speaks, or the authority—this mind finds that as long as there is a seeking, which means finding, that state of seeking and finding is the essence of the positive mind, which does not mean that the negative mind does not seek, does not find, does not do.

Question: Excuse me, sir, while we are in the present state, the present level of consciousness, isn't any question we ask a positive question?

KRISHNAMURTI: Why shouldn't we think and function positively? What is wrong with that? If we find that it is not worthwhile, if we find that it does not clear up our confusion, we will then look for something else; but if we accept the positive way of life, which is, "I will, I will not," according to the image which has been created through pleasure—which means the avoidance of pain, though the cultivation of pleasure breeds pain—from that image we determine to be or not to be, to do or not to do. This positive, assertive, directive, determined pursuit of seeking and finding in itself creates contradiction. As long as we do not learn about it, we will not come upon the other.

Comment: When we look at life with a positive outlook, with a positive mind, we divide life into the 'me' and the 'not-me'.

KRISHNAMURTI: The positive approach to life breeds competition because the positive approach inherently is to seek and to find, and therefore there must be competition, aggressiveness. Can a positive mind know what affection is, what love is? A positive mind demands experience. Because it is tired of all the experiences it has had, it seeks out new experiences. When they are not sufficiently acute, strong, then through imagination it creates experiences, visions; and if that too does not satisfy, then it takes to drugs, not only marijuana, but stronger forms of drugs: opium, the derivatives of opium, and LSD. Through these drugs it induces a negative state of mind, which has certain experiences through stimulation, but such a mind is still a positive mind, seeking experience.

What is wrong with having wider and deeper and stronger experiences? What is wrong with self-created experiences, projections from one's own conditioned mind, longing, seeking, searching, wanting? That's the way we live. There is a dependence on drugs, whether the particular drug be drink, sex, amusement, going to church, or attending Mass with all its rituals. A mind which is seeking to escape from the past, which has been cultivated through experience into the future must inevitably be in conflict. A mind that is seeking, experiencing, wanting more experience, is always in a state of contradiction.

We see the nature and the structure of a positive mind. It is aggressive, competitive, jealous, vain, superstitious, ambitious, and in despair. It seeks and therefore finds. It is dissatisfied with what it has found and wants more because it wants to reach a certain point of eminence, or excellence, where it can be undisturbed and certain. Our concern is to find out if the mind can be free from contradiction, not temporarily, not for a certain period, but completely free. It is only then that there can be clarity, and clarity is not something to be found.

But I am discovering that a mind that is seeking may find clarity which is merely self-created, and therefore within itself inherently contradictory. Such an activity can only produce more contradiction. It is only a mind that is completely negative that can be in a state of noncontradiction. I've learned it! No one has told me. I haven't read a book, I haven't been to a philosopher, I have no guru, teacher, and all that silly nonsense. In doing I have learned, the mind has learned.

So, a negative mind, the negative state, is not a contradiction of the other, is not the opposite of the positive. It is very important to understand this point. I may deny, sacrifice myself and reject property, money, and fame because I want to find God, truth, or bliss. If I reject anything because I want something else, it is not really a rejection, it is part of the same movement.

Question: I look at something, a face, the movement of the river, a mountain, a tree. I look at something, and through that very observation there is an experiencing. Is that still a positive mind?

KRISHNAMURTI: I say it is. You are going to discover something if you pursue it, but as long as there is an experiencing, for whatever cause, it is still within the field of the positive.

Question: How will we get it?

KRISHNAMURTI: I have very carefully explained that you can't get it. (Laughter)

Comment: Create it.

KRISHNAMURTI: You can't create it. Sir, look. When you understand that a particular snake is poisonous, you have understood the whole thing, haven't you? You move away from it. When you see poison, you don't drink it because you see it is destructive. So, in understanding the positive, which is very complex, it isn't just a matter of saying, "Well, I've got it"; it is a tremendous understanding. It means having a mind that has no authority, and therefore no experiencing as recognition.

I see a beautiful face, and I experience pleasure. That pleasure has arisen through recognition of what I consider to be beautiful. The experience is through stimulation of a pleasure which I have established as beauty.

By understanding the whole nature and structure of the positive mind, as I understand poison, my mind moves away from it totally. The mind doesn't have to do anything about it. If it does, there is a contradiction. But if the mind understands the poisonous nature of the positive, it automatically moves away into the so-called negative.

Question: Therefore, isn't that an experience of the negative?

KRISHNAMURTI: Oh, never. The mind has no experience of the negative. It has experience only within the field of the positive. This requires tremendous understanding. Don't agree or disagree. I have been told that there is a whole school of thought in Buddhism which is based on negation, and there are people who have given all their lives to find out what this negation is. You have given half a day, or an hour, and are now trying to say that you agree or disagree. You have to understand a most profound thing, whether it is possible for the mind to be in a state where it is clear. It can only be clear in negation, when it has no experience at all.

Question: We ask questions because there is a challenge and a response; and the response is always according to the background, according to our experience, according to our knowledge. The answer is always within the question. Is it possible to remain only with the question, and not seek an answer?

KRISHNAMURTI: Why do you ask a question?

Comment: In order to renew, renovate, add to the storage as experience, as knowledge.

KRISHNAMURTI: From that storage, from that knowledge, from that past you experience, you act; and that action, that experiencing, creates contradiction.

Comment: We ask questions only about the part.

KRISHNAMURTI: Obviously. We ask questions fragmentarily. Only when the mind is functioning in fragments does it ask questions. When it is functioning as a whole, is there any need to ask questions? The whole is not the positive but the negative. The positive question is a fragmentary question, within the field of the positive, because the mind is functioning fragmentarily, and therefore contradictorily. When we understand the nature of that positive structure—the understanding is the learning and the doing—the mind has moved away, as it moves away from poison; and that movement is negation.

Question: Does self-assertion come with questioning?

KRISHNAMURTI: Self-assertion, desiring fame, wanting self-expression, wanting to be somebody, a great writer or painter—all that is still within the field of the positive. But surely, I can question without self-assertion. I can ask you what love is, what death is, what life is, and it is not because I'm self-assertive. I lead a miserable, sordid life, within the field of fame and success and all the rest of it, and I say, "By Jove, there must be something else." That is not self-assertion. But it becomes self-assertion if the positive tries to seek and find it. All religions have said, "Seek and ye shall find," but we are cutting at the root of all that. How you can accept it, I don't know!

Question: Can we be conscious of the negative state of mind?

KRISHNAMURTI: Obviously not. We have to find out what we mean by that word *conscious.* When are we conscious? That airplane is making a noise; I want to listen to you, and I feel disturbed. Then I become conscious. I suffer; then I become conscious. I want to be famous, and I'm frustrated; in that frustration there is pain, and I become conscious. I become conscious either through the demand for the continuance of pleasure or through the avoidance and the pushing away of pain.

Sir, look. When I do something as a journalist, as an engineer, as an artist, which are all functions, is there any consciousness of being a functionary? You become conscious as a functionary only when out of that function you are seeking status. You are a good writer, or something else, and through that function you seek fame; then all the mischief begins.

Comment: Consciousness seems to be synonymous with awareness, or the opposite of being sound asleep.

KRISHNAMURTI: Consciousness is synonymous with words, with symbols, with experience, with deriving status from function, with ambition, greed, struggle, and effort. This is clear. What we are talking about is understanding the whole positive, learning about it; the very learning is a new movement. It is not a question of "How am I to live without experience? Won't I die?" Of course you'll die. Anyhow, we are already dead, so it doesn't really much matter! (Laughter) Such questions have no meaning. But if we see what the nature and the structure of consciousness is, if we understand and learn, that very act of learning is the doing, and the doing is the movement that comes—which is not related to the positive.

Question: You say that in seeking there is no understanding. How about without seeking it, do you understand it?

KRISHNAMURTI: We are asking why we seek, not that we mustn't, or must. Why do we seek?

Question: Is there not a difference between seeking and inquiring?

KRISHNAMURTI: Oh yes, surely, but don't complicate it; take things one after another. We are discussing the question of seeking.

Why do I seek? I'm unhappy, I'm miserable, my life is shoddy, petty, small, though I may have a great reputation and many titles. My life is ugly. I'm struggling and I want to get away from it, find something more. Also I'm dissatisfied with everything I've touched; dissatisfied with my family, with my wife, with myself, with the world, with everything. Out of that flame of dissatisfaction I want to find something, and I generally do. I may become a communist, a socialist, a Roman Catholic, a Zen Buddhist, or whatever it is.

Can the mind which has lived on experience, adding more and more to itself, expanding itself through knowledge, through fame, through aggression, and finding all that to be empty, giving no significance to life—that mind which is the outcome of time, and therefore a tremendous positive process, with its "I will; I must; this isn't right; this is wrong; this is the line which no one is going to cross"—can such a mind, which has been brought up for centuries upon centuries on positive, competitive, aggressive seeking and finding, can that mind understand all this and move away by learning about the positive? If the mind does not move away from the positive, it will always remain in conflict. If you derive pleasure from conflict, go on. Don't say, "I want the other," yet swallow this poison.

Question: Sir, isn't that dissatisfaction with what you call competition also the motive power which leads people to seek for what you call the negative state?

KRISHNAMURTI: Yes, sir. Dissatisfaction is so easily satisfied, and being easily satisfied is simply going to try to find the negative state. Before, I found pleasure in the positive; now I am going to find pleasure in the negative. But the mind is still the rotten, little, stupid mind which has functioned within the positive, and is now going to try to function within the negative. It is the same mind, wanting fame, wanting success, wanting to find, wanting to experience; only it says, "I'm negative."

Comment: That is why we are attracted first by one, and then by the other.

KRISHNAMURTI: Sir, we have to live in this world.

Comment: Yes, we are affected by thought, by all sorts of things.

KRISHNAMURTI: We are saying exactly the same thing that you are saying. We have to live in this world, we are influenced, we have our jobs, we have our families, we have our beliefs, dogmas, fears, anxieties, quarrels, jealousies, ambitions. That's our world, and that is a world of the positive state in which we live, kicking each other, killing each other, doing everything in that state. That is what we call life. If you say, "That's good enough for me," carry on with your gods, with your superstitions, with your leaders, with your gurus, with your saviors, priests, or whatever it is, carry on! But if you say, "Look, is there a way to end contradiction and live totally differently, not the opposite of this?" then you must understand this whole business of living in the world.

Question: We are so busy with family life, with our children, with our jobs, and all the rest of it. Can we really do this, not in some vague, idealistic, utopian way, but actually do it in life?

KRISHNAMURTI: You've asked the question. Are you waiting for me to answer it? If you wait for an answer, and I say, "Yes, you can do it," then what? Where are you? But if you say, "Look, let me understand this whole structure, let me look at it, let me understand this mind''; if you give ten minutes, then you will see that you can live in this world totally differently. If you cannot live totally differently in this world, then it's not worth it. Throw it in the garbage. One must be clear, ruthless with the understanding of this structure. Then one can go into the question of the state of the mind that lives and has its being in negation. But if you have not understood the positive, you can never go into the other, you can never flow into the negative.

Take the question of beauty. What is beauty? Volumes have been written by professional artists, professional theoreticians, about what beauty is—beauty according to the East, beauty according to the West, the Greek ideal, the Egyptian ideal, and so on and on. How do you find out? If you answer it from knowledge, then it is the answer of a petty mind, for all knowledge is within the petty mind. Does that mean that you are not to have any knowledge?

I'm asking you. Are you going to seek an answer? If you seek an answer, and find an answer, it will be in terms of what you already know; but if you listen to that question, and have no answer, then what is your response?

Question: May I ask one question more?

KRISHNAMURTI: Yes, sir.

Question: How can one live in negation and still carry on with the practical problems of life?

KRISHNAMURTI: We have just answered that question, sir. I can go into the mountains this afternoon, come back home and answer the telephone. In the mountains I have understood, and therefore learned and acted; there was a movement which was not of the positive. I can now pick up that telephone and hear someone say, "Will you come to dinner tonight?'' I'll answer what is suitable at that moment, either that I want to or that I don't want to, and there is the end of it. Understanding the negative state demands something else. One has to understand what it is to be alone, for beauty is aloneness.

August 5, 1965

Third Dialogue in Saanen

I think it is very important to understand this question of a positive activity, and the negative which is not the opposite of the positive. We must understand this question very fundamentally because there is need of a tremendous, radical revolution in our lives. We need to change. Our whole way of living, thinking, and feeling must undergo a radical mutation. This is fairly obvious to anyone who is at all sensitive and aware, living in this rather mad and insane world.

Man has suffered endlessly, tried various subterfuges, escapes, but he hasn't really, fundamentally gone beyond elementary suffering. We either worship suffering, as is done in Christianity—try to escape through various forms of inventions, drugs, and ideas, as is done in the Western world, or through images and symbols, as is done in the East. I feel that unless one understands the positive and the negative, a radical mutation will not take place. We may change in areas that are of little value—change the economic world, or the social world, or make a change in our relationships—but that means very little.

We are talking about a mutation that is not brought about by will or by the principle of pleasure. To bring about this mutation, one must understand the enormous problem of what the positive is and what the negative is; and one must understand that the negative is not in contradiction to the positive, the opposite of the positive, or a reaction to the positive. One must understand the structure, the nature, and the meaning of the positive. Without understanding that, one can't go into the other. One can only escape into a kind of negative, bland, mystical, sentimental, devotional nonsense, which has no validity at all. So we must explore still more this question of what the positive is, without seeking an end to it.

We were saying yesterday that the very essence of the positive is seeking and finding. This question interests me tremendously. I am very much excited about this; I have never before thought about this point—not thought about it, it has never happened to me. The positive, as we said yesterday, is the self-centered activity which identifies itself with a formula, with a utopia, with a social activity, and so on. We also said that it is the positive that follows, believes, conforms, obeys, possesses, dominates, and accepts domination. In the area of the so-called positive one feels secure, one feels safe; and the mischief begins when we deny the impermanency of everything we touch. The positive mind wants a shelter at any cost, so it establishes an ideological area, as God, atma, or some other Hindu, Christian, or Buddhist ideal. It establishes a formula and holds on to it like grim death, but to be without shelter, without anchorage, without comfort, is to be without fear.

There is another area which needs great exploration, understanding, unfolding, and that is: Where there is seeking, there is always a finding. The seeking implies distance, and the reaching, finding, is also a further distance.

Please, I'm not making a speech; we are simply going to talk this over. Please stick to the point, and not talk about how to stop the war in Vietnam. Perhaps we shall stop a war in Vietnam by approaching it differently.

When the mind admits distance as the time involved in seeking and the time involved in finding, there is a duration. We are caught in that mode of thinking. We use time as a means of overcoming or annihilating distance, but time itself is distance.

Let me put it differently. I have an image of myself, an extraordinary being—our images of ourselves are always most extraordinary, lovely, divine, spiritual—but I am just what I am—crude, vulgar, ambitious, worldly, with plenty of money, or lacking money and wanting it, craving position and prestige. I am that, but the image is something entirely different. To reach that image, and to be totally identified with that image, requires time in which to cover the distance; and the covering of that, the reaching of that is a positive action. We soon realize that the image is self-fabricated, manufactured by ourselves; we want a center which is permanent, beyond the image—God, reality, or utopia. We cross the space between the actual and the ideational, and beyond the ideational. All this involves distance, and to cover that distance, time is necessary.

Time, as you will find if you go into yourself and observe it realistically, not mythologically, is a most detrimental thing. The ideal, the image, is nonfactual; it is based on pleasure, and inherently in it is the seed of sorrow. I cannot face the fact of what I actually am. Facing the fact of what I am, *what is,* needs no time, but the other needs time. So we have invented time as a means of avoiding *what is.* To look at *what is,* we need no distance between the observer and the thing observed, but we need distance between the fact and the image. So, time breeds disorder in helping us not to face *what is.* The time needed to cover that distance is not only a waste of energy, but inherently it is breeding disorder. The positive is the way of disorder.

What we are concerned with is the radical mutation of the human mind. Can that mind be completely transformed through time, or is it to be transformed immediately? I see time, which is the distance between the fact and the image, as an element of disorder. Time creates the distance between the fact and the image, the space around the image, and the space around the fact. I see that completely, not as an idea, not as a particular, as a fragment, but totally. So I reject time totally as a means of bringing about order, but I don't know what comes next.

Please don't listen to me. Listen to yourselves as we are talking.

Question: Shouldn't we move from the positive to the negative?

KRISHNAMURTI: You're quite right. But I want us to understand completely the nature and the structure of the positive before we go into the other because I feel there is a distance of a different kind, which is not this distance. I didn't want to start with that.

Look. There is no mutation possible as long as I am functioning within the field of the positive, which is of time, which is covered by the distance between the fact and the image. There is no mutation possible as long as there is this reaching out, this searching and finding—all of which are forms of greed and pleasure, breeding pain, suffering, anxiety, and fear. When there is an understanding of that, which we call the positive, there is a moving away from it to something else. The moving away does not involve distance. The negative is not an idea to which you are moving, away from the positive.

One must understand this question of distance. You are sitting there, and the speaker is sitting here. There is a distance between us. There is a distance between you and the person who is next to you, between you and the mountain. Those are actual facts. To reach the mountain, you need time. There the object is very clear: you want to get to the top of the Diablerets and you walk, or take the lift. But inwardly, inside the skin, inside the whole structure of consciousness, within the limits of consciousness, is there a distance? Distance between what? There is a distance only when there is a center which creates space around itself. If that center, driven by pleasure or by pain, moves to another center, the movement is still the continuation of that center in a different field.

Question: Doesn't a center create space around itself?

KRISHNAMURTI: What does space mean to you—space between where you are and where that mountain is, the space created by the tent, within the tent, and outside the tent? We only know space when there is a center. There is a tree; the tree creates space around itself. A building creates space outside and inside because the building is the center. We only know space where there is a fixed point round which there is space, and beyond. We know that when an image has been put together by pleasure, we call the idea a center, and that center creates space around itself. Is there any kind of space other than that? If space is only the outcome of an object, an idea, a center or an image, then within that field there is no freedom. A man who wants to find out what freedom is, not through curiosity, but actually, must understand this question of space. He must know whether it is possible to be free of the center, which is the image put together through pleasure. As long as there is activity within that space which has been created by the image, or by the center, there can be no freedom, and therefore there can be no mutation.

Question: If thought has created space and time, why can't thought end it?

KRISHNAMURTI: Can thought end anything, sir, actually? I am greedy, violent. Can thought end it? It can run away from it, it can find a substitute for it, it can suppress it, it can control it. Thought is a reaction to memories of accumulated pleasures; thought has created greed, and so thought itself is greed. Can that end greed?

Comment: Water cannot wipe away water.

KRISHNAMURTI: All right, but let's go on. We have so far been considering the nature, meaning, and structure of what we call the positive in life; this is productive of disorder because it admits time. The mind sees that as a whole, not a fragmentary disorder, but total disorder. Then one moves away from it, naturally, as one moves away from poison. If one is neurotic, one may play with poison, take a little bit of it and get used to it, but if one observes with a healthy, clean attention, one moves away. The movement is not a reaction to the positive. The movement is not towards anything. If it moved to a point, that point would still be the projection of the positive as a reaction.

The mind, having understood the nature of the poison, has moved away, naturally. This movement is negation; because when I reject something, either I reject because I react to it, the reaction being pleasure or pain, or I reject it totally because it is finished, it has no meaning any more. The total rejection brings about the movement of another quality which we call the negative.

I must understand very clearly whether I'm rejecting because of a pleasure and pain reaction, or whether it is a natural movement away because I see its whole nature. I know most intimately exactly what takes place within the field of the positive; there is no deception, no illusion, no covering up. I have very clearly seen every angle, every recess, every secret movement, every pursuit, search, and finding. There is no movement which breeds illusion because the pleasure principle is totally absent.

Question: What about space?

KRISHNAMURTI: Sir, may we for the moment forget about space? You see, it is very important to understand this rejection, this putting away, this falling away. When you see a poisonous thing, you move away, both physically and psychologically. I wonder if you have ever rejected anything which gave you pleasure? Have you?

Comment: I eat something which gives pain; therefore, I reject it. (Laughter)

KRISHNAMURTI: I am afraid we must leave that and go on. Do you do anything without motive, give up smoking, or whiskey, or whatever you are a slave to? Will you give it up without any motive? Have you ever done it? Not because a particular food gives you pain, and therefore you give it up; but have you ever given up anything which is pleasurable, not because of a greater pleasure, but without motive? You have never done it. That is our tragedy. You will give up something because of a greater pleasure; it is still within the field of the positive. The understanding of the nature, the structure, and the significance of the positive is in itself a moving away from it; there is no motive to move away, but when you see the structure itself has no meaning, you are already out of it.

Comment: Before one can see the meaning of the positive and be able to reject it, one must have gone through a lot of self-knowledge.

KRISHNAMURTI: Sir, we've asked a very simple question. Have you ever done anything without a motive, such as pleasure or pain? Can you do anything without a motive? Can you be kind, generous, nongreedy, nonacquisitive, without violence—not because you want heaven, not because you want peace, not because you want to live a comfortable life, but just do it? If you have not done it, then I'm afraid you can't go any further because we are entering into a dimension, into a field in which there is no motive, but only action. Motive is the positive, and it brings disorder. Unless you have understood that completely, you can't go into the other, do what you will. You might say, "Well, go on talking about it; I like to listen," but that has no meaning. When you have done an act without motive, then you will know about the negative.

Comment: Spontaneity is without motive.

KRISHNAMURTI: That is a very dangerous word. We think we are spontaneous when we are not. To be spontaneous is a most extraordinary thing. To jump into a river when you see someone drowning, without calculation, without heroism, without the onlooker, is a very rare incident. To be really spontaneous demands an immense understanding of the positive. The world of the positive is totally unrelated to the world or to the dimension of the negative. That is the first thing one has to realize.

Comment: But it is not the opposite.

KRISHNAMURTI: It is not the opposite, under any circumstances. In the world of the negative there is only action, not motive and action, not idea followed by action.

As far as I understand electricity, it seems that only when the positive and the negative meet is there an explosion. There is never an explosion in the positive. In that field which is total negation, there is a positive movement which is the meeting of the negative and the positive, which is action.

Question: Should we do nothing but look at it?

KRISHNAMURTI: Do nothing? We have done a tremendous lot. We have found out that the positive, as we know it, is most destructive; that's why human beings are so monstrously ugly and destructive. In that field which we call the negative, which is a totally different dimension, unrelated to the positive, and not a reaction to the positive, there is a totally different positive, which is action. It is not thought and action, or the idea created by organized pleasure and action; these are in the field of the positive. There is only action, and that action can only take place when there is that positive which is not related to the other positive, and the total negation.

Comment: You asked us earlier if we have ever acted without a motive.

KRISHNAMURTI: Sir, haven't you moved away from that?

Comment: But you asked us that question.

KRISHNAMURTI: I've asked another question.

Comment: The first question is very difficult to answer. The question was whether I have ever done anything without a motive. I sometimes think I have, but then I always discover that there is a motive, some hidden motive.

KRISHNAMURTI: Probably we have never done anything without a motive, conscious or unconscious.

Comment: Not always. When you really love, there is no motive. I don't mean physical love! (Laughter)

KRISHNAMURTI: The questioner says that when you really love, there is no motive. I don't know what that means.

Comment: I could put it differently.

KRISHNAMURTI: You can put it in different ways, but it is still the same thing. Physical love, sensual love, false love—all these are divided, fragmented, but in true love there is no motive.

But we were talking about something that is really quite extraordinary.

Comment: Excuse me, I didn't understand what you said about the positive state. I thought you were talking in general. I say that almost anything you want, you can do without motive.

KRISHNAMURTI: Look, when what we call love shows itself as jealousy, possessiveness, obstinacy, vanity, and domination, even though we may call it that, it is not really love. It is our daily life, with the agony of it all. You love me, I don't love you, jealousy, and all the rest of it. If we accept that as the only thing, we will make the best of it. Living in a prison, we will decorate the windows, or we will go into terrific despair. We don't say there is "real" love, or "real" spiritual love, and all that. We don't know. If the mind says, "Look, I want something which is not enmeshed in all this jealousy, possessiveness, mine, yours, physical love, spiritual love, divine love, and profane love; I want to find something which is not all this," is there something else? The fact is, we *are* this. Unless the facts are faced and we are free, there is no possibility of anything else.

We all know about action based on idea, action derived from approximating or adjusting oneself to an idea, the idea being organized pleasure, memory, experience, or knowledge, which are always positive. Just now I was speaking of something entirely different, action not based on an idea. In a state of negation, in that state of the negative which is not positive, there is only action, and therefore no idea. There can be action without idea. And thought has no place in that dimension.

Comment: When you say that thought has no place in that dimension, I don't follow you.

KRISHNAMURTI: Sir, when do you use thought? Or if thought is taking place, when are you aware that thought is functioning? I ask you a most familiar question, what your name is, and your response is immediate. "Immediate" may be divided into seconds, but it is almost instantaneous because you are very familiar with the answer to that question. Let us move a little further. You are not very familiar with some such question as the mileage between here and Zurich. You say, "Well, I don't know, but I'll look it up, or ask someone who knows, such as the garage man." You have taken time. Between the question and the answer there is a time interval in which you have tried to find out. Then there is the question to which you don't know the answer, or to which there is no answer. So what do you do? During the time interval between the question and the answer, you are thinking, you are investigating, asking, waiting, demanding, looking up in books, going to a professor, a scientist, or a priest. In the interval between the question and the answer, there was a lapse of time, which was thinking.

Now, if a question is asked in which thought doesn't function at all, and you say, "Really, I don't know," in that state there is no expectation, no waiting for an answer, because there is no one to answer you. You don't know a thing about death, do you? You have seen death, but if you are asked what is beyond, what is the nature of death, the whole structure of that extraordinary thing, if you are really honest, not wanting to invent theories, you say, "I don't know."

What is the state of mind that says, "I don't know"? Is there thinking? Is there really thinking? You're not waiting, you're not expecting, your brain is faced with something it cannot possibly answer; the brain cells are quiet because there is no response, there is no reaction. Either you become indifferent to the question and walk away or you remain with the question, not knowing the answer. There you don't accept. Your mind, your brain is completely quiet because it doesn't know. So is there any thinking? Your mind is tremendously active. Your brain is active; it hasn't gone to sleep, it hasn't become blank.

That mind, that brain is now completely alive. Previously it was waiting for an answer. It was asking, demanding, looking, expecting—all that. When there is no answer at all, it doesn't mean that you are asleep. On the contrary, your whole body, your whole organism, your mind, your brain cells are tremendously active; but then thought is absent. To listen with that sense of intense aliveness to that car, to that train going by, what happens? Is there a thought? There is a state of mind in which thought is totally absent; it is a state of action. When that state of mind has to do something, what it does is not based on an idea.

So, one knows then the poisonous nature of positive action. When that is totally understood, not verbally, but completely, not fragmentarily, but wholly, then comes a natural state which is negation, a negative mind which is not a blank mind, which is not a reaction, which is not a rejection of the positive; such a mind is intensely active, and therefore it is action. The mind itself is action.

August 6, 1965

Fourth Dialogue in Saanen

What shall we talk about together this morning?

Question: We started out to see if the thinker could actually be known. Is there anything more we can do along that line?

Question: Can you not speak about the "now"?

Question: Is it possible to see ourselves as we are, without condemnation or justification?

Question: Sir, you said that the moment the positive and the negative meet, there is an explosion. Does it mean that at that moment the whole positive is exploded?

KRISHNAMURTI: Oh, no, we were talking about something completely different. Let us leave to yesterday what we discussed yesterday. One questioner wants to know what is the "now." Another question is, "Why do we always condemn or justify, without actually observing *what is?*" Shall we talk over the question of the now? In doing that, perhaps, sir, we will answer your question, and probably yours, too, madame. The now, the active movement of the present, involves the understanding of time, doesn't it?

Question: Is time a movement of the mind?

KRISHNAMURTI: We will go into what time is, not only chronological time, but also the other areas where thought creates or breeds or puts together this thing called time. Time involves distance, a movement. . . .

Comment: If we keep on using the mind, we are going to be leaving the now. Every thought we have takes us out of the now.

KRISHNAMURTI: Ah, yes. Every thought one has is a movement away from the now. But to understand the now, whatever that is, mustn't we regard the whole area where time is employed? Mustn't we consider time as the past, the present, which is the now, and the future, which are all one movement? Can we separate the now as something distinct and apart from the past or the future?

Comment: The now contains within itself all the past.

KRISHNAMURTI: I understand all that. Are we talking things over verbally, intellectually, argumentatively, and dialectically, or are we trying to find out actually how to live in a state where time doesn't breed disorder?

Comment: Well, you see, if you are living in the now, then there is order.

KRISHNAMURTI: My lady, how am I to live in the now? What does it mean?

Comment: Well, you are already in the now.

KRISHNAMURTI: Oh, oh!

Comment: But the mind keeps interfering with that.

KRISHNAMURTI: All right, you say I am really living in the now, but the mind interferes. How am I to stop this interference? How am I to stop the mind from interfering?

Comment: By being aware and seeing that every movement of thought is taking you out of the now.

KRISHNAMURTI: Why does the mind move away from the now? If the now is so extraordinarily important and all-significant, why does the mind, or thought, or desire move away from the now? To understand the now, or to live in the now, I have to understand the whole area of time, the whole field of the movement of thought, the movement of the mind, the movement of desire, and all that.

Question: Isn't that going back again the old way?

KRISHNAMURTI: I am not going back the old or the new way. Look, madame, does one understand what it means to live completely in the now?

Comment: You don't have to understand it, you have to live it. It doesn't need any understanding, it only needs constant and immediate awareness.

KRISHNAMURTI: But unfortunately one has not this constant awareness. How is one to cultivate it? How is one to get at it?

Comment: Well, you see, if you are living in the moment, you are always knowing what it is to live in the now.

KRISHNAMURTI: All right, all right. But if I live in the now, what does that mean? What does it mean to live in the now?

Comment: It means not to have a problem. There is no problem. If you do have a problem, the mind creates it. I have listened to you, and I have tested this in my life.

KRISHNAMURTI: I understand, madame. Practicing is not living.

Comment: A great deal depends on the meaning one gives to the words one uses.

KRISHNAMURTI: I know; that's why we are trying to clarify the meaning of the words that we are using. I want to find out what it means to live in the now.

Comment: You don't have to find out; you just live it.

KRISHNAMURTI: Look, let's all have a little patience about this. Please don't get irritated with that lady, or amused by her. Let's all find out together what it means to live in the now. What does it mean?

Question: Are you asking me the question?

KRISHNAMURTI: I am asking everybody.

Comment: It means you have no problems. All the problems are created by the mind moving out of the now.

KRISHNAMURTI: Then if I have no problems, I might be either totally asleep or totally awake. Which is it?

Comment: Totally awake.

KRISHNAMURTI: Now, what does that mean, totally awake? Don't say, "No problems." Don't say, "You will know when that state arrives," and all the rest of it. What does it mean to have a mind that is living in the present and has no problems? Does it mean that it is totally asleep, or totally awake? Wait a bit! What does it mean to be totally awake?

Comment: You live only one moment at a time. You only have one moment at a time in life, only the mind makes you think there is a past and a future. If you can live this one moment properly, you do not need to be concerned about anything else.

KRISHNAMURTI: I understand, madame. I'm afraid I have already talked a great deal about all that.

Comment: But you have to live it.

KRISHNAMURTI: Now, wait a bit! I may or I may not live it.

Comment: I'm not saying that you are not living it.

KRISHNAMURTI: I don't know; I may be. I am saying to myself, "I may live it or I may not live it; I don't know." But I am saying to myself, "What does it imply to live in a single moment totally?" What does it imply?

Question: Why do you want to know what it implies? (Laughter)

KRISHNAMURTI: Ah, wait! My lady, I want to find out whether I am deceiving myself. I want to find out whether my living is so verbal that when I say, "Well, I just live so completely in the moment," this is a form of self-hypnosis. I may be creating the illusion that I am living totally in the now, in the moment; but actually I may be very dull, and have no sensitivity to anything that is happening, not only within the moment, but round it.

Question: What instrument are you using with which to find out if you are self-hypnotized?

KRISHNAMURTI: That's right. What instrument am I using to find out? Generally we are using the instrument that has been created through reaction, through condemnation, through justification, as the instrument which is the censor—the intellectual background which has been cultivated along the line of a certain culture. That's the only instrument we have. Do we use that instrument to find out what the moment actually is? Or is there another movement, another instrument totally different, which is not born of time? I don't quite see how one can live completely, totally, in the present, without being free, both consciously and unconsciously, of the psychological social structure of greed and envy, and all the rest of it. I don't know what it means to live so completely in the moment. If you say to me, "Live," I say I do live; but I don't know, I can't know what it means to live completely in the moment. If I think I am doing so, I may be deceiving myself; I may be fooling myself about something which is not actual.

Perhaps, if you will kindly permit me, we will be able to come upon this now without trying to twist the whole of life into one moment.

Comment: You cannot twist it into one moment. You are the whole of life up to that moment.

KRISHNAMURTI: My lady, I understand. How am I to stop this dreadful mind that is going, that is wandering, twisting, creating illusions, that is battling with itself? How am I to put an end to it?

Comment: It is necessary to be aware of it.

KRISHNAMURTI: In being aware of all that, I am not living in the present. The present has gone away because I am living. I am being aware of something which has already gone.

Comment: You are watching every movement of the mind; you are paying attention and watching how the movement is trying to take the opposite view now.

KRISHNAMURTI: I understand all that. I have talked and, as you have said, you have read about all this. If I may suggest, please don't come to any conclusion. Let us start all over again because perhaps that way we will come upon it anew. Let us start again to find out what it means to live in the now, in a moment which is total. Let's find out again. Don't tell me, "Be aware of the past, be aware of the movement of the mind," and so on and on. That I know; we have done all that during the last fifteen talks. Leave all that aside; let's find a different approach to this. There may be a new, a different movement which will come naturally.

What is the essence of time?

Comment: A succession of events.

Comment: It's merely a movement.

Comment: It is the nature of duration.

Comment: Distance.

KRISHNAMURTI: Look, I have asked a question. I don't know. I really don't know. One person says, "It is a movement, a succession of events"; another says, "duration"; still another says, "distance." But is that the essence of time? I am not saying that it is not. I want to find out, don't you? You have given opinions, you have verbalized. It may be the truth, a fact, the essence, and you may have found it. But I also want to find it. And another man wants to find it. So, give us a chance. Give that other man and me a little space between the question and the answer. A little space—not what you think and what I think, what your opinion is, what you find to be a fact. Just give that person and me a little space to discover for ourselves.

Why do I demand space? And what do I mean by that space? I mean an interval, don't I? Don't push me; don't give more and more ideas, more words. Give me a little space, give me a little time in which I can probe, investigate, ask myself, look. A question has been asked, "What is the essence of time?" You have given answers. Perhaps you are much quicker than I am and see much more quickly than I do. But I also want to see. So I say to myself, "What is the essence of time, and how do I find it?" But if you are pressing in all the time with your opinions, with your ideas, with your knowledge, with your facts, I have no freedom in which I can discover for myself.

So I need freedom, freedom from your opinion, from your knowledge, from your facts, from your ideas of truth, which may be true, or may not be true. These are all trying to influence me, push me in a corner where I say, "Yes, you are right," and I accept it. I don't want to do that. I want to be free. There must be freedom, not only from your opinions, your judgments, your truth, but also freedom from my own prejudices and conclusions, from what I have understood, what I have read—I must be free from all of them.

I am beginning to find out that to answer that question as to what the essence of time is, there must be freedom. I must also have space not cluttered up with noise. I must have freedom, and space which is silent. It is a new question to me. So there must be freedom, there must be a sense of silence in which there is no demand, no impingement of immediate answer, no pushing, no asking.

I must have freedom, and there must be space in the mind which is completely quiet, not waiting or expecting an answer, but completely quiet. Then one may find out for oneself, not opinion, but the truth of what the essence of time is. I may find it tomorrow, I may find it next year, but that doesn't matter. What matters is that the field must be right, the foundation must be laid.

Question: What is time?

KRISHNAMURTI: Sir, we are not asking what time is. We are trying to find out the essence of time, like the essence of a pine tree or the essence of a flower.

Question: Is time a quantity or a quality?

KRISHNAMURTI: The gentleman wants to know if time is a quantity or a quality. Someone suggested yesterday that questioners should be taxed. (Laughter) And the reply to that suggestion was, "You are a fascist." (Laughter) Not that we are taxing here, not that there is a Mussolini or a Hitler here, but I think it was an amusing idea.

All right. I've got it! Have you? Any movement, in any direction, involves a center and an object toward which it is moving. I go from here to the chalet, to the rooms in which I live. There is a movement from here to there. That involves time, not only physiological time, but also the time that says, "I am hungry; I want to get there." So any movement, in any direction, from the center to the periphery, is of time. So the essence of time is nonmovement. What do you say? It is very interesting. Please listen.

I only know time as movement, as thought, as the movement of an idea in action. I don't know any other time. I know time as the past, with all the memories, knowledge, and experience, through the present, through the now, which we call action, which creates the tomorrow. So time is that, is this movement, endless movement from the past to the future, from the center to a particular object, from the object to the center as a reaction. All that we know is only a movement within the field of time. And if there is no movement at all, is that time? The essence of time is the cessation of all movement, and therefore no-time. The essence of time is no-time. I think that will hold right through. And the lady means that the now is that no-time in which there is no movement.

So, this movement which is put together, which has been bred through time, which is the whole of me—not only the physical, but the conscious and the unconscious, the whole structure of me—is movement in the field of time. How is that movement to end—not in sleep, not in illusion, not in an ideological formula—without any kind of effort from the mind?

If you like, put it the other way round. Each one of us, each human being, is the result of time—two million years, more or less—and he has a lot of history behind him, not only factual history, but fictitious history, communal history, the story of his fathers, his mothers, his traditions, all that he is. That story has a life of its own, a tremendous life, the unconscious, the past. The conscious mind also has its own activities—going to the office every day, following a certain routine, a certain pattern. So there is a hiatus, a division between that immense, unexplored part, and the casual living of daily, conscious life. That is what is taking place in each one of us. Each has a movement of its own; each has its own life, drive, purpose, fear, anxiety, and despair. Can this division be done away with so that it is one movement, and not contradictory movements? This means a total consciousness of the past and the present, not a fragmentary past and a fragmentary present.

The mind is aware of, perceives, or listens to the history of the past, which has a life of its own, moving, living. The mind is also aware of the daily life. The two are not completely divided; they have a certain rather tenuous relationship. One has to be totally aware of these two processes, the conscious process and the unconscious process. Is it possible to be aware of this whole structure without introducing time?

Are you interested in what we are talking about?

Audience: Yes.

KRISHNAMURTI: Why? We are interested because that is the only life we have. Any other life is merely speculation, a field in which the theologians can have a thundering good time. But this is the only life one has; and in this life there is such misery, confusion, anxiety, ill-health, disease, death, wanting to be well—all that is going on in each one of us. The mind is tormented, and naturally wants to find a way out of it all. But to find a way out may be an escape; one has to be extremely careful not to escape. One has to find out what escape means. I may say that I don't want to escape, but I may be escaping all the time. So, the mind has to find out how it is escaping.

One sees that the first escape is to verbalize, and that's what we are doing all the time. We are aware of this movement of the total consciousness, and the escape comes when we say, "I like it, I don't like it," or "That is jealousy, this is anger, this is greed, this is the observer, this is condemnation, this is justification." Any movement away from the fact—a verbal movement, a movement of condemnation, justification, or interpretation—is an escape.

So, escape is degeneration of the energy that is needed to face the fact. Whether I deliberately escape through amusement, through sex, through drink, through marijuana, or this, or that, any deliberate escape is an avoidance of the fact. I see that escape dissipates energy, and I need complete energy to face the fact. To understand the fact, there must be no escape; therefore, I don't escape. There is no escape. It is not a question of how I am to stop escaping. I realize that any form of escape—condemnation, verbalization, justification, saying, "I don't like it, I like it; it is pleasure, it is pain; I want to escape"—any form of escape is a dissipation of energy.

The mind realizes the dissipation of energy through escape, and therefore there is no escape. You don't condemn; you don't justify. You are concerned with the fact of *what is.* There is no interpretation, no trying to say, "But I don't like it," because condemnation, justification, and interpretation are based on pleasure, on the idea that it will give you pain, and not pleasure. Seeing all that is a natural focusing of all energy to observe the fact alone. The fact is *what is.*

To observe the fact, the *what is,* is there a distance between the observer and the thing which is? I am escaping through worship, through reading, or something else, and because you have talked to me, I suddenly realize how absurd it all is. My energy is centered, focused. I wonder if there is another form of dissipation of energy. I discover that there is much more of a dissipation than mere escape into something infantile, like fame or success. The mind discovers that between the *what is* and the observer, there is a space. There is a distance. That distance is a dissipation because it involves time. But when there is a total cessation, naturally, voluntarily, easily, without denying, there is not the space but only the fact, not the observer looking at the fact. If there is an observer looking at *what is,* then there is a distance. That distance is a waste of energy because it involves time.

The mind discovers how extraordinarily subtle these forms of escape are, and in the discovering, the mind itself has become extremely subtle and sensitive. There must be an extreme sensitivity and subtleness to observe the fact.

Now, proceed a little further. Then the fact becomes unimportant. What is important is the mind that is looking at *what is,* not the fact. Look at that tree. What is important? The mind that looks at the tree is the important thing. The tree has its own importance, but when you are looking at the tree, when there is no movement of any kind—therefore complete energy, the highest form of sensitivity, extremely swift in its movement—then you will see that facts have very little meaning.

Suppose I am angry. All right. It is over and I don't hold on to it. That's the end of it. Not that I must end anger, that is too silly. But in understanding this whole process, the mind has become extraordinarily alive, sensitive, subtle—not partially sensitive, fragmentarily sensitive, as an artist, a poet, a writer, or whatever it is, but totally sensitive—and a mind that is totally sensitive has no movement at all. Such a mind has no time; it is the essence of time, but it has no time.

That is the now. That means living in complete emptiness, an emptiness that is tremendously active, because the mind has not just gone to sleep and become empty, like an empty cup; the mind is empty because it has no movement. And from there, that functions. Then the question arises, is it possible to live a daily life in that state, going to the office with all the details of business? That state is the now; that is the very essence of time, which is no-time. Is it possible to live a daily life with that in mind? That, I'm afraid, you have to find out for yourselves.

Question: When there is distress, is it always caused by self-pity?

KRISHNAMURTI: I wonder, madame, if you have listened to what has been said—not that we are avoiding your question. But you have remained with your problem and have not listened to the things that have just been said. If you are following what is being said, distress is nonexistent because you meet it and don't translate it as pleasure, which breeds pain and distress. That's why one has to understand this question of pleasure, which is not easy, because our image of ourself, our attitude, and our work are all based on this demand for pleasure, not on a demand to face the facts as facts.

So, is it possible to live a life other than our daily, boring, strenuous life, which apparently has no meaning at all? Is it possible to live a life which is not based on pleasure? Again, you have to find that out. That opens the whole field of what love is. Because without that being, pleasure will continue, and the mind becomes a breeding ground of pain. One has a lot of work to do, not only within this tent, but there is a tremendous work to do all the time; that needs great energy, and therefore no escaping.

August 7, 1965

Fifth Dialogue in Saanen

What shall we talk about this morning?

Question: Sir, I wonder whether it would be worthwhile considering what discussion is. What is the basis of discussion? I do not know whether it is possible to discuss with so many people, but some of us discuss, when you are not available, in small groups, and it might be important to talk about what discussion is. Related to that I have a question: How can a person learn who is not as brilliant as another? I have found that in a discussion group where the speaker is quite brilliant, he gives what he learns so quickly that I can't follow.

Comment: I wonder if you might talk further about meditation in daily activity.

Question: Sir, as the essence of time was traced yesterday, would it be possible to trace down the essence of dying to every moment?

KRISHNAMURTI: One questioner has asked what we mean by discussion. As he discusses with various groups, he finds that one or two people are brilliant, and the rest are not; and from that discussion, because of the brilliance of the few, there is hardly any learning. And so he says, what is discussion, the intention of discussion, and what is learning?

Then someone asked to go into the question of meditation in daily life, not as an abstraction, not something that one does occasionally, but whether it is possible to be in a state of meditation throughout the day, naturally and easily.

The other question is: "As we traced yesterday the whole movement of time, could we this morning go into detail into the question of dying to everything, dying so as to be fresh and new every day?"

Question: How can one deal with the unconscious, traumatic, compulsive urges?

Question: What do you mean by the essence of anything, essence of time, essence of love, and so on?

Comment: When you are aware of conflict, one of three things can happen: it might disappear, it might continue, or it might increase.

Comment: One difficulty is having motives. Would you please speak about motives.

KRISHNAMURTI: Now, there are enough questions. Let us see if we can't include all these in one question.

First of all, what is the meaning of these talks? Why do you and I come here every morning to talk things over? Either you treat the speaker as your authority from whom you are going to learn, which is not the intention of the speaker at all, at any time, at any level, or we come together to talk things over amicably, exposing ourselves inwardly to ourselves, because this offers an opportunity to uncover and discover and go beyond. That is the intention when I come here and talk, not that the speaker is laying down a law, a dogma, an authority, a belief, a way, but rather in speaking together we are listening to ourselves rather than to someone else. In listening to ourselves we discover an infinite lot, a great depth to all our words and meanings. At least, that is the intention of these discussions here the last four or five days, and also the talks that we have had the ten times previously.

If we treat these discussions merely as an intellectual, verbal battle of opinions, then I'm afraid they will be of very little value. What we are concerned with, seeing the misery within ourselves and in the world, the confusion, the incessant battle between man and man, is whether there is a different way of living altogether, not merely in certain economic or social areas. Can one live a totally different life in all the areas? That is why we have these meetings here. To learn is to listen, not only to the speaker, but to that river. Listen to it as we are talking; listen to the boy who is shouting; listen to your own thoughts, to your own feelings, so that you become completely familiar with them. Becoming familiar is to understand, and to understand there must be care to listen, not only to your opinions, because you know very well what your opinions are. Your opinions are your prejudices, your pleasures, the conditions under which you have been brought up. One must also listen to all the impacts, if one can, of the outward influences and reactions; and through this listening, seeing, there comes a learning. That is the intention of these discussions and talks.

The next question was whether it is possible to meditate throughout the day without making meditation into some squalid affair of an hour or two, or ten minutes, but to sustain it throughout the day, and through this meditation to understand the nature of dying, and what it means to live anew.

The question was also asked, whether it is possible to put an end to all the unconscious or conscious traumas, drives, compulsions. We will limit ourselves this morning to those questions. If we begin to discuss, talk things over about meditation, then perhaps we shall include the question about the way of dying to everything so that the mind is made new, and we may also understand the compulsive urges that we human beings have.

That word *meditation* must be used most guardedly, with a great deal of hesitation, because in the Western world—and it is a great pity that the world is being divided into the West and the East—in this part of the world, meditation has very little meaning. One knows here the word *contemplation.* I think contemplation and meditation are two different things. In the East, meditation is something that one practices day after day, according to a certain method, a certain pattern laid down by some authority, ancient or modern; and in that, in following the pattern, one learns to conquer, control thought, and go beyond. That is the meaning generally implied by that word. The West is not fully acquainted with the word. So let us for the moment forget what the East means by the word, put away both the East and the West, and try to find out not how to meditate but the quality of a mind that is awake, aware, intense, that has no trauma, no suppression, no indulgence, that is not controlling itself all the time or at any time, that is free and therefore never lives in the shadow of yesterday. That is what we are going to consider.

We must begin to understand this right from the beginning because the first step matters much more than the last step. Freedom is not at the end but at the beginning, and that is one of the most difficult things to understand. Without freedom there is no movement except within a very, very restricted area, that restriction being based on the image or the idea of organized pleasure.

I am not laying down the law or telling you what to do, or what not to do, or that you must agree or disagree, but we have to see the idea, the principle, the image from which all thinking begins, from which all our reactions come. Without understanding that, it is not possible to be free to go far beyond the limitations of the mind, or the limitations of the society or culture in which we have been brought up. So, if I may suggest, as we are listening, you each have a double task, not only to listen to the speaker, but also to listen to yourself, who *is* the speaker.

We all want wider and deeper experiences, more intense, more alive, not repetitive; and so we seek experiences through drugs, through meditation or through visions, through becoming much more sensitive. The drugs help one, for the time being, to become extraordinarily sensitive; the whole organism is heightened; the nerves and the whole being are liberated from the pettiness of daily existence, and that brings about a great intensity. In that state of intensity, there are certain experiences where there is not the experiencer or the experience, there is only the thing. There is only the flower, if you are watching that flower, not the watcher watching the flower. These drugs in various forms give to the body, to the whole organism, and so to the brain, an intensity, an extraordinary sensitivity. In that state, if you are a poet, if you are an artist, if you are this or that, you have an experience according to your temperament.

Please, I have not taken any drug because to me any form of stimulant—any form, listening to the speaker and therefore being stimulated, or drink, or sex, or a drug, or going to Mass and getting into a certain state of emotional tension—is utterly detrimental, because any stimulant in any form, however subtle, makes the mind dull because it depends upon that stimulant. The stimulant establishes a certain habit and makes the mind dull.

Most of us do not use drugs, but we do want wider and deeper experiences; therefore, we meditate. We hope by meditation, by control of thought, by learning, by getting into some peculiar, emotional, psychological, mystical state, having visions, experiences, to reach an extraordinary state. If you are using meditation as a means to something, then meditation becomes another drug. It creates a habit, and therefore destroys the subtlety, the sensitivity, the quality of the free mind.

Most of us like systems to follow, and there are so many systems in Asia which have been transported, I don't know why, to the West. Everyone is trapped in those systems; there are mantras and all the rest of it. Constant repetition of words, in Latin, Sanskrit, or any other language, makes the mind quiet, but dull and stupid. A petty, little mind repeating the prayer of a Christian is still a petty, little mind. It can repeat ten million times a day; it is still a narrow, shallow, petty, stupid mind.

Meditation is something entirely different. In order to understand it, we must put away drugs and reject all methods, including the repetition of words in order to reach some peculiar state of silence, which is really stagnation. We must put away every form of desire for further experience. This is very difficult because most of us are so saturated with the ugliness, the brutality, the violence, and the despair of life that we want something more. We are longing for new experiences, whether outward experiences such as going to mass or inward deeper experiences. But one has to put all these away; only then is there freedom. The manner of putting away these things is of great importance. I can put away wanting this or that because it is too silly, but inwardly I may still want experiences. I may not want to see Christ or Buddha, or this or that person—that's too obviously silly because it's a projection of one's own background. I may rationally, logically reject that. But inwardly I want my own experience which is not contaminated by the past. But all experiences, all visions, are contaminated by the past.

I have to understand the depth, the height, the significance, the quality of the past; and in the understanding, I am dying to it, the mind is dying to it. The mind is the past; the whole structure of the brain, with all its associations, is the result of the past. It is put together by time, two million years of time, and you can't put it all away by a gesture. You have to understand it as every reaction arises. Since most of us still have a great deal of the animal in us, we have to understand all that; and to understand it, one has to be aware of it. To be aware is to watch it, listen to it, not condemn it or justify it.

By becoming aware outwardly and inwardly, by being aware and riding on that awareness of the outward movement as a tide that goes out and a tide that comes in, riding on that, the mind then begins to discover its own reactions, responses, demands, compulsions; and to understand these demands, urges, responses, you must not condemn; if you do, then you don't understand. It's like condemning a child because that's the easiest way to deal with the child. We condemn, and we think we understand, but we don't.

We have to find out why we condemn. Why do you condemn? Why do you rationalize? Why do you justify? Condemnation, justification, rationalization are forms of escape from the fact. The fact is there, *what is;* it is there. Why should I rationalize it? Why should I condemn it? Why should I justify it? When I do that, I am wasting energy. Therefore, to understand the fact, you must live with it completely, without any distance between the mind and the fact, because the fact is the mind.

You have rejected drugs and the urge for experience because you understand that when you want to escape from this ugly, monstrous world into something extraordinary, you invite experiences, and they again become escapes from the fact. Since the mind and the brain are the result of the past, one has to understand the conscious as well as the unconscious past. One can understand it immediately, not take time, months, years, going to the analyst, or analyzing oneself; one can understand the whole thing immediately, with one look, if one knows how to look. So we are going to find out how to look. One cannot look if there is any sense of condemnation, any sense of justification of what one sees. That must be completely clear. To understand a child you can't condemn it; you must watch it, watch it while it is playing, crying, laughing, sleeping. What is more important is not the child but how you watch the child.

We are now considering not how to look, not the method. We are trying to understand whether it is possible, by one look—not with your vision, not with your eyes only, but an inward look—to understand the whole structure and be free of it. That is what we mean by meditation, nothing else.

The mind has come to this point because it has rejected drugs, experiences, authority, following, repetition of words, control, forcing oneself in one direction. It has looked at it, studied it, gone into it, observed it—not said it is right or wrong. What has happened? The mind now has become naturally alert and sensitive, not through drugs, not through any form of stimulant. It has become exceedingly sensitive.

Let's go into that word *sensitive.* Do you want to ask questions? Are you listening to the speaker, or are you listening to yourself as the things are being said?

Comment: As you speak, I can't see myself.

KRISHNAMURTI: When do you see yourself? Do you ever see yourself as you are, not here, but when you go out of the tent? Do you ever see the poses, the mannerisms, the pretensions, the vanities, the wanting to impress, the 'what you are'?

We are now trying to see what we mean by sensitivity. This is of great importance—sensitivity of the body, the organism; sensitivity of the brain; total sensitivity. The essence of sensitivity is to be vulnerable. Organically, physically, when one is in good health, one is vulnerable. And one can reject any disease that comes near. But if one is weak, has disease, one is not vulnerable. So vulnerability implies great health, physically, organically. You may be ill, but you have vitality.

To be vulnerable inwardly means not having any resistance, not having any image, any formula; not saying, "This is the line I draw," and reacting from that line. That is merely a resistance. Such a mind, such an inward state of defense, resistance, acceptance, obedience, following authority, makes the mind insensitive. Fear of any kind—one of the most difficult things to be free from—makes the mind invulnerable, makes it dull and insensitive.

There is no sensitivity when you are seeking fame, when you are dogmatic, when you are violent, when you are in a position of authority and misuse that authority by being rude, vulgar, oppressive. All that obviously makes the mind, the whole being insensitive. Only a mind that is vulnerable is capable of affection, love—not a mind that is jealous, possessive, dominating. We understand now, without going too much into detail, more or less what sensitivity means. It is another thing to be in that state, not intellectually agree, or say, "How am I to come to that state where I'm totally vulnerable, and therefore totally sensitive?" You can't come to it by some trick; you'll come to it naturally, sweetly, easily, without effort, if you understand all that we have said previously about drugs, experience, ambition, greed, envy.

There is sensitivity only when there is freedom. Freedom implies freedom per se, not freedom from something. Having understood the past, we are now considering how by one look one is free of the whole structure. To look, to observe, to be aware of the whole structure instantly, there must be sensitivity. That sensitivity is denied if there is any form of image about oneself or about what one should be, that image being based on pleasure. The mind that is seeking pleasure in any form is inviting sorrow.

The mind that is sensitive—in the sense that we are using the word, not only neurologically and biologically, but vulnerable inwardly, totally, without any resistance—has an extraordinary strength and vitality and energy because it is not battling with life, neither accepting life nor rejecting it. When one understands this whole phenomenon, when one has gone through it all, then one look is enough to destroy the whole structure. This whole process is meditation.

In understanding meditation, one has to understand control and identification. Control of thought implies resistances to every other form of thought. I want to think about one thing, but thought wanders away, like a leaf aimlessly wandering. I concentrate, I control, I make a tremendous effort to push all thought away, except that one thought. That one thought is based on an ultimate pleasure. Concentration implies exclusion, narrowness, focusing on one thing, and keeping everything else in darkness. But when one understands what it is to be attentive, with the body, the nerves, the eyes, the ears, the brain, the whole total being; to listen to the irritating noise of that airplane when one wants to listen to the speaker; to be attentive to color, to thought, to one's speech—then, in that attention, there is a concentration which is not exclusion. I can attend, I can look, I can work on something without exclusion.

One must also understand identification. A child is absorbed by a toy. The toy is more fascinating than anything else, and the child is completely lost in that fascination; he becomes quiet, not mischievous, not naughty, he doesn't tear and run about. The toy has become the thing that takes his mind, his body, everything. The toy has absorbed him. And we also, as the child, want to be absorbed by an idea, by our images, or by the images that have been given to man, such as Buddha, Jesus Christ. Where the mind is being absorbed, either by a drink or by an image made by the hand or by the mind, there is no sensitivity, and therefore there is no love. The mind that is free is really an empty mind.

We only know emptiness as space with an object in it. We only know this emptiness in the tent because there is the outward structure of the tent, and that we call emptiness. We do not know space—not between the earth and Mars, we are not talking about that—without an object, and therefore, we don't know what emptiness is. A mind that is not totally empty, without an object, is never free. One can understand intellectually that all desire, all relationship, all action, takes place within the space created by the object, or by the center, or by the image. In that space there is never freedom. It's like a goat tied to a post, who can wander only the length of its tether. To understand the nature of freedom, one must understand the nature of emptiness and space, and again, all that is meditation. Only when the mind is totally empty and there is no center which creates space, and therefore there is space, is the mind completely quiet. The mind then is extraordinarily still, and it is only in stillness, which can only take place in the emptiness which is space without the object, that all energy—all energy—comes into being without movement.

When energy is no longer dissipated, and comes about without any movement, there must be action. A kettle that is boiling, if it has no escape, must burst. Only when the mind is completely still, not the stillness of stagnation, but of tremendous vitality and energy, is there an event, an explosion which is creation. Writing a book, writing a poem, becoming famous, is not creation. The world is filled with books. I believe four thousand or more books are produced every week. Self-expression in no manner is creation. And a mind that is not in that state of creation is a dead mind. One must begin, if one would understand meditation, right from the beginning, and the beginning is self-knowledge. Self-knowing is the beginning of wisdom, and the ending of sorrow is the beginning of a new life.

Question: How can you look at a tree without having distance between the tree and you?

KRISHNAMURTI: How do you look at a tree? How do you look at it? Do you look at all at anything? Do you look at your neighbor, at your wife, at your children? Do you look at your job? Do you look? Or do you look through your prejudices, through your ambition to fulfill, to become famous? Do you look at life as a Christian, as a Catholic, as a Protestant, as a communist? How do you look? Do you look with knowledge, which is your past, or do you look openly? Just to look, sir, is apparently one of the most difficult things to do; to look at a tree, and not have distance between you and that tree.

Look at that tree, do it please, as we are talking. Do you look with a resistance, with a line that you have drawn around yourself beyond which you will not go, from a platform which you have created for yourself through your belief, fear, dogma, greed? When you do look in that way, there is a distance between you and the tree; therefore, you are not looking, you are not observing, you are not listening. But when there is no line, no wall around yourself, of which you may be conscious or unconscious, when there is no line, wall, image, or center from which you are looking, then is there a distance between you and the tree? Find out. When there is no distance, you're not the tree or you're not yourself; therefore, distance has quite a different meaning.

Look, sir. If one is married, with a family and a job, like most of us, one has built around oneself walls of isolation, conscious or unconscious; one has collected knowledge as experience. I know more, and you know less; I am the great man, you are the lesser man. We build around ourselves enormous structures, and through those structures we look at life. Whether the structure be knowledge, or self-importance, or a craft, a technique that you have learned as a writer, as a poet, as a scientist, or as a lawyer, through that you look. Therefore the distance between you and the tree and your family and your neighbor is quite a different distance from the distance in which there is no center, no line, no fortification.

Question: In what sense do you use that word distance?

KRISHNAMURTI: There is a distance when there is a center of condemnation, justification, the censor apart from the fact, the *what is*. But when there is no center as the censor, is there a distance between the fact and oneself? Is there a distance?

Look. I am angry. Anger is a reaction, and I know I'm angry. It is something outside of me. I don't say, "I am anger," but "I am angry." When I say "I am anger," there is no distance. That is *what is*. But when I say,

"I am angry," there is a distance; and I then try to cover that distance by trying to do something about it. But when I realize I am anger, there is no space to do anything, but only the fact. Then *what is* becomes immensely important—not how to get rid of it. Therefore, *what is* is completely transformed when there is no distance created by the censor.

Question: What is the value of a human being who is liberated?

KRISHNAMURTI: What significance has such a human being? What's the value to society, to the family, to culture; what importance has he as a human being? None whatever! We want to transform society, we want to alter it; we say we must help each other. So, what is the function of a man who is free? What is his relationship, what can he do? Why do we ask that question? Why does that question arise at all?

Comment: We only see the death of ourselves, and therefore we don't see beyond that.

KRISHNAMURTI: Not quite, sir. The question was: "You are liberated, you are free, you are sensitive, alive, tremendously in the state of meditation; what is the value to me of your state? I am suffering, anxious. What is the use of you to me in my human travail?" Why do I ask that question? You are there, like a flower, like a sun, like some extraordinary sense of beauty. You are there. Why do I say, "Well, what will you do to help me; what is the use of you?" I say it because I want to get something of that. I put out a hand, a begging bowl, so that you will fill it. That's all our relationship is. But if I realize that you cannot possibly help me, if I realize that the beginning and the end of sorrow is the understanding of myself—not through you, not through anybody, or through any philosophy, or any system—then I am delighted that you have reached the 'something'. Our relationship is entirely different.

August 8, 1965

Sixth Dialogue in Saanen

What shall we talk over together this morning?

Question: What is the essence of pain?

Question: Why do we crave pleasure more and more?

Question: Haven't you gone rather easily and quickly into the question of time by saying that the essence of time is no-time? And also, could we discuss vulnerability a little further?

Comment: To be healthy is to be vulnerable.

KRISHNAMURTI: Yes. To be healthy is to be vulnerable, not only psychologically, but physically. And what's the other question?

Question: Why haven't you spent more time at the schools in India?

KRISHNAMURTI: Why have I spent so much time. . . .

Question: Why have you not spent more time?

KRISHNAMURTI: Oh! (Laughter) Why haven't I spent a much longer time at the schools in India, to which I go for a month every year? Is that it?

Question: Is it possible to discuss more deeply the question of conserving energy?

Question: Would you please explain motive, and give an example of an action which is without motive?

Question: What do you mean when you talk about a new society?

Question: We go through life and death alone. Would you please talk more about that aloneness?

KRISHNAMURTI: Now, there are enough questions. How do we answer them all? What do we mean by a new society, aloneness, life and death? And have you not slurred over and simplified time too much by saying "no-time"? Why don't you spend a much longer time in those two schools in India? And the other question about vulnerability. How do we answer all those questions?

Question: What is the difference between seeing and not seeing?

KRISHNAMURTI: Ah! Sometimes one sees, and most of the time one does not see. What is the reason when one does see?

I wonder if we cannot answer all these questions—I am just suggesting it—by considering the question of what we mean by a new society. May we explore that together? Perhaps in that exploration we shall be able to answer all these questions, except the question of why I don't spend a much longer time (Laughter) in the two schools I go to every year for a month or much longer. For a very simple reason: I haven't the time. You know, there are two schools in India, one in the north and one in the south, and I spend about a month in each place. I also spend nearly a month each in Bombay, Delhi, and Madras. So about four and a half months are spent in India, and that's enough.

What do we mean by a new society? We mean by society the organized customs, habits, of a so-called civilized nation. That is the generally understood meaning, according to the dictionary, which by chance I looked up this morning. That's what it says.

The society in which we live is based on acquisitiveness, greed, the search for power, prestige, position. We are concerned, not only with the transformation of the human being, but also with bringing about a radical change in society, because the human being cannot possibly exist outside of society. He is part of society, society being the organized customs and habits of a nation. That society is based psychologically on greed, envy, and all the rest of it, of which each one of us is a part. Is it possible to bring about a change in the human being apart from society, or must we wait for society, which includes every human being, to change, and then only shall we change as individuals? The thing we must find out is whether society, which is organized according to a certain pattern of behavior, conduct, organized communication, and so on, will permit freedom to a human being. You may not be interested in all this, but I am afraid we have to go through it.

Society, as we know, does not consider freedom necessary because society thinks or feels that freedom implies disorder, that if there is complete freedom, the human being will do what he likes. There is a fear of free enterprise and aggressive individualism, so society inherently tries to prevent human beings from being free. Can a society exist with a group of people who are free and yet part of society? This question is very important, for society as it is now is not the ground, the area in which human freedom can easily grow. So, must a human being seek freedom outside the area of society, or can he find out what freedom is while still living in society?

We have been talking about freedom, freedom which is not a reaction, freedom which is essentially a state of mind that has put away greed, envy, ambition, self-fulfillment, aggressiveness. By negating the positive there is freedom. The other day we discussed sufficiently what the positive is, the area of the human being, of society, which is positive. By negating that, not intellectually, verbally, idealistically, theoretically, but actually negating it—that is, when the human being is in a state of freedom in which aggressiveness, domination, the search for power, self-fulfillment, does not occur, does not take place—only then is there freedom. Then what is the relationship to society of a human being or a group of human beings who have come to this freedom?

To understand that, one has to explore this question of life, death, and the futility of a life that faces inevitable death. Please bear in mind all we have said previously about society. Our society is based on life and death, living and dying. The theory of reincarnation and the theory of resurrection are merely hopeful, suggestive ideas. If you accept reincarnation—which is to be born over and over again until the whole mind and heart are purified and reach the highest point of intelligence and Brahma—then you must accept the fact that you must behave in this life completely, not postpone.

If you accept or believe in reincarnation, continuity in the next life, then it is of tremendous importance what you are now, not what you will be tomorrow, in the next life, because the next life is shaped by what you are now. Reincarnation not only says that there is continuity of the human mind, but it implies that you must behave with such extraordinary understanding that in the next life you will have reached a tremendous height, not fallen behind. So, the next life is not important, but what you are now. The comfort that you derive from reincarnation is denied when you have to face life now. Therefore a society that gives significance to life according to a pattern, and not life itself, loses the true significance of life.

Our society is based on life and death, and the futility of a life that ends in death. Life becomes very superficial, meaningless, frustrating, despairing, without significance to a human being in a society that gives no significance to living because there is death. Therefore we say, "What is the purpose of life?" or establish a satisfying purpose, which is not living. Please, this requires not agreement or disagreement, but attention and tremendous inquiry.

This society in which we all live only breeds more superficial activity, such as amusement, entertainment, the Mass, and so on; and life becomes meaningless because there is death. I may go to the office every day for the next forty years. Just think of it! Just think of a human being going to an office every day for the rest of his life! I do not know if you see the extraordinary sorrow in that. Such a human being, spending his days in an office and his nights at home, asks, "What is it all about? Why should I live? What does it mean? I write a book, become famous for a few days, and die; what then?"

Unless we find a significance—not substitute an ideal—unless we find a different way of living, a different outlook, a different feeling about life, a different inward state of mind, though there is death, there will not be a total cycle. Am I making that clear? I want to go step by step.

Comment: That point is not clear.

KRISHNAMURTI: Look, sirs. Civilizations in the past have lived, like Egypt—not that I'm an Egyptologist; I don't know, I just watch things in life—in order to die. All living is an ending; therefore, they prepared, while living, for death. Other civilizations knew birth and death only as a movement in the whole of life, the whole of existence. Most modern people belong to life. They don't prepare for death; they don't treat life and death as a movement in living. For them there is only a routine living, a mechanical living, a frustrated self-fulfillment, followed by inevitable death. Life and living lose all significance in themselves because death is there.

Others may not be interested in all this. You and I are here. We are talking together. Therefore you and I are interested in finding a new way of living—outside society, not inside society, though living inside the area of what we call society, not belonging to it, but outside it. To live outside it, there must be freedom from the psychological structure of society. One must be free of greed, envy, ambition, the urge for self-fulfillment, the pursuit of pleasure, and so on and on, which we have discussed sufficiently.

Is it possible for you and me—as human beings capable of having enormous energy, capable of understanding this movement of life in which there is death, but not death as the ending, not as continuity in the next life—is it possible for us to untangle ourselves from the structure of society?

One of our major problems, living in this society, is the utter boredom of life. One may have pleasures, one may have cars, one may have many other things, but this boredom, this indifference, this mechanical living leads to further misery, and so one has to understand as a human being a life in which there is death, but not a continuity as the 'me' in the next life. One has to see. I am going to try to answer the question of seeing.

Do we see this thing which the speaker has described in words, which, if we are at all intelligent, aware, we know? Whether in the communist world, in the Christian world, or in the Asiatic world, this is the way we live. Now, do I see this as an idea, something apart from me, because you have described it to me, or do I see it totally? What do I mean by seeing, and when does seeing take place? I know that I see in fragments. My behavior isn't good today. I'm moody, I'm angry, I'm obsessive, rude, dominating. The next day I see something else and try to deal with each fragment as it arises. When do I see, not only visually, but psychologically, inwardly? When do I really comprehend totally, not in fragments? When do I see life totally, in which is living and dying, and a life which is not merely ending, not merely living for sixty years and then dying? I do not understand death because I am so frightened of it, and therefore I am not living.

When do I see the whole of it, both the living and the dying, not only as a human being, but also in relation to society, so that I am free from society psychologically? When do I see this whole thing so completely that there is no death, no living as misery, no striving, trying to come to some superhuman state, or making tremendous effort to reach greater pleasures? When do I see all this as a total thing?

Are you waiting for me to give you the answer?

Comment: The constant companion is the observer.

KRISHNAMURTI: We have been through that. I do not know if you have been here from the beginning of these discussions, and the ten previous talks. We went into that, and if you don't mind, sir, it would be a pity to go back to it. If I may put it very briefly: When there is a thinker, the observer, the experiencer, which is the censor, the companion, there cannot be total observation. If you don't mind, we will proceed.

I asked if you are waiting for an answer from the speaker, telling you how to see totally. Will my description help you to see totally? Or is there a total action in which there is neither the fragment nor the observer, nor an idea as the observer, but only action?

I don't see life as a whole—life as living, not fearful, anxious, despairing, miserable, in conflict. And in that life there is death also. And that dying is not an ending, but living. Don't translate it in terms of Christianity, the eternal life. In the dying is the living, because I am living. There is no fear of dying, no sorrow at all; the mind has totally understood this question of sorrow, which breeds pain. How do I, who am accustomed to seeing everything in fragments—living and dying; living in misery, squalor, and poverty; inwardly and outwardly struggling; and then dying—how do I see this whole thing totally, immediately? There is no process of seeing totally. It is useless to say, "I will practice constant awareness; I will meditate; I will be; I will do this; I will do that," but if I understand why the mind functions in fragments, and negate it, then I have something else.

Until now I have divided life into office, sex, family, the neighbor, the religious life, the life of amusement—the various departments separate from each other, as the professor, the artist, the scientist, the housewife, the monk. Why do I do this?

Comment: I have never realized that there can be total action.

KRISHNAMURTI: No, madame, please listen. I have put the question. Don't try to answer it immediately. Let it soak in, let it boil inside you a little bit. Let it simmer, so that you know, as you know when the pot is simmering because you smell it. So let it simmer, and let it come naturally. Don't have one idea which you are trying to convey.

I am asking why it is that we live in fragments, in departments—the artist, the writer, the scientist, the businessman, the religious man, the professor. Why? I really don't know. I have never thought about this, I have never felt my way into it; I am doing it now. So are you; we are doing it together. I want to find out why we live in fragments. I am not interested in some opinion, an idea; it must be the truth.

Comment: Perhaps the mind cannot see the totality.

KRISHNAMURTI: Then you have blocked yourself, finished. When you say, "Maybe the mind can't," you have stopped. I don't know whether it can or cannot! If it cannot, then life is a torture. If it cannot function totally, life becomes fragmentary, contradictory, inharmonious, destructive, with the army on one side, and the priest on the other, both of them talking peace and preparing for war and destruction. So don't say the mind can't do it.

Comment: It may be so.

Comment: Go beyond the mind.

KRISHNAMURTI: Please listen. I don't know how to go beyond the mind. Don't say that only beyond the mind is there a perception of the total! I must begin right from the beginning. When do you see anything? Not when you are deliberately trying to see something, do you? When you want to understand somebody, or yourself, you look; but if that look is deliberate, purposive, full of effort, then you have spent your energy in effort, in deliberation, in a purpose. To look, those must be absent; your look must be effortless, easy; there must be no motive. We are trying to find out why the mind lives in fragments, in departments; why the mind has divided life as death and living.

Question: Why do you separate the outer life and the inner life?

Comment: We live in fragments because we have different attractions.

Comment: We give substance to the ego by clothing it in different ways.

Comment: If the mind could be perfectly quiet, then we could see the total.

KRISHNAMURTI: But how do I get the mind to be perfectly quiet?

Comment: By rejecting positive thinking.

KRISHNAMURTI: Sir, make it much simpler than that. Let us for the moment leave the question of when you see anything totally. Let's approach it differently.

What is beauty? Do you know what beauty is? Please don't answer. Don't jump to words and say something. Is beauty brought about by any stimulus? When you see a beautiful mountain, a magnificent building, a lovely face, or read a poem, listen to music, or see the light on the snow of an evening, and say how extraordinarily beautiful it is—is that beauty? Does beauty depend on stimulus? Don't agree or disagree, because if you are not going to go through this, it has no value. You have to feel what beauty is, not agree with words, nor disagree. You have to find out. You are all in agreement or disagreement, and therefore you are not inquiring. That's why I close my eyes. If beauty is dependent on a stimulus, then the reaction to that stimulus depends on the various characteristics, conditionings, temperaments. It becomes merely a question of individual taste, which has nothing whatsoever to do with beauty.

Is there beauty without a stimulus? I can see the lake, clear, blue, or green, with extraordinary life in it, and the reflection of the mountain on it. Does that make me feel beautiful? Do I know beauty from that, or is beauty independent, something entirely different from any stimulus, whether that stimulus is a reflection in the water, a mountain, or a face? I can read a poem and get emotionally ecstatic, shiver over it. That is stimulation through imagination, through words, but surely it is not beauty. And if it is not beauty, then how does a mind see beauty, without being dependent on a stimulant which gives one a certain excitement, a certain sense of heightened energy, which makes one say, "That's a beautiful building," or "That's an ugly building"?

With most of us the mind has been dependent on stimulants: drink, sex, pleasure, mountains. How is such a mind to see beauty without dependence on a stimulus? Leave it there for a moment. I am getting at the problem in different ways.

What is love? We know what is usually considered to be love: jealousy, possessiveness, domination, my family as opposed to your family, my country opposed to your country, my God and your God, the profane and the spiritual, which are all fragments. Do I know love without jealousy, without possessiveness? So I have to find out what love is.

Now there are three questions: What is love? What is beauty? and What is seeing?

What is total, not fragmentary seeing? When I see, I see life totally: death, birth, the whole of it, not in fragments. I say to myself, "Living in this world, what is beauty?" There are so many museums, so many paintings, so many books, all influencing, or stimulating, or trying to shape my mind; some say that a thing is beautiful, and others that it is not. I depend on a stimulus, and is that stimulus beauty? I say, "No, it is not; it can't be." Seeing a beautiful building, or a beautiful face, or a mountain, or a reflection on the water, and saying that it is beautiful—I know that is not beauty. I have rejected negatively, not knowing what beauty is, rejected what has been considered beauty, which is a stimulus. I've rejected it completely.

I also see what love is, as we human beings know it: jealousy, anxiety, a sense of loneliness, not feeling love and wanting to be loved, sentimentalism, emotionalism, possession—all the ugly turmoil of despair is in it. I see that it is not love. This is a fact, not an idea. If love is mere torture, then call it what you like, but it is not love. The mind tells us to reject it, totally.

When I reject without motive, without reaction, what has taken place? You answer me, sirs, what has taken place? My mind is in a state of negation, isn't it? I haven't yet found out what the positive is. The positive is the fragment. By denying all that, my state is a negation. My mind is empty because it doesn't depend on any stimulus, such as sex, jealousy, or position. I see beauty is not a stimulus; it must be something entirely different.

Also I see that living in fragments can never bring about the total. I see all that, and I am in a state of negation. The mind is in a state where it is completely negative, but not blank. It is full of vitality, full of energy, but there must be another element. In electricity there must be two, the positive and the negative. I have only one side of it. Now, what will bring about the other? The negative has its own movement. It is not still. When there is no movement at all, there is a positive which comes to meet it. Look at it yourselves, sirs, don't listen to me. Do it, and you will see in a second. It's marvelous, so come on! The mind has lived on fragments, and is in a state of continuous conflict, effort, and competition. That mind now says, "Finished; I am not going to enter into that field at all." In not entering into the field because the mind sees the foolishness, the absurdity of it, it has become negative. Because the negative state has its own movement, it is only when that negative state is completely still, not blank, but full of energy and therefore of stillness, that positiveness comes into it, not from any direction, but in itself. This needs a little careful thinking.

Look, sir. Sit very quietly, without any movement. What happens? Your mind wanders off, you try to control it, try to resist it; go through all that, and then your mind, your body, your nerves, your brain cells, all of them, are quiet. Then if you sit with your mind completely quiet, which is a stage of negation, what happens? Another factor is coming in, another movement is taking place in it, which is not created by any stimulus; but because the mind is so completely in a state of void, emptiness, negation, passiveness—in which there is no movement at all created by a negation which says, "I must go further"—there is a movement which is not created by the mind. The mind has no place to go; it is not expecting an answer, waiting, hoping, searching, looking, finding. So when there is an absolute negative, passive stillness, in that comes a different movement. The positive and the negative are meeting. The two have met. With that mind which knows both complete negation and complete positiveness, not the positiveness of fragments, with a mind which knows this extraordinary positive and negative, look. Look at beauty, love, and the nature of a mind that sees totally.

Only a mind that is completely still, with this passive, negative state, can totally see life without sorrow. It can see that life dying is not an ending, because dying then is a renewal, a new thing. If I die to yesterday, to all the memories of yesterday, my mind is fresh, innocent, alive. I'm no longer afraid of death. I've found a new way now, found out how to look at everything totally, out of the complete emptiness which is positive.

August 9, 1965

Seventh Dialogue in Saanen

As this is the last discussion, what shall we talk over together this morning?

Question: How do we observe in this state of negation in which there is a positive movement?

KRISHNAMURTI: Really, I can't go over it again. We said something yesterday with regard to how to observe, what it is to see or listen. I can only put it in different words, and not in the same words.

Question: When one looks out of silence, out of emptiness, is that look from love, from affection?

Question: Could we perhaps talk this morning about the possibility and the necessity of a human being living totally within the terms in all his relationships?

KRISHNAMURTI: I am afraid that I haven't understood the question, sir. Will you please repeat it?

Question: May I put it this way: Can we live true to life and true to nature?

Question: In seeing oneself, or gaining self-knowledge, how does one know that one is not being deceived?

KRISHNAMURTI: Ah, how does one know that one is not caught up in an illusion, or how does one know that one doesn't deceive oneself?

Question: Sir, will children have to go through the positive mind of knowledge and then arrive at the negative, or can they start out with the negative from the beginning?

KRISHNAMURTI: Must children go through the positive acquisition of knowledge to arrive at a different state, or can they jump into it right off? Is that what you wish to discuss?

Question: Could you clarify the significance of the self-hypnosis that takes place when one watches fire or running water?

Question: What is this energy that is needed for total attention, and how does it come about, when most of our life is a waste of energy?

KRISHNAMURTI: Perhaps by talking that question over together, we might answer the other questions. May we proceed with that question? Would that be of interest to everybody?

Audience: Yes.

KRISHNAMURTI: When you listen to that stream, to the breeze among the leaves, how you listen, it seems to me, is of great importance because the listening is the doing, and therefore the listening and the doing bring about energy; but listening and then doing is a waste of energy. Let's go into that.

Every action demands energy. To do anything: to think, to feel, to talk, demands energy. In the doing, if there is effort, or if there is a division between the idea and the doing, there is dissipation of energy. If I do something because I see clearly, then there is no waste of energy; seeing and doing together, instantly, is not a dissipation of energy. If I see something dangerous, that perception of danger and the immediate action is not a waste of energy. But with us, the doing is usually separate from the idea; the approximation of action to the idea is a waste of energy.

This is, I think, very important to understand because all of us function with a formula, either a Catholic formula, a Protestant formula, a communist formula, or some other formula which one has developed for oneself through experience, through knowledge. That formula may be the image which each one of us has of himself, or what society is, or what it should be. The formula is not action. The formula is the desire, the demand, to be secure in action. When there is an action in which there is no friction, there is no waste of energy; but action in which there is friction as idea, as pleasure, as formula, is a waste of energy.

So we must not be concerned with action but with the question of why it is that we have formulas, images. That is the question, not how to act in such a way that there is no friction, but rather, why it is that we have developed, cultivated, nourished formulas. The more complicated, the more subtle, the more based on knowledge, on experience the formulas are, the stronger they become. Is it possible to act without the formula? That brings up a question: What is maturity? Is maturity age, a matter of growing, ripening, and dying, or has maturity quite a different significance?

In order to ripen, a fruit needs sunshine, darkness, rain, nourishment from the tree; when it is ripe, it falls from the tree. That is what we call maturity, ripeness, in fruit. To us, maturity apparently comes only through friction, through conflict, through constant battle within and without. What we call maturity in human beings is the deepening of conflict, and the expression of that conflict in action or in disorder.

What is it to have a mature mind? Must the mind go through innumerable experiences, conflicts, battles, all the influences that a human being lives under in modern society—must he go through all that in order to ripen? Must he be in a constant state of conflict in order to become mature? This is the same question that gentleman asked; I am trying to answer it in a different way.

Must one go through all the experiences of life to be mature, to be capable of action in which there is no element of friction? Must the human mind, like yours and mine, go through every form of struggle, conflict, dissipation of energy, control of energy, in order to arrive at a ripened state? We generally say yes. Now we are going to question that yes.

Question: Isn't there a completely different type of experience?

KRISHNAMURTI: I don't know. You are asking if there is not a different type of experience. Please, that's an avoidance of the fact, avoidance of *what is,* when we are looking for a different kind of experience. I've been through all that; don't let's go over it again. Sir, let me put the whole thing differently. Can a mind which has lived for so long in time, has accumulated so much experience, which has certain values in certain areas—can that mind become totally innocent, and from that innocence, act? Let's forget all that we have said during all these seventeen talks, and look at it anew.

Must the human mind, as it is now, go through years and years of struggle, bitterness, fear, hatred, vanity, and then put it all away in order to be innocent, or can it be innocent right from the beginning, and sustain that quality of innocence? It is only a fresh mind, uncontaminated, not broken into fragments through experience and then put together—a mind that is clear, without any scratch of memory—only such a fresh mind can see anything new. If I want to see something new in life, I can't come to it with my cluttered brain, cluttered ideas, confusion, misery. It is absolutely imperative to have a fresh mind.

How is this to come about? Obviously, not through methods, systems, practices, doing, practicing awareness; all those only make the mind more conditioned in its particular pattern. My question is: Though the mind has lived for so long, under so many influences, so many kinds of conditioning and so many types of environment, can it free itself instantly and be fresh? It may be an absurd question because I am asking myself why I should go through any experiences, or if I do, why should they leave any mark? It is the mark, the remembrances, the pleasures that make the mind heavy, cluttered, not free, not fresh.

I want to find out if it is possible—and I don't say it is possible—to have a fresh mind all the time, in spite of all the incidents, accidents, and experiences. Has that question any validity? I think it has validity because I see that without a fresh mind I cannot solve any problem, even the least complicated scientific problem. There must also be a fresh mind to cope with the ever-increasing complexities of modern society and understand the relationships of human beings with that society. It is a valid question because, as I have explained, it is only the fresh outlook of a fresh mind, a mind that is not heavily conditioned, that can create a new human society, a new human existence. How is this to come about? Well, sirs, please go into it. If you think that question is valid, let's talk together about it.

I had an experience yesterday—one cannot avoid experience. To have no reaction is to be dead, paralyzed; and reaction is experience. When one sees a beautiful mountain, to be completely paralyzed, without reaction, has no meaning. But how is it possible for the reaction, which is an experience, to take place and yet strike no root at all in the soil of the mind? How is it possible to have an experience, and finish it immediately? Living in this world, with all its complexities, with all its experiences, with all the reactions, conscious and unconscious, that are taking place all the time, that are impinging, is it possible for a mind to experience and not have the experience leave a mark as memory—and from that memory, that remembrance, to act? The action then is merely in conformity with, or an approximation of the memory, and the reaction does not release or free the mind from the past.

I must find a clue to this, for otherwise I shall live constantly in the increasing of experiences, being heavily conditioned in sorrow, in pain. I must find a key which will open the door to every experience, and leave no mark, or a state of mind that has no experience at all.

There are three questions involved in this. First, one sees very clearly that there must be death to the past so as to have a very fresh, clear, innocent mind that is capable of dealing with everything in life. It is as much a necessity as food, as drink, as exercise; it is an absolute necessity. Then is it possible to live in this world, experiencing, and not have those experiences leave a single mark? The third thing is: Is there a state of mind which, living in this world, functioning, has no experience at all? This doesn't mean that it is paralyzed, blind, or isolated; it has so separated itself that it avoids every form of experience. You are following? First, the necessity for a fresh, new mind; second, a mind that experiences, functions, acts, without leaving a scratch behind; and third, a mind that is so tremendously alive that it needs no experience.

We will leave the third question out for the time being. For most of us, there are only two things involved. We don't see that a fresh mind is necessary, not seeing intellectually or verbally, but actually demanding it. We don't really want a fresh mind because that means leaving all the pleasures that one has accumulated, dying to the past—not fragmentarily, but totally, dying not only to our sorrows, pains, and fears, but to all pleasures; otherwise, one can't have a fresh mind. We know, deep down, that a fresh mind is necessary, but we don't want it with urgency, immediacy, and passion, and the passion, the urgency cannot be stimulated by this talk or by another.

The energy that is needed to have a fresh mind is the energy that comes when one dies to the past. We began by asking how it is possible to have this energy, which is being in a state of constant heightened sensitivity, and in which there is no contradiction, no dissipation. We are answering that question.

One sees intellectually, verbally, the necessity for a fresh mind. The mind asks, "How am I going to come to that state where there is a fresh mind?" The demand, the question really is: "How am I to come to that fresh mind, which will give me great pleasure?" It is not that you want a fresh mind for itself but for the pleasure that you are going to get out of it. The demand for that pleasure is a dissipation of energy. I want to be healthy, but I want to eat all the foods I like; I want to drink and smoke, but yet have good health. The two can't be matched. I have discovered something: that to have a fresh mind I must understand and put an end to, die to the pleasure principle. Because if I don't, I ask, "How am I to find pleasure in that new mind?"

I see that most of us don't want to die to all the pleasures, the accumulations, the hatreds, the vanities that we have had. We want to treasure them, and yet have a fresh mind. You can't. So how am I to die to the past? Will I put that question? I won't because I really don't want to give up the past. I have written books, I have been somebody, I have talked on many platforms, I have a history, a reputation; I don't want to die to all that because if I die, what happens? I'm nobody; I'm in a state of vacuum, emptiness.

You see, if I die—and I mean die—not care two pins about reputation, what people say, whether I've talked in different parts of the world, all the rest of the rubbish; if I really don't care, there is a state of emptiness, a state of complete emptiness. In that state of emptiness there is tremendous energy. You don't know this unless you have done it. It's an emptiness charged with tremendous sensitiveness and intelligence. That energy, that intelligence, that sensitivity cannot possibly be brought about through the accumulation of knowledge, experience, memory.

That emptiness feels, "I have lost everything: friends, reputation, the demand to talk and use the audience for my pleasure." When you have understood the pleasure principle, the demand for the continuity of pleasure, there is no record of memory as memory. I hold to memory because it is pleasurable; and because it is pleasurable, I don't want pain. So the pleasure creates pain. I see the necessity of a fresh mind, and realize that to be in a state of mind which is always fresh, not because it is pleasurable, there must be a total emptiness in which thought as pleasure, as the image, as expression has no meaning. The mind has come to that point through intelligence, reason, logic, sanity, health—not because it wants pleasure.

It is a natural sequence, if you can call something a sequence which is not of time.

Experiences can go through that emptiness. It is not that I am experiencing, and therefore the 'I', the observer, the thinker, the experiencer, retains what is being experienced. It's not like putting a pin in your leg, and if the leg is paralyzed, there is no reaction. There must be reaction. In fact, every reaction is heightened, but in passing through that emptiness there is no recording of the experience, and therefore no past based on pleasure and the avoidance of pain.

All this demands intelligence, not "I want to get it." It is not the accumulation of knowledge; it is not reading books or listening to talks. Nothing will do it. The mind sees the necessity for clarity and a fresh mind, and a fresh mind and clarity can only come through tremendous intelligence. Intelligence is energy because intelligence then acts, but its action does not breed an idea, which would be a dissipation of energy. Intelligence is energy.

The mind has come to that point. It doesn't say, "How am I to die to the past? How am I to die to the memories that I have had, to self-fulfillment with its pleasures, frustrations, and pain?" It doesn't ask the method. It sees the necessity for a fresh mind. It has to tackle that; it has to come to grips with that.

To reject a pleasure without the motive of a greater pleasure, to die to that pleasure completely needs an awareness which is intelligence. This comes when there is an understanding that there must be a fresh morning, not yesterday's evening carried over into this morning. When that is absolutely clear, everything follows easily. One can have experiences without leaving a mark when one has rejected every form of pleasure, and therefore pain and sorrow, because that rejection is an awareness of the whole structure of pleasure and pain. Out of that awareness comes energy, which is intelligence.

A motive has energy, but it is not of the quality of intelligence. Total awareness, without choice, of pleasure and therefore of pain, brings order and that energy which is intelligence. Intelligence is always empty. Therefore energy, which is intelligence, is essentially simple. Simplicity has become such a loaded word that it has lost its meaning altogether. Saints, monks, and teachers have limited simplicity to such tawdry matters as money, clothes, and food. To them simplicity is to have few clothes, one meal a day, and a few miracles thrown in. Miracles are the easiest things to do. If you are very simple in a certain direction, you can do miracles. It has been done. This extraordinary halo is given for nothing, but true simplicity is something entirely different. One must be extraordinarily simple, and not only in regard to clothes, food, and shelter.

Where there is this intelligence, which is energy, and the individual lives in a state of complete emptiness or aloneness, that intelligence functions always with facts, and therefore is simple. It has no opinions, no dogmas about the fact. There is only the fact, the *what is.* The space between the fact and the image, the formula, the opinions which we have about the fact, is a waste of energy. This is the last talk, so go into it, drink it in, so that your mind, your whole energy becomes astonishingly alive and intelligent, and therefore extraordinarily simple. That simplicity is the state in which there is no space between the observer and the fact. There is only the fact, the *what is.* Whether it is painful or pleasurable doesn't matter.

We see all that. Then is it possible, one asks, to live in this world, go to the office, have a family, go for holidays, do all that one does, live, and yet have this intelligence functioning all the time? That's a wrong question. That's not a simple question. That's a question based on the desire for pleasure. But if you were to say, "Can I face the fact, the *what is,* every day without an interval between the fact and me?" then that would have meaning. If you ask, "Can I maintain this sense of intelligence all the time?" then you're asking the wrong question.

What you have come to now is the fact, the *what is,* the experience. You are forcing the mind to look at it as it is, not through your opinions and ideas. Your opinions and ideas produce the experience with regard to the fact, but when you see the fact as a fact, as *what is,* there is no experience. If I am angry, I am angry. It is a fact. It is so. But the moment I say, "I must not, it is bad, it is not good for my health, for my liver, for my heart, for my spiritual life," then I am beginning to experience in the field which is not factual at all. How extraordinary it is that a mind can look at a fact, at *what is,* without any experiencing; if I am a liar, to look at the fact without any explanation, justification, condemnation. The mind which gives itself over to explanation, justification, condemnation—all of which are based on the past, on pleasure, pain, and memory—that is the mind which experiences, not the mind which faces the fact that it is not telling the truth.

What happens to the fact that I am telling a lie? Is there a puzzle about this? I am telling a lie because I am frightened. Keep it on a very simple level. The fact is fear, not the lying—the fear that has caused me to tell a lie. The fact, the *what is,* is fear. And fear I must get rid of; I don't like it, it causes disturbance, makes the mind dull, heavy, cunning. So I try to get rid of it. The getting rid is wasted effort, whereas the fact is fear. Any action, any movement in any direction about fear is a waste of energy; the interval, the gap between the observer who says, "I am afraid," and the fear is also a waste of energy. Can the mind, without any movement, stay with that fear? I'm afraid of death, or a dozen other things. Can the mind stay with that fear without any activity? Can it be aware of the whole structure of fear, and not try to condemn it, translate it, or justify it, but be completely aware of it so that there is no movement, and therefore there is an energy which is intelligence? In this complete awareness, there is no fear.

It is not a question of sustaining a state of mind that is not afraid. I may be afraid tomorrow, or the next instant, but if I meet that fear now, totally, in complete, choiceless, passive awareness, there is an energy which is intelligence, hence no fear.

Don't try to learn the trick! It's not a trick. If you try to learn the trick, and apply it to get rid of fear, goodbye; you will never get it. But if you see this whole thing, there will be no fear. There is no practicing of awareness, no demand for its continuity; you don't demand, and you don't practice because the mind is intelligent through awareness.

The next question is: Is it possible for a mind to be in a state where experiences—visions, what people say, what they don't say, whether you're talking or not talking, whether you write or don't write, whether you are famous or not famous—have no meaning? Unless one has understood the first question completely—the necessity for a fresh, clean mind—and gone into it thoroughly, one can't answer the next question. Because the second question—whether it is possible to live in the world without experiences leaving a mark—comes naturally from the first.

We think awareness is something that has to be maintained, but anything that has a continuity is not fresh. What we are talking about is a mind that is fresh, greatly intelligent; it is intelligent because it understands, and the understanding is the energy that creates that intelligence. When you have lived that way, the attention, the awareness can go to sleep, can be quiet; and when necessary, you can act in that state of intelligence.

But if you say, "I must maintain the thing constantly," then you are back again; there will never be a fresh mind. The fresh mind is not an idea. It is a fact, but only when we have understood the structure and the nature of pleasure, which is the breeding ground for sorrow. So one must begin very near. The first step, which is very near, is sorrow, pleasure in little things, not in vast, tremendous ideas. By moving from there you will find out for yourself whether a mind can live in this world, function, go to the office, and all the rest of it because it is so tremendously awake that it has no experience; it is only such a mind that is innocent. Innocency is the highest form of simplicity. In that mind that is completely intelligent, where there is an energy which is silent—for energy that is not silent can never be intelligent—then there is quite a different movement altogether. But that becomes speculative, and therefore useless, unless one has gone through this first and has a mind so alive that it needs no experience.

August 10, 1965

New Delhi, India, 1965

First Talk in New Delhi

If I may, during these four talks here, I would like to talk about order, violence, and peace.

We are not merely theorizing, or merely giving various explanations for various causes. What we are trying to do is to understand the whole movement of life, this vast panorama of conflict, not only in this country, but also throughout the world where man is in conflict with another man; where man has lived for so many millennia of recorded history, fought over fourteen thousand wars, and has not been able to live peacefully with his neighbor; where nationalism, destructive and disorderly, is rampant throughout the world; where, though man endeavors everlastingly to find order within himself and also order outwardly, apparently it has been almost impossible for him to live peacefully.

It is only in peace that a human being can flower in goodness—not in war, not in violence, not in disorder, but only when there is a deep, abiding peace. And to understand this whole phenomenon of hate, destruction, and disorder, one has to inquire not merely intellectually—because such an inquiry is futile, worthless, and has no meaning whatsoever—but actually inquire what order means, what violence means, and the significance of peace; one has to inquire nonverbally, nonintellectually, which really has very little meaning because most of us have read or indulged in theory what peace should be, how to get rid of violence, how to establish order; books, volumes, have been written about it.

In the first war that took place about fifty-five hundred years ago in recorded history, man must have thought that that would be the last war. And we are still at it. And so there must be something radically wrong, destructive, in human beings who divide themselves into nationalities, break their minds into fragments as religious sects with dogmas, beliefs, politics, into classes, divisions of every kind, and thereby hope to bring about peace and order. So apparently after these thousands upon thousands of years, we have not found peace. As we said, there have been fourteen thousand six hundred wars; that means two and a half wars every year. And yet we are going on living in the same stupid, destructive manner, hating each other, calling each other names, labeling ourselves as Hindus, Muslims, Sikhs, Russians, communists, and so on.

So you have to look at all this dispassionately, factually, not emotionally or in any prejudiced way; you have to regard it as a fact, not interpret it according to your particular likes and dislikes, according to your favorite war which you call righteous, or unfavorite war which you think is evil; you have to look at it as a phenomenon, as something animalistic, which must be solved by each human being. Because war, violence, disorder—along that path there is no peace, do what you will; there, a peace is an interval between two calamities, between two wars, two destructions.

So one has to find a new way of living, not theoretically, not discussing everlastingly about it. We have to find actually in our daily life a way to live totally differently—which means a total revolution in our ways of thinking, living, feeling. And unless we discover that for ourselves as human beings, we shall never find order, peace, and a state of mind that can flower in goodness. So, we are not indulging in words, in theories: what should be, what must be. But we are investigating actually *what is,* because it is only when you are capable of facing the fact that you can do something about it. If we refuse to face the facts, then we get completely lost in opinions. And opinions—however clever, however erudite, however dialectical they may be—have very little meaning when you are confronted with hate, disorder, violence. And that is what we are faced with now, throughout the world. The war that is going on in Vietnam is your war, my war; so also the war that has been in this country, on the border.

Man has suffered indefinitely, infinitely. And as human beings who have lived so many millennia, you and I, as human beings—not as a Hindu, not as a Christian, not as a communist or a Mohammedan or whatever you call yourselves—have to find order because order is necessary not only within but outwardly. And it is one of the most difficult things to find this order. Because the word *order* has an extraordinary depth if you go into it; it has an extraordinary significance, if you can unravel it, if you can look into it deeply. Order is not according to your order or my order; nor according to the politician, this person or that person. But the word itself has an extraordinary significance and an extraordinary depth if we can go into it. And that is what we are going to do together.

We are not doing any propaganda. I have a horror of propaganda. I am not trying to convert you to any belief, any dogma, or any way of life—that would be too stupid. But what we are trying to do is to point out, investigate, talk things over together as two human beings confronted with the same enormous, complex problem. And if you cannot look at it dispassionately, then we shall live as human beings another five thousand years fighting each other, tearing each other's hearts out, destroying each other. And it is very strange: all the ancient teachers have talked about peace, not to hate another, to be kind, to be generous, to be forgiving; all that has been overthrown throughout the world. And in this country, which is supposed to be so old and ancient and full of wisdom—which is nonexistent at the present time—that tradition, not the tradition practiced by politicians or by the semipolitical saints, that reality where you must not hurt another, where you must love another—all that has been set aside. And as human beings, you and I have to find out for ourselves a new way of living, a new order, the ending of violence, and therefore bring about in ourselves, outwardly as well as inwardly, peace.

So we are going to talk over together, first, this question of order. Our life is very disorderly, both outwardly and inwardly. We are in conflict, both outwardly and inwardly. We are in contradiction, outwardly as well as inwardly. And order is not possible when there is conflict, when inwardly there is a battle going on—hate, envy, greed, competition, brutal thoughts about somebody else. When there is this national prejudice—which is a poison—how can there be order? And you need order, you need an enormous order.

And to have order you must have immense space, inwardly as well as outwardly. You cannot cut yourself off into a little country, or cultivate your own backyard and bring about an order in that little space, as an individual within yourself. Because the individual is a very limited mind and being; and if he brings about order within himself, it has no meaning whatsoever. But what has meaning and significance is that the individual becomes a human being not belonging to any religion, to any nationality, to any class, to any political party—a human being with his problems, suffering, aching, in agony, greedy and envious, seeking power, position. And we are such human beings, and therefore we have to bring about order.

We can only bring about order negatively. I mean by that: Order cannot be brought about by or through imitation or conformity. Please do listen to this, not because I am talking about it, but because you have to find out the truth of all this; it is your life, it is your misery, your desperation. When you are living so close to disaster, you have to solve it. So listen to it with a passionate eagerness to find out how to live a different kind of life.

As we have said, order can only come about negatively. If you deliberately set about to bring order within yourself, you attempt it either through suppression, control, or through conformity. Do you understand? We want order; we see the importance of order, outwardly as well as inwardly; and there is no ideal pattern of orderliness. You cannot say, "This is order and this is not order. I will follow this path which will bring about order within myself." Order must begin within oneself first and then outwardly manifest itself. You cannot bring about order outwardly as every politician, every reformer does throughout the world—he is concerned with bringing about order outwardly. But there is order only when there is orderliness within. And then every action, every movement of life is orderly, sane, rational. So to find this order, one must approach it negatively. We will explain what we mean. It may be a little complex, but it is not really so, if you will listen.

You know, it is one of the most difficult things to listen. We hardly ever listen. We listen to our opinions, we listen to our knowledge of what we have experienced, we listen to what other people have said or written. We listen to all the promptings of our own prejudices, but we never listen to our life. I am going to talk about something which needs acute listening. You will have to listen to it, not counter it by your own knowledge, by your own information—you can do that much later. If you want to listen to somebody, you have to give attention. And you cannot give attention if your whole mind, your body, your nerves, your eyes, your ears do not listen totally. And one has to listen to life that way. Life demands this attention, not your casual, irresponsible, disorderly attitudes or opinions. Life demands that you listen to every movement of it. Life is yourself, your thoughts, your feelings, your activities, your ways of life. How you react to all that is the movement of life. And you have to listen to it passionately, completely, totally with all your being. Then only does one understand the actual fact of life and the movement of life in which thought and mind can flow.

So, kindly listen to what is being said, not accepting—that would be too immature—nor denying, which would be equally juvenile; listen to find out. To find out, you must listen with freedom. It is only a free mind that can find out. So we said that orderliness, order, comes about negatively—that is when you understand what does not bring about order. Order cannot come through compulsion, through discipline— please listen carefully, I will explain all this. Order cannot come through conformity because conformity denies freedom. Conformity implies fear. In conforming there is subordination, obedience to authority. A mind that is ridden with authority, with compulsive fears, cannot possibly have order. So one begins to see that conformity to a pattern, however good, however noble, however sufficient, does not bring order. Therefore, one has to investigate within oneself this whole process of submission to a pattern of life, and that is what actually is taking place. You are submitting to an idea as a national, as a Hindu, as a Muslim, and God knows what else. It is an idea, and you are submitting to it and therefore conforming to a tradition which has no value.

So, when you understand this whole significance of conformity, in which is involved authority, fear, and the accepted norm as the way of life, then out of that understanding comes order. That is, when I see something as being false—not because somebody tells me, not because it is convenient for me, not because circumstances influence me, not because propaganda forces me to think in a certain way—actually when I see something as false, unreal, which has no validity at all in life, then that very perception of what is false brings about order. Therefore, order comes only through negation, not through the positive assertion of will. I hope I am making myself clear. If not, we are going to talk about it for the next three or four times, and I hope by then we shall be able to communicate with each other.

You know, to communicate with one another is one of the most difficult things to do. I want to tell you something. I am passionately interested in what I am telling you because I think that is the only way to live in life, a different way. And to communicate with you, you must also be passionately interested, not when you go home, not when you are sitting in your office or in your business, but actually now. So, communion can only take place when you and I are both intense at the same time, at the same level; otherwise, there is no communion between us. That intensity, that passionate attention is after all what we call love. When you love somebody intensely and that person also loves at the same time, at the same level, at the same intensity, then there is communion; then words have a different perfume, a different significance, a different value. And that is what we are doing.

If you do not want to listen so completely, with such intense passion, you won't understand this at all. Because our life is very short, we have to live so completely today and not tomorrow. So we have to understand this movement of life with its tradition, with its brutality, with its agony, with its violence, disorder; and in understanding this movement of confusion, conflict, out of such understanding comes order. So, order is only possible without your desiring it, and it comes about naturally. If you desired it, it would be an act of will and therefore would essentially create conflict. That is, I want to be orderly—which means what? I do not understand what has brought about disorder, but I am merely resisting disorder; so I can understand neither disorder nor order. I am only making a conceptual perception of what order should be and conforming according to that pattern. Therefore that very concept of order brings about disorder. So will, conformity, or the ideal as a pattern according to which order will be brought about, can only bring about disorder.

You have to understand that completely, and you can only understand it completely, not verbally, by examining actually what is taking place within yourself, inside the skin—not trying to bring about order, but understanding the actual fact as it is, what is actually taking place within yourself. Then you will see that out of this understanding of what is the actual fact comes order.

How can you have order if you are completely divided, if you have divided yourself into nationalities, into sects? How can you have order if you call yourself a Hindu, and I a Muslim? How can you have order if you are a communist and I am an imperialist, and I hold to my opinions and you hold to your values? We destroy each other. That is what is actually taking place in the world. There have been religious wars which have been called righteous wars. How can any war be righteous? To kill another—how can it be righteous? And our daily life of hate, competition, antagonism, ambition, seeking power, position, prestige—these bring about war. And war which is violence is the very essence of disorder.

You know, there is a great deal of the animal in us. The biologists tell you that, and we do not have to listen to the biologists if we observe ourselves and observe the animals. There is a great deal of the animal in us. We are authoritarian, brutal, violent, pushing others aside, aggressive—which the animals are. There is always the top animal, the dominant animal. All the characteristics of man, most of the characteristics of the human being are shown in the animal. Unless there is a transformation in each one of us as a human being—that is, freeing ourselves from the animal—we shall live everlastingly in conflict.

So, order is only possible when we understand the ways of disorder. Obviously, nationalism is a disorder. I know how the majority of you feel. When there is a war, the national spirit is very strong. Through hate we can unify ourselves, but that unity does not last. What brings about unity is the understanding of disunity. Nationalism, religious organizations, beliefs, dogmas, conceptual attitudes towards life—all these bring about disunity. You and I notice this; any intelligent man reading history, observing daily facts, knows all this; and yet we keep on repeating this pattern over and over again. So we do not learn through suffering, we do not learn through experience, we do not learn through history. But apparently we just want to live for the moment, suffer and die and not recreate a new world, a new sense of being.

So orderliness comes only when you understand the causes of disorder, when you cease to be a Hindu, or a Muslim, or a communist, or a socialist, belonging to this party or that party, or belonging to this group or that group—which are all such infantile business. When you see how the world is divided by religions, by sects, by politicians, by hate; when you see actually, not verbally, not theoretically; when you feel it in your blood, with your complete being, then you will do something. Then out of that perception comes order. Therefore, order is only possible negatively, not positively.

You know, the question of the positive and the negative is very important to understand in life. The positive, as we know, is conformity, doing something because somebody has told you, or because you have experienced and the experience tells you that you must do it, or because you are afraid and therefore you are aggressive and so on. All such pursuit of pattern as tradition, as conforming to a particular public opinion, and so on and so on, is what we call positive action. But such positive action is destructive action because it breeds disorder. So, it is only when you begin to understand what brings about disorder, only when you understand that—not intellectually, there is no such thing as intellectual understanding; either you understand it or you don't—if you understand it, then out of this extraordinary clarity comes order.

And one of the causes of disorder is violence. Why are we human beings violent? Do you understand, sir, the word itself? Why are you violent? Not why somebody else is violent, the Muslim, the Hindu; but you as a human being, why are you violent—violence being anger, hate, fear, accepting authority, asserting oneself constantly, hating—why? Because mostly each one of us wants security. When your security is threatened, when your country, when your ideas, when your concept of what God is, what truth is, what should be, or what should not be, when that conceptual attitude is threatened—which makes you feel so completely insecure—then you become aggressive, violent. This means that as long as you are satisfied, as long as you are left undisturbed in your little backyard, as long as nothing threatens you, you live peacefully. But the moment there is any kind of threat, any kind of uncertainty—uncertainty about your relationship with your wife—you become violent. When there is uncertainty about your position, when you are not capable of fulfilling yourself, being somebody, having a position, prestige—when all those are threatened, then you become violent.

So what you really want is not the ending of violence; what you really want is to be completely secure, both inwardly and outwardly. You want to be secure inwardly with your ideas, secure in your relationships, secure in your concepts. But unfortunately you can never be secure. That is one of the first things to realize: that life is not for the secure—which does not mean that you must be insecure or that you must seek insecurity. That is, each one of us, as a human being, wants to be secure within the pattern which we have created for ourselves as being secure, and that pattern will invariably contradict the pattern of another, and so there is a battle between us. And if you observe, not idealistically but factually, life is never secure. Your wife may run away, or my wife may die; there is disease; there is death; nothing is secure.

Do think about it, do reflect about it honestly, and you will find it for yourself—which means, to understand it is to be afraid. And we are frightened human beings, dreadfully frightened—frightened about insecurity, frightened about our relationship, frightened about our job, frightened about death, frightened about our love, our affections, our attitudes. So out of this fear comes violence. And we have lived that way for thousands of years, and we seem to be incapable of breaking through that darkness of fear. So that is why we are violent. As a human being, can you understand for yourself—observing life, the everyday incidents—that there is no such thing as security, that life is a movement, an endless movement? And a man who can move with it and go beyond this movement—he will find that peace, that joy, that eternity.

But that means one has to be rid of fear. And fear is one of the most difficult things to be free from. Therefore one has to investigate the whole structure, the psychology of fear. You know, to understand something like fear you have to observe it in yourself—not to deny it or run away from it or suppress it, but just to observe it. And to observe it you must have clear eyes, you must listen to it completely. But you don't listen to it, you do not see the whole structure of fear. If you try to develop courage, it is an escape from the fact which is fear—I hope I am conveying all this. So first there is no escape; there must be no escape from fear. One has to observe it totally, completely. So there can be no escape. And you are caught in the network of escapes; your gods, your pujas, all the circus that exists around you is the network of escapes.

And a man who would really understand this and be free of fear has no escape, not merely verbally—which is very difficult because the word *fear* is in itself the cause of fear, if you observe it. Therefore, one must be free of the word, and therefore of the explanations of fear, of the cause of fear, the searching out, or the analyzing of the process of fear, of the causes of fear. You must look at it totally, silently, completely. Then there is no escape; therefore, you are confronted with a fact. You know, you have to be confronted with the fact of hate, not the justification of hatred because somebody hates you, but the fact of hate in the world. This hate is mounting, it is not decreasing. Every war, every conflict, every inward struggle is an expression of hate. And to look at it demands that you look at it nonverbally. You have to come directly in contact with this feeling of hate, which you cannot come directly in contact with if you have a verbal concept of it—that is, you must hate, or you must not hate.

To understand something, sirs, you must look at it. To understand this whole phenomenon of violence in the world, you must understand the psychological structure of man, who has immense fears. That means you have to look at your own fears, which no God, no system, nothing will dissolve, except yourself. So you must become astonishingly serious. And seriousness leads to efficiency, clarity. It is only the serious, earnest man that lives, and the rest become merely either canno fodder or useless human beings. And it is very difficult to be serious—not grow beards or put on a loincloth, or a sannyasi's robes, or become a monk, or join an ashram; such a person is not a serious man at all. A serious man is one who sees the facts of the world as they are, who is not caught in concepts, in formulas, or in ideals, but who sees things as they are in the world and faces them and resolves them. Such a man is a serious man. And it is only such serious men that can bring about a different society.

And we need a different society because society as it is, is always in a state of disorder, because there are classes, the rich and the poor, the man who knows and the man who does not know, the leader and the follower, the guru and the disciple. Think of all that and see how totally disorderly all that is. And out of that disordered society you try to build a new society, or try to reform it. It is not possible. A new order can come into being only when we understand ourselves and bring about a total change within the human mind.

And the mind is extraordinarily capable of anything. Look at what they are doing—going to the moon, going under the sea, living under the sea—consider the electronic brain, automation, the extraordinary scientific facts, and the discoveries. The mind is capable of anything. But not your mind, as your mind is small, petty, concerned with itself, with its dogmas, with its fears, with its pursuits of its own pleasures—all that has to come to an end; then you will know for yourself what truth is. Then you will know for yourself whether there is infinite joy or not. It is not someone else's joy, someone else's peace that matters; it is yours that matters infinitely because you alone, as a human being in relation with another human being, can bring about a revolution, not an economic or a social revolution—which again is an outward thing. Revolution must begin within oneself. And then you will have peace, a state of nonviolence, a state of freedom from violence and order. Without these we are not human beings; we are violent, destructive, incapable of order, and therefore we have no love.

Sirs, I have said at the beginning of the talk that we are not doing propaganda. I am not trying to convince you of anything. All that we are trying to point out is that you, as a human being, can change and must change, not through any form of compulsion, not through some influence, but out of the necessity of it. And then only, out of that necessity, out of that understanding, there will be a freedom. And it is only the free man that can bring about a new world, a new society.

November 7, 1965

Second Talk in New Delhi

We were saying the other day when we met here how urgent it is that there should be a radical mutation of the human structure psychologically, because outwardly there are so many changes taking place, not only in size—economic and so on—with which we are all quite familiar. But apparently after these many centuries our human mind has undergone very little change. We are what we have always been—violent, ambitious, greedy, seeking power, prestige, and so on. We can change outwardly and adjust ourselves to environmental conditions. And perhaps through pressure, economic and so on, we can bring about in ourselves a little change, be less greedy, be more free, be less afraid, be less anxious, and feel less guilty. And perhaps we can remove some of the strains. But it seems to us that such superficial changes are not good enough. We need a tremendous revolution in ourselves, and to bring about such a great revolution psychologically in the mind, we must go, it seems to me, beyond the limits of our own mind. And whether that is at all possible is what we are going to discuss this evening.

We lead a life of mediocrity. Our lives are very repetitive—office, sex, family—and within that we ask questions. When anything disturbs us, we think that we are concerned with it. And all our questions are answered from that narrow, limited, conditioned feeling of our human mind. We never ask fundamental questions, and we never meet the challenges that life presents all the time to each other. And when we do meet, we meet them according to our limited knowledge, our limited experience, and information. But it seems to me that we have to meet all these challenges quite differently—the challenges of poverty.

What is implied in radical change, mutation in the human mind? What is implied in being free? What does it mean to be greedy? What is mutation, and what is death? These are the challenges which all of us are confronted with every day, and we respond rather casually or indifferently, or let it go by. You have had this great challenge, in this country, of the war on the border, and you have responded like every other country in the world. There have been, since 1945, forty wars. Do you understand? Forty wars! And we are still going on thinking in terms of war.

And so, man who has lived for so many millennia has not been able to solve these problems, the immense problem of poverty, war, violence, what it means to be free, if there is God or no God, what is implied in religion. All these things are pressing on us constantly. And we apparently have neither the time nor the inclination to respond to them seriously; and we assert vaguely that we must change, that the human mind must undergo a tremendous mutation to meet all these challenges. And such change is merely verbal, or when we do answer these challenges, we answer them theoretically, or with a tradition in which we have been brought up—either the tradition of the past, the immense past, or the tradition of a few years, according to the pattern in which we have been brought up, or according to a particular activity—communist, socialist, and so on—to which we are committed. But such answers are not sufficient because we are what we are: we are violent, envious, greedy, fearful, feeling occasionally guilty; and we face death when we must and casually inquire or believe in God.

So seeing all this, not theoretically, but factually—because we are dealing with facts and not with theories, not with beliefs and opinions—seeing all this one must obviously demand how a human mind can undergo a tremendous change. And that change is urgent; it will not admit of time. And so we have to find out what is implied in the question of change, that is, if you and the speaker see the urgent necessity of change, of bringing about within himself a mutation. Then the question arises: How is a human mind—yours and mine—to undergo this transformation?

First of all, what do we mean by change? For us mostly it means a modified continuity, what has been is modified in the present and changed a little bit in the future. And in this change there are the influences, social pressures, economic strains, and so on and so on. Outwardly there are so many pressures taking place, straining us, that we invariably modify or adjust ourselves to the pressures. Surely that is not change at all. That is, you can be forced through propaganda, through environmental influence, through economic conditions to change yourself a little. Because in that change there is a motive, the motive of fear, the motive of a better life, the motive of more comfort. All these motivations, however necessary, do not bring about a radical change. And, I think, this we must understand very clearly. What makes one change? What makes you do something voluntarily? If you do it through fear, it is not a change at all, is it? If you do it through compulsion, it is no longer a change. So one must find out how to bring about a mutation in the human mind without a motive, without a purpose, without an ideal as a means of bringing about a change, because all these admit time.

So one has to inquire into this question of time. Please, I do not know if one is interested in all this—because this is a very serious matter which we are talking about—and whether one is really capable, or has a deep intention to understand these problems. Because our life is petty, shallow, empty, repetitive. There is great sorrow, not only individual sorrow, but the sorrow of the world; there is pain; there is suffering. And apparently we have not been able to be rid of them. We have not thrown off the shackles—the pain, the misery, the suffering. We are talking about psychological suffering, not merely physical suffering only. So to understand a mutation in the human mind, we have to understand this whole question, the structure of time, the significance of time and what importance it has in relation to action as change.

We know time as duration, that is yesterday—the experiences, the memories, the knowledge of yesterday—functioning through today forming a tomorrow. That is duration. That is one type of time. Then there is time as will: I am this, I should be that; and to become that, I need time. That is, through gradualness, through tomorrow, through day after tomorrow I shall achieve, I shall become. Then there is time as effort. That is, to become that, to change ourselves according to some ideal, some utopia, some pattern, we make an effort, and that involves time. And there is time as thought.

So we are going to examine these; first of all, our mind which is the machinery of thought. Thinking is the result of time, obviously. The brain, the whole structure of the brain is the result of time, many, many—two million—years. And it has taken time to be what we are. And thought—the whole process of thinking—is based on time, time being knowledge, experience, the accumulated information as memory. So when any challenge, any question is asked, we respond according to our knowledge, information, which is memory, and that process involves time.

Please, you have to understand this. I mean by that word *understand,* not intellectually, because you can listen intellectually, agree or disagree or add more to it; but such understanding is not total comprehension. When you understand something, from that understanding, that very understanding is action. There is not first understanding and then action. When you understand, that very understanding is action. So what we are doing is not intellectually, verbally discussing this question of time. We are trying to find out whether it is possible for a human being as he is, living in this world, functioning in this world, to find out how to comprehend and act totally—not in the past, not as an artist, as a scientist, as an economist, as a communist, as a religious person, and so on and so on, broken up in fragments.

So what we are trying is to investigate and discover for ourselves, not theoretically, but actually—which is, factually find out for each one—how a mind, so heavily conditioned as a communist, as a socialist, as a Hindu, as a Muslim, and all the rest of it, how such a mind can transform itself, break away from its conditioning totally. Because only then in that freedom is it possible to find out what truth is. And it is only in that freedom there can be peace and order, not through disorder or violence, not through the fragmentation of human minds as the communist, the socialist, the Catholic, and the Hindu, and so on, nor through nationalism. It is our world. You have to live in it as human beings, not as Americans, Russians, Hindus, or Muslims. And to live peacefully there must be order. And order can only come about through freedom. And this freedom can only come when we understand this whole psychological structure of the human mind.

So it is important, I think, that one should listen to all this, neither agreeing nor rejecting, just listen. You know one of the most difficult things in this act of listening is that we are incapable of giving attention to anything for a period, for a length of time. You come after a long day of work in ugly offices, doing routine things which have little meaning, tired out, and you try to understand what is being said. To understand what is being said, you need a fresh mind, a mind that is active, clear, sane, not committed to any pattern of action—because if you are, you are incapable of examining, looking, observing; then you are prejudiced.

So what we are trying to do this evening is to find out for ourselves actually the nature of time, because we are so conditioned to think in terms of time—that we must go through certain stages, like going through nationalism and eventually coming to internationalism and later on to something else; that is, thesis, antithesis, and synthesis; all that takes time. And if we examine the whole structure of time, you will find that time breeds disorder, not order. And therefore to bring about order in ourselves and in society, there must be an immediate action, not action in terms of time as duration.

So, as we have said, thought is time. The whole machinery of thinking is the result of time. Thinking is the response of memory. That memory is experience, tradition, the established routine, the condition in which we have been brought up. And with that background we respond to any challenge. And therefore these responses are always conditioned, limited. And we have to free the mind from these limited responses because the challenges are immense; and we have to respond to these challenges totally, not partially. And it is only when we respond to these challenges partially, inadequately, that there is conflict, there is pain, there is suffering. It is only the mind that can respond totally to a challenge, which means adequately—it is only such a mind that can be free from sorrow, from conflict.

So all our thinking is never free. It is always conditioned by the past, by our experience, by our knowledge—thinking in words, or thinking nonverbally. And thinking is a duration in time. That is, any response we give to any challenge, if it is familiar, is immediate. I ask you something you know very well, and your response is immediate. "What is your name; where do you live?" And you respond very quickly, because you are already familiar with it, and therefore your answer is immediate. But if you are asked something much more complex, your response will take time, there is a lag. During that interval, thought is operating as memory, looking, asking, demanding, trying to find out the answer. In that interval is thinking. And that thinking is based on our knowledge, on the past, on the information and experience that we have had.

So thinking is always limited. We are not saying that you must not think. Please do not jump to the other conclusion. On the contrary, you have to think tremendously to find out the limitations of thought. You have to think rationally, sanely, logically. And when you understand this whole structure of thinking, then perhaps you will understand a state of mind in which there is only perception and so action. That is a fact, like poverty, war, hate, violence—which are facts and not opinions. Facts do not need opinions, judgments, evaluation. Facts demand that you look at them. And to look at them, opinions and experiences do not matter. What matters is that you look at them clearly.

Look, sirs, there is this question of poverty, this appalling, destructive, degrading poverty in this world with which we are all familiar. It is a fact. And we deal with that fact through opinions, through political parties, as a communist would deal with it, or as a socialist, or as a congressman, or as this and that. We are not concerned with poverty. What we are concerned with is how to deal with poverty, what to do about poverty in terms of our prejudice, of our inclinations, of our political bias. After all, poverty can only be solved on a world basis, not as a Hindu, not as a nationalist. So to remove this poverty one has to be nonnationalist, not committed to any party—because then you are concerned with a method of solving it, and therefore other methods are opposed to your method, and so on and so on; and in the meantime poverty goes on. So what is necessary is to see the fact, not in terms of your prejudice, of your nationality, of your religion, of your particular upbringing. And when you look at a fact actually, then you will find that in that perception there is love, not an intellectual formula of how to solve the problem.

So time is a fact in your life. Time is necessary at a certain level; otherwise, you will miss your bus; otherwise, you will not be able to go to your office and so on and so on. But time becomes destructive, time creates disorder when we use it as a means of bringing about a change within ourselves. Look, I am greedy. Let us suppose you are greedy and you create the ideal of nongreed, and you hope through that to change yourself. That is, the fact is you are greedy, and through time, through many days, through many months you hope to achieve that result. Now, what has happened between *what is* and 'what should be'? There are many other elements entering into it, many other factors. And these other factors, elements, create disorder. Look, this country has preached nonviolence for many, many years, many decades. That has been a tremendous ideal, something irrational. An ideal has no meaning whatsoever. What has meaning is the fact, not ideals. The fact is human beings are violent. Why do you need an ideal? You use an ideal as a means, as a lever, to uproot violence. You use an idea, a concept, a formula to change the fact. You use a myth to wipe away *what is,* and it is never possible. You have talked of nonviolence, but actually you are violent, and you can only deal with violence nonidealistically. You can only deal with it actually, find out why you are violent and go into it with all your being. And ideals are merely an escape from facts, from *what is,* from what you are. It is only when we can look at what we are that it is possible to bring about a radical transformation within ourselves.

So thought is never free. And thought is always making an effort determined according to a pattern, according to a norm, according to an ideal, to achieve a change. So time is necessary for such thinking as a means to bring about a change. I hope I am making myself clear. As we said in the beginning, we are not agreeing or disagreeing; we are examining. We can go into it much more in detail, but this is not the occasion to go into very deep detail.

So thought implies will, the will to change; the determination implies effort. That is, I am this and I will become that. And to become that there must be an effort, which is will. That is all we know. And will is resistance. And through resistance, through conformity, through compulsion we hope to bring about a change within ourselves. And that is why we are making everlasting efforts, in the office, at home, in schools; all the time we are making effort, effort.

And is there a different way of living in which effort is not involved? That is an essential question, because effort implies violence, effort exists only when there is a contradiction. Please do not listen to the speaker merely verbally but listen so that it reveals your own mind and heart, so that you see what actually is within yourself, inside your skin. Because the psychological change is far more important than the outward change. The outward changes are not possible fundamentally unless there is a radical transformation, a revolution within the psyche. The outward changes, reformations, reforms are necessary; but they are always destroyed by the inward state of confusion, disorder, violence.

So if we would bring about order in the world outwardly, there must be order within. And this order cannot possibly be brought about through any form of will, through any form of thought—will being effort, thought being time. So what is one to do? Do you understand the problem?

Look, sir; let me put it differently. There is the unconscious and the conscious. You all know that. The unconscious is the residue of the past—tradition, racial inheritance, the innumerable experiences of man, deeply hidden, which give occasional intimation through dreams and all the rest of it. And there is the conscious mind, the mind that functions every day, going to the office, struggling, adjusting, acquiring new techniques, learning capacities, and so on and so on. Between the conscious and the unconscious there is a conflict. Obviously, the greater the tension, the greater is the conflict and the greater the neurosis. And in that tension you may produce great literature, you may write poems, you may compose; but it is the outcome of this tremendous contradiction which is in each one.

You know what I mean by contradiction—thinking one thing and doing another; thinking marvelous thoughts, how you should be this and that and the other, and living contrary to them. So there is this contradiction. The more intellectual, verbal, theoretical, political you are, the greater is the contradiction, because you are living in theories, but not in facts. So this contradiction breeds conflict. Doesn't it?

Do examine, sir, do listen to what is being said. We are dealing with your life. You are not concerned with my life. We are concerned with the life of each one of us because each one of us has to live in relationship, and relationship is life. And when there is conflict in that relationship, then it is destruction, it is disorder. And in that contradiction, in that conflict, love is not possible. It only produces more fear, more anxiety, more guilt. So in our lives there are contradictions, various obvious and subtle forms of contradiction—doing one thing and thinking another. And being in conflict indicates, brings about, effort. A man who is not in conflict with himself or with society—he has no conflict and therefore he is essentially peaceful. Because, a human being has produced the society in which he lives, and society is the human being. So the two are not separate. And this contradiction in our life breeds disorder.

So, we see all this—effort, contradiction, imitation, conformity to a pattern, this everlasting thinking, thinking which has very little meaning; that is our daily life, our daily problem of anxiety, of fear, of greed, of envy. Seeing all this, how is a human mind which is the result of time, which is the result of violence—how is such a mind to bring about a mutation within itself? And you will say: What importance has this mutation of a human being in relationship to the whole? How will one human being bring about a change within himself so radically, and how will it affect society? Inevitably that is asked. That is one of the most stupid questions asked. Because when you radically change, you are not changing because of society, you are not changing because you want to do good or you want to reach heaven or God or whatever it is. You are changing because it is necessary for itself. And if you love a thing for itself, then it brings about tremendous clarity, and it is this clarity that is going to bring about salvation to man—not doing good works and reforms.

So this challenge is demanding your complete attention. What is the challenge? The challenge is: One observes all this, this complex way of life inwardly; one may be outwardly very simple; one may have a few clothes or eat one meal a day, but inwardly may be boiling—as most saints and most religious people are; outwardly they garb themselves in simple things and inwardly they are in turmoil—how can a mind, observing this extraordinary, complex phenomenon, bring about order; or rather, how can such a mind live in a state of mutation? Do you understand my question?

First of all, having put that question to yourself, find out how you respond. Because mutation is necessary, a revolution, a psychological revolution is absolutely necessary. Because the world is much too chaotic, disorderly; there is tremendous violence and hatred, all of which breeds disorder. And so seeing all this, this question is imperative; and you have to answer it. You cannot say, "It is not my business, it is for the religious, it is for the philosopher, for the scientist"—this is an escape. It is your problem. How will you answer it? How do you answer it? How are you answering it?

Now, what is necessary is to answer a challenge so completely that your answer is adequate to the challenge. Otherwise your answer will only breed some more conflict. It must correspond to the challenge. Do you understand? You know what is meditation? I do not mean the stupid repetition of some words, sitting cross-legged and breathing and all the rest of that business. Meditation is something entirely different. Meditation is not self-hypnosis, as most people indulge in, seeing visions, stimulating various forms of excitement, taking drugs. For example, you can take a certain drug and that produces extraordinary results, much greater results than self-hypnotic meditation.

Now to answer this question adequately, completely, with all your being—that is the only way you can answer a fundamental question—you have to give your complete attention, not partially, not when it suits you. To answer it completely, the mind must be in a state of meditation, which means that the mind must be tremendously active—not the stimulated activity of an idea, or of an examination. You know the mind is capable of anything, as we said the other day. And a mind when opposed, when challenged with this problem, can only look at that problem in silence. A problem which you have never put to yourself, a question which you have never asked yourself—you cannot answer it except out of silence. Can you? You know what I mean? Look, there are the religious people throughout the world who want to know if there is God. I am not talking of those people who believe in God. They are not religious people at all. It is just an idea. They go to a temple, church, mosque, or whatever it is. That is merely a form of conditioning. They may attend innumerable ceremonies, twiddle their thumbs, and all the rest of it, attend Mass and all that. That is not religion at all. That is just an escape from the facts of life.

Now, to find out whether there is a reality called God or some other thing, your mind—which is only petty, small, conditioned—when it meets such a problem, must be completely silent. Do you understand what I am saying, sir? Look: this is an immense problem which we are putting to you, a very complex problem which we cannot answer with yes or no in a minute. To meet this challenge, you need a mind that is completely quiet. That is, sir, take for example a complex, mathematical problem, or a scientific issue. You have thought about it, you have investigated it, you have pulled it into pieces, inquired, searched, asked, examined, and you cannot find an answer. Which means what? Your mind has been tremendously active in the sense of looking, asking, searching, examining to find out the answer, and it has not been able to find it. Therefore it becomes quiet. It leaves that problem alone. But the problem is still there. So out of that silence you have the answer to that problem.

So this question can only be met by a mind that is meditating—that is, a mind that is completely quiet, not induced to be quiet, not made quiet, not disciplined to be quiet. When the mind has examined this problem widely, a problem which is so complex, in the very examination of that problem there is a process of discipline. And that examination and that discipline which is not conformity, which is not compulsion, which is not pursuing a pattern, which is not drilling the mind to think in a certain way—only such a mind can answer this question. For a mind to examine this very closely, attentively, to be aware of all the implications of all the things like time, change, sensitivity, what is implied in effort, to examine it factually, not according to one's opinions—that demands attention. And an attentive mind has its own discipline. And, therefore, a mind that is attentive is a silent mind.

To put it very simply, when you look at anything, that microphone or that tree, when you look at your wife, your children, or your husband, you can look through your memories; you can look at your wife or your husband through the past memories of hurts and all the rest of it. Or you can look without the interference of the past. To look without the interference of the past is to look in complete silence. And out of that silence comes about a mutation, not thought out, not planned, not conditioned. And it is only such a mutation that can bring about order in the world.

November 11, 1965

Third Talk in New Delhi

I think one of our big problems is communication. Words in a sentence are sounds leading to an idea. And when we use a word, each one of us has a different association with that word. A word is, after all, a sound, and each sound is associated with a memory, with a prejudice, with a concept. And so when we use words, which is perhaps the only way to communicate with one another, each one of us creates, or has an image associated with that word, or with that sound.

And so communication becomes extraordinarily difficult, and especially so when we are dealing with problems that need clear, objective thinking—observation.

And communication becomes still more difficult, not only when we are dealing with abstract problems, but when most of us refuse to think clearly, directly, and simply, because we are very complicated human beings. We have so many concepts, formulas, experiences, according to which we function, according to which we act. And as these talks here are meant not merely to convey an idea but rather to participate in what the speaker is trying to convey, the problem becomes still more difficult. Because we have to walk together. After all that is the function of any good, sane talking over together—that you and I, both of us, walk together, share together, partaking in what is being said not merely verbally but actually. Because you have to walk and I have to walk. But most of us when we go to a meeting of this kind, a gathering of this kind, refuse to walk together, but listen casually, accepting or denying and go on. But when your responsibility is as great as the speaker's, when we are walking together, then our communication becomes much more intense, much more vital and significant.

Communication is not merely verbal; but if we penetrate the word—not merely the meaning of it, just the dictionary meaning of that particular word—if we could go beyond, penetrate, delve deeply into the significance of the word, then I think communication becomes extraordinarily easy and simple. Because after all, we are not only trying to communicate with each other, talk over together the various human problems, but also we are trying to be in communion.

I think there is a difference between communication and communion. When you are in communion with something, you are very intimate with it, you are partaking of it, you are not merely intellectually examining it, but your whole being flows with it. That is when you commune with yourself, if you ever do—which is quite an art—that is when you are quiet, observing yourself, watching your thoughts, your feelings, your activities, objectively as well as inwardly, not denying or accepting but merely watching, flowing with it, with a sense of ease, a sense of great affection, care, and attention: in that there is a communion, not only with yourself inwardly, but also outwardly—like watching a tree.

I do not know if you have ever watched a tree—or perhaps you are too busy and occupied with your own problems. If you have ever watched a tree, you have watched it botanically, giving it a name, the species it is; but if you want to commune with it, be with it, really see the beauty of it, enjoy it, see the lovely shape of it, the feel of it, the vitality, the intensity of the tree, then you have to be in communion with it, you have to flow with it. And you can only flow with it when there is no barrier between you and the tree, which is after all a sense of great affection, a sense of great sympathy, love. And it is only in that state of communion that there is real penetration of the problem, of the word, of understanding, feeling something most profoundly. And from that sense of communion there is action, and that action is never contradictory. And that is what we are going to try this evening to talk over together.

I may put it into words: the speaker may put it into words, into sentences, into ideas. But those ideas, those sentences, the sound, the word, have very little meaning if we are only in communication with the meaning of those words; but if we could together commune—that is, together feel the problem—we see the complexity of the problem, we see what are the implications. And you cannot see the implications, the intentions, the beauty, the quality, the inwardness of something unless you are in communion with it, unless it is a problem to you—not to be resolved, not quickly to find an answer, which is too immature; but you inquire into it, flow in it, let it open as a flower opens in the morning, showing all its beauty, its perfume.

So, similarly, if we could together this evening commune with each other, not think together—you cannot think together, that is the ugliness of thought; but we can commune together, which takes place only when you and I are both vitally concerned, responsive, eager to feel the problem, to touch it, to smell it, to taste it, to go deeply into it—then communication has an extraordinary significance. It is like communing with oneself, so that in that communication, in the communion you see the hidden things, you see the beauty which you had never felt before, you see the quality, the intensity. Then from that communion action takes place. And in that action there is no contradiction because that action is not based on an idea.

So, what we are going to talk over, commune over together, this evening, is this question of contradiction. Because it is only possible with a mind that is mature, when there is not only a state in which there is no contradiction but also there is in it a movement as a whole. Now, there is a contradiction not only outwardly but also inwardly, contradiction as violence and peace, the family and the community, good and evil, the truth and the false. And we all know the various forms of this contradiction, the individual and the collective, tyranny and freedom, and so on and on. Please remember what I said, that we are in communion with each other. That is, you are observing, you are in communion with yourself, not with the speaker. The speaker is irrelevant; because if we could totally eliminate inwardly and therefore outwardly this sense of contradiction, then life would be a movement, then life would be something to be lived with joy, with tremendous attention and vitality.

And one has to become aware of this contradiction. The fragmentation of our lives as the bureaucrat, as the family man, as the politician, as the religious man, as the man who has given up the world, as the man who is caught in the world, as the businessman, as the artist—they are all contradictions. There we live in departments, and each department is in contradiction with the other. And so our life is a series of contradictions and therefore conflicts, therefore misery and confusion. One knows this.

If one is at all aware of the whole structure of one's own mind, the meaning of that structure not only verbally but nonverbally, not only psychologically but objectively, then one asks oneself—is there an action, a total action which is never contradictory? And merely to ask that question is not enough. One has to find it. One has to work very hard to find it. It is much harder than going to the office and working there nine hours a day. This requires tremendous inquiry. Because we must find an action that is not contradictory—right through life, not at an occasional moment when the action seems to flow without any resistance, without any contradiction—but is an action that is full, rich, complete, a movement right through without contradiction. To find that out requires great awareness, great attention.

We are using the word *awareness* in its very simplest form, meaning to be aware: to be aware of that sound, of that hammering. You cannot be aware of that hammering if you resist that sound because you want to listen to the speaker. Therefore, there is a contradiction. You want to listen to the speaker and at the same time that hammering disturbs you. So, there is a resistance against that noise, and so that resistance is a contradiction which prevents you from being aware of the noise, of the movement of the person sitting next to you, and also listening at the same time. It is after all what is attention;

that is, to be attentive to what is being said without resistance, to listen to the sound of that hammering without resistance, so that attention is a state of noncontradiction. If you can listen, if you can see without any form of resistance, then out of that observation, out of that listening, out of that perception and understanding comes action which is not contradictory.

Now there is contradiction not only within but outwardly. All our life is a terrible, brutal contradiction. And so one asks oneself: Is there a source, a something, a state of mind, from which—having touched it, having seen it, felt it—all action flows inevitably without contradiction, without resistance? And that is what we are going to find out this evening.

But to find out one has to inquire very, very deeply. One has not only to inquire into what is desire and pleasure but also to inquire into the thinker and the thought—in which there is also contradiction. And perhaps that is the very essence of contradiction. Because, you see, we live in a world where there are national, linguistic, religious divisions, where there are wars going on, where man is killing man in the name of peace, in the name of country, in the name of God, in the name of—dozens of names! There is violence all over the world. And observing that, one feels that human beings walking along that path can never find peace, can never be in a state of mind where there is love, where there is sanctity of being, unless they solve this problem as human beings, not as Muslims, Hindus, Pakistanis, Indians, or Russians, but as human beings. And unless we solve this problem for ourselves, we shall always be in a contradiction and conflict and therefore in sorrow. A man who would resolve and end sorrow has to understand this contradiction. And what we do is to try to put the fragments of these contradictions together and make something whole out of them. Do you understand? We live—our life is in fragments and we say, "Let us bring about integration between the fragments, let us put all the fragments together and make a whole out of them," which is not possible. Because a fragment will always remain a fragment, even though you add other fragments to it. It is only possible—this sense of noncontradiction—when the mind works as a whole.

So we are going to inquire, commune together, over this question of pleasure and desire. Because most of us function, live, act through pleasure. Pleasure for most of us is tremendously important: the pleasure of belonging to a country, to a particular group, the pleasure of domination, the pleasure of a certain prestige, the pleasure of having capacity, the sexual pleasure, the pleasure of having talent, being a genius, and so on. To us pleasure is the ultimate valuation.

Please don't deny it. If you deny it, we are not in communion with each other—not that the speaker is persuading you to think along his lines. I belong to a certain political party, why? Essentially it gives me pleasure; through joining that party I hope to achieve all kinds of things. I go to the temple or the mosque or the church because it gives me an extraordinary sense of pleasure, excitement, and sensation. I associate myself with some form of political activity, or religious activity, or social activity; I commit myself to something, to a formula, to a concept, because deep down I like it. The like, the pleasure, is not according to facts, but the facts create an image in me of the pleasure. Watch it in yourselves. If you are a communist, if you are a socialist, if you are a Hindu, if you are this or that, why? There is not only the fear of being thrown out of it, of standing alone, but also in it there is the pleasure of belonging. So one has not only to see the significance of pleasure but also to understand what gives continuity to pleasure. Do you understand? I look at a sunset, or a beautiful face, or a quiet evening, and there is tremendous enjoyment, there is great joy in it. If I do not feel that joy, that intensity, that beauty, I am dead, my senses are paralyzed. I must see the beauty of a tree. If I don't, something is wrong with me. But when the perception of that beauty becomes a pleasure and that pleasure demands a continuity, a duration, a lengthening of that pleasure, then our problems begin. I hope I am making myself clear.

So one has to find out the nature of pleasure, what gives it continuity, and the whole structure of desire. What is desire? Do you understand? We are not saying that desire is wrong, that you must suppress desire, that you must kill it, that you must be free from desire. We are talking about something entirely different, because if you suppress desire, as the so-called religious people do, then you are in perpetual battle with yourself, you are boiling within yourself your desire, and each suppression only strengthens that particular desire. So one has to understand desire, neither control it—please listen carefully—neither control it nor suppress it, nor make it conform to a particular pattern which you have established as righteous behavior, or twist it according to a certain norm, a certain pattern.

So this requires tremendous understanding. And that very understanding of desire is its own discipline, in which there is no conformity, no suppression. Because a mind that has suppressed, disciplined, twisted, tortured itself—such a mind is a worthless mind; it is not a good, rich, sane mind. And you need a sane, healthy, clear mind, a good mind, to find out what reality is.

So what we are talking about is the understanding of desire and not the suppression, not the control, not putting it aside. So this requires investigation, attention, seeing all the intricacies of desire. Now what is desire? Probably most of us have not gone into it. Or when that question is put to you, you say such and such a philosopher or a teacher has said this, or a psychologist says that, and you trot that out as though you have understood it. But if you have put away all that others have told you about desire, then you have to find out for yourself. And that is what we are going to do; because to discover something for yourself, you have to be free of all authority, not only the authority of the past, of the teachers, but the authority of a mind that has remembered its own experience and translates according to that experience the fact which occurs now. So you need a very sharp mind, not a dull mind, not a tortured mind. You need a very, very sensitive mind.

So what we are going to do is to find out for ourselves the nature of pleasure, what gives it continuity; and therefore where there is pleasure, there is its contradiction as non-pleasure, and from that contradiction there is sorrow. And the very essence of this sorrow is this feeling of loneliness in which there is no pleasure. And to find out what desire is, one has to observe oneself in action. You know, what we are talking about is something with which there is neither agreement nor disagreement. As I said, we are in communion with the question. Therefore, there is no question—either you agree or disagree—but inquiry. You say, "What is desire? How does it come about? How does it arise?" And why have people said—the so-called teachers and all the rest of it—why have they said, "destroy, suppress, control, or sublimate it?" Why? Why do you do it? Not what they have said—what they have said has very little meaning. Because we think desire breeds trouble, breeds various forms of anxieties; desire expends itself in waste of energy, and desire to us is something ugly, something to be put away. So to understand desire one needs clarity. And that is what we are going to proceed with.

What is desire? How does it arise? There is a car outside your window, a nice, polished, new car, long lines, good cylinders, many cylinders, working beautifully, driving perfectly. You see that. There is this seeing, then there is the sensation out of that seeing. Then there is contact with the object which we have seen and from that contact, sensation; that sensation is desire. It is very simple. Don't complicate it. Perception, contact, sensation, and desire: this is what is happening instantly with all of us. I see the flag—the English flag, your flag, the communist flag, or some other flag. Then there are the associations with that flag, the pleasure of that flag, the commitment to that flag, and all the rest of the phenomena of pleasure, pain, desire, and everything. I see a beautiful tree in another's garden and I want to possess that tree in my garden. I see a beautiful face and I want to be equally beautiful. I see somebody very clever, high in position, prestige and I want that—perception, sensation, contact, desire. That is happening instantly all the time, consciously or unconsciously. When you become conscious of it and the pleasure, and when that desire gives you pleasure, you want it to continue. Sex: there is the act, there is the thought, and that thought gives desire a continuity.

So we are inquiring to find out what gives to a desire a duration, a continuity, what makes it continue day after day. Surely, it is thought. There is the seeing of that car, the desire, and you say, "I wish I had it"—thought giving to desire a continuity as pleasure. Now, why should you suppress it, why should you say it is wrong or right, "I must have it" or "I must not have it"? What becomes enervating, what is disturbing, what is destructive is to give to desire thought as pleasure. Do you understand? Am I making myself clear? I can look at that tree, see the beauty, enjoy the shade, the depth, the color, the proportions, the symmetry of it. But the moment desire comes in and says I must have that pleasure continuously, then begins the problem of how to retain it, how to capture it, hold it, and all the rest of it, and effort and pain come in. And so one can observe the tree without the interference of thought.

So this very observation, if you are at all aware of all this, this seeing of the interference of thought with desire—how thought interferes with desire and gives it a strength, a continuity, a dynamic quality—this seeing is in itself discipline, and that discipline is much more vital. Because that discipline gives energy, but the other forms of discipline only diminish this quality of energy that you need for action.

Then there is also this contradiction between the thinker and the thought. In all of us there is this duality. It is important to understand this. You may be a communist, or a socialist. If we have to create a new world, a new society, a new human being, a society must live in a state of noncontradiction; to flower in goodness, there must be peace, you understand, not war, not hate. And you will live in hate, you will live in agony, despair, anxiety, if action is not a total action.

So now we are inquiring into this contradiction between the thinker and the thought—the thinker who says I must control thought, the thinker who is the censor, the thinker who is the experiencer, who is the observer—the observer and the thing observed. Unless we understand this—that is, the rich and the poor, my wanting to be bigger than the other fellow, having more prestige, more power, and so on—unless we understand the structure of this, human beings will always live in pain and misery, in contradiction and conflict. And the inward contradiction only produces a society in which there are greater, more violent contradictions. So the reformation of a society, however necessary, however imminent, can only begin within oneself, for oneself is the society. The two are not separate.

You know what beauty is, the beauty of a tree, the beauty of a sunset, the flow of a river, the sunlight on it, a beautiful building, well proportioned. Is beauty in the object, or is beauty in the observer? If the observer sees beauty in the object, then the observer himself has the pattern, the design of beauty. Perhaps we will discuss that too, the whole question of what is beauty, because without beauty man cannot live. Your saints, your religions have denied beauty. They write about beauty in some sacred books because beauty is associated with desire. And desire, apparently, for a religious man is a curse, something to be destroyed. And we are saying that unless you and I as human beings living in society which is so contradictory, so terrible in its ugliness and monstrosity—unless you and I understand the nature of this contradiction, we shall always live in sorrow. And a man who will end sorrow must end this contradiction. And one of the roots of this contradiction is this division between the thinker and the thought. Why is there a thinker at all? Don't ask the question whether the thinker came first and thought afterwards, or thought first and the thinker afterwards. That is one of our pet ways of discussing, which is rather immature, if I may point out.

Is there a thinker at all without thought? Do you understand? Is there space without the object? Do you understand? There is this object, the microphone in front, it creates space round it and it is in space. Please, I am not going off the subject. You have to understand this too, this whole, very extraordinary question of space. There is the object which creates space round it, and that object also lives in space. Do we know space without the object? Unless you know space without the object, your mind will always remain in limitation, and therefore there is never freedom. In the same way you have to find out—you have to be in communion with yourself, to find out—whether there is a center which is the thinker, the censor, without thinking. Surely, there is only thinking, which creates the center, not the other way round. If there is the other way round, that there is a center, a censor, a thinker, then that is an object which creates space round itself and therefore is never free.

As I was saying the other day, meditation—when there is meditation—is the most extraordinary thing; don't get excited about that word. We do not know how to meditate. To meditate is not only to find out this question of thinker and thought, pleasure and pain, but also to go beyond thought so that there is no center at all—which means no center which creates space round itself, and therefore its space is always limited, therefore it is always living in a prison which it calls space. So there is only thinking. That is, I ask you a question. You reply; you reply according to your prejudice, your knowledge, your experience, your background. Your background, your experience, your knowledge is the center from which you are replying. That center is created by thought as memory and so on and so on. And that center, thought has created because in that center there is security, there is certainty—I exist, I am good, I am bad, I must reach whatever it is I reach.

So one has to understand again this structure of thought, not deny it. When you deny something, or when you suppress something, you create contradiction. But when you understand something, then there is no contradiction. So one has to understand the nature of thinking. And the nature of thinking is the background, the tradition, the experience from which you react; and that reaction is based on pleasure or pain, or on facts which will give you pleasure. And according to that pleasure you respond, and the response is thought. And thought is a process like desire cultivated.

So you see the nature of pleasure and desire, and what gives it continuity is thought: thought which has established a center as the observer, the censor, the background from which there is operation in action. And so action is always divided as the idea and action—the formula, the concept, and action. If you are a communist, you have a concept, you have ideas according to Marx or Engels. And this concept you try to fulfill in action. And this concept becomes the utopia which gives the person who is operating in that framework the pleasure to bring about that utopia in the world. It does not matter what it means; he wants that to be carried out. And if you are associated—a socialist, a Hindu, and God knows what else may be the labels that one has—you are also operating the same way. So, our action is based on an idea, a concept, a formula, and then from that formula we act, from that idea we act. And so there is a contradiction. I feel I should be noble—an idea which is rationalized thought. Then according to that idea I try to live. My living is contradictory to what should be. So I never throw out of the window that idea, the formula, the concept, the conclusion. But I keep that and try to act according to that. Observe it, you are doing it all the time. But if you threw that out of the window completely—the concept—then you would only be in a state of "acting," the present participle "acting," and not "have acted" or "will act." So, that action is not contradictory because you are dealing with facts, not with opinions, not with conclusions, not with what Shankara or Buddha or Marx or somebody else has told you.

So you will find, if you inquire into this, that action without idea, that is, without concept, is possible when you are only dealing with facts and not with conclusions. And when you are only dealing with thought and not what thought should be, and when you are aware of the nature of pleasure and desire, then you will find that maturity is action in which there is no contradiction. You are not going to tell me that I am in contradiction or not, nor will somebody else tell me. Because I have investigated it, gone deeply within myself, I have found out how to live in this monstrous, stupid world of destructive violence, how to live without contradiction. And to find out, one has to go through all this; and to inquire into this is meditation, not sitting in some corner and breathing deeply and holding your nose and repeating some silly words. Because it is only the mature mind that does not function in fragments, as a communist, as a socialist, as a religious man, as a nonreligious man, as a Muslim, and all the rest of that human invention which has separated man and destroyed man.

It is only this mature mind that does not function in fragments. It is only such a mind that can bring about a different world. It is only such a mind that can have love. And love is not a thing to be cultivated. Either it is or it is not—like humility. But you come upon it darkly without your knowing it when you have been in communion with yourself infinitely and deeply; and then out of that comes the joy of love.

November 14, 1965

Fourth Talk in New Delhi

It seems to me that one of our great difficulties is that we seem to be incapable of learning. And we are using that word *learning* not in the sense of accumulating mere knowledge, or gathering experience from which to act; but we are using that word in a different sense. We see around us not only in this country but all over the world that man suffers, not only outwardly, through outward incidents, accidents, ill-health, and misfortune, but also inwardly, much more, not only physically, but psychologically. There is great poverty outwardly as well as inwardly. And there are wars—one group, or one community, or one tribe against another. There have been wars, immemorial wars—beyond memory. Seeing all this and knowing all this, we do not seem to be able to learn. We are capable of adjusting to misfortune, to wars, to hate, to poverty, to tyranny.

Adjustment is not learning. The difference between man and an animal is that man is capable of adjustment to any climate, to any food, to any condition, to any environmental influence: animals cannot. And this constant adjustment to our environment is not learning. Learning is something entirely different. Learning is not accumulative. We don't learn and having learned, act. That is what most of us do.

There is a learning which comes from the very acting, which is from the very doing, not having learned and then doing, but in the very doing is the learning and the acting. And to learn from all our misery, from the innumerable frustrations, from conflict within and without—we do not seem to be able to learn so as to bring about a radical revolution in ourselves. And it seems to me it is imperative that there should be this learning from the very doing, and therefore there is no pattern or authority which tells you what to do. I do not know if you have read that they are experimenting in America in factories because they want greater production. And when you keep doing, or when a man does the same thing over and over again, it gets monotonous, and he does not produce more. Whereas if he learns in the very act of production, in the very act of doing, then he produces more.

And though we have suffered for millennia, both inwardly and outwardly, we do not seem to be capable of learning. And it indicates, does it not, that we are not tremendously interested in living, in living freely, totally, in living a life without conflict, without sorrow. We do not want to know the structure of sorrow, or the nature of fear. We just accept it, or we adjust ourselves to it and we put up with anything, unless of course it gives a great deal of physical pain—then we go to a doctor, or something or other. But we accept psychological pain.

And it seems to me that fear is one of our major problems. Because a mind that is fearful, timid, anxious, is incapable of clear thinking; it lives in darkness, it has various forms of neurosis, various forms of contradictions. And most of us, if we are at all aware that we are frightened, that there is fear—we either escape from it, run away as far away from it as we can, or we submit to it; we accept it and live within that shadow.

We do not know how to deal with fear because we have lived with fear for millennia. And because we do not know the nature of fear and how to resolve it, we turn to religion, to drink, to aggressiveness, to violence, and so on. So, one may have fear of different kinds—conscious as well as unconscious. And to be rid of fear totally, not partially, requires the investigation and the understanding of fear, not developing a courage, but the understanding of fear, which is much more important than creating resistance against fear, which is courage. We are afraid of losing a job, we are afraid of darkness, we are afraid of death, we are afraid of public opinion, we are afraid of so many things, and we live with this fear. Now, one can listen to what is being said. But mere words, intellect, cannot possibly solve this fear. What one has to do is to apply, come directly into contact with fear, and not escape. Because religions throughout the world have offered man an escape from the final fear of death. They have given him hope in the hereafter in different forms. Religions have tried to tame man, civilize him, make him more humane; but religions have not been able to stop wars. As we said the other day, there have been fourteen thousand and more wars, two and a half wars every year throughout the world. And we have not learned to stop wars. And religions have said: Don't kill, love your neighbor, be kind, be gentle, think of another. And we have not done that either. Religions have become merely rituals, like big corporations without any meaning.

And it is absolutely necessary for human beings to have that religious mind, not the religions of belief, dogma, church, rituals, but a religious mind that is totally unafraid. And a mind that is unafraid is always alone, not isolated, but alone. It is only the mind that is frightened, anxious, guilty, greedy, envious that is always seeking company, afraid of being alone. And it is only the religious mind that is capable of being totally alone, because it is totally free from all fear.

And we are going to talk over together this evening this question of death. Because that is what most of us are frightened of, though we try to avoid it, though we do not want to think about it, though we treat it as an unpleasant thing to be put away, to be sidetracked. Because we are frightened of it, we have a belief—belief in resurrection, in a continuity, in immortality, or in reincarnation. But this belief does not solve the problem of fear. Scientists are saying that man can live indefinitely. They will probably find ways and means to prolong human life. But such prolongation does not solve the problem of fear.

And a society, a human being, that has not solved this problem of death lives a very superficial life. Because if there is death, an annihilation, a destruction, a coming to an end, then one lives as one can through life miserably, anxiously, and therefore life has no meaning; life becomes a meaningless thing, without much significance—which is what is happening in the modern world. And many civilizations have tried to solve this problem of death.

And because we are not capable of understanding it, we try to invent theories which will be satisfactory, which will give us comfort. So, if we may, this evening, we would like to talk about this, talk over together—together; that is, you and I are going to think over together, investigate, search out—commune with each other over this question of fear, death, and love, and something much greater, beyond all religions, which is creation.

And as we said the other day, communion with one another over a problem of this kind does not mean that you and I agree, that you should agree with the speaker, or disagree. This is too vast a problem to be categorized, to be classified. And to inquire into something of this nature demands on your part a great deal of searching inquiry, not acceptance or denial. It requires intelligence, not clever, cunning, dialectical reasoning of opinion, but rather you and I together take a journey into this enormous problem of life and death.

And we cannot possibly take a journey together if there is not the vitality, the energy, the intensity to search out and to discover for oneself the truth of this matter. This energy, this intensity, this vitality does not come by gathering energy; but through the very act of investigation there is energy, through the very act of inquiry energy comes. But for most of us we think energy must first be gathered, accumulated through various means and then, from that energy, proceed. What we are saying is quite the opposite: that energy to inquire comes through search, through asking, through demanding, through questioning, through doubting, not through accepting. We are not accepting a political formula or a religious formula, not accepting the authority of anyone or any book. And then out of that nonacceptance, which is a very positive action, comes energy. We inquire, we ask, and in that very asking is energy. So that is what we are going to do together, we are going to take a journey, and you are going to work as hard as the speaker. Because for most of us a talk of this kind is generally the work of the speaker, and you become merely listeners. I am afraid this evening you have to work as hard as the speaker.

We never come directly into contact with fear. Please follow this a little bit carefully. To be in contact with something is either to feel it with your senses, or to have no psychological barrier between the fact and yourself. To come into contact means to touch, to come directly into touch with something, with facts, as I would touch that microphone. I cannot touch that if there is a hindrance, a barrier. That barrier may be words, the desire to escape so as not to face facts, or intellectually rationalize the fears or be unaware of the barriers, conscious or unconscious. These prevent directly coming into contact with a fact. And we are trying this evening to come into contact with the fact of fear, not intellectually, not what you should do or should not do about fear, but to come to know the nature of fear. Then that very coming into contact with something is the understanding of that fact. And therefore when you understand something, it is no longer the false.

We are afraid of many things. Naturally we have not time nor the occasion to go into the many forms of fear, conscious as well as unconscious. Especially, unconscious fears are much more difficult to deal with. Conscious fears one can do something about. But unconscious fears are much more strong, more deep—which fears take the form of dreams in your sleep, and so on and so on. I won't go into all that now. But there is for every human being, however long he may live, this question of death. Unless he understands it, comes directly into contact with this question, with this problem, his life is very superficial and will always remain superficial. And a superficial mind then tries to give significance to living according to its conditioning, to its environment, to the society in which it has grown. Please do listen to this, give your attention for a while.

So there is this question of fear with regard to death. Now to understand this question one has to be free from all belief, from all your ideas of reincarnation or resurrection or personal immortality. You don't know anything about it. Even if you do, it is a tradition, a verbal conditioning. You have not come directly into contact with death, or the fear of that fact. And as we said, it is imperative for a human being, living in this ugly, brutal, terrifying world with its wars and antagonism, to understand this fact. Otherwise our life becomes utterly meaningless. Going to the office every day for the next thirty years, twenty years, or forty years, repeating, repeating the same old stuff, breeding a few children, and everlastingly being in conflict with oneself—this has no meaning whatsoever. The more intellectual you are, the more you are aware of the world, of what is taking place, the more you try to run away from the superficiality through drink, through various forms of amusement, or invent a philosophy, or go back to some philosophy of some book. So what is necessary—if you will make life a significant thing in itself, a life that has a meaning, a life that is rich, full, complete—is that you understand this question of fear and death.

Now we know what fear is—a reaction, a reaction to something of which we do not know, to something of which we have not direct experience or knowledge. We have seen death, it goes by every day; this war has brought it home. But a human mind, living, healthy, sane, not neurotic—such a mind has not come into contact with it. And it is only when you come directly into contact with something that you see the meaning of it, you begin to understand the significance, the depth, the beauty of it.

So to understand this question of death, we must be rid of fear which invents the various theories of afterlife or immortality or reincarnation. So we say, those in the East say, that there is reincarnation, there is a rebirth, a constant renewal going on and on and on—the soul, the so-called soul. Now please listen carefully.

Is there such a thing? We like to think there is such a thing because it gives us pleasure, because that is something which we have set beyond thought, beyond words, beyond; it is something eternal, spiritual, that can never die, and so thought clings to it. But is there such a thing as a soul, which is something beyond time, something beyond thought, something which is not invented by man, something which is beyond the nature of man, something which is not put together by the cunning mind? Because the mind sees such enormous uncertainty, confusion, nothing permanent in life—nothing. Your relationship to your wife, your husband, your job—nothing is permanent. And so the mind invents a something which is permanent, which it calls the soul. But since the mind can think about it, thought can think about it; as thought can think about it, it is still within the field of time—naturally. If I can think about something, it is part of my thought. And my thought is the result of time, of experience, of knowledge. So, the soul is still within the field of time. Right? Please, we are not accepting or denying. I am not doing propaganda of some theory—which is too immature and childish. We are taking a journey of investigation. And investigation, which if you follow step by step and go into very deeply, will bring you into contact with something of which you are afraid.

So the idea of a continuity of a soul which will be reborn over and over and over again has no meaning because it is the invention of a mind that is frightened, of a mind that wants, that seeks a duration through permanency, that wants certainty, because in that there is hope. So man clings to that and therefore he must have many lives, everlasting business. That is, it matters immensely how you behave now, if you believe in reincarnation, because next life you are going to pay for how you behave now. But you are not concerned with behavior which is righteousness. If you really believed in reincarnation, your acts, the way you think, the way you live, your callousness and indifference to everybody would disappear because next life you will pay, you will suffer. But you don't believe in all that. Actually you don't. It is just an idea, an idea which you think is very spiritual, which is sheer nonsense. But the fact remains that there is the fear of death and in the West it takes a different form of resurrection, of a continuity in a different field of renewal.

So there is this question of fear, and of fear of something which we do not know, which we call death. So we separate life, living, from death. We have not understood living, nor have we understood death. Because to understand life means to enter into life, to come into contact with life—life being greed, envy, brutality, hate, wars, escape, the bestiality, the craving for power, position. That is what we call life. That is the life you lead every day, whether you are a sannyasi or a businessman or an artist. There is a boiling going on inside, and that we call life. And we have not understood this, we are not free of it; we are not free of our anxieties and guilt, anguishes, nor have we understood this enormous thing called death. So we have not understood living, nor have we understood the enormous significance of dying.

Now you have to understand living—living, not battling, not being in conflict, not being tortured, not torturing yourself to find God. A human being who tortures himself to find God—such torture is not worth it. He will never find God or whatever that is. By distortion, you cannot find truth. You want a clear, sane, rational, healthy mind, not a tortured, twisted mind.

So you must be free, free from fear of life itself, free from your anxieties, from your conflicts, from your avarice, greed, envy, whether it is for money or for God. You must be free of that; then you come directly into contact with life; then living is related to dying. Please follow this. Surely, a man who has no love is always in despair; he is seeking authority, position, prestige; he is envious, callous; such a man is not living. He does not know what life is. All he knows is the little mind, whether he is the politician, or the sannyasi, or the businessman, or the artist—the little mind, the petty, little mind and its worries. That is all he knows. And it is only when he is free of that pettiness, of his fears, that he will know what it is to live. And when he knows what it is to live, then he will know what it is to die. Because we have separated living from dying—dying being coming to an end, psychologically, physiologically. And we think we are living. And our living is sorrow. So unless there is an ending to sorrow, there is no understanding of death.

So one has to find out for oneself, not because somebody else says so. You have been fed, you are fed, on other people's discoveries; you are bound by tradition, by authority, by fear; you have not found out as a human being—living in this world, tortured, suffering—how to end suffering. We know how to escape from suffering through drink, through amusement, through sex, through going to temple, reading—a dozen ways we have. But we have to come into contact with it, and end it. It is only the mind that ends sorrow that can have wisdom. And it is only the mind that is free from sorrow that can know what it means to love.

So our question then is: Is it possible, not in some distant future—is it possible living in this world now, today—is it possible to be free of sorrow and come into contact with something which we do not know, which we call death, which is the unknown? What we are afraid of is not the unknown but letting go of the known. Is it not? You are not afraid of death, the ending, but you are afraid of losing what you have, what you know, your experience, your family, your little pleasures, your knowledge, your technology—you know, the things that you know. And you say, "By Jove, I have learned so much, I know so much, and when death comes, I shall lose everything." And that is what you are frightened of, not the extraordinary nature of death. And what are you holding on to?—the known. What is the known? Your family, your little house, the squalor of that house, the dirt of the street, the lack of beauty, the effort, the jealousies, the anxieties, the pettiness of the office, the boss, you know. That is all you know and that we are afraid to let go. So when you let that go happily, easily, with grace and beauty—that is to die to the known. Then you will know what it is to die, so that you will know the unknown.

Now, please listen to this. Can you end immediately, not through time, not through gradual process, discipline, torturing yourself—can you end your fear immediately? That is really the question, not what will happen after death. But can you end a habit, the sexual habit, psychological habits, physical habits—end them immediately? To end them is to be free of them, to put an end to your worries, to your fears, to your greed, to your wanting to be powerful, strong, to your imagining you are a great shot. Because if you do not know how to end these petty things of life, the things that you know, to which the mind clings, then you will be living in a state of turmoil all the time, and therefore confused. And it is only the confused mind that is in sorrow, not the mind that thinks clearly, that comes directly into contact with facts.

So, dying is the dying to the things that you know, not to the unpleasant things known, but to the pleasant also. You would like to put aside, die to the memories of pain, to the insults; but you would like to keep the memories which are pleasant, which give you satisfaction. But to put an end, to die to the pleasure as well as to the pain—you can do it if you give your attention completely to every thought, to every feeling; attention, not contradiction; not say, "I don't like it, I like it"; just give attention.

You know what it is to give attention to something. Attention is not concentration. When you concentrate, as most people try to do—what takes place when you are concentrating? You are cutting yourself off, resisting, pushing away every thought except that one particular thought, that one particular action. So your concentration breeds resistance, and therefore concentration does not bring freedom. Please, this is very simple if you observe it yourself. But whereas if you are attentive, attentive to everything that is going on about you, attentive to the dirt, the filth of the street, attentive to the bus which is so dirty, attentive of your words, your gestures, the way you talk to your boss, the way you talk to your servant, to the superior, to the inferior, the respect, the callousness to those below you, the words, the ideas—if you are attentive to all that, not correcting, then out of that attention you can know a different kind of concentration. You are then aware of the setting, the noise of the people, people talking over there on the roof, your hushing them up, asking them not to talk, turning your head; you are aware of the various colors, the costumes, and yet concentration is going on. Such concentration is not exclusive, in that there is no effort. Whereas mere concentration demands effort. So, if you give your attention totally—that is, with your nerves, with your eyes, with your ears, with your mind, with your brain, totally, completely—to understand fear, then you will see you can instantly be free of it, completely. Because it is only a very clear mind, not living in the darkness of fear, or in the confusion of many wants—it is only such a clear, lucid mind that can go beyond death. Because it has understood living. Living is not a battle, is not a torture; living is not something to be run away from to the mountains, to the monastery. We run away because living is a torture, an ugly nightmare. And if you give your attention to one thing totally, out of that freedom you will see, you will know what love is. Because for most of us love has very little meaning. For most of us love is surrounded by jealousies, by hate. How can there be love when you compete with another in the office? Please listen. Without love, without this feeling of beauty, life naturally becomes utterly empty. And being empty, we seek the gods which are man-made; being empty, beliefs, dogmas, rituals become very important; and we fill that emptiness with these tawdry affairs of things, tawdry affairs which have been put together by man. So if you would know what love is, there must be freedom from jealousy, from conflict, from the desire to dominate, the desire to be powerful—which means you must live peacefully to know what love is, not outside of life, but actually every day.

Then there is one other important thing in our life—creation. We do not know what creation is because we are bound by authority. The word *authority* means the author, the one who originated something, an idea, a concept, a vision, a way of life thought out or lived by another. He is the originator of that, and we see that person living in a certain way, feeling, thinking in a certain way, and we want that and therefore we imitate that. Therefore that person, or that idea, that concept, that ideal becomes the authority, the authority of tradition, the authority of your particular pet religion. And a mind that has authority, that is bound by authority, can never be in a state of creation. Because, you see, authority breeds fear; all that we are concerned with is to be told what to do, and we do it, technologically as well as psychologically. That is why all these innumerable gurus exist in this world: because we are frightened. They know, you don't know. They tell you what you should do as a scientist, as a doctor; so you depend on authority.

Now the authority of law and the authority of fear are two different things. One has to obey the authority of law which says: Keep to the left; when you are driving, go on the left side. That must be. You must pay your tax, you must buy a stamp to post a letter, and so on and on. But the authority set by a pattern of a society as what is the religious idea—the concept which has been established by tradition as what is God, what is this, and so on and so on; the authority of religion, the sanctions of religion which you blindly accept, or you think you have investigated but have not because you are frightened—such authority, in any form, psychologically is the most destructive thing. Because then it makes you follow; then you follow, you don't investigate, you don't find out, you don't search out and discover for yourself.

But after all, truth is something that cannot be given to you. You have to find it out for yourself. And to find it out for yourself, you must be a law to yourself, you must be a guide to yourself, not the political man that is going to save the world, not the communist, not the leader, not the priest, not the sannyasi, not the books; you have to live, you have to be a law to yourself. And therefore no authority—which means completely standing alone, not outwardly, but inwardly completely alone, which means no fear. And when the mind has understood the nature of fear, the nature of death, and that extraordinary thing called love, then it has understood, not verbalized, not thought about, but actually lived. Then out of that understanding comes a mind that is active, but completely still. This whole process of understanding life, of freeing oneself from all the battles, not in some future, but immediately, giving your whole attention to it—all that is meditation; not sitting in some corner and holding your nose and repeating some silly words, mesmerizing yourself, that is not meditation at all, that is self-hypnosis. But to understand life, to be free from sorrow—actually, not verbally, not theoretically, but actually—to be free of fear and of death brings about a mind that is completely still. And all that is meditation.

And it is only a very still mind, not a disciplined mind, that has understood and therefore is free. It is only that still mind that can know what is creation. Because the word *God* has been spoiled. You can call it the other way, dog; it has no meaning any more. Hitler believed in God, and your politicians believe in God; they destroy each other, kill each other, torture. There are those who torture themselves to find God. So it has no meaning any more; it is just a word. But to find out that something which is beyond time, you must have a very still mind. And that still mind is not a dead mind but is tremendously active; anything that is moving at the highest speed and is active is always quiet. It is only the dull mind that worries about that is anxious, fearful. Such a mind can never be still. And it is only a mind that is still that is a religious mind. And it is only the religious mind that can find out, or be in that state of creation. And it is only such a mind that can bring about peace in the world. And that peace is your responsibility, the responsibility of each one of us, not the politician, not the solider, not the lawyer, not the businessman, not the communist, socialist, nobody. It is your responsibility, how you live, how you live your daily life. If you want peace in the world, you have to live peacefully, not hating each other, not being envious, not seeking power, not pursuing competition. Because out of that freedom from these, you have love. It is only a mind that is capable of loving that will know what it is to live peacefully.

November 18, 1965

Banaras, India, 1965

First Talk at Rajghat

If you will allow me, I will talk for about half-an-hour or more, and perhaps then you will ask questions or discuss points for further clarification.

It seems to me that one of our great problems is order and disorder, freedom and conformity. Until we resolve this question within ourselves, not as a group, not as a community or by organized acceptance of a certain formula—unless we, as human beings, as individuals, resolve this problem, our revolt or freedom will only be a further process of confusion and conflict. We conform—that is fairly obvious—right through the world, hoping that conformity will bring about order. We must have order. No society, no individual—within or without—can have disorder; there must be order. And order is not possible by merely stating what order is, in terms of a categorical or a patterned order.

Order, it seems to me, can only come about when we discover for ourselves what breeds disorder; out of the understanding of what brings about disorder, naturally will come order. That is fairly simple. When I know what brings about disorder in a family, in myself, or in society, and if I wish, as a human being, to bring about order, first I must clarify or put away disorder. So, the order of which we are talking is not a positive act, but rather it comes about through the understanding of the negation of what is disorder. If I understand what is disorder and negate it, put it aside, clarify, inquire into all the implications involved in that, if I understand all of what is disorder, this may appear superficially as negation. But out of this understanding of disorder comes a natural order, not the other way round, not conforming to what is considered as order—such conformity only breeds greater disorder because we are human beings in conflict, in fear, in anxiety, with a great many problems of obedience, acceptance, anxiety, seeking power, and so on. And so merely to seek order, or the pattern of order, and then conform to that pattern essentially breeds disorder.

Please, we must understand this, not verbally. Because, you know, it is one of the most unfortunate things that we all preach endlessly, write books, have theories, formulas, and concepts, and there is no action at all. We are masters, especially in this unfortunate country, at verbalizing, theorizing, having concepts, formulas, and exploring these concepts dialectically, hoping that through the discovery of the truth in theories, we will come to action; and therefore there is inaction, we do not do a thing. So, we must at the very beginning understand that order cannot possibly be brought about through conformity to a pattern, under any circumstances—whether it is a communist order or a religious order or a personal demand for orderliness. This order, which is extraordinarily positive, can only come about through understanding the negation of disorder. Please understand this issue very profoundly because we are going to go into things with which you will presently not agree at all—at least I hope you will neither accept nor discard; that leads nowhere.

So, we have to find out what causes disorder in the world outside and within. The understanding of the disorder outwardly brings about the understanding of the disorder inwardly. But this disorder which we divide as the outer and the inner is essentially one and the same; they are not two separate disorders because each of us, as a human being, is both society and the individual. The individual is not separate from society; the individual has created the psychological structure of society, and in that psychological structure he is caught. And therefore he tries to break away from that psychological structure, which is a mere revolt and therefore does not resolve any problem.

We have to inquire into what creates disorder because out of disorder nothing can grow, nothing can function. You must have tremendous order to bring about the understanding of truth, or whatever one likes to call it. You must have great order, and this order cannot possibly come about through revolt, or through conformity, or through acceptance of a formula—socialist, capitalist, religious, or any other formula.

So, what brings about disorder? You understand? There must be order in the world. There is no order now in the world. War is the essence of disorder, whether it is in Vietnam or here or in Europe; war at any level, for any cause, is disorder. And why is there this disorder in the world—in this world in which we have to live and function as human beings? We are going to examine that; we are not examining it verbally or theoretically or statistically but actually, factually. When you understand the fact, then you say that you prefer either to go that way or not to go that way.

So, what brings disorder in the world, psychologically, inwardly? Obviously, one of the reasons for this enormous, destructive disorder in the world is the division of religions—you a Hindu and I a Muslim; you a Christian: Catholic, Protestant, Episcopalian—a multitude of divisions. Obviously religion has been put together by man in order to help to become civilized, not to seek God—you cannot find God through beliefs, dogmas, through rituals, through repetition, through reading the Gita or the Bible, or through following a priest. This world is divided into religions—organized religions with their dogmas, with their rituals, with their beliefs, with their superstitions—throughout the world. And religions do not bring people together at all. They talk about it; they say, "If you see God, we are all brothers." But we are not brothers! We are looking at facts and not at hopes and theories.

So, religions have separated man, and that is one of the factors of great disorder. You are not agreeing with me, you see the facts. You see how, in Christendom, for two thousand years they have been fighting each other, Catholics and Protestants, Catholics amongst themselves, and there have been tortures. And this has happened in this country—the Muslims against the Hindus and the Hindus against the Muslims; one guru against another guru; one guru having fewer disciples, the other having more and wanting more!

Please do listen to all this because we are reaching a great crisis in our lives, not only as individuals, but as a community. And any man who wants not only to bring about order in himself but to bring about a good society—not a great society, but a good society—needs to resolve this problem. So, we can see factually in the world that religions have separated man, and that there have been tremendous religious wars in the East as well as in the West. So that is one of the roots of disorder. The organized beliefs with their churches, rituals, have become a tremendous corporation, a business affair, which has nothing to do with religion.

And nationalism, a recent poisonous growth, is also the cause of disorder. This country probably has never been nationalistic. Europe has divided itself into many sovereign states, fighting each other, and tearing at each other for more land, for greater economic expansion, and so on. They have had recently two tremendous, destructive wars within the memory of man. Nationalism has divided the people—the Englishman, the Frenchman, the Indian. And now you are becoming nationalistic in this country also. It is hoped that, through nationalism, human beings can be united. Worshiping the same flag, a piece of cloth—that has no meaning. (Laughter) Please do not laugh. This is not a rhetorical or amusing, entertaining gathering. We are very serious; we are concerned with immense problems.

War has brought disorder in the world. War is always destructive; there is never a righteous war. And there have been within the recorded history of mankind, I believe, something like fourteen thousand six hundred wars and more. Since 1945 there have been forty wars! In the first war, the people might have said, "Let us hope this will be the last war!" The mothers, wives, husbands, children, must have cried. And we are still crying, after these five thousand five hundred years. People have accepted war as the way of life. Here in this country you are also accepting war as the way of life—more armaments, more generals, more soldiers. And as long as you have sovereign governments—that is, nationalistic, separate governments, sovereign governments with their armies—you are bound to have wars. You may not have your son killed at Banaras, but you will have a son killed in Vietnam, whether he is an American or a Vietnamese. So, as long as there are sovereign governments, there must be war.

And, what is a man to do who says, "I will not kill"? You understand? In this country, for generations upon generations, a certain class of people has been brought up not to kill, not to hurt an animal, a fly. And all that is gone. They will write volumes about the spiritual inheritance of India, but the actual fact is that we have destroyed all that inheritance; we are just verbally repeating something which is not real.

So, we have two issues involved: What is a human being to do in a country like this, or in Europe, or in America, when he asserts he will not kill? And strangely, in this country for several years, perhaps thirty years or so, you have been preaching nonviolence—you have been shouting it from the housetops; that has been the export from this country to the West—"Don't kill," "ahimsa," and so on. Now you are brought together, united by war! Somebody told me yesterday with great enthusiasm, with great pleasure, that war has united India as never before! I have been told this in several places, by several people. You know, this is not very strange. This has happened in England, where class division is as strong as here; they all slept together in the underground, they were all terribly united through hate! And you have the spurious arguments: What would you do, if you were in the government; would you not fight if you were attacked? Obviously, if you are in a government, if you are the head of a sovereign state with an army, with all the paraphernalia of uncivilized existence, you are bound to attack or to defend. Nowadays nobody talks about being attacked or defending. You are at war; do not justify war!

Please, sirs, listen to all this, it is your life. In this country, in spite of its nonviolence, its preaching of nonkilling for thousands upon thousands of years, there has not been one human being who has said, "We will not kill." There have been whispering campaigns; you and I privately tell each other in our rooms that we won't kill. But publicly we never get on a platform and say, "I won't kill," and go to prison, or get shot for saying it. There has not been one boy or girl or one human being who has stood up against the stream. When it was popular to preach nonviolence, we all supported it. Now that war is popular, you also go for it. I am not talking of such individuals.

What is a human being to do, who says that he will not kill? What is he to do? He cannot do anything, can he? Either he can go to prison or be shot, killed by the government because he is a rebel, disloyal—you know all the words put out by the politicians and by the religio-political entities. Please inquire into yourselves: Why is it that there has not been one human being in India who said, "This is wrong, killing is wrong"? Not as governments, but as a human being, why is it that you have not said it? Must you be challenged? Through all the various organizations created for nonviolence, why have they not stood up? There is something very radically wrong in this country when they have not got that conviction of what they believe. So nationalism is disorder, it breeds disorder. War breeds disorder. Obviously, religions also breed disorder. So civilized man, a man who is really human, will not accept sovereign governments. You understand? You say, "I am a Hindu"—who cares whether you are a Hindu, a Chinese, or whatever you call yourself? What matters is what you are, not what your labels are.

So, unless you, as a human being, are free from all these labels—socialist, communist, capitalist, American, Englishman, Indian, Muslim—as long as you are labeling yourself in any way, secretly or openly, you are breeding disorder in the world. And also you are breeding disorder outside and inside when you belong to any religious group, or follow any guru. Because truth is not to be found by following somebody, by making it all easy for you as a pattern: doing this, following this, meditating this way, disciplining this way. You will never get it that way. To find truth you must be free. You must stand alone, swim against the current, battle. You know, I was told the other day that this war that India has had is justified because the Bhagavad-Gita said so! I thought that was rather lovely—don't you?

So, what are you going to do about it—not as Indians? What are you, as a human being, confronted with this problem—what are you going to do about it? There is poverty in this country, tremendous poverty—you know it as well as I do. And this poverty is going to increase because of this war. There is lack of rain, also inefficiency, corruption, and national divisions. We will accept food from one country and not from another—all politics! So, as a human being, what are you going to do? Either you accept disorder and continue to live in disorder and therefore inefficiency and therefore wars, therefore poverty, therefore hunger, or, as a human being, you reject it totally, not partially. You cannot reject something partially; you do not reject poison a little bit, you reject the whole thing. And that means you have to stand alone. Then you will be despised by society. You will be shot, probably. In this country, it is not too efficient yet, fortunately. In Europe, during the last war, many were killed. A mother we know had a son, a boy of eighteen—not a grown-up like you—who refused to go to kill, and he was shot. That boy did not talk about nonviolence, ahimsa, Gita, nonkilling, none of that. He did not want to kill, and he was killed.

So, seeing all this, the outer disorder and inward disorder, merely to become a pacifist is not the answer. The answer is much deeper than all this. But to find that answer, one has to reject the obvious things. You cannot keep the obvious things that are poisoning you, and then try to see much deeper. You cannot say, "I will have my pet guru and follow him, accept what he says and meditate, and then try to seek an answer much deeper." The two cannot go together. Either you reject the total thing or not at all—reject as human beings but not as a collective body. Because, when you become a collective body and reject, then you are merely conforming, and you may have the support of a hundred or a million people behind you—that is a mere following of another, in a different way. But to stand out completely alone—that is a very difficult thing for most people, because they are frightened of losing their job. You know all this.

So, seeing all this enormous disorder in ourselves and in the world, how is one to bring about any order? As we said, order will come when we understand disorder, when we cease to be nationalist, when we are really seeking truth, freedom—not through some organization, not through some belief, not through some guru.

Now, what makes each one of us change—you understand? That is the real question. What makes you, who have been nationalistic, or a tremendously devout person with regard to some guru, change? To me the word *guru* is poison, and there is something ugly in human beings following anybody. Now, how will you drop all this? How will you drop your Hinduism, your gurus, your nationalism? How will you stand alone, not follow what everybody says? What will make us, as human beings, do this? That is the real issue. You understand, sirs? What will make you divest all this at one blow, one breath, and say, "I am out"? Probably, most of you have not thought of all this at all. You have never said to yourself in your heart, "Why have I not stood up with tears in my eyes not to kill anybody?" Why have you not done it? Don't invent reasons. Why have you not done it?

And what will make you change? That is the real issue. You say, "I do not want to change, I will accept the things as they are. That is good enough for me; there is disorder, poverty, there is starvation; there will be wars. There have been wars for five thousand years and more, and we will have some more wars. What does it matter? The world is maya anyhow, and what does it all matter?" You accept it, as most of you apparently do. Because we human beings have an extraordinary capacity to adjust to anything—to living in a small room for the sake of God, doubled up, having one meal, a tortured mind; or to the appalling, bestial conditions of war, not at Banaras but in the front, at Vietnam, whether American or Vietnamese. Human beings can adjust themselves to anything, to dirt and squalor in the streets, open gutters, a corrupt municipality; they can put up with anything. After all, adjustability is the difference between animals and human beings—animals cannot, but human beings can.

So, we accept things as they are and go along miserably, torturing ourselves, unhappy, killing and being killed, seeking fulfillment and being frustrated, wanting to be leaders, restless, unhappy—which is what we are doing. If you accept that, there is nothing more to be said. You understand? You say, "That is my life, that is the way my father lived, my grandfather lived, my sons will live. And generations will come that will live likewise." If you accept that, that is all right. Don't introduce another problem. If you don't accept it, as a man of affection who feels strongly, who feels this whole monstrous thing, then what are you to do? How is such a man to change? How is he to bring about a mutation within himself? And that mutation perhaps will not, or will, affect society—but that is irrelevant. Society wants this disorder—not wars, but greed, envy, competition, seeking for power, position. That is what society is. And when you see all that, how will you change? You understand my question, sirs? How will you change?

May I proceed to point out what brings about this enormous mutation in a human mind? May I go on with it? Wait, sirs. I will go on. But it is not a verbal statement, it is not a thing about which you say, "I agree" or "I disagree." Because you see there is disorder and you are passionate, you do not say, "Show me the way and I will follow it." We are not talking of like and dislike, what is convenient, what is not convenient, nor in terms of a communist, a socialist, a Hindu, a Buddhist, or whatever you are. We are talking nonverbally, factually, about the necessity of tremendous, human change. Because, you see, the electronic brains, automation, and other technological things are going to bring about a certain change in the world. Man is going to have more leisure—it is not yet in this country; it is coming in Europe, and the beginning of it is already in America. So, all these things: automation, computers, wars, nationalism, these religious differences, to face all these and to break through all these, there must be in each one of us—not as a collective group belonging to some organization, but as human beings—a tremendous mutation. How will you change? What is the thing, what is the element, what is the energy that is necessary to break down this tremendous, destructive chaos in which one lives?

What makes one change, even a little bit? Say, for instance, you smoke—if you do. What will make you drop it? Doctors state that your lungs will be affected, and that is one of the ways of making you drop smoking—through fear. Punishment and reward—those are the only things that will force us to change. Punishment and reward; heaven and hell; next life and therefore behave in this life; therefore, the carrot and the whip—that is, punishment and reward. That is the only thing we know—"It gives me greater profit, greater satisfaction, greater energy, greater amusement, greater excitement, greater adventure; therefore, I will do it!" Now, any change taking place through punishment and reward—is that change? Please, sirs, you have to answer this question, not I. So, don't go to sleep! Is that a radical change, not a superficial change? Superficial change—we have done that for centuries, and that has not brought any mutation in human beings, any revolution in the human mind. We are asking the question much more fundamentally.

If there is no punishment and reward, what will make you change? And there is no punishment and reward. Who is going to punish you, who is going to reward you? All those things are overt. God is not going to reward you for righteous behavior; He does not care two pins for your behavior, right or wrong. The Church no longer has any importance. You may go to confession and so on, in Europe that is Catholic. But all that is disappearing, all that is being thrown overboard, except in the most backward states. Perhaps, in India where you say a little but not too much, you pretend to be a little more careful; that is all. But actually there is nobody to punish and reward. On the contrary, society says, "Come along; be greedy, be envious, be competitive, fight, quarrel; kill the Muslim and the Muslim will kill you." Society loves that, and the politicians play up to it! So there is nobody who is going to reward you or punish you—nobody. Neither your guru—you don't believe in gurus anyhow—nor your gods and goddesses will reward or punish you. Probably your wife or husband can only punish you. When you have a family, your wife says, "I am not going to sleep with you tonight"; or, "I am not going to do this or that"—that is all!

So, as there is no reward and no punishment—and there is not any actually when you investigate—how will you bring about this change? You understand the problem that is getting more and more complex for each one of us? Is this a problem to you? It must be, if you are at all thoughtful, serious, if you have watched the world's events. Seeing what is taking place in this country; knowing that religions have no meaning anymore—probably they never had it—seeing the futility of sacred books; seeing the absurdity of following any guru, however profitable, however pleasant; seeing that nobody can give you freedom, nobody can give you a mind that is healthy, strong, and deeply silent; seeing that no society, nobody is going to punish you or reward you—seeing all this and realizing that human beings must change radically, fundamentally, deep down, how will this change come about?

Shall we stop there this morning? Let us stop here this morning and continue on the twenty-fifth morning. You will perhaps be good enough—I am not asking you or trying to persuade you—to ask questions or discuss what we have been talking about.

Comment: I see all that you have said this morning. But there is no change.

KRISHNAMURTI: Let us go slowly and clearly, without any sentimentality involved in it.

Comment: I am not sentimental. I see clearly . . . .

KRISHNAMURTI: I want to clarify your question to myself. There are two ways of looking at things. Either one sees intellectually, verbally, all that we have been talking about. Verbally, that is superficially. Then the question, "How am I to change?" will never occur to that person. He will say, "It has been like this and it will go on like this." Or, he says, "I see it, I smell it, I taste it, it boils within me; I am burning with it, and yet action does not come out." And there is the other who sees it, and the very act of seeing is the act.

Comment: Sir, this has not happened at all, though you have talked about it for forty years.

KRISHNAMURTI: We know very well, perhaps just as you do, that for forty years we have talked about all this, and many of you here have listened to me for forty years. And you go your way and we go our way. We are not discouraged, nor are you! Basically you are not discouraged; you want that way, you go that way.

And the gentleman says, "You have talked for forty years and what a waste of time!" I do not feel it that way at all. We have other problems.

Comment: You have isolated yourself from the world altogether, and therefore you are happy.

KRISHNAMURTI: Why don't you do the same?

Comment: We are all ordinary human beings.

KRISHNAMURTI: We cannot afford to be ordinary human beings anymore. It was all right at one time. You cannot afford to be an ordinary, mediocre, dull, stupid, human being anymore. The challenge is too immense. You will have to do something. So, let us go through this slowly, sir. If you see it intellectually, there is no problem to you. If you see this whole thing from a comfortable easy chair—of course you happen to have a little money or a good job or . . . .

Comment: Let us have it out, sir.

KRISHNAMURTI: I am glad we know each other, we can fight it out. And if you belong to some socialist organization, communist, or whatever it is, then you want the world to change according to that pattern because you play an important part or you are a leader, you are this, and it gives you a certain importance—you all love that. That is one kind. Then there is the other kind—intellectuals who talk, who preach, who write books, who go to meetings, who cannot be kept away from any meetings, who always want to talk, talk. Then there are the others who see this mess, this confusion, this disorder, this misery, this agony that is going on in the world, and don't know what to do. They cannot break away from their nationalism, from their religion, from their gurus, and so on and on.

Then there are very few who say, "Look, I see this chaos, actual chaos"; and the very perception of it is action—not that they see it and later act. It is like seeing something poisonous and dropping it. There are very few of this kind because that demands tremendous energy, inquiry, application, attention, stripping yourself of all your vanity, of all your stupidity, of everything.

The intellectual obviously will have his own kind of armchair; he takes away this armchair, but he will invent another armchair. If you take away his organization, he becomes a super-communist or something else. So, there is only the middleman left, who says, "I see it, I do not know what to do, tell me what to do. Tell me the next step; step by step tell me, and I will follow it." That is his difficulty. He is looking for somebody else to tell him what to do. Instead of following the old, bearded gentlemen and ladies who have been your gurus, you throw them away and you come to me and say, "You are my guru, please tell me what to do." And I refuse to be put in that position.

Question: Still the question remains: Why, in spite of your talking about this for forty years, not a single human being has become different?

KRISHNAMURTI: The gentleman asks why is it that though I have talked for forty years more or less of the same thing in different words and expressing it differently, there has not been one human being who is different? Why? Will you answer it, sir? Either what is being said is false and therefore has no position in the world—it is false and has no validity, and therefore you do not pay attention; your own reason, your own intelligence, your own affection, your own good sense says, "What rubbish you are talking about!" Or, you hear what is being said, but it means nothing to you because the other is much more important.

Question: Why should truth be so impotent?

KRISHNAMURTI: Because truth has no action. Truth is weak. Truth is not utilitarian, truth cannot be organized. It is like the wind; you cannot catch it, you cannot take hold of it in your fist and say, "I have caught it." Therefore it is tremendously vulnerable, impotent like the blade of grass on the roadside—you can kill it, you can destroy it. But we want it as a thing to be used for a better structure of society. And I am afraid you cannot use it, you cannot—it is like love;

love is never potent. It is there for you, take it or leave it.

So, sirs, the problem is not that we have spoken for forty years. But the problem is: How is a human being, who has listened for forty years with a dry heart, without a tear in his eyes, who sees all this and does not do a thing, whose heart is broken up, whose heart is empty, whose mind is full of words and theories, and full of himself—how is he to make his heart alive again? That is the real question.

November 22, 1965

Second Talk at Rajghat

We are going to talk over this morning, together, the question of change: What moves a human being to change?

We are not talking about change at the peripheral level—that is, merely on the outward level, at the level of the frontier or at the edges of one's mind—but rather about change at the very center of the human mind and the human heart. We are going to consider this morning the change in relationship, because relationship is the very center of all human existence—relationship, to be related, to be in contact, not only the relationship between human beings and the state, but also the relationship between human beings themselves.

We are now confronted—especially in this country, which has been talking, preaching, theorizing about nonviolence and the question of war—with the question of relationship between a sovereign state, that is, the so-called government, and the human being. What is the relationship of the human being with the state, with society? Until we understand this question very deeply and very seriously, mere theorizing about the state and the reformation of the state or of society and the various speculations that are taking place with regard to the human being really have no meaning at all to a serious mind. We are confronted with this tremendous problem, not only in India, but throughout the world—this question of violence, not only the violence in the individual, in the human being, but also the violence, the organized violence which inevitably leads to war, of a state, of a sovereign government.

What is your relationship, as a human being, to the state, to society? You cannot, anymore, dodge, hide behind theories; you may not because there is the challenge thrown right at you. You say, "It does not concern me because I am beyond forty; I will not be called to serve the country; therefore, I preach, I talk and live the way I have lived." But it is a tremendous, vital, urgent problem for each one of us. We may not escape it, either saying "I have nothing to do with the state, I am a religious person and I am going to withdraw into the mountains, a monastery, or something or the other," or hiding behind the words, theories, speculations, intellectual froth which have no meaning. If you are at all serious, you have to face the issue.

What is your relationship with your neighbor, with your wife, husband, another human being? And also what is your relationship, as a human being, with the state, with a sovereign government that goes to war? You have to answer this; that is, the relationship of yourself with your neighbor, your relationship with your intimate family, your relationship with the so-called collective, which is society, and your relationship with a sovereign government or a state. And please do not theorize, do not speculate—that is one of the most dreadful escapes that the so-called intellectual people have in this country; they spin a lot of theories about nonviolence, violence, your state and your relation to it, and all the rest of it and they do not act. We have got to act.

So we are going to consider the change in relationship, not how to change a sovereign government, or the state, or the social structure of which each one of us is a part, the social structure which every human being has contributed to build up. Society is yourself and yourself is society. If you are born in communist Russia, you will believe that there is no separation between you and the state and all the rest of it. So we are now considering what is the nature of the thing that makes a man change in his relationship.

Why is it that this country, which has talked infinitely, for centuries, about "don't kill, be kind," which believes in so-called reincarnation, the unity of life—why is it that not one human being in this country, not one of you who has talked of violence and nonviolence, who has practiced nonviolence, who has gone to prison for independence, for this and that, has risen and said, "I will not kill," publicly? Do you understand? It is a very serious charge. You cannot just say, "It is not my business."

Not one has said, "I will not kill." Why? Please, sirs, put this question to yourselves, not to somebody else. Is it that you just follow what the popular opinion is? Popular opinion was, five to twenty years ago, for nonviolence, and you have been told to be nonviolent. In another decade something changes, and you run with that; there comes a war and you follow that. So it indicates that you do not believe or that you are not really convinced about anything. Do please listen to this. For you, neither violence nor nonviolence matters as long as you are completely safe, as long as you carry on with your popularity; whether you are a leader, whether you are efficient here or cheating there, whether you talk to this group or to that group, you carry on, repeating what is popular and just flow with the current. And how is such a human being to change his relationship, not only with himself, but also with another? Because it is a matter of relationship.

What makes you change? That is where we left off the other day. What makes me or you change—not at the outer edges of our activities, but right at the center? All the reformers are concerned about change at the periphery, at the social, extremely superficial level. We do change a little bit here and there because that is the fashionable thing to do. Some immature saint comes along with some cantankerous opinions and talks about all this outward, peripheral change, and you talk about it and you try to reform a little! But we are not talking at that level at all. We are talking at a different dimension, at a different level of the conscious human mind, and of the heart, which is the center from which all relationship takes place. Unless there is a change there, do what you will, you cannot bring about a society, a human being, tremendously sophisticated, highly civilized, and really religious.

So, what makes us change? If you are not interested in this question, don't bother, do not make another problem of it. You have enough problems as it is, whether you are conscious or unconscious of it. But if you are a really serious and thoughtful person in this world—which has become so violent, so brutal, so competitive, so nationalistic, dividing itself into families, groups—you are confronted with this problem, whether you like it or not. You can say, "I will not touch it, I will spin my theories and live in a cocoon of my own ideas." But, if you are concerned, you have to find out what makes each one of us change, and change at the center; what brings about a revolution right at the core of our being—not whether we travel third-class or first-class, fly, or we eat one meal a day and put on a loincloth; all that is a trivial thing when you are confronted with an immense problem.

Now, what makes us change? And do we want to change at the center? The center is the very essence of pleasure. For pleasure we will do anything, believe in anything, strive for anything, conform to any pattern as long as it is pleasurable, as long as it suits us, is convenient, gives us a certain position, a certain satisfaction, a certain fulfillment. Don't quickly brush aside this question of pleasure. After all, that is what all activities are based on—pleasure. I like a certain theory, a certain formula, and I act on it. Because I like it, it appeals to me, it is attractive, I believe. Or, I discard that and take up another—again that same principle. Or, I deny pleasure and say, "I must not have pleasure at all in life," and force myself, torture myself not to react to pleasure—which is what is called a religious pursuit. You can call this pleasure by any name, give it a marvelous-sounding word in Sanskrit or in Latin, or give a coating to that image and try to destroy it, try to break through, without understanding the whole structure of pleasure.

So, what makes us, you and me—as human beings, living in this terrible world, which is not illusion, which is terribly alive, brutal beyond words, with the utter callousness that is going on—what will make you and me change radically at the root which is based on the structure of pleasure and the avoidance of anything that is painful or not pleasurable? You believe in God because it gives you pleasure, because it makes you feel safe; that gives you some stability. Or, when you do not believe in God, that also gives you another kind of pleasure. So the whole structure is based on this.

Now, how will you, as a human being, bring about a change which is not another form of pleasure—a superior pleasure, a more subtle form of pleasure? So, we have to examine the nature of pleasure, not try to break it down or transform it or try to find a substitute for it, but to understand it. Right? To understand—what does it mean to understand something? We use that word *understanding* very easily when we say, "I understand it." A boy says, "I understand this mathematical problem. I understand the nature of human beings, the structure of society or of the government, and so on." But we are using the word understand in a different sense. We are using the word nonintellectually, nonemotionally. Obviously, the intellectual understanding of something is no understanding at all. Also, an emotional reaction to a given problem is no understanding. Please, when you have a very, very serious problem, as we have, you cannot approach it intellectually because it is a fragment of the whole of your human being. It is a segment, it is a section of the human structure. So, when we say that we understand something intellectually, it is not understanding. Intellectual understanding is a destructive understanding because you are dealing with a tremendously complicated problem with a fragment of your being, which is the intellect. Or when you emotionally get stirred up, when you sentimentally feel about something, again it is partial; therefore, in that there is no understanding.

So, there is understanding only when there is the intellect, the emotion, the nerves, the ears, the eyes, everything responding totally to the problem, not partially, not fragmentarily. When your whole being, whatever that whole being is—however little, however petty, however stupid, however narrow, however shallow—when that whole being responds to it completely, then there is a possibility of understanding that issue. That very understanding is action—not understanding and then acting. I hope that is clear—that is, we are approaching this problem totally, not fragmentarily; and the problem is: How is the human mind, how is this human being, who is so complex, to understand this complexity? One has also to comprehend that action is not different from understanding, that the two things are not separate. When I understand that it is a poisonous snake, I leave it. There is not: I understand it first, and then leave it; the thing itself is dangerous, and the understanding of the danger of it makes me act. So, the action is a total action, not a partial, fragmentary action.

You, as a human being, are a very complex entity. There is not only the conscious, educated, sophisticated mind, the brain of superficial consciousness of everyday activities—going to the office, family, and all that—but also there is the unconscious, the deep down, which is the racial, the communal, which is the traditional, all the past, the history of the civilization in which the human being exists, is educated and functions. So, one has to understand this whole structure, not partially, and not say, "I will begin to understand the unconscious or the conscious, little by little, and then put it all together and then see the whole of it as a whole!" I hope we are communicating with each other.

That brings up the question of communication. Relationship is communication. I do not know if you see this. If I hide behind the mask of my own ambitions, greed, envy, my own pettiness, and all the rest of it, I have no communication with you. You may also be petty, greedy, envious, behind your own mask. Each one of us lives behind masks. And so, though you may be married and have a wife, children, all the rest of it, every one of you lives in a prison of his own, behind the mask of cunning, deceit, and all the rest of it, and hopes to establish a relationship with another. It is impossible. Communication or communion can only exist when there is relationship. You understand, sirs? That is, if you say, "I am a Hindu," it is a mask, it is just a tradition, it has no meaning in the modern world—and never had anyhow—and you live behind that mask. And I, a Muslim, live behind my mask, my tradition, my bigotry, my upbringing. Is there a communication between you, a Hindu, and me, a Muslim? None at all. And this relationship is no communication. Now, between you and the speaker, we have to establish this relationship; otherwise, there is no understanding of each other. If you listen, while you are here, indifferently, casually, or because you have a certain idea about the reputation of the speaker, a certain false respect, how can there be a communication, which is relationship, between you and the speaker? We must both meet at the same level, at the same time, with the same intensity; otherwise, there is no communication. I do not know if I am making myself clear on this issue. I may pretend; I may be tremendously nationalistic; I may be inwardly, deeply Hindu, and talk about unity, and so on; I have no communication with you. Or, you may be out of this category of human labels.

So, to establish communication and deeper communion, there must be a relationship, not merely at the verbal level—that is absolutely necessary; I speak English, as I do not know any Indian language, and you also understand English; therefore, there is a verbal communication. But the verbal communication is not a relationship. Relationship can only take place when you meet the fact nonverbally, nontheoretically, without abstraction. It is only when both of us are going to meet the fact that there is communion or communication between us; both of us have to see the same thing factually, not emotionally, not according to our opinions, beliefs, dogmas, hopes, fears, not as a Hindu, as a Muslim, as a Buddhist, as a communist, and so on. We have both to see the actual fact at the same time—not you go home and see the fact, but see the fact as it is said, at the same moment—with the same intensity; then only is communion or communication possible; and then only is relationship possible. And it is only when there is a relationship between you and the speaker about the fact that there is a possibility of bringing action to the fact, or the fact bringing action. Please follow this, it needs attention.

We are talking about change in relationship, and that is absolutely necessary, not at the superficial level, but at the very root of our being. And we are going to discover the fact—discover it, not be told what the fact is. And when we discover the fact for ourselves, we look at the fact nontheoretically, without opinions; then that very look brings action. And therefore that very observation is the factor of change. I wonder if you understand all this. Am I making myself clear? Don't agree, sirs. You are not pacified. Either it is clear or it is not clear. If it is not clear, we will discuss it, we will debate, we will go into it, because you have to see the tremendous importance of this. It is the observation of the fact itself that brings change, not your volition, not your desire, not your memory which says, "I must change, I must be happy"—which are all conclusions based on pleasure and, therefore, not a factor which brings about in itself the energy to change. It is the observation of the fact itself, being totally in communion with the fact—it is that communion or that relationship with the fact itself that brings the change. Human beings are violent because they are still animals. Now I am going to go into it; please follow.

I am violent; from childhood I have been trained to be violent, to compete, to assert myself, to fulfill myself, to conform to society, to adjust. So from childhood, through various cultures and all the rest of it, this violence continues. I hate people. I do not like people, I am cunning, I want position, I want to be famous, I want to be regarded as a very good man, very capable—you know the image that we build about ourselves: I am this or I am that. I see I am violent. As long as it is pleasurable, as long as it gives me satisfaction, I continue to be violent. It is only when that violence becomes painful that I begin to say, "I must change"—not because of any theory; not because of any God; not because of society, doing good to society, following this saint or that saint. I like to be violent when it pays, and I don't like to be violent when it does not pay. That is a fact.

I see that violence, in itself, is destructive; in itself, it destroys the human mind because if I am competing, fulfilling, struggling, battling with you and with everything, the brain wears itself out. There is no affection, there is no tenderness, no grace, no beauty. I see that, but I do not know how to change this thing called violence. I see that, and I ask myself, "How am I to bring about a radical transformation at the very root of violence, which is the 'me', the 'me' of accumulated memories, hopes, fears, anxieties, spiritual concepts—that I am the soul, that I am the atma, that I am God—which are essentially based on pleasure and therefore violence?" I do not know if you are following all this. I must come into relationship with the fact, which we have talked about earlier. The mind or the brain must come into contact directly with what it calls violence. Right?

I can only come into contact with you when I hold your hand. I must come directly into contact; otherwise, there is no contact, physical contact. I must come into contact with that thing which I call violence. I cannot possibly come into contact with that feeling called violence as long as I have explanations about violence, or as long as I have intellectual explanations for why I am violent: I am an animal; society is violent; I am part of that society, and because of society, I am also violent; circumstances force me. Those explanations prevent me from coming into contact with the fact. I see that, and I see also that it is imperative that I have relationship with the fact; therefore, I have no theories any more. You understand? I have no theories of any kind—communist, socialist, this saint or that saint—which is a difficult thing for a man to do because he lives by words. So, I will not have a theory about violence; I want to come into contact with it. I cannot have a theory about love if I love you. Love is not a theory. Theory exists only when the heart is empty, and you hope to fill the empty heart with words and theories. And theoreticians, these saints—you know, this country is so full of them—have no love.

So I can only come into contact with a fact when I have no theories, no beliefs, no opinions about the fact. Also, I have no relationship with the fact if I am trying to escape from it. I escape from it when I say, "What is the answer to this problem?" because I am more concerned with the answer, the resolution, or the substitution of the problem, and not with coming into contact with the problem itself. I hope you are following all this.

So, I come into relationship with the fact, with neither opinion nor theory. Opinion, theory, will prevent one from coming into relationship with the fact. And escape in any form prevents me from coming into contact with the fact—and a very subtle form of it is the word about the fact. You understand, sirs?

Look, sir, the word is very important. For us, the word *Hindu* is very important because behind that word or for that word we will fight and kill. We do not investigate what that word means. We just accept that label, and we are willing to slaughter, or be slaughtered by, anybody who stands in the way or is against that label. So, the word—communist, socialist, my way, the class I belong to—is extraordinarily important to people. We live by words, and therefore our hearts are empty, dry, cruel. So the word *violence* prevents you from coming into contact with that feeling which you call violence.

Look, sirs, let me put it round another way. I want to understand, to know, to feel, to come into what love is, and let love flower in me. I do not know what love is. But I have opinions about it: godly love; physical love; saintly love; lust for man. Do you love God? Do you love your neighbor? Do you love everybody? I have concepts, formulas: pure love, ignoble love, no sex. I have quantities, volumes of opinions about love. To come into contact with the fact of what love is, I must eschew, put away, burn all the books about what love is. In the same way, to find out, to come directly into communion with violence, the first thing is: no explanations, no escape—escape being trying to find out the cause or trying to find an answer. Also I must be tremendously aware of the danger of the word itself. It is only then that my whole being can come into contact with that thing which I call violence. There is the 'me' who is looking at violence. I have not given explanations, I have not escaped, I have not understood the word. So I look at the fact which I call violence. Is that violence different from the observer? It is not different. The observer is the observed; the observer is violence, not that he is apart from that thing which he calls violence. So there is contact with that which we have called violence.

All this must be understood, not gradually. You follow? It must be understood immediately. That is the whole issue.

We were talking the other day about the question of order and disorder. Time is disorder, not chronological time, not time by the watch. If you do not keep time by the watch, you create more disorder. If I do not come by the watch exactly at half past nine, there is disorder. So, time and order exist chronologically—the bus, the train, the airplane, the appointment, when the factory starts working, and when I must be there. Any other time except that time breeds disorder. Do not agree; see what is implied in it. Because, for us, time is a gradual process, a continuation of yesterday through today to tomorrow—a duration. I haven't the time to go into it too much.

When I say to myself, "I will understand violence slowly," it is a gradual process. When you say you will eventually come into contact, into relationship between you and the fact—you understand?—when you say, "I will take my time to understand violence," you are postponing your relationship with the fact. And when you postpone your relationship with the fact, you are creating more disorder. Isn't that so? Do see the very simplicity of it now; it gets tremendously complicated and subtle later. But do see the simplicity of it first. That is, I am greedy; and I say I am greedy because it is painful. As long as it is pleasurable, I go on with my greed, calling it by different names, covering it up, pretending, being saintly, and all the rest of it. Whether it is for God or for things or for success, it does not matter; it is still greed. When I say to myself, "I will get rid of it presently," I have postponed my relationship with the fact. And in this interval which I call gradualness, in which there is the lag of time, in that interval, there are other influences going on: I am pretending to be nongreedy, I am pretending to accept; there are many, many factors involved in that postponement; you can see all this for yourself.

So that postponement, that gradualness, that lag of time, is the factor of disorder. So time, as a postponement, is the avoidance of the fact. When one says, "I will do something tomorrow, I will be good, I won't be angry," all those statements are postponement and avoidance of the fact. And when you avoid something, you are creating more confusion, more sorrow, more trouble, more conflict and therefore, more disorder. When you understand this thing really—not verbally, but actually—when you see how time creates disorder, then your action is immediate.

So the relationship to a fact is only possible when there are no opinions, explanations, theories, when there are no escapes—such as trying to find an answer or trying to find a cause—when the word no longer interferes between the observer and the observed, and when you see that the observer is the observed. When you understand this whole problem of time, which we have briefly explained, then you are directly in contact, in relationship, with the fact. And it is this relationship with the fact that brings about the energy that brings complete change.

What is real is the fact, and any abstraction is a barrier. All explanations, theories, opinions, trying to avoid the fact, the time element, the observer saying that he is observing the thing—these are abstractions, and have to be eliminated. As long as you have a barrier as an abstraction, you are not in relationship with the fact. Therefore, it is only when you are completely, with your whole being, in contact with the fact that the fact is going to bring this revolution—not will, not decision, not saying, "I will do something about this"—none of these, if you have observed yourself, will bring this revolution. You will see the fact only when you are confronted with the fact. If you say, "I do not want to face the fact"—which is perfectly all right—you are not serious. But if you are really serious and come into contact with the fact, then you will see that this operates always.

I do not know if you have ever considered why we attend meetings at all, why you sit there, and the speaker sits here and talks. Why do you listen at all? It is a peculiar phenomenon in life: whether it is a talk by a politician, or by a guru, or by anyone else. Why do you listen to a talk?

Why do you listen and how do you listen? I wonder if you have ever gone into this question, or even thought about it: why we listen at all to what another says. I can understand my listening to a technological talk by a technological professor about the computer, about science, about mathematics, and so on—technological knowledge. But why do you listen to me? Are you actually listening to me? Or are you observing yourself through me? You are following? After all, when one listens—if one is at all serious—one is actually listening to oneself. The speaker expounds, explains; but that is irrelevant. What is relevant is that you are observing yourself, how your mind is operating, what your reactions are. When the speaker talks about nationalism, Hinduism, what are your reactions to it? You begin to discover yourself, your reactions, your cunningness, your deceptions, and all the rest of it, when you are actually sitting quietly and listening to a talk of this kind. Otherwise it has no value at all. I can go on spinning about violence, I can tell you about the structure of violence and so on. But if that does not reveal to yourself what your own mind is, what your own heart is, then such a talk as this morning's is absolutely worthless. It is your life. You have to live your life. You are called upon to find out how you respond to this war. Do you just flow with it, as almost all the people do, including the saints and all their disciples?

In listening one discovers for oneself how shallow one is, and the discovery is not depressing. On the contrary, one discovers a fact; and when you discover a fact and react to that fact as being depressed or as saying, "I wish I weren't that," then you are avoiding the fact. It is only when you discover by listening to yourself through listening to the speaker or anyone else that you will unfold an extraordinary treasure, and open a door to such things as you have never even dreamed of. And out of that comes great affection, great love. And without love, do what you will, you will have no order, no peace. And with love, you can do what you will.

November 25, 1965

Third Talk at Rajghat

I would like this morning, if I may, to talk over together several issues. But before we proceed with them we have, after all, to understand what real communication means. When we attend a talk or a gathering like this, we are really, aren't we, trying to communicate with each other over several problems. We are not merely intellectually dissecting opinions, or comparing knowledge, or interpreting what somebody else says—whether it is Shankara, Buddha, Christ, or anybody else—but rather are trying to discover for ourselves the sources of all our problems. Because we are inundated, drowned, by so many problems, not only outwardly, economically, socially, environmentally, but also inwardly; deep within ourselves there are so many contradictions, both conscious as well as unconscious, so many conflicts unresolved, so many problems that have taken such deep roots within ourselves. And we are communicating together about those problems. We are not trying to overlay these complex problems by another issue, by another solution, by another way of looking at life, by another philosophy, by a system, and all the rest of it. What we are actually doing is to unfold the complex nature of our being and to look at it—really to look at it with our hearts, with our minds, with our ears, eyes, with all our being, so that we come directly into communion with them and thereby resolve them.

And, therefore, you who are listening to the speaker—you have not only to listen to what is being said, but also to listen, observe, to what actually is, to what actually is going on within this human mind. Because that is the only thing we have—the mind, however little, however small, however petty, tyrannical, or brutal. That is what we have, and we have to understand it, not try to deny it, not try to say that this is an illusion, not try to go beyond it. We have to understand this thing which is our life, which is our relationships.

And, therefore, it is important to listen, not only to the speaker, but to all the various movements of life, because life is a movement in relationship. We have to listen to this movement, day in and day out, all the time; we have to listen to it attentively—not try to translate it, not try to say, "This is right, this is wrong; this is good, this is bad; this must be, this must not be"; but just listen to the song of this extraordinary movement of life. And in listening to it one begins to understand it.

Because life is not something outside, something that is flowing by, which we look at. Life is this movement in ourselves, of which we are a part; it is that which we have to understand, which we have to unravel, comprehend, love, pursue; and we have to imbibe deeply the full significance of it all. Otherwise, our minds remain extraordinarily shallow. You may be very learned, quote all the religious books of the world, practice a great many systems of yoga, expound this or that philosophy, show off your erudition, but your mind will still be very small and petty. And it is that pettiness that has to be understood, and in the very understanding of that pettiness the thing is broken.

So, what we are going to talk over together this morning is this question of conflict within and without, sorrow and the ending of it, and life as action. These are the things, if we may, we would like to talk over this morning. When the speaker is talking, you are also participating, you are not just listening to what is being said, agreeing or disagreeing; both of us are sharing, partaking; you are working as hard, as intensely, as vitally, as the speaker. And it is only when you are working so intensely that this has meaning. But if you sit down there, to be entertained by casual talk or listen to confirm what you believe or deny and so on, then you are merely listening to a series of words, sentences, and phrases which have very little meaning.

Man has lived for over two million years of suffering—that is, with physical pain and psychological pain, outward pain and inward pain. Please observe yourself. Pain is not some abstraction; we are suffering, human beings are suffering. There is the physical as well as the psychological, the inward pain; and, apparently, we have not been able to solve it at all, we have not been able to be free of this ache, of this anxiety, of this fear, of this contradiction. Unless there is freedom from that contradiction, conflict, pain, sorrow inwardly, it is not possible to have a mind that is clear, and that by its very clarity is still. And it is only the still mind that is creative; it is only such a mind that understands what is truth and the creation of what is true. Truth is not something abstract, something final, but it is a living thing, it is perpetually in creation.

We are using the word *creation* in its deepest and widest sense, not merely writing a poem, a book, or an article, or making a speech, or doing some outward thing.

So, our human concern is with regard to effort, sorrow, and action. They are all interrelated. You cannot say, "I will understand effort, then conflict, and then come to sorrow, and then come to action." They are all closely interwoven, and in understanding one of them you are already comprehending the other.

We know, as we observe, without being told by any philosophy or any ideology, that we are in conflict. That is a fact. And we do not know what to do with it. If we are intelligent enough and know what to do with it, then we will be out of it and be free from conflict and therefore from sorrow. Action then becomes a total movement. It is not an action based on fragmentation, it is a total action.

So, conflict is part of our daily existence. From childhood until we die, we are always in conflict, tortured, torturing, in contradiction. And until we die, this problem is apparently never solved. From the sannyasi, down or up, from the businessman to the man of power, position, everybody is in conflict.

And is there a way out of it? Is it possible for a human being, like you and me, to be completely free from this agony of conflict? The more intense the conflict, the more that conflict expresses itself—if you have a certain capacity—in action, as writing a book, a clever book, a very clever poem. Or, if you have a talent for music, you express it that way. So, the greater the conflict, the greater the tension; if you have a certain capacity, the expression takes all the importance, not the ridding or the understanding of that conflict. If you are slightly intellectual, if you can quote books, though you may be intensely in conflict inwardly, you can get up and make speeches, you become a politician, a writer. You escape that way, or you escape in so many different ways. But it is essential for us to be free from conflict. I do not think we feel the necessity or the urgency or the importance of being free from conflict.

You know, freedom is an extraordinary thing. It is not freedom from something. If you are free from something, that freedom is merely a reaction, and therefore it is not freedom. Please understand this—not intellectually, but feel your way into it. If I am free from anger, that freedom from anger—not being angry any more—is another form of resistance, another form of suppression or sublimation, and therefore it is not real freedom. Freedom means freedom in itself, and not from something.

So, is it possible to be free from conflict? Conflict exists because we are in contradiction—want and no want; pleasure and pain; ambition and at the same time trying to find out what love is. Seeking power, position, fame, notoriety—none of those things can exist with affection, with love, with kindness, with goodness; and so there is always contradiction. We know it, but we get accustomed to this contradiction. We are used to it, so our mind becomes dull. You can look at that river. When you see it for the first time, you rejoice in it, you see the light on the water, the ripples, the beauty in the light, the current, the fish; you see the extraordinary richness, the fullness of the movement of that river. But when you come back to it and look at it again, you have already got used to it! Your memory has accepted that first vision, that first rejoicing; and now, because it has accepted it and has got used to it, when you look at it again, you have lost the flavor, the sensitivity to all that.

Similarly we have got used to this conflict and we accept it. I think that is one of the most destructive things a human being can do: to accept, merely to adjust. We accept poverty, the squalor on the road, the dirt, the corruption, the terrible things that are going on in the world. We accept all that and say, "Well, it has been like that and will always be like that." So this acceptance prevents action. Acceptance, mere adjustment, getting used to things, not only prevents the understanding of conflict, but makes the mind dull. You have always been a Hindu, and you will always be a Hindu, until you die—or a Muslim. We get used to it and keep on repeating the same pattern of existence day after day, until we die.

So, one of the major issues in understanding conflict is this gradually becoming accustomed to it, putting up with it; and that is the first thing to guard against. When you do not accept suffering, when you do not accept conflict, your mind is disturbed; then your mind can ask radical questions; then your mind can not only ask but be in an intensive state until it finds out the way out of this—not escape into some ideology, or into some theory, or escape from life altogether by running away to some mountain, becoming a monk, and so on. When you do not accept it, your mind becomes alert, sharp, and therefore you can investigate and find out a way out of it. That is the first thing one has to learn.

You know, learning is different from accumulating knowledge. A mind that is merely accumulating knowledge as experience, cultivating memory from which it acts, is no longer learning. Learning implies a mind that is constantly, actually learning, not accumulating. I hope I am making the point clear. Because learning is always fresh. I do not know a language, and I am learning it; the moment I have learned, which is the past tense of that verb, I have ceased to learn. After all, the verb "to learn" is always the active present. Do listen to this. Learning is always in the active present—not "I have learned," or "I should learn." The moment you say, "I have learned," you have already accumulated, and from that information, from that knowledge, you act; and therefore action then is conforming to the pattern of your conditioned knowledge. But when the verb is always the active present—which is "learning," not "having learned" or "will learn"—the active present of that verb is always fresh; it is never tinged by the past, and it is therefore tremendously active. And therefore a mind that is always learning keeps itself strongly alive and is capable of meeting any situation afresh, because it is learning.

So, one has to learn, in the active present, his habit formation, getting used to conflict. Therefore a mind which is always learning—which is the active present—is capable of meeting conflict, and therefore learning about it. The more problems we have, the more conflict we are going to have; and we have to meet them, we have to learn all about them, not the accumulated past; the learning process must go on. A mind that is always learning is never in conflict—do see the beauty of that! But when a mind has accumulated a set pattern of behavior, conduct, and meets the present—which is always active—it has a contradiction. And from that contradiction, there is conflict. And where there is conflict, there is this incessant effort, a rat race that is going on all the time.

So, we have to understand this process of a mind that gets used to things. You can get used to beauty as well as to ugliness. The mind is so capable of adjusting itself to anything. You will accept war, as Western Europe and America have accepted war, as the way of life. You are now beginning to accept war as the way of life. And the moment you have accepted war as the way of your life, then you get used to it. You will have military service, drilling in your schools, soldiers—the more you have soldiers, the more will be the poverty of the country; the whole cycle will begin, and you will say that all this is natural, inevitable! Do consider all this, please. It is your life, not my life; it is your daily living.

And when the mind is not fresh, is not actively present as learning, then either sorrow becomes something that you worship—as they do in the Christian world—or you try to escape from it, or you find a causation in the past. So, your mind is incapacitated to find out, to learn what sorrow is. Until you learn what sorrow is, you will never be free of it. Please do go with the speaker a little bit, feel your way into it. Because wisdom does not lie with the mind that is sorrow-ridden. However cunning, however erudite it is, whatever its capacity is, a mind in sorrow is a source of mischief. If there is to be social order, human beings must be free from sorrow. And we need order—tremendous order. Because it is only when there is order, which comes when the human being is free from conflict and therefore from sorrow, that out of that order, a new society, a new way of living comes into being.

So, there is an ending to sorrow. And you are the only person who can find out, not somebody else. Some teachers have said that sorrow can be ended, and you may repeat it; that has no value at all. What has value is to find out for yourself, and to learn the whole structure of sorrow—that is, to observe your daily movement, your daily activity, your daily relationship. And out of that observation, out of that learning, which is always in the active present, you will find for yourself that sorrow can be ended. And it can be ended only when you watch—not when you say, "I must end sorrow, sorrow must end," and find a system to end that sorrow; that does not end it. What ends sorrow is a close observation of everything you do, not only in the family, but in the office, in the factory, in the bus—the way you talk, the way you gesture; everything matters. And from that observation there is the beginning of learning.

And there is this question of action. I do not know if you have noticed in the morning, high up in the sky, the big vultures, the big birds, flying without a movement of their wings, flying by the current of the air, silently moving. That is action. And also the worm under the earth, eating—that too is activity, that is also action. So also it is action when a politician gets up on the platform and says nothing, or when a person writes, reads, or makes a statue out of marble. That is also action when a man, who has a family, goes to the office for the next forty years, day after day, doing drudgery work without much meaning, wasting his life endlessly about nothing! All that a scientist, an artist, a musician, a speaker does—that too is action. Life is action from the beginning to the end; the whole movement is action. But, unfortunately, we have divided action into fragments: noble action, ignoble action, political action, religious action, scientific action, the action of the reformer, the action of the socialist, the action of the communist, and so on and on. We have broken it up, and therefore there is a contradiction between each action, and there is no understanding of the total movement of action.

And in our own lives, the activity in your house is not so very different from the activity in your office. You are equally as ambitious in the office as you are at home. At home, you dominate, oppress, nag, drive—sexually and in so many different ways. Also you are doing the same outside the home. There is the action of a mind that seeks peace, that says, "I must find truth." Such a mind is also in action.

Now, maturity is the comprehension of action as a whole, not as fragments. I am not defining maturity, so do not learn the definition by heart, or learn another definition. You can see that as long as action is fragmentary, there must be contradiction and therefore conflict.

So, how does one come to discover or to feel or to live in the active present, in an action that is total, whole, not partial? Have I made my question clear? We have to understand this question because our actions are fragmentary—the religious, the business, the political, the family, and so on; each is different, at least in our minds. And so the worldly man says, "I cannot be religious because I have to earn a livelihood." And the religious man says, "You must leave the world to find God." So everything, every action, is in contradiction. And therefore out of that contradiction there is effort, and in that contradiction there is sorrow, fear, misery, and all the rest of it.

So, is there an action which is total—so that it has no fragmentation as action—which is life, total life? Unless one understands that, all our actions will be in contradiction. So, how does one learn about it? Not "having learned" or "going to learn," but actually "learning" about action which is total, which is not fragmentary. Right? I have put the question. If the problem is clear, we can go on.

There is only one action that is total: that is death. Right? There is no argument, no intellectual quibbling about death. There is no opinion, you do not cite your religious books, you cannot escape from it, you cannot avoid it. You do not ask death, "Give me another day." So there is only one total action, which is to die—dying.

Now, dying for most people, is negation; dying is like suicide! And because we have not comprehended the extraordinary nature of death, we—the clever, the intellectual people—make life into something that has no meaning at all. Life, then, has no meaning anymore. Has your life any meaning anymore? Please, sirs, do look at it! Has your life any meaning—going to the office, earning a livelihood, supporting a family, having sexual pleasures, driving in a big car or in a little car, or walking? What does it all mean to you—writing a book or not writing a book, doing some petty, little social reform, belonging to some little society, and all the rest of it? What does it all mean? And the more you question living, the torture of it, the less meaning it has. And all the clever people write useless, meaningless books; out of despair they write about philosophy, they invent a philosophy. But we are not talking of a suicide, we are not talking of a despair as the ultimate action. We are pointing out that death is the only action which is total and complete—like love. Love is also total action. Love has no contradiction. But our love is hedged about with jealousy, with anxiety, with loneliness; it is "my love" against "your love," "my family" against "your family," "my nation," "my tribe" against "your tribe," the "South" against the "North." And we say we love; our love is a contradiction.

So, we have to understand death. And it is only in the understanding of death that you will know what love is. Or, if you understand the whole nature of this contradiction, which exists as pleasure, then you will understand the total action of love, because love and death go together. You have to understand this extraordinary mystery of death.

And meditation is the understanding of death and love. Not sitting on the banks of a river, muttering a few words; or in your room silently sitting cross-legged, breathing in some way, repeating some mantras or some words—all that only hypnotizes you; that is not meditation. Meditation is the understanding of life in which there is love and death and sorrow—understanding, not intellectually, but learning about it. The understanding of the extraordinary nature of death and of love is meditation. And to understand it, there is no method, there is no system, there is no practice, because you are learning. You cannot learn through a method. You understand? The two are contradictory. Learning, as we have said at the beginning, is always in the active present—you are learning. You cannot be learning in the active present if you have a method, a system: first step, second step, third step. So, one has to learn about death. And to learn about death is to die to the things that one has accumulated psychologically, every day, every minute. You understand? That is what is pain for most of us: to die, to put an end to one's pleasure. Have you tried it ever? Just to die—without argument, without pro and con, without saying, "Why shouldn't I?" without all the clever, cunning things we invent to protect ourselves.

You have to die naturally, easily, to some pleasure that you have—try it; do it, without will, without exertion, without effort, without detachment, without cultivation of this and that in order to achieve something. You know, in the cold weather, in the autumn, the leaf drops from the tree to the ground and the leaf is multicolored, beautiful, rich; in its death also it is as beautiful as when it was living, fluttering in the wind, in the sunlight. And to die psychologically, don't begin at the physical end—to die to your clothes, which is nothing; putting on one loincloth, which is nothing. Don't begin at the wrong end; begin at the right end, which is the inward end; inwardly die to your beliefs, to your knowledge, to your petty, little ambitions, your cunning, your deceptions, your pleasures and pains; just die simply, naturally—which you are going to do when you grow older. Without understanding death, old age is a pain, a distortion.

And when you know this thing named death, then you will know also what love is. And in this country we do not know what love is—nor in other countries. Because we are frightened of beauty—to look at a tree, to look at a bird on the wing, to see the lovely face of a woman or a man or a child. Because you have been trained, you have accepted, adjusted; it has become a habit that a religious man must be completely insensitive to beauty because beauty for him means a woman, the sensation, the pleasure, and therefore it has to be avoided. Therefore your lives are empty; your minds may be full of words, but your heart is empty. Therefore you allow things that are intolerable for any really religious mind.

So, where there is the understanding of conflict, there is the ending of sorrow. And the ending of sorrow is the beginning of total action. And total action can only come about when there is dying psychologically to things that you hold as pleasure and pain. And then only is there love. If you do not have this, do what you will, walk up and down the Himalayas ten times, a hundred times, go round the world, do all the reforms, there is no way out.

And when you understand all this, the mind becomes extraordinarily quiet. In the understanding of all this there is discipline—not a discipline imposed outwardly or inwardly. And that discipline is order. And when there is this extraordinary living, dynamic stillness, then in that stillness there is creation. Call that creation what you will—God, or dog—any name would do! But until we come to it as human beings, there is no way of bringing order, peace in the world. And you must have peace, because in peace alone can you flower in goodness.

November 28, 1965

Questions

London Dialogues, 1965

Paris, 1965

Saanen, 1965

Saanen Dialogues, 1965

Banaras, 1965

Index

Printed in the USA
CPSIA information can be obtained
at www.ICGtesting.com
LVHW081751190324
774699LV00002B/5